THE FOUNDING MYTHS OF ISRAEL

THE FOUNDING MYTHS
OF ISRAEL

NATIONALISM, SOCIALISM, AND THE MAKING OF THE JEWISH STATE

Zeev Sternhell

Translated by
David Maisel

PRINCETON UNIVERSITY PRESS   PRINCETON, NEW JERSEY

Copyright © 1998 by Princeton University Press

Translated from Zeev Sternhell, *Aux origines d'Israël:*
Entre nationalisme et socialisme. Copyright © 1996 Fayard, Paris

Published by Princeton University Press, 41 William Street,
Princeton, New Jersey 08540
In the United Kingdom: Princeton University Press,
Chichester, West Sussex
All Rights Reserved

Library of Congress Cataloging-in-Publication Data

Sternhell, Zeev.
[Aux origines d'Israël. English]
The founding myths of Israel : nationalism, socialism,
and the making of the Jewish state / Zeev Sternhell ;
translated by David Maisel.
p.   cm.
Includes bibliographical references and index.
ISBN: 0-691-01694-1 (cl : alk. paper)
1. Zionism—History.   2. Zionism—Philosophy.
3. Jewish nationalism—Philosophy.   4. Labor Zionism—
History.   5. Jews—Palestine—History—
20th century.   I. Title.
DS149.S69513   1997
320.54′095694—dc21   97-15871   CIP   r97

Princeton University Press wishes to express its appreciation
to the French Ministry of Culture for its assistance
in the preparation of the translation

This book has been composed in Caledonia

Princeton University Press books are printed
on acid-free paper and meet the guidelines
for permanence and durability of the Committee
on Production Guidelines for Book Longevity
of the Council on Library Resources

http://pup.princeton.edu

Printed in the United States of America

1   3   5   7   9   10   8   6   4   2

For Ziva, Tali, and Yael

Contents

Preface   ix

*A Note on the Transliteration of Hebrew Names and the
Translation of Hebrew Book Titles*   xv

Introduction
Nationalism, Socialism, and Nationalist Socialism   3

Chapter One
The Primacy of the Nation: Aaron David Gordon and the Ethos
of Nation-Building   47

The Negation of the Diaspora   47
What Is a Nation?   52
*Nationalism versus Socialism: The Amelioration of Man,
    Nation, or Society?*   59
The Right to the Land: The Power of History   68

Chapter Two
The Worker as the Agent of National Resurrection   74

The Heritage of the Second Aliyah   74
The First Stages of the Shift to the Right   80
The Elimination of the Marxist Po'alei Tzion Party   92
The Founding of Ahdut Ha'avoda   107
Experiential Socialism   121

Chapter Three
Socialism in the Service of the Nation: Berl Katznelson and
"Constructive" Socialism   134

The Legend and the Reality   134
The Nation above All   146
From "Productivist" to Nationalist Socialism   153

Chapter Four
Ends and Means: The Labor Ideology and the Histadrut   178

The Bases of Power   178
*Taking over the Collective Settlements: The Establishment
    of the Nir Company*   192

The Cult of Discipline and Authority: The Destruction of
   Gdud Ha'avoda (the Labor Corps)   198

Chapter Five
The Triumph of Nationalist Socialism: "From Class to Nation"   217

   What Is a Class?   217
   The Collaboration with the Middle Classes   233
   The Struggle over Workers' Education   244

Chapter Six
Democracy and Equality on Trial   264

   The Hegemony of the Apparatus and the Poverty of
     Intellectual Life   264
   Oligarchy and Conformism   270
   Equality: Principle and Practice   282
   The Failure of the Family Wage   290
   Class Warfare in the Histadrut   306

Epilogue
From the State-in-the-Making to the Nation-State   318

Notes   347

Glossary   391

Bibliography   399

Index   409

Preface

THIS BOOK, which appeared in Hebrew in June 1995 and in French at the beginning of 1996, immediately provoked a lengthy and continuous debate. Some of the reactions deserve a study in themselves, but since the debate is still proceeding, as vigorously as ever, I feel it fitting to postpone this task until later. For the moment, I will simply point out that the intensity and scope of these exchanges show the degree to which this work goes to the heart of the controversy over the nature of "Israeliness." I feel that, very often, major questions concerning the nature of Jewish nationalism and the character of Zionist socialism (including its origins and its place in the development of Israeli identity) have been formulated incorrectly, and in many cases important issues have been evaded. It is precisely these issues that this book attempts to reformulate and analyze.

This work began with a critical reflection on Israeli society in the past and the present. Throughout my academic career, my professional field of research lay in Europe, mainly in France and Italy, and where Israel was concerned, I had to rely either on my own impressions, intuitions, and personal experiences or on the work of others. In either case, I was on unsteady ground and my perspective was necessarily limited. In one place the facts were missing, and in another their interpretation was insufficient. My curiosity failed to be satisfied, especially as quite early I began to have serious doubts about a number of accepted ideas sanctioned by Israeli historiography and social science, which are still very much part of the Weltanschauung of the Israeli cultural elite.

That is why one day at the end of the 1980s I decided to find out for myself. I wished to proceed in the only way that is really proper for a professional historian: to search the archives, to reread the texts, and to test social and political realities against the ideologies designed to guide policies. The study of Jewish society in Palestine (1904–48) is comparable to the study of any other society, and the methods of investigation should be the same whether one is writing the history of the twentieth century or of more distant periods. To analyze social and political realities, one has to give priority to the raw material of the period and not to the eyewitnesses' memories of it. Those who take part in unfolding events often have an unfortunate tendency to wax sentimental about their far-off youth and to embellish the realities of those years. Memory is not only a filter; it also has a regrettable way of reflecting the needs of the present.

Another unfortunate aspect of traditional Israeli historiography is the damage caused by the prevailing separation in universities of Jewish history from general history. The view that Jewish history is a separate area of study has already had many negative results, but in twentieth- century history and especially the history of Zionism, its consequences have been truly appalling. Very often this approach has paralyzed any real critical sense and any effort at comparative analysis, has perpetuated myths flattering to Israel's collective identity, and has led many historians of Zionism to lock themselves up in an intellectual ghetto where there are no means of comparison or criteria of universal validity. Such exclusiveness can lead to ignorance. When the subject of the labor movement is touched on, emotional blindness is added to other weaknesses.

But even professional historians cannot profess absolute detachment. Even if they wanted to, it would not be possible to attain this. But they at least have the duty to offer the reader a well-made piece of work. They know they have to maintain a certain distance, suppress their emotions, look with skepticism at even the most accepted ideas, and constantly scrutinize the most unquestioned certainties. This is often a thankless task, and it will not please everyone. It will certainly not please those who feel an understandable nostalgia about a period that they have come to look upon as a golden age and who consider themselves the best interpreters of their own story.

Others—for example, the children and grandchildren of the pioneering elite whose ideas and deeds are examined here, or all those who regard themselves as the jealous custodians of the national myths, group portraits, and statues of the founders—may look upon the scholar who brings to light unpleasant truths, who challenges the myth and comes up with unorthodox interpretations, as a fly in the ointment or even an enemy of the people. This phenomenon is not unique to Israeli society; it is also very common in Europe. In Europe as well the emotion-laden memories of some people and a certain apologetic historiography constantly try to distort the perception of a past that is ever present.

Despite these strong defensive reactions, and sometimes precisely because of them, the historiographical and sociological debate in Israel in recent years has assumed unprecedented proportions. A distance of some fifty years was needed to examine the relationship of the Yishuv (the Jewish community in Palestine) to the Holocaust, the War of Independence, the creation of the problem of the Arab refugees, or the social differences in Jewish Palestine with sufficient detachment. These subjects still carry a heavy emotional charge, but they are no longer taboo. Israel is growing up and learning to look at itself and its past.

The debate for and against people who are described by themselves and others, whether in a positive or a negative sense, as the "new historians" or the "critical sociologists" is already part of the Israeli cultural discourse.[1] An ambiguous epithet is applied to both these groups: they are called revisionists by those for whom this concept is a way of lashing out at any new approach, any refusal to toe the line and faithfully repeat accepted formulas. There are some who prefer to forget that all valid historiography is anticonservative and revisionist because it reevaluates existing sources or searches for new ones. Progress in scholarship always depends on criticism and pitting oneself against existing scholarship, and thus automatically gives rise to new interpretations. Without successive generations of revisionists, the history of Rome would still be written from the perspective of Theodor Mommsen, we would still see twentieth-century Germany through the eyes of Friedrich Meinecke, Italian fascism would be studied through the lenses of Benedetto Croce, and Alphonse Aulard would to this day be our only guide to the French Revolution. Thus, all true scholars ipso facto became revisionists as soon as, by virtue of their critical approach, they made a significant contribution of their own. They themselves were soon the object of the next revision and were liable to find themselves part of a new conservative camp. Revisionism is a natural process and is so self-evident a phenomenon that there would be no point in drawing attention to it here if recent progress in this field had not produced a sense of crisis among broad segments of the Israeli intellectual establishment.

In contemporary Israel, as in Germany, Italy, and France, when problems connected with the more complex aspects of the history of the twentieth century come up for discussion, the historiographical debate assumes a particularly intense tone. In Israel the reason is that this academic debate merges with the public debate on the future of Israeli society. Thus, the Israeli intellectual establishment tends to blur the distinction between two totally different phenomena: the progress of scholarship and the emergence of what are called post-Zionist tendencies. This lack of clarity in many ways is a consequence of the fact that the primary objectives of Zionism have been so splendidly achieved and that the state of Israel has already existed for half a century.

Broad segments of the Israeli political and cultural establishment have a great fear that any criticism of the ideas that have been commonly accepted over a long period, whether positivistic, relativistic, or purely political and ideological, will undermine the basis of Zionism. In this connection, I should explain that post-Zionism derives from two completely different sources: first, the debate about Jewish identity and the character of the future Israeli society (this takes place against a background of struggle over the future of the territories conquered in 1967), and second, the appearance of postmodernist tendencies in Israeli society. This is not the place to discuss the virtues and weaknesses of postmodernism and its connection with post-Zionism. Here I will only say that because postmodernist tendencies stress cultural pluralism and the rights of minorities, they are often regarded as hostile to the classical concept of Israel as the state of the Jewish people and as a melting pot in which the Jews lose their various former identities and gain a single new identity. Moreover, placing the emphasis on minorities' rights immediately raises the problem of the Israeli Arabs, constituting about 20 percent of the population, and brings up the question of the Jewishness of Israel and the place of religion and tradition in Israel's national identity in the coming generations. In addition, relativistic values undoubtedly have a very central position in postmodernism, and in its extreme form this trend tends to blur the basic distinction between causes and effects, facts and values. All this is liable to arouse understandable fears among those who are unshakably attached to the total and unquestioning worldview of the founders and who wish to base Zionism on the eternal historical right of the Jewish people to Eretz Israel.

There can be no greater error than to associate scholars' questioning of accepted ideas about Jewish nationalism, Jewish socialism, or the place of universal values in the Jewish national movement with post-Zionism. Similarly, there can be no greater distortion than to view intellectual developments deriving from the very existence of the state of Israel as undermining its moral foundations. And nothing could be more erroneous than to regard all attempts to make Israeli society an open, liberal, and secular society as an attack on Zionist objectives.

This represents the real focus of the cultural and political controversy in Israeli society. The state of Israel is a classical product of modern nationalism as it materialized in Eastern Europe and the Third World. After a long and difficult struggle, the nation was able to acquire a state. But during the years of struggle to set up the state and defend it—a struggle that has not yet ended—Israeli society refused to consider the significance of the necessary changes that would take place after independence. The normalization sought by the first pioneers who came to settle the land, apart from some isolated ideological groups, was conceived first in terms of power. The "new Jew" was a fighter and conqueror who won the land through hard work, boundless self-sacrifice, and the force of arms. Only a few people understood that the founding of Israel would constitute a revolution whose consequences would be felt only after a long period. Now the bill has to be paid: only in our time has the realization begun to penetrate Israeli consciousness that a liberal and free state worthy of the name is not only a military, economic, and technological power structure that can provide the nation with the means to ensure its security and achieve its objectives. It is also a framework in which one can decide which way of life is most suitable, what political and social system is most desirable: one in which the state is merely the operative arm of a cultural-religious community, or one in which it is based on the concept of citizenship and the idea bequeathed by the French Revolution that all those living within the boundaries of a state are free individuals and citizens with equal rights.

Those who wish Israel to be a truly liberal state or Israeli society to be open must recognize the fact that liberalism derives from the initial attempt, in the seventeenth century, to separate religion from politics. A liberal state can be only a secular state, a state in which the concept of citizenship lies at the center of collective existence. Kant and the "philosophes" of the French Enlightenment have taught us that the only free and open society is one that recognizes the independence of reason and the autonomy of the individual. Reason determines the frontiers of knowledge, and reason, not religion, should form the basis of our moral and political decisions. Kant and Rousseau believed that human will is the source of morality, so that the only laws one needs to obey are those one has created. Thus, a state cannot be liberal as long as religion plays a major role in governing society and politics, or as long as the state is defined as the operative arm of the nation, conceived as a living organism, a unique creation, one of a kind.

Finally, I have tried to approach the subject of the formative years of the state of Israel with the same degree of detachment that I have devoted to the treatment of European history in the past. I do not claim to offer my readers a work free of all value judgments. Certainly not! If this were a criterion for producing scholarly works, I would have sought another career long ago. My predilections are clearly expressed in these pages, but I have done all I can to keep my intellectual views separate from the historical analysis.

I started writing this book in 1991–92, when I was a fellow at the Woodrow Wilson Center in Washington, D.C. I thank the director of the center, Charles Blitzer, and his colleagues for the opportunity of working at this outstanding research institute.

Before and after my stay in the United States, and until the book was published, the Leonard Davis Institute and the Levi Eshkol Center of the Hebrew University and the Israeli branch of the Ford Foundation (Israel Foundation Trustees) provided me with the financial assistance necessary for me to complete my research. The staff of the Central Zionist Archives in Jerusalem, of the Labor Movement (Histadrut) Archives in Tel Aviv, and of the Archives of the Labor Party (Mapai, in the period that concerns us) at Beit Berl in Zofit were extremely helpful, as was the staff of the National Library in Jerusalem and the University Library on Mount Scopus. The help of my students Gal Betzer, Anna Bosheri, Ayelet Levy, and Dan Tadmor was equally invaluable. My special thanks are due, finally, to my editor at Princeton University Press, Brigitta van Rheinberg, for her warm support and advice, to David Maisel for an intelligent translation, and to Dalia Geffen for her skillful, careful copyediting.

A Note on the Transliteration of Hebrew Names and the Translation of Hebrew Book Titles

There are various ways to transliterate Hebrew terms into other languages—especially Hebrew names. Transliteration into English takes pronunciation into account, but there are no general rules. Moreover, usages have sprung up over the years that have become entrenched, although they do not always correspond to the rules that are nevertheless accepted.

First names present a special problem. Various people spell, or have spelled, the same name in different ways. Weizmann and Arlosoroff have spelled their first name as CHAIM, while many other people, including Israeli scholars whose works are mentioned in this book—Barkai or Golan, for instance—spell it as HAIM. I choose to write YOSEF HAIM BRENNER, although Brenner's Israeli publisher, Dvir, spells it JOSEFH CHAYIM; and Arthur Herzberg, in his anthology *The Zionist Idea* (New York: Atheneum, 1977) prefers JOSEPH HAYYIM. Syrkin's first name is spelled equally often as NAHMAN or as NACHMAN, as his daughter spells it in her biography of her father. The same problem exists with such names as NAHUM and NACHUM, ISRAEL and YISRAEL, AARON and AHARON, as well as many others. It can also happen that the same name appears in different forms because the owner himself is inconsistent. And finally, inconsistencies themselves are common in writing.

Translating titles of books written in Hebrew that have not been translated into English poses another problem. These books include those that have been given English titles by the Israeli publisher for commercial reasons or for the purpose of cataloguing in foreign libraries. Such titles are sometimes completely different from the original ones. A case in point is a book by historian Anita Shapira, the translation of whose Hebrew title would be *Going toward the Horizon* (Tel Aviv: Am Oved, 1989), but which the publisher called *Visions in Conflict*. In this case, as in others, I have preferred to give the translation of the original Hebrew title, which is more expressive of the nature of the book than its English alternative.

THE FOUNDING MYTHS OF ISRAEL

Introduction

Nationalism, Socialism, and Nationalist Socialism

IN THIS BOOK I seek to examine the nature of the ideology that guided the central stream of the labor movement in the process of nation-building and to investigate how it met the challenge of realizing its aims. In many respects, the purpose of the book is to analyze the way in which the ideology and actions of the labor movement molded the basic principles of Jewish society in Palestine (the Yishuv) and its patterns of development in the period before the War of Independence (1948–49). In this sense, this book is a study of the intellectual, moral, and ideological foundations of present-day Israel and a reflection on its future.

Speaking of the Israeli model of nation-building, however, raises a question of general significance: is a national movement whose aim is a cultural, moral, and political revolution, and whose values are particularistic, capable of coexisting with the universal values of socialism? The leaders and ideologists of the labor movement used to answer this question unhesitatingly in the affirmative. They maintained that the movement's synthesis of socialism and nationalism was its main historical achievement and its claim to uniqueness among labor movements. From the beginning of their political careers, the founders persistently claimed that in Eretz Israel (Palestine) the aims of nationalism and socialism were identical, and that they complemented and supported one another.

In this book I examine this position and counter a number of current opinions. I ask whether a unique synthesis of socialism and nationalism was ever achieved in Palestine; I also examine a more complex and difficult problem, namely, whether the founders actually intended to create an alternative to bourgeois society, or whether very early on they realized that the two objectives were incompatible, and therefore, from the beginning, they renounced the social objective. Was equality a genuine goal, however long-term, or was it only a mobilizing myth, perhaps a convenient alibi that sometimes permitted the movement to avoid grappling with the contradiction between socialism and nationalism? Here I question one of the founding myths of Israeli society and its national epic.

Another fundamental question concerns the nature of Jewish nationalism as understood and developed by the founders. Was the nationalism of the labor movement and its practical expression, the pioneering ideology of conquering the land—first by means of a Jewish presence and Jewish labor and later by force, if necessary—in any way special? Did it have a universalistic, humanistic, and rationalistic basis that distinguished it from the nationalism flourishing in Eastern Europe, where Zionism originated, or was Labor Zionism simply one of the many variations of the historical, ethnic, and religious brands of European nationalism? Did it ever have the potential to overcome the religious substance of Jewish nationalism and thus establish a liberal, secular, and open society, at peace with itself and its neighbors?

For the sake of brevity and convenience, I use the term *labor movement* to refer to the central stream of the Histadrut (the General Federation of Jewish Workers in Eretz Israel), and not to the whole movement. The labor movement consisted of two parties—Ahdut Ha'avoda (United Labor) and Hapo'el Hatza'ir (Young Worker)—which in 1920 founded the Histadrut as a comprehensive social, political, and economic organization, gave it its purpose, and enjoyed unchallenged domination of it until these two parties fused in 1930 within the framework of Mapai, the Workers' Party of Eretz Israel. The defection of Hakibbutz Hameuhad (the United Kibbutz Movement) and the urban Faction B in 1944 and the establishment of a new political party, which symbolically adopted the name Ahdut Ha'avoda and in 1946 merged with the small left-wing party Po'alei Tzion (Workers of Zion), did not really change the balance of forces and the general lines of development. Similarly, the existence of the Marxist Hashomer Hatza'ir (Young Watchman) did not diminish the dominance of Mapai in the Histadrut and in the Yishuv, the Jewish community of Palestine. Likewise, the establishment in 1948 of a unified Mapam (United Workers' Party), comprising the "new" Ahdut Ha'avoda–Po'alei Tzion and Hashomer Hatza'ir, did not have significant effects on the power relationships in the labor movement. Mapai controlled the movement and molded it in its image. The founding of the Labor Party in 1968—the result of the tripartite union of Mapai; Ahdut Ha'avoda, which in 1954 had split from Mapam; and Rafi, the Ben-Gurion group that in 1965 broke off from Mapai—and the creation in 1969 of the common front with Mapam (Maarach) only had the effect of demonstrating even more clearly the hegemony of the central ideological force, which had persisted for nearly seventy-five years.

Every society is ruled by an elite. In this book I hope to reconstruct the saga of the labor elite and its long march toward a nation-state.

Israeli society was molded and assumed its present form in the decisive years of the British mandate. At the end of the 1920s, a few years before they gained official control of the Zionist movement, the labor elite had already acquired a position of unquestionable moral, social, and cultural authority in the Yishuv. In 1933 Mapai became the dominant party in the Zionist movement: in the elections to the Zionist Congress, it received 44 percent of the vote. Two years later Ben-Gurion became chairman of the Zionist Executive and of the Jewish Agency's Executive. From that point on the labor movement provided Israeli society with such a strong model of development that even after its fall from power in 1977 no real changes occurred in the economic, cultural, and social life of Israel. After more than forty years of continuous political activity, the original leaders of the movement founded the state of Israel and shaped its first twenty years. Representatives of the original and now expanded nucleus of the movement, members of the Second Aliyah (the immigration wave of 1904–14) and the Third Aliyah (1919–23), fixed its objectives, laid its organizational foundations, and built its political and economic power structures. They both formulated its ideology and put it into practice themselves. The theorists were also political leaders who controlled the political, social, and economic institutions they had set up. In the democratic world, this phenomenon was unprecedented both in its depth and in its continuity.

Thus, it is particularly significant that at the end of these long years of dominance a movement that claimed to be socialist had not created a society that was special in any way. There was no more justice or equality there than in Western Europe, differences in standard of living were just as pronounced, and there was no special attempt to improve the lot of the disadvantaged. An informality in personal relations and other characteristics typical of an immigrant society lacking class consciousness and a traditional elite could not hide the dry statistics that accurately reflected wide differences in standards of living.

Moreover, by 1977 not only was Israeli society not different from any other developed society, but its social policies lagged far behind those in France or Britain under the Labour government. In secondary and higher education, in the advancement of the poorer classes, and in the provision of assistance to the needy and the "nonproductive" elements of society, Israel in the first twenty-five years of its existence was guilty of conscious neglect, continuing the policies that the same elite had maintained in the days of the Yishuv. Secondary education, a prerequisite of upward mobility in a modern society, was expensive and inaccessible to large numbers of laborers, salaried employees, artisans, shopkeepers, and new immigrants. Until the revolt of the Black Panthers in the early 1970s, Israel did not have any social policies at all. This was not due to lack of sensitivity but derived from ideology.

The Third Aliyah was the only immigration wave with a revolutionary potential, but this potential was never realized, and its members adopted the conceptual outlook of their predecessors. Members of the Gdud Ha'avoda (the Labor Corps, see chapter 4), an original creation of the Third Aliyah, who refused to submit to the modes of thought and principles of the old leaders of the movement were thrust aside, abandoned politics, or left the country.

However, the generation of the War of Independence proved to be conformist and unoriginal. None of its leaders, writers, poets, and fighters had anything important to add to the heritage of the Second Aliyah. Where ideology was concerned, this was a sterile generation. Due to this ideological stagnation and continued attachment to the Second Aliyah's aims, Ben-Gurion's Mapai, even though it led the Jews of Palestine in their War of Independence, did not effect any social changes; nor had it any intention of doing so. Moreover, the lack of universal values explains the moral, political, and intellectual paralysis of the Labor Party, which was founded immediately after the great victory in the Six-Day War of June 1967.

Since independence, Israeli society has been engaged in a struggle over the future of the territories conquered in June 1967. If we wish to understand why Israelis have not yet succeeded in ending their hundred years' war with the Arabs, in drafting a liberal constitution and a bill of rights, we must examine the world of the founders and their legacy. The historical struggle between the labor movement and the revisionist Right was a struggle over the methods of implementing national objectives, not over the objectives themselves. It was a struggle for the control of a society which Ben-Gurion's Mapai, by exploiting the ideological polarization of the interwar period, turned into a war between good and evil. Indeed, the nationalist ideology of the Jewish labor movement was to conquer as much land as possible.

Moreover, under the auspices of the mandatory government, a free-market economy flourished in Palestine, which was a paradise for capitalists, businessmen, and members of the liberal professions. This policy included an absence of direct taxation of income and large-scale importation of private capital (75 percent of the capital that entered Jewish Palestine between the two world wars was private). The entire Zionist movement, including the labor movement under the leadership of Mapai, supported this policy enthusiastically for national reasons: those who favored the Jews' immigration sought economic development at any price. No social consideration was allowed to stand in the way of national interests. Due to this policy, promoted by Mapai, the Jewish Yishuv of the 1930s became a typical bourgeois society, with significant social and economic discrepancies.

I contend that the inability of the labor movement under the leadership of its founders and immediate successors to curb aspirations to territorial expansion, as well as its failure to build a more egalitarian society, was not due to any objective conditions or circumstances beyond its control. These developments were the result of a conscious ideological choice made at the beginning and clearly expressed in the doctrine of "constructive socialism." Constructive socialism is generally regarded as the labor movement's great social and ideological achievement, a unique and original product, the outstanding expression of the special needs and conditions of the country. But in reality, far from being unique, constructive socialism was merely an Eretz Israeli version of nationalist socialism.

To avoid any misunderstanding or confusion, I have used the term *nationalist socialism* despite the fact that it does not figure in an American dictionary, where the more usual term *national socialism* is preferred. But *national socialism*, which was commonly used at the beginning of the twentieth century, has been contaminated by its association with the Nazis. However, the adjective *nationalist*, although not traditionally used, in its strict sense describes one of the variants of socialism accurately. There is a nationalist socialism just as there is a democratic or revisionistic socialism, often known as social democracy. Here let us remember that until the second half of the twentieth century, European social democracy remained faithful to the basic premises of Marxism. Similarly, in contrast to the so-called utopian socialism, Marxist socialism was also known in the old communist circles as scientific socialism. Later we shall see that Chaim Arlosoroff (1899–1933), one of the major leaders and theoreticians of the Zionist labor movement, strongly promoted the idea that Jewish socialism cannot be anything but national.

Nationalist socialism, properly understood, appeared in Europe in the last years of the nineteenth century and the beginning of the twentieth as an alternative to both Marxism and liberalism. In contrast with social democracy, this ideology of national unity par excellence was the product of an encounter between anti-Marxist and antireformist tendencies in socialism on one hand and ethnic, cultural, and religious nationalism on the other. The uniqueness of European nationalist socialism, whose origins can be traced to the pre-Marxist socialism of Proudhon, in relation to all other types of socialism, lay in one essential point: its acceptance of the principle of the nation's primacy and its subjection of the values of socialism to the service of the nation. In this way, socialism lost its universal significance and became an essential tool in the process of building the nation-state. Thus, the universal values of socialism were subordinated to the particularistic values of nationalism. In practice, this was expressed by a total rejection of the concept of class warfare and by the claim of transcending social contradictions for the benefit of the collectivity as a whole. This form of socialism preached the organic unity of the nation and the mobilization of all classes of society for the achievement of national objectives. According to the theory, this process was to be led by natural elites, whose membership was determined not by class, origin, or educational qualifications but by sentiment, dedication, and a readiness to make sacrifices for all. Nationalist socialism quite naturally disliked people with large fortunes, the spoiled aristocracy, and all those to whom money came easily and who could allow themselves to be idle. It lashed out mercilessly at the bourgeoisie whose money moved from one financial center to another and whose checkbook, close to its heart, served as its identity card. In contrast with all these, nationalist socialism presented the working man with both feet firmly planted on the soil of his native country—the farmer, whose horizons are restricted to the piece of land he tills, the bourgeois, who runs his own enterprise, and the industrial worker: the rich and poor who contribute the sweat of their brow, their talents, and their money to increasing the collective wealth.

According to this school of thought, the only real social distinction is between the worker and the person who does not work, that is, the "parasite." These social categories replaced the Marxist division of society into a class that owns the means of production and a class that does not. This form of socialism was careful to speak not of "proletarians" but of "workers," and to distinguish not between the proletariat and the bourgeoisie but between "producers" and "parasites." Nationalist socialism taught that all kinds of workers represented national interests; they were the heart of the nation, and their welfare was also the welfare of the nation. Thus, workers standing beside the production line and the owners of the industrial enterprise were equally "producers." Similarly, nationalist socialism distinguished between the "positive" bourgeois, the producer, and the "parasitic" bourgeois, between "productive" capital and "parasitic" capital, between capital that creates employment and adds to the economic strength of society and speculative capital, capital that enriches only its owners without producing collective wealth. So we see that nationalist socialism fostered a cult of work and productive effort of every kind. All workers were regarded as deserving of protection from the incursion of foreigners. Nationalist socialism wished to close its country's borders to foreign labor, and also to foreign capital when it competed with national capital, and considered the right to work as the right of every member of the nation. Nationalist socialism sought to manifest a natural solidarity between productive national wealth and the worker, between the owners of capital, who provide jobs, and the native-born workers. This was a partnership of interests, but also an ideological partnership: all social classes were to unite in an effort to increase national wealth. All had to contribute to the capability of their society to compete against other nations. According to nationalist socialism, the fate of each social group was organically linked to that of all other classes, and all members of the nation were responsible for one another. Class warfare was obviously out of the question.

Indeed, nationalist socialism was based on the idea of the nation as a cultural, historical, and biological unit, or, figuratively, an extended family. The individual was regarded as an organic part of the whole, and the whole took precedence over the individual. The blood ties and cultural ties linking members of the nation, their partnership in the total national effort, took precedence over the position of the individual in the production system. To ensure the future of the nation and to protect it against the forces threatening to undermine it, it was necessary to manifest its inner unity and to mobilize all classes against the two great dangers with which the nation is faced in the modern world: liberalism and Marxism in its various forms. Liberalism views society as a collection of individuals forever struggling for a place in the sun, a sort of open market in which the sole driving force is personal gain. Marxism views society as a place of conflict between hostile classes, groups driven by the inner logic of the capitalist system to fight one another relentlessly. The originality of nationalist socialism was that it refused to accept society as a theater of war. It also refused to contemplate any intermediate or partial solutions. Nationalist socialism rejected neo-Kantian reformism, out of which democratic socialism developed; it rejected Austro-Marxism, which tried to deal with the national question within the Marxist framework; and it also rejected attempts to bring Marxist economic thinking in line with technological and scientific developments at the beginning of the century. Nationalist socialism repudiated all this mighty intellectual effort for one basic reason: all schools of thought involved in it belonged to a conceptual universe rooted in the principle of class warfare.

However, at the same time as it denied class warfare, nationalist socialism actively favored a solution to the social problem. No one who had the nation's future at heart, it claimed, could remain indifferent when large segments of the national body were sunk in poverty and degradation or when one segment of society existed through the exploitation of another, and it made no difference whether the exploiters constituted a majority or a minority. Although nationalist socialism detested the owners of fortunes and abhorred uncreative, egoistic, and speculative capital, it never objected to private capital as such. If capitalists did not sink their money in production, contribute to the enrichment of society, or employ workers, they were incorrigible parasites, but the fault lay with unproductive capitalists, not private capital itself. When various forms of private capital were productively invested in enterprises serving national objectives, they fulfilled their purpose and were not to be touched. When, however, capital served only the interests of its owners, when the capitalists were motivated only by personal gain, the well-being of the community required that the capitalists be disciplined and brought under control. Thus, the aim of nationalist socialism was not the socialization of the means of production, and its attitude to private capital was solely functional. In the same vein the attitude of nationalist socialism to the individual was always based on the following criterion: the benefits he or she was able to confer on the various strata of the national community. These principles of nationalist socialism were the main, if not the only, features of the constructive socialism of Ahdut Ha'avoda and later Mapai.

From its inception, the rise of nationalist socialism resulted from three concurrent and partly overlapping phenomena: the retreat from Marxism, the crisis of liberalism, and the emergence of organic nationalism as a social force that swept away the masses. Thus, nationalist socialism was, by its very nature, hostile to democratic socialism. Democratic socialism renounced the prospect of social revolution in the foreseeable future, but it did not abandon the Marxist conceptual framework and did not adopt an order of priorities in which national objectives were given first place. Similarly, democratic socialism regarded itself as the heir to liberalism and not its grave digger, and it considered democracy a positive value in itself. Finally, democratic socialism opposed tribal nationalism, which emerged as the antithesis of the liberal nationalism of the beginning of the nineteenth century, and refused to accept its worldview, which contradicted the historical philosophy of Marxism.

Marxism was the heir to the rationalism of the eighteenth century, and Marx can be regarded as the last philosopher of the Enlightenment. The new nationalism, however, constituted a total reaction to the principles of the eighteenth century. Tribal or organic nationalism swept over all of Europe, and by the end of the nineteenth century it had supplanted liberal nationalism, based on the principles of the Enlightenment and French Revolution. The rise of organic nationalism was a pan-European phenomenon, and it found expression not only in Germany, where unification had come very late, but also in France, the oldest and best-established nation-state on the European continent. The new nationalism was a nationalism of "blood and soil," a cultural, historical, and, finally, biological nationalism. This form of nationalism undermined the foundations of liberalism and offered a total alternative. It fomented anti-Semitism in Western Europe and transformed the Dreyfus Affair from an ordinary trial for treason into a world drama. Organic nationalism condemned liberalism on moral, intellectual, and political grounds; for many people, it symbolized the bankruptcy of the Enlightenment. In Central and Eastern Europe, however, in the multinational empires, this cultural and biological nationalism reflected the will to revival of downtrodden peoples—peoples whose political independence had been taken away from them and whose cultural identity had in many cases been suppressed.

But the two types of nationalism did not always develop in reaction to each other; their growth was often parallel, and their degree of success depended on cultural, social, and political conditions. These conditions were radically different in Western Europe and in the eastern part of the continent. In Western Europe nationalism appeared first as a political and legal phenomenon. The nation came into being through a long process of unification of populations, which were very different in their ethnic origins, cultural identities, languages, and religions.

To the east of the River Rhine, however, the criteria for belonging to a nation were not political but cultural, linguistic, ethnic, and religious. German, Polish, Romanian, Slovakian, Serbian, and Ukrainian identities came into being not as the expression of an allegiance to a single independent authority but as the result of religion, language, and culture, which were very readily regarded as reflecting biological or racial differences. Here the nation preceded the state. The thought of Johann Gottfried von Herder was most relevant to Eastern Europe, not the teachings of Locke, Kant, Mill, or Marx. In particular Marxism, which deliberately ignored the national question, which it saw as a relic of the past that would vanish with the onset of modernization and industrialization, never penetrated beyond a thin layer of the intelligentsia. For the same reason, democratic socialism, which recognized the strength of tribal nationalism but refused to submit to it, was never really a force in Eastern Europe.

In Central and Eastern Europe the concept of citizenship lacked significance, and the idea of a civil society never carried the weight that it did in the west of the continent. Thus, liberal democracy was also unable to develop into a real force in that part of the world. In those regions the individual was never regarded as standing on his or her own and as having an intrinsic value; a person was never anything but an integral part of a national unit, without any possibility of choice, and the nation claimed absolute allegiance. Any other allegiance could be only secondary and necessarily subordinate to national objectives. The entire collective energy was directed to the attainment of these objectives, and the supremacy of particular values over universal ones was firmly established.

This was the historical and intellectual context in which the modern Jewish national movement came into being. Organic nationalism is far more relevant to its history than the revolutionary socialist movement. Zionism was born into a world of violent and vociferous nationalities, a world with no national or religious tolerance, a world in which the distinction between religion and nation, or between religion, society, and the state, was unknown and perhaps inconceivable. Such distinctions were luxuries that only the Western European societies could afford. In this respect the peoples of Eastern Europe were not dissimilar to those of the Near East at the beginning of the century: the struggle for national revival was paramount, and each nation knew that all its gains were necessarily achieved at the expense of other nations. This situation was regarded as the natural order of things. Thus, neither Marxism nor liberalism could really succeed in that part of the world. In fact, the opposite was the case: both Marxism and liberalism were considered a mortal danger to the nation. Both threatened to tear apart its fabric of ethnic and cultural unity. The rationalism of Marxism and of liberalism, the view of the individual as the final object of all social action which was common to Marxism and liberalism, the concept of class warfare which gave Marxism its meaning, or the principle of individual competition central to liberalism obviously menaced the very foundations of national identity.

That is why Marxism and liberalism stirred so strong an opposition in these areas. In the last decade of the nineteenth century, however, such an opposition also emerged in Western Europe and began to be a real force in

France, the land of the great revolution of 1789, the land of the rights of man, and the home of the most progressive liberal society on the continent. In the last decade of the nineteenth century it became apparent that in French society too there were forces that rejected the individualistic and rationalistic concept of the nation. If the nationalism of "blood and soil" had begun to demonstrate its power even in France, what could be expected in Eastern Europe? The fact that Zionism appeared at a time when the universal and humanist principles of the national movements, as a distant legacy of the eighteenth-century revolutions, had been shattered even in Western Europe is tremendously important. From the point of view of the educated and the assimilated, Zionism was a natural response to the failure of liberalism as a rational and antihistorical system, to its inability to neutralize tribal nationalism, or at least to keep it within reasonable bounds. The Dreyfus Affair dramatically highlighted the crisis of liberalism and of modernity. Where the Jewish people were concerned, the Dreyfus Affair placed an enormous question mark over the future of emancipation in Europe. In the liberal circles to which Theodor Herzl (1860–1904) and Max Nordau (1849–1923) belonged, France was not only the accepted model of a liberal society but also an example of future developments in Central and Eastern Europe. That was why this rebellion against modernity shocked them so profoundly and brought them to such radical conclusions. Herzl represented that segment of the Jewish intelligentsia that looked to the West, and not only hoped for emancipation's success but was prepared to pay full price for it. That price, as we know, included the obliteration of Jewish national identity.

This, however, was not the situation of Eastern Europe, where the great majority of the Jewish people lived. In the Russian empire, which was the Second Aliyah's point of origin, in Austrian Galicia, and in other parts of the two multinational empires, emancipation was only just beginning. But, already at that early stage, the Jewish intelligentsia realized that emancipation's underlying principle presented the Jewish people with an entirely new challenge. For the first time in their history, Eastern European Jews, faced a real danger to their collective identity. For the first time there was the possibility that the future of the Jewish people depended on each individual's personal decision. Liberal individualism suddenly appeared as a real threat to the continued Jewish people's existence as a homogenous and autonomous unit.

Thus, Zionism was not only a reaction to increasing insecurity but also a Herderian, not to say tribal, response to the challenge of emancipation. For David Ben-Gurion (1886–1973), Zionism was not only an answer to the Jews' distress but a solution to the loss of identity that threatened the Jewish people.[1] There is no doubt that in a most basic manner, Zionism came into being because of the breakdown of security in the Pale of Settlement, the gradual destruction of the Jewish economic infrastructure, and the rise of anti-Semitism in Western Europe. But until the beginning of the 1920s, there was a simpler and easier solution to pogroms and economic discrimination: emigration to the United States. And, in fact, among the masses of Jews who left Eastern Europe in the thirty or forty years prior to the passing of the American immigration laws in 1922, only about 1 percent or slightly fewer came to Palestine. For this minute minority, a pioneering elite in all respects, Zionism was more than an attempt to save themselves or their possessions; it was a response to the degeneracy with which the processes of modernization threatened Jewish society. Moreover, ideological Zionism was, from the beginning, the preoccupation of a minority, which understood the Jewish problem not in terms of physical existence and the provision of economic security but as an enterprise for rescuing the nation from the danger of collective annihilation. Only with the closing of the gates of the United States did Palestine become a land of immigration, although even then it was not an entirely ordinary land of immigration. Even someone who had no choice but to land on the shores of Jaffa and Tel Aviv was viewed as fulfilling a national mission.

In this sense, Dan Horowitz and Moshe Lissak's assertion that Israeli society "sprang up as a result of ideology" and that "immigration to the country was motivated by ideology" is perfectly true.[2] But the creation of Israeli society was also due to the existential necessity of rescuing European Jews from destruction. The first three waves of immigration were a consequence of an ideological decision, but the number of immigrants and of those who remained was small. A Jewish society capable of standing on its own feet would never have come into being in Palestine if the first two waves of mass immigration had not occurred in the 1920s and 1930s. The Polish Fourth Aliyah (1924–26) and the German Fifth Aliyah (1933–39) were definitely motivated by distress, and it was these that laid the true infrastructure of Israeli society. These waves of immigration provided the necessary foundation for building the Jewish state and enabled the Jewish Yishuv to conquer the country. Zionism found its moral justification in existential necessity. The fact that Palestine was the only place in the world to which European Jews could escape in the 1930s and 1940s gave the Yishuv a moral credibility and political support without which the state of Israel may not have come into being. From the time the Nazis came to power until the wave of immigration from the former Soviet Union in the 1990s, Palestine and later Israel were first a place of refuge. Thus, even if Israeli society was largely an ideological creation,[3] one should not forget that it sprang up to an equal extent as a result of the upheavals that took place and are still taking place in Europe.

But even more important, all national movements of the last two hundred years were nurtured by norms and values that over time were translated into concrete political categories. There was never a national movement that did not try to realize "ideological" aims: the definition of national identity in cultural and historical terms, self-rule as a step toward independence, the realization of independence, and the founding of a nation-state. In this respect Zionism was not unique. The unification and independence of Italy and Germany, the long war of the Poles—full of revolts with no chance of success, from the division of Poland into three parts at the end of the eighteenth century until their resurrection at the end of the First World War— and the struggles of the Slovaks, the Czechs, the Ukrainians, and the Baltic peoples resulted from the kind of ideological impetus that led to the growth of the Jewish national movement. Israel is a society in which a national consolidation and a sense of ethnic, religious, and cultural particularity created by a common history preceded the realization of independence and the construction of a national state. In this respect Israel is not dissimilar to other states in Central and Eastern Europe.

Horowitz and Lissak were amazed by the fact that "the Hebrew language became a living tongue through deliberate nurturing, the result of an ideological decision."[4] But if there is anything special about that, it is the scale and depth of the operation rather than its principle. The languages of the peoples of Central and Eastern Europe—especially the smallest among them—also had to be nurtured through an ideological decision after long periods of political and cultural oppression, when they had degenerated into the languages of the masses of ignorant peasants and the urban poor. The languages of culture in multinational empires were German and Russian, and among the elite French was also common. At the end of the eighteenth century even German needed ideological nurturing; Herder, the progenitor of cultural rebirth as the basis of national rebirth, viewed language as a medium through which people become conscious of their inner selves and can enter into communion with their ancestors. Thus they can not only take part in the working of the ancestral mind but perpetuate and enrich the thoughts and feelings of past generations for the benefit of posterity. In this way language embodies the living manifestations of historical continuity and is the expression of the "spirit of the people." Herder encouraged the conquered peoples on the shores of the Baltic and in the inner regions of Central and Eastern Europe to revive their original languages and to make them languages of culture once again. The local elites, from Riga and Lvov to Prague, were enjoined to speak to their children in their national tongues. Manifestations of this kind, which accompanied the activities of the "defenders of the language" in Tel Aviv in the days of the Yishuv, had not been unusual in regions of the Austrian empire two or three decades earlier.

The same applied to what Horowitz and Lissak saw was special for the Zionists. "Ideological commitment," they wrote, "encouraged the tendency to self-sufficiency of the Jewish Yishuv in Eretz Israel to the point that it became an autonomous social framework."[5] The question must be asked: has there ever been a national movement in which the aspiration to self-sufficiency was not a declared aim? Can there be a national movement whose objective is not to create an autonomous social, cultural, and political framework? Is that not the very aim of nationalism as one of the main cultural and political manifestations of the last two hundred years?

The kind of national and cultural unity that distinguished the Yishuv was not, after all, dissimilar to the one found among other peoples engaged in a daily struggle of defending their collective identity and existence. The degree of discipline, conformism, and readiness to shoulder burdens and make sacrifices resembled what exists in developed societies in a state of war. Similarly, the extent of evasion of the burden of struggling for independence was not very different from similar situations in other places. Obviously, this does not detract from the importance of the enterprise or from its historical significance. Undoubtedly, unless the founders had been equipped with very sharp ideological tools from the beginning, they would not have been able to function. But the decisive point here is that the conceptual framework in which they operated was molded by historical, cultural, and romantic nationalism. Moreover, the veneer of secularism was very thin; beneath it, the burning embers of Jewish tradition continued to smolder. All over Central and Eastern Europe, the nation preceded the state, and ethnic units fought for their cultural survival and political independence. The Jewish national movement was similar. All other elements, beginning with socialism, were additions of secondary importance.

In this respect, the Jewish national movement was no worse than other national movements, no more aggressive or intolerant but also not much better. It did not develop a sense of ethnic superiority to the Arabs, and that in itself was a considerable achievement. From many points of view, one can say that the Arabs' weakness prevented Zionism from becoming a brutal movement, such as occurred in various European national movements. The Zionist movement went from achievement to achievement, from strength to strength, whereas the Arab national movement experienced continual defeats. But beyond the hypocritical rhetoric and naive phraseology, one basic fact stands out: the significance of Zionism was the conquest of land and the creation of an independent state through work and settlement, if possible, or by force, if necessary.

When nationalism is used for state-building, it is generally incompatible with liberal democratic values. In this respect, the Israeli version of nationalism was unusually moderate; nevertheless it failed to avoid an essential contradiction between universal values and the particular requirements of state-building by a nation engaged in a continuous struggle with another nation for the same piece of land.

As it began to be implanted in the country, Zionism developed the classic features of organic nationalism. The experience of contact with the soil, the desire to strike roots in it, and the need to lay a foundation for the legitimation of a return to the country led to a blossoming of the romantic, historical, and irrational aspects of nationalism. The cult of ancient history, from the conquest of Canaan to the rebellion against Rome, and the "sanctification" of places where Joshua Bin-Nun or the kings of Israel had fought were not very different from similar phenomena in the Czech, Polish, or German national movements of the nineteenth and twentieth centuries. The founders' love of the country and its landscapes, enthusiasm for its vegetation, and sense of the soil's holiness had a truly mystical quality, which was paralleled in Europe. The organic nationalism of Aaron David Gordon (1856–1922), chief theorist of Jewish nationalism in Palestine in the first two decades of the century, corresponded to the teachings of tribal nationalism in Europe. Gordon's thought dominated the ideology of the labor movement throughout its existence.

Such was the outlook of the founders of the labor movement, which also determined the future development of the state of Israel. The founders were true revolutionaries, but their revolution was national and cultural rather than social. The fact that the Second Aliyah took place in the shadow of the Russian Revolution of 1905, and the most organized and united group among its members was the small Jewish Russian Marxist party Po'alei Tzion (Workers of Zion), created the impression that this was a socialist aliyah, which came to build a new society in Eretz Israel. In reality, even at this early stage, the national element was dominant; it was no accident that the Marxists in Po'alei Tzion became progressively less influential and the disciples of Ber Borochov (1881–1917) ceased all large-scale activities, until the movement completely disappeared even before Britain had received its mandate over Palestine. In the tense atmosphere of building up the country, where the main preoccupation of Jewish workers was the "conquest of labor," in other words, the dispossession of Arab workers in order to take their place—and thus the establishment of a solid infrastructure for an autonomous Jewish existence—Po'alei Tzion was doomed. In this national struggle, a movement grounded in the universal values of socialism could not survive. The problem with Borochov's disciples was not their Marxist determinism but the universal, humanist nature of democratic socialism.

To a greater degree than liberalism, whose chances of succeeding in areas densely populated by Jews were slim, Marxism offered a conceptual system for the liberation of humankind from social, national, and religious oppression. There is no doubt that Marxism represented a more serious threat to the traditional Jewish frameworks of survival owing to their national and religious character. Outside the large cities of the Austrian empire, and in particular Vienna and Budapest, liberalism was a potential rather than an actual danger. But Marxism, in its various forms, recognized only social and economic categories, and this threatened the sense of identity of the Jewish masses in all areas where modernization had begun. Yet, at the same time, socialism, in the same way as liberalism, regarded assimilation as the true end of emancipation. Liberals and socialists saw both Jewish particularity and anti-Semitism as relics of an obscurantist past that was bound to disappear. They considered the suppression of ethnic and cultural barriers and the eradication of all forms of Jewish particularity as one of the great achievements of modernity. Progressive European circles regarded any attempt to define the Jew on any basis other than religion, which rightly belongs to the private sphere, as totally reactionary. A liberal true to his principles sees human beings as autonomous individuals free to define themselves as they wish, and a socialist places them according to their objective membership in a social category. Even if these distinctions were not always observed and were not realized with exactitude, the definition of Jews as a nation was contrary to the liberal and socialist outlook rooted in the rationalism of the eighteenth century.

Thus, the founders could regard liberalism and socialism based on Marxism only with suspicion. Moreover, among the Jewish masses, a bitter struggle was taking place between the earliest members of Po'alei Tzion and the Bund, which was rapidly gaining wide support among Jewish laborers. The anti-Zionist Marxist Bund reflected socialist teachings to the letter and accepted the principle that individuals are defined first by their place in the system of production and not by their national or religious affiliation. Borochov succeeded in creating a conceptual framework that provided an alternative to the exclusively class-related approach of the Bund, but even this brand of Marxism, adapted to the needs of Jewish nationalism, failed to take root in Palestine. Here, in the realities of the Third World, in conditions of technological, scientific, and economic backwardness on one hand and of incipient national struggles on the other, nationalist socialism flourished.

This form of socialism was far more realistic and far less optimistic than democratic socialism. It did not put its trust in long-term social and economic processes, and it did not have excessive faith in the masses. It did not have an idealistic view of the human being; its attitude to the individual was quite suspicious and its belief in democracy very limited. Nevertheless, this form of socialism believed in the capability of human beings, if properly led, to change the world through the exercise of will, faith, and determination. But, above all, nationalist socialism believed in power: political power, economic power, and organizational power. Ben-Gurion, likewise, did not rely on spontaneous action and believed far less in democracy than in elites' possessing political and economic power and imposing discipline on the masses through a strong and inclusive organization. This form of socialism sought to place the strength of the organized masses at the disposal of the nation.

That is why this form of socialism was so self-involved, so far from the universalism of democratic socialism. All the life force of the labor movement was directed toward the conquest of the country. Thus, a tribal view of the world grew in Palestine. Similarly, and in contrast with European democratic socialism, which always eschewed the use of political force, all the attention of the labor movement was focused on the attainment and exercise of power, not in order to bring about a social revolution, nor to realize universal values, but for the sake of a national revolution.

According to the traditional and largely labor-inspired historical and sociological interpretation, an interpretation I would not be too wrong in calling mythological, the founders believed that "a new society would now be constructed from top to bottom." Their aim, wrote Anita Shapira, was "truly and sincerely to build a socialist society in Eretz Israel."[6] Horowitz and Lissak support this view: "The labor movement . . . had an ideology of dual commitment—to the nation on one hand and to a class on the other."[7] About twenty years later, in an autobiography that appeared after his death, Horowitz wrote that "the hegemony of the labor movement . . . was intended to serve as a means to bring about social change."[8] In *Troubles in Utopia*, the sequel to their first book, *From the Yishuv to the State*, Horowitz and Lissak expressed a similar view and stated that the Histadrut, as well as being "a major tool for achieving national objectives," was also meant to be "the nucleus of a socialist society." Horowitz and Lissak stressed the "orientation toward the future in the social sphere, which was conspicuous in the ideology of the labor movement before the founding of the state."[9] In the same spirit, Anita Shapira entitled her collection of articles published in 1989 *Going toward the Horizon*.

This point requires particular emphasis. Eli Shaltiel also wrote that "the socialist element was as important and decisive in the Histadrut as its national element," but his interpretation is more complex. He acknowledges that when there was a "conflict of interests between the rights of the worker as a worker and his supreme national duty, the building of the land, the national task generally prevailed."[10] But the main problem here is not the interests of the wage earner. What fell victim to national objectives was not only the rights of the workers but the very aims of socialism as a comprehensive vision of a changed system of relationships between human beings.

When one studies the growth of the labor movement, it soon becomes clear that it was no accident that Ber Borochov's work, a unique attempt to incorporate nationalism into the conceptual framework of Marxism, had no real influence. Indeed, from the time of their arrival in Palestine, the people who were to become the prime creators of the Histadrut, the pillars of the labor movement, and the founders of the state of Israel were first and foremost nationalists. Some were purely nationalist and even violently anti-socialist: these were the founders of the Hapo'el Hatza'ir Party. Others claimed to be both socialists and nationalists but were fully conscious of the contradictions this dual allegiance implied. These were the "nonparty" people, who had a definite bias in favor of the nation's primacy. Among these was Berl Katznelson (1887–1944), who became the ideologist and the "conscience" of the labor movement in Palestine. Others, again, genuinely wished to reconcile their socialism and nationalism, a goal they did not consider impossible to achieve either in theory or in practice. These were the Borochovists of the Po'alei Tzion Party. Among these, two people stood out: Yitzhak Ben-Zvi (1884–1963), who became the second president of Israel, and David Ben-Gurion.

Ben-Gurion's membership in Po'alei Tzion was to only a very small extent a matter of conviction, and to a very large extent, if not entirely, due to the circumstances that prevailed in czarist-occupied Poland during the Russian Revolution of 1905 (more on this later). Ben-Gurion knew that a national movement does not function in a void and that Palestine was not an uninhabited territory. Even before he disembarked at Jaffa, he knew that these two facts made the Borochovistic teachings invalid. From the beginning he was convinced that settling Jews on the soil of Eretz Israel would mean a conquest of land and a rivalry with Arabs. He did not believe in the Borochovistic concept of working-class collaboration, which supposed that the Jews and Arabs in Palestine could attach at least as much importance to their common condition as workers as to their respective nationalisms. If Ben-Gurion was the first member of the Eretz Israel Po'alei Tzion to reach this conclusion, it was because he was only formally a member of the party. Ben-Gurion, however, was not the only member of Po'alei Tzion to realize that the universalistic nature of the Borochovist theory precluded it from taking root in Palestine.

That was why, at the end of the First World War, the Po'alei Tzion Party suffered a great reduction in support, not on account of its Marxist determinism but because of the universalism and humanism of its socialism. That was also why orthodox socialism was so little represented in the ranks of Ahdut Ha'avoda, a party established in 1919, of which Po'alei Tzion was a cofounder. When the Histadrut was established in 1920, and the labor movement was founded simultaneously, the principle of the nation's primacy was dominant. In 1920 true believers in Borochovism were so few in the Histadrut that they could do little except throw up their arms in despair every time there was a greater or lesser infringement on the organization's "commitment" to socialism. With the founding of the Histadrut, socialism became merely a tool of national aims, and the labor movement unhesitatingly took the path of nationalist socialism. This explains the fact that the Histadrut made no large-scale attempt to create a society essentially different from a normal capitalist one. Even more significant is the fact that the Histadrut made no real attempt to promote egalitarian values either in its own economic institutions and system or, after independence, in the state of Israel.

Anita Shapira expressed the classic opinion that "mass emigration changed the composition of the Jewish population in Palestine, and at the same time brought forward groups with a petit bourgeois, individualistic, or traditional-religious outlook. This was a population to which socialist ways of thinking and the order of priorities derived from them were strange and alien."[11] This assertion represents a convenient explanation of the facts, perhaps too convenient. It was used a great deal even in the time of the Yishuv. All waves of immigration subsequent to the Third Aliyah were regarded as unworthy of the generation of giants, and they were depicted as unwilling to be satisfied with a life of hard work, few needs, and equality, values that the earlier immigrants were supposed to have brought with them. The founders, incomparably gifted at self-promotion, assiduously nurtured this myth. This assertion is repeated in our day as well, but now it is not only the days of the first pioneering waves of immigration that are depicted as a golden age but the entire period of the Yishuv. Anita Shapira does this, and so do Horowitz and Lissak, who also, in a more modest and cautious way, declare themselves unhappy with "the demographic changes that took place in Israel in its early years."[12] In fact, the trouble was not only that egalitarian forms of existence were few in the Yishuv but that the Histadrut itself failed to serve as a counterculture to society as a whole and was run according to criteria that were not so different from those of the general society. Hevrat Ha'ovdim, the Society of Workers, registered with the mandatory government in 1924, was the umbrella organization of the Histadrut economy, which developed into an enormous holding; it was not, as its name might suggest—*hevrat ovdim* means "community of workers"—the model of an ideal society that organized its life in a particular fashion and wished to bequeath its values to society as a whole.

The socialism of the labor movement was most of all a mobilizing myth—a "social myth" in the sense that Georges Sorel gave to this concept at the beginning of this century. The Sorelian "myth" is a neutral phenomenon that can be used for various purposes. The Zionist labor movement—and it was not unique in this— used this myth as a tool to bring about a national and cultural rather than a social revolution. Nobody stated this more openly and clearly than Ben-Gurion.

Already at the third Ahdut Ha'avoda convention, which took place in Haifa in December 1922, Ben-Gurion, the head of the Histadrut, made a declaration of the intentions to which he adhered throughout his life.

We must clearly decide on the starting point from which we can judge our work in this country. And it seems to me that the starting point of Comrade Levkovitch is wrong. It is not by looking for a way of ordering our lives through the harmonious principles of a perfect system of socioeconomic production that we can decide on our line of action. The one great concern that should govern our thought and work is the conquest of the land and building it up through extensive immigration. All the rest is mere words and phraseology [parperaot umelitzot], and—let us not delude ourselves—we have to go forward in an awareness of our political situation: that is to say, in an awareness of power relationships, the strength of our people in this country and abroad.

And, as a result of this awareness, we can come to only one conclusion: we are facing a catastrophe. We are facing the bankruptcy of the Zionist movement, a terrible crisis in this country. The possibility of conquering the land is liable to slip out of our grasp. Our central problem is immigration . . . and not adapting our lives to this or that doctrine. We are not yeshiva students debating the finer points of self-improvement. We are conquerors of the land facing an iron wall, and we have to break through it. Where shall we find the strength and resources necessary to conquer the land in the short time that history has allotted us?

The established Zionist movement has failed, the time of crisis has come. It has lacked the willpower and the energy that this catastrophic moment demands. We in this country have seen this, and we have come to the conclusion that this movement is incapable of achieving the great things we expected of it.

Now, in this hour of crisis, the full scope of this question appears before us. How can we run our Zionist movement in such a way that it will be a movement of great willpower and ability, steeped in a sense of historical responsibility, which will be able to carry out the conquest of the land by the Jewish worker, and which will find the resources to organize the massive immigration and settlement of workers through their own capabilities?

The creation of a new Zionist movement, a Zionist movement of workers, is the first prerequisite for the fulfillment of Zionism. Without such a movement, our work in this country will come to nothing. Without a new Zionist movement that is entirely at our disposal, there is no future or hope for our activities.[13]

These guidelines for action left no room for misunderstanding. The aim of Ahdut Ha'avoda and the Histadrut was the conquest of the land. The failure of the First Aliyah of the 1880s and 1890s and its traditional modes of colonization obligated the worker to take upon himself the task of conquest. The movement's main concern, said Ben-Gurion, was not "adapting our lives to this or that doctrine" but the danger that "the possibility of conquering the land will slip from our grasp." This concise, concentrated, programmatic, and important speech, contained not a single word about equality, justice, universal values, or the creation of an alternative society. Only one objective was mentioned, and all the energy, strength, and capabilities of the young movement were directed toward achieving it. Ben-Gurion, in his inimitable style, told those who still indulged in dreams of social reform: "We are not yeshiva students debating the finer points of self-improvement. We are conquerors of the land facing an iron wall, and we have to break through it." For those who still, perhaps, failed to understand the true meaning of his words, Ben-Gurion added: "The one great concern that should govern our thought and work is the conquest of the land and building it up through extensive immigration. All the rest is mere words and phraseology." This was Ben-Gurion's basic conception, which guided him to his last day as a political leader.

Judging from this convention, one of the most important in the movement's history, the leadership accepted this line of thought. Similarly, there was no sign of rebellion among the party members of the second rank, although in connection with the debate on the status of Ahdut Ha'avoda, a rank-and-file Po'alei Tzion veteran observed: "Among us, people have even begun to be frightened of the word 'socialism.'"[14] When ten years later Berl Katznelson compiled a collection of writings representing the ideological legacy of Ahdut Ha'avoda leaders, he was alarmed by Ben-Gurion's speech, and censoring the words of his friend, he omitted the questionable passage quoted earlier.[15] One might conceivably reveal one's true opinions to an elite circle, but the rank and file had to be provided with a mobilizing myth.

In the same vein Katznelson stated unequivocally, at the third Histadrut convention in 1927, that the organization existed "to serve the cause of conquering the land, which we have taken upon ourselves."[16] "We came here as the standard-bearers of the national revival," he said,[17] immediately adding that the Labor movement should recognize the fact that "no single class has the power to accomplish this task alone."[18] Thus, he said, although "the fulfillment of Zionism does not take place independently of practical reality and does not obscure conflicts of aims and interests," it nevertheless "requires interclass cooperation."[19] Since the principle of the nation's primacy had been agreed upon and accepted among them ever since they were adults and decided to immigrate, it was not difficult for them, as the leaders of the country's only real political organization, to decide on their order of priorities. At the top of the list was the final goal, conquest of the land and the creation of a Jewish state. This goal was to be achieved with the organization of workers through the Histadrut, and the means to control the Histadrut was the political party. To those who thought that the establishment of the Histadrut was sufficient in itself to accomplish the task, and who wished to regard Ahdut Ha'avoda as merely a kind of vague "association," Ben-Gurion declared: "We want to found a party, and let us not delude people, but call things by their names."[20]

Thus, the party and the Histadrut regarded the organized wage earner as a soldier in the labor force, the army of the national revolution. The founders' conception of socialism was essentially instrumental: it was understood not as relating to universal objectives but as a means of achieving Zionism. In the view of Ahdut Ha'avoda, only the worker was a true Zionist: he was liberated from sectorial interests and fully devoted to the national mission. As he did not possess anything, he did not develop class interests. The well-being of the worker was necessarily identical with the well-being of the nation. By contrast, the danger of "acquisitiveness," which Ben-Gurion warned against so often, was said to harm national objectives.[21] Social differences and exploitation were also defined mostly in terms of the harm they caused the nation's ability to function. Capitalist exploitation was described as a mortal danger to the nation, and materialistic egoism, which found its outstanding expression in the employment of Arab labor, was denounced as a fatal blow to national solidarity.

The founders did not reject private property as such, but only the misuse of it. As long as he absorbed immigrants, the private farmer could enrich himself as much as he pleased, but the moment he refused to employ Jews he contravened a principle that the leaders of Ahdut Ha'avoda regarded as a sine qua non for the fulfillment of Zionism. For them, Jewish labor had always represented the infrastructure for national rebirth. The interest of someone like Ben-Gurion in the laborer, however, was extremely limited; the worker was important only as long as he successfully furthered national objectives. Universalistic ideals such as justice and equality interested Ben-Gurion only insofar as they served national objectives and did not interfere with their attainment. Because he did not regard them as having any intrinsic value, it was not difficult for him to dispense with them at the first signs of incompatibility.

The same principle applied to the Histadrut's economic enterprises. Economic power was built up to serve national objectives, not the well-being of the worker. Histadrut institutions were not expected to practice equality, and they were soon freed from the burden of the egalitarian "family wage" system. The Histadrut economy was not mobilized to overcome the severe unemployment of the second half of the 1930s, and thus it did not have to part with its financial reserves. From its earliest years, building up the Histadrut economy took precedence over social values, and economic considerations were given priority. This principle, like the party's dominance of the entire socioeconomic system, was transferred directly from the Histadrut, as a state in the making, to the state of Israel.

The labor movement did not come into being in consequence of a revolt against exploitation, and its development was not characterized by strikes or violent incidents. Rather it was born from a protest against a shameful national existence. The founders did not see the wretchedness of the Jewish condition in exile as being due to the capitalist order and economic exploitation; instead they viewed it as resulting from national impotence. As in all nationalist socialist movements, leaders of the labor movement avoided the term *proletariat*. Except in the initial period after his immigration, when in a personal letter he used phrases such as the "Jewish proletariat" and "proletarian persons,"[22] Katznelson refrained from using this expression. In a collection of essays (*Neglected Values*), he specifically recommended avoiding the phrase "proletarian outlook"; a member of the Histadrut, Katznelson insisted, was not the helpless proletarian of the nineteenth century.[23] The European worker of the 1930s, however, had also come a long way since the days of the wild capitalism of the mid-nineteenth century, but all socialist parties nevertheless continued to champion the cause of the "proletariat." More than representing a social category, it was a flag, a code word, a concept charged with emotional significance, and in the period between the two world wars, its abandonment generally signified a betrayal of the basic principles of socialism.

Already in 1926, Chaim Arlosoroff declared that "the organized labor movement in Eretz Israel is not 'proletarian.' The Histadrut is the Yishuv aristocracy."[24] Thus, he inferred, class warfare did not and could not exist in Eretz Israel; the idea of class warfare, he believed, was imported from abroad and lacked any significance or basis in Palestine. This attitude necessarily led to the conclusion that there was no need for real structural changes in Jewish society. If the organized wage earner dominated society or at least dictated its norms of behavior, if he was an object of envy for the bourgeoisie with whom he stood together in a single front against the mandatory power and the Arab enemy, who would be so foolish as to expect the labor movement to offer a total alternative to bourgeois society? "The socialism of Eretz Israel is a socialism of producers and not of consumers," said Arlosoroff,[25] thus repeating one of the classic formulas of the nationalist socialism of the beginning of the century.

Indeed, anyone reading the celebrated book *Der Jüdische Volkssozialismus* (The popular socialism of the Jews), in which Arlosoroff, in 1919, laid the conceptual foundations for his political and journalistic activities, and compares it with the principles put forward by the European school of nationalist socialism, must necessarily conclude that this gifted man sprang from an intellectual soil very similar to the one that nurtured anti-Marxist nationalists. The latter sought to create a new kind of socialism, a socialism for the entire people. "Our nationalism," wrote Arlosoroff, "is a nationalism of the hungry . . . for all of us, the entire people, are, nationally speaking, proletarians."[26] His was a socialism of the marginals, those who could not afford waiting for the maturation of long-range social and economic processes. Ten years before Arlosoroff, Enrico Corradini had spoken in a similar vein and in similar terms. The founder of the Italian Nationalist Association described his compatriots as a proletarian nation fighting for its right to feed its children. All nonconservative nationalists believed that "social and national liberation will be the common product of all the productive classes of the nation";[27] hence the need for an all-out struggle against both Marxism and liberalism, two outlooks that tore the fabric of the nation apart. Arlosoroff adopted the language of the French nationalist Maurice Barrès, very commoon at that time in Western Europe, who in the 1890s had created the concept of nationalist socialism in opposition to Marxism. In Arlosoroff's view, Marxism "had been defiled with the evil of class economic interests" and had turned socialism "into an affair of the stomach."[28] He rejected not only class warfare but the "materialistic" outlook of socialism; at that period this was a code name for rejecting the rationalistic content of all varieties of Marxism. It is no accident that Arlosoroff assailed "social democracy for using class incitement and class warfare as a terrible instrument of propaganda."[29] He objected to the principle itself, and not only to its application to Jews, among whom, in his opinion, there were no "clear class differences."[30] This point must be stressed: class warfare was unacceptable not only because it was unsuited to the needs of the Jewish people but because it genuinely represented the materialistic basis of Marxism and consequently of social democracy.

Here Arlosoroff adopted a purely nationalist socialist approach. He abhorred social democracy because it "diminished the value of the spirit, was insensitive to its essence, and disdained its creativity."[31] "Spirit," he wrote, "is the main thing. It is not factories, nor great industries, nor financial systems, that constitute capitalism, but the spirit through which they were created and by means of which they exist. . . . Everything depends on spirit."[32] This general outlook was alien to all branches of democratic socialism and all varieties of Austro-Marxism, from Bernstein and Jaurès, who wished to assimilate Kant into Marx's system, to Otto Bauer, who made a great effort to adapt Marxism to the reality of national differences. To readers who are familiar with the anti-Marxist and antiliberal cultural critics of the beginning of the century, the following passage will be of particular interest: "The European-American civilization has made the life of humanity mechanical. Everything has become technical. The whole life of humanity has become one great machine: not an organism, but an organization. Urban civilization and the division of labor—these are the two pillars of the modern temple of idolatry."[33]

The condemnation of the city and the cult of a return to nature, to the simplicity, authenticity, and rootedness of the village, was always one of the myths of radical nationalism, not of socialism. Socialism was oriented toward the modern world, industrialized and urban. The enemies of modernism, even when they utilized all the achievements of technological civilization, continued to preach a struggle against it and saw it as a sickness eating away at the body of the nation. The myth of a return to nature was nurtured by the labor movement even in the 1920s and 1930s, when Jewish society was already an urban society. In fact, Jewish Palestine under the British mandate was one of the most urbanized countries in the world: eight out of ten Jews lived in the cities (see chapter 5). At the same time, the Zionist consensus continued to preach the virtues of contact with nature and distrust of urban life, bureaucracies, and experts. The "new Jew" who embodied the Zionist myth, the depository of all the virtues of the national revolution, was the farmer, the conqueror of wilderness. Like the other members of Hapo'el Hatza'ir, Arlosoroff bemoaned the development patterns of the Fourth Aliyah. When it was demonstrated that four out of five Jews settled in the cities, Arlosoroff complained: "Facts and numbers show that the attraction of the cities for the wave of immigration of recent years has reached frightening proportions."[34]

Arlosoroff rightly saw Hapo'el Hatza'ir as the backbone of "the popular Jewish socialist movement."[35] He was attracted by the teachings of Aaron David Gordon, for Gordon too made Zionism dependent on a cultural revolution brought about by a reformation of the human being, two concepts alien to the world of democratic socialism. Indeed, socialism was interested in changing social and economic structures, not in the amendment of the individual. But like the founders of Hapo'el Hatza'ir at the time of the Second Aliyah, who came from the shtetls of Russia and Poland, this disciple of the German nationalist school was a spokesman for cultural rebirth, enthusiastic about the Bible, and zealous about historical rights to the land.[36] In his opinion, the reform of society could result only from national rebirth, and it could take place only on a basis of national cooperation and on behalf of the national interest. Every social goal was, from the beginning, conceptually subordinated to the needs of the nation. Thus, wrote Arlosoroff, "Jewish socialism has to be clearly and unequivocally national."[37] Arlosoroff's position was undoubtedly close to Gordon's, but also, and no less, to the ethical and "voluntaristic" socialism of Oswald Spengler and the "German socialism" of Arthur Moeller van den Bruck and Werner Sombart. Like Nachman Syrkin (1867–1924), the Jewish socialist theoretician who had a decisive influence on Katznelson and on other leaders of the Eretz Israel labor movement (see chapters 2 and 3), Arlosoroff was deeply rooted in the cultural environment that produced German nationalist socialism. He said nothing about the nature of socialism with which Spengler or Moeller van den Bruck would have disagreed. Indeed, the slogan repeated throughout chapter 2— devoted to socialism—of Moeller van den Bruck's book *The Third Reich* declares, "Each people has its own socialism." Elsewhere, Moeller tells us, "Socialism today must transform itself from a class socialism into a socialism of the people."[38] *Volkssozializmus* (socialism of the people) was the term Arlosoroff used in his essay of 1919, at the end of which year Spengler published *Preussentum und Sozialismus* (Prussianism and socialism). Moeller van den Bruck's *Third Reich* came out in 1923.

Underlying nationalist socialism was the Herderian idea that each culture had a unique character and a rejection of the "materialist" content of Marxism. Nationalist socialism taught that each people possesses a unique "soul," has needs specific to itself, and gives every general concept its own interpretation. According to Spengler, Marx never understood the spirit of German socialism, which is expressed in the saying "Every true German is a worker." At the same time, Gilbert Merlio has demonstrated that "Prussian socialism," like all other forms of nationalist or organic socialism, led to an antirationalist and antimaterialist revision of Marxism. This was achieved by abandoning class struggle and proletarian internationalism and making the national community's aim not a collective search for happiness but the heroic realization of its imperial vocation.[39]

It is here that the enormous difference between German nationalist socialism and the nationalist socialism of German Jews such as Arlosoroff or Germanized ones such as Syrkin is perceptible. Zionism was not a movement of imperial conquest, nor, essentially, a revolt against the heritage of the Enlightenment, but simply a path of rescue for an endangered people. Zionist socialism went off in search of not new forms of Caesarism or will to power but ways of saving a group of humans that Europe was casting out. However, this defensive reflex resulted in the adoption of a touchy nationalism, tribal, strongly tinged with religious elements, and little drawn to individualistic and universalistic values. Like all nationalist socialisms, Zionism was also a new revolution.

After his arrival in Palestine in 1920, Arlosoroff, like Katznelson and Ben-Gurion, was content to control society and had no desire—not even a theoretical one—to change it. His frame of reference was not social or economic but cultural. The use of cultural and psychological formulas rather than social ones was, once again, a distinctive feature of nationalist socialism. Nationalist socialism always saw the worker's exploitation and sense of inferiority as subjective and not the result of his position in the production system. Accordingly, a worker who enjoys a respected position in society, who considers himself as performing a necessary social function, and who believes that he belongs to the social and political elite feels no need for general social change. Arlosoroff apparently realized that the replacement of social concepts with cultural ones was always accompanied by an abandonment of the idea of offering an alternative society.

Thus, constructive socialism was different from democratic socialism, with its Marxist origins and Kantian and liberal elements. Because it set itself the goal of building the nation and redeeming it through independence in a hostile environment, the labor movement acquired a great belief in power. This belief distanced the revolutionaries of Jewish Palestine from social democrats. Whereas nationalists all over Europe believed first in force, social democrats were always apprehensive of, and often abhorred, the use of force. This was one of the major reasons for their impotence. The founders were no daydreamers; they believed foremost in a strong organization. They were much closer to Spengler, who at the end of *Preussentum und Sozialismus* wrote: "Socialism means power, power, and again power." Spengler took that famous formula from Heinrich von Treitschke; for the

German historian of the end of the nineteenth century, the state was first power, second power, and third power.

Essentially, it was democratic socialism, and not Bolshevism, that was true to the original Marxism; socialists believed in social and economic processes that, by their very nature, were slow and gradual. Social democracy was wary of the use of force because it was conscious of the fact that Marxism does not recognize sudden leaps of development. Particularly in the period between the two world wars, social democracy's faith in Marxism, mingled with liberal democracy, quite often paralyzed its ability to act. For revolutionaries, however, time was pressing. Neither group of revolutionaries, the Bolsheviks or the nationalists, believed it could afford to wait until deterministic processes had run their course. Nobody was more contemptuous of a belief in these processes than Katznelson and David Ben-Gurion.

This was sufficient reason for the founders of the labor movement not to adopt Marxism. Their feeling was always that the ground was burning under their feet. In their vocabulary, no terms recurred more often than "catastrophe" and "crisis." They could not permit themselves to wait for relationships of production to develop and for the proper social stratifications to come into being in Palestine. For that reason, they rejected Borochov's teachings, and soon after nothing remained of the intellectual heritage that the original members of Po'alei Tzion had brought with them from Russia. Similarly, democratic socialism, with its complex syntheses, was also alien to them. Even Syrkin's teachings were not considered really necessary.

The nationalist outlook of the founders placed them from the beginning in a very difficult position with regard to the socialist movement. At the beginning of this century, no European socialist claimed that the task of the socialist movement was to lead a national struggle. On the contrary, socialism, whether of the rigid Marxist variety or of the social democratic variety, abhorred the tribal nationalism that was beginning to dominate all of Europe. Only in the nationalist socialist variety was the working man supposed to lead the tribal struggle. This form of socialism played an important role in the first half of the twentieth century because it corresponded to the social and economic needs and to the emotional, cultural, and psychological requirements of many different societies. Nationalist socialism was particularly suited to the needs of societies in which the struggle for national unification and independence had not yet ended, or had ended only a short time earlier, and where national feeling was still very high. This was the situation in Eastern and Central European countries, including Germany, and later in the Third World. Nationalist socialism was also suitable to poorly developed areas, such as southern Italy, Portugal, and the fringes of the Mediterranean, where all social classes were required to make a concerted national effort to overcome economic and technological backwardness. Nevertheless, nationalist socialism also flourished in France, a country whose national unification was completed by the end of the wars of religion in the sixteenth century and whose technological level was one of the highest in the world. There, a strong nationalist socialism declared the primacy of the nation and the necessity of promoting national unity on a cultural and ethnic basis, and it mobilized all social strata, regardless of class differences, in an effort to ensure national survival.

We must consider another point. When Mapai was founded, not only did it fail to meet the intellectual criteria of continental social democracy, but it also did not have a single thinker comparable to Harold Laski, who contributed a great deal to the promotion of Marxism in the British Labour Party, or to Anthony Crosland, author of *The Future of Socialism*; it also did not have the social policy of the British Labour Party of the 1940s and 1950s.

Unlike social democracy, the labor movement was not drawn toward intellectual struggle or the play of abstract ideas. Institutions and parties created by the founders, the Histadrut, Ahdut Ha'avoda, Hapo'el Hatza'ir, and Mapai, as well as their conventions, councils, and central committees, promoted few ideological debates and were primarily concerned with the burning political and organizational issues of the hour. There was never any question of the kind of discussions that preoccupied Syrkin or Borochov and his friends. It would obviously be unfair to compare the leaders of young groups who immigrated from the shtetls of Eastern Europe in order to conquer Palestine with figures such as Rudolf Hilferding, Max Adler, Saverio Merlino, Jean Jaurès, or even Léon Blum and Émile Vandervelde, but we should remember that socialism depends on a fusion of theory and practice, and thus, in the first half of the twentieth century, socialist parties were still deeply preoccupied with theory. Too great a gap between theory and practice usually leads to an abandonment of theory, and the divide between Marxist teachings and their realization is the reason that from the time it seized power in Russia, Russian communism failed to produce a single thinker worthy of the name. In the West, however, the gap between theory and practice made a mockery of the socialist parties' ability to act, and their discussions about final objectives, when they knew of the great distance between theory and the realities of daily life, seriously impaired their capacity to function.

Like most nationalists, leaders of the labor movement despised abstract principles and had only contempt for universal norms and values. They were also afraid of becoming entangled in unnecessary ideological difficulties. They felt that intellectual debates might undermine not only the self-confidence of the movement but also the organic unity of the nation and perhaps harm its determination in the long and bitter struggle for independence. Nevertheless, there is no doubt that the intellectual horizons of the dominant elite were extremely narrow, and its thinking was not distinguished by any talent for abstraction. Borochov never reached the country, and Syrkin did not settle there. None of the official leaders of the movement felt the need to write down his ideas in an orderly and systematic manner. Their writings are made up of speeches, conversations, newspaper articles, and memoirs. Even Katznelson, who was considered the ideologist and the "conscience" of the movement, did not leave behind a single systematic essay. He was a gifted speaker, with an emotional style that drew a deep response from his audience, but, if one reads him, one is often reminded of a fireside chat rather than anything else.

Similarly, Ben-Gurion was not a theoretician, not even a frustrated intellectual who was forced to deal with day-to-day political affairs through force of circumstances. Shabtai Teveth has pointed out, in his wonderfully precise and detailed biography, that even in his youth the subjects that most interested Ben-Gurion were organization and politics. All his articles (compared with Yitzhak Ben-Zvi and his other friends Ben-Gurion did not write much) in the Po'alei Tzion newspaper, Ha'ahdut, were concerned with purely political and organizational matters.[40] In this early period, Ben-Gurion did not stand out particularly and did not make an impression; he also did not demonstrate any unusual intellectual capacity. He was overshadowed by Ben-Zvi.[41] Ben-Gurion rose to dominance in the movement after he built up the Histadrut power structure. His ascent began only when the organization whose foundations he had helped lay and which he led was established. Ben-Gurion's success was the direct result of his extraordinary ability to maneuver among party institutions, economic bodies, interest groups, and organizations of various kinds and to create ad hoc coalitions that supported him. Not only did Ben-Gurion and Katznelson not participate in the intellectual debates taking place at that time in international socialism, but only a faint echo of them reached their ears.

Unlike all socialist parties in Europe, in which intellectuals and thinkers held key positions, the labor movement in Palestine was dominated by professional politicians. These were people who had entered public life when they were very young, and politics was the only art they knew. They practiced this art to perfection and thus ensured for themselves long years of uninterrupted control. At the same time, they well understood the power of ideology to mobilize the masses.

If an ideology may be defined as a relationship between culture and politics, in other words, as a body of principles guiding political actions, it may be observed that the political actions of the labor movement, from the beginning of constructive socialism in the 1920s until its fall from power in 1977, remained true to the body of principles that took final shape in the decade after the First World War.

The starting point of constructive socialism was a pernicious critique of the life of the nation. It was characteristic of nationalist socialism that this criticism was primarily cultural. Nationalist socialism was always marked by its rejection of bourgeois values and the supposed characteristics of a bourgeois way of life, from physical degeneracy to a taste for an easy existence and the pursuit of wealth. In place of bourgeois individualism, nationalist socialism presented the alternative of team spirit and the spirit of comradeship; instead of the artificiality and the degeneracy of the large city, it promoted the naturalness and simplicity of the village. It encouraged a love of one's native land and its scenery. All these were also the basic values of the labor movement. Socialist Zionism, however, went further than any other national movement when it rejected the life of the Jews in exile. No one attacked Eastern European Jewry more vehemently than the young men from the Polish shtetl who settled in Palestine, and no one depicted traditional Jewish society in darker hues than the pioneers of the first immigration waves. Consequently, Jewish communities in the diaspora were viewed primarily as suppliers of manpower. Ben-Gurion was not the only one uninterested in the fate of the Jews outside the Zionist context. The belief of the movement's leadership in the supreme importance of the Zionist revolution was so great that immigration to Palestine was regarded as the final aim of Jewish existence. A Jew who did not intend to settle in Palestine, and who did not prepare his children to do so, was considered a useless Jew. All other matters, including social problems, were viewed as insignificant in comparison with national rebirth.

On 11 September 1939, when Hitler's troops were overrunning Poland, there was a debate in the Histadrut Executive Committee about the role of the Jews in the war. Eliyahu Golomb (1893–1945), leader of the semiclandestine Hagana, the Jewish defense force, and Yosef Sprinzak (1885–1959), another towering figure who would become the first speaker of the Knesset, wanted an immediate general conscription of the Jews in all countries where they lived. Ben-Gurion replied:

> For me, Zionist considerations take precedence over Jewish sentiments, and I only heed Zionist considerations in this matter—that is, what is required for Eretz Israel. And even if my Jewish feelings urge me to go to France, I shall not do so, even if, as a Jew, I would have gone. Zionism is the most profound thing in Judaism, and I think we should act according to Zionist considerations and not merely Jewish considerations, for a Jew is not automatically a Zionist.[42]

Even in that fateful hour, Zionist considerations took precedence over Jewish sentiments; this was the case even though Ben-Gurion, on the same occasion, also forcefully expressed his awareness of the danger of catastrophe hanging over Poland's Jews.

The revolution presided over by the founders was a national revolution whose success depended on a cultural revolution, but it was not a social revolution that required drastic change in the forms of the ownership of wealth. This fact is crucial for an understanding of the rise and development of the labor movement, its culmination in the founding of the state of Israel, and its consolidation during the first twenty years of independence. The labor movement presided over the process of nation-building, which involved a major revolution for every immigrant. In this respect, the Jewish national movement was significantly more far-reaching than any other national movement in the modern world. This revolution required a metamorphosis: emigration to a distant land, a change of language, often a change of profession, and a dramatic change in lifestyle. Thus, according to the founders, building the nation involved a change in the Jew himself, and this required a profound cultural transformation but not a change in the general social and economic system.

Thus, socialism was always a secondary factor. Undoubtedly, the founders would have been pleased to realize an egalitarian society had there been no contradiction between socialism and nationalism. But this contradiction was insurmountable. Despite the rhetoric and the repeated claims, especially by Ben-Gurion and Katznelson, that this contradiction did not exist, leaders of the labor movement resolved this contradiction by abandoning the universal aims of socialism for the particularistic aims of nationalism. Let us recall that until the end of the 1950s, democratic socialism adhered doctrinally to the main teachings of Marxism, including the concept of class warfare and the socialization of the means of production. The Jewish labor movement in Palestine abandoned these teachings in principle as well as in practice in the 1920s. With the founding of Mapai in January 1930, this process reached its conclusion.

At this early stage it became apparent that the labor movement did not claim to offer a general alternative to the capitalist system and had no intention of endangering or restricting private property. Indeed, its only social frameworks—the kibbutz, the moshav (smallholders' cooperative settlement combining private initiative and collective action), and the urban cooperative—further strengthened the capitalist economy by furnishing proof of the fact that constructive socialism had no answer to capitalist forms of property ownership except for isolated pockets unable to influence society as a whole.

Here I draw attention to a point of which even Israelis are often unaware, despite the fact that the founders always emphasized it: collective settlement was a pragmatic rather than an ideological choice, and raising national funds for that purpose did not imply a rejection of private property as such. The *kvutza* (small kibbutz) and the moshav resulted from the old capitalist agriculture's inability and unwillingness to give priority to national considerations and to take on Jewish workers in place of Arab ones. Independent collective settlement was not a conscious ideological choice but a solution arrived at after some years of attempting to employ members of the Second

Aliyah as salaried workers on farms created by the Zionist Organization. The kvutza, the kibbutz, and the moshav (the first moshav, Nahalal, was the outcome of at least thirteen years of groping, thought, and experiment), which were set up on national land with the aid of national funds, constituted a pragmatic Zionist solution to the problems of conquering the land, lack of work, and the need to absorb immigrants; it was not an ideological solution aimed at eliminating inequality or combating private property.

Nobody gave a better account of the first gropings of collective settlement than the founders themselves. People like Katznelson always boasted of the Second Aliyah's capacity for invention, in other words, their own capacity for invention.[43] However, twenty years before Katznelson, Arthur Ruppin (1876–1943), head of the Palestinian office and later director of the colonization department of the Zionist Organization, in a book he wrote in 1926 about settlement in the country, specifically described the beginnings of collective settlement as a solution to three basic problems that prevented immigrants of the Second Aliyah from continuing the methods of private settlement of the First Aliyah. The first two problems were the lack of funds and the lack of candidates with the ability and experience to settle as independent farmers. To this, Ruppin added a third problem: the failure of the managers of national agricultural farms. The problem of bad relations between young workers of the Second Aliyah and professional agronomists who ran the farm at Kinneret, in the north of the country, on the shore of Lake Tiberias, could be solved only by giving part of the land owned by the farm at Umm-Djuni to a group of five or six workers. That is how Kvutzat Degania came into being. "The kvutza was not created with the intention of making a social experiment," concluded Ruppin.[44] In 1909–10, in his reports to the central administration of the Zionist institutions, then situated in Germany, Ruppin described establishing the "mother of the kvutzot" as a modest experiment and a matter of chance, which all those involved asked to keep secret until its success was assured. The first kvutza, whose members received a wage and shared half the profits, was organized according to the system (which was not socialistic) worked out by Franz Oppenheimer (1864–1943), a German Jewish economist. The experiment was successful, and in 1910 Ruppin planned to apply it in other parts of the country as well.[45] Three years later, when he appeared before the eleventh Zionist Congress, which met in Vienna in 1913, Ruppin was able to say with assurance: "Without the workers, settlement would have died, but thanks to them it received new life."[46]

In this way a collaboration began between the agricultural workers of the Second Aliyah and the Zionist Organization. This collaboration continued after the founding of the Histadrut, and it grew stronger over the years, when it became clear beyond any shadow of a doubt that the labor movement was interested in political power rather than in social change, and that it wished to control society, not to create a model one.

This state of affairs made possible the enduring collaboration between the socialist Left and the bourgeois Center. The middle class understood very well that it had nothing to fear from the labor movement. It permitted its domination of the Yishuv and saw no reason to replace it with its only real rival, the revisionist movement. The labor movement gave proof of its practical abilities: it organized salaried workers and concerned itself with their relative well-being; the labor movement also curbed radical tendencies and prevented wildcat strikes, or wage demands that were exaggerated from the viewpoint of the enterprise's owner. Thus, the discipline the Histadrut imposed was invaluable not only for its own enterprises, which functioned as employers in all respects, but also for private concerns. The declared struggle of the movement's leaders against the propertied classes of Tel Aviv, especially at election time, could not hide the truth: in practice, a collaboration existed between the two sides, both in the national sphere and in economics. Both sides needed each other, and they knew it. Zeev Jabotinsky (1880–1940), the revisionist leader, also understood this very well and did not look to the Jewish bourgeoisie in Palestine as a power base for his movement. He loked toward the Jewish masses in Poland, who did not always agree with the elitism of the pioneering movements and their contempt for traditional Yiddishist culture.

The decision to favor national objectives rather than social ones was reflected throughout the history of the labor movement, from the end of the Second Aliyah to the founding of the Labor Party in 1968. In many respects, the history of the labor movement may be seen as a continual drift to the right, a process in which more radical principles, those closest to the aspiration of creating a more egalitarian society, were progressively eroded. The series of unifications, which led first to the founding of Mapai and forty years later to the founding of the Labor Party, all had the same result: an increasing commitment to national goals rather than to those reflecting an aspiration to equality. Thus, from one unification to another, socialist identity was lost.

The founding of Ahdut Ha'avoda, after the liquidation of the Po'alei Tzion movement in Palestine, marked the conclusion of the first stage of the drift to the right and the triumph of the viewpoint known in the days of the Second Aliyah as nonparty. The nonparty people were close to Hapo'el Hatza'ir, a strongly anti-Marxist party. Aaron David Gordon, a militant anti-socialist, well expressed the nationalist and cultural approach of the Hapo'el Hatza'ir Party. The nonparty, anti-Marxist group led by Katznelson, Yitzhak Tabenkin (1887–1971, founder of the United Kibbutz Movement), and David Remez (1886–1951, Ben-Gurion's successor as head of the Histadrut) collaborated with Ben-Gurion, who represented Po'alei Tzion only in theory and even at that time led its nationalist wing. Ben-Gurion presided over the liquidation of the Po'alei Tzion movement, and with this process he began to attain the dominance that led him to the Histadrut's leadership.

The founding of the Histadrut as a partnership between Ahdut Ha'avoda and Hapo'el Hatza'ir and the declaration of its "general" (that is, comprehensive, nonparty) character constituted the second stage in the process of asserting the primacy of national objectives. Ten years later the founding of Mapai offered a unique spectacle in the socialist world: two parties, one of which had an avowed antisocialist past, fused into a single party on the basis of rejecting the principle of class warfare. After ten years of the Histadrut coalition, the leadership of Hapo'el Hatza'ir knew well that the nonbinding socialist ideology of Ahdut Ha'avoda, once it had completely abandoned Marxism, class warfare, and the socialization of the means of production, was not very different from that of their own party. Sprinzak, Arlosoroff, Eliezer Kaplan (1891–1952, the first minister of finance in Israel), and Levi Shkolnik (Eshkol, 1895–1969, the third prime minister, in office during the Six-Day War) understood that there was no difference between themselves and Ben-Gurion, Katznelson, Remez, and Ben-Zvi. Each stage in the "unification of the labor movement" ('unification" being a magic formula employed by Katznelson and Ben-Gurion throughout a whole generation) always, once it was accomplished, ended with the victory of rightist principles.

Finally, Ben-Gurion's famous principle of the primacy of the nation and supremacy of the state over civil society, of political power over social action and voluntary bodies— called *mamlachtiut* in Hebrew (derived from *mamlacha*, kingdom)—represented the true nature of the Eretz Israel brand of socialism. It is often regarded as a product of the 1950s, symbol of the lost innocence of the prestate period, the end of socialism's golden age. The truth is that by the 1920s the foundations of mamlachtiut had already been laid, and in the 1930s the whole system was at work. Here Ben-Gurion was consistent and true to the aims he had set for himself and his movement. From the time he presided over the liquidation of the Gdud Ha'avoda (Labor Corps), Ben-Gurion never deviated from this path. If at times it seems that until 1923–24 Ben-Gurion's thinking developed in an uneven manner, there can be no doubt about his consistency from the struggle against the Gdud Ha'avoda in the mid-1920s until his resignation from political life in the mid-1960s. In reality, Ben Gurion's basic position was already established with the liquidation of Po'alei Tzion. It was this position that was adopted by the leadership of Ahdut Ha'avoda. Constructive socialism constituted the basis of mamlachtiut; from the beginning of his career as a political leader, Ben-Gurion viewed himself as the founder of a kingdom, as an armed prophet, and not as a social reformer. The essence of socialism, after all, had always been the fact that it offered universalist solutions; but Ben-Gurion, like Katznelson, Gordon, Arlosoroff, Tabenkin, and all the other key figures of the labor movement, was primarily interested in a specifically Zionist solution for the Jewish people.

The heart of the Zionist revolution was the reform of the Jew as a person. The disgust and shame the pioneers felt about their people sunk in poverty, exposed to the blows of gentiles, or held captive by alien cultures was boundless. The founders believed that national revolution necessitated an absolute social and emotional break with exile. Immigration to Palestine was supposed to represent a new birth, a rupture with the past whose chief symbol was the obliteration of Yiddish culture and the shift to physical labor. Gordon was the prophet of physical labor, and two generations of young people—the children and grandchildren of the members of the first waves of immigration—were reared on the cult of agriculture and work in the fields. Even Arlosoroff saw the future of Jewish Palestine as being in agriculture and not in industry.[47] But in the long run this cult of physical labor had a number of harmful weaknesses.

First, the idea of reforming people by turning them into agricultural laborers was applicable only to a few. Those engaged in agriculture had always been a minority, and the pioneers in collective settlements were a tiny minority, between 6 and 8 percent of the Jewish population. The concept of the pioneer was elitist and from the start was addressed to only a handful. Second, already in the days of the Third Aliyah, physical labor could no longer be taken seriously as an ideal. For the overwhelming majority of manual workers it was an existential necessity and not a moral value. Indeed, how could working as a builder in Tel Aviv be regarded as ideal when one was exposed to every possible hazard? The first victims of economic crises, they could suddenly, without any warning, become unemployed with no alternative means of support. Work conditions at the building sites of that period were harsh and sometimes humiliating. In contrast, workers in the service industry, including the Histadrut's office workers, enjoyed far more comfortable working conditions, a much higher salary, and, even more important, security that shielded them from life's vicissitudes. The situation of the farmhand, whose salary was usually at the bottom rung of the Jewish economy, was comparable to the builder's, his urban counterpart. How could the farmhand regard his situation as ideal for himself or for his children? How could he see the preaching about physical labor of office workers in Tel Aviv as anything other than hypocrisy?

Over time, laborers who were not members of kibbutzim or moshavim, that is, the overwhelming majority of workers, perceived that this idealization of physical work was a myth fostered by ideological orthodoxy, and the perpetuation of this myth beyond its time revealed all the more clearly a situation that was perceived as an intolerable discrepancy between theory and practice. In the 1920s this gap was already very wide. But more important, the cult of physical labor represented a regressive factor, perpetuating the backwardness of the urban worker. The principle of productivization and the reformation of the human being through labor in practice led to a blocking of the horizons of social progress.

An outstanding illustration of this phenomenon was the Histadarut's failure to develop a system of secondary education for its members' children; workers' children were expected to remain workers. And when eventually secondary schools were established in the cities, continuing the primary education of the labor system (see chapter 5), tuition fees were beyond workers' means. In theory workers were regarded as the aristocracy, but the reality was quite different, and workers were conscious of that reality. Where living conditions were concerned, laborers were at the bottom of the social and economic scale. That was their real status in society in general, and that was also their true status in the society of the Histadrut.

In theory the social status of the office worker was lower than that of the laborer, but in practice the Histadrut and party apparatus were made up of workers who had abandoned work in agriculture or the factory as soon as they could or of people who had never done any physical labor. The preaching of self-fulfillment did not prevent a drift toward cities and offices. Leaders of the Histadrut and party were the first to flee physical labor, agriculture, and the kibbutz. Whereas members of the Second Aliyah, through force of circumstance, had spent some time working in the fields, members of the Third Aliyah, who soon constituted the second and third echelons of the leadership, were careful not to do so. Thus, in an atmosphere of sanctimoniousness, preaching to others, and continual castigation of sin, a great chasm opened between ideology and reality. Leaders of the movement who returned from the spas of Europe, where they recuperated from the strain of their Zionist missions, never ceased praising the glories of pioneering and self-realization. In the collective settlements where, contrary to the carefully nurtured popular myth, the kibbutz or moshav member never shared the lot of the farmhand in Galilean villages or the harsh conditions of the laborer in the port of Tel Aviv, things were taken more lightly than in the first Jewish city. However, in Tel Aviv at the end of the 1930s, victims of the economic crisis reached the point of rebellion. Perhaps that was why, in the labor movement, the poor in general and the unemployed and discontented in particular were regarded with suspicion. Conformism was one of the essential characteristics of the ideal member of the movement.

The Histadrut sought to provide its members with a comprehensive framework of life. As the organization matured and reached its final form, the Histadrut became a power structure that mobilized all members for the supreme national goal. That is why it was built from the start as a multipurpose organization, centralized and capable of providing essential social, economic, and cultural services. In order to achieve its aims, the organization was set up as a "general," nonfactional and nonideological, Histadrut and not as a socialist Histadrut. In volume 11 of his works, devoted to the history of the labor movement in Palestine, Katznelson quoted Yosef-Haim Brenner (1881–1921), a member of the Second Aliyah and the greatest Hebrew writer of his time (some say of all time). There was no need, wrote Brenner, for the Histadrut to be "specifically called Socialist-Zionist. The title 'Histadrut of the Workers in Eretz Israel' is sufficient."[48]

On one hand the Histadrut wished to own the means of production, and on the other hand it was also a trade union. This was unique. It cannot be denied that the Histadrut had great achievements to its credit and, among other things, was a powerful and effective trade union; at the same time there can be no doubt that in this way an interdependence was created between the individual and the organization, which greatly restricted workers' freedom of choice. This dependence was especially pronounced among workers in the weakest position, for although the Histadrut was theoretically a voluntary institution, freedom of action among the majority of members was extremely limited. The likelihood that they could dispense with the Histadrut's employment bureau or sick fund was minimal. Only the strongest categories of workers, members of the liberal professions, people in senior management positions, and skilled workers in great demand, could break away. The Histadrut was conscious of this danger and was careful not to harm the interests of the stronger elements, even at the expense of mutual aid. This situation was particularly marked in periods of economic crisis.

Thus, the Histadrut can be regarded as a wonderful organizational body reflecting the collective strength of the working population, or it can be seen, if one wishes, as a powerful tool for regimenting salaried workers and for mobilizing them in the nation's service. Essentially, it constituted a power structure that never offered workers a real alternative; first and foremost it required discipline from its members, and in exchange it provided them with social, economic, and cultural services. Indeed, there is no doubt that the Histadrut's basic demand was submissiveness and not ideological support. Some among the members were not socialists, and others were not even Zionists. All that was required of either group was to abide by the Histadrut's decisions and submit to its discipline.

In the absence of a vision of far-reaching social change, of any real aspiration to equality, great attention was paid to fostering the laborer's sense of cultural superiority—that is, to myths and symbols. The labor movement's nationalist ideology set up the manual worker as an ideal to follow, but there was no intention of creating an alternative to the capitalist system and no attempt to institute a policy that would change the laborer's standard of living. In this respect, the Histadrut's behavior was in complete accord with the normal practices of nationalist socialism. It often seems that the Histadrut leadership, like nationalist socialists in general, viewed inequality and exploitation primarily as a psychological problem and only secondarily as an economic problem. The supposed cultural superiority of the laborer served as a kind of compensation for his low standard of living. His exalted position as the instrument of national revival made his predicament bearable, at least in periods of affluence. In times of economic crisis, however, one can hardly claim that workers in agriculture, in ports, and in construction found that their supposedly lofty status in the national hierarchy satisfied their need for food.

The ideology of workers' cultural superiority had far-reaching consequences. First, this view legitimated existing social structures. If the aristocrats in this land of immigration were the laborers and not the educated middle classes living in relative comfort or the private farmers of the coastal plain north of Tel Aviv or the landlords in Jerusalem, then from a cultural or national point of view there was no need to seek a change. The son of an agricultural worker, if he did not join a new kibbutz, was expected to follow in the footsteps of his father, a pioneer developing the country, and to continue to work for a wage that was unlikely to be much higher than his father's. If it was not the well-paid managers of the Histadrut industrial sector but the construction workers who were the cream of society, the fulfillment of the Zionist dream, and the model for the new Jew growing up on the sands of Tel Aviv, how could one offer the workers' children possibilities of advancement that would lead them astray from physical labor, the true path to the reformation of man, self-realization, and the building of the land? In this way, the attachment to national aims contributed to social conservatism. Such were the practical results of nationalist socialism, everywhere and always.

In addition to legitimizing the prevailing social structure, the doctrine of workers' cultural superiority provided an excellent basis for building up the political strength of the labor movement. The fact that the struggle against the bourgeoisie was cultural and not social paved the way for the labor movement's successful strategy for the conquest of power. The struggle in the cultural sphere was accompanied by the usual socioeconomic struggle over wages and work conditions, but the economic battle was waged with great caution; it did not represent a danger to the real status of the propertied class, and it did not attempt to close widening social gaps. Leaders of the labor movement never had any real objection to private wealth or to social and economic differences. However, they had two demands: on one hand, they expected preference to be given to public capital, that is, Histadrut enterprises, from agriculture to industry to banking; on the other hand, they firmly insisted that private capital be used to fulfill its task of developing the country and absorbing immigrants. On this basis, social tranquillity and a division of labor prevailed between the labor movement and the middle classes.

The labor movement's focus on settlement rather than on creating a new society greatly facilitated its relations with the middle classes. Jabotinsky realized that this orientation made it economically dependent on the Jewish middle classes in the diaspora, which provided the money.[49] The public funds that provided the basis for the labor movement's power structure—collective agriculture, industry, services such as Bank Hapo'alim (Workers' Bank), and all the other Histadrut institutions—came from private hands, and the leadership of the movement was careful not to endanger this source of financing. Both sides reaped an advantage: the bourgeoisie had the assurance of dealing with an abstract form of socialism that did not threaten its existence, that never demanded the "socialization" of private property, that never interfered with its economic activities, and that in fact consolidated its status because of the major part it played in the economy as a whole. The labor movement gained the bourgeoisie's cooperation in the area it believed was most important: the financing of the agricultural settlement that was conquering the land. Settlement served as a common denominator for the salaried workers of the Histadrut and the middle and upper-middle classes. Both sides were united in their national aims, and both presented a common front against the Arab threat and against the possibility of a blow to national interests by the mandatory government.

The entire Jewish bourgeoisie, including the emerging one in Palestine, knew that collective settlement had grown as a response to the needs of the time, as a necessary improvisation, and not as the model of an alternative society. Members of Degania, the first kvutza, where Gordon resided, were identified with Hapo'el Hatza'ir, and as such they were regarded as avowed antisocialists. Collective settlement arose out of the need to find an unconventional solution to the problem of unemployment in agriculture. It was a tool of Zionism and not a spearhead of socialism seeking to conquer Tel Aviv. But, most of all, the idea of settlement as the ultimate socialist enterprise led to a renunciation of concern with society as a whole. The concentration of its energies on collective settlement absolved the labor movement from the need to devote itself to the problem of inequality in the cities.

From the beginning, the kibbutz had a special place in the Zionist ethos. Agricultural collectives fired the imagination of millions of Jews throughout the diaspora and were a source of pride for the Tel Aviv bourgeoisie. Their ideological enemies among the radical bourgeois Right were helpless in the face of the spirit of sacrifice and the pioneering fervor of the conquerors of the wilderness, the builders of roads, and the drainers of marshes. The weapon-bearing farmers were an outstanding symbol of the land's conquest and its settlement with the economic and moral assistance of the entire people. This wonderful vanguard, which also realized in itself the dream of an egalitarian society, was the labor movement's supreme weapon. In its name budgets were provided by the Zionist Organization, and in its name national funds were collected for the Histadrut's enterprises. Agricultural collectives were exhibited with great pride to all visitors from abroad, and all of them, Jews and non-Jews, socialists and members of the European nobility, were thrilled and excited at the sight of the egalitarian utopia coming to life in the land of the Bible.

But still more important, the bourgeois Zionist movement accepted the view that no one could compare with the young, ready pioneer, free of money and possessions, enlisted in the Histadrut's army of labor, as the agent of the enterprise of national renewal. Indeed, for the Zionist movement, collective settlement was proof of the labor movement's practical capabilities. Was anyone comparable, as an example of Zionist values, to the farmer-soldiers of the newly founded kibbutzim? On this basis, an alliance was forged between the leadership of the labor movement and the chief representatives of the liberal bourgeoisie, from Chaim Weizmann (president of the Zionist Organization), Ruppin, and Menachem Ussishkin (a Russian Zionist leader and a key figure in the process of acquiring land for agricultural settlement) to Zalman Shocken (the owner and the editor of the liberal newspaper *Ha'aretz*). This alliance was based on an acknowledgment of the superiority of the worker organized by the Histadrut as the bearer of the national enterprise. Thus, a division of labor was created between those who provided the resources and those who carried out the task. The collaboration between the body responsible for settlement—the Zionist Organization—and the pioneers who performed the labor by the sweat of their brow was a basic fact of national life. The liberal bourgeoisie acknowledged the dominant position of the forces bearing the physical, practical, and emotional burden of the conquest of the land, and the labor movement's dominance of the Zionist Organization derived first from this acknowledgment by the Jewish bourgeoisie in Eretz Israel and abroad of the superiority of the pioneer as a nation builder. Even those elements of the bourgeoisie who fought against the collectivistic principles exemplified by the kibbutz movement could not refrain from being excited by the settlers' achievements.

However, on the eve of independence, at the end of 1947, in a general population of more than 600,000 and a Histadrut membership of 175,659 people, only 23,962 lived in kibbutzim and 8,149 in moshavim. It should be quite clear now that it was not a radical social ideology or an egalitarian way of life that triumphed when the labor movement gained control of the Yishuv and the Zionist Organization. The labor movement was built up not through its social achievements but through its ability to bear on its shoulders the construction of the nation. But the egalitarian ideology did not really succeed in the society as a whole; neither did the kibbutz form of settlement succeed in imposing its values on the Histadrut society. Although kibbutz members always remained an insignificant minority from a numerical point of view, the kibbutz served as an alibi for the whole movement, which almost from its inception was contrary to the lifestyle of an egalitarian society. The kibbutz was a kind of magnificent showcase, behind which a very different reality was taking shape. Agricultural communes were admired throughout the Jewish world, and they served as an example for youth in the pioneering movements of Eastern Europe. At the same time, the kibbutz lent legitimacy to the existing social order, and the focus on it permitted the movement to avoid concerning itself with the necessity of making structural changes in the general society.

As is always the case with nationalist ideologies, the conceptual system of the labor movement was elitist. The activist minority engaged in collective settlement was held to represent the hard core of the conquerors of the land. In the same way, only the pioneering minority among the Jews of the diaspora really interested the leadership of the labor movement: the Jews of Eastern Europe were to furnish the pioneers, and the Jews of the United States were to provide the means for settling the country. Everything else was secondary. The same applied in Palestine: in principle, the city worker's concerns could not be regarded as equal in importance to settlement matters. This attitude led to a lack of interest in structural changes in the society as a whole. Agricultural settlement was isolated from it, and it could still achieve its aims even though social differences were on the rise in the cities. But, in addition, there can be no doubt that the main reason for the movement's conservatism was the fact that any attempt to prevent the Yishuv from developing into an ordinary capitalist society would have involved a struggle that would have endangered national solidarity. Similarly, there can be no doubt that any such endeavor within the society of the Histadrut would have involved an internal conflict that would have ended with the dissolution of the organization.

Moreover, of all the young people reared on "self-realization," only a minute minority joined a kibbutz. The Histadrut youth movements helped provide for their members a happy childhood, which to this day is an unfailing source of nostalgia for many cultural, administrative, and political elites. But only a small minority of the country's youth belonged to these youth movements, and even fewer remained in the kibbutzim. The great majority, after participating in the War of Independence and the succeeding wars, took up advanced studies and academic research, a military career, or a career in the higher echelons of public administration or private business. From the early 1940s on, agriculture was relegated to the Holocaust refugees from Europe, and after the founding of the state, to the new immigrants from Arab countries.

It soon became apparent that behind the facade of a frugal, pioneering kibbutz society, a social reality had developed within the Histadrut which was not essentially different from that of society as a whole. There was a considerable difference between the stratum of workers in demand, managers and senior officials who formed part of the leadership of the ruling party, and laborers in towns and villages, especially on the lower echelons. Every society is ruled by elites: it was the labor movement that provided the Yishuv and later the state of Israel with its political, cultural, and military elites. The evolution of the Histadrut is a classic illustration of Robert Michels's well-known ideas, and of Milovan Djilas's more recent ones, about the oligarchic tendencies of organizations. The labor oligarchy was undoubtedly a "new class" in the strictest sense of the term. The "family wage" (see chapter 6) was already a fiction from the mid-1920s on, and in periods of crisis, like the late 1930s, there was an enormous gap between the managers and officials of the Histadrut economy, who enjoyed a guaranteed income regardless of the economy, and the masses of the unemployed. The hostility between those waiting in line for a day's work and begging for assistance for their undernourished children on one hand and the heads of the Histadrut and party on the other broke through the barriers of conformism, discipline, and dependency which had hitherto confined most of the members of the Histadrut, especially those with the lowest levels of income. Archival materials paint a dark picture of economic distress and moral alienation. Not only was there conflict between the Histadrut's managers and political leaders on one hand and the workers on the other, but the entire Histadrut society was fragmented into various strata, and the differences between them were no smaller than those found in the Yishuv as a whole.

The building of the Yishuv was accompanied by a constant struggle with a stubborn Arab opposition to Zionist goals. Contrary to the claim that is often made, Zionism was not blind to the presence of Arabs in Palestine. Even Zionist figures who had never visited the country knew that it was not devoid of inhabitants. At the same time, neither the Zionist movement abroad nor the pioneers who were beginning to settle the country could frame a policy toward the Palestinian national movement.[50] The real reason for this was not a lack of understanding of the problem but a clear recognition of the insurmountable contradiction between the basic objectives of the two sides. If Zionist intellectuals and leaders ignored the Arab dilemma, it was chiefly because they knew that this problem had no solution within the Zionist way of thinking. Among those who sought to hold a dialogue with the Arabs, some hoped that Arabs would feel that rapid development would compensate them for loss of control of the country or of large parts of it, and others entertained ideas of coexistence within a binational state. Still others considered a federation with neighboring Arab states, then on the road to independence, but in general both sides understood each other well and knew that the implementation of Zionism could be only at the expense of the Palestinian Arabs. The leadership of the Yishuv did not conceal its intentions; nor was it able to do so. Similarly, the Arabs, who knew from the beginning that Zionism's aim was the conquest of land, made perfectly clear their refusal to pay the price for the Jewish catastrophe. The pioneers well understood that the Arab national movement regarded Zionism as an enemy, even though it was obvious that the Jewish presence could contribute to the country's rapid modernization and the improvement of its economy.[51]

In 1891 a group of Arab notables from Jerusalem approached the Turkish government with complaints about the Jewish acquisition of lands,[52] and in the years before the First World War, the Arab opposition began to acquire definite features of a national struggle. This fact of life could not be ignored. Representatives of the World Zionist Organization, however, made various attempts before and during the war to reach an arrangement with the Arabs. The activities of Nahum Sokolov, one of the heads of the Zionist Organization, in Beirut and Damascus in the months before August 1914, and the meeting between Weizmann and King Faisal in Aqaba in May 1918 are the best known among them. The Zionist movement was impressed by the fact that in Cairo, for instance, the Balfour Declaration of November 1917 was not received with total hostility, and two Arab representatives participated in the large meeting held by the Zionist Organization in London on 2 December 1917 to celebrate British recognition of Zionist objectives.[53] But in general it was clear to everyone that the chief aim of the Zionist movement was to find allies to help it conquer the land.

What may have been acceptable to the Egyptians, the Saudis, or the Syrians was obviously not always acceptable to the Palestinians. After all, they had to have the last word, and they viewed the Balfour Declaration as a supreme danger, because they realized that it meant they could lose their land. The violent disturbances of 1920–21 in Upper Galilee, Jerusalem, and Jaffa, in which two of the best-known figures of the period—the writer Yosef-Haim Brenner and the soldier-pioneer Yosef Trumpeldor—were killed, were an immediate reaction to the declaration, badly led and organized but perfectly clear.

The next stage was marked by the uprising of 1929. From then until the great revolt that began in April 1936 and lasted until the Second World War, the Arab national movement did all it could to prevent the consolidation of the Yishuv and the creation of a Jewish state. In the "disturbances" of 1929, all Jews in Hebron were murdered, some Jews in Safed were slaughtered, and a number of isolated settlements were wiped out. The Arab revolt of the second half of the 1930s was a guerrilla war, and like all wars with irregular forces, it was accompanied by Arab acts of terror against Jews. Chronic insecurity arose in the country, but from the Arab point of view the uprising's results were the opposite of what its perpetrators had intended: the revolt not only contributed to the military capabilities of the Yishuv and its internal unity but led in July 1937 to the first Partition Plan, devised by the Royal Commission (the Peel Commission) appointed to investigate the situation. Britain retracted the plan, but the idea had nevertheless been given currency, remained at the center of public debate in the country, and was implemented after the Second World War, when the Jews' distress reached its peak.

The Arab struggle continued more vigorously after the Second World War, when hundreds of thousands of Jewish refugees needed a home in which they could rebuild their lives. The Arabs' refusal to agree to the immigration—however restricted—of Holocaust survivors languishing in refugee camps in Germany was absolute, no less absolute than their rejection of Jewish immigration in the early days of the mandate, and it caused immeasurable damage to the Arab cause. After the Holocaust, the Zionist endeavor to set up a Jewish state gained a moral basis, an urgency, and an international support that it had never had in the past. The opposition to the partition proposals of 1937, the Palestinian guerrilla war that began immediately after the UN decision of 29 November 1947 to partition the country, the invasion of the Arab armies at the end of the British mandate on 15 May 1948, and the Arab threat of extermination in May 1967 form a single chain of Arab acts of refusal to accept the existence of a Jewish state in Palestine.

So profound was Jewish distress in the 1940s that the Yishuv reacted to the decision to divide Palestine into two independent states with an extraordinary explosion of joy. On the night of 29–30 November 1947 Jews danced in the streets of Tel Aviv; on the same night the War of Independence broke out, formalizing a conflict that half a century later has not yet ended.

Six months later, on Friday, 14 May 1948, the fifth of Iyar 5708, in the afternoon, one day before the end of the British mandate, Ben-Gurion, as president of the Executive Committee of the Jewish Agency, proclaimed the founding of the state of Israel. He was surrounded by all the major figures of the labor movement. The state was established, and the goal of the young pioneers, who in the earliest years of the century had "come up" from Poland and Russia, had been achieved. The Zionist movement had been tireless in its efforts and single-minded in its obsession. It had triumphed over all adverse circumstances, inspired by the principle of the primacy of the nation.

During the long and difficult years of struggle, there developed a Jewish, and later an Israeli, refusal—especially after the Six-Day War of 1967—to recognize the legitimacy of the Palestinian national movement. Many members of the Jewish political and cultural elite, both of the Right and of the Left, considered an agreement to partition the country and the acknowledgment of a Palestinian nationality as a denial of three thousand years of history, a mortal blow to the rights of the Jewish people in the land of its fathers, and consequently an undermining of the foundations of Zionism. This view has been as destructive for Israel's policies since the Six-Day War as for the spiritual and moral climate in which Israeli society has developed in the last generation. The origins of this view go back to the days of the Second Aliyah and form an inseparable part of the founders' heritage.

With the conclusion of the mighty task of establishing national independence and bringing in masses of immigrants, the lack of a social vision rooted in a comprehensive outlook and universal values became fully apparent. All the particularistic solutions of nationalist socialism had the purpose of building up the strength of the nation-state; apart from preserving the entire land of Israel, all major objectives had been achieved. Objectives that were not achieved were not really intended to be achieved. Over the years, however, the price of particularistic, elitist solutions inevitably increased. The pioneering ideology, with its central principles—the conquest of land, the reformation of the individual, and self-realization—was not an ideology of social change; it was not an ideology that could establish a secular, liberal state and put an end to the war with the Arabs. With the end of the War of Independence and the completion of the great waves of immigration, it became apparent that the labor movement was not equipped with a conceptual framework that permitted it to move beyond the national revolution it had led and presided over with such conspicuous success.

CHAPTER ONE

The Primacy of the Nation: Aaron David Gordon and the Ethos of Nation-Building

THE NEGATION OF THE DIASPORA

Most national movements and parties that managed to translate their historical and cultural aspirations into political terms in the late 1800s and early 1900s viewed themselves as fighting not only for their nation's liberation from a foreign yoke, for its unification, or for the return of its separated brethren but also for protection from assimilation, loss of identity, and cultural annihilation. Zionism was also of this nature. Physical danger, which was a real threat to Eastern European Jews, was not the only peril. The danger of a loss of identity—the result of a modernization process that had begun to spread to Eastern Europe as well—was even more serious. A seemingly paradoxical situation had arisen. Although liberalism had suffered serious setbacks in Germany, Austria, and France—as a result it appeared that the Jews' emancipation was in jeopardy—the assimilation process continued at full strength. Most Jews continued willingly to pay the price for emancipation and gave up their national identity without difficulty, even when it was perfectly clear that this provided no solution to anti-Semitism. Despite the fact that society as a whole increasingly opposed their absorption even as individuals, cultural assimilation continued. The process of loss of identity was very rapid in Central and Western Europe, but signs of it also began to appear in the east, in the Russian empire. It could easily be supposed that in a short time assimilation would gain as much ground there as it had in Western Europe.

A concern for the fate of the nation, which for the first time in its history found itself in a situation in which the traditional frameworks that had held it together for so long were disintegrating, and whose destiny had begun to depend on the personal decision of each member, was accompanied by another, no less important phenomenon: a loathing of the diaspora. No one was more disgusted with their people, more contemptuous of its weaknesses and its way of life, than the founders. These stern individuals, who permitted no self-indulgence, described exiled Jews in terms that at times resembled those of the most rabid anti-Semites. Aaron David Gordon, for instance, wrote that the Jewish people was "broken and crushed . . . sick and diseased in body and soul."[1] This great disability, he said, was due to the fact that we are a parasitic people. We have no roots in the soil; there is no ground beneath our feet. And we are parasites not only in an economic sense but in spirit, in thought, in poetry, in literature, and in our virtues, our ideals, our higher human aspirations. Every alien movement sweeps us along, every wind in the world carries us. We in ourselves are almost nonexistent, so of course we are nothing in the eyes of other peoples either.[2]

Indeed, said Gordon, "It is not our fault that we have reached this point, but that is the fact: that is what exile is like."[3] This destructive criticism was very widespread at the time of the Second Aliyah and, no less than the danger of pogroms in Russia, was fundamental to Zionism.

From the beginning, Zionism faced stiff competition from two factors that played a powerful role in Jewish life: on one hand the instinctive urge to save one's skin and ensure one's economic existence by leaving Eastern Europe for the New World, and on the other hand the attraction of movements with a strong universal and humanistic component, bringing the promise of full emancipation: socialism and liberalism. Emigration to America was a response to the blows anti-Semitism inflicted, a consequence of modernization. The only barrier Zionism could place before this mass exodus was a rejection of the diaspora as such: not merely a rejection of the European diaspora, where the Jewish ability to survive had disappeared, but a total opposition to the concept of life in the diaspora. It was therefore necessary to demonstrate that Jewish life outside Eretz Israel was in its death throes. The Jews, wrote Gordon, were "a people hovering between life and death,"[4] and if they had not yet vanished from the face of the earth, it was only because "the body of the people of Israel existed in a mummified state." But now that "the walls of the pyramid have been breached . . . the body has begun to crumble, and the fragments are dispersed in all directions."[5] Thus, "In exile, we do not and cannot have a *living* culture, rooted in real life and developing within itself. We have no culture because we have no life, because the life that exists in exile is not our life."[6]

This concept of the diaspora was quite common among the leadership of the Second Aliyah. In 1915 Ben-Gurion repeated Gordon's statement almost word for word: "We cannot develop a normal and comprehensive culture in exile, not because we do not have the right but because we are physically and spiritually dependent on the alien environment that consciously or unconsciously imposes its culture and way of life upon us."[7] Thus, from the point of view of Zionist activism, there could be no compromise with exile. "Not to condemn exile means to perpetuate it," wrote Berl Katznelson at the height of the Second World War. In this connection he mentioned an article by Yosef Aharonowitz, one of Hapo'el Hatza'ir's founders, written a few years earlier. Aharonowitz, wrote Katznelson in December 1940, "contrasted Eretz Israel with the diaspora, not because he thought Eretz Israel could rescue all the Jews of the diaspora but because he saw that destruction was coming over the diaspora, and only the remnant of Israel in Eretz Israel would be rescued, and that would become the Jewish people."[8] A hatred of the diaspora and a rejection of Jewish life there were a kind of methodological necessity for Zionism.

This had two consequences. First, the explanation of anti-Semitism given by Jew haters of the school of social anti-Semitism fell on fertile soil here. Typical of this way of thinking was an article that appeared in *Ha'ahdut* in 1912.

> Modern anti-Semitism, which the Jews have suffered from during this last century, in politically free countries as well, is largely a consequence of the abnormal economic positions that the Jews have occupied in the diaspora. . . . Today, the Jewish people has many more shopkeepers, businessmen, teachers, doctors, etc., . . than the small and impoverished masses of Jewish workers is able to support. Thus, our shopkeepers, businessmen, and members of the liberal professions are obliged to gain their livelihood at the expense of the hard toil of the non-Jewish workers.[9]

Similar ideas may be found in abundance in all modern European anti-Semitic literature, and they underlie the claim that modern anti-Semitism is not an expression of religious or racial hatred but an attempt to root out parasitic elements that prevent the proper functioning of social systems. Thus, anti-Semitism has been represented as a defense of the working masses against their exploiters, and hence as a legitimate political phenomenon. It has been seen by many as a manifestation that does not necessarily contradict universal, humanistic, or egalitarian values. At the beginning of the century, the views of those who sought Jewish political independence and those who sought to purge their countries of the Jewish presence were often quite similar.

The second and most important consequence of the rejection of the diaspora, however, was that all hopes and efforts focused on Palestine. The country was regarded as the sole center of not only Jewish existence but also Jewish history, the source of inspiration and the elixir of life. As with all national movements, history played a decisive role in Zionism. As with all national movements, Zionist interpretations were very selective: not only was the favorite period always that of the kings and Maccabees, but it sometimes seemed that between the far-off days of independence and the beginning of the return to the land at the end of the nineteenth century, very few events worthy of mention had taken place in the nation's life. Not only was Jewish history in exile deemed to be unimportant, but the value of living Jews, Jews of flesh and blood, depended entirely on their use as raw material for national revival. The Jewish communities scattered across Central and Eastern Europe were important to the founders chiefly as a source of pioneers. They were considered to have no value in themselves.

Thus, even at the height of the Second World War, there was no change in the order of priorities: it was not the rescue of Jews as such that topped Berl Katznelson's order of priorities but the organization of the Zionist movement in Europe. In December 1940 Katznelson lashed out at Polish Jewry in areas conquered by the Soviet Union because they were unable to cope with the situation and "unable to fight even for a few days for small things like Hebrew schools. In my opinion," wrote Katznelson, "that is a terrible tragedy, no less than the trampling of Jewry by Hitler's jackboots."[10] Indeed, this was the founders' order of priorities from the beginning, and the tragedy of the Jews in the Second World War could not change it. Zionism was an act of rebirth in the most literal sense of the term. Thus, every event in the nation's life was evaluated according to a single criterion: the degree to which it contributed to Zionism.

This concept of Jewish history explains what, in itself, is quite astounding. On the eve of his death, the Kishinev pogroms of 1903 held a more important place in Katznelson's thinking than the Holocaust. In a famous series of lectures on the history of the labor movement in Palestine, given in the summer of 1944, Katznelson dwelled at length on the pogroms at Kishinev, on the reactions of Hayyim Nahman Bialik (1873–1934), the national poet, on the historian Simon Dubnow (1860–1941), on Ahad Ha'am (pseudonym of Asher Zvi Ginzberg, 1856–1927), the father of "spiritual Zionism," and on the heroic action of the youth Pinhas Dashevsky, who attacked one of the main instigators of the pogroms. Katznelson equated Dashevsky with Yosef Trumpeldor, the legendary hero killed by Arab guerrillas in 1920 during the battle for Tel Hai, the Jewish settlement on the Lebanese border. Dashevsky's deed, he said, was "the first revolutionary manifestation of Jewish national consciousness." This youth was particularly exemplary because "he understood the true nature of Zionism and adhered to it throughout his life."[11] Judging from volume 11 of Katznelson's *Writings*, the story of Pinhas Dashevsky had far greater importance for the ideologist of the labor movement than the Warsaw Ghetto Uprising. In June 1944 one could not yet know the place the revolt would have in the history of Zionism, but at that time—a whole year after the destruction of Polish Jewry—every child in Jewish Palestine knew about the effect of the Kishinev pogroms on national revival; the Kishinev pogroms had released the mechanism of the Second Aliyah. "Nevertheless," said Katznelson, "*this event* of Kishinev was central in Jewish history. It was decisive for Zionism."[12] Thus, one is hardly surprised to learn that in 1944, as in 1924 or 1914, the main problems on the movement's agenda remained the same: immigration and maintaining the movement's solidarity. When Katznelson spoke of a "disaster," he meant the internal difficulties of the labor movement, the "disaster of the Gdud Ha'avoda" or the "disaster of defection that befell Hashomer Hatza'ir,"[13] not the events taking place in Europe under Nazi rule.

For the people of the Second Aliyah, Zionism was not only an answer to the Jews' distress, and Eretz Israel was more than one night's shelter. In this matter, there were always two schools of thought in Zionism. The first, which can be described as the liberal or utilitarian school, viewed the Jews' gathering in Eretz Israel as a solution to physical and economic insecurity in Eastern Europe on one hand and as a response to liberalism's failure in Western Europe on the other. The second school viewed immigration to Eretz Israel as the culmination of Jewish history and the rescue of the nation as a historical entity. From the point of view of the first school, a Jew who clung to exile endangered his property or his person. The Jew—this was the logical conclusion to be drawn from the outbreak of anti-Semitism in France at the time of the Dreyfus Affair—carried anti-Semitism about with him like a piece of personal luggage. Jew hatred was an inseparable part of Jewish existence, and now there was no longer any reason to assume it would disappear with emigration to America. If emancipation had failed in France, there was no reason to suppose that it would succeed on the other side of the ocean. Thus, a concern for the safety of each individual made it imperative to find a territorial solution to the Jewish problem, which would ensure the nation first self-rule and later political independence. Zionism was the most rational solution, an empirical solution suited to the thinking of liberals steeped in Western culture such as Herzl and Nordau.

But Herzl and Nordau never reached Palestine, and liberal values never took root in the founders' ideology; this was not the thinking of groups of young activists who came from areas where tribal nationalism ruled unchallenged. From their point of view, Zionism's justification was not that it provided the most rational or effective solution to the Jews' need for security. The question of security, apart from their sense of shame at Jews' inability to defend their lives and honor during pogroms, was not central to their thinking. As they saw it, Zionism was an operation to rescue the nation and not an operation to rescue Jews as individuals. For them, the quantitative aspect was always secondary, and the founders knew from the beginning that only a few would be attracted to the task of building the nation. Thus, all efforts were directed toward the few thousand (toward the end of the 1930s there were tens of thousands already) who were organized in the Halutz (Pioneer) movement and in various youth movements. All their hopes were centered on this pioneering minority. To them, the masses of Jews who were not Zionists or who were not organized for immigration to Eretz Israel were of minor importance.

WHAT IS A NATION?

Aaron David Gordon, it is generally agreed, has a special place among the people of the Second Aliyah. To the pioneers who got off the ship at Jaffa, "this Jew of about fifty,"[14] as Katznelson described him after their first meeting, was already very old. But more important, Gordon was a man of intellectual stature. Among the young pioneers, he stood out as a giant. He was familiar with the dominant cultural trends of his time and knew how to adapt them to the needs of Zionism. Like Ahad Ha'am, Gordon was not an original thinker, but he was one of the few links between the young leadership of the labor movement and European culture as a whole. Katznelson was especially close to Gordon and absorbed his influence directly. At Kinneret, the legendary settlement on the shore of Lake Tiberias, they shared a room, and long afterward Katznelson related that he was the first person to see all of Gordon's manuscripts at that period.[15] There is no doubt that Gordon's influence on Katznelson was decisive and profound. In the struggle between the heritage of Borochov represented by Po'alei Tzion and the pure nationalist current represented by Hapo'el Hatza'ir, Gordon's presence in the country carried special weight for those semi-intellectuals who began their political activities before the First World War.

Gordon gave these young people, who lacked the intellectual equipment of a traditional Torah education and had not yet acquired any real European culture, the first solid basis on which to construct their national outlook. He developed a form of semisecular nationalism that in many respects, although in a far more moderate way, reflected some of the basic principles of European integral nationalism. "A complete and absolute nationalism," "a nationalism complete and absolute through and through," was how Gordon, in 1921, described the conceptual framework and modes of behavior that he deemed necessary for the nation's survival in the open and secular world of the future. For him, the existential danger was not anti-Semitism but liberalism. Since national life in exile, as we have seen, was not considered a life worth living, Gordon proposed a radical solution.

> If we do not have a complete and absolute national life embracing our entire existence, it is better that there should be full and total assimilation. If the national ideal is not the loftiest of ideals, which puts all other party and non-party ideals in the shade and which compels us to devote ourselves to it body and soul, it is better that there should be a total end to things, and that we should disappear in the midst of nations among whom we are scattered and dispersed. For it should be clear to us that if we do not take steps to secure our existence, assimilation will automatically prevail in consequence of the decline of religion in our time, especially if the position of the Jews in the lands of

the diaspora really improves. But if we cannot renounce nationalism, it must be complete and total, embracing everything, because this is the only kind that can give us a profound life as a people. This should be clear to us.[16]

The integral nationalism of Gordon is based on the assumption that the nation is "one great family,"[17] an organic body from which the individual draws not only his culture but his very existence. A nation, wrote Gordon, unlike a society, "is not a mechanical conglomeration of individuals from the general pool of humanity."[18] Unlike a society, "which is a mere artificial conglomeration, devoid of the spirit of life," a nation "is bound up with nature. Its living connection with nature is its creative force, which makes it a living entity."[19]

The nation is the source of life. "The nation created language (that is, human thought), religion (that is, man's conception of the world, the expression of man's relationship to the world), morality, poetry, social life. In this sense, one can say that the nation created man."[20]

On several occasions Gordon expressed his absolute rejection of the liberal conception of the nation as a collection of individuals. He called this a "society," that is, an "artificial conglomeration, devoid of the spirit of life,"[21] as opposed to the nation, "which created human nature and human life."[22] Moreover, "The nation represents the spirit of the individual."[23] And elsewhere he said that one should always remember that the soul of the people "is the source of the soul of each one of us, and that its life is the source of our life."[24] Finally, since it is a living body, a nation cannot exist for any length of time uprooted from the soil in which it grows. It receives its creative power from its roots in the soil. "This is the root of its soul," which sometimes it can preserve even after "being uprooted from its soil," but only if "it is not completely dried up or is not overlaid with the spirit of another nation."[25] Thus, a nation has to preserve its purity of soul, and it can do this only by settling on a piece of land, which is the inheritance of the nation. "Purity of spirit" was always one of the shibboleths of tribal nationalism. There is no doubt that one finds in Gordon's teachings, as Shlomo Avineri has pointed out, an echo of Slavophile nationalism.[26] In fact, one finds there not only echoes but a real intellectual affinity with integral nationalism.

Gordon was well acquainted with the liberal, individualistic, and universalistic way of thinking. He mercilessly attacked those who insisted on seeing the nation as a "fortuitous creation, a survival of the past, an unnecessary partition between men which was set up before the light of Higher Thought shone upon mankind," so that it now only remained "to destroy it and to leave it for the wide world, for humanity at large."[27] But Gordon was also aware of the perversions and dangers to which nationalism was prone. In this respect, Gordon has a special place among the theoreticians of integral

nationalism. He understood that Marxism, as well as Nietzschean individualism and Tolstoyan "altruism," could drive nationalism further and further
into the clutches of the "darkest forces." Nationalism was transformed into
a "brutal, vulgar chauvinism," and conditions were ripe for "the wild and
vulgar national egoism to explode in all its savagery."[28] Similar considerations applied to the relationship between the individual and the nation. "It
is forbidden to sacrifice man even on the altar of the nation," said Gordon.[29]
Yet, at the same time, "Individuals are like cells in the body of the nation."
A deterministic relationship defines the individual's behavior and his way of
thinking even when he is not aware of the importance of the "national character in his soul."[30] Gordon concluded that "the national 'I' is in this sense
the progenitor of the individual 'I,' or, at any rate, it plays a large part in its
formation and existence."[31] Gordon repeated this assertion in various forms,
together with the principle, which was one of the cardinal tenets of organic
nationalism, that this natural and organic relationship between the individual and the nation exists on an unconscious level, independently of the
individual's volition. This was a key concept: even when the individual constitutes a value in himself and is not called upon to sacrifice himself on the
altar of the nation, the relationship between himself and the nation remains
totally independent of his own powers of decision.

> Thus, we see in reality that each individual "I," to the degree that it is authen-
> tic—that is, to the degree that it draws from the depths of life, from the depths
> of the infinite—always draws from the wellspring of the nation: it is national in
> its productions and in all its manifestations, whether their progenitor is aware
> of it or not, and quite often despite the fact that their progenitor consciously and
> knowingly rejects nationalism (thought, it seems, does not always acknowledge
> its source even when it is genuine. Authenticity does not belong to conscious-
> ness but to below the level of the conscious. Thought is genuine only to the
> degree that it derives from that source).[32]

Thus we reach the conclusion that only members of the same nation
can participate in a common cultural tradition. This conception of the
relationship between the individual and the nation is inseparable from integral nationalism.

According to Gordon, the nation is the element linking the individual to
humanity at large. Humanity is made up not of individuals but of nations:
"The nation, so to speak, represents the spirit of the individual. . . . Through
the nation, the soul of each individual becomes a kind of reflection of cosmic
existence." The nation "is the link between the soul of the individual and the
soul of the world."[33]

There is no doubt that throughout his career Gordon was deeply influenced by Johann Gottfried von Herder. Herder's thinking had tremendous

importance in Eastern Europe. Shmuel Hugo Bergmann has already drawn attention to the similarity between Herder's and Gordon's views. Bergmann observed that "Herder's definition of the people and the state recurred in Gordon's 'people-state' concept. And, like Herder, who stressed the organic nature of the people (*Volk*) and the mechanical nature of the state, Gordon claimed that the people reflected the life of the cosmos, whereas the state was merely a machine." Bergmann regards Herder the father of a pluralistic concept of nationalism, advocating a comradeship between nations, believing in spontaneity, and disparaging both the state and a closed society. He writes that Zionism, in the beginning, drew from the same "sources of humanism as those which Herder offered the awakening peoples of Europe."[34]

There is no doubt that Herder's teachings, especially in their immediate context, in the second half of the eighteenth century, had a humanist dimension. But, at the same time, Herder's conception of the Volk community as an organic whole, his stress on tribal roots and on community's distinct collective consciousness, to which he also referred in terms of "national character" and "national spirit," his discussion of the conflict between "climate" and the "genetic force," had a different connotation at the beginning of this century. Herder's organic concept of the nation, the cult of the *Volksgeist* (the spirit of the people), his historicism, his assertion that the proper foundation of collective identity is a common culture, fostered a cultural nationalism that as early as the second half of the nineteenth century gave rise to the historical-biological form of nationalism. By contrast, liberal nationalism was inspired by the doctrine of natural rights and the idea that the individual had priority over society, and that civil society, as a collection of autonomous individuals, had priority not only over the state but also over the nation.

Neither liberal thought, which centered on civil society, nor Hegel's system, which was based on the state, corresponded to the needs of the Eastern European intelligentsia. This was even more applicable to the Jewish-nationalist intelligentsia: an acceptance of the liberal concept of society would have meant the end of the Jewish people as an autonomous unit, and Hegel's philosophy of history and philosophy of law had little significance where the Jews were concerned. However, the concept of nation offered by Herder, the father of *volkisch* thought, had much relevance in Eastern Europe. The definition of the nation not in political or judicial terms but in cultural, historical, linguistic, and religious terms raised the stature of all those peoples who had lost their political independence hundreds of years earlier. The idea that the individual owed his being to the nation, that unique cultural unit which derived its existence from nature and was rooted in the soil of the motherland, created a human identity independent of a person's political or social status.

In nationhood there is something cosmic, as if the spirit of nature of the nation's motherland fused with the spirit of the nation itself. . . . And that is what is all-important. This is the nation's source of life and creativity, its supreme source of abundance, and it constitutes the difference between the nation, a living and creative collective body, and a society, a mere functioning mechanism.[35]

This form of nationalism had a religious component. A cultural-organic conception of the nation necessarily included religion, which it saw as an inseparable part of national identity. This was the case in Eastern Europe, but also in Western Europe, in France and Spain. French integral nationalism was no less Catholic than Polish nationalism, and religion played the same role in it as it did in Poland or Romania. It was a focus of unity and identity, over and beyond social divisions. In integral nationalism religion had a social function, unconnected with its metaphysical content. Generally, it was a religion without God; in order to fulfill its function as a unifying force, religion required only external symbols, not inner content. Thus, it was natural that Gordon would reject anticlericalism and seek a rapprochement between the religious and the secular. He regarded Jewish anticlericalism as an imitation of European phenomena, an expression of spiritual servitude. Jewish anticlericalism, in his opinion, had no justification because "our religion does not give anyone power over anyone else." If certain rabbis aspired to clerical status, he said, they were in principle no more to be blamed than those who sought power "in the name of the Haskala [Jewish Enlightenment] or in the name of the proletariat."[36] Gordon admitted that the Haskala's negation of religion had been necessary to national revival, but now that it had taken place there was no reason to continue emulating others,

> for the simple reason that our religion is not, like the religion of the European peoples, of alien origin, but is the creation of our national spirit. Our religion permeates our national spirit, and our national spirit is to be found in every part of our religion. To such a point is this true that it is perhaps not too much to say that our religion is our national spirit itself, only in a form that has come down to us from primeval times, and it is no accident that we have survived on the strength of it until today. Its form has grown old, but its spirit seeks renewal.[37]

This was also the view of Katznelson and the great majority of the leaders of the Second Aliyah. They all regarded religious heritage or "tradition" as having a value in itself, without any connection to ceremonial or metaphysical beliefs.

Eliezer Schweid has examined the place of religion in Gordon's thinking. Gordon's expectation "that Zionism would prove to be a movement of religious renewal," wrote Schweid, "that only as such would it have a chance of succeeding, his prayer for the revival of prophecy among the people, is simply an expression of his belief in the existence of an eternal stratum of basic religious experience." Religion, according to Gordon, is "one of the basic factors that have made man what he is ever since he has been man." Schweid concludes with two observations that are particularly interesting from our point of view: on one hand, he points out Gordon's positive attitude not only to "the traditional requirements of religion: its beliefs, its rituals, its commandments as a whole," but also to "the historical manifestations of tradition"; on the other hand, he draws attention to "the paradox of religiosity without belief in God" in Gordon's thinking.[38]

In fact, this is not a paradox at all. European integral nationalism also regarded religion as an essential component of national identity. Consequently, its attitude to tradition, ritual, and, generally, the church as an institution was extraordinarily positive. Its affirmation of religion as a source of identity had no connection with metaphysics. At the end of the nineteenth and the beginning of the twentieth century, religion divested of a belief in God was considered an unrivaled basis for mobilization and a component of national identity not only in Eastern Europe but also in the West. This was an outstanding example of the common ground between all national movements.

Essentially, Gordon, and Katznelson after him, accepted Ahad Ha'am's view that "someone who says 'I have no connection with the Jewish religion, with the historical force that gave life to our people and influenced its life, spirit, and observances for thousands of years' . . . may be a decent man, but he is not a national Jew even if he lives in Eretz Israel and speaks the national tongue."[39]

In the Zionist context, the religious element was reinforced by a supremely important factor: for the founders, the Bible was not only a tool to cement the inner unity of society but an indispensable weapon in the struggle for the land. "We in this country," said Gordon, "created the saying 'Man is made in the image of God,' and this statement has become part of the life of humanity. With this statement, a whole universe was created." From this he drew the following political conclusion: "With this, we gained our right to the land, a right that will never be abrogated as long as the Bible and all that follows from it is not abrogated."[40]

It may be said that the religiohistorical element as a focus of national identity had even greater importance in Zionism than in other national movements. In the final analysis, it was religion in the broadest sense, with all its national and historical connotations, that provided the justification for the conquest of the country and the legitimation of Jews' return. As in all expressions of integral nationalism, there is in Gordon a turn to irrationality.

We have seen the importance Gordon attached to the unconscious, both individual and collective. Like all theoreticians of tribal nationalism, he abhorred an excessive inclination toward reason and skepticism. National rebirth was supposed to be a remedy for that weakness as well, a weakness that Gordon very typically viewed as the cause of modern degeneracy.

> Is this not the very thing, the very defect for which we hope to find healing in a new life? Being sick with too much cerebralism and lack of life, and eaten up by doubts to the point of despair? One could say that all cultured humanity is clearly sick with excessive cerebralism, for the whole tendency of the present culture is toward excessive cerebralism at the expense of life, and it is this, in fact, that is responsible for the decline of humanity.[41]

To counter this "excessive cerebralism," Gordon, like Brenner and all the cultural critics of the period, turned to *élan vital*, mysticism, the forces of the soul. In fact, his work reflects the intellectual revolution of the turn of the century. Menachem Brinker has pointed out the feverish preoccupation with Nietzsche in Russian literature between 1890 and 1905. The currents that were active among young Jewish intellectuals at the end of the nineteenth and the beginning of the twentieth century found their way into the work of Brenner, and Nietzsche is no less present in his narratives than Tolstoy or Marx.[42] These European influences are also very recognizable in Gordon. Even when it is difficult to know whether these are direct influences or were absorbed from the prevailing Zeitgeist, there is no doubt about the way in which these influences molded Gordon's vision of history. His 1920 article, "A Clarification of the Basis of Our Ideas," is an adaptation of Nietzsche to the needs of nationalism, very common at that time among nationalist intellectuals in Europe. The taste for spontaneity, the cult of "life," and the rejection of the "mechanical" and the "herd instinct" will be familiar to any reader of the post-Nietzschean synthesis, anyone whose ears are attuned to the expression of the reaction against modernity, socialism, and liberalism which swept over Europe at the beginning of the century. Whether such an interpretation was faithful to Nietzsche's teaching is irrelevant in this context.[43]

When he asked himself the basic question put by every thinker and writer at the beginning of this century—"How can people be mobilized?"—Gordon accepted the conclusions of the Sorelian doctrine of "myths." He did not call it that but embraced its view that in order to mobilize people one must appeal to their instincts and emotions rather than to their intellect. "An idea has little influence on the public," he said, "as long as it is the property of individuals, or as long as the public has only a cerebral understanding of it but does not grasp it emotionally. But one has no greater power over life than when the idea becomes everyone's property, the property of all." For Gordon, the great, the one-and-only question in history and politics was:

"How does one get the public to accept the idea until it becomes its own property, part of its very being, working naturally and constantly within it as an inalienable force?"[44] As early as 1904, in his "Letter from Eretz Israel," Gordon claimed that nothing can be achieved by realism, or without self-sacrifice: material interests have no power to move people. Only the spirit, the consciousness, and the will can do this.[45] Even socialism, wrote Gordon, had power only because of the idea it contained, because of its ability to turn "the idea from a spirit hovering upon the surface of life into a movement, a mighty current within life itself."[46] Gordon's explanation of socialism's success shows that he did not underestimate it, which made him all the more determined to fight it.

NATIONALISM VERSUS SOCIALISM: THE AMELIORATION OF MAN, NATION, OR SOCIETY?

Gordon regarded socialism as the diametrical opposite of nationalism and its greatest enemy. Socialism's appeal to emotions made it all the more dangerous. Gordon realized that because of its essential nature and its principles, no synthesis between socialism and nationalism was possible. In his view, socialism held that "the basis of life is matter," and the human unit on which it depended was society, the "mechanical collectivity," whereas nationalism represented "the living collectivity, the collective personality, collective man."[47] Gordon not only understood the nature of Marxism but knew that there was also another form of the "mechanical," another type of "materialism," namely, capitalism and liberalism. He thus rejected with equal force both of these individualistic systems, which represented the domination of "the mechanical" over "the natural." He complained that capitalism, "with its advanced technology and cities cut off from nature[,] . . . has finally destroyed the collective cell, the nation . . . and reduced the individual, the private personality, to an isolated atom."[48]

Gordon rebelled against the sense of urban alienation that industrial societies and large cities necessarily produced by tearing individuals away from their natural roots, soil, and landscape and by the modernization process that shattered the organic unity of the community, turning an individual into an isolated molecule without an identity. Gordon's view of the individual was essentially anti-individualistic and communitarian. The individual was considered a cell in the body of the nation, an inseparable part of the whole.

We see that Gordon grasped the point that socialism and liberalism had in common: the concept of society as a collection of individuals and the view of the individual as the final object of all social activity. These were precisely the social principles that integral nationalism abhorred, seeing them as a mortal danger to the nation. In this struggle, Gordon was totally uncompromising. He was consistent in the positions he adopted, and in the best traditions of integral nationalist ideology he attacked socialism and liberalism with the same vehemence. As he saw it, the nature and purpose of socialism and liberalism were completely opposed to the nature and purpose of nationalism. "In the world of mere matter there is room only for isolated individuals, who together are called humanity," wrote Gordon. He hated this idea, which he saw, with some justification, as one of the foundations of modernity. "Modern thought," he wrote, "which bases everything on observation and experiment, has come to the general conclusion that the basis of life is matter. It sees the economic factor as the motive power of life, as if soul and spirit were not important." He deplored "the tendency to make people envisage the future in mechanical, materialistic terms, in terms of the economic well-being of the individual."[49]

Thus, Gordon rejected the individualistic, hedonistic, and utilitarian content of both liberalism and Marxism. On one hand, he condemned "the teachings of socialism," which, he said, were "the doctrine of a human collectivity whose members have only a mechanical relationship, and whose collective life has only a mechanical economic basis"; on the other hand, he attacked "modern individualistic teachings," because "individualism shrinks into its skin like a tortoise into its shell."[50] Gordon repeatedly said that "in these teachings . . . the principle of contraction . . . is so profound that it can only give rise to materialism. It is the principle of contraction that produces the mechanical quality in human life, its separation from the life of the cosmos."[51]

However, in the context of Jewish Palestine, Gordon believed that the true enemy was socialism and not liberalism. Thus, his whole struggle was directed against a single objective: Marxism, which the first members of Po'alei Tzion had brought with them from Russia. Although Borochov had already adapted this socialism to allow it to be assimilated by the national movement, Gordon rejected this solution, declaring that "between nationalism and socialism there is an essential opposition, a contradiction that cannot be resolved. Those socialists who violently oppose nationalism are undoubtedly consistent."[52]

Gordon repeated this claim many times in various forms while adhering consistently to the principle. The ultimate argument was always that "if one pairs socialism with nationalism, one is pairing one kind with another, and the pairing cannot be successful."[53] In 1909 Gordon insisted on his total opposition to socialism, giving the following as his reason: "I am as distant from socialism in the form in which it exists today as Judaism is from materialism."[54] This, indeed, was an essential principle of his, and it is of paramount importance for an understanding of his teachings and their influence on the labor movement. In his rejection of the materialism of socialism, he employed the classic terminology of romantic, volkisch nationalism.

At the beginning of the century, *materialism* was a code word describing the rational and utilitarian nature of both socialism and liberalism. The idea that society and the state were tools to serve the good of the individual was regarded as materialistic. The term *materialism* denoted a hedonistic and utilitarian concept of society, a readiness to accept the pursuit of wealth and happiness as a legitimate goal, and a belief that human weaknesses and the darker side of human existence were the products of social factors rather than personal ones. No opinion was more despised by the integral nationalist school than the idea that the reform of civilization necessitated the reform of society rather than of the human being. In many respects, Gordon was a moralist who was bound to be revolted by the political culture of modern materialism. "It is no accident," he wrote, "that the founders of socialism based socialism on materialism and class warfare. The very fact that they based their whole argument on one aspect of human life shows how mechanical their thinking was."[55] The "mechanical" nature of socialism particularly repelled Gordon. Although he was aware that socialism had nonmaterialistic currents, he condemned all forms of socialism as mechanical.

In Gordon's terminology, the "mechanical" denoted first individualism, which contradicted the idea of the individual as a cell in the body of the nation, an organic part of a whole. All representatives of the various organic or communitarian approaches hated individualism, in the sense that this concept had possessed since the seventeenth century, when the founders of Western liberalism, Hobbes and Locke, compared man to a molecule and society to a collection of units grouped together for their mutual advantage. In many ways, there is a great similarity between Gordon's point of view and that of the communitarian thinkers who flourished in Europe at the beginning of the century in the Catholic, antiliberal, and anti-Marxist Left. Gordon, whether consciously or instinctively, was in agreement with these cultural trends, which, although they contained oppositions and contradictions, had the same disgust for both the individualistic and the materialistic bourgeois culture and for Marxism, which was basically no less materialistic and individualistic. Adherents of the communitarian philosophy promoted organic concepts, which negated both capitalism and Marxism. But Gordon was also well grounded in the principles of romantic nationalism, which detested the "dryness" of liberalism and Marxism. He yearned for the spiritual exaltation, the outbursts of vitality and altruism of romantic nationalism, which, for him, represented the antithesis of the various kinds of Marxist socialism.

> One feels this mechanical quality in all the actions, in all the public activities of the socialists, and in all that they write. One sometimes seems to catch sight, here and there, of signs of breadth, flights of imagination and song, but when one looks more closely one sees that this is only the sweep of an exhibi-

tion, of a large battlefield, of a public procession, but not the expanse of a universe; that it is the flight of an aeroplane, of some advanced Zeppelin with all its sound and noise, but not the flight of an eagle, nor of a dove, nor even of a small free bird; that it is the sound of a gramophone, of some extraordinary singing machine, but not the song of a living person.[56]

And on the previous page, he observed:

> The greatness of nationalism is its cosmic dimension. Socialism is totally different. . . . It is the absolute opposite of nationalism, being entirely based on production and technology, whereas nationalism represents life and creativity. . . . For this reason, the reforms and innovations in human life proposed by socialism depend chiefly on the reform of the social order and not on the reform and renewal of the spirit of man.[57]

Gordon regarded the socialists' ambition of reforming society as merely an aspect of the hated "mechanical" approach. Their preoccupation with society rather than with the individual as a cell in the body of the nation reflected, in his view, a preference for quantity over quality. Socialism's exploitation of the power of the masses—in Gordon's terminology, the exploitation of "determinstic force, or, one might say, the force of the herd"— its concern with class consciousness, and its doctrines of class warfare and the dictatorship of the proletariat betrayed its essential unhealthiness.[58] Its practice of making social change the focus of human endeavor hindered the improvement of human beings, encouraged their egoistic and utilitarian tendencies, and finally imposed the "spiritual coercion" of a minority on the majority.[59] Instead of developing the workers' sense of creativity and personal responsibility, socialism fostered a "herd psychology," utilitarian demands, materialism, collectivism, and an obsession with class warfare. It did not matter whether workers' claims were right or wrong.[60] Socialism made it impossible to "change man's life and improve his character"; thus socialism's bankruptcy was revealed in all its starkness.[61]

This total war against socialism did not, however, imply an acceptance of social injustice. A conservative who rejected socialism in the name of history and the natural order might have abandoned the idea of seeking justice and equality. The integral nationalists did not do this; they wished to do justice for the sake of the indivisibility of the nation, but while completely dissociating themselves from socialism. "As if justice and socialism were synonymous!" cried Gordon, repeating a formula used by all European integral nationalists.[62] Moreover, the problem of exploitation was said to be not only of the workers but "of the people."[63] Capitalism was not only the enemy of wage earners but the enemy of the people as a whole. Gordon declared that "our nationalism is all-embracing."[64] Nationalism, which by definition represented the life of the nation in all its aspects, embraced the social side as well. A nationalist ideology could not be indifferent to the fate of any part of the people. Thus, in order to defend workers, in order to support their demands, there was no reason to resort to socialism. It was enough, for this purpose, to adhere to the principle of national solidarity. "We demand justice—justice in all its forms, between a man and his fellow human beings and between one people and another—not in the name of socialism, but in the name of nationalism,"[65] wrote Gordon. He appealed to justice for the simple reason that "a robber is a robber, and a perverter of justice is a perverter of justice, whether the robber is a capitalist or a proletarian."[66]

We have already seen that Gordon's main objection to socialism was that "it bases human life *chiefly* on the reform of social order and not on the reform and renewal of the spirit of the people."[67] Indeed, the entirety of Gordon's nationalist ideology was focused on the reform of the human being and the reform of the nation. If the individual is a limb in the body of the nation, the improvement of the nation clearly depends on the reform of the human being, and the reform of the human being can be achieved only through labor. "In order to renew life and reform the human being," wrote Gordon,[68] one must "wage war against parasites and parasitism, and not against this or that class or this or that group. We must wage war against parasitism of every kind, parasitism that is also rooted among us, the workers, and also against spiritual parasitism, parasitism on the spirit, the thought, the creativity of others, the universes and lives of others, and so on."[69] For Gordon, like all socially aware nationalists, "parasitism" was first a cultural rather than a socioeconomic phenomenon. For him, a parasite was anyone, an individual or a group, who did not stand on his own two feet, who did not provide for himself, and who was dependent in some way on his fellow human beings. This, he claimed, was the situation of the Jewish people as a whole, including the Yishuv in Eretz Israel. It was a parasitic body living off the labor of others. And finally, it fell into spiritual parasitism as well: "We are parasites living on the handiwork of strangers and we do not feel it, for we have been parasites exploiting the minds of strangers, the souls of strangers, and the lives of strangers."[70]

Thus, humanity—individuals, social groups, and peoples—was divided into two basic categories, the only ones that were really significant: those who created material and spiritual wealth, people living on their own labor, and the others, that is, all those whose dependence on their fellow human beings made them material and spiritual cripples. Gordon rejected the Marxist conception of society, the class conception subscribed to by all streams of world socialism. He dismissed the theories of socialism on the grounds that they were trivial or absurd. In explaining the relationship between capitalists and proletarians, Gordon's ultimate argument was that "the power of the capitalists does not reside in their wealth, and indeed, they do not have any real power. Their power is simply the individual weakness of the workers."[71] And farther on he wrote that "the war between capitalism and the proletariat is not so much a war between capital and labor as a war between the individual and collectivity in its modern form."[72] The solution to class struggle, as to all political, social, and cultural problems, lay in the reformation of people by developing their "sense of creativity and responsibility."[73]

In the reform of the human being, the essential first step toward the reform of the nation and the normalization of Jewish existence, physical labor had a special role. Katznelson even went so far as to say that his life in Eretz Israel and the work of Gordon had been entirely consecrated to the promotion of physical labor.[74] Physical labor was for Gordon the means to the solution of all the problems of humanity and society. First, it was the prerequisite of all spiritual life: "The ultimate foundation of all works of the spirit is physical labor. That is, it is their foundation not in an economic sense but in a *moral sense*, in the sense of constituting a foundation of *truth* for all constructions of the spirit."[75] Second, physical labor was the prerequisite for the reform of humans and the renewal of national existence.[76] Similarly, Gordon viewed physical labor as the solution to the problem of exploitation and the realization of social justice. If everyone, he wrote, agreed "to abandon a life of parasitism, and if all potential idealists . . . went to work and lived a life of labor, . . . they would constitute a body that, through their multiplication, would slowly shift the center of power and activity in economic life and public life in general from the sphere of the capitalists to that of the workers."[77] And finally, labor was a tool to redeem the land: the true instrument for conquering the land and restoring it to the Jewish people.[78] "Thus, in saying 'labor,' we have said everything. And if we add that labor must be free, on the basis of the nationalization of the land and the tools of labor, we have no need to seek the support of any mechanical socialism."[79]

In these circumstances, not only was socialism unnecessary, but in Gordon's opinion it stood in opposition to all personal and national renewal. Socialism denied the primacy of the nation, loathed nationalism in its organic and cultural forms, and saw a change in the ownership of wealth as the prerequisite to a change in life. It focused on the need for a social revolution and regarded all attempts to "reform man" as naïveté and bourgeois hypocrisy, if not sheer deceit. It was bound to be described by Gordon as the great enemy of Zionism. Thus, Gordon stated categorically: "We did not come to Eretz Israel on behalf of socialism, and it was not for its sake that we came here to labor and to live on the fruits of our labor."[80] Gordon endlessly repeated this assertion, and at the same time he provided the truest description of the real situation: "We all came here to be the nation and to be ourselves. A small minority came here in the name of socialism, bringing its teachings."[81]

Moreover, socialism, with its universal and international dimension, represented a mortal danger to Jewish nationalism, as it threatened to bring the hated exile to Eretz Israel. The founders' hatred of the exile knew no limits, and socialism represented an "exilic demon" that led astray "a rootless people hovering between life and death."[82] Socialism, wrote Gordon in 1920, in an article entitled "Building the Nation," split the unity of the pioneering force that came to Eretz Israel, shattered its ideological cohesion, and weakened its purpose by promoting class interests and links with the international proletariat. He claimed that if socialism had triumphed, instead of a nation being built in Palestine, everything would have remained "as in the cities and shtetls of the exile." Socialism, wrote Gordon, was based on the opposition of classes, but the well-being of the nation required a solidarity transcending social divisions. One should seek unity with "our 'bourgeois.' Are they not the multitudes of the house of Israel: the shopkeepers, the merchants, etc., etc.?"[83]

There is no doubt that Gordon's position was entirely consistent and of an unassailable inner logic. To those who hoped that one day "a suitable compromise would be found between nationalism and socialism," Gordon answered, "Here, no compromise is possible. Here, the only thing possible is a slow, imperceptible transition from socialism to nationalism in its new form."[84] The new nationalism, for its part, understood that "all attempts to renew human life by means of new social arrangements and social education without beginning everything afresh, from the foundations, are only palliatives, perhaps able to provide a superficial and deceptive alleviation of the sickness for a time, and are in fact harmful, in that they distract attention from the cause of the illness and the necessity for a radical cure."[85]

A radical cure was possible only through labor. Labor had both a spiritual and a national value. It created the new human being and the new nation; it was the expression of self-realization and of national rebirth; it symbolized a separation from the exile and was the supreme moral and practical instrument for conquering the land. It also represented a direct contact with nature. "To work in nature, to experience nature in Eretz Israel," and to feel part of the country, wrote Gordon, were one and the same thing.[86]

In Gordon's opinion, the idea of physical labor "as a natural value in our lives,"[87] as a condition for "the renewal of life here,"[88] that is, the redemption of the individual and the nation, and "the war against parasitism through labor" necessitated "the nationalization of the land and the tools of labor."[89] Gordon laid great stress on the fact that there was no connection between his call for nationalizing the means of production and socialism or class warfare; nor, he wrote, was there any connection between the war against "parasites" and the war against the bourgeoisie. However, he claimed there was an inalienable connection between "the idea of labor and the nationalization of the land."[90] Just as labor was the inescapable prerequisite of the reformation of man and national redemption, so "the primary foundation of national creativity . . . is the land."[91] Gordon was in total agreement with those who thought that "all the land should be national, just as all industry should be national. And there is no need," he wrote, "to be exploiters or exploited, but simply Jews working and living on their labor."[92] The nationalization of agricultural and industrial resources was both an "economic necessity" and a means of redeeming the people.[93]

Thus, Gordon can be ranked among the theorists of modern nationalism who on one hand developed a violent anti-Marxism, which also meant rejecting democratic socialism, yet on the other hand opposed capitalist exploitation and demanded public ownership of the means of production on behalf of the nation. The unity of the nation required the elimination of the exploitation that tore it apart, just as it necessitated an uncompromising struggle against the principle of class warfare. Gordon entirely opposed the policy of promoting "Jewish labor" in Palestine to serve any class interests whatsoever. In 1920, after the founding of Ahdut Ha'avoda and the Histadrut, he saw fit to declare, on behalf of those who rejected the idea of the unification of Hapo'el Hatza'ir and Po'alei Tzion, that Hapo'el Hatza'ir "did not seek socialism—either political socialism or productive socialism (if its activities in any way resemble productive socialism, that is, life; but the way of socialism is not its way, nor is the spirit of socialism its spirit)."[94] The only union he recognized was "the complete union of soul of the entire people, without any differences of class, party, or sect."[95] Although Gordon regarded the reform of the human being as a value in itself, he considered the nation the sole criterion of all social and political action. It was the national "I" that prescribed the nature of the individual "I";[96] he did not view the individual as having any existence outside the organic framework of the nation.[97] Thus, the moral arguments that Gordon used in favor of public ownership of the means of production were nationalist.

In 1920 Gordon summed up his nationalist outlook in two articles. In "Building the Nation," an essay that can be counted among the classics of nationalist socialism, he demonstrated his awareness of the deeper implications of his teachings.

> I do not mean that we must be segregated from all other peoples, but the interaction and hence the comradeship between peoples must be an interaction of complete bodies, like the interaction of celestial bodies. There can be no question of an interaction of parts of these bodies *against the other parts*. Any union of parts of different bodies *against the other parts* of those bodies necessarily produces a division in those bodies and harms their wholeness of spirit, vitality, power of creativity, and inspiration. This means that such a union unwittingly destroys in the depths, from within, the subjective spiritual foundation of the structure that this type of unification is intended to create.[98]

In the second article, "On the Unification," Gordon gave us another classic example of nationalist socialist doctrine.

> The socialists can say what they like, but I say quite openly: we are closer to our own "bourgeois" than to all the foreign proletariats in the world. It is with them, with our bourgeois, that we wish to unite, and we seek their resurrection as we seek our own. We shall fight their parasitism: perhaps we shall fight it more than the socialists themselves, just as every one of us would combat his own weaknesses more than the weaknesses of others. But even in the midst of this war, we shall never forget for a moment that they are our own brethren and flesh and blood, whose sins and transgresssions are our own, which we have to correct, just as we have to correct our own sins and transgressions.[99]

Like all nonconservative, or revolutionary, nationalists, Gordon knew that economic oppression, like great social differences, tears the nation apart and places its future in jeopardy. He rejected the rule of finance and class warfare in equal measure. The perpetuation of the existing social and economic order was almost as dangerous, in his opinion, as a socialist revolution. Gordon condemned the "rotten order of the domination of work by capital," but he claimed that capitalists and "those living on the work of others" who are interested in maintaining that order "constitute a very small part of any people." The great majority of the population, including the middle classes, has no reason to want "that rotten order to continue." In the best traditions of nationalist socialism, Gordon maintained that "from the national point of view, the war between labor and capital is not a class war and is not only an economic conflict but a war of the people against its parasitic elements, a war of life against corruption." He continued: "The power of the people is in labor, and the people wants the worker to eat the fruit of his labor in its entirety but does not want the power of his labor, the power of the people, to come to nothing."[100] The worker, wrote Gordon, is the people, and workers as a class constitute the majority of the people, as opposed to a small stratum of exploiters. The war against exploitative capital is not a war against the bourgeoisie (a social category that in Gordon's oeuvre generally appears in quotation marks) but against parasitical elements, for the true struggle of all times and places is between producers and parasites.

Finally, Gordon asked the workers not to waste their energies on a war against capital, "which is essentially international, or a-national and inhuman," but "to concentrate on work, which is essentially national, and to fight against capital within the limits of the nation." Farther on, Gordon added another principle, which would become basic to constructive socialism and would be a chief feature of the cultural revolution as interpreted by the labor movement: "The emphasis should be not on the workers' portion of the immediate material benefits of labor but on the work itself—that is, its creativity and the spiritual benefit contained in it."[101]

Thus, in addition to possessing a moral value, labor also had a national value: the reformation of the individual and the rebirth of the nation would come about through labor, as would the conquest of the land. Here, the workers played the role of "a vanguard going before the people." However, in a letter to Brenner in 1912, Gordon was careful to point out that although in his teachings "the main emphasis is on the actions of a few," he was not advocating a Nietzschean morality.[102] These few are "the first to go forward and reach the place where the people are to be gathered," but this group should not "regard itself as a special class among the people, or as one part in opposition to another part."[103] It serves as an infrastructure for the national edifice; it assumes responsibilities and experiences hardships, but unlike the proletariat in socialism, it has to remain an inseparable part of the nation as a whole. The Yishuv in Eretz Israel, the prototype of such a pioneering group, was "the first living cell of the national body in the process of resurrection."[104] Its task was to bring to fruition the rights of the Jewish people over Eretz Israel.

THE RIGHT TO THE LAND: THE POWER OF HISTORY

Like every other system of thought, Gordon's thinking, which helped order the outlook of the labor movement, developed not only through its own inner logic but in response to historical necessities. In 1909 Gordon declared that "the land of Israel is ours as long as the people of Israel lives and does not forget its country. But, on the other hand, we cannot maintain that the Arabs have no part in it. The question is: in what sense and to what degree is it ours, and how much is it theirs? And how can one reconcile the claims of the two sides?" It is especially interesting that after he recognized the validity of these conflicting claims to the land and the necessity of finding a balance between them, Gordon was careful not to decide in favor of either of the two peoples. "The question," he wrote, "is not so simple and requires much study." In those far-off days of the Second Aliyah, Gordon refused to enter this minefield and formulated an opinion that corresponded to his concept of national rebirth: "One thing is certain, and that is that the land will belong more to the side that is more capable of suffering for it and working it, and which will suffer for it more and work it more. . . . That is only logical, that is only just, and that is how it should be in the nature of things."[105]

There is another interesting point here. Gordon made land ownership contingent on its redemption through labor—"One sees here, once again, the power of labor and the place it has in our resurrection and redemption"[106]—but this was not the only prerequisite of ownership, which at that stage was in any case partial and shared between Jews and Arabs. The other prerequisite was the awareness of this right; the right existed as long as the people of Israel "did not forget its land." Yet, however that may be, the fulfillment of that right required national determination, spiritual strength, and persistence in pursuing one's objectives.

But most of all the right of ownership would be retained only if the nation passed through a process of individual and collective moral renewal, which could be attained only through labor. In these years before the First World War, the belief in the necessity of moral renewal as the basis for national renewal had such an important place in Gordon's thinking that in 1914 he declared: "If I believed that our renewal and redemption would come about only through the labor of others, I would run away from here as one flees in a revolution to any place one can see and to wherever one's legs will carry one. Give me the worst exile or the worst calamity, but not a parasitic renewal and a parasitic redemption!"[107]

With the end of the war, Gordon changed his tune. Gordon's thought, as well as Po'alei Tzion's, underwent a modification. On one hand, labor still held to its central position as a means by which a people shaped its universe and created its redemption. A people, wrote Gordon, could lose its freedom, "but the land, in fact, always remains in the possession of those who live on it and work it. . . . Land is acquired by living on it, by work and productivity."[108] On the other hand, a new argument was now put forward, which from then on held an increasingly important place: that of an unquestionable and inalienable historical right, which did not, in itself, depend on the will and capability of that generation, the eternal right of the people of Israel to the land of Israel. This right was confirmed by the inability of the Arabs to cultivate and settle the country.

> We have a historical right to the land, which remains with us as long as another living and creative force does not wrest it from us. Our land, which in days gone by was "flowing with milk and honey" and which in any case was the seat of a high culture, has become more poor, desolate, and abandoned than any other civilized country, and it is also almost uninhabited. This is a sort of confirmation of our right to the land, a suggestion that the land awaits us.[109]

The first year after the British victory in Palestine and Allenby's entry into Jerusalem (December 1917) was one of hope for messianic redemption. The Jewish Battalions of the British army were still stationed in the country. The optimism that prevailed with its liberation by the forces of the government that had just given the Zionist movement the Balfour Declaration was expressed in the expectation of a wave of pioneering immigration of unprecedented proportions. A completely new situation had arisen: a God-forsaken province of the disintegrating Ottoman Empire had turned into a center of international attention. The Middle East had been divided into spheres of influence, Britain and France determined the land's frontiers, and the

British Empire recognized the rights of the Arab national movement. This movement also began to claim Palestine for itself, and the more perspicacious leaders of the Second Aliyah, especially Ben-Gurion, began to recognize the depth of the opposition of the Arab national movement to Jewish settlement.

Gordon was not a politician in the sense that Ben-Gurion, Katznelson, Tabenkin, and Ben-Zvi were. In addition to being one of the most interesting thinkers of the new Jewish nationalism, he was also a humanist. But he too recognized that the claim of the Jewish people to Palestine required a stronger foundation than the one provided by redemption through labor. Thus, during and after the final year of the First World War, he made the historical argument the main one to justify the activities of the pioneers of the Second and Third Aliyahs.

The conceptual framework that Gordon elaborated in 1918 to encourage the hoped-for wave of settlement was still based on a delicate balance between historical rights and the right of moral conquest through labor.

> The problem is expansion. The question is: who has more right to expand on a soil that has not yet been acquired through work and creativity? Quantity is not the main factor here but quality: the force of life and growth (as we see in the vegetable kingdom) and the force of work and creativity. Whoever works the most, creates the most, and shows the most dedication will gain the most moral right to the land and the most power over it. A peaceful rivalry is taking place here, and our right to participate is due especially to our historical right to the land. And in this we should be joined by the whole Jewish people in all the lands of the diaspora. This right to a peaceful rivalry, to an expansion in the land, does not belong only to the small community that lives here but to a people of twelve million souls.[110]

Here the scales began to tip in favor of history. When Gordon stressed the right of the entire Jewish people to Palestine, he meant that historical right had precedence over a right based on labor. He also recognized the Arabs' historical right to the country but denied them the right to rule the land because political control had never been theirs. In this respect, there was equality between Jews and Arabs, and the land was open to a free rivalry. In the final analysis, Gordon recognized that the Arabs had "a historical right to the country, just as we do," but he immediately qualified this by writing that "our historical right is undoubtedly greater."[111] This was the solid foundation on which Gordon based the Jewish right to own the land. The realization of that right depended on the worker; it was necessary to treat the Arabs with the greatest possible fairness and even to be ready to pay "two or three times the proper value" of the land purchased, but one must always remember that in practice, in daily life, "there is no other right to the land and no other form of possession of it than the right and the power of possession through labor." Thus, concluded Gordon, "From now on, we have an objective, real, political categorical imperative: to work. And to the degree that we work, the country will belong to us, and if not, no 'national homes' or 'blood and fire' will be of any avail."[112] Two years later, in 1920, Gordon again insisted on the need "to confirm and renew our right to our land through real physical labor."[113]

Gordon continued to maintain this position but knew that, following the Balfour Declaration, a more complex form of reasoning was required. "If, until now," he wrote, "until the outbreak of the war, we needed only to acquire the right to the land through labor, now, in this new situation, we must make clear to ourselves and others our right as a nation to this land and our political rights as a people of this land."[114] He rejected rights based on conquest, the argument that power confers rights. Gordon was a consistent antimilitarist. He hated naked force and regarded military organizations as a "vast, perpetual hypnosis."[115] He condemned those who claimed that "the use of the fist [was] a supreme heroism" and believed that brute force was "a desecration of the true spirit of devotion."[116] To his friends who had enlisted in the Jewish Battalions and who seemed to have allowed uniforms and arms to go to their heads, Gordon declared that the army was the source of the "rule of wickedness and parasitism."[117] In this, Gordon differed from European nationalists and made a decisive contribution to preventing the development of a cult of force, if not the use of it, in the Zionism of the Left.

But Gordon was no unrealistic dreamer. He fully realized that the principle of redemption through labor, in addition to possessing a moral value, also had a quantitative aspect. The country could not be redeemed through labor if there was an insufficient number of Jews to perform labor. When it became clear that the construction of a national home under a British administration acting under a mandate from the international community did not fire the imagination of the Jewish masses and did not bring them to the shores of Palestine, Gordon increasingly sought to base Jewish claims to ownership on the historical argument. From the time of the British conquest, the future of the land was open to question, and the Arab majority made every effort to press their own claims.

Like all Zionists, Gordon did not recognize the principle of majority rule, and he refused to acknowledge the right of the majority to "take from us what we have acquired through our work and creativity."[118] Moreover, he had confidence in the spiritual vitality of the Yishuv, its energy and motivation, and believed it was supported by the entire Jewish people. In 1921 he spoke in much stronger terms than he had done between 1909 and 1918: "For Eretz Israel, we have a charter that has been valid until now and that will always be valid, and that is the Bible, and not only the Bible." The Gospels, the New Testament, he claimed, were also the work of the Jewish people: "It all came from us; it was created among us." And now came the decisive argument: "And what did the Arabs produce in all the years they lived in the country? Such creations, or even the creation of the Bible alone, give us a perpetual right over the land in which we were so creative, especially since the people that came after us did not create such works in this country, or did not create anything at all."[119] The founders accepted this point of view. This was the ultimate Zionist argument. The centrality of the Bible was responsible both for the importance of historical factors in the thinking of the movement and for the place given to religion and tradition. The dependence of the Jewish movement of national rebirth on history and religion necessarily gave it from the start a radical character that was unavoidable.

The concept of the Zionist revolution as a personal revolution and a national revolution, but not as a universal social revolution, was passed on to the labor movement. "Judaism is one of the foundations of our inner being," wrote Gordon without hesitation, "one of the foundations of the 'I' of every one of us."[120] Gordon did not believe in the complete disappearance of religion as a social force, and he did not think that nationalism was capable of replacing it entirely.[121] In other words, he did not believe in a secular nationalism, because he did not believe in a liberal nationalism based on the principle of natural rights. Just as a liberal nationalism was possible only in a situation where the individual was seen as self-sufficient, an autonomous unit with its own raison d'être, so a true secular nationalism could not develop in a culture steeped in the Bible, in a country whose landscapes were those of the Bible, and in a situation in which return to one's homeland meant a return to the land of the Bible.

Thus, the revolution Gordon envisaged had two aspects: rebirth and a complete break with exile on one hand and an attachment to one's historical roots and to the religious content of national life on the other. The "return to the point of departure,"[122] which he advocated so eagerly, was rooted in national history, and as a result Gordon's worldview was limited. Essentially, his thought was anti-universalistic and anticosmopolitan and favored tribal segregation: "From the time I came here, I have never looked outward, for I know that external forces are not what is most important to us."[123] He wanted "to construct our national edifice not on rotten foundations, and not on foundations borrowed from others, but on our natural human national foundations." For Gordon, biblical culture constituted the infrastructure of Jewish nationhood; it was complete in itself and contained all the values necessary for the reborn nation. Gordon complained bitterly of "our hypnosis by others," of "the rule of other people's spirit over our own souls."[124] He regretted the disappearance of "national egoism, the attitude of 'Thou hast chosen us,' which was characteristic of the Jews of former generations."[125] As part of this attempt to increase the sense of national tribal identity, the strong self-criticism for which Gordon's writings were noted was toned down, and their emphasis shifted to a struggle against assimilation resulting from emancipation. Gordon began to be conscious of the price demanded of the Jews by the liberal, open society of Western Europe, namely, the destruction of all the Jews' "national, independent thoughts and feelings."[126]

Whatever might be said about the "cosmic" dimension of Gordon's "people-man" concept,[127] as Bergmann described his national and social philosophy, it was not cosmopolitan in the true sense of the term. It was rather the opposite; Gordon represented an organic, closed, and tribal form of nationalism, and this became the hallmark of the nationalist socialism of Ahdut Ha'avoda and subsequently of Mapai. Gordon's teaching had a real political content, and it is worth reading his work in the same way as one reads Fichte, Mazzini, Michelet, or Mickiewicz: without idealization, and perceiving their true contribution to the national ideology and the national struggles in which they participated.

Gordon's importance in molding the labor movement can scarcely be exaggerated. Not only were Hapo'el Hatza'ir members in Israel and abroad, especially in Germany, Gordon's disciples,[128] but Katznelson declared that Gordon was "the man I admire the most," despite the fact "that he described the creation of Ahdut Ha'avoda as 'something infernal.'"[129] Finally, it was precisely Ahdut Ha'avoda, most of whose major leaders, from Ben-Gurion and Katznelson to Tabenkin and Remez, were close in spirit to Hapo'el Hatza'ir, that brought Gordon's nationalist conceptions to fruition. His teaching, and not Borochov's, served as the intellectual foundation for the struggle of the labor leaders to forge the tools of national independence. From Gordon, the founders learned the principle on which their system was based; namely, that a moral and cultural revolution depending on an existential revolution is the best means of achieving a national revolution and at the same time dispenses with any necessity for a social revolution.

CHAPTER TWO

The Worker as the Agent of National Resurrection

THE HERITAGE OF THE SECOND ALIYAH

On 20 January 1955 the Mapai Central Committee met in Petah Tiqwa to discuss the forthcoming party convention and the elections that were to take place that year: the elections to the Histadrut in the spring and the general elections in July. But this was not a normal gathering; the whole leadership of the party and the Histadrut were present, and among the dozens who were invited many people in the second and third echelons of the leadership were later to take their place at the top of the ladder. Although nothing on the formal agenda suggested it, this was an especially festive occasion; Ben-Gurion, temporarily out of office, also took part, and as was usual since the early 1920s, he made the opening speech. In this speech, the first part of which was devoted to the fiftieth anniversary of the Second Aliyah, Ben-Gurion made a historical evaluation of the labor movement and a personal evaluation of his relations with his rivals on the Left. The speech filled about fifty pages of minutes and lasted for two and a half hours. It was a classic Ben-Gurion speech: a jumble of brilliant perceptions; crystal-clear historical insights; petty settlings of accounts; and cheap, hurtful, provocative, and superficial polemics. But the importance of this fascinating document lies especially in Ben-Gurion's interpretation of the nature and achievements of the labor movement, with an account of its development from the beginning of the century until the birth of the young state.[1]

As Ben-Gurion saw it, the special contribution of the Second Aliyah to Zionism was not the founding of Jewish settlements. In this area, priority went to the immigrants of the 1880s and 1890s who founded the villages of Petah Tiqwa, Rosh Pinna, Metulla, Hadera, and Rehovot. The first workers' organizations also preceded the Second Aliyah. In 1891, he said, "The first workers' organization in the country was founded," which according to Ben-Gurion already had "some of the basic ideas of what we call the Second Aliyah, and they were signed by Meir Dizengoff."[2] The special contribution of the Second Aliyah, however, was the "concept of labor as the key idea of the Jewish revival." The search for a way "to guarantee Jewish labor" led to the birth of communal settlements, and not any theory. Ben-Gurion did not forget to point out that the theorists of Hapo'el Hatza'ir and Po'alei Tzion, Yosef Aharonowitz and Borochov, had opposed this type of settlement. Even after fifty years, Ben-Gurion did not hesitate to place Aharonowitz, a major figure of the Second Aliyah but a publicist lacking in originality, and Borochov in the same category. It is true that he called Borochov "the great teacher and theoretician of the Po'alei Tzion Party," but nothing whatsoever was said in this speech in favor of socialism or the heritage of Po'alei Tzion, and Ben-Gurion repeatedly stressed that the building of the land had been achieved "without any preconceived theory."[3]

This, however, was not indicative of a disdain for ideology as such; nor was it a reconstruction of the past for present purposes. This was a faithful expression of Ben-Gurion's way of thinking at every period. Already in his speech at the festive assembly to mark the twenty-fifth anniversary of the Second Aliyah, which also took place in Petah Tiqwa, on 28 April 1929, Ben-Gurion read a long passage from the introduction to the statutes of the Ha'aretz Veha'avoda (Land and Labor) association, written in 1882 by Arieh Lieb Gordon, Meir Dizengoff, Moshe Rattner, and Aaron Eisenberg. "The question of workers," he read, "is of greatest importance, for it is not only a social question but also, and especially, a national question, a question concerning the whole Yishuv. Experience teaches us that without Jewish workers there can be no Jewish agricultural settlements. . . . The Jewish workers are to the Yishuv what blood is to a healthy body. It is they who give it life, and it is they who preserve it from destruction and decay." In these words, Ben-Gurion saw a complete and wonderfully accurate summary of the goals that the Second Aliyah had set for itself. He had no doubt about it: in these words from the founders of the old moshavot, from the people of the First Aliyah—people for whom socialism, if not detestable, was totally alien— Ben-Gurion saw the essence of the Second Aliyah ideology: "Almost the whole philosophy of the Second Aliyah labor movement is vigorously expressed here years before it took place. And not only did they have such ideas, but from the days of the Biluim [the pioneers of the First Aliyah], Jews came to work the land and to consecrate their lives to this sacred task."[4]

After he had discounted socialism as part of the founders' heritage, Ben-Gurion drew attention to the quality he considered most important in politics and that he saw as the secret of the Second Aliyah's success: the ability to confront reality without any restricting ideological preconceptions. He called this "independence of thought." This, he believed, was the greatest virtue of the Second Aliyah and the basis for its leaders' claim to the right to lead the labor movement, a claim substantiated with the founding of Mapai. Mapai, according to Ben-Gurion, was the only political body to represent the aims of the Second Aliyah so completely that it was totally identified with it: "The Eretz Israel Workers' Party [Mapai] embodies the Second Aliyah. It represents its values and the spiritual, human, creative, and belligerent qualities of this aliyah, which were also characteristic of those that came after it."

The Second Aliyah, according to Ben-Gurion, was able to absorb the waves of immigration that came after it, beginning with the third. Whatever was good, positive, or true in these other waves or of the bodies and organizations that they created had its origin in the modes of thought and action of "these torchbearers of the labor movement in this country." He believed that those who strayed from the path laid down by the Second Aliyah and exemplified by Mapai were doomed to failure.

Among these "strayers from the path," Ben-Gurion listed Yitzhak Tabenkin, one of the six members of the unification committee that founded Ahdut Ha'avoda and the founder of Hakibbutz Hame'uhad. Ben-Gurion wished to deny this man the right to belong to the heroic nucleus of the fathers of the nation. This man, he wrote, "belonged to the Second Aliyah chronologically," but "he arrived late and came when everything was finished, two years before the First World War." The exclusion of Tabenkin, who came to the country "only" in 1912, was not due only to personal resentment or political animosity against someone who had dared, at the end of the 1930s, to challenge Ben-Gurion's leadership and endanger his power base in the country. The erasure of his memory from the golden book of early pioneers was necessary in order to support Ben-Gurion's theory of the two great "positive commandments" of the Second Aliyah: to avoid all clear political and ideological positions and to preserve the unity of the labor movement at all costs. Similarly, Ben-Gurion sought to demonstrate that all the "separated bodies," beginning with part of Gdud Ha'avoda (the Labor Corps) and followed by Hakibbutz Hame'uhad, Hakibbutz Ha'artzi, and finally Hapo'el Hamizrahi and Ha'oved Hatzioni, were products of the spirit of later waves of immigration. All political elements originating with the Second Aliyah were found in Mapai, fulfilling its historic mission and continuing to realize its ideals.

Essentially, Ben-Gurion was right. His assertion that the values, modes of action, and rules of conduct of the Second Aliyah were embodied in Mapai was basically correct. Mapai was founded by the leadership of the Second Aliyah and represented the final victory of Hapo'el Hatza'ir, a notable creation of the Second Aliyah. The principles for which Gordon had fought and that Hapo'el Hatza'ir wished to bequeath to all the young workers of the Second Aliyah were in 1930 the official property of Mapai. In fact, at the beginning of the 1920s, soon after the liquidation of the Po'alei Tzion Party and the founding of Ahdut Ha'avoda, conditions were already beginning to lend themselves to a unification of all political bodies created by the members of the Second Aliyah.

The common factor between these disparate elements was a recognition of the nation's primacy and the subordination of all social values to that principle. Gordon laid a theoretical basis, which Katznelson and Ben-Gurion reinterpreted in terms of politics. The beginnings of the violent clash with the Arab national movement in its initial stages caused the Histadrut leadership, with its two main factions—Ahdut Ha'avoda and Hapo'el Hatza'ir—to jettison the universal, humanistic dimension that Gordon's teachings still retained when his nationalism hardened after the First World War. With the liquidation of the Po'alei Tzion Party as an autonomous body, the ideological balancing of nationalism and socialism, which was Borochov's great achievement, also came to an end. Borochov's teachings were not assimilated into Ahdut Ha'avoda; those of Syrkin, far less conceptually binding and focused on agricultural cooperation, were better suited to the ideological leadership of Ahdut Ha'avoda, of which Katznelson was becoming the main representative. As for Ben-Gurion, this political leader and outstanding organizer ceased at an early stage in his public career to need a theoretical framework that would enable him to overcome the incompatibility between socialism and nationalism.

It is also difficult to see what was especially socialistic about the intellectual heritage that the other leaders of the Second Aliyah, with the exception of Yitzhak Ben-Zvi, brought with them: the cult of physical labor and self-realization is not identical with socialism and does not guarantee the creation of a different kind of society. For the vast majority of people, work is an existential need, not a universal value, but in the Palestine of that period, physical labor was held to be a national value and had a special character: this also was the instrument par excellence of the conquest of the land. True to the practical implications of the principle of the nation's primacy, the leaders of the young workers never rejected capitalism or capitalist society as such. Their attitude to private property was eminently functional. The cult of personal fulfillment and of redemption through physical labor took the place of the socialization of the means of production. The Zionist revolution was personal and national: it was a cultural, not a social, revolution.

Another attitude that became established in the days of the Second Aliyah was the recognition of the right of the original pioneering nucleus to dominate later waves of immigration. The pioneering ideology required the authority of the founders in order to be accepted. Although the builders of the first moshavot, the people of the First Aliyah, had preceded them, the real founders were the members of the Second Aliyah. They were the first immigrants to know how to fashion the political, organizational, cultural, and economic tools for the Zionist enterprise. These were the founding fathers in the full meaning of the term, just as the creators of American independence and the shapers of the political system in the United States bear the title Founding Fathers instead of the first immigrants who descended on the coasts of Virginia and Massachusetts. It was the leaders of the Second Aliyah who gave the labor movement the power to govern, it was they who established the rules of the political game, and it was they who supplied the leadership of the Yishuv in mandatory times and of the state of Israel in its first twenty years. Those who came after them can be divided into two groups. The vast majority accepted the authority of the pioneering nucleus and under its leadership blended into the system set up by their predecessors; the second group, which fought to preserve its special character and its independence, was roundly defeated.

From the sociological point of view, the liquidation of Gdud Ha'avoda represented the victory of the old-timers, and from the ideological point of view it was the victory of the out-and-out nationalists over the revolutionary enthusiasm of the generation of the Soviet Revolution. The elimination by the leadership of Ahdut Ha'avoda of the radicals among the people of the Third Aliyah convinced Hapo'el Hatza'ir that it no longer needed to have any doubts about its ideological identity. Thus, the way was now open to the founding of Mapai. A political culture came into being marked, among other things, by a habitual suspiciousness of radical principles emanating from the Left, an acceptance of the supremacy of the founding generation, and a voluntary acquiescence in their values. Even after the Yom Kippur War, when power was transferred from the founding generation to younger people, this was done to ensure that the government would continue along the same path. This acquiescence in the outlook, norms of behavior, and political conceptions of the founders was largely responsible for the impotence of the second and third echelons of the leadership, and in the second and third generations it made a decisive contribution to the ideological and organizational stagnation of the movement.

Among the people of the Second Aliyah, suspiciousness toward speculative thought and disdain for theories that brought no immediate benefit were cardinal principles. Yet its leaders, despite the fact that most of them lacked a formal education, recognized the value and importance of culture. Moreover, they had a profound understanding of the connections between politics, economics, and culture and an awareness of the tremendous advantage an organization can derive from providing all possible essential services to its members. This comprehensive vision made members of the Second Aliyah the builders of the nation.

The Second Aliyah undoubtedly consisted of a very small group of people. The term *Second Aliyah*, as used here, applies not to most of the immigrants to Palestine in 1904–14 but to a group of young workers, the vast majority of whom worked as farmhands. These young workers constituted only a small percentage of the forty thousand souls who were added to the Yishuv in those years. Israel Kolatt, citing the figures of the Odessa Committee on immigration from Russia to Palestine via Odessa in 1905–9, provides this picture: the number of immigrants registered was 10,986, and of these only 25 percent were aged sixteen to thirty. Twenty-four percent named the moshavot as their destination.[5] Here it must be pointed out that those leaving Odessa were not obligated, on getting off the boat at Jaffa, to go to the destination they had named on setting out. The number of workers may therefore be larger or smaller, but they were undoubtedly a minority. Moreover, the number of dropouts among the arrivals as a whole was enormous. At the meeting of the Mapai Central Committee in January 1955 to mark the fiftieth anniversary of the Second Aliyah, Ben-Gurion estimated the number of those who remained at "perhaps 10 percent of those who came."[6] Ben-Gurion had already given this estimate in 1929, on the twenty-fifth anniversary of the Second Aliyah.[7] He did not give specific figures, as they were not known to him, and they are not known for certain even now. It is generally thought that among the workers who immigrated to the country in the ten years before the First World War, about twenty-five hundred people remained. This number includes a few hundred immigrants from Yemen, and it is based on a census taken by the Histadrut in 1922. Two thousand five hundred nineteen people were counted as having come to the country in 1904–14, 759 in 1904–8 (1908 was the year of the Young Turks' revolution), and 1,760 in 1909–14.[8]

Here too I must add a reservation: not all workers who came before the First World War necessarily joined the Histadrut. They may have been more numerous: some workers joined the middle classes or simply remained marginal. But all this does not alter the fact that what really mattered was the workers in the Histadrut. As none of the workers from Yemen reached a position of leadership (over time, the "Yemenite worker" became a concept denoting a modest man who works hard and is satisfied with little—qualities that did not especially characterize the leadership of the Second Aliyah), I must conclude that about two thousand young people from Eastern Europe produced from their midst the political elite that brought the Yishuv to independence and ruled the state of Israel until the beginning of the 1970s. This, as Ben-Gurion said in 1955, was "the chosen remnant, the selection that remained."[9] In this connection, let us remember that until the gates of the United States closed in 1924, Palestine received only a minute proportion of the European Jewish emigration. The collapse of security and the destruction of the traditional Jewish economic infrastructure, whether due to modernization or the policies of the Russian imperial government, which encouraged Jewish emigration, brought to Palestine no more than forty or fifty thousand Jews out of the 2,400,000 who left Russia, Russian-occupied Poland, Galicia, and Romania. Only from the mid-1920s on did the country have a real place in Jewish emigration from Europe. Between the two world wars, about 340,000 people settled in Palestine.[10]

All this explains a sense of chosenness among the people of the Second Aliyah. They regarded themselves as a tiny minority carrying on their shoulders the fate of the entire people. Because they were the chosen few who had passed through the crucible of the first years of suffering—years of hard physical labor, loneliness, and uncertainty about the future—they gained the conviction that they had the right to dictate the path of those who came after them. This attitude was always typical of activist minorities: they looked with disdain at the large amorphous masses of those lacking in will-power. The leaders of this pioneering nucleus, which set up the political and economic institutions of the state in the making, knew from the beginning how to translate the pioneer spirit and the sense of superiority that went with it into political terms. They knew how to exact the full price for the fact that they had volunteered and led the way, first from the Zionist Organization and later from the entire society of the Yishuv. There were very few of them—an infinitesimal minority among the Jewish people, and a no less insignificant minority among Jewish emigrants from Europe and among members of the Yishuv. They were distinguished by a capacity to translate this situation into terms of power, displaying a political sense of a special kind. This activist minority knew wonderfully well how to achieve a unity of theory and action. The leaders of the Second Aliyah were the first to make the primacy of the nation the goal and to separate Jewish nationalism from universal principles—the socialism of Borochov or the liberalism of Herzl and Nordau—which they saw as a weakening factor. Yet at the same time they were able to provide this nationalism with the tools necessary for its realization.

THE FIRST STAGES OF THE SHIFT TO THE RIGHT

The Second Aliyah began in December 1903 with the immigration of a Po'alei Tzion group from Gomel in White Russia. In Jewish history that region was known as part of Lithuania. This group, made up of self-defense corps that were active in Russia, played an important role in the founding of Hashomer (the Guardian), the first Jewish self-defense force in Palestine. Another Po'alei Tzion group immigrated in 1905 from the Russian town of Rostov, after pogroms there. The Rostovians founded the Po'alei Tzion Party in Palestine. Po'alei Tzion, led by Ber Borochov, favored a Palestinian solution to the Jewish question but constituted only a tiny minority among the Jewish Left in Eastern Europe. Most of the Jewish proletariat was faithful to the non-Zionist Bund, and after the Sixth Zionist Congress in August 1903, where Herzl made his Uganda proposal, the Zionist Left split into three branches. The central branch, which tended to support the Uganda plan, based its Zionism on the need to provide a quick and effective solution to the distress of a population sunk in poverty and in perpetual fear of the next pogrom. Most of its members accepted the territorial solution, as they understood that Eastern European Jews were not in a position to wait for the kind of solution that Zionism, either of the "practical" or of the "spiritual" variety, was able to provide at that period. In January 1905 the committee of the Po'alei Tzion organizations that supported the territorialist idea met in Odessa and announced the creation of a socialist Zionist party. At the seventh Zionist Congress, which met in Basel in 1905, this party was represented by thirty delegates, headed by Nachman Syrkin. They joined Israel Zangwill's Jewish Territorialist Organization.

Another group, consisting of intellectuals attracted to socialist Zionism, friends and sympathizers of the various Po'alei Tzion groups, after the failed revolution of 1905 set up an organization that demanded Jewish national autonomy, with a territory and the right to an independent existence. This entity was to be governed by a parliament, *Sejm* in Polish. Hence they were known as the Sejmists. In 1905 they organized themselves as the Jewish Socialist Workers' Party. These two branches were lost to Zionism, and most of their members went over to Russian communism.[11] The third branch was the Borochovist one.

According to letters sent by immigrants from Eastern Europe to Russia and the United States, the Po'alei Tzion Party in Palestine was founded in November 1905. At the beginning of 1906, the party consisted of approximately 60 members, divided into two groups. About 30 people belonged to the Rostov group, whose leaders had an excellent understanding of Marxism; there was also a group of 25 in the north of the country, the Galilee, for whom Marxism, at best, was only an adjunct to their nationalism. When the first Po'alei Tzion convention took place on 4–6 October 1906, membership in the party reached about 150 people, divided into the same two groups. About 70 people attended the convention. A month earlier, on 7 September, David Gruen emigrated to Palestine from Płońsk, a small town about forty miles northwest of Warsaw, and rapidly took his place at the head of the nationalist faction. At the October convention, he was elected to the Central Committee and was made chairman of the drafting committee. On the same occasion, Gruen (Ben-Gurion) proposed a general federation (*histadrut*) of all Jewish workers in Palestine. This proposal contradicted the Marxist approach, which required a single organization for all workers in the country without exception, including the Arabs. After a few days of discussion, the nationalist group won. On the same occasion, a drafting committee was elected, which met between 7 and 9 October 1906 in Ramle and issued the Ramle Platform, the first ideological declaration of the party in Eretz Israel. It was approved at the first party convention in Jaffa in January 1907. This convention also gave the party its name, the Jewish Social Democratic Workers' Party in Palestine–Po'alei Tzion. At the sixth convention, in April 1910, the name of the party was changed to the Jewish Social Democratic Party in Eretz Israel–Po'alei Tzion.[12] The word *Palestine* had been dropped.

The Ramle Platform was based on the Poltava Platform, which had been accepted at the inaugural meeting of the Po'alei Tzion Party in Russia in March 1906. Poltava, in the Ukraine, was Borochov's hometown. In the

Poltava Platform, entitled "Our Platform"—his best-known text and the most influential—Borochov wrote, "The realization of political and territorial autonomy in Eretz Israel will come about chiefly through class warfare, and the movement of liberation will be headed by the proletariat."[13] The "Platform" continued: "Already from the beginning of the 'stychic' aliyah [aliyah occurring through a deterministic process] of Jews to Eretz Israel, a violent struggle will take place there between Jewish labor and capital." This refers, of course, to "class warfare between Jewish labor and capital."[14]

Here we should pause to consider the place of "Our Platform" in Borochov's thought. For many years, writes Jonathan Frankel, Borochov's name was inseparably linked with the principles presented in that famous "Platform." The "Platform" was regarded as the essence of Borochovism, and it thus became usual to see Borochov as a somewhat monolithic figure. However, Frankel, basing himself on the study by Matitiahu Mintz, drew attention to the change that took place in Borochov's thinking at the end of 1905. In the previous period, in 1904–5, Borochov had been Menachem Ussishkin's right-hand man, he had been a General Zionist who had fought with great determination against the supporters of the Uganda proposal, and he had written a long essay entitled "The Question of Zion and Territory." At the end of 1905 Borochov, whose approach to Zionism had been basically voluntaristic, became a determinist, an outstanding theoretician of class warfare, a proletarian revolutionary. In the previous period, when he had agitated on behalf of Tzionei Tzion (Zionists who insisted on settling in Zion rather than any other territory), Borochov had thought it absurd that the Jews should expect a mass redemption to come about through a social revolution. As a marginal group of aliens, the Jews, he believed, would undoubtedly find themselves caught in a cross fire between the forces of the revolution and those of the counterrevolution. He viewed anti-Semitism as a cultural phenomenon ingrained in people's soul, and not only in the sociopolitical order. Thus, there was only one solution: removing the Jews from their midst and giving them a territory of their own. For objective reasons, the most suitable territory, he believed, was Palestine. This was the only alternative to destruction. At that period Borochov not only called for an immediate Jewish colonization of Palestine but was also indifferent to the Russian Revolution of 1905. From the organizational point of view, wrote Frankel, Borochov was an elitist who ascribed a decisive role to the avant-garde and had no belief in action by the masses whatsoever. Philosophically, he maintained a balance between determinism and voluntarism, materialism and "ideologism," and psychological and socioeconomic interpretations.[15]

At the end of 1905 Borochov's thinking changed direction decisively. He organized the "Palestinian" Po'alei Tzion as a party—The Jewish Social Democratic Workers' Party–Po'alei Tzion—whose first convention took place at the end of February 1906 in Poltava, where Borochov lived. Here Borochov drafted the outline of "Our Platform." This text had a completely different point of view from the one he had espoused a year earlier. Although the new party continued to declare its belief in a Palestinian solution to the Jewish question and supported aliyah, the voluntaristic, emotional, and idealistic approach was dropped from its program. Now Borochov put his faith in long-term developments, in socioeconomic processes. The new doctrine maintained that the proletariat and its role in class war were the key factors in the Jewish question. At the center of his teaching was the conviction that the Jewish question would be resolved not primarily through political action but by virtue of an inevitable socioeconomic process. "Anyone," he wrote, "who thinks we are calling for emigration to Eretz Israel is making a great mistake. That, as we have said many times before, we leave to the 'stychic' [deterministic] process." But, in the same breath, in the next passage but on the same page, Borochov corrected this statement, making the following declaration: "We call upon the Jewish proletariat to assist anything that can encourage or facilitate Jewish mass immigration to Eretz Israel . . . and to oppose anything that can hinder such an immigration."[16]

In August 1907, at the party's second convention, which was held in Kharkov, a violent ideological confrontation took place between the delegates from Russia under the leadership of Borochov, who had just ended five months' imprisonment there, and the Polish faction under Nahum Rafalkes (Nir), who in 1959 was to serve for a few months as speaker of the Knesset (due to the Left's revolt against Ben-Gurion). Among the delegates from Poland were also David Bloch (Ephraim Blumenfeld), mayor of Tel Aviv in the late 1920s and one of Ben-Gurion's chief political victims at that period, and Yitzhak Tabenkin. It appears that his ideological struggle with Borochov persuaded Tabenkin, after his immigration to Palestine in 1910, not to join Po'alei Tzion. The Polish faction stressed the special place of Palestine in the consciousness of the Jewish people. A Marxist, they thought, could not ignore the fact that economic marginalization and political ostracism for two millennia had compelled the Jews to develop a profound identification with their ancient homeland.[17]

Two possibilities may account for the 1906 change in direction: a simple illumination comparable to a religious conversion or, as Mintz believes, a shrewd political maneuver designed, against the background of the 1905 revolution, to save Po'alei Tzion from destruction by joining the international revolutionary camp. It may indeed be true that Borochov saw himself as having the duty of developing an ideology that would answer the needs of revolutionary youth and give it an attachment to Eretz Israel.[18] From that time on, Borochov's name has been linked to "Our Platform," an expression of his adherence to orthodox Marxism. In Palestine this was a bone of contention between Po'alei Tzion and Hapo'el Hatza'ir, the ideological and psychological source of a rivalry that ended only with the liquidation of the Po'alei Tzion movement in Palestine.

The Ramle Platform, divided into four paragraphs—slightly more than three hundred words—was to some degree a compromise between Borochov's teachings as they had crystallized after the turning point of 1906 and the nationalist line represented by Ben-Gurion. Its authors, led by Ben-Gurion, began by correcting the *Communist Manifesto*, writing that "the chronicles of humanity consist of national and class wars," and then stated their belief in the power of the deterministic process. The Jewish worker and Jewish capital, read the platform, would move to Eretz Israel through an inevitable process. "Large-scale capital" would arrive there because it is always in search of new places for investment in noncapitalist countries, and "medium-scale capital would move there because, more than large-scale capital, it is forced out of the countries of exile by local competition." Also, "The Jewish masses are being excluded from all areas of production, and they are forced to emigrate." The only option for them will finally be Eretz Israel, because "the countries that have received them until now are increasingly setting obstacles in their path."[19] This analysis and this prediction clearly had the great virtue of fully supporting the national imperative of emigration and conquest of the land of Israel.

One can assume that the declaration that the struggle between nations is as important in the history of humanity as the struggle between classes was not simply a sign of ingenuousness or a lack of culture on the part of the Po'alei Tzion in Palestine. At the beginning of the century, every person, regardless of ideological tendencies, knew that a view of history in terms of class struggle formed part of a complete and comprehensive system of thought. One might criticize this system, but to combine it with a conception of history as consisting of national struggles was absurd. The drafters of the Ramle Platform knew this very well. However lacking in culture they may have been, they were aware that struggles between nations were a recent phenomenon in the history of humankind, scarcely a hundred years old. If they knowingly decided to commit such a gross error, it was because they had no other means of reconciling the two schools of thought, which at the end of 1906 divided the little socialist community in Palestine. Ben-Gurion's biographer Shabtai Teveth writes that the coupling of class struggle and international struggle in the Ramle Platform and the equal weight given to both should be seen as a retreat on the part of Ben-Gurion and the nationalist right wing of Po'alei Tzion.[20]

However, the opposite was the case. It needed considerable powers of persuasion to urge convinced Marxists like the Rostovians to combine national struggles and class struggles in the same interpretation of history. Ben-Gurion would no doubt have liked the preface to the program to have indicated the greater importance of the "dialectic" of national struggle rather than class struggle, but he knew he could go only so far without splitting the Rostovians and losing them completely. In Ramle Ben-Gurion was not so much trying to find an intellectually coherent explanation of history as to gain a political victory over the left wing of the party, and in this he succeeded. Moreover, at this period Ben-Gurion had already ascribed only a limited importance to ideology.

As long as ideology was an important factor among the Po'alei Tzion in Palestine, the leader of the party was Yitzhak Shimshelevich (Ben-Zvi), who had arrived a few months after the convention in Jaffa in January 1907, which approved the Ramle Platform. Ben-Zvi had been a leading personality in the Russian party, a member of the committee that drafted "Our Platform," and one of the Central Committee's five members. Throughout the period when the Po'alei Tzion Party was engaged in ideological debates and expressed an opinion on speculative questions, the leadership was in the hands of Ben-Zvi. This man was far from being a thinker of the first rank, but his wide general education and his grasp of the principles of Marxism were enough to make him an intellectual leader for the small group of young people who constituted the Po'alei Tzion Party in Eretz Israel.

Ben-Gurion came into his own only when the party's main preoccupation shifted to organizational and political matters. Then his full stature was revealed, and Ben-Zvi was gradually thrust into relative obscurity. But in the years between his immigration and their joint exodus to Constantinople in November 1911 to study law, Ben-Gurion, leader of the right wing, or Eretz Israeli faction, was overshadowed by Ben-Zvi. Finally, in order to overcome the left-wing faction with its Marxist orientation, Ben-Gurion had no choice except to destroy the party. This was the significance of the founding of Ahdut Ha'avoda. The new party was not interested in Borochov's search for a synthesis of socialism with nationalism, nor in Ben-Zvi's attempt, based on Borochov—an attempt that ran into insoluble theoretical difficulties—to prove that the interests of the wage earners were identical with the national interest. To all these questions, if they were raised, Ben-Gurion found the perfect solution: the subordination of socialism to nationalism. Thus, all theoretical difficulties were resolved and all obstacles were removed, including the need for "universal working-class solidarity," which Ben-Zvi had advocated on the eve of the First World War.[21] This first stage in the shift to the Right was crucial, for at that period (the end of the First World War) the conceptual framework of the labor movement was established.

Ben-Gurion never considered himself bound by the Ramle Platform. Eventually, wrote Shabtai Teveth, he was ashamed of the platform whose chief drafter he had been, and he did not mention it in his memoirs at all.[22] It is probable that one of the main reasons this series of doctrinal statements troubled him was that it constituted living proof of his inability, at that early period, to provide a global "national" or "Eretz Israeli" alternative to the

Borochovistic system of thought. His writings in *Ha'ahdut*, the Po'alei Tzion journal, do not show any particular intellectual depth. The twelve articles he contributed deal mainly with workers' practical problems: employment, housing, security, and Jewish labor in the moshavot. When he went beyond daily issues, the terms of reference were entirely national; not only was there no trace of Marxist thought or even of the idioms usual at this period among socialists, but there was not the slightest concern with social questions that were generally of greatest interest to European leftists. Ben-Gurion's horizons at that period were remarkably narrow and restricted. Not only is it difficult to believe that he was a labor leader, but one does not have the impression that this writer had any intellectual interest in social problems or culture.

At the same time, Ben-Gurion knew the basic Marxist terminology, and when he wanted to he was able to use it. This was the case in his somewhat programmatic article "Our Sociopolitical Work," dated October 1911. Here Ben-Gurion claimed to represent the "Zionist proletarian idea" in "Hebrew socialism," but the context was nationalist: his objection to the growing tendency of "the Jewish socialists in Constantinople and Salonika . . . to oppose Jewish nationalism, and especially Zionism."[23] He was acquainted with the distinction between "bourgeois and proletarians," and he spoke of "Jewish proletarians" whose Zionism was a "proletarian Zionism." He praised that "small section of the Jewish proletariat in the workers' party, Po'alei Tzion."[24] When in the years before the First World War there were tensions between the Palestine branch of the movement and the international Po'alei Tzion, Ben-Gurion stated that this "conflict of principles is quite unnecessary, and it could never have happened except through a temporary misunderstanding to the detriment of one or other of the two principles we mentioned earlier: the international unity of the interests and ideals of the Jewish workers, and the role of the Eretz Israeli worker in realizing those ideals." The worker himself is described as "the instrument and the fulfillment of the Zionist proletarian ideal."[25] Statements so unequivocal in spirit and language were no longer made after the liquidation of the Po'alei Tzion Party in Eretz Israel. When this happened, the pioneering Eretz Israeli nucleus lost touch with a comprehensive worldview. The abandonment of key terms in Marxism meant a retreat from ideological and political concepts of universal significance. This concept of "proletarian Zionism," for instance, was forgotten when the shift to the Right began.

Similarly, in the publications of Ahdut Ha'avoda or Mapai one never again encounters certain other aspects of the socialist ardor found in *Ha'ahdut*. In an editorial—"At the End of the Third Year"—dated September–October 1912, the editors declared with pride that "*Ha'ahdut* is not just a proletarian newspaper. *Ha'ahdut* is the only labor newspaper in the world that has set out to spread scientific socialism in the language of the first prophets of social justice."[26] When the paper first appeared, Ben-Zvi spoke in the same spirit when he wrote that the "first principle" of socialism is "class warfare."[27] Ideas of this nature completely disappeared from the intellectual horizons of the Second Aliyah leadership with the rise of Ahdut Ha'avoda and the Histadrut. The debates that accompanied their establishment were not "inological" discussions but concerned the nature of the two bodies, now the spearhead of the Zionist enterprise.

Ben-Gurion, for his part, always counterbalanced any socialistic tendencies he may have had with the adoption of clearly nationalistic positions. For instance, he began to advocate a cooperation with the Old Yishuv in order to harness it to the national effort, and once again on nationalist grounds he attacked the ethnic discrimination from which the Yemenite workers suffered in the moshavot. He regarded the ill-treatment of the Yemenites as especially reprehensible in view of the fact that they were the only Jewish workers able to compete effectively with Arab labor. Moreover, he claimed, ethnic discrimination tore the nation apart, just as the division of the Yishuv into the Old Yishuv and the New also harmed national unity.[28] And finally, he gave his view of the national function of the labor movement: "The Jewish worker must always remember that he is not only the builder of the Yishuv but also its guide, in the broadest and deepest sense of the concept. And just as he creates new products through his physical labor, so, through his spiritual life, he must create new social values of truth and justice."[29]

Such was the spirit of Ben-Gurion's writings in the years before the founding of Ahdut Ha'avoda and the Histadrut.[30] Even at that period, when he was not engaged in practical tasks and had time to think and write, Ben-Gurion's primary interest was in day-to-day politics and organization. An exception that proves the rule is perhaps his article "Ba Midron" (On the slope), in which he defended Brenner against the anger of Ahad Ha'am. An article by Brenner considered hostile to Judaism aroused the indignation of the Odessa Committee, which, in protest, dropped its support of the journal *Hapo'el Hatza'ir*, where the offending article had appeared.[31] Where quality of writing and interest in theoretical questions were concerned, the young Ben-Gurion was an anomaly among the leaders of the labor movements.

An examination of *Ha'ahdut* definitely leads one to the conclusion that Ben-Gurion never internalized Marxism. He was acquainted with its terminology and knew how to play with it, but that was all. That is the answer to the question Teveth asked in the first volume of his monumental biography: "When did Ben-Gurion, to use his own expression, join his socialism to his Zionism? When did he become a Zionist Marxist?"[32] Teveth's own detailed description of Ben-Gurion's early years in the country makes it clear that he had never been a Marxist: a revolutionary, yes, but not a Marxist. Teveth's question stems from a common conceptual error, namely, that at the beginning of the century a revolutionary was necessarily a Marxist, whereas there was another kind—the nationalist—who was no less radical than the Marx-ist. Ben-Gurion was the leading Jewish national revolutionary.

His joining Po'alei Tzion was not motivated by an ideological decision but resulted from a combination of circumstances. In the summer of 1905, Ben-Gurion was in Warsaw. The Po'alei Tzion Party in Warsaw, as else-where, was an activist Zionist body that fought against territorialism and the Bund and at the same time dealt with self-defense. The year 1905 in Poland was one of violent struggle against the Russian empire. Warsaw was the center of disturbances that swept over the country, but at the end of that year the Russian government initiated pogroms against the Jews. Ben-Gurion returned to Płońsk and organized the youth of the local Ezra Zionist organization as a self-defense group. He called for assistance from the Po'alei Tzion in Warsaw, who immediately sent instructors. That was how Ben-Gurion joined Po'alei Tzion; he regarded himself as joining not a social-ist party but a self-defense organization. Two of his close friends who went to the country before him, Shlomo Levkowitz (Lavi) and Shlomo Tzemah, were among the founders of Hapo'el Hatza'ir. Teveth writes that if Ben-Gurion had made aliyah in December 1904 with Shlomo Tzemah, he too would have joined this party.[33]

In making this assertion, Teveth goes some way toward answering the question he asked about Ben-Gurion's socialism. Ten years after the appear-ance of his book, he elaborated on this theme on the centenary of Ben-Gurion's birth. "Marxism and Borochovism," wrote Teveth, "were more of an affair of fashion for Ben-Gurion than an all-encompassing belief'; they were a sort of "thin . . . coat of paint, a changeable outer layer." Teveth suggested that Ben-Gurion's spiritual universe was shaped by his native town, its heder, and its synagogue. At the heart of it, there was "a trinity of loves: love of the Bible, love of the Hebrew language, and love of Eretz Israel."[34] Ben-Gurion was a member of Po'alei Tzion in Poland for only one year, and when he arrived in Palestine, he was already an integral national-ist. But because he had belonged to the Po'alei Tzion Party in Poland, when he got off the ship, he turned to the parallel organization in Palestine.

Ben-Gurion's concept of Zionism was in total contradiction to Borochov's principles of the 1906–7 period. In Warsaw and Płońsk this was not noticed, or it hardly mattered. When attention was on the struggle against the Bund and against the territorialist tendency within Zionism, there was little point in being oversensitive about inner contradictions. Those who favored a Palestinian solution were divided into different factions, but their preoccupation with self-defense and their devotion to the Jewish homeland united them despite their differences. This was not the case in Eretz Israel, however; there the bundle broke apart and the unifying factors were no longer effective. Ben-Gurion had a voluntaristic conception of Zionism; to his way of thinking, aliyah, when it resulted from a personal decision, gave settlement in Palestine a special value, which was lacking in a mass exodus resulting from a combination of circumstances over which no one had any control. Borochov based his theory of Zionism on a deterministic process, which for him was an element of strength, but which from Ben-Gurion's point of view was a weakness. On this point, all the Eretz Israelis—Gordon, Ben-Gurion, and Katznelson—were unanimous. They all believed that aliyah, when voluntary, had a value in itself; it was the first step toward the accomplishment of a great personal and cultural revolution. The deterministic concept of immigration, however, lacked this revolutionary dimension. Someone who fled to Palestine in consequence of modernization in the European continent or because of other peoples' wars of independence was not a pioneer but a helpless pawn of history. Similarly, nationalism, in Gordon's opinion, when mingled with socialism, ceased to be "integral." In the same way, Katznelson described a member of the Second Aliyah as "someone who wanted to be whole."[35] This cult of "wholeness" represented the local version of European organic nationalism, which was incompatible not only with Marxist determinism but with a social democratic vision of society.

Thus, it was not only the realities of a backward country that disqualified Borochov in the eyes of someone like Ben-Gurion and made Gordon and Katznelson into adversaries of Marxism; it was not only this experience that prevented Tabenkin from joining the Po'alei Tzion movement in Palestine.[36] The rejection of Borochov resulted from a conscious ideological decision. The founders realized at an early stage that there was a contradiction between socialism and nationalism, and since the first meaning of Zionism was the building of the nation, one had to make a decision. This problem also existed in Europe, and there too a similar decision was made.

If, in the first decade of this century, the deterministic process failed to bring Jews to Palestine in appreciable numbers, and if, in the period of the Second Aliyah, it was possible to claim that Borochov had been mistaken, that only a chosen few came to the country and remained there and that these were motivated by national sentiment, from the mid-1920s onward Borochov's predictions have been largely realized. Jews were driven out of Eastern Europe, the former Soviet Union, the Near East, and the Mediterranean countries through processes over which they had no control, and most of them reached Palestine and Israel through lack of choice. The influx of Jewish capital into Palestine in the period between the two world wars also was due to a lack of choice. But the founders' view of Zionism led them to continue to uphold the illusion that aliyah was always a voluntary act of self-elevation and an expression of national consciousness and pioneering spirit. Aliyah was supposed to be an act of resurrection, a miraculous new beginning "from the foundations upward," but this radical new beginning, which necessitated the abandonment of the alien ideological baggage imported from abroad—and this included the universal principles of social-ism—was not regarded as requiring a liberation from Jewish tradition, as this was considered an inseparable part of national identity.

Essentially, the activists in the days of the Second Aliyah were divided into two groups: the Eretz Israelis and the others. The Eretz Israelis had immediately abandoned the universal elements of socialism and were "full Zionists," that is, integral nationalists. In principle, there were no limits to their nationalist extremism; the limits were fixed by conditions prevailing at a given time, by the limits of power and by that of the Yishuv. The others, like the Rostovians, were said by the Eretz Israelis to be "alien," as their allegiance was divided between the nation and the universal values of social-ism. Tabenkin, Katznelson, and Ben-Gurion always viewed them with suspi-cion. Thus, it is incorrect to regard constructive socialism as a pragmatic school of thought; its creators adhered to a definite ideology, but its princi-ples were those of integral nationalism.

This was the main reason that the development of the Po'alei Tzion Party in Palestine was marked by an ever more radical nationalism. This process of retreat from Borochovistic thought was slow, lasting about ten years. The transition to what some called a "practical and flexible view of things" and the creation of a "specifically Jewish socialism"[37] were nothing other than a gradual shift to the Right, a retreat from moderate social democratic posi-tions and the formation of a nationalist socialism. The zealotry concerning the Hebrew language, the total war on Yiddish culture, and its progressive elimination from the lives of the pioneers were a necessary stage in nation-building, but they were also a striking, uncompromising expression of the national-revolutionary trend. The abandonment of the principle of class war-fare, to which all socialist parties adhered until the second half of the twenti-eth century, even when it was not applied, took place simultaneously with the beginning of the conquest of labor. By the eve of the First World War, the Po'alei Tzion Party had already moved quite far to the Right, and its liquidation in 1919 ended a process that had continued for a number of years. This was the first formal stage in creating the nationalist socialist force that later was to lead the Yishuv.

The theoretical problems the founders faced were by no means unique. They also existed in Europe, in the west and in the east, though in the two regions their causes were different. In Western Europe modernization did not bring the results the socialist movement had hoped for, and in Eastern Europe the process of modernization had hardly begun. Despite this, the socialist parties did not think it necessary to abandon Marxism as a general system of criticism of the capitalist order and as a compass.

The "reality" of life in Palestine was not as special as some people claim. The suggestion that this reality led to the demise of every social democratic principle has no foundation, and the idea that a specific "Jewish socialism" was an adaptation to a "specific reality" is mere apologetics. Whatever adjustments may have been made, Marxism at the beginning of the century remained what it always had been and was always intended to be: first and foremost a critique of capitalism. It is hard to understand how Marxism could have been relevant to Russia, Poland, and Romania but not to Palestine. In Western Europe as well, Marxism had been and continued to be revised by socialist theoreticians and leaders. Many thinkers of the Left had come to the conclusion that particular points of Marxism needed adaptation or revision; even Karl Kautsky, the guardian of Marxist orthodoxy, was of this opinion. But no socialist believed that the time had come to revise the entire theory, or that it could be separated from its central core, class warfare. None of them—whether Eduard Bernstein, the revisionist who viewed socialism as the heir to liberalism; Jean Jaurès, the patriot deeply attached to his national culture yet a great assailant of tribal nationalism; Rosa Luxemburg and Rudolf Hilferding, who sought to complete Marx's economic theories; Antonio Labriola, who paved the way for an interpretation of Marxism as a "philosophy of praxis"; the Austro-Marxists, who reexamined every aspect of Marx's thought; or Antonio Gramsci and György Lukács, Labriola's successors—thought that the Marxist system could cease to be regarded as an integral whole or that capitalism should no longer be criticized.

Thus, the fact that history did not develop according to Marx's original predictions did not diminish the system's value but was believed to necessitate its adaptation to a changing reality. Social democratic parties regarded Marxism as a conceptual framework, an analytical tool for transforming bourgeois society. They did not draw up a timetable for this objective, but they never renounced the aim. European socialists who proclaimed the irrelevance of Marxism were precisely those who drifted to the Right. This process had been unfolding since the last decade of the nineteenth century, and it greatly accelerated between the two world wars.

Even the schism that followed the creation of communist parties and the foundation of the Third International in 1920 did not undermine the faith in the fundemental norms of Marxism of those who refused the twenty-one principles that Lenin placed before the socialist parties. Socialist parties that continued to claim that a Marxist party can be democratic and can work for the transformation of bourgeois society by democratic means persisted in their criticism of capitalism and never abandoned the principle of class warfare. The fact that the 1920 events in the Marxist world failed to shake the socialists' convictions shows how important the theory was in providing stability and a sense of direction. Although the cleavage between theory and practice was obvious, the theory was respected, and tremendous efforts were made to remain true not only to the interests of the worker but also to his universal mission. This adherence to principles made the socialists the spearhead of the struggle against tribal nationalism and the cornerstone of ideological modernity. That is why democratic socialism was the direct heir of the Enlightenment and a defender of freedom.

During the period of the great split in the world socialist movement Ahdut Ha'avoda and the Histadrut were established. There was no reason that the party of Ben-Gurion, Katznelson, and Tabenkin should not have been established on a theoretical basis similar to the one on which the European socialist parties reorganized in 1920. It was no accident that Ahdut Ha'avoda was set up on different principles. The Marxist element in the labor movement in Palestine had already disappeared, and the founding of Ahdut Ha'avoda was preceded by the liquidation of a socialist party. The dissolution of the Po'alei Tzion Party was a precondition for the founding of Ahdut Ha'avoda. The existence of the Po'alei Tzion Party had represented a link with world democratic socialism with all its problems, hesitations, and compromises. If the party had continued to exist, it would have experienced the same ideological upheavals as European socialism in that period, and that was exactly what Ben-Gurion wished to avoid. After all, if the founders had wanted to found a socialist party, why was the liquidation of the moderate social democratic party that the Po'alei Tzion Party had been considered necessary? Why did one have to set up Ahdut Ha'avoda?

THE ELIMINATION OF THE MARXIST PO'ALEI TZION PARTY

Ben Gurion's programmatic speech at the Po'alei Tzion convention on 22 February 1919 is a fascinating document. It not only emphasizes the difference between his thinking and that of other socialist leaders in the world, but it also indicates what his outlook was in subsequent years. Like all Zionist leaders, Ben-Gurion was aware both of the global changes that were taking place at the time and of their social significance. Following the Russian Revolution of 1917, he too expected dramatic developments. "Everyone is full of the socialist idea," he wrote, "and everyone hopes for reforms in social life, especially now, when the socialist revolution is taking place."[38] With regard to the Jewish people, he believed that there was now, with the change to "an enlightened regime with an incomparable experience in settling desolate countries," a special opportunity to realize on a large scale what the pioneers had already realized in their daily lives: "The organic fusion . . . of two worlds: Jewish national redemption and the social liberation of man."[39] This "hoped-for synthesis of Zionism and socialism" was, according to Ben-Gurion, a phenomenon possible only in Eretz Israel. It was impossible in exile, where an insuperable contradiction between nationalism and socialism existed. Ben-Gurion believed that this contradiction was the result of the social situation in Russia and of the Jews' dependence on Russian culture. Only their settlement in Eretz Israel made possible their liberation from foreign influences. "Here, our thinking has been renewed," he wrote, "and we have found new directions for the realization of our work." Here, an enterprise had taken shape, "which the greatest of our comrades, Ber Borochov, never imagined in his place outside the country."[40] In his appearance before the Po'alei Tzion convention, this party's last in Palestine, Ben-Gurion used language appropriate to the setting. The few words in praise of Borochov were necessitated by the situation: one could not give less than that to the people assembled in Jaffa in February 1919, while the Jewish Battalions of the British army were still in the country, and among the large crowd were members of Po'alei Tzion from America. The number of participants from abroad was sufficiently large for Ben-Zvi to provide a summary of his speech in Yiddish. It is significant, however, that Borochov was mentioned only in passing in a context where one might have expected a little more. Who else had done as much as Borochov to create a synthesis of socialism and Zionism? But the synthesis Ben-Gurion had in mind was very different from Borochov's. Characteristically, Ben-Gurion did not relate to Borochov's teachings but dismissed them as alien and irrelevant to the reality in the country. The way he dealt with the problem was similar to the way he overcame the obstacle presented by the existence of Po'alei Tzion as an independent entity in Palestine: he eliminated it by denying its existence.

> The interests of the Jewish working class are the interests of the Jewish people in Eretz Israel, and thus our life in this country is not torn between conflicting positions. We have only one problem: deciding on the proper role for the worker in building the country, and here one cannot distinguish between national aspirations and the private aspirations of the worker. We do not have two souls within us, one socialist and one national. One cannot ask the Jewish worker whether the national ideal or the socialist ideal is dearer to him. Such a question would be like asking an individual whether he prefers his father or his mother.

The conclusion, as ingenuous as the claim itself, was incisive and left no room for doubt: "In any case, the whole question is pointless."[41]

There is a special interest in examining the development of Ben-Gurion's thought, for here, in the winter of 1919, the conceptual framework for his actions in the following fifty years was already present in all its essentials. He endlessly repeated his basic assertion: "A distinction between the needs of the individual and the needs of the nation has no basis in the lives of the workers in Eretz Israel." Consequently, he said, "Our movement makes no distinction between the national question and the socialist question: there is no such distinction in life, and in this we are different from other groups whose interests do not always correspond to the general interest."[42] According to this way of reasoning, Ben-Gurion's only significant complaint against private capital was that the moshavot employed cheap—that is, Arab—labor. Capitalists, he maintained, did not favor Jewish labor and always preferred the cheaper Arab workers, whom they "mistreated . . . like slave dealers." He believed that this policy would have the direst consequences.

> We have the danger not only of a hostile alien element in our midst but also of national degeneration. . . . We do not only have to be frightened of a social revolution on the part of the Arabs; even before we reach that stage, when the enlightened peoples see what the Jewish people has made of the country, they will say that they made a bad bargain, for it was not their intention to help exploiters of workers, and they will regret what they did on our behalf. If the building of the land is entrusted to private capital, even if it is Jewish, one may expect the destruction of our whole dream, and it will end in shame and disaster. We thus see to what an extent the national question depends on the social question.[43]

Obviously, there was no tension, let alone a contradiction, between nationalism and a socialism of this kind. At best, socialism was simply a means of achieving national objectives. There is no suggestion here of the teachings of social democracy, its way of thinking, or its concepts. Ben-Gurion had no sense of a universalist mission. This state builder was entirely preoccupied with the only objective that had any real significance for him, and the mission of the working class was limited to building the nation, not changing social structures. It is significant that Ben-Gurion hardly ever used the word *proletariat*. The proletariat, according to the Marxist view accepted by all socialist parties, was universalistic; it was not representative of national interests at all.

In accordance with this nationalist outlook, Ben-Gurion proclaimed the unity of all groups in the population. Although he knew very well how great an aversion the people of Hapo'el Hatza'ir had for social democracy, and although nobody knew better than he did the deep, instinctive anti-Marxism of the nonparty faction led by Katznelson, he sought a fusion with these elements and once again declared that their differences of opinion were only the result of "exilic fears." The truth, he said, was that in Eretz Israel, "in the harmonious unity of socialist and nationalist aspirations which we achieve in our work, we have fused the working population into a single unit."[44] What mattered, he believed, was daily existence, not ideology. This was the basis for his call in this speech for the founding of a "new organization [histadrut]," but it is obvious that the harmony between "socialist and nationalist aspirations" Ben-Gurion was talking about existed only for someone who defined socialism as providing for the needs of the nation and not as the ambition of creating a different kind of society. Understood in this way, there was truly no contradiction between socialism and nationalism: Ben-Gurion described the prospective organization as encompassing the entire existence not only of laborers but of all wage earners, all those who live by their labor. The organization would "embrace all the economic, spiritual, cultural, and political interests of the workers." The organization would assume the burden of building up the land, and it would be "the only contractor for all the work carried out by the Jewish people in the country." It would also be a supplier of services and commodities, from a health care organization (Kupat Holim, the sick fund) to stores for food, clothing, and footwear.[45] Thus, Palestine would be built "on socialist principles" harmonized with the needs of the nation. This presumed identity between the needs of the worker and the requirements of building the land was the only basis for Ben-Gurion's insistence that in Eretz Israel a synthesis between nationalism and socialism had been achieved.

Like Aaron David Gordon and various branches of the Zionist Organization that did not claim to be socialist, such as the Zionist Organization of the United States at its conference at Pittsburgh in 1918, Ben-Gurion proclaimed the principle of the national ownership of the land and of natural resources.[46] But at the same time he refrained from making too specific a demand for a rejection of private property as such. There was only one place in this major programmatic speech in which he said, among other things, that the task of the cooperatives was to "reduce the influence of private capital" and to "create an example of a miniature socialism, which will serve as a model for what must be built in Eretz Israel."[47] In contrast to the relative detail with which he described the actions that the movement should take and the economic enterprises it should set up, Ben-Gurion did not devote more than two sentences to the matter that should have been his main subject. Moreover, he spoke only of the need to "reduce the influence of private capital," not to abolish it, and there was no explanation of how the country would be built on a socialist foundation. One gets the impression that these things were said chiefly to conciliate members of the Jewish Battalions. Their representatives at the convention were often intransigent, like the delegate Ben-Yemini, "who passed on the instructions of his company in the battalion that the union with Hapo'el Hatza'ir should be accepted 'only if they do not ask us to compromise on principles.'"[48] And, in fact, the differences of opinion between the "Eretz Israelis" under the leadership of Ben-Gurion (Ben-Zvi had already adopted most of his colleague's positions) and all those who had a strong suspicion that they were expected to yield on essential matters were very real. They knew that it was not merely the name of the Po'alei Tzion Party but its very existence that was in question. "In no case can we abandon socialism," said another soldier from the Jewish Battalions. The civilian delegate from Jaffa, a Dr. Mitman, announced his voters' decision to oppose the name Ahdut Ha'avoda. They asked for "the word 'socialist' to appear in the name of the new formation." In the Jaffa branch, some demanded the inclusion of "the phrase 'social democratic,' which has been used until now."[49] As we saw at the beginning of this chapter, the full name of the Po'alei Tzion Party was the Eretz Israel Social Democratic Workers' Party–Po'alei Tzion.

In his usual way, Ben-Gurion brushed aside criticisms, without addressing any of them. Here is a typical example:

> With regard to the criticism of Comrade Blumenfeld, who wants to call our federation 'The Socialist Workers' Federation in Eretz Israel,' it is unfortunate that he does not know English. In that language, 'labor' means not only 'work' but also the body of workers as a whole. We wish to introduce this concept into our language. We wish, as far as possible, to build the land not as salaried workers but as free workers. 'Labor' is a broader concept than 'worker.' I am making this formulation not from a linguistic but from a sociological point of view.[50]

Later in his speech, Ben-Gurion enunciated his main principle. He said he was primarily concerned not with theories but with finding a way of developing the power with which the nation could be built. Many of the rank and file were no doubt disturbed by the idea of creating a new organization in place of Po'alei Tzion, an organization that would include nonparty people, people who, for as long as Po'alei Tzion had existed, had refused to join it on principle. Ben-Gurion, however, went still further toward these people and called for the creation of an even more inclusive organization. "We would like all workers to belong to a general organization, which would be based on nonpartisan principles." He wished "to incorporate the whole working class—all those who do not live by exploiting others—in a single organization. We wish to unite and organize all productive elements living on their own physical or spiritual labor."[51]

In the collapse of Po'alei Tzion's ideological basis, the cooperative program of Nachman Syrkin, Franz Oppenheimer, and Shlomo Kaplanski played a major role. In 1895 Oppenheimer, a physician from Berlin whose main interest was economics, published a long essay entitled *Cooperative Settlement*. The book had an interesting subtitle: *Toward a Constructive Rejection of Communism through a Solution to the Problem of the Cooperative and the Agrarian Question*. Oppenheimer saw cooperative settlement as the highest form of social organization and regarded himself as the continuer of the utopian tradition of Charles Fourier, Étienne Cabet, and Robert Owen. He was also close to Ferdinand Lassalle. The kind of cooperative colony he envisaged was a mixed rural-urban settlement, and its members were allowed to decide, after the initial investment had been made, the form the colony would take, including the way the land would be divided into private holdings. There is no doubt that an affinity existed between Oppenheimer's program and Syrkin's. They established contact in 1901, and at the end of that year, after Oppenheimer had published a series of articles in the main Zionist journal, *Die Welt*, which appeared in Vienna, he began corresponding with Herzl. At the sixth Zionist Congress in August 1903, Herzl invited Oppenheimer to present his plan. He was aware of its importance to the Zionist movement and wished to adopt it. Although Oppenheimer was described in the March 1903 issue of *Die Welt* as someone who advocated "cooperative settlements on land under permanent public ownership"[52] and who said he was a Zionist because he was a socialist, in reality the Oppenheimer plan was a Zionist, not a socialist, program. It was a solution to problems of employment and of creating an economy, not a method of transforming social relationships.

Shlomo Kaplanski, a member of Po'alei Tzion from Austria, was the great advocate of cooperative settlement in the Zionist movement. However, he did not claim that cooperation constituted a socialist plan in itself. "We are talking about the principles and consequences of this colonization from the point of view of its role in national settlement," he wrote in *Ha'ahdut*.[53] Kaplanski was careful to point out that Herzl was the one who "had emphasized collective settlement as the form of colonization most suited to us." Herzl, he wrote, "reached this conclusion through an intuition of genius, whereas Oppenheimer and Po'alei Tzion reached it through research and the study of other peoples' successful attempts at colonization."[54] For Kaplanski, the situation in Palestine furnished decisive proof of the value of the agricultural collective as a form of settlement serving the higher national interest. Kaplanski's involvement in the question ought particularly to be noticed, as in the period between the two world wars he was a central figure in the struggle of the left-wing opposition to the leadership, and he was finally thrust aside and appointed president of the Technion, the Haifa Institute of Technology, thus disappearing from political life. Even someone considered particularly a man of the Left evaluated forms of colonization by their capacity to absorb immigrants and provide them with a livelihood.[55]

Syrkin's approach was also primarily national and pragmatic, but it had a liberating aspect as well. It is impossible within the scope of this chapter to analyze Syrkin's doctrines, but a few observations are necessary in order to fill out the general picture. Even if his ideology was less original than Borochov's, it undoubtedly possessed a conceptual value far beyond anything the young people who immigrated to Palestine in the first twenty years of the century were able to provide. Katznelson considered himself his disciple; if his thought lacked the conceptual depth of Syrkin's, he took from Syrkin his anti-Marxist, voluntaristic approach, his belief in the ability of the national will to perform miracles. Syrkin, wrote Jonathan Frankel, at-

tacked one by one the metaphysical theories of history as the manifestation
of a predetermined logic. He rejected Marxist determinism, positivism, and
social Darwinism. But Frankel also insisted that in his struggle against
the various deterministic schools, including Marxism, Syrkin's thinking was
derived from Wilhelm Dilthey and Georg Simmel, Dostoyevsky and
Schopenhauer, in other words, from the conservative school of historiography and sociology, and not from socialist schools of thought. Nevertheless,
wrote Frankel, Syrkin remained true to the eighteenth-century notion of
progress and claimed that the theory of progress was equally applicable in
the moral sphere.[56]

Here, it is worth drawing attention to something Frankel overlooked:
it is no accident that Syrkin ignored the contribution of Bernstein and
Jaurès. The synthesis of Kant and Marx, the conception of socialism as the
heir of liberalism, the emphasis on individualism on one hand and on thinking in social rather than cultural terms on the other were foreign to this
Russian-Jewish nationalist looking for a solution to his people's plight.
Moreover, for social democratic circles true to the principles of the French
Revolution and to the idea of the emancipation of the Jews on the basis
of natural rights, Zionism was a suspect ideology. Zionism exacerbated religious and racial differences and was consequently classed as a right-wing,
nationalistic movement, which democratic socialism, after the Dreyfus Affair, violently opposed.

In fact, there was a very problematic side to Syrkin's thought. His anti-
Marxism went hand in hand with a belief in the determinant role of heroic
characters in history. An affinity with Thomas Carlyle is very obvious here.
Another belief of Syrkin's was that human progress occurred as the result of
an ideological revolution that took place from time to time among minorities.
He sought explanations in places that social democracy avoided like the
plague: the collective national soul, the Volksgeist, and the various peoples'
mysterious cultural and historical symbolisms. Syrkin was not content with
maintaining that human beings are motivated by religious and semireligious
impulses and visionary manifestations, in addition to material interests. He
went so far as to claim that the more absurd a plan appears to be from a
utilitarian point of view, the more likely it is to succeed. The true test of a
political strategy, wrote Syrkin, is not the degree to which it corresponds to
the situation or to reality but its power to penetrate the souls of the masses
and to activate the will of the people. This was obviously not very different
from Sorel's theory of myths. Frankel admits that by ascribing such an important role to mass unconsciousness, he was following a line of thought that
could lead to the relativism of the German historicist school or even to racial
chauvinism.[57] Just such an approach led many people of the Left to abandon
the universal values of socialism. The retreat from these values was the usual

path to the most extreme forms of nationalist socialism at the turn of the century. Frankel wrote that if Syrkin did not take this route, it was because he continued to be attached to the rationalist philosophy of the eighteenth century. But Frankel fails to acknowledge that despite this Syrkin deviated from the main tradition of social democracy and adopted the belief that the path to socialism passes through nationalism.

Here the highly problematical aspect of his thinking is apparent, for the social democrats would not have agreed with Syrkin that "nationalism, among the proletariat, necessarily takes a socialistic form."[58] And they would not have accepted Syrkin's account of the character of peoples and races. "In the prehistoric period," he wrote, "racial, physical, and psychic characteristics appeared and developed among the various groups of human beings into which mankind was divided." Nor would they have accepted the idea that "the concrete manifestation of racial-psychic characteristics can be found in the principles of language, the foundations of religion and life, and the division of prehistoric peoples into groups and families."[59] Unlike the democratic socialists, Syrkin believed that a nation is a fact of nature. Thus, in his system of thought, the nation is given greater importance than class interests. However, Syrkin knew that "a conflict of economic interests makes national unity, the precondition of Zionism, impossible."[60] This statement, like his view that "Zionism, being the Jewish enterprise of national construction, does not conflict with class warfare but simply transcends it,"[61] is a classic nationalist socialist formulation.

This outlook does not make Syrkin, as Frankel believed,[62] a pre-Marxist type of socialist; rather it makes him a post-Marxist, anti-Marxist socialist who has moved toward nationalist socialism. This same utopian tradition deriving from Proudhon, whose kinship with Syrkin Frankel insists on, was at the beginning of the twentieth century the major source of inspiration for the most extreme forms of nationalist socialism. It was a combination of nationalism, of an attachment to religion as a focus of national identity, and of a worship of the traditional heroes of the nation. This ideology did not necessitate the socialization of the means of production, and it even consecrated private capital. In many respects, the developments of Syrkin and Sorel were similar: essentially, Syrkin also believed in the ability of belief, willpower, and the emotions to move the masses. The rationality of a political program for him was not a criterion of its seriousness. An absurd program, but one with the capability to fire the imagination of the masses, was the one that would prove to be a historical force.

In the final analysis, what prevented Syrkin from moving to the Right was not an attachment to universal principles but a fidelity to the rejection of capitalism. Syrkin entered the path that led to nationalist socialism but stopped halfway. In this he differed from Sorel, but this was also the great difference between himself and Ben-Gurion and Katznelson. With them, the defensive wall that prevented Syrkin from moving to the Right soon disappeared. The leaders of Ahdut Ha'avoda never rejected capitalism per se.

Syrkin wrote that "the socialist proletariat is the only ally of the Jews"[63] and that "a Jewish state built on the basis of private capital like the other states in history is logically inconceivable."[64] After expressing his conviction that "in a socialist form, Zionism can be the property of the entire Jewish people," Syrkin explained his vision in detail: the Zionist Organization would embrace the entire people and would gain possession of the land by means of a national fund and a national bank.[65] The Jews would make an alliance with "the oppressed peoples of Turkey. . . . They would support the rebels with money from the national fund and even provide volunteers to fight." If necessary, the land could also be acquired by other means: not only with cash but also by gaining "the sympathy of European democracy and the proletariat" so that they would bring pressure to bear on Turkey, or by using "the indirect methods of diplomacy."[66] Syrkin's arguments are not uninteresting.

> Through their influence in journalism, in the stock exchange, and in diplomacy, the Jews could reach a solution of the Eastern question which they would consider desirable. The European states are interested in the settlement of Eretz Israel by the Jews. On one hand it would enable them to rid themselves of the Jews, who are in any case a source of social disturbance and a destructive element in the life of the nation, and on the other hand the economic and cultural development of Asia would be carried out by others.[67]

And finally, he wrote, "Eretz Israel, which is very sparsely populated, and where today the Jews constitute 10 percent of the population already, has to open to the Jews."[68]

These declarations were straightforward, clear, and unequivocal, without the dialectical gymnastics typical of social democracy in general and Borochovism in particular. They were accompanied by analyses of the nature of anti-Semitism which are not particularly surprising: "The Jewish masses have the right to impose the realization of Zionism on these people (the wealthy). They, the rich, with their wealth, assimilation, and intrigues bring hatred and persecution on the Jews, which is borne exclusively by the poor, for only the masses suffer from the anti-Semitism occasioned by the rich Jews."[69] Syrkin also made more subtle analyses of the anti-Semitism of the middle classes, but on the whole his writing was very uneven.[70]

Syrkin acquired from classic socialist thought the idea that there is a class struggle in every society; however, his stress on nation and race, his ideas about the historical, physiological, and psychological development of nations, and his claim that "human progress is the result of the struggle for existence, like the development of the various species in nature, although naturally in a different way,"[71] lent his socialism a very ambiguous and sometimes extremely nationalist quality, far removed from even the most moderate social democracy. No socialist around the year 1900 would have agreed with the following statement:

> The aim of the struggle for existence in nature is the survival of the individual. This leads to the existence of the generality—that is, the masses—for the masses only possess what the individual does. The aim of the struggle for existence of the human collectivity, the individual members of whom, as the old saying goes, are social animals, is the existence and strengthening of man in society—that is, of society itself, of the community. This struggle for survival, in short, is the basis for the existence and development of the individual.[72]

In this context, Syrkin drew conclusions concerning the differences between one people and another: "Each and every people has a special function in history . . . because each and every people has its own life, different from the lives of the others."[73] These cultural, physiological, and psychological differences between peoples, he wrote, produce not only different societies but also, of necessity, different socialisms. It follows that "the socialism of the Jews must be a purely *Jewish* socialism."[74] Syrkin was aware of the serious implications of this idea and tried to defend himself against possible reactions to it by saying that there were those "who would see in this particular combination of words a reactionary form of socialism, especially because the word 'Jewish' is usually comparable to words like 'Christian,' 'national,' 'German,' and so on. But this would be merely a matter of polemics, for logically and where truth is concerned, a Jewish socialism would be in the same category as a proletarian socialism, for both of them have common roots in bondage and an unjust distribution of power."[75]

At first glance this explanation could simply be an answer to the criticism that Syrkin expected, but in fact this argument on behalf of a socialism of the oppressed was very common and widely accepted at that period among nationalists with a developed social consciousness, as well as among anti-Marxist socialists belonging to peoples who regarded themselves as victims of the existing order. This was the socialism of Proudhon and Corradini, and the Prussian socialism of Spengler also derived from a general outlook not very different from Syrkin's.

Syrkin also had a practical plan for colonizing Palestine by means of cooperatives. This idea was based on a project he had elaborated in 1898, but it had never reached the point of actualization. According to his plan, the Jewish proletariat would be divided into groups of ten thousand people who would settle in successive order. The land and the other means of production, industrial buildings, and houses would be common property. The right to work would be guaranteed, and nobody would have to work longer than the time required to pay his debts and interest to the national bank. Each member of the group would receive a work voucher. With this voucher the worker would buy the necessities of life and would pay rent and taxes for the running and maintenance of schools and other services. The rest was similar to other utopias: in the absence of any reason for conflicts between individuals, there would be no crimes in the Jewish state; there would be no need to enforce laws; there would be no power struggles; and the state would not intervene in external conflicts. The "opposition between town and country would be eliminated," and finally, "the running of the country would be confined almost entirely to the management of its economic life. . . . The state would become unnecessary and be replaced by an association of free producers."[76]

To promote the idea of cooperatives, Syrkin contributed articles on the subject to the Po'alei Tzion newspaper, *Ha'ahdut*. The cooperative movement, claimed Syrkin, was not solely the concern of the workers. It reflected a need for collective colonization common to them and the middle classes. This was because there was "no other way for Zionism, if it was true to its main idea." Only cooperation could provide the infrastructure for "a new mass movement toward Eretz Israel" and bring to pass the "great dreams" of the Herzlian era.[77] The cooperative system "provided the solution to the question of Jewish labor," but at the same time it represented a great opportunity "to become completely liberated from the opposition between the man of property and the worker, between Boaz the colonist and the Canaanite or Hebrew slave, between the exploiter and the exploited. In the future colonization of the land, the worker would also be the property owner, and the cooperative form of labor would sweeten the bitterness of work in bondage and would free this activity from the eternal curse upon it."[78] The gospel of social liberation, though expressed here with suitable pathos, was secondary to national objectives nevertheless. Cooperation, he wrote, also provided an ideal solution to the "historical affliction of civil war which has plagued mankind" since the dawn of history and which, if proper measures were not taken, "would destroy the Yishuv in Eretz Israel even before it has begun to blossom."[79] This was the language of nationalist socialism, not of social democracy, and these statements were very acceptable to Katznelson and Ben-Gurion.

The question of building up the land by cooperative means was the main subject of discussion for the delegation of the Po'alei Tzion World Union that visited the country from January to May 1920. The Union decided to organize the delegation at the third and last session (from 23 September to 5 October 1919) of the Council of the Union, which met in Stockholm and held discussions there in three consecutive sessions: 21–29 July, 23–30 August, and, finally, the last days of September and the beginning of October.

The task of the delegation was to report to the Union—which was founded at the first world conference at The Hague in August 1907—on the situation of colonization and to propose a plan of action. The leaders of the recently founded Ahdut Ha'avoda—Ben-Gurion, Ben-Zvi, Tabenkin, Rubashov (Shazar), and Yavnieli—were appointed to the delegation, plus Syrkin and another delegate from the United States, two from the Ukraine, one from Poland, and one from Lithuania. The gathering at Stockholm decided that the report would be discussed at the sixth world conference of Po'alei Tzion, which was to take place in Vienna in July 1920.[80]

Judging from the reactions of Katznelson, the editor of *Kuntras*, and Brenner, the editor of *Ha'adama* (the monthly journal of Ahdut Ha'avoda), the initial decision to send a delegation was received coldly by the leadership of the newly founded party. Ahdut Ha'avoda, which demanded for itself the place in the World Union previously given to the Po'alei Tzion Party in Eretz Israel, was well aware of the criticism to which its founding gave rise, as well as its principles and ideas. Ahdut Ha'avoda members recoiled from the words of condemnation published in the Po'alei Tzion journals in Poland, Austria, and the United States. Katznelson at first tried to avoid going to Stockholm and wanted to invite the delegates of the Union to London, where the Executive Committee of the World Zionist Organization was meeting. But finally, apparently out of adherence to Ahdut Ha'avoda's rule of never abandoning a position, he went to the Swedish capital. In Stockholm Ahdut Ha'avoda joined the Union, but Katznelson and Brenner, the chief spokespersons of the former nonparty faction, as mentioned earlier, received the matter of dispatching a delegation with reserve.[81]

The only member of the delegation who was given a friendly welcome in Palestine was Syrkin. When he made a speech entitled "Constructive Socialism in Eretz Israel" at the Council of the Union in Stockholm,[82] he created a concept that corresponded to the hopes and requirements of Ahdut Ha'avoda members, especially those who had come from the nonparty group, without whom it would have been impossible to found the new party. This group was made up of workers (their numbers continually increased in the years before the First World War) who refused to join either of the two parties but who were generally close to the anti-Marxist Hapo'el Hatza'ir Party. But in his celebrated speech "Toward the Days to Come," delivered in 1918, Katznelson had already hailed Syrkin as a true Zionist "whose fire has not been extinguished: a vital man with tremendous national feeling and a deep sense of the future."[83] Katznelson was referring not to the socialist aspects of Syrkin's teachings but to their Zionist qualities. Brenner, who was always suspicious of socialist ideologists and who at the Ahdut Ha'avoda convention in Haifa on 10 December 1920 said once again that his "relationship to Po'alei Tzion is generally negative," also received Syrkin warmly. It was likely that the visitor from America was cordially welcomed not only because he was "endowed with a prolific pen"[84] but in his capacity as the father of constructive socialism, which relieved Ahdut Ha'avoda of the liability of Marxism and dependence on social democracy. Before the members of the delegation who held an intensive seminar with fifty-three plenary sessions, Syrkin explained his vast program for rural and urban cooperation, to be financed by national funds and to be implemented within ten years.[85] It was a grandiose scheme, and some people said it was utopian. Syrkin parried the criticism of the Left—"I don't know which is more realistic, utopian socialism or materialistic socialism"—thus winning the favor of the Eretz Israelis.[86] His zealous advocacy of Hebrew also helped him here. One of those present even accused him of comparing Yiddish to pornography.[87] In general, the leadership of Ahdut Ha'avoda realized that despite his fiery declarations in favor of socialism ("We want to build Eretz Israel in the socialist way"),[88] Syrkin had reached practical conclusions that were not that different from theirs.

> Let us consider three different types of society: the socialist, the cooperative, and the communist. We wish only to build cooperatives. In a communist society each person produces according to his needs, but this cannot apply in Eretz Israel, as it would take us even further away from current trends in human thought. A socialist society is also impractical, because people have been talking about it for a hundred years, and we still do not know what it is. Cooperative experiments, however, have already been made in present society, and we are able to build on them.[89]

Thus, Syrkin knew very well that his plan "to turn the whole country into cooperatives" was not a socialist program but rather a substitute for a socialist program. He also knew that to mobilize funds in sufficiently large amounts for the program to be carried out he could not apply to the labor movement. He did not suppose that the Socialist International would supply the means, nor did he think, like Nathan, the delegate from Lithuania, that "the meager resources we can obtain from the proletariat have greater value than billions donated for nonsocialist purposes."[90] For him, the implementation of Zionism would be the affair of the whole Jewish people: fifteen million people would have to shoulder the huge undertaking. "And if one sees that the worker alone cannot carry out this plan," he said, "we shall enlist the help of the entire people. . . . How we shall do so is a question to be discussed at this meeting."[91]

Ben-Gurion's thinking was along the same lines, although his focus was not cooperatives but establishing "a Jewish state in Eretz Israel."[92] As far as he was concerned, "A Jewish Eretz Israel is the essence of our action. It is Zionism itself."[93] That was how Ben-Gurion answered Nahum Rafalkes

(Nir), the delegate from Poland, who represented the views of the Po'alei Tzion leftists at the convention. Thirteen years earlier, at the Kraków convention, Nir had been the spokesman of Polish rightists against the Russian leftists, led by Borochov. At the meeting on 17 March, Nir challenged Tabenkin, who had made one of his rare appearances at the convention the previous day. "Yesterday," he said, "I heard that what you are proposing is not a socialist Yishuv but a Jewish one, and this is supposed to come about with the consent of the workers. Now your true intentions have finally been revealed! We shall on no account agree to this. We will not agree to merely building Eretz Israel."[94] Nir took up a clear, unequivocal position, but Ben-Gurion's diametrically opposed position was no less clearly expressed. "We must not break away from General Zionism," he said, "because that would amount to a separation from Zionism as such." But, in the same breath, he ventured to say that "the idea of linking the fate of building Eretz Israel with the fate of world revolution is not to be totally dismissed."[95] In these early years Ben-Gurion was prepared to accept any solution provided it served the national interest. He declared himself a supporter of the Soviets—"I personally am in favor of the Bolsheviks"—but at the same time he said that he did not think "the socialist revolution would be brought closer by class warfare."[96]

Ben-Gurion knew how to take the bull by the horns. "The comrades have the wrong idea," he said. "They think they have to show us how to organize a socialist society, but what they must show us is how to create a Jewish society in Eretz Israel." He also thought that no program would be realistic without a solution of the Arab question: "In any plans concerning Eretz Israel, we shall not ignore this question."[97] Socialism and cooperatives were in his view only means to the goal of transforming the "Jewish people . . . into a single political unit." In addition to domination by the bourgeoisie and the dictatorship of the proletariat (both of them equally absurd, in Ben-Gurion's opinion), there was also, he thought, a third possibility, "the dictatorship of the Jewish people."[98]

Thus, in the years after the delegation's visit to the country, the Histadrut was established as a system that in no way resembled Syrkin's cooperative ideal. It was the most concentrated, disciplined, and power-driven system imaginable. Collective agriculture—the jewel in the crown—was based on two principles: control of the settlements by a central administration and the absolute dependence of the individual on the system. Outside the collective settlements, an ordinary capitalist society grew with the full encouragement of the labor movement. The likelihood that the entire new Jewish economy would be reorganized on cooperative lines was no greater than the likelihood that it would be the arena of a liberating class struggle. We should remember that at that period the great majority of Jewish workers lived in cities, and this situation never changed. Also, among this class there never was a movement from the city to the countryside; in fact, the opposite was true. Many farmhands left the settlements as soon as the possibility of working in the cities arose. But most important, the cooperative program was never seriously intended to apply outside the agricultural settlements. In the cities normal conditions of working-class life prevailed, but without the ideological infrastructure that at that time and in other countries usually lent itself to left-wing politics, including the idea of class warfare as its symbol. Thus, most urban laborers—a genuine proletariat—were organized within a framework that provided them with essential services and an excellent professional protection in exchange for an agreement not to challenge the prevailing social and economic order. From the point of view of the society as a whole, the cooperative system was a stabilizing element, and in the long run it proved to be one of the most conservative elements in Israeli society.

Cooperative principles, inasmuch as they applied to the Histadrut economy, had nothing in common with the principle of self-management. Sollel Boneh (originally the Bureau of Public Works), the most important building and road-making concern in the country, one of the pillars of the Histadrut economy, was not managed by the workers. The journalists and the print-shop workers of *Davar*, the Histadrut daily, likewise had no say in the running of the newspaper. The same applied to other institutions, whose managers were subservient to the political leadership if they did not belong to it themselves.

From the point of view of the pioneers who set up Ahdut Ha'avoda and the Histadrut, collective agriculture proved to be an ideal solution. On one hand it was a means of building the nation, and on the other it was a method of organizing the labor movement as an autonomous force, embracing all wage earners in the economy. No wonder that Katznelson always regarded Syrkin as the great teacher of the "socialist Zionist movement."[99] Socialism, here, was subordinate to national requirements and was free from most of the ideological principles to which social democracy adhered. It was owing to the theoretical basis he gave to cooperative agricultural settlement that Syrkin was Katznelson's hero. Thus, both his support of the Uganda proposal and his leadership of the territorialist Left were overlooked. By contrast, Borochov's fidelity to Eretz Israel and his stubborn fight against both the Bund and the territorialists were to no avail. He and his followers were tainted with the sin of Marxism, and they were never forgiven.

The liquidation of the Po'alei Tzion movement had become a necessity, for anyone who wanted a different kind of socialism could not act within the framework of a social democratic party, faithful to the universalist principles of socialism. The creation of a nationalist socialist force was not possible as long as there existed a social democratic party true, like all social democratic parties of its time, to the essential teachings of Marxism.

THE FOUNDING OF AHDUT HA'AVODA

The formal decision to found Ahdut Ha'avoda was made at the Convention of Agricultural Workers, held in February 1919. This was the first country-wide gathering of all regional agricultural workers' organizations. The elections took place according to the system of proportional representation, with 1 representative for every 25 people; small settlements were allowed to send 1 representative for every 12 people. Altogether, 58 representatives were elected to the convention, 28 of whom were nonparty, 11 from Hapo'el Hatza'ir, and 19 from Po'alei Tzion. Thus, a clear majority supported non-socialist, if not antisocialist, principles. Prior to this agricultural gathering, the two political parties also held conventions, and at the Po'alei Tzion convention in Jaffa on 21–23 February, the party disbanded in order to clear the way for the founding of Ahdut Ha'avoda. The Hapo'el Hatza'ir convention was held simultaneously, and the agricultural convention met the day after the party conventions had ended. A short time later, after the people of Hapo'el Hatza'ir had refused to take an active part in establishing the new organization, the inaugural convention of Ahdut Ha'avoda took place in Petah Tiqwa in March 1919. Eighty-one delegates took part, representing 1,871 people. On this occasion, representation was according to sectors: 47 delegates were from the agricultural sector, 15 represented the urban workers, and 19 were volunteers from the British army's Jewish Battalions.[100]

Agricultural workers constituted the infrastructure of the newly founded organization, although even then they were already only a minority among the country's workers. Among the six founders of the new party, four came from the leadership of the nonparty agricultural workers: Berl Katznelson, Shmuel Yavnieli, David Remez, and Yitzhak Tabenkin. One—David Ben-Gurion—was close to them, although he formally belonged to the Po'alei Tzion Party, and only the sixth—Yitzhak Ben-Zvi—was a true representative of the Po'alei Tzion Party. All six were political activists for whom politics would soon become their sole occupation. Three of them—Remez, Ben-Gurion, and Ben-Zvi—had already had interesting careers. They not only abandoned physical labor as soon as they could, or never did any at all, but they left the country to study law in Istanbul with a view to preparing themselves for political leadership. For them the idea of redemption through labor seems to have been open to a very wide interpretation.

The leadership of Ahdut Ha'avoda included a number of other members of the Second Aliyah, only one of whom remained in the leadership after the founding of Mapai, in 1930, playing an important role. This was Eliahu Golomb, one of the founders of the Hagana, the semiclandestine Jewish defense force in Palestine. Golomb was younger than the others, came to Eretz Israel with his parents, and like his future brothers-in-law, Dov Hoz, another prominent figure, and Moshe Shertok (Sharett), the second prime minister of Israel, was in the first graduating class of the first Hebrew high school, Gymnasia Herzliyya in Tel Aviv, in 1913. The three others were Shlomo Kaplanski, David Bloch, and Neta Goldberg (Harpaz). Kaplanski came to the country in 1912, after a short time went abroad again, and in 1924 returned as director of the Department of Colonization of the World Zionist Organization. He was the main liaison between the labor leadership and the Po'alei Tzion World Union. David Bloch (Ephraim Blumenfeld) also came to the country in 1912, as secretary of the Eretz Israel Workers' Fund, which the Po'alei Tzion World Union had set up to finance its activities in the country. Neta Harpaz was also a member of Po'alei Tzion.[101] The three of them were progressively excluded from the leadership. It was not by chance that those who were progressively excluded from positions of influence in Ahdut Ha'avoda and who in the 1930s disappeared completely from political life were former members of Po'alei Tzion.

Ahdut Ha'avoda was not founded as a party in the usual sense of the word. The founders, having learned from the experience of the First Aliyah, believed that the historic task of building the infrastructure of a Jewish state had fallen on their shoulders. In practical terms, they felt that it was necessary to prepare the ground for the absorption of the immigration wave that everyone expected. Ahdut Ha'avoda was intended as an organization that could mobilize the manpower and resources to absorb and settle immigrants. Katznelson was quite correct in saying: "We are not a party and do not wish to be a party. We are a professional workers' organization, and our task is to fully accomplish the task of the workers."[102] The main emphasis was naturally on the last part of the sentence. However, the leaders of Ahdut Ha'avoda, despite the impression that some of them attempted to give for the sake of appearances, did not keep away from politics. It was Ben-Gurion, once again, who gave the clearest picture of the situation. In the debate on the name to be given to the new organization, he said: "I object to the name 'party.' The name is divisive, but that is not the only reason I object to it. A party is a political concept, a body dealing with politics. Not that we object to politics: we shall deal with it as the need arises; but the concept 'party' makes politics the main point of emphasis, whereas we want the main emphasis to be on productive labor, and I therefore propose the title 'Socialist Federation.'"[103]

Thus, Ahdut Ha'avoda (United Labor) was founded as a federation (*hitahdut*). This concept was much broader than the concept of a party. The founders' intention was to mobilize all wage earners by providing for their needs and all the services they required in order to facilitate the construction of the nation. Thanks to this comprehensive system, the workers, like the soldiers of a well-organized army, would be able to concentrate their efforts on this all-important task. As political action was impractical at that stage, the country being in the hands of the British, the first priority was action in the social and economic sphere. Thus, Ahdut Ha'avoda set up institutions such as a health care organization (Kupat Holim), workers' kitchens, a buying and selling cooperative (Hamashbir), and a workers' bank (Bank Hapo'alim). The collective settlements, originally a solution to unemployment, soon became an outstanding example of the workers' independence, a source of political strength, and an unrivaled organizational tool. The founders generally realized that there was no point in creating a classical political organization whose purpose was to engage in a struggle for power.

At that period the mandatory government wielded political authority, and the Zionist Organization was dominated by forces immeasurably stronger than the few thousand Jewish workers in Palestine. But these workers had one great advantage: they lived in the country, on the front line; they were young, on call, and ready to shoulder the practical burden of settling the land. To achieve this objective, a comprehensive organization and leadership were necessary. The organization they required was broader than a political party but also needed to fulfill a political function. Just as national rebirth could not be a purely political phenomenon, so Ahdut Ha'avoda could not be purely and simply a political body. The word *party* implied fragmentation, as Ben-Gurion pointed out, and the founders wanted to create a single power structure based on an existential partnership in the process of building the nation.

Because the founders intended to establish a single organizational structure common to all, the refusal of Hapo'el Hatza'ir to participate in Ahdut Ha'avoda led to the founding of the Histadrut, which was created to circumvent this obstacle. The Histadrut was founded as the General Federation of Jewish Workers, and the criterion for membership was national and organizational, not political. After a few years of coexistence within the framework of the Histadrut, Hapo'el Hatza'ir was finally convinced of the acceptability of Eretz Israeli existential socialism and decided that it constituted no danger to the national enterprise. After negotiations lasting a few years, the Eretz Israel Workers' Party (Mapai) was founded in 1930. Thus, the process that began with the liquidation of the Po'alei Tzion Party and the founding of Ahdut Ha'avoda had reached its conclusion.[104]

At the time Ahdut Ha'avoda was founded, a heated debate arose about the name to be given to the new body. This debate, however, was of more than purely semantic interest. The Po'alei Tzion leftists became alarmed when they saw that the word *socialism* did not appear once in the document, dated the end of January 1919, which the unifying committee submitted to the Convention of Agricultural Workers in Jaffa. Instead, it spoke of a "Union of the Working Class in Eretz Israel" and a "Union of Labor."[105] The leaders of the nonparty group—Katznelson, Tabenkin, and Remez—regarded the debate in Petah Tiqwa as part of the struggle that accompanied the liquidation of the Po'alei Tzion Party. These individuals—especially Katznelson and Tabenkin—asked for the offending word to be omitted on the grounds that this controversy over definitions was meaningless and futile. By contrast, Ben-Zvi, the last of the Po'alei Tzion diehards in the leadership of the new formation, immediately realized that matters of substance were at stake. This would affect the future. Ben-Zvi wanted the new party to be socialistic.

Ben-Gurion, for his part, adopted an intermediate position. He was inclined to the position of the nonparty people but knew that one could not ignore the claims of Po'alei Tzion members who still adhered to classical socialism. Accordingly, a compromise was reached: Ahdut Ha'avoda was founded not as a party but as a socialist federation. The nonparty group, essentially nonsocialist if not antisocialist, disliked this formula but accepted it for lack of choice. Years later Katznelson acknowledged that he and his friends had been very close to Hapo'el Hatza'ir; he had even collaborated in their newspaper.[106] Anita Shapira described Po'alei Tzion as "an abomination to Berl [Katznelson]," and Ben-Gurion later said that Tabenkin was "the greatest hater of the party [Po'alei Tzion] among the nonparty people."[107] In Tabenkin's speech at the founding convention in Petah Tiqwa, there is nothing that can be interpreted as contradicting this claim. If we take into account that Ben-Gurion was much closer to this group than to the members of his former party, we can see that the real power was concentrated in the hands of those elements opposed to the founding of a new socialist party.

In reality Ahdut Ha'avoda was founded by the nonparty group, and it was dominated by them. This was apparent in its institutions, particularly its Executive Committee. Of its first nine members, two had no particular affiliation, and two—Ben-Zvi and Blumenfeld—adhered to the Po'alei Tzion Borochovistic tradition. It is perhaps not surprising that both were gradually thrust aside. Of these two, Ben-Zvi fared the best. He accepted a post in the Va'ad Leumi (National Council), a public institution of secondary importance in comparison with the Histadrut's Executive Committee. Thus, not only was Ahdut Ha'avoda in its first year a party dominated by the nonparty group,[108] but this dominance increased until it triumphed completely when Blumenfeld and Kaplanski, the only people from Po'alei Tzion who still wished to preserve some kind of independence, were driven out.

There was no precedent for the founding of a European socialist party on such a basis. Although in Germany and France the founding of socialist parties involved a compromise between Marxist and non-Marxist principles, in Germany the right wing eventually accepted the orthodox line, whereas in France the "independent" socialists, or right wingers, were absorbed into a body in which the majority were Marxists or Marxist-Kantians. In both cases there was no doubt about the nature of the party or its fidelity to the tradition shared by all socialist parties that founded the Second International in 1889 or joined it in subsequent years. In Palestine, however, the right wing reacted to the "compromise" on ideological matters with revulsion and did all it could to divest it of significance. It did not find this difficult to do, since it dominated the new party.

At the inaugural convention, Katznelson gave the principal speech. Anyone examining this fascinating document and comparing it with his lectures and "conversations" of the 1920s and 1930s will quickly see how little his outlook had changed since the Petah Tiqwa convention. The speech focused on the primacy of the nation and his conception of socialism as nationalist socialism. To all doubters, to all opposers of the union, to all those who thought that socialism and nationalism do not always coincide, he replied as follows: "It is as if, in the reality of the worker in Eretz Israel—and not in the deceptiveness of words—there could be a nationalism without socialism, or a socialism without nationalism! As if there were workers among us whose Zionism condoned the oppression and exploitation of workers, or there were workers in this country whose socialism looked toward alien horizons and was indifferent to the revival of the people or the building of the land!"[109]

The idea that nationalism could be only socialist and that socialism could be only nationalist was widespread in Europe at the beginning of the century, but not in the socialist camp among parties belonging to the Second International. At the turn of the century the idea increasingly gained ground among national revolutionaries that national interests were not identical with those of the capitalists, the nation was not identical with the bourgeoisie, and a nationalist ideology was not identical with conservatism. At the same time, there was a common belief that true socialism was not Marxist internationalist socialism, the socialism of class warfare, but a socialism that aimed at unifying the nation and increasing its strength by creating a new system of social relationships. Thus, nationalist socialism opposed the exploitation of the worker and advocated solidarity and mutual responsibility. It was the worker and not the bourgeois—who lived by exploiting his brother—who sustained the nation, it was the worker and not the capitalist—with his selfish, particularistic interests—who constituted the cornerstone of national strength. Thus, the real socialism, the true socialism, the living, existential socialism, had to be national. Democratic socialism, however, with its Marxist roots, was often regarded as an abstract phenomenon or, to the degree that it was concrete, as a danger to the nation's existence. These ideas were strengthened by the First World War. At the end of the war, in areas in which the national struggle dominated collective existence, this was the only form of socialism that stood a chance of becoming a historical force. This is how it was in Palestine: all essential principles of nationalist socialism were expounded at the first conventions of Ahdut Ha'avoda.

In Palestine no one formulated these principles better than Katznelson, and no one based his idea of socialism more on experience and less on ideology. Katznelson stressed the principle of national unity as basic to any harmonious social organization, saying that "socialism must necessarily be national and nationalism must necessarily be socialist." Social organization, as envisaged by Katznelson, had to be based on the ideals of "national rebirth, the liberation of the worker, and the revival of our language." Anything that failed to contribute to the realization of this threefold objective was regarded as alien, a "remnant of the exilic spirit."[110] He claimed that although the pioneers required a loosely defined ideology, there was no need to take the definition any further, for socialism was one of those "national possessions" which were not "the prerogative of any one party."[111] Whatever one may say, he declared, "We are all in the same boat,"[112] and the nation would never reach port unless it "gave the worker a key position in this country, discovered the liberating qualities of our national movement, and fought the mercantile system that sustained oligarchy and careerism until it was overcome."[113] He further claimed that the worker in Eretz Israel ought not to "aspire to be a part, a majority, or a class," but "his desire and objective should be to be the people, the Jewish people living from its labor."[114] Here he was referring to salaried workers, but soon after this principle was extended, through the inner logic of the argument, to all those participating in building the nation. Thus, socialism—in Katznelson's words, a national possession—was an instrument in the long process of building up the nation returning to its land. Tabenkin, in an equally interesting speech that he gave at the Petah Tiqwa convention, said: "This assembly brings together the Jewish people working in this country. The aim of the labor movement is not just to lead a class but to lead the nation, and not just to lead the nation but to be the whole nation, to create a working Hebrew nation."[115] Ben-Gurion, as usual, defined most precisely the situation of those present: "We are gathered here on this occasion as Jews and national Zionists to define the particular status of the worker in Eretz Israel."[116]

The idea of Eretz Israel as the inheritance of the reborn people, as presented at the Petah Tiqwa convention, did not mean an aspiration to equality. It seems that the concept of equality was never mentioned. Nothing whatsoever was said, or even hinted at, about providing an alternative to the capitalist economy. Tabenkin insisted on the necessity of nationalizing "the land and its resources,"[117] but not by way of criticizing the capitalist economy. Ahdut Ha'avoda was set up to mobilize manpower, without any direct connection to a general philosophical theory, in order to overcome the disadvantages that the system of individual settlement had bequeathed to Zionism. The immigration of individuals, the absorption of individuals, except in particular cases, was declared not to be viable. "In a country like ours," said Katznelson, "in conditions like those we work in, the life of the individual cannot exist in the individual sphere alone; the life and activities of each individual are closely linked to the life and organization of our society."[118]

About four years later, Ben-Gurion said the final word on the subject. "Our main problem is immigration, large-scale immigration: the large-scale immigration of workers, finding them employment, settling them on the land. That is the all-important question and not adapting our lives to this or that doctrine," he declared at the end of 1922.[119] This was the principle guiding the leadership of the movement from the time Ahdut Ha'avoda was founded, during the entire period when it dominated the Yishuv, and under the state of Israel. The founders learned from their experience during the Second Aliyah that ideological discussion divides, but a shared existence unites and is thus a source of strength. Their conviction that ideology (which in this context meant socialism as an expression of universal values) was a source of weakness grew stronger due to their service in the Jewish Battalions during the First World War. From that time on, ideological unclarity, in all matters not directly connected with the implementation of Zionism, became a political tool of the utmost importance.

It would be wrong, however, to assume that this deliberate lack of clarity applied to all their thinking. The founders' conception of nationhood was crystal clear. At the same time, the "socialist" aspect of their thinking lacked the universalist side of socialism, leading historians of the period to gain the false impression that the unification of 1919 took place without any real ideological content. The new party deliberately refrained from giving an ideological definition of itself—except where general national objectives were concerned—in order to avoid having to confront the issue of the nature of socialism. The leaders justified this approach by claiming that achievements were more important than theories. This enabled the founders to create, as an infrastructure for the construction of the nation, a single comprehensive political framework for all types of wage earners and for the small-scale self-employed. Such an organization was disdainful of socialist principles. Thus, the controversy over the name of Ahdut Ha'avoda was in reality a struggle over its nature. The founders of the party had intended to include within it Hapo'el Hatza'ir, an antisocialist body that was composed of manual workers and therefore also "labor" in an existential sense. How could such a party be expected to seek a new social order?

Never before had a socialist party been founded on the basis of a shared "existence" and not on the basis of a common ideology. At all times and places, from the beginning of the socialist movement, workers in the socialist trade unions and socialist parties were a minority, and sometimes a small minority, not only of all wage earners but also of manual workers. Their common basis was ideological, their common values were universalist. A labor "existence" was never considered a guarantee of a commitment to changing society, and it never took the place of ideology. In reality,

Ahdut Ha'avoda also had a common ideology, but the ideology was national-ist, not socialist.

Thus, in the platform of unification, the usual Marxist analysis of the social and economic reality was missing, no use was made of the key concept class in the sense accepted in all the socialist parties of Europe, and the principle of class warfare was nowhere in sight. Another key concept, the socialization of the means of production, was totally absent. The main point that can be considered socialist in the program related to private property, but here too nothing was proposed beyond the nationalization of land and natural resources such as water. However, we must remember that most members of the Second Aliyah considered the nationalization of land and water resources necessary to settlement, the creation of employment, and the ab-sorption of immigrants. The members of Hapo'el Hatza'ir, declared anti-socialists though they were, demanded the nationalization of land for reasons that had nothing to do with revolutionary social philosophy. Their experience had taught them that private capital did not have the capacity to absorb immigrants. National ownership of land and water and the guarantee of national credit were practical steps toward the objective of a national revolution based on a personal and cultural revolution.

The formula "Ahdut Ha'avoda" had two senses. Ben-Gurion regarded it as a general description of the body of workers, like "labor" in English, whereas Tabenkin viewed *avoda* (labor in the sense of "work") as the basis for unity; Katznelson also stressed the principle of the unity of all the work-ers in the country.[120] However, the term *socialist*, although it appeared in the full title of the new formation (Zionist Socialist Federation of the Work-ers of Eretz Israel), was deliberately left undefined; at any rate, the leaders made no attempt to interpret or define it. This tendency to leave things undefined derived from a mentality common to all nationalist ideologies. The advocacy of unity on the basis of a shared culture or existence is a regular feature of nationalist thought. By contrast, nationalist thought de-tests abstract principles; intellectual abstractions are thought to sow divi-sion, whereas existential partnerships unite. The nationalists not only used this argument as political ammunition but really believed in the extraordi-nary value and creative power of a shared existence and common action. A disdain for theory and a rejection of abstract principles on one hand and a cult of action on the other characterized all nationalist movements, both conservative and revolutionary. Thus, it was not extraordinary if Ahdut Ha'avoda was founded on the basis of a conscious avoidance of a clear ideo-logical content. The founders, especially Katznelson, Ben-Gurion, Taben-kin, Remez, and Yavnieli, had no real ideological affinity with socialism. Kolatt already drew attention to the fact that the concepts "socialism" and "class" do not appear much in Katznelson; the broad, indeterminate, and unifying concept of a "labor movement" suited him much better. But Kolatt also claims that Katznelson was not satisfied with the principle of "unity of existence" alone and laid down three other principles.[121]

Indeed, in his long programmatic speech at Petah Tiqwa he formulated the three principles—socialist Zionism, pioneering action, and the Hebrew language.[122] The last two were purely nationalist, and socialist Zionism, to the degree that it had real content, was also essentially nationalist. Katznelson explained his point of view: "We have no need to label our ideology: it is a matter not of Zionism or socialism but of our existence as Jewish workers. That says it all."[123] That did indeed say it all; he knew very well that in the life of the workers at that period, the greatest common factor was Zionism and not socialism. For those present at the Petah Tiqwa convention, Zionism was not an ideology but represented the very essence of their existence. The renunciation of ideology had only one practical significance: the abandonment of socialism.

If anyone had any doubts about the meaning of socialist Zionism, Tabenkin's speech would have enlightened him.

> And now let us speak of the socialist-Zionist alliance. We want to unite with all those elements in the people who wish to create a socialist Zionism. Foremost among these is the workers in this country. But it is not only them, not only the workers, but the majority of the people. The part of the people that wishes to immigrate but does not have great material resources—and this is the majority of our people—agrees with our view of the proper way to build the land, which is the way that makes it possible to bring the largest possible number of people into the country and ensures the harmonious development of the people. That is socialist Zionism.[124]

Just as the controversy about the name of the party was not about terminology but about content, the use of concepts was also revealing. Katznelson wanted a union "based on the unity that exists in life," not a socialist party but a general organization "based on life, not ideology."[125]

Thus, all traces of Marxist socialist Zionism had disappeared, and Ahdut Ha'avoda was founded on a set of principles that contradicted those which the Po'alei Tzion newspaper, *Ha'ahdut*, had only a short while earlier declared as the basis of socialism. The principle of class warfare had vanished completely, nothing remained of "scientific socialism," and the socialism that remained was divested of universal significance. In place of these, Katznelson provided new definitions: "The socialist Zionism of the worker in this country is not a collection of sayings and projects unconnected with life and serving the purposes of polemics and philosophizing. Its aims and achievements are concrete: they came into being in consequence of his life and work."[126] This idea was not limited to the period of the founding of Ahdut Ha'avoda. It was endlessly repeated in the 1920s and 1930s by Ben-Gurion, head of the Histadrut and of the dominant party in the Histadrut.

"Our socialist Zionism," he wrote, "is not the abstract, artificial doctrine of the socialist Zionist theoreticians in exile, but an ideology arising out of the life and activities of the Jewish workers in this country."[127]

The founders had no more insulting epithet in their vocabulary than "exilic," and ideology, in the sense of a set of abstract, binding principles, was often represented as inseparably linked to the conceptual universe and modes of behavior that the new Jew had left behind him forever. Ben-Gurion boasted of the fact that "the Histadrut was not bound by any program or progammatic intention," and he repeatedly stressed the lack of ideological commitment on the part of Histadrut members. The Histadrut member was not even asked to make a commitment to the nation, "as long he does not infringe on its discipline in practice. The only obligation the Histadrut imposes on its members is the discipline of action."[128] Years later, when Ben-Gurion was about to assume the leadership of the nation, he once again extolled the principle of existential partnership that had guided him throughout his years as head of the Histadrut. It was an incomparable tool for the concentration of power: "Every Jewish youth desiring to work in this country, every pioneer and every laborer, whatever his ideological outlook, is a true partner in the national enterprise and in the labor movement in Eretz Israel. Not because there is no value in ideologies and theoretical concepts, but these are not decisive for a movement that depends on action. The criterion here is action, not theory."[129]

Nationalist socialism always sought to correct social distortions in order to ensure the unity and stability of the nation. It believed that there was an inseparable connection between national problems and social problems, and that the solution to social questions depended on a solution to the national question. This was the rationale for the founders' repeated claim that not only was there no contradiction between socialism and nationalism but socialism could only be nationalist and Zionism could only be "social." But nationalist socialism did not reject the capitalist economy and never proposed an alternative to it.

On this basis, there was a division of tasks between the workers and the bourgeoisie. Each group made its contribution to nation-building in the area in which it had a relative advantage. The founders knew that the person providing work had a definite advantage over the person looking for work, but they also knew that no one could take the place of the worker in carrying out the work. They were aware of the tremendous power organized labor represented. Accordingly, Ben-Gurion began to transform the labor movement into an organization to be reckoned with by the Jewish trade unions in the world at large and by the Zionist Organization. This had been Ben-Gurion's approach before the first World War, before he studied law in Constantinople. In an article he published in the fourth issue of *Ha'ahdut*, at the end of 1911, Ben-Gurion discussed the tasks of the Eretz Israel Workers' Fund, the modest financial tool created by the Po'alei Tzion movement for the use of its members in the country. "Proletarian Zionism in Eretz Israel faces two tasks," he wrote. "One is to consolidate the position of workers already in the country, and the other is to attract new workers from outside."[130] There is no suggestion here of any concern about the nature of the social order or about the moral or "universal" role of the working class. Thus, it was hardly surprising if the social achievements of the collective settlements, urban cooperatives, and institutions of the Histadrut were mere byproducts of the intention to realize the supreme national goals. The founders saw communal settlement as the most effective tool for the conquest of the land and regarded financial institutions and assistance funds primarily as means of ensuring the ability of the worker to carry out his task. This does not mean that they were unaware of the human aspect of aid, but principles such as justice and equality were always secondary to national objectives.

This attitude was expressed in particular in a key concept in the vocabulary of the labor movement: pioneering. Pioneers were those who devoted themselves of their own free will to the great objective of building up the land. This, however, was a relative concept. The Second and Third Aliyahs were considered pioneering aliyahs for two reasons. First, those who came to the country in those years had the option of going to other places more suited to the absorption of immigrants. Second, these immigrants came to a country whose development was only beginning. Construction workers who built the first houses of newly founded Tel Aviv (1903) were considered pioneers, but in the 1930s the leadership of the movement regarded these workers as having turned their backs on colonization and settlement. Because the definition had narrowed over time, by the end of the 1930s the concept of pioneer related solely to members of communal settlements. Only the conquerors of the wilderness were deemed worthy of that exalted title.

Despite the very "national" character of Ahdut Ha'avoda, Hapo'el Hatza'ir refused to participate in the unification of the two parties. Hapo'el Hatza'ir, the Federation of Young Workers in Eretz Israel, was founded at the end of 1905 by ten youths, four of whom came from the Polish town Płońsk, Ben-Gurion's birthplace. Among them was Shlomo Tzemach, a close friend of Ben-Gurion's. In February 1906 the party numbered ninety members.[131] On the face of it, the two parties in Eretz Israel at that time, Po'alei Tzion and Hapo'el Hatza'ir, had a common basis. They not only waged a war against colonization based on philanthropy, but they also believed in the capitalist dynamic as the key to progress. They believed that the Zionist enterprise in Palestine could succeed only in consequence of a rapid and constantly expanding capitalist development. An inflow of capital in quest of profit, a ferment of private initiative, an expansion of the internal market, and an increase in exports—only these could bring real progress. Capitalist initiative would bring to Eretz Israel the masses of workers who in the meantime were going to the United States. The young immigrants in the two parties regarded themselves as the vanguard and general command of the masses of Jewish workers who would stream into the country.[132] The parties expected mass immigration and called for it: the Ramle Platform of October 1906 viewed immigration as a historical necessity that would bring in the masses,[133] and the Central Committee of Hapo'el Hatza'ir in December 1907 issued an appeal to Jewish youths in Eastern Europe to settle in the country and occupy the new places of employment that were coming into being.[134]

This belief in the efficacy of capitalism, wrote Jonathan Frankel, derived from an experience of conditions in Russia.[135] In reality, in the first years of this century, this belief was common in Western Europe as well. Even the greatest enemies of liberalism saw no alternative to a capitalist economy, and social democrats, for whom socialism was the heir of liberalism, accepted a reality in which capitalism went from strength to strength. Revolutionary-syndicalist revisionism also began with a revision of Marxist economics: it was based on the assumption that there is no alternative to the capitalist economy.

Despite this common basis, it was hardly surprising that these few dozen politically minded pioneers who arrived in the first years of the Second Aliyah, after the 1905 events in Russia and Poland, had formed two parties. In volume 11 of his writings, devoted to the history of the labor movement in Palestine, Katznelson maintained that in those early years "there was no real difference between Hapo'el Hatza'ir and Po'alei Tzion, as there was at a later period." Thus, the two parties agreed on everything "and then split up because of the name. I say specifically *because of the name!*"[136] The reality, however, was different: the split took place not because of the name but because of content. Hapo'el Hatza'ir was derived from General Zionism, and most of its members came from the youth organizations of the General Zionist movement, and especially from the Tza'irei Tzion and Hatehiya groups.[137] According to Yosef Gorny, there were no real differences in the social origins of the two parties' members.[138]

No, the difference between them was ideological. For the members of Hapo'el Hatza'ir, nationalism was an all-embracing ideology that was not to be adulterated with socialist principles, whereas Po'alei Tzion, true to Borochov's approach, wished to implement Zionism while adhering to the basic principles of Marxism. Whereas Hapo'el Hatza'ir was strongly anti-Marxist, Po'alei Tzion tried to be faithful to the revolution at the same time as being true to the nation. The ideological difference required a separate organization, and the rivalry between the two parties was over matters of substance. Thus, in their formative years, 1906 to 1909, both of them made a great effort to create a network of activists, to publish newspapers, and to gain the support of as many workers as possible.

In accordance with its ideology, at the end of the First World War members of Hapo'el Hatza'ir in Jaffa, where a party convention was held from 29 December 1918 to 4 January 1919, proposed to call it the National Socialist Workers' Party in Eretz Israel–Hapo'el Hatza'ir. This proposal gave rise to much controversy, which centered on the question of whether the party needed a platform at all. Until that time Hapo'el Hatza'ir had no written program, and many people at the convention thought it better to continue that way. There were those who asked: "Why do we need socialist teachings when we have the teachings of Moses and the prophets?" There were those who thought that the Zionism of Hapo'el Hatza'ir constituted an answer to socialism, and others claimed that "whatever is natural triumphs in the end. Zionism, which was a natural phenomenon, triumphed over those who fought it, and we too must be natural and not seek out things that do not suit us. The Jewish people has suffered a great deal from the socialist parties within it, because they did not originate with us."[139] Many thought that instead of being concerned with a program, it would be better to concentrate on the main issues: pioneering, the conquest of labor (a concept originating with Shlomo Tzemah), and immigration. These issues were most important to the party, apart from the zealous promotion of Hebrew, on which Hapo'el Hatza'ir had insisted from its inception.

Thus, the programming committee elected in Jaffa, which was given the task of formulating ideological guidelines, never met, and Hapo'el Hatza'ir never advanced beyond the two one-page documents it had from the beginning. One was "Drafts for Programs," formulated in the summer of 1906, about a year after the founding of the party. It stated that "the task of Hapo'el Hatza'ir in Eretz Israel is the implementation of Zionism in general and the Jewish conquest of labor in particular." The second document, which was never brought out into the open and was never even discussed, was written in 1908 and entitled "Principles (Platform)." Interestingly, just as the programming committee, which was to discuss the Hapo'el Hatza'ir platform, did not meet after the First World War, so the 1908 platform never came up for discussion because the committee that was to deal with it never met, and the one that came after it did not discuss the matter at all.[140] This was the soil in which the teachings of Aaron David Gordon gained acceptance: the focus of the cultural revolution, which preceded and supported the national revolution, was above all labor.

Israel Kolatt writes that on the eve of the First World War, Hapo'el Hatza'ir was "an organization without a program."[141] This is true only if one reads this word in its most narrow and technical sense. There was indeed no platform in writing, but the statement is quite untrue if it is taken to mean that the party had no guidelines for political action. The party had no need of a written platform, for the ideology of Hapo'el Hatza'ir was crystal clear. All social values were subordinated to an extreme, exclusive, and all-embracing nationalism. At a very early stage, members of Hapo'el Hatza'ir had dissociated the idea of cooperation and collective settlement from any suggestion of socialism. The same applied to the nationalization of the land and of natural resources. Nationalization was not the socializing of private property but bringing land, particularly government land, under the control of the Jewish people.[142] In practice, these lands could just as well have been transferred to private individuals and not to national bodies. The members of Hapo'el Hatza'ir, those close to them in Po'alei Tzion, such as Ben-Gurion, and their sympathizers in the nonparty group, such as Katznelson, did not ascribe to the word *nationalization* its usual significance in the socialist world. They had no intention of transferring ownership of land or of any other form of property from private individuals to society or the state. Similarly, the founders of the first collective settlements, members of Degania and Nahalal, who were close to Hapo'el Hatza'ir or identified with it, recoiled from any connection with social democracy. All nationalist socialists in Europe at that period kept their distance from systems of thought they considered rigid, from social theories they regarded as abstract, and they praised all that was "living," "real," and "tangible." This had never been characteristic of democratic socialism, just as the establishment of isolated cooperative enclaves, without any intention of making general social changes, was meaningless where the socialist movement was concerned.

Because of the refusal of Hapo'el Hatza'ir to join Ahdut Ha'avoda, the Histadrut was founded as a "general," nonpartisan organization, nonsocialist by definition. The mutual aid institutions run by the party—Kupat Holim (the health care organization), Hamashbir (the buying and selling cooperative), and the workers' kitchens—were soon transferred to the Histadrut. The Histadrut soon gained complete control of the lives of the salaried workers who belonged to it. But the presence of the nonparty people in the Histadrut was not a sufficient guarantee of nonpartisanship. Another ten years had to elapse before the people of Hapo'el Hatza'ir were fully convinced that behind the seemingly innocuous terminology of Ahdut Ha'avoda there did not lurk some revolutionary intention. The only difference between the nonpartisan Katznelson, Remez, and Yavnieli on one hand and Sprinzak, Aharonowitz (editor of the party newspaper), and Shkolnik (Eshkol)—members of Hapo'el Hatza'ir—on the other is that the nonparty people had already been convinced when serving in the Jewish Battalions that Ben-Gurion's positions lacked any real Borochovistic content. Hapo'el Hatza'ir therefore needed a few more years' experience. As an alternative to the tripartite union, which never came about, the Histadrut was founded.

Some of its supporters thought that after the creation of the Histadrut, the task of Ahdut Ha'avoda had come to an end. The leaders of the party rejected this point of view completely. They had not set up an organization whose entire purpose was to provide services to its members and to absorb new immigrants. They had created the operative arm of the national movement whose aim from the beginning had been to establish, in due time, a Jewish state. Yonathan Shapiro has pointed out that Ben-Gurion and his associates needed a party that would protect the national interests in case the Histadrut favored sectorial or partial interests. Thus, there was a danger that if a conflict arose between the material interests of Histadrut members and the national interests, Histadrut members would prefer their own. Or, in a period of economic crisis, the Histadrut might prefer to halt immigration rather than to create unemployment. Ben-Gurion did not trust the national sensibility of Histadrut members or their ability to always put the well-being of the nation at the top of their list of priorities.[143]

Due to his adherence to this principle Ben-Gurion opposed the founding of moshavim, because they did not have the capability to absorb a large aliyah. His attitude to all forms of settlement was determined by a single criterion: the degree to which they served national interests.[144] At a gathering of Ahdut Ha'avoda members at Kinneret, Ben-Gurion said: "We must examine our lives in light of our essential national requirements. We must set up a thriving economy that is self-sufficient and at the same time corresponds to all our national needs. If the economy is antithetical to our national needs in this country, it is better that it should not come into existence. We have no need of an economy that, even if self-sufficient, is not suited to our national requirements."[145] For the same reason, Ben-Gurion opposed the creation of private farms on national land, as this would make national ownership of land merely nominal. "The nationalization of land," said Ben-Gurion, meant that "the land would be utilized for the good of all and not just for the benefit of a particular individual or group."[146]

EXPERIENTIAL SOCIALISM

At that early period, Ben-Gurion's ideas were dominated by his general belief that salaried workers should be gathered together on a collective basis in a *hevrat ovdim* (workers' community), which would ensure the control of the individual by the community. At a meeting of the Ahdut Ha'avoda secretariat, Ben-Gurion said: "A single community of workers, a single economic organization for all workers—that would be unity of labor [ahdut ha'avoda]. . . . The kibbutzim would continue to exist and supply the Histadrut with as much grain, milk, etc., as possible. Tailors and shoemakers would also produce for the Histadrut. In return, the Histadrut would not pay a salary but would supply everyone's needs."[147] The hevrat ovdim would have total control of the labor economy to facilitate the implementation of national goals.

This was also the reason for Ben-Gurion's enthusiastic support of Gdud Ha'avoda (the Labor Corps) when it was first created. The Gdud sought to exemplify the collective ideal. Ben-Gurion's proposal to organize the workers of the Histadrut on the lines of a collective, however, had nothing to do with the realization of a social utopia; it was an attempt to find a solution to a problem before it occurred. Ben-Gurion was apprehensive about the individualistic tendencies revealed in the demand to set up moshavim, and he feared the emergence of sectorial interests, which would lead moshav members to adopt positions similar to those of the farmers of the First Aliyah. These too had been Zionists, but they had yielded to their private economic interests. Ben-Gurion therefore wished to form an organized army of labor subject to the discipline of a general command, with a collective way of life that would facilitate mass colonization, a primary Zionist objective that, he believed, was impossible to achieve within the framework of the moshav. To those who questioned his opinion, including Tabenkin—who did not share his colleague's enthusiasm for communism and was alarmed by it—Ben-Gurion replied: "My communism comes from Zionism."[148]

Indeed, Ben-Gurion wanted to regiment the Histadrut in order to make it into an elite of public servants free of special interests. Anyone who reads young Ben-Gurion's writings with perception will have a better understanding of the well-known liking of the first prime minister of Israel for Plato. If it were up to him, Ben-Gurion would have established the Histadrut society on the lines of the guardians in *The Republic*; that is, as an elite group without property, living a communal existence and dedicated to community service.

This state builder understood from the beginning that a strong economic infrastructure was essential to the realization of political objectives. The economy had to absorb immigration; for this purpose, the leadership of Ahdut Ha'avoda favored the purest form of collective settlement, the kvutza or the kibbutz. From the beginning it was clear that the kvutza and the kibbutz, with their disciplined members and fully cooperative forms of life, constituted unique "regiments"; moreover, they were unrivaled political tools. Tabenkin placed such hopes in the kibbutz that at the end of 1921 he left Tel Aviv and joined Kibbutz-Ein Harod. In the long run, this caused him to lose some of his political influence, but he apparently believed he had chosen a path that would lead him to the top posts in the Histadrut and thus to a position of command among the Jewish elite.

Ben-Gurion not only opposed moshavim but also refused to grant collective settlements their independence. The national objectives of immigration and absorption required a centralized organization. As it was unlikely that every kibbutz and urban cooperative would make decisions that accorded with national interests, political control was needed, but political control depended on economic control. This situation led Ben-Gurion to the conclusion that one had to have a single central management to implement national objectives. Thus, the idea of concentrating all economic units under a single authority stemmed not from any social philosophy or from considerations of economic efficiency but from the need to place national interests above the economic interests of various units.[149] In the first year of the Histadrut's founding, Ben-Gurion claimed the leadership's right to impose its will on various units. Thus, for example, he asked that the leadership be allowed "to decide on the location of a moshav and control its relations with the Arabs, the education of its children, and its size and composition." He knew that the best way of operating such a system of control was through communism. To Ben-Gurion's way of thinking, communism, like socialism, was nothing but a means of control. But since a communist regime could not be set up in Palestine because the political situation was unsuitable, the alternative was economic domination. Ben-Gurion sought to achieve this through an organization with exclusive control of the development of the country.[150]

Hence the opinion he expressed in writing at the second convention of Ahdut Ha'avoda in September 1921. The Histadrut, he wrote, should be "the sole contractor of all public and private work in the country," and it should be organized as a "disciplined army of labor" in which all Ahdut Ha'avoda members would be immediately enlisted. They should be "irreversibly committed to carrying out any task that the leadership of the army of labor deemed necessary, and in any place they decided." To facilitate this, Ben-Gurion declared that "agricultural collectives and urban cooperatives should become the sole property of the Histadrut, and the produce of these enterprises should belong to the Histadrut." "All those working for the government, the Zionist Organization, the national enterprises, and the private sector would be working for the Histadrut, and their salary would go into the Histadrut fund. All the needs of the workers—food, clothing, housing, culture, children's education, and so on—would be provided by the Histadrut."[151] Even Gorny acknowledges that "David Ben-Gurion's point of departure was not moral or concerned with values but utilitarian and national."[152] Ben-Gurion regarded the egalitarianism of the commune not as a value in itself but as a means of unifying those engaged in building the land, in other words, as a means of regimenting the Histadrut society.

Thus, the well-being of the worker was not considered a desirable goal if it conflicted with the building of the economy. In the Histadrut Council, which met on 17 and 18 January 1923, Ben-Gurion toned down the radicalism of his demands but still insisted on placing the creation of employment at the top of his list of priorities, even when it conflicted with cheap imports, and on creating a closed economy in which the wage earner would be under the complete control of the organization. "Every man who receives his wages from the general fund," he said, would be provided with "a voucher from the distribution center equal in value to his salary. This is the first change we must make in our lives. This method of payment infringes on the freedom of the individual, but it is essential and has to be carried out."[153] Here it is no longer a matter of a general commune of the workers of Palestine but of a type of dependency on the employer which every trade union and socialist party in the world bitterly opposed. This kind of system formerly existed in Europe, especially in coal-mining areas, and was considered a form of slavery. Ben-Gurion did not regard the creation of this kind of dependency as contrary to "the organization of all our work in this country on the basis of a self-sufficient economy and of the control of all labor and markets by the working population."[154] By no means. An outstanding expression of the view that a self-sufficient economy acted as an instrument for controlling the workforce, thus ensuring that resources would not be dispersed and would not be diverted to purposes not directly serving national interests, may be found in his "Notes for a Proposal," which he placed on the agenda at the Ahdut Ha'avoda convention in 1921. Here Ben-Gurion violently attacked cooperative enterprises, both urban and agricultural.

> Urban cooperatives, most of which were set up through the Eretz Israel Workers' Fund, are really the private ventures of groups that exploit the public, including the workers, as much as any capitalist enterprise. The Histadrut's control of the assets of these cooperatives is a legal fiction devoid of reality. The funds intended to strengthen the working class are invested in a private concern managed by people who are not dependent on the working class. The members of the cooperatives use the workers' money solely for their own benefit. The existence of the cooperatives and their development do not improve the situation of the working class but, on the contrary, harm it . . . and the same applies to agricultural cooperatives."[155]

Ben-Gurion's chief complaint against the cooperatives was the autonomy the various groups enjoyed. Ben-Gurion described this absence of central control in all areas of the Histadrut economy as anarchy. This was the cause of the Histadrut's great weakness, and, as he put it, "We must now put an end to this anarchy."[156] Ben-Gurion judged all forms of social life by a single criterion: the extent to which they ensured control of the leadership responsible for building the country and absorbing immigration.

In accordance with this way of thinking, at the end of 1921 Ben-Gurion and Tabenkin supported the Gdud Ha'avoda (Labor Corps). This decision of the Ahdut Ha'avoda Council was not based on social or moral considerations. Whereas the Gdud Ha'avoda wished to implement a social philosophy and realize a noncapitalist form of economy, Ahdut Ha'avoda was concerned only with building the land. Gorny calls this the "principle of national functionalism,"[157] a euphemism that conceals a far simpler truth. The mentality of Ahdut Ha'avoda's leadership excluded any consideration except Zionism. As long as it thought that Gdud Ha'avoda served the national interest by being an organized and disciplined army of labor, which placed its "regiments" at the disposal of the Histadrut, it considered it its foremost representative. Could one have imagined a more Zionistic element than this band of young people, living in a commune with a common fund and totally dedicated to building the land?

A year later, at the third Ahdut Ha'avoda convention, Ben-Gurion summarized the party's attitude to communal settlement as a means of building the land: "The one great preoccupation that dominates our work and thinking is the conquest of the land and building it up through large-scale immigration. . . . About fifteen years ago, we came to realize that the colonization that had taken place until then had weak foundations, and we attempted a new path. We did this not out of a desire to assert our independence or to create something new, but out of a realization that what was being done was not Zionist and contradicted the very essence of Zionism."[158] Ben-Gurion and Katznelson always acknowledged with some pride that cooperative settlement had been a sort of improvisation, a solution to the needs of a new wave of immigration. Only when it became clear to the members of the Second Aliyah that private farms, for economic reasons, were unable to absorb them and would always prefer cheap Arab labor did they decide on self-absorption by forming groups of workers settling on their own account. Only when members of the Second Aliyah realized the immensity of their predecessors' failure to lay an economic, organizational, and political infrastructure for the implementation of Zionism through the absorption of new immigrants did they take matters into their own hands.

The inability of the traditional agricultural economy to realize national aims led them to two conclusions: there was a need to discover an economic alternative to private agriculture, and one had to find, in place of the independent farmer, someone to take charge of the Zionist enterprise. Thus, members of the Second Aliyah saw themselves as starting from the beginning: collective settlement was the solution to unemployment, and the wage earner began to depict himself as someone who had wrenched the torch of national renewal from the hands of the landowning settler. In 1911 Ben-Gurion had already said: "The cornerstone and very basis of our national revival is Jewish labor. And foremost among the architects and warriors of the national revival is the Jewish worker. And anything that makes for his strengthening and development, increases his social and political rights, and improves his material and spiritual condition contributes to the general good of the nation."[159] Thus, Ben-Gurion already expressed the point of view of Hapo'el Hatza'ir and laid down, once and for all, the principle of the identity between the social, economic, and organizational interests of the labor movement and the national interest. This process of shifting the center of gravity from the independent settler to the organized salaried worker occurred in the second decade of the century and became more pronounced until, at the beginning of the 1920s, the leaders of the organized salaried workers, who now headed the Histadrut, began to claim the leadership of the Yishuv.

Again national interests governed Ben-Gurion and Katznelson's relationship with the international labor movement. Their original suspiciousness of Marxism and internationalism did not diminish between the two world wars. The desire of the Ahdut Ha'avoda leadership to join the Socialist International was motivated not by ideological reasons but by the political benefits they could gain. The need to demonstrate a national presence in this international organization drove Ben-Gurion and his colleagues to seek representation in this body.[160] Again, national interests dictated the relationship of Ahdut Ha'avoda with the Soviet Union. Eliahu Golomb perceived a parallel between the Bolsheviks and Ahdut Ha'avoda, arguing that Lenin's faction, like Ahdut Ha'avoda, had adapted itself to social realities and was concerned solely with the interests of the Russian people, coopting the other communist parties into the service of the nation.[161] This point is very important and has been frequently misunderstood. The admiration of the founders of Ahdut Ha'avoda for the Soviet Union was due not to any ideological sympathies but to their great respect for the practical abilities of Lenin and the other leaders of the revolution. They believed that the Bolsheviks' relationship with the Comintern was quite similar to their own relationship with the Socialist International.

Once again the principle of the primacy of the nation dictated the attitude of the leaders of Ahdut Ha'avoda to their own party. Shlomo Kaplanski, a "classical" socialist who headed an opposition group, wished Ahdut Ha'avoda to function as a normal socialist party. He wanted the party to have a clear and unequivocal ideology and to influence the Histadrut, moving it in the correct direction. He protested against "the attempt to obscure the political character of Ahdut Ha'avoda and the blurring of its socialism" and objected to "the calls for unity that have been heard again recently in Ahdut Ha'avoda and are mainly directed at the Right, which dislikes the idea of international socialism." At the same time, Kaplanski complained of the "lack of democracy in Ahdut Ha'avoda. There is not enough sustained contact," he wrote, "between the members and their representatives in the party institutions and the Histadrut, and there is a lack of full and objective information."[162]

All the failures of Mapai from the 1930s until the time it broke up in the late 1960s were already discernible at that early period. This was also true of Mapai's relationship with the diaspora. Kaplanski spoke of "the tendency to claim the absolute sovereignty of Eretz Israel over the diaspora, and to speak arrogantly of 'domination,' 'hegemony,' and 'control' when we ought to be cooperating with the diaspora and exchanging ideas."[163] The leadership of the movement, however, considered such small matters as beneath its attention. It was interested only in building up a center where it would have undivided power. "The Histadrut," said Ben-Gurion, "is not only a workers' federation but the supreme embodiment of the Jewish people's renewal process."[164]

In practical terms, the Histadrut was a center of power and control, which the party was never able to rival. Moreover, the Histadrut encouraged the fiction of class unity. From the time of the founding of Ahdut Ha'avoda and the Histadrut, the leadership of the movement made tremendous efforts to give their notion of class a semblance of reality. They used intellectual casuistry, material blandishments, and in extreme cases economic pressures, threats, and coercion. But what was necessary most of all was the abandonment of any ideology apart from nationalism; for the leaders of the movement, a class could be a single, unified body despite the fact that it contained extreme differences of opinion. The Histadrut contained every possible ideological viewpoint, just as the founders had intended. That is why they reacted so strongly to the assertion that "Ahdut Ha'avoda was founded as a party." David Remez even declared this a "blood libel," saying that "anyone can be a member of Ahdut Ha'avoda, except for those who want to destroy Ahdut Ha'avoda."[165] To be a member of Ahdut Ha'avoda or the Histadrut, it was enough to subsist on one's own labor. Membership had nothing to do with class consciousness, allegiance to social ideals, or a universal scale of values. The class included all salaried or self-employed people who were not employers, regardless of ideological or philosophical differences.

Thus, membership in the Histadrut never depended on an ideological commitment to socialism. On the face of it, the Histadrut did not require an identification with Zionism either, but one should remember that on one hand it was not open to Arabs and on the other hand all the Jews, including the communists, were de facto Zionists by their very presence in the country. In this respect, the Histadrut leadership consistently adhered to the principle that what mattered was the existential situation, not the ideology. In accordance with this point of view, Moshe Beilinson, an important columnist for *Davar*, asked the members of Ahdut Ha'avoda to abandon their opposition to broadening the Jewish Agency: "We have before us a single objective, special of its kind, and that is building up the country. And we have to attain this objective *by any means*. This necessitates a broadening of the Jewish Agency. In view of this principle, all other principles have to be set aside." Here democratic principles were sacrificed to national objectives. Because the birth of democracy had preceded the Zionist enterprise by only a short while, Beilinson did not think it necessary to give it too much validity. In his opinion, the Zionist movement did not need to alter its policies merely to preserve "the purity of democratic principles."[166]

Let us remember that immigration to Eretz Israel, until the mid-1920s, was in itself an ideological decision. The Second Aliyah, which provided the labor movement with its top leadership, and the various waves of immigration of the 1920s, which gave it most of its elected officials, managers, and bureaucrats, were made up of people whose immigration resulted primarily from their attachment to their national identity. This was the element that bound them together. Regardless of social or ideological differences, these people were united by this basic decision of carrying out a dramatic personal revolution in order to participate in the great national revolution. Because of this profound involvement in the Zionist enterprise, these idealistic young people soon made their influence felt. Unlike other groups in the Yishuv, they recognized the importance of organization and leadership. After the founding of the Histadrut and the arrival of the Third Aliyah, settlers and their urban associates constituted a movement unrivaled in the local political spectrum.

At the same time, the Histadrut leadership was careful not to give the impression of threatening private enterprise. The secret of the coexistence and partnership between the labor movement and the Jewish bourgeoisie in Palestine, which despite some mutual mudslinging grew ever stronger, was not only the acquiescence of the labor movement in the burgeoning of the private sector but the fact that the movement viewed the success of the private sector as Zionism's success. The supreme goal of building the country included everyone in a partnership, wage earners and employers alike. Constructive socialism favored the development of all sectors of the economy; it was interested in the general accumulation of wealth, not in its distribution. The Eretz Israeli bourgeoisie knew that it had nothing to fear from the labor movement. It was not disturbed by its socialist jargon, for it too was more impressed by actions than by symbols. No one who carefully watched the leaders of the movement needed to worry about their vocabulary; everyone understood from the start that the labor movement never questioned the right of private capitalism and private property to exist, and it never even threatened them. On the contrary, as long as private wealth fulfilled its national role, the bourgeoisie of the Yishuv could rely on the support of the labor movement. All that was asked of it was to agree to the idea that "as soon as the Jewish working class appeared in the Yishuv, it became the main vehicle for the implementation of Zionism in the country."[167] Already at the end of the 1920s Ben-Gurion was careful to describe the wage-earning class not as the sole instrument for the implementation of Zionism but as its main instrument. Whereas Shlomo Kaplanski, writing in *Ha'ahdut* at the beginning of the First World War, had not hesitated to describe "the toilers and the propertyless" as the nation itself,[168] Ben-Gurion was far more cautious. In the January 1918 issue of *Der Yiddisher Kampfer*, Ben-Gurion acknowledged that "Eretz Israel can of course be built on entirely capitalist lines, like other countries, but building a country that is entirely capitalist will not bring about the implementation of Zionism. In a purely capitalist economic system, there would be no Jewish labor and the soil would not be in Jewish hands. Without Jewish labor and Jewish land, Zionism would be a mere hoax."[169]

This, according to Ben-Gurion, is where the wage earner has an advantage over the capitalist. Capital and labor are equally necessary to Zionism, but although there is always an alternative to the supplier of capital, there can never be an alternative to the supplier of labor. Capital can come from various sources, private as well as collective, but nobody can supply manpower except the worker; nobody can replace him as a settler and conqueror of the land. Nor can anyone rival the quantitative importance of the wage earners as a whole; it is owing to them that the Yishuv grows. "Zionism is not possible without capital, and it is not possible without labor. Both are necessary to the building of the country and the existence of our people. However, the value of the *capitalist* to the nation is not equal to that of the *worker*. If all the capitalists in the country were Jews, the country would not be more Jewish than it is now. On the contrary, even the Jewish sector would lose its Jewish character. But if all the workers in the country were Jews, the country would be entirely Jewish."[170] In these statements and those that follow, representing the mature thinking of Ben-Gurion, there is not a single word about the wage earner as the instrument of a social philosophy, or about the moral superiority of a society that has abolished private property over one that is entirely based on it. There is not a single word of criticism of private property as such, regardless of its task in Zionism. Where Ben-Gurion was concerned, the only criterion that mattered was and remained a functional and utilitarian criterion: "Private capital fulfills a Zionist mission if it creates Jewish employment, and public capital falls short of Zionism if it does not serve this purpose. The public capital invested in the building of Zichron and Binyamina [two settlements where Arab labor dominated] failed Zionism. The private capital that built Magdiel and Ra'anana [two settlements that employed Jewish workers exclusively] fulfilled a Zionist mission a hundred percent."[171]

From this one may conclude that in Ben-Gurion's view there can be situations in which private capital is preferable to national funds. Private capital that provides employment and absorbs immigration will always be preferable to national wealth that employs Arab labor and thus closes the country's gates to Jews. For Ben-Gurion, all other considerations were and remained irrelevant. One can imagine a situation in which Ben-Gurion had to choose between two places of work. One is a Histadrut enterprise employing Jews and Arabs on a cooperative basis, treating them with equality and providing fair wages and good working conditions, and the other is a private business employing Jewish labor exclusively. The first, exemplary in all respects, is defective in its capacity to employ Jews. One can say with certainty that such an enterprise would not fulfill its function where Ben-Gurion was concerned. There is no doubt that he would have preferred a moshava or an industrial enterprise that employed only Jews in harsh conditions such as in fact existed; the farmhand in the 1930s—the period Ben-Gurion was talking about when he mentioned Magdiel and Ra'anana—was at the bottom of the wage scale. Exploitation (no one can take issue with this word in connection with the farmhand) was less shameful to Ben-Gurion than the employment of Arabs. In the final analysis, exploitation concerned only the well-being of the worker. It involved only the individual and was a point of negotiation. The concept of exploitation was contingent on changing economic circumstances, whereas the employment of Arabs constituted a threat to Zionism.

Here we reach one of the key points in our understanding of constructive socialism. From the point of view of Ben-Gurion and the labor elite, all class interests, those of the capitalists and of the working class alike, were narrow, selfish, and divisive. The difference, where Ben-Gurion was concerned, was a functional one: "The worker too has interests," he wrote. "He too has class needs and a class outlook. But the essential difference between the worker and the capitalist . . . is that the class interests of the worker coincide with general national interests, and his historical requirements correspond to the needs of Zionism in the making, whereas the class interests of the capitalist clash with general national interests, and his aims are inconsistent with the needs of Zionism."[172] As he wished to control society rather than change it, Ben-Gurion constantly reiterated this theme in the same words, although with variations of emphasis owing to the need to stress the workers' special role in the implementation of Zionism without estranging the productive bourgeoisie that provided employment and investment.[173] His ultimate statement on the matter was a classic of nationalist socialism, dating from 1927: "The Jewish worker's concept of class is identical with the concept of political sovereignty held by political Zionism."[174]

Ben-Gurion maintained that in order to control society one must identify with the national objectives of one's period. He saw the economic selfishness of the middle class as the chief reason for the political failure of the bourgeoisie.

This inner vacillation between his class interests and his national interests has rendered the Jewish bourgeois in Eretz Israel incapable of implementing Zionism. In effect, the bourgeoisie has disqualified itself.

No class is able to lead the people, to take political control, or even to gain spiritual hegemony if it is not seen to act as a guide to the nation and if it does not, in its class activities, advance the interests of the entire people. If it does not have the interests of the nation at heart and a sense of national destiny, a class cannot unite and impose its social and spiritual authority on the other classes of people. . . . Among other peoples, the ruling classes always led the way and were instruments of progress. In their hour of greatness, they not only were exploiters and business people but also built states and enriched the national economy and culture.[175]

Ben-Gurion knew that in order to "act as a guide to the nation" and "impose its authority" on the other classes, the class of organized salaried workers would have to create around itself as broad a consensus as possible. He also knew that one could create a consensus not on the basis of radical social change but only on the basis that was common to the whole Yishuv: the struggle for national independence and a Jewish state. Thus, he and his friends in the leadership, especially Katznelson, made a tremendous effort to form a conceptual system that on one hand would mobilize the wage earners and raise a pioneering elite in the service of the nation and on the other hand would not arouse the opposition of the capitalist middle class. An intellectual framework was thus created which preserved the basic mobilizing concepts of the period—socialism, the working class—at the same time altering their meaning. Socialism, according to Ahdut Ha'avoda and Mapai, was a socialism of national unity which offered the wage-earning class psychological benefits in return for a renunciation of structural changes in society. The middle class, for its part, recognized the tremendous contribution made by the organized wage-earning class; it disliked socialism even in its national form but knew that the national part of this nationalist socialism was far more significant than the socialist part. Bourgeois leaders such as Weizmann, Ussishkin, Ruppin, and Moshe Glickson, the editor of the liberal daily *Ha'aretz*, never had any doubts about the real nature of this form of socialism. They supported the leadership of the movement and rightly saw it as a national treasure. They understood the true meaning of Ben-Gurion's definition of socialism: "Our movement has always stood for the socialist idea that the party of the working class, unlike the parties of other classes, is not only a class party concerned solely with the affairs of its class but a national party responsible for the future of the entire people, and not just a sector but the nucleus of the future nation."[176]

If one accepts this definition of class, all contradictions and oppositions between nationalism and socialism, between nation and class, disappear once and for all. Obviously, such a solution can be reached only if the concept of class is divested of the significance it possesses in even the mildest socialist interpretations. Only nationalist socialists could have imagined a conceptual system like this one, in which the idea of class is dissociated not only from class warfare but also from the wish to achieve a classless society by peaceful means and by means of a majority decision. In fact, European democratic socialism had renounced class warfare in the period preceding the founding of Ahdut Ha'avoda, but it never abandoned the hope of bringing about a structural change in capitalist society. Class warfare was regarded as a tool belonging to the predemocratic period, which could be given up when the proletariat had gained another instrument: political democracy. But a renunciation of the means never meant the abandonment of the final goal. This remained what it had always been: transforming capitalist society, drastically changing the system of ownership, and when the time came creating a classless society. All these normative aims of democratic socialism had disappeared from the ideology of Ahdut Ha'avoda and Mapai, and the accepted terminology reflected this development. *Proletariat* and *bourgeoisie*, terms that suggest conflict, made way for *the worker* and *the property owner*. Workers and property owners were able to coexist within the existing order much more easily than the bourgeoisie and the proletariat. From the end of the nineteenth century, this was the path nationalist socialism generally took.

In this situation, it was indeed possible to speak of an identity between the interests of salaried workers and national interests. After the movement had abandoned the struggle against capitalism, after it had contented itself with control of the society as it was on a basis of cooperation and a division of tasks between itself and the bourgeoisie, there no longer was any contradiction between the "class interest" and the national interest. This contradiction had disappeared because the labor movement had renounced all particularistic class interests and instead had taken upon itself the supreme national mission of building a state. Here the leaders of Ahdut Ha'avoda and Mapai were right: the bourgeoisie did not renounce its own class interests, and thus, as far as it was concerned, the usual contradictions between national interests and class interests remained.

From that moment, it was inevitable that, with the consent of all other classes, the labor movement would assume the leadership of the society. All capitalists, great and small, knew already in the 1920s that they had nothing to fear from the Histadrut. This was the secret of the dominance of the labor movement: it was an arrangement of truly historic importance. The labor movement renounced the struggle against capitalism and the existing social order and was content with managing the national struggle. In exchange, the middle and upper-middle classes renounced the struggle for power and assented to the labor movement's claim to political leadership.

The educated upper-middle class also appreciated the national revolution presided over by the Histadrut. It, too, applauded the personal revolution "that had taken place among the workers of the country" and that "involved a total fusion of will and intelligence, creativity, and consciousness, as a result of which the first cell of Hevrat Ha'ovdim [the Society of Workers as a holding company and not a workers' community], sustainer of the national economy and harbinger of Jewish statehood, came into being."[177] It realized that the vaunted political and cultural "hegemony" of the movement had been gained at the cost of surrender on the social front.

The labor movement agreed to confine its social experiments and innovations to a single sector, which enjoyed great prestige but which never, from the quantitative point of view, amounted to more than a minute part of the population. The socialism accepted in Palestine was a "productive socialism," which concentrated on the creation of wealth but not on the equitable sharing of it or its transference, at least in part, from the "haves" to the "have-nots." This acceptance of the capitalist order had not only a social and economic significance but also a far-reaching cultural significance. In reality, the labor movement never succeeded in passing on its values to society as a whole; Tel Aviv remained to a large extent outside its control, and to the extent that the movement dictated social norms, it was affected by the covert influence of the bourgeoisie.

Thus, the labor movement developed two very different kinds of socialism simultaenously. Constructive socialism, which was a socialism for the masses, was and remained a tool of national construction. As such, it was a consolidating factor, and in the long run it also proved to be conservative. Parallel with this, the movement encouraged and sustained the kibbutzim, ideal models of an egalitarian way of life. But the socialism of the kibbutz had an elitist character, its benefits were available only to a few, and it never affected more than a small minority. The population as a whole continued to live its life outside the framework of the value system of the kibbutzim or the youth movements. This was the main reason for the failure of the movement to assimilate the mass immigration of the early years of the state. It was able to administer the masses of immigrants, but it was unable to serve as a home to them.

Socialism in the Service of the Nation: Berl Katznelson and "Constructive" Socialism

THE LEGEND AND THE REALITY

Berl Katznelson has a unique place, not only in the history of the labor movement and its historiography but also in the collective memory of the Israeli political and cultural elite. His death in 1944 at the relatively early age of fifty-seven, at a time when all his friends of the Second Aliyah, from Ben-Gurion, Tabenkin, and Ben-Zvi to Eshkol, Remez, and Sprinzak were approaching the zenith of their careers, his reputation as an ideologist and educator who did not "soil his hands" with day-to-day politics, and his long and sentimental lectures called "discussions," full of reminiscences of the early days, resulted in an image in which reality and imagination, truth and legend, have been indiscriminately intermingled for more than sixty years. In the collective consciousness of the native-born generation that reached maturity in the 1940s and early 1950s and that was reared on the legend, Katznelson was the embodiment of the pioneering Yishuv, of the heroic and pure society, frugal in its ways, swamped by waves of mass immigration and the modernization process of the early years of the state. That generation longed for an image that would immortalize its lost innocence and that in many ways would serve as an alibi.

In recent years the most interesting expression of the cult of Berl Katznelson is Anita Shapira's biography.[1] More than a history book, it is a labor of love, and the responses of Israeli readers reflect a nostalgia for a golden age that has vanished beyond recall. For the children and grandchildren of the immigrants who came to the country before the Second World War, graduates of the famous high schools in Tel Aviv, Jerusalem, and Haifa, products of youth movements and kibbutzim, and, generally speaking, the children of the educated upper-middle class close to the labor movement, Katznelson represented an inseparable part of the vanished days of their youth, together with the sand dunes of Tel Aviv, the campfires that lit up their nights in the summer camps in Galilee, and the comradeship of the youth groups. The fact that this nostalgia has more to do with myth than with the gray realities of that period makes little difference. It is necessary to discuss Katznelson's thought not only because he was a key figure in the formation of the labor movement's ideology but because he embodied all the strengths and weaknesses of the movement, all the tensions, contradictions, and ambiguities it contained from the beginning.

Katznelson's thought was not remarkable for its depth or originality. This man, who was regarded as the spiritual mentor of his generation and was its foremost ideologist, did not leave behind a single systematic essay. In the socialist world, this was an unparalleled phenomenon. His writings consist of newspaper articles, lectures, and "discussions." All his work—frequently repetitious—deals with day-to-day matters and represents a response to the immediate concerns of the hour. It may be that more cannot be expected of an autodidact from Bobruysk, in White Russia, but the matter deserves to be looked into. Katznelson was not a political leader but a kind of secular rabbi whose strength lay in a direct contact with a sect of believers and not in the leadership of a mass movement. Katznelson did not feel the need to devote himself to theoretical writings. From this point of view, his lectures are disappointing. Israel Kolatt describes his famous speech, "In Preparation for the Days to Come," delivered at the seventh convention of the Organization of Agricultural Workers in Judea on 26 January 1918, shortly after the British conquest of the country, as a "programmatic lecture." Shapira regards it as one of his greatest speeches, and according to Kolatt, this speech became a sort of Second Aliyah visiting card and a declaration of its social intentions.[2] One cannot avoid the impression, however, that this speech, mingling references to the ancient dreams of the Jewish people with a discussion of the day-to-day affairs of the agricultural worker, was a warm, friendly talk such as those attending the conference needed rather than a serious statement of policy.[3] Today the speech has lost much of its appeal, but it must have made a strong impression on the gathering of workers from Judea.

Katznelson's two major speeches, which begin the first volume of his writings—"In Preparation for the Days to Come" and his long speech "Ahdut Ha'avoda," delivered at the inaugural convention of the party, about one year later, on 24 February 1919—were outstanding examples of Zionism as nationalist socialism. The appeal to sentiments, feelings, instincts, life forces, and existential experience, the affirmation of faith as the chief if not the only motive power of organized social action, and the recognition of the need to give nationalism a social content were all typical of post-Marxist or anti-Marxist nationalist socialist thinking. Shapira remarked on Katznelson's affinity with "the world of Georges Sorel in his syndicalist period"[4] but failed to consider the significance of this fact.

Sorel's work, in the early years of the century, constituted a challenge to both Marxist and liberal rationalism. Sorel viewed myth as the only force able to drive people to action. He regarded myth "as identical with the beliefs of a group, and . . . the expression of these beliefs in the language of movement." Through myth one could appeal to people's hearts and sentiments. This strongly antirationalistic approach derived from Bergson and

Nietzsche and was opposed to all forms of Marxism, including the social democratic form. It was significant that Sorel particularly detested Jean Jaurès and French social democracy, and in the last years before the First World War he allied himself with the Action française nationalists led by Charles Maurras. Shapira's account leads one to the conclusion that Katznelson's general view of the forces driving human beings was similar to Sorel's. "One might think, at first," wrote Sorel, "that it would be enough to say that we are ruled by our feelings, but everyone today agrees that the essence of emotional life is movement."[5] This idea was common to the anti-rationalistic revisionism of Sorel, which was directed against Marxism, and the nationalist intellectuals in Western Europe who rebelled against positivism and against the rationalistic dryness that, they said, sapped the life force of a nation.[6]

These factors also existed, in varying degrees, in the reviving Hebrew culture. The Jewish national movement, like all other national movements, culled these ideas from the cultural revolution of the period. When this cultural revolution was translated into political terms, it took the form of a revolt against the rationalism, hedonism, and utilitarianism of socialism and liberalism. Thus, a frequently destructive "ideology of denial" came into being, whose consequences lasted throughout the twentieth century.

In a society in the process of construction and incapable of translating the principles of cultural rebellion into government policy, this ideology was unable to reach fulfillment, but it was sufficient to contribute to the elimination of the Marxist heritage and the inhibition of the universalistic characteristics of social democracy during the critical period of laying foundations. The special Jewish character of Eretz Israeli socialism was sufficient to make it a form of nationalist socialism. The anti-intellectual, vitalistic, and organicist tendencies one finds in Gordon and Katznelson, the devotion to the cult of life forces, of existential "rootedness," as opposed to rationalistic detachment, were very important factors in the development of this ideology.

Katznelson himself realized the special status his 1918 speech enjoyed among his contemporaries. In another speech, on the tenth anniversary of Ahdut Ha'avoda, he repeated the same formula but added an exhortation to preserve the heritage of the Second Aliyah unchanged: "And also in preparation for the days to come we should not abandon the tools of labor and reflection we have forged, the resources of strength we have discovered in ourselves, but, on the contrary, hold on to them and continue on that path."[7] The conservative ideological attitudes of the leaders of the movement, which would prove to be a stumbling block in the future, were already operative at the end of the 1920s.

Even in the peak years of his activity and influence, Katznelson did not express ideas essentially different from those of his speech to the seventh agricultural workers' convention. The lectures he gave in 1928 to members of the Ahdut Ha'avoda youth movement, which was founded about two years earlier, do not demonstrate any special breadth of vision. The subject was the history of the labor movement in Eretz Israel from the early years of the Second Aliyah until the founding of Ahdut Ha'avoda.[8] Sixteen years later, in May–June 1944, Katznelson again lectured on the same subject to the Young Guard of Mapai. The stenographed notes of these lectures were included in volume 11 of his writings, and since then they have occupied a place of honor both in the heritage of the labor movement and in studies of Berl Katznelson. Judging from these notes, it does not seem that there was any real development in his thought. The somewhat methodological preface and the evaluations of the international labor movement are extraordinarily banal, and the lectures consist chiefly of Katznelson's reminiscences of the Second Aliyah.[9] The members of the Second Aliyah, wrote Shapira, were in love with the members of the Second Aliyah. Indeed, since immigration to Eretz Israel began, there has never been a group of people as much in love with themselves and as self-absorbed as the members of the Second Aliyah. "The Miracle of the Second Aliyah" was the modest title Katznelson gave his speech on the aliyah's twenty-fifth anniversary in April 1928. On its fiftieth anniversary, in 1955, Ben-Gurion boldly declared that "in the future," the anniversary of the Second Aliyah would "be a national holiday, and one of the important dates in our history."[10] But if in 1928–29 this point of view was understandable and in many ways justified, in 1955 this self-absorption was already a sign of blatant conservatism.

In most of Katznelson's major lectures, the reader will find a combination of simplistic formulations with flashes of penetrating insight. These lectures, when they were not polemical, like those, for instance, in which he criticized the Hashomer Hatza'ir kibbutz movement at the end of 1939, when it was reluctant to form a union with Mapai's Kibbutz Hame'uhad,[11] were a type of discussion. These "discussions" with Histadrut activists or with the leaders of youth movements did not provide a setting particularly conducive to theoretical thought. Nevertheless, this was a better environment for the exercise of his talents than the party and Histadrut institutions, where his polemical side was mainly revealed. The well-known lecture "In Favor of Perplexity and against Whitewashing," which he gave in early August 1940 to the leaders of Youth Aliyah, is considered one of his most impressive pieces of writing.[12] It was precisely in the last period of his life, when he decided to fight the influence of communism, that he succeeded in rising above the political and party polemics that had been his usual concern throughout his career. Only when he realized that the sense of certainty that he and his friends had formerly possessed had now passed to his rivals, when he understood that the scales were tipped in favor of Hashomer Hatza'ir and that Hakibbutz Hame'uhad was about to slip from Mapai's grasp, did Katznelson begin to advocate perplexity. The object of his perplexity was socialism, and the sense of certainty he wished to undermine was the young people's uncritical faith in the Soviet Union. When he felt that his own camp was in a defensive position, Katznelson began to encourage doubt and call for independent thinking, for an abandonment of accepted formulas, and for a readiness to look at historical events with fresh eyes. He complained of the "distortion and madness of nationalism in our days'; because of his strong opposition to accepted Marxist interpretations, he understood that fascism was not a "conservative" or "reactionary" phenomenon but a "destructive revolutionary force." But, above all, Katznelson encouraged perplexity as a defense against communism: "A generation such as this, which sees the distortion of class motivations and perceives what becomes of the idea of class when it is in power, negating all its promises and making a mockery of all its values . . . why should such a generation not be perplexed?"[13] By contrast, he felt that the existential socialism of Eretz Israel was more valid than ever. While barbarity ran amok in the Soviet Union, Jewish youth, he said, from the moment it set foot in Eretz Israel, "breathed an atmosphere of socialist idealism that is not mere lip service here but truly a matter of life."[14]

In general, it seems that Katznelson's intellectual scope did not extend far beyond the limits reached at an early stage.[15] In 1937 he met Rudolf Hilferding, then a refugee from Nazi Germany, in Switzerland. He knew Hilferding was "one of the great European socialists," but in his account of this meeting there was nothing to suggest that he was acquainted with his work.[16] It is doubtful whether any leaders in the European socialist world had not read Hilferding's *Das Finanz Kapital* and were unaware of the importance of this work in socialist thought. This difficult book, the work of the most eminent Marxist economist since Marx himself, was published in Vienna in 1910, and two years later was translated into Russian, Katznelson's language. Lenin was inspired by it to write *Imperialism: Last Stage of Capitalism*, which appeared in 1916, and in Western Europe Jean Jaurès praised the work of the Viennese Jewish doctor in the French parliament.

Katznelson's writings not only reveal the dearth of analytical depth in his thought but also reflect the intellectual shallowness of Eretz Israeli political life and its provincialism and conservativism. The intellectual level of the labor movement never rose very high, and its nationalist ideology encouraged isolation as a means to tribal unity. "The people of my generation who came to this country first had to resist liberal and socialist assimilation," said Katznelson in the summer of 1940 to the leaders of Youth Aliyah, when urging them to fight against "communist assimilation" and "fascist and Nazi assimilation."[17] This was the logic of modern nationalism, and Zionism was not the first national movement to take this path. All national movements of the nineteenth and twentieth centuries sought cultural autonomy and cherished the glories of their own particular past and national productions. The alien was not only "other," but by definition hostile. With Gordon, as with

Katznelson, there was a suspiciousness of the outside world, and alien cultural influences were considered harmful to the life of the nation.

Another aspect of this strong suspicion of the outside world was a distrust of any fixed theoretical framework. At the beginning of the 1940s, Katznelson returned to the arguments he had used in the ideological struggles of the Second Aliyah. Once again he directed his barbs at the "idle discussion" he so hated. The need to erect protective walls against alien drafts was as strong as ever. At the fifth Histadrut convention, in April 1942, at the height of the controversy with the Left, Katznelson warned of the danger "of the spiritual influence of the outside world" and spoke of the high price the movement had paid "for its inability to resist the ideas prevailing in the world."[18] Freedom from ideological dependence had always been considered a kind of guarantee of nondependence on universalistic systems of thought, which were essentially alien. At the beginning of the 1930s, Katznelson still claimed that "we are fortunate in not being tied to a theoretical tradition that comes between an understanding of things and the things themselves." In his speech before the council of Mapai at the beginning of 1931, Katznelson said he regarded the founding of Mapai without any clear ideological basis as a great achievement: "We have no need whatsoever to be sorry that, once again, we have begun with 'doing' rather than with 'hearing.'"[19] (This is a reference to the people of Israel at Sinai, who said, "We shall do and hear," Exodus, 24:7.) His call for a theoretical clarification at the end of the union process does not alter the fact that in a matter of supreme importance such as the founding of Mapai, Katznelson felt it possible to restrict oneself to a common existential basis without any theoretical infrastructure. Also in this context Katznelson condemned the dogmatism of Borochov's followers, who, he said, "lacked any capacity for thought." Thus, Katznelson, in his speech before the Council of Socialist Youth in December 1927, managed to reject Borochov's legacy while praising his personality.[20] From a political point of view, however, it was undoubtedly his ideological legacy and not his personality that was significant.

Katznelson always praised the members of the Second Aliyah for rejecting socialism "out of an opposition to the various forms of Jewish socialism, which led to assimilation and anti-Zionism and a perpetual readjustment to the outside world," while "having in their hearts a socialist existence and socialist values."[21] Here, "existence" was the key word. Thus, Ahdut Ha'avoda members had an irrefutable argument with Hapo'el Hatza'ir members. When, in the 1920s, the latter refused the proposed union, saying, "What do you want from us? We're not socialists," this factor of "existence" enabled the leaders of Ahdut Ha'avoda to answer with total self-confidence: "You are no better or worse than we are, and you are no less socialist than we are."[22] If the sole criterion was existential and not ideological, then common participation in the Histadrut or a collective settlement was enough. If action always preceded thought, just as "the form of settlement and the institution of the kibbutz preceded the theory of settlement,"[23] there was no point in theoretical definition or ideological content. A striking example of this point of view was Katznelson's attitude when Mapai was founded.[24] Nobody insisted more obstinately than Katznelson that nothing prevented union with Hapo'el Hatza'ir, although it persisted in describing itself as an antisocialist body. Socialism as a system of universal values had no meaning for him. The humanistic principles he adhered to were not special to socialism, and the principles that were specifically socialist were precisely those that Katznelson rejected and Ben-Gurion disregarded.

This way of thinking persisted in the 1930s, and Katznelson spoke in the same way at the end of 1935, in a speech he made at the inaugural conference of the General Zionist youth group in the Histadrut. The warm, fatherly tone in which he addressed the new antisocialist members of the Histadrut is especially noticeable when compared with one of his usual attacks on the Po'alei Tzion leftists he made a few weeks later. At the Histadrut Council, which met on 9 February 1936, Katznelson assailed his adversaries on the Left for again committing what in his eyes was an unforgivable sin: instead of focusing on immigration and creating an infrastructure to absorb it, the Left wanted to discuss "the question of tomorrow," in other words, the relationship with the Arabs.[25] If anyone in 1936 thought that the "main questions" confronting the Histadrut were not limited to the organization of an unemployment fund, Katznelson had nothing whatsoever to say to them. At the same time, he beamed affection on the General Zionist youth, and he made special efforts to show them, as he formerly did to Hapo'el Hatza'ir, that "our vision" is in reality "your vision" also: "Among us, members of the Second Aliyah, there were also some people who never stopped declaring that they were not socialists. This declaration did not prevent them from striving with all their might to create here a life of labor and a society of a new kind, and from being among the founders of the collective settlements and the labor movement in this country." He was convinced that the General Zionists, with their "pure unadulterated Zionism," had the same ideals as Gordon, which Mapai wished to embody; thus they could not be indifferent "to social questions and questions of social reform." There was therefore no reason they should not identify with an outlook whose main tenet was the following: "One class should not dominate the other classes, but there should be a working people, a liberated people free of the domination of other nations and free of class domination."[26] Moreover, he said, "The meaning of socialism is to impose the authority of the nation on ever wider areas of life in the community, and not only to mediate between classes and achieve a compromise between them, but also to impose on them the popular will to such a degree that classes are eliminated."[27] Was it not Gordon who "saw the redemption of man and the reform of society in nationalism itself"?[28] One can hardly say that this mode of thought—even if we attach due importance to the elimination of classes—ever reflected the social democratic outlook.

On innumerable occasions, Katznelson stressed the uniqueness of the labor movement in Eretz Israel and the originality of the solutions it offered. He always saw its special creations—collective settlement and the Histadrut—as the crown of the whole enterprise. These solutions, he said, were not arrived at via an intellectual understanding but were responses to immediate needs: the isolation and alienation that made it hard for members of the Second Aliyah to remain in the country gave rise to cooperative settlements and mutual aid. They resulted from an existential need and not an ideological decision. Similarly, the kibbutz was the answer to unemployment and the pioneers' strong desire to take root in the country.[29]

This point requires special emphasis. The founders did not conceal the aims of Zionism, and to their credit, they did not attempt to present members of the Second Aliyah as seeking to lay the foundations of a socialist utopia. "I want there to be no misunderstanding concerning the Second Aliyah. You probably imagine that the Second Aliyah had a clear, preconceived notion of what it had to do, or an agreed-upon and ready-made ideology, as people think they had," said Katznelson in 1944 to the Young Guard of Mapai in that same series of lectures, which may be regarded as a kind of ideological testament.[30] Communal settlement was not the result of a conscious decision, said Katznelson. In the atmosphere of that period, there were indeed dreams of communes, of a shared life and equality, but the founders of Zichron Ya'akov and Rishon-le-Zion (private agricultural settlements) had similar ideas. The first agricultural settlement that began to be run on communal lines, the "collective in Sejera," came into being "not because the founders' dream was to create a communal settlement. They had political intentions. Their idea was *guarding*. Farming and agriculture were merely an addition to guarding. Their dream was to create a Jewish force that would change the regime in the country and end dependence on the Arabs." The original motivation, according to Katznelson, was "the idea of Jewish political sovereignty."[31] Katznelson made it clear that the first kibbutzim were founded not to realize a socialist utopia but to lay the groundwork for the conquest of national independence. It was also an improvised solution to the problem of strained relations between the owners of Jewish farms and members of the Second Aliyah: "The people who founded Umm Juni [which became Degania, the first kvutza] did not intend to be settlers. In reality, [Umm Juni] was a revolt against the regime of the functionaries. The proposal of the workers at [the farm of] Kinneret to be allowed to manage their own affairs in a portion of the estate at Umm Juni laid the foundations for collective settlement. It was a practical solution to the bitter dispute between themselves and the manager of the estate at Kinneret."[32]

On this point, Ben-Gurion was as unequivocal as Katznelson, and his description of the birth of collective settlement at Sejera and Umm Juni and the creation of Hashomer entirely confirms Katznelson's account. Ben-Gurion concluded: "Only through the search for a solution that would guarantee Jewish labor did they arrive at the idea of the collective settlement— that is, colonization on a completely different basis from that practiced during the previous twenty-five years."[33]

Like Ben-Gurion, Katznelson was always proud of the original practical solutions that Eretz Israeli socialism found, and he viewed this as a unique trait. His continual emphasis on this uniqueness strengthened the self-confidence of the labor movement—and often its belief in its superiority to other socialist movements.[34] This was an extraodinarily effective means of preventing an intellectual dependence on the outside world and of avoiding criticism by orthodox socialists.

The determination of the founders to keep Eretz Israeli socialism outside the sphere of influence of the world socialist movement was largely due to their fear of the internationalist implications of socialism and its doctrines of class warfare. It was also due to the necessity of protecting themselves from the extreme suspiciousness of all socialists toward socialist parties unduly concerned with religion, culture, history, and ethnic origins and overinvolved with themselves. Thus, the organized labor movement in Palestine had nothing to say when civil war broke out in Spain; it had very little interest in subjects that did not affect it directly. Socialism and all other universal values were in the service of the nation. Nobody typified this outlook more than Katznelson and Ben-Gurion. The two men complemented one another and divided the work between them. It would be wrong, however, to suppose that one was the man of dreams, ideals, and principles and the other the political leader who made difficult compromises. This was not the case. The teacher, educator, and preacher of morals was also a shrewd politician. As though at the touch of a magic wand, the saint with an anguished soul (according to Shapira's biography) could cast off his image of the tortured prophet and turn into a hardheaded political activist who knew all the tricks of the trade—vindictive and able to fight for power. His self-righteous manner immediately gave way to a merciless onslaught on his foes.[35]

By present-day standards, Katznelson did not play an outstanding role where democratic values in the party were concerned, but if we are to judge by the criteria accepted in Ahdut Ha'avoda, the editor of Davar was true to his task. Even Shapira admits that he was not generous in his treatment of minority groups in the Histadrut. He demanded and received exclusive control of Davar, which he founded in June 1925, after a long period of internal power struggles.[36] It was Ben-Gurion's support that decided the matter. Katznelson and Ben-Gurion stood side-by-side in the two great internal crises of the 1920s: the crushing of Gdud Ha'avoda (the Labor Corps), which will be discussed in the next chapter, and the corruption scandal in the Histadrut (the affair of the "advance payments," discussed in chapter 6). Katznelson did not use his control of the paper to turn it into an open forum of opinion, a platform for freedom of expression where the weaknesses of the movement would be debated with courage and candor. In general, the paper was closed to voices of the opposition. Katznelson's pretexts were hypocritical and self-righteous, but his adversaries were impotent. *Davar* did not even commemorate the fifth anniversary of the founding of the Gdud. Even Shapira agrees that when one considers that every workers' weekend gathering was recorded in the newspaper, *Davar*'s silence on the Gdud's fifth anniversary was significant.[37]

This state of affairs deserves careful scrutiny. Katznelson excluded his rivals' opinions from his columns, and even Hapo'el Hatzair members who did not support the positions of Ahdut Ha'avoda preferred to use their own newspaper and not to have to contend with *Davar*'s editor. However, *Davar*'s exclusion of those who disagreed with the positions of its party did not spring from a petty desire to make the newspaper the property of Ahdut Ha'avoda. Katznelson was convinced that his positions and those of his party corresponded to the objective will of the workers as a whole and served their interests and those of Zionism. For Katznelson, *Davar* was a weapon of war. It was "his" newspaper and his weapon,[38] and to put it at the disposal of an adversary was inconceivable. Katznelson denied Gdud Ha'avoda expression in his newspaper, seeing it as a source of "rebellion and sabotage against the Histadrut."[39] He detested the Po'alei Tzion leftists and complained of the freedom of expression granted to members of the Communist Party at the second Histadrut convention. He disliked democratic debate as practiced in Western Europe. He would have preferred to deny the extreme Left the right of debate altogether, and he intended to restrict freedom of discussion in the Histadrut by a rule allowing members to be dismissed from the organization "for spreading slander, in Eretz Israel or anywhere else, about the Histadrut and its institutions." Spreading slander about the Histadrut included, for instance, the complaint of the extreme Left about the Histadrut's refusal to include Arab workers in its ranks. Katznelson claimed that the Histadrut should not have to tolerate the presence of those who accused it of chauvinism or, as he put it, caused hostility between Jewish and Arab workers.[40] Hence, the slogan "Freedom of debate and unity of action" was a fiction: the Histadrut was a tool for building the nation, and anyone who disliked the way it functioned was to be put outside the pale. Representatives of the pacifist Brit Shalom movement were treated in the same way in the internal debate following the first Arab revolt of 1929.[41] Censorship was then a normal working tool for the editor of the Histadrut journal.

Moreover, with the same fidelity to what he believed were the needs of the movement with which he repressed left-wing opinion, Katznelson defended those involved in the great corruption scandals of the 1920s. His excessive indulgence toward those who rifled public funds in a period of distress, unemployment, and hunger was not only due to his feelings of friendship toward Remez and the other members of the Second Aliyah.[42] Katznelson thought it inadvisable to reveal the truth, thereby hoping to protect the party and the Histadrut. The behavior of the man whom Shapira described as the symbol of integrity, the man who was considered "a pillar of morality, the very soul of the movement,"[43] was no better than Ben-Gurion's, for both had the same motivations and the same basic outlook. As they saw it, the smooth functioning of the Histadrut preceded moral integrity, freedom of expression, or democracy—often dismissed as "formal" democracy—in the national scale of values.

Thus, within the Histadrut, Katznelson opposed any deviation from the official line and over time, despite his repeated calls for moral stocktaking, became a strong conservative figure. Similarly, Katznelson always refused to relate to the bitter complaints of the left wing of the Histadrut about the movement's leadership. He was evasive, he insulted, he was scornful, but he did not really come to grips with the question.[44] To those Po'alei Tzion leftists who in 1934 had doubts about dismissing Arab workers because of the principle of Jewish labor, that principle which had been sacred from the beginning of the Second Aliyah, Katznelson replied with a verse from the national poet Hayyim Nahman Bialik: "I abhor both the aggressiveness of dogs and the timidity of rabbits." This was how Katznelson interpreted the ideological difficulty of the Zionist Left: as the "cowardice and impotence of rabbits" on one hand and as "parasitism" on the other. Katznelson said that he understood and respected those who refrained from making aliyah for fear of taking employment away from the Arabs. But in his view, there was no greater "baseness" than to persist in this moral hesitancy after coming to the country while exploiting "the situation we have created" and "benefiting from the conquest of labor we have achieved." A person who did not accept the principle of Jewish labor condemned the Jewish Yishuv to being "a population of cheap dealers, either real estate agents or revolution brokers; it is all the same."[45]

Katznelson was quite often given to prevarication instead of dealing with problems. For example, at the Mapai convention at Rehovot in 1938, he explained his support for Ben-Gurion in the Gdud Ha'avoda affair as having been due "to the great injustice that was being done to Lavi and Tabenkin."[46] Less than four years later, however, at the convention in Kfar Vitkin in October 1942, Katznelson's account of the reasons for his intervention in the Gdud Ha'avoda affair was quite different. He had just come back from America, he said, and had no preconceptions or knowledge of the matter. He proposed to help and investigate the problem, but his offers of service were rejected.[47]

On another occasion when the leadership of the movement was criticized, he said he did not know who the leadership that was the object of such bitter complaints was. At the Kfar Vitkin convention, Katznelson, at a time of dissension in the Tel-Aviv branch of the party, said he did not know "what they are talking about and what they are arguing about" in Tel-Aviv. But immediately afterward he declared that "what has happened in Tel-Aviv is not factionalism. It's putschism" and "defiance of the party and its institutions." Asked to intervene in the dispute, Katznelson admitted that he was very far from being an "automatic apologist for the apparatus," but he lashed out fiercely against these "unholy alliances between the pioneering agricultural sector and the salaried workers."[48] All of a sudden, the celebrated partnership between kibbutz members and workers in the cities, which had been the pride of the Histadrut and one of its chief claims to uniqueness and originality, had become an unpardonable sin.

But these were more than mere rhetorical tricks. In this case, Katznelson's outburst expressed his genuine feelings. Precisely in the hard political struggle that led to the split in Mapai in 1944—the most difficult one the movement's founders had been involved in since they had arrived in the country—was Katznelson's conception of the movement most clearly revealed. "The individual worker has not become a partner in anything with the pioneer!" shouted Katznelson, agitated and frightened at the collaboration between the opposition in the Tel Aviv branch of Mapai and the representatives of Hakibbutz Hame'uhad.

> What you are doing does not raise the individual workman to the status of a full partner in the pioneering enterprise but places it in the hands of those who have refrained from pioneering. Pioneering does not count for anything in the lives of members of the leagues and factions; it does not bring them a new ethic or a different cultural life, but it brings the pioneer, hitherto free and independent in his own sphere, down to the level of a mere cog in the political "machine," ignorant of how it runs or functions.[49]

"The hands of those who have refrained from pioneering," let us remember, belonged not to local party functionaries, whom Katznelson generally referred to respectfully as long as they served the party and did not slide to the opposition, but to the construction workers and port workers who suffered from hunger during the economic depression of the late 1930s. Katznelson, like all the leaders of the movement, was not too sympathetic toward the simple, rebellious workers of Tel-Aviv. The opposition group in the Tel-Aviv branch, which at the end of the 1930s constituted a majority there, was led by Dov Ben-Yeruham, a true workers' leader. It was regarded as irresponsible, vulgar, and prone to demagogy, and its members, terrible to say, still sometimes spoke Yiddish! Could anything more uncultured be imagined?[50] These were the people who had built Tel Aviv with the sweat of their brow, but for Katznelson they were mere workers and not a vanguard of Zionist colonization.

Thus, in a moment of truth, the low status of the urban laborer in the eyes of the labor movement was suddenly revealed. This basic fact was central to Israeli society throughout the second half of the century. Ideologically, the labor movement was not equipped to deal with the problems of a normal society. It was able to settle empty areas of the country, or areas that had been emptied of their inhabitants, but it was unable to mold a different kind of society. Its spiritual mentor was uninterested in the wage earners in the cities, and in fact in workers in general; he viewed them only as auxiliaries to the vanguard of Zionist settlers. Similarly, Katznelson lacked perspicacity in another existentially important issue: the Arab problem. On one hand, he described Zionism as a colonizing but not a colonialist movement, which had no need to account for its actions; on the other hand, he justified Arab opposition to Zionism as being due to the stratification of Arab society and the rule of effendis.[51]

At the same time, Katznelson did not accept the myth of the country's conquest through bloodshed,[52] and in the "disturbances" of 1929, the usual Jewish euphemism for the Arab revolt, he condemned the writer and poet Aaron Reuveni for his insulting references to the Arab people in his poem "The War of Jerusalem, Poem of Victory." The poet David Shimoni (Shimonovitz), a native of Katznelson's hometown of Bobruysk, came to his colleague's defense, and Katznelson in a private letter rebuked this friend of his youth for praising a poem with a harsh nationalistic tone, which placed a collective guilt on all Arabs and called for a vendetta.[53] From a political viewpoint, however, there was no doubt that Katznelson, relatively unconcerned with the Arab problem,[54] was closer to Tabenkin, who did not recognize the existence of the Arab national movement at all, than to Ben-Gurion. The latter, who unlike Katznelson was extremely conscious of the Arab question, adopted at that time a characteristically pragmatic position. "The question of whether an Arab national movement exists or not," he said, "is a mere matter of terminology. What matters to us, however, is that the movement attracts the masses. We do not see it as a movement of renewal, and its moral value is dubious, but from a political point of view it is undoubtedly a national movement."[55]

THE NATION ABOVE ALL

The concept of the nation's primacy was basic to the ideology of the labor movement. Aaron David Gordon gave integral Jewish nationalism its theoretical basis, and the liquidation of the Po'alei Tzion Party marked the end of an attempt to find a balance between national and universal values.

Katznelson accepted Gordon's basic concepts but went beyond them to create the practical and intellectual infrastructure of the labor movement. Whereas Gordon rejected socialism and fought it bitterly, Katznelson accepted an edulcorated version of socialism but subordinated it to national ends. From his perspective, socialism was a myth that mobilized the masses. Instead of wondering how socialism and nationalism could be combined (something that, from a theoretical point of view, was difficult to imagine, and from a practical point of view caused many ruptures and crises in the socialist movement throughout the half-century before the Second World War), the leadership of the Second Aliyah found an ideal solution: placing the universal values of socialism at the service of the particularistic values of nationalism. According to an identical logic and for the very same reasons, the individual was subordinated to the nation. On a practical level, the individual was required to accept the authority of organizations: the Histadrut, the party, or the institutions of the settlement movement. The kibbutzim and moshavim as individual units of settlement also had to accept the authority of the collectivity, represented by the Histadrut.

In this way, each individual and social group was directly or indirectly enlisted in the nation's service. We have already seen that in Gordon the collectivity took precedence over the individual. Gordon viewed the individual as constituting an organic part of the nation, from which he derived his very existence. This had always been the viewpoint of integral nationalism. This principle was immediately translated into practical terms. "We believe that the building up of the land will come about through society's authority over the individual, and not by some anarchistic means," said Eliahu Golomb to the members of Gdud Ha'avoda in June 1921.[56] Golomb considered society's authority over the individual as the essence of socialism. The founders also adopted this principle when they abandoned the idea of building Jewish Palestine as an egalitarian society.

Similarly, the Histadrut was not regarded as an end in itself; it was only a tool for conquering the land and building the nation. The same applied to the kibbutz. At the council of Ahdut Ha'avoda on 25 February 1927, Katznelson explained why he had opposed Gdud Ha'avoda, and he described the task of the kibbutz as he saw it: "The ideology of the Gdud, which saw the kibbutz as its chief purpose and subordinated agriculture and politics to its interests, was a negative and dangerous ideology. But I approve of the kibbutz as a tool for the Histadrut."[57] The topic of discussion was the organization of Kibbutz–Ein Harod as a nucleus of Kibbutz Artzi, a countrywide group of kibbutzim, the organization from which Hakibbutz Hame'uhad had sprung up. Tabenkin, the head of Hakibbutz Hame'uhad, also viewed the kibbutz primarily as a tool for the conquest of the land. "What is the idea of the kibbutz?" he asked. "It is to participate in the rapid development of the land via the commune, and via the uplifting of each one of us through work in expectation of the arrival of a large aliyah. What exists today must serve as the basis for what will be tomorrow."[58]

The founders attached great importance to the smooth functioning of the institutions they had set up. They were not willing to tolerate any tendencies toward self-management. This was the main reason for the disbandment of Gdud Ha'avoda. Similarly, individual kibbutzim were not allowed to self-manage in any matter other than internal work arrangements. The kibbutz did not control the right to settle on the land; it was not free to market its produce, to obtain supplies or equipment, or to receive credit. The Histadrut used all possible means to prevent the kibbutzim from developing an independent relationship with the Zionist Organization. The Histadrut system was all-embracing, for that was essential to its ability to fulfill its national mission. "Our movement is a movement of state-building," declared Katznelson. "Our struggle within Zionism was directed against anarchy, arbitrariness, lawlessness, and capriciousness, as it still is. We all realized that we could not build a society on the basis of unlimited freedom. We knew we needed rules and restrictions, and for many years we asked the kibbutzim to observe them as well."[59] These demands were not in fact directed against anarchistic tendencies; these hardly existed, and nobody asked for unlimited freedom. Even though Eliezer Yaffe, one of the originators of the moshav and a founder of Nahalal, requested a little more freedom, the movement as a whole was extraordinarily disciplined and conformist. When centrifugal forces appeared within it, the leadership of the movement fought them to the bitter end. The unity of the movement was regarded as decisive, an indispensable prerequisite for the realization of national goals.

Essentially, Katznelson rejected the conception of society as a collection of individuals. This individualistic concept was common to liberalism and socialism, and it was one of the main features of the heritage of the eighteenth century. Because of this shared view that the individual was the measure of society, people such as Bernstein and Jaurès considered democratic socialism as liberalism's heir. This universalistic, rationalistic, and individualistic approach, however, was alien to the national revolutionaries. Katznelson devoted much time and effort to thinking about the place of the individual in society, especially in the pioneering society. This question preoccupied him particularly in view of the opposition, especially among moshav members, to Nir, a stock company controlled by the Histadrut, to which the founders wished to cede ownership of all collective and semi-collective farms (see chapter 4). The leadership's proposal made the individual settler a captive of the organization. Yaffe led the struggle against this manifestation of the centralizing tendencies of the Histadrut. Arguing with Yaffe at the agricultural convention in February 1926, Katznelson expressed to the opposition the views of the leadership: "Our movement wishes to create a new society, which recognizes the freedom of the individual, but an

exaggerated individualism, which regards the individual as its aim and purpose, is not suited to our movement; nor is it appropriate to our culture and
requirements."[60] Obviously, such a view was alien to socialist thought. For
all types of socialism except for nationalist socialism, the individual was indeed the "aim and purpose," and such an individualism was not regarded
as exaggerated. The Marxism of Marx and his immediate successors never
rejected this principle. This principle was never realized in the Soviet
Union, just as Marxism in general was never carried out there. This was one
of the chief sources of conflict over which the socialist movement split up.

However, for nationalist socialists, individualism was the greatest danger.
In their view, individualism endangered the unity and strength of the national community, and there was an absolute curbing of individualistic tendencies. Like all ideologists of the new nationalism, Katznelson identified
individualism with degeneracy: "In Europe, in periods when regimes were
coming to an end, there was an escape from society, a phenomenon of By-
ronism and Nietzscheanism." This, according to Katznelson, was not the
case in societies fighting for their existence. But for nationalists, all societies,
even the most solidly based ones, like the German or the French, were
always struggling for their existence. Such societies needed a heroic ethos
that placed the individual at the service of the collectivity. "When there was
no place for heroism and character," continued Katznelson, "longings arose,
an ideology of individualism and separation from society, romanticism
(which, incidentally, produced neither heroes nor men of action)." This
brings us to his conclusion: Zionism was far removed from romanticism.
"Zionism is a social movement. It gave rise to the 'Halutz' [pioneer] movement, heroes like Trumpeldor, and these were the product not of an individualistic aestheticism but of a demanding social ideal of duty."[61] Thus,
Katznelson reiterated a concept found in all major European languages in
which the ideologists of the new nationalism wrote.

In this matter, as on all really important issues (apart from the independence of the workers' educational system), there was full agreement between Katznelson and Ben-Gurion. "There is no place here for the interests
of the individual. It is the interests of the majority that take first place,"
stated Ben-Gurion at a meeting of the Executive Committee of Ahdut
Ha'avoda in October 1921.[62] He said this in connection with the debate
about the nature of Ahdut Ha'avoda. Immediately after the founding of
the party and the Histadrut, Ben-Gurion wanted to turn Ahdut Ha'avoda
into an army of labor, a service community headed on a sacred mission. In
1926, at the time of the great debate on Nir, Ben-Gurion was once again
on the same side as Katznelson. "Through the use of the word 'sacred,'" he
said, "we express our deep spiritual attachment to the thing that is dearest
to us, and there are some things that are dear to the labor movement; its
unity, the unity of the Histadrut, is especially dear to the movement."[63] At

the same time, the principle of the primacy of the community, the organization, or the nation in relation to the individual was established. In addition,
there arose the political principle that anyone questioning this idea sen-
tenced himself to political death, unemployment, and if not starvation then
having to leave the country.

The founders were revolutionary nationalists and not social reformers.
They were conscious of having been chosen by history to perform a historic
task. "We have consciously and voluntarily taken upon ourselves the burden, the mission of the redemption of the people and of carrying out the
labor revolution in this country," said Ben-Gurion.[64] All other considerations
were necessarily subordinated to this mission, which Ben-Gurion spoke
about in terms of the sacred. It is significant that Katznelson and Ben-
Gurion used the religious or quasi-religious terminology of national redemption rather than speaking about society's transformation. In Katznelson, one
feels a sort of Jewish puritanism, which was also expressed in his attitude to
private property. His views on equality, national wealth, or private property
depended on circumstances and could change with the situation, but his
sense of the sacredness of the national mission was immutable.

"The Histadrut is a detachment of the nation's force and the nucleus of
Jewish sovereignty," declared Katznelson.[65] This definition helps elucidate
the meaning of the concept "the unity of the Histadrut" or "the unity of the
labor movement." By *unity* the leaders of the movement really meant an
acceptance of the organization's authority. Members of the Histadrut were
obliged not to identify with its aims but to accept the decisions of its institutions and never to question the system, under any circumstances. The inte-
grality of the system and its exclusive authority were the secret of its
strength and the basis of the leadership's power. The Histadrut never regarded itself as one voluntary body among others but demanded for itself the
kind of exclusive authority generally accorded to the state. In the absence of
legal means of compulsion, social and economic pressures were brought to
bear. For the founders, this was a perfectly legitimate form of action, no less
than sanctions used against lawbreakers. Thus, the Histadrut soon became
a center of authority that sometimes dispensed with legal restraints and the
rules of fair play characteristic of a democratic society; sometimes it was
more brutal than a state based on the rule of law. Reliance on force was a fact
of life, tactfully concealed behind formulas such as "public responsibility"
and "voluntary self-discipline."

Ever since Ahdut Ha'avoda and the Histadrut were established, the
founders indefatigably sought to consolidate their power. Ideological deviations not translated into political action were regarded as having no real
importance: theoretical debates, which in any case were few, were not considered significant. However, any attempt on the part of a body within the
party or the Histadrut, or in the political or economic sphere, to achieve any

degree of independence met with a strong reaction. Ideological opposition, such as the opposition of Po'alei Tzion leftists or Hashomer Hatza'ir, did not trouble the movement's leadership. It had no difficulty relating tolerantly to differences of opinion in its conventions and councils. But when social bodies such as Gdud Ha'avoda came into being, or when political opposition organizations, like the Kaplanski-Kolton group, appeared within the party, or when David Bloch, the mayor of Tel-Aviv in 1925–27, tried to preserve a degree of independence in the activities of the Eretz Israel Workers' Fund, the machinery of destruction launched into operation. Among the opponents, some were driven to hunger.

Nevertheless, someone like David Remez, who led Sollel Boneh to bankruptcy, thus threatening to undermine the foundations of the whole Histadrut economy, was treated with extraordinary leniency. He was pushed into a tiny office in the basement of the Executive Committee, only to emerge a few years later as Ben-Gurion's successor as head of the Histadrut, a position he held for thirteen years. Similarly, no one was hurt by the notorious corruption scandal of the late 1920s—the affair of the advance payments (actually gifts from public funds) that the leadership awarded itself; yet members of Gdud Ha'avoda who refused to toe the line were forced to surrender. No sin was unforgivable, from managerial failure to personal corruption; only political or organizational threats were unpardoned. Thus, a conception of public life came into being in which political loyalty and group solidarity—"haverut" (comradeship)—were the supreme norms of behavior.

Katznelson never thought there could be any doubt about the nature of Zionism. "The Zionist enterprise," he said in 1929 when summing up the first ten years of Ahdut Ha'avoda, "is an enterprise of conquest." And in the same breath he added: "It is not by chance that I use military terms when speaking of settlement."[66] All other considerations—social, economic—were subordinated to national considerations: "For us, *aliyah* is the supreme criterion, and every economic system will be judged according to its ability to create employment."[67] And elsewhere he wrote: "The success of the movement of national redemption of our time depends—perhaps in a final and decisive way—on two things: on the capabilities of the new aliyah and on the capability of the country and the national leadership to receive it."[68]

Like all the nationalists of his time, Katznelson knew that "the national will as manifested in life, being a concrete phenomenon, can never be neutral or devoid of social awareness." Here is the key to the general outlook of the labor movement. Like all national movements fighting for independence, and like all nationalist parties struggling to attain office in their respective countries, the Jewish national movement understood the necessity of a progressive social policy. "Our national movement is the child of its generation and reflects the image of its representatives. Are not the desire for the redemption of the people and the desire for the liberation of the worker fused into a single ideal in the hearts of the pioneers?" asked Katznelson. He also asked for "Jewish society to be built on healthier, freer, and more fruitful foundations."[69] These reflections from "In Preparation for the Days to Come" do not contain anything to which a twentieth-century nationalist thinker would not have subscribed. On the contrary, the recognition that nationalism would never be complete or integral without a social consciousness, without taking the side of the working man against the rich, the strong, and the famous, was already an accepted idea in all European nationalist movements.

While adhering to this principle, Katznelson lashed out mercilessly at anyone who regarded private capital as such as a danger to the labor movement. He considered the value of private capital to be relative to its task in the conquest of the land. If it helped colonizate and create places of employment, private capital was a constructive element.[70] For Katznelson Zionism was foremost a "movement of settlement."[71] He repeated this definition many times: "As I said, the purpose of our movement is settlement." This, he said, is "the beginning and end of our desires."[72] Sometimes, and especially in the last period of his life, Katznelson seems to have been assailed by doubts, and he recoiled at placing the whole focus of the movement on agricultural cooperatives, but it is significant that his reservations—or was it a change of heart?—appeared mostly in the context of the great controversy with Hakibbutz Hame'uhad and Hashomer Hatza'ir. At that time, Katznelson suddenly began to feel that the spiritual and emotional guidance of the youth movements was gradually slipping into the hands of the spiritual leaders of the kibbutz movement, "secular rabbis" like himself. "I admire the kibbutz movement," he wrote, "and I believe it has a historic task, but romanticism about this form of life cannot replace romanticism about the very fact of settlement in Eretz Israel."[73] He now regretted the failure of the urban cooperatives, and he was sorry that the movement had never invested in the creation of new forms of social organization in the cities even a minute part of the energy and effort that had been put into rural communal settlement.[74]

At the council of Hakibbutz Hame'uhad at Na'an in the summer of 1939, Katznelson asked three questions that troubled him: "What is the real importance of the cooperative sector in the lives of workers as a whole? Is there any likelihood of its reaching the great masses and affecting large areas of life? What do the workers think of it?"[75] On the whole, however, he viewed settlement as the focus of the movement and the crown of its endeavors. The story of the Second Aliyah, as he related it at the end of his life to the Young Guard of Mapai at the beginning of the summer of 1944, developed like a grandiose epic toward its climax—collective agricultural settlement. Katznelson described the ideological heritage of Mapai as the heir to Ahdut

Ha'avoda and Hapo'el Hatza'ir as "suited to the race of pioneers."[76] On the threshold of the split in Mapai and at the height of the Second World War, Katznelson's main interest was still the unity of the kibbutz movement.[77] Thus, shortly before the founding of the state and the beginning of mass immigration, the dominant ideology condemned the whole movement to impotence where the creation of a new social order outside the islands of settlement was concerned.

FROM "PRODUCTIVIST" TO NATIONALIST SOCIALISM

The term *constructive socialism* was coined, as mentioned earlier, by Nachman Syrkin after the First World War, at the council of the Po'alei Tzion World Union, which met in Stockholm in the summer and autumn of 1919.[78] Thus, the ideology of the newborn Ahdut Ha'avoda received the sanction of the most respected socialist theoretician in the Jewish world. Until that time, Syrkin's thought had developed parallel with the fluctuations of doctrine in Palestine, but one can hardly say it was a direct source of those changes. Syrkin, who called Borochov's intellectual efforts "high school exercises,"[79] deliberately ignored the intractable problems that had preoccupied him, and in so doing helped produce a form of socialism that became the operative arm of Jewish nationalism. This was the true significance of the claim that the labor movement's socialism was unique and original. Katznelson expressed this idea when he wrote: "It was possible to regard European socialist thought only as a tool, a method, but not as a possession."[80]

Gordon was not enthusiastic about this Eretz Israeli form of socialism. To appease Gordon, who was firmly opposed to socialism, Katznelson and Brenner told him, "Your argument with us is only about terminology."[81] At the time of the preparations for the founding of the Histadrut, Brenner published a celebrated short article entitled "Concerning Matters of Terminology," which stated "that if he [Gordon], who devotes his life to manual labor and writes his articles 'Out of Impatience' [the title of one of the articles], is not a socialist, then . . . there is no socialism in the world."[82] Brenner could not fathom how "a man so extreme in his condemnation of all forms of parasitism, who wishes to bestow the duty and blessing of labor on all human beings, who is committed to creating a culture of labor, who calls and works for the triumph of natural social feeling in the life of humanity, and who predicts and demands a nationalization of the soil and its resources" could refuse "to call all this 'socialism' but calls it 'nationalism' instead." Gordon's persistence in "regarding this terminological difference as all-important"[83] was beyond Brenner's comprehension.

The difference was not only one of terminology. Gordon was well aware of the difference between socialism and nationalism, and he was perhaps the only founder who was careful about conceptual definitions. But from the point of view of the founders of the Histadrut and Ahdut Ha'avoda, the conceptual clarity that Gordon strove so hard to achieve was a difficulty and an obstacle that had to be circumvented when it could not be eliminated. Gordon understood that a synthesis of socialism and nationalism was impossible; one could only reach a compromise, and that was exactly what he refused to do. By contrast, Katznelson's whole approach was based on the assumption that in the reality of Palestine not only did contradictions disappear but a natural identity was formed between the two, because socialism was an inseparable part of the national experience and an operational tool for Zionism.

"Socialist Zionism is not a mechanical combination of the two words 'Zionism' and 'socialism,'" wrote Katznelson. "Nor is it a compromise between two opposing principles. Whoever thinks it is has never understood its conceptual and spiritual essence, its inner wholeness."[84] In his opinion, this wholeness resided in the revolutionary nature of the movement, as a rebellion against both classical socialism and classical Zionism. He never ceased to bitterly ridicule those who had "found satisfaction in the Erfurt doctrine" (in the Erfurt Program of 1891 the German Social Democratic Party had pledged itself to Marxism) or had hungrily devoured the Russian revolutionary literature. Katznelson believed that in contrast to these teachings, socialist Zionism represented a true revolution, as its founders had rebelled against exile in all its manifestations, and they had also realized that the Russian Revolution of 1917 and the abolition of the Pale of Settlement would not save the Jewish people. Unlike exilic socialism, socialist Zionism knew that "the supreme question was ensuring the existence of the Jewish masses through labor."[85] Katznelson repeated this formula at every opportunity. "I will not attempt to define Zionism and socialism," he told instructors of new immigrants in October 1940. "I will only say this: there is an organic chemical fusion and not merely a mixture. . . . It is not a mixture, and the elements simply cannot be separated."[86]

Although he tried to avoid definitions, Katznelson nevertheless had to answer questions that he himself asked: "Why am I a socialist? Or why does a young man become a socialist? Is it because he cannot bear the fact that in London a worker does not receive a fair wage, and most of his earnings go into the pockets of his employer? To me, that would be rather surprising. Just as a worker in London does not become a socialist because Jews are being expelled from Germany, we too in this country did not become socialists because a worker in America or England did not receive his salary."[87] Such were the thought processes of Berl Katznelson, which easily allowed a blurring of distinctions between universal and national principles, stressing now this principle and now that one, and without taking the argument to a conclusion, going back to the beginning. Here we see once again:

There is a great difference between the views of socialism held by different peoples, but I think that at the starting point there are no great differences between the majority of people. I think that Lenin and Kautsky and Mac-Donald and Trotsky all came to socialism for a single reason, and that is the desire to correct injustices. A religious person might maintain that the world is sunk in sin, and therefore has to be redeemed. A moralist might say that we are living in falsehood and have to discover the truth. Someone else might say that there is social injustice or oppression, and we therefore have to fight for freedom, equality, or truth. All these are different expressions of ideals revealed to us in one way or another. I do not imagine that any socialist thinker has made a distinction between truth and freedom, or between equality and freedom. At any rate, I can't think of any. I am not referring to isolated people outside the movement who had different ideas. But generally, a man comes to the socialist movement because he has ideas on sin and injustice and wants to correct whatever needs to be corrected.[88]

Katznelson continued:

We believe that freedom, justice, and equality can be achieved in people's lives. These things can be attained, and we want to attain them. A truth that is not the whole truth is a lie; freedom that is not absolute freedom is not freedom.

This, for me, is also the starting point of Zionist thought. . . . Not only is a socialism that accepts that a single child should cry not socialism, but a socialism that accepts that a single people should not be redeemed is not socialism.[89]

This brought him to his final point, which is worth quoting at length.

For me, the Zionist idea is inseparable from socialism. The meaning of socialism is not just improving the lot of workers through trade unions. We reject those in the labor movement all over the world who ignore problems in India or the question of the Negroes and so on, and are only interested in improving the situation of workers in Europe. We say they are merely narrow trade unionists, for they have ceased to regard socialism as an ideal that calls for the solution of world problems and think its only purpose is to protect the narrow material interests of the working class. Why should this be true in the case of other peoples but not with regard to the Jews?[90]

All the inner contradictions, all the logical difficulties of which these texts are full, derive from a single problem: the inability to acknowledge the contradiction between nationalism and socialism, and hence the impossibility of finding a point of equilibrium where one will not overshadow the other. Katznelson refused to acknowledge the fact that socialism is by its nature universal, whereas nationalism is by definition particularistic. He wished at all costs to clothe Zionism in universal values, and he attempted to do so through the principle of the equality of all peoples. Here Katznelson came upon another difficulty, which he refused to recognize: if a socialism that "accepts that a single people should not be redeemed is not socialism," how does one relate to the Arab question? It would appear that for Katznelson the principle of "a single unredeemed people" applied only to the Jews, and for that reason the Arab problem could be neither national nor socialist. The idea of an organic connection between Zionism and socialism necessarily produced a type of nationalist socialism cut off from universal principles. But this organic connection was possible only on two conditions: first, one had to accept the principle of the primacy of nationalism over socialism, and second, socialism had to be given the new meaning that Katznelson wished to give it—the change to a life of labor in Eretz Israel. Only then could socialism be freed from the condition of "slavery within revolution"[91] in which, according to Katznelson, all non-Zionist varieties of Jewish socialism were immersed.

As we have seen, the founders regarded Jewish labor as a sine qua non. It was not primarily a moral or an economic question, and it was not exclusively a Zionist question. It was the one factor without which nothing would have been possible: the "question of questions, the principle of principles."[92] It was the cornerstone of Eretz Israeli integral nationalism. Physical labor was a way of both conquering the land and transforming the Jewish individual, the supreme expression of moral revolution and the prerequisite for the great national revolution. The idea of Jewish labor permitted the principle of the primacy and the exclusivity of the nation to be translated into practical and concrete terms. Anyone expressing any doubts about the consequences of applying this principle placed himself beyond the pale.

Katznelson expressed his arguments in terms very similar to those of the most representative of the nationalist socialist ideologists, Enrico Corradini. Like all nationalist socialists, Katznelson wished to uphold the cause of "oppressed peoples," and he maintained that "the war of Jewish labor must be fought on behalf of future immigrants, those masses uprooted from labor and lacking any means of subsistence, in order to ensure work for an unemployed people. Anyone who denies us the right to work denies us the right to live, not only as individuals but also as a nation."[93] "Jewish labor," he concluded, "is a question of life for the entire Yishuv. . . . Without Jewish labor, there is no Jewish homeland."[94] Thus, the principle of Jewish labor was a practical realization of the nation's primacy.

On this point Katznelson launched his main offensive against the Left, against all those who, in the name of equality and class solidarity in its normal sense, denied the validity of the Jewish worker's struggle for Jewish labor. The equality in question, wrote Katznelson, was false because the Arab economy was closed to the Jewish worker, as was the governmental sector of the mandatory administration, which fixed a wage on which a Jew was unable to manage. Equality, he wrote, was only a whip with which to scourge the concept of Jewish labor.[95] But Katznelson realized that nevertheless there was a problem here because equality was a universal principle, and one could not evade the question by saying that it is necessary to distinguish between real equality and formal equality. After all, the task of a socialist party was to correct injustice, not to perpetuate it or to make it worse. Thus, Katznelson was placed in a position where he was obliged to attack not only "false equality" but also the principle of equality itself.

Katznelson assailed the "terminological routine" and "cosmopolitan approach," which ignored the complexity of the human condition and related to people either as autonomous units or as humanity at large. This view, he believed, was "excessively simplistic" and belonged to the Enlightenment and to socialism's infancy. He claimed that ignoring history was a dangerous tendency.

> The reality of peoples, the fate of peoples, their special historical circumstances, their particular sufferings and tribulations, do not exist for this school of thought. There is the human being, there is the human race, and that's all. There is one rule and one law for all men: all questions are solved automatically, and before the world achieves the equality of all men in life, the representatives of cosmopolitanism achieve it in their imagination. They blur all particularities, level everything out, and skip over the vast complexities of human history as if they did not exist.[96]

Katznelson's attitude was shared by all nationalists who rebelled against the rationalistic and universalistic heritage of the Enlightenment. What followed could have been written by any European nationalist socialist.

> This view is especially suitable for members of humiliated peoples wanting to escape from their inferiority and to shed the yoke of their particularity, and who wish to find redemption for themselves by fleeing from their peoples, and, on the other hand, this cosmopolitan disdain for national realities is also suitable, in another way, for the socialist parties of dominating peoples. Instead of recognizing the justice of the claims of oppressed peoples and abandoning the advantages that even the worker enjoys by belonging to the dominating people, they tell the workers of the oppressed peoples, in the name of this precious cosmopolitanism, to give up their demands, renounce their nationalism, and acquire the "higher" language and culture.[97]

Just as Katznelson, when defending the cause of the Jews, depicted them as an "oppressed people," so Corradini described Italy as a proletarian nation, preached amity between the nation and the proletariat, and asked nationalism to adopt socialism for itself. Similarly, Katznelson described the Jewish people as an "unemployed people," and just as Corradini wrote that the status of Italy as a proletarian nation justified foreign wars in order to give this oppressed nation its place in the sun,[98] so, for Katznelson, the lowly status of the Jews justified their struggle for the conquest of the land, their freedom, and their independence. In the same way as Katznelson, Corradini only asked that Italy have the right to feed its inhabitants. Why had rich nations spread over the face of the earth while this proletarian people was confined to its barren hills and had to supply immigrants to the United States? In the name of what principle did anyone have the right to prevent this nation of immigrants from conquering neighboring Libya in order to provide food for its inhabitants and to prevent them from having to leave their homeland? Katznelson was also thinking along these lines when he said: "Should we bow our heads before this type of equality? We said that true equality means that the Jewish people has the same right to feed and find employment for its seventeen millions as other peoples have."[99]

For Katznelson, nothing was more abhorrent than "cosmopolitanism." Not only did cosmopolitanism spread the dangerous illusion of equality among men and persist in promoting this false and illusory equality while ignoring all hierarchical relationships, but it "did not want to understand that no individual can live and work outside his people."[100] Here Katznelson reflected the view of organic nationalism that the individual is inseparable from the national community. He repeatedly stressed the exclusiveness of membership in a nation. The nation, he believed, is undoubtedly the primary group to which a person belongs, and all social or class affiliations are of secondary importance or are even to be regarded as dangerous. This leads one to the conclusion that because cosmopolitanism did not understand the centrality of the nation in human experience, it also "failed to understand that equality between men is a futile concept as long as there is no equality between nations. No regime can act justly toward an individual if it does not act justly toward the people to whom that individual belongs."[101] Although all nationalist socialists would have agreed, no social democratic thinker would have subscribed to such a view.

Katznelson expressed the principle of the primacy of the nation and its corollary—the subordination of socialism to nationalism—in a variety of ways. On the tenth anniversary of the founding of Ahdut Ha'avoda, for instance, he made the following remarks:

> Political Zionism in its true sense—the ingathering of the exiles, popular immigration, and national rebirth—is the soul of our movement. It is the stem from which all our dreams of man and society have sprouted; it is the source of all our class energy, all our creative force. Without this Zionist faith, we would not have been able to create our Jewish socialism, with all the riches it contains. You are familiar with Jewish socialism in exile. Despite all the devotion

put into it, and despite the warm temperament of our people, how poor is its content, how weak are its roots, how bowed is its crest! What has given us our life and creativity, our unity, persistence, and expansion outward and in depth is our Zionist faith.[102]

The very expression "Jewish socialism" would have been distasteful to social democrats, but it lent credence to the idea "that our movement has the advantage of not knowing any contradiction between socialism and nationalism."[103]

The elimination of the contradiction between socialism and nationalism becomes possible only if one believes that "socialism is the full and complete expression of the preeminence of the nation."[104] In reality, the contradiction was not eliminated, simply because it is ineradicable. There was only an illusion of eliminating the contradiction, which was made possible by a dual operation: on one hand, there was the subordination of socialism to national objectives, and on the other hand, socialist doctrines, which Katznelson called "a string of theoretical declarations divorced from reality and of use only for polemics and philosophizing," were superseded by a program aimed at satisfying the worker's "social desires." These had the merit of being "concrete" and "derived from his work and life." "The realization of these aims," wrote Katznelson, "is determined by his actions themselves. This is not hypothetical or abstract but is naturally, organically alive."[105]

A disdain for theory and a stress on action, a subordination of social concerns to national objectives and a denial of universal values, described with the dismissive term *cosmopolitanism*, were characteristic of Eretz Israeli socialism. Katznelson called the Eretz Israeli form of nationalist socialism "revolutionary constructivism." He explained that "every single people makes its revolution in accordance with its life and experience."[106] Thus, in the situation of the Jewish people, "constructive revolution"[107] took the form of a revolution of labor. Katznelson contrasted "professorial socialism" with "our socialism," which was "a socialism of labor."[108]

Here we reach the crux of Katznelson's argument. "I have been speaking about cooperativeness and not about socialization," he wrote when the Nir company was set up, "for everyone puts his own ideas into the word 'socialization.'" He was referring to the "cooperativeness that should manage our settlement of the country."[109] In plain language, Katznelson was saying that the socialization of the means of production was not an objective of the labor movement. Its socialism focused on building up the economy; Katznelson described it as a "productive socialism."[110]

Indeed, this was the heart of the matter. "It is necessary to make a fundamental distinction," said Katznelson in his important lecture to the Council of Socialist Youth at the end of December 1927, "between a socialism of producers and a socialism of consumers, between a socialism based on national production and a socialism based on the distribution of products."[111] And elsewhere, he said:

> There are two kinds of socialism: the socialism of consumers and the socialism of producers. The consumer is primarily interested in delivery, a redistribution of consumer goods produced by the community. It is in this way that socialism is understood by a man who does not stand on his own two feet in the process of production. He is attracted by equal distribution. The long road by which it is reached does not concern him; he is unaware of the difficulties. He directs his whole social strategy toward creating a consumer's socialism, but there is a productive socialism, which sees the basis of society in production, and which understands that one cannot create a new order if production is deficient. This socialism is more prudent and circumspect and does not aim at easy solutions. It is concerned above all with the problems and life requirements of the productive sector.[112]

And again:

> Many of the weaknesses of European socialism are due to the fact that, in general, it did not venture sufficiently far beyond the problem of the consumer. . . . We, in this country, with its special conditions, have corrected this because we came here through our Zionism, not as consumers but as producers. Zionism is entirely a movement of producers.

And he ended this passage with a key sentence:

> Zionism, from the beginning, caused our socialism to be a productive socialism.

Katznelson immediately passed from the sociological sphere to the political and drew practical conclusions. Every nonproductive brand of socialism, he said, would in the Jewish context lead to "fractionalism." This was the case with Borochov's socialism.

> From him one may learn that the outlook of the whole Jewish labor movement in exile was not that of a productive socialism but of a socialism of impoverished, rebellious Jews wishing to improve their lot—a consumer's socialism.
> But our socialism in Eretz Israel was productive, and could not have been otherwise. Any socialism here would have been ridiculous if it were not based on the producers. It would have inevitably led to fractionalism. Fractions [Marxist or communist left-wingers] are not only a present-day affair: twenty years ago there were also such phenomena—the Rostovians, for instance.[113]

Thus, in the 1920s, the idea of a socialism of national unity, or "constructive" socialism, attained its final form. It had a decisive influence on the development of the labor movement, and both theoretical and practical consequences. But before we examine these consequences, let us investigate

Katznelson's claim, erroneous from the start, that a socialism of production was an invention of Eretz Israel.

A definition of socialism in terms of production rather than of distribution was already well known in Europe. It derived from a turn-of-the-century revision of Marxism, which was based on two assumptions: there was no alternative to a capitalist economy, and the true opposition of social forces followed not the traditional Marxist pattern of a division of classes into the proletariat and the bourgeoisie but a division into producers and parasites. According to this view, the producing class was made up of all sectors that shared in the process of production, from the workers standing in the production line to factory owners and shareholders. This was also the nature of the distinction between productive capital and parasitic capital. Productive capital was capital invested in an enterprise. Such capital contributed to an increase in national wealth; it created jobs and competed with foreign industries. Thus, the productive worker had an interest in the success of the factory in which he worked, and there came into being a communion of interests between all the productive elements in society. Thus true class polarity was not between the possessors of the means of production and those without such means but between producers and parasites. This was the contribution of the European revolutionary syndicalists to the revision of Marxism and the retreat from it.

This conception of social divisions and the role of capital contradicted European social democracy and was well suited to a view of the nation as one's primary object of allegiance. If a man's position in the social order is determined not, as traditional socialism claimed, by ownership of the means of production but by his contribution to the increase of national wealth, then ethnic, national, and cultural affiliations once again become relevant and are of primary importance. This is how the meeting between socialism and nationalism came about, and on this basis a new synthesis arose. The originators of this synthesis also did not see a contradiction between socialism and nationalism. From their viewpoint, they were right. There was indeed no contradiction between socialism, in the sense they gave this concept, and nationalism.

Katznelson's thinking was along the same lines. Because he had a nationalist frame of reference, and because he held that the task of the production system was to serve the national effort, there were no clear-cut distinctions in his thinking between capitalism and socialism or between the proletariat and the bourgeoisie. In his debate with the Po'alei Tzion leftists in 1928, Katznelson adamantly refused to be bound by theoretical definitions or "opposing formulations."[114] Reality, he said, is many-sided and complex, and the future is uncertain. Katznelson was aware of the fact that the labor movement had not made Eretz Israel a socialist society: "All the great things we have accomplished—cooperatives, workers' enterprises, and workers' banks—are not socialism, but they are pockets of socialism." These, said Katznelson, constituted the foundations of a new regime existing in a period of twilight and "protracted struggle."[115] He believed that categorizations such as capitalism and socialism, bourgeois and workers, were to be judged according to their contribution to the national interest. Productive socialism had "a special ethic, connected with a proper attitude to work. . . . The attitude of consuming socialism is wasteful; it is not economically minded. Productive socialism has an attitude of thrift, of concern for collective property and national property."[116]

Constructive socialism, whose advocates saw themselves as bearing responsibility for the entire national economy, was thus a natural ally of all productive elements in society. For Katznelson, a socialist was not someone who adhered to socialist ideology or who advocated equality or the socialization of the means of production. A true socialist was someone who worked for immigration and settlement: "When Weizmann or Ussishkin purchase plots in the country and set up agricultural settlements on them, they participate in the historic mission of the Jewish nation in search of employment and share the mission of the Jewish worker and the immigrating Jewish masses." His conclusion is not without irony and originality: "In this they are far more socialistic than a party that professes an ultrasocialism but does not understand the duty of helping the worker to consolidate his position, to conquer a place of work, and to set up a working economy."[117] In such a situation, it was absurd to think of changing the social structure or of socializing the means of production. This functional approach also dictated Katznelson's attitude to private capital and to collaboration between the classes.

Katznelson naturally always preferred public capital. But the salient question, in his eyes, was not the nature of the ownership of capital but the purpose it served. Thus, private capital used for colonization was quite as "positive" as public capital.[118] Katznelson even boasted of the fact that the labor economic sector had already reached the stage in which private capital was invested in it for profit.[119] Again, in his address "In Preparation for the Days to Come," his only complaint about private capital was that the private sector was slow to utilize innovations and to finance research owing to its wariness of investments that did not yield an immediate profit. He had a purely utilitarian approach to private capital.[120] Capital, for him, was an instrument for achieving national objectives, and his attitude to property was entirely puritan and thus totally alien to a socialist attitude. "There grew up among us," wrote Katznelson, "a type of man who saw capital not as a means to enjoy an 'easy life' but as a working tool."[121] Nowhere is it said or even suggested that it is possible and desirable to use economic power to create a different society.

All this brought him to an immediate practical conclusion. "The task as defined from the beginning by socialist Zionism," he said to the leaders of the Hano'ar Ha'oved youth movement in August 1934, "cannot be carried out by a single class of the people,"[122] which means that "the implementation of Zionism . . . requires interclass collaboration."[123] This was a supreme patriotic necessity. He reminded the youth leaders that in the French Revolution, the Paris Commune, and the 1917 Russian Revolution, social values went hand in hand with love of the homeland. "With us, too," he wrote, "the defense of the country and the building of it go together with defense of the worker and striving for his regeneration."[124] And finally, "Interclass collaboration, necessary for the implementation of Zionism, means mobilizing maximum forces for building up the homeland through labor."[125] Thus, Katznelson unceasingly attacked the Po'alei Tzion leftists and never stopped advocating national unity. "I will warn over and over again," he wrote, "of the false attitude of seeking to substitute part of the people for the whole people. Although one part has the capacity to lead and volunteer, it does not have the capacity to replace the whole people and fulfill all its tasks."[126] From his point of view, everything that helped to foster unity and a sense of partnership was positive, including religion and religious tradition. Katznelson asked the youth movements to regard the ninth of Ab, the eleventh month in the Jewish calendar, the day the Second Temple was destroyed by the Romans in September 69 A.D., as a national day of mourning. He rebuked their leaders for leaving for summer camp "on the night Israel bewails its destruction and servitude and remembers the bitterness of exile."[127] There is no doubt that his attachment to the national religious tradition not only represented an inseparable part of his inner consciousness but was also an expression of his deep awareness of the national vocation of the labor movement.

Building up the land was possible only through a collaboration between the pioneering movement and those who provided the means. Not only could the labor movement not claim exclusivity in this matter, but it carefully refrained from demanding it. This was the supreme test and sole criterion for judging political conduct and ideological positions. "There are people who according to their class or party allegiance are alien to the workers, but in their lives are very close to them," said Katznelson to Ussishkin, president of the Jewish National Fund, and as such one of the main promoters of collective agricultural settlement.[128] People and their actions were judged according to their contribution to the nation and their role in the implementation of Zionism. Thus, anything that helped the organized worker conquer the land and build it up was regarded as desirable, and anyone who helped him do so was considered an ally; all other considerations, especially ideological considerations of a "cosmopolitan" kind, were irrelevant. Katznelson felt much closer to the bourgeoisie that contributed to colonization on national grounds than to the Po'alei Tzion leftists who questioned it on ideological grounds. His relationship with Hashomer Hatza'ir—an outstanding pioneering movement—was ambivalent. He greatly admired its kibbutzim, its dedicated youth, but disapproved of its Marxism.

Katznelson, as we have seen earlier, was always ill disposed toward Marxist Zionism, burdened as it was with the universalistic heritage of socialism, looking with one eye in the direction of communism, and subject to strange ideological struggles. He also disliked being drawn into ideological debates; this was still the case in the latter part of his life, when he was far better intellectually equipped than in the days of the Second Aliyah. In this later period, he still avoided theoretical discussions by the method he had used in the 1920s and 1930s: he contented himself with a few sneering and stinging remarks.[129] At the same time, he advocated the union of the two Mapai kibbutz movements, Hakibbutz Hame'uhad and Hever Hakvutzot, and after that the union of the Mapai kibbutzim with Hashomer Hatza'ir. He regarded the unification of the kibbutz movements as a "great principle" and never ceased recommending it wherever he could.[130] He considered the union of Mapai kibbutzim with Hashomer Hatza'ir possible because he did not regard their ideological differences as important. He claimed, in the early 1940s, that the successful experiment of the days of the Second and Third Aliyahs might be repeated. Did not the founding of Ahdut Ha'avoda, followed by the partnership with Hapo'el Hatza'ir, lead to excellent results? Did not Zionism in action prove stronger than all ideological differences? Katznelson hoped that the joint organizational and political apparatus plus economic interests would finally yield the desired result. But he failed to take two factors into consideration: first, the ideological difference between Hashomer Hatza'ir and Mapai was a real one, whereas the differences between Ahdut Ha'avoda and Hapo'el Hatza'ir were only apparent; second, the founders of Hakibbutz Hame'uhad headed by Tabenkin were experienced in unification matters. They knew how all previous unifications had ended, beginning with the union of the nonparty people with Po'alei Tzion. They also had no intention of abandoning their only effective weapon—their independent organization—and of being subsumed into a large body in which their influence would inevitably be reduced, and which would be dominated by Ben-Gurion because decisions would depend on the automatic majority he had at his disposal.

Katznelson's relationship with the General Zionists was much easier. The movement was poor in ideological content, and for that reason it regarded the nationalism they had in common as sufficient. Like him, General Zionists were not unduly troubled by the question of Arab workers, and they had no leanings toward internationalism. Between the Histadrut and the Jewish upper-middle classes in the diaspora there was a division of labor that satisfied both sides: one side provided the means, and the other carried out the work. Both sides shared the view that just as there was no alternative to the labor movement as a vehicle of colonization, so there was no alternative to the Zionist Organization as the mobilizer of financial resources. Both sides needed and complemented each other.

Consequently, Katznelson recognized the essential role of the middle classes, and he never thought of doing anything to harm them. The socialization of the means of production was never an issue, even as a long-term proposition. On the contrary, at every opportunity, Katznelson stressed the responsibility of the movement for the future of the middle classes. He clearly distinguished between these people and the "landlords."[131] Like all nationalist socialists, Katznelson loathed the egoistic and unproductive part of the upper bourgeoisie and ceaselessly bewailed the "rule of the pluto-crats" developing in Tel Aviv, its "immigrant upper crust," those "well-to-do refugees who evade every public duty." Their "behavior was swinish."[132] By contrast, he had only words of praise for bourgeois settlement enterprises, the independent farmers of Nes Tziona, Magdiel, and Yavne'el who were careful to employ only Jewish labor.[133] None of these farmers had any doubts about the moral correctness of Zionism.

This attitude to the middle classes that worked or that supplied work was in keeping with nationalist socialism. Like the workers, these bourgeois be-longed to the class of producers. Katznelson's understanding of the working class was also identical with that of other nationalist socialists, and it was the opposite of the definition of *class* prevailing in the socialist movement at that time. Between the two world wars the accepted definiton of *class* was still faifthul to Marx's thinking. A class was a group with a common relationship to the means of production, a relationship that brings it necessarily into conflict with another group, which has a different relationship to the same means of production. By definition, an owner of the means of production and a person only using the same means of production could never belong to the same class of producers.

By contrast, all nationalist socialists regarded the urban worker, the farmer who owned his land but lived by the sweat of his brow, or the bourgeois whose small factory created employment and contributed to national wealth as the backbone of the country. The farmer always had a privileged place in nationalist socialist mythology; all nationalist socialists abhorred parasites and exploiters, and saw simple toiling folk, linked to the land and its scenery, as the eternal embodiment of the nation. Katznelson, too, asked his friends to strive to be "faithful representatives of Jewish history."[134] He believed whole-heartedly "that our movement is responsible for the implementation of Zion-ism, for a people's destiny."[135] On the tenth anniversary of Ahdut Ha'avoda, he described the labor movement as the "vehicle of our sovereignty"; it was "a precious possession, which had to be carefully guarded."[136]

In this struggle for the conquest of the land, an alliance between the labor movement and the productive middle classes, and all the nonsocialist elements that joined it in building the nation, came into being. On one hand Katznelson tried very hard to convince the movement that "if we don't do it, no one else will,"[137] and on the other hand he never failed to acknowledge that the movement did not and would not have the ability to shoulder the enterprise alone. In his debate with the Zionist Left, he explained this in terms of historical necessity. "The implementation of Zionism," he wrote, "took place in a period in which two systems were in conflict. This conflict also exists within Zionism."[138] In this period in which capitalism and socialism were engaged in a struggle yet existed side by side, there was no point, he believed, in raising the troublesome "question of the worker in a capitalist environment."[139] This would lead only to the "idle discussion" Katznelson so detested. The struggle, he wrote, is taking place throughout the world and within the Jewish people. In this situation, "Our aim should be to increase socialist production, and the more we increase our strength . . . the nearer we shall bring the victory of socialism, which is nothing other than the victory of the working people."[140] However, to the question of whether one may conclude from this that "there are such contradictory economic class interests in this country that it makes a national collaboration impossible and perhaps irrelevant," Katznelson emphatically replied, "I don't believe it."[141] This was the bottom line in his thinking and one of the main causes of his long and bitter dispute with the Zionist Left.

Katznelson's war against the Zionist Left close to Marxism, and, generally speaking, against all the forces to the left of Mapai, began in his first days in Palestine and ended only with his death, at a time when the Soviet Union's attraction for the Zionist Left was at its height. It began with his confrontation with the socialists of Po'alei Tzion: the Rostov group made an indelible impression on him. He believed they were one of the most serious ideological threats Zionism had to face in Palestine. They were no less reprehensible, in his view, than the communists; he was haunted by this memory from the distant past many years after the Rostov group had been scattered. Later, Ben-Zvi related that when he arrived in the country in early 1907, there were no more than remnants of the "Rostovim," who had come in the winter of 1905.[142] Despite this, the danger first embodied in this little group of early arrivals of the Second Aliyah was a permanent factor in Katznelson's consciousness. As he saw it, its essential characteristic was its ideological and spiritual servitude to world socialism, and hence its tendency to judge the labor movement in Palestine by universal criteria. In his view, there could be no greater sin than that.

Katznelson was apprehensive not only of world socialism but of all major ideological developments in the outside world. "Every major new movement that comes into the world," he wrote, "first causes us to assimilate, until it is absorbed and digested by us." From the Enlightenment to Bolshevism via the first socialists, there was a repetition of the same phenomenon, a "complete denial of the right of a Jewish conception of life to exist."[143] "Until a few years ago," he wrote, "socialism did not even recognize the existence of the Jewish nation." According to Katznelson, the denial of Jewish national existence was also encouraged by the activities of assimilated Jews in various socialist movements. These circles regarded Zionism as a reactionary movement.[144] For years Katznelson never stopped trying to settle accounts with "assimilationist socialism" and with the Socialist International, which closed its doors to the labor movement, and he complained of the "hostility and ostracism" that the Eretz Israeli labor movement encountered in the socialist world.[145] In a public meeting of Ahdut Ha'avoda in 1928 in honor of Émile Vandervelde, Katznelson demanded "'compensation' for thirty years of isolation and orphanhood in the world labor movement."[146] He requested help in explaining the Eretz Israeli case in the Socialist International and asked the International to use its influence on behalf of Jewish workers everywhere. He said that some major socialist figures such as MacDonald, Bernstein, Blum, and Longuet were to be counted among the friends of the Zionist enterprise. He apparently did not realize that the French socialist Jean Longuet was Karl Marx's grandson.

However, this was not the end of his struggle with the Left. The greatest and most significant enemy he faced was Bolshevism. In his later years, Katznelson was aware that the true problem was no longer a "Zionism of idle discussion" and endless wrangling but the dark shadow cast by the Soviet Union. He feared the attraction of the Soviet Revolution for wide circles of Eretz Israeli youth. "The great light in the East," which impressed so many people in the European Left, also had an influence in Palestine. But here this new struggle was a successor to the long war against Po'alei Tzion, which never ceased to accuse Ahdut Ha'avoda and Mapai of class betrayal. What should one do, Katznelson asked them ironically, when it seemed that "there had been an error in the historical process" (a heavy allusion to Borochov's teachings), and things did not work out as expected?[147] What was one to do when the Second Aliyah came to the private agricultural sector, and "it vomited us up?"[148] But no sooner was the controversy with the Marxist vulgarization of history over than Bolshevism reared its ugly head: "The influence of Bolshevism . . . on the Jewish labor movement," he wrote, "was totally destructive."[149]

In the last years of his life, Katznelson concentrated his efforts on this fight against communism. The need to oppose the influence of communism on youth and the necessity of counteracting the attraction of the Soviet Union, which had borne the brunt of the war against Nazism in the soul-stirring epic of the Red Army, led him to revise his thinking about several basic political principles. One can hardly say that his thought reached a high theoretical level, and there was no indication that Katznelson had deeply considered problems of political philosophy. A new situation, however, had arisen that demanded a response. The turn to the Left in the labor movement, the kibbutzim, and the youth movements constituted an unprecedented challenge. Until then, it had been possible to overcome these tendencies by organizational means. The crushing of Gdud Ha'avoda and most of the leftist opposition in Tel Aviv had been possible without any need to raise the disagreements to the level of a theoretical debate.

Usually, the opposite was the case: the leadership of the party was frequently interested in representing the confrontation as a simple power struggle, a revolt of frustrated elements, or just one more expression of what they liked to call the "sickness of division." Katznelson and Ben-Gurion were extraordinarily skilled at sticking the label of sectarian divisiveness on any expression of dissatisfaction, independence, or refusal to toe the line. This time, however, Katznelson had to take the bull by the horns, and he was thus given the opportunity to reactivate his long war with Marxism. In the process, some of his positions were given the theoretical basis that they had lacked in the past or that had not been sufficiently stressed.

The ideological war against communism in which he engaged centered on questions of freedom and equality. His starting point was economic equality. Here Katznelson adopted a clear position with a deep inner logic despite its apparent inconsistency. "There is something that is a prerequisite of economic equality," he wrote, "and that is the elimination of private property. You may think it strange if I say that I consider economic equality a valid aim, but the elimination of private property is not a valid aim. I can imagine regimes in which private property is eliminated, but which have neither equality nor freedom."[150] He was aware of the problematic nature of this assertion, and so explained that Hitler or Mussolini was also capable of eliminating private property. Did Hitler not "requisition a great deal?" he asked. "Did he not place all industry at his disposal, or at the disposal of the state?" One could readily imagine, he continued, a situation in which, "seeing that England was winning the war, Hitler decided to eliminate private property. Doesn't he claim that Germany is an anticapitalist country?" His conclusion was that "the elimination of private property in a dictatorial regime merely reinforces the dictatorship." This rule, he wrote, applies to all societies, all regimes, and more to socialist societies and socialist regimes than to capitalist societies. Katznelson was of the opinion that "socialism, in general, has a greater capacity to repress freedom, to repress opposition, than existing capitalist states."[151]

Thus, he saw an organic connection between freedom and private property, in this way adopting the classic liberal conservative position—a position not accepted by even the most moderate socialists. With regard to Germany, Katznelson's reasoning was a repetition of the more simplistic arguments of the Right. Socialism was concerned with the question of the compatibility of freedom and equality, freedom and interventionism, and was consequently aware of the problematic nature of the use of political power. Social democrats were suspicious of the state and thus always tried to base the use of political power on the will of the majority, but democratic socialism never made the attainment of political freedom dependent on private property. It can be said that in many ways it was Katznelson who ended the labor movement's aspiration to economic equality. Someone who both claimed that the elimination of private property is the prerequisite for economic equality and rejected the elimination of private property because of the inherent danger to political freedom had in practice renounced all changes in the social order.

Here one should note Katznelson's avoidance of the word *proletariat*, cornerstone of social democracy's vocabulary and system of ideas. He viewed *proletariat* as being too closely associated with Marxism, and he repeatedly told his listeners that the Eretz Israeli worker could not be a proletarian because he was a property owner. He recommended the avoidance of terms "that are open to various interpretations." He wrote that he did not understand what it meant to educate youth in a "proletarian vision." A "proletarian vision," he wrote, "can mean anything on earth."[152] Did Gordon have a proletarian vision? he asked. Does a kibbutz member have a proletarian vision? And what, he asked, can one say about "those wretchedly poor members of the oriental communities" in Jerusalem who have "a terrible hatred . . . for the Ashkenazim," despite the fact that "they are true proletarians"? Obviously, "In this case, considerations of race prevail over those of class." Having made this rather curious assertion, Katznelson returned to the attack.

> The word "proletarian" suits the European worker in 1940, just as it suited him in 1840. But from the human point of view, the worker in Eretz Israel does not lack for anything. He does not lack culture, does not lack a homeland, and does not lack property either. He has the enormous Histadrut and kibbutz properties, and we all wish to increase this collective class property. How can one call our workers' spiritual universe a "proletarian vision"?[153]

In this passage one finds the heart of Katznelson's mature thinking. These few sentences contain all the ideological ambiguity of the labor movement at its peak. The difficulty undoubtedly stems from the principle of constructive socialism, a socialism of "producers," which in reality could be said to be a "nationalist socialism of ownership." Katznelson claimed that this fact of ownership was reflected in the workers' spiritual outlook: how could a property owner have a "proletarian vision"? Similarly, the concept of class was not given its usual socialist significance. Whereas in classical socialism the criterion of the class one belongs to is the degree of control one exerts over the means of production, in the illusory system of the Histadrut, these distinctions lose their meaning. But the fiction of collective ownership connected with the Histadrut achieved the classic aims of nationalist socialism: the elimination of class friction, the strengthening of national solidarity, and the creation of a sense of responsibility for the national economy among workers. However, all this did not prevent hunger, unemployment, and huge differences in standards of living among Histadrut members. All this did not make the workers' ownership of Bank Hapo'alim, the Nir company, or the Mashbir cooperative anything other than a miserable fiction, a mockery of the poor. But this was nationalist socialism's way of thinking, and it proved to be an effective means of mobilizing the masses for as long as the country did not embark on a course of accelerated modernization.

The struggle for the soul of youth was a holy war for Katznelson, and it was responsible, in his last years, for some of his finest definitions of socialism. All his life he had stressed the values of social discipline, accepted the supremacy of the collectivity, and fought against individualistic tendencies, which he frequently described as "anarchy." Values such as freedom, democracy, or the rights of the individual were not of primary interest to him in the period between the two world wars. His basic outlook was rigid and puritanical: the individual was merely a soldier in the army of national liberation, and his duty was to accept the rules of the regimented Histadrut society. But now, when the attraction of communism had increased, the only way of gaining the hearts of the young was by stressing the humanistic aspect of socialism. "The meaning of socialism," he wrote, "is the elevation of man, the creation of conditions that elevate man."[154] Already in 1927, in his lecture to the Council of Socialist Youth, Katznelson had said that "socialism is the highest expression of humanism."[155] But one had to wait until the Second World War for him to come to the defense of those values which at the end of his life he described as essential to socialism: democracy, political equality, political freedom, freedom of expression, and universal suffrage.[156] Against revolutionary violence, mass arrests, and executions in the Soviet Union, Katznelson enlisted the aid of Marx and Rosa Luxemburg. Lenin and Kautsky both served him in his defense of democratic rights and political and judicial equality.[157] Katznelson's desperate tone reveals how great the admiration for the Soviet Union must have been among the youth in Palestine.

In order to salvage whatever could still be saved, Katznelson retreated from some of the positions he had held since the days of the Second Aliyah and the founding of Ahdut Ha'avoda. Thus, for example, nobody in the formative period of the labor movement attacked anarchists more than Berl Katznelson. Now he eulogized Gustav Landauer and complained that only Karl Liebknecht and Rosa Luxemburg were remembered among those killed in the failed German revolution. Nobody was as expert as the communists, said the man who all his life had looked at the world through the spectacles of the Second Aliyah, at commandeering history for their own purposes.[158] To the young people gathered around him, Katznelson said: "One cannot attain freedom through lack of freedom, nonviolence through violence."[159] He asked for an explanation of how the dictatorship of the proletariat could ever be brought to an end. Katznelson warned them against the cult of personality; he settled accounts with the Russian Revolution in general and the Comintern in particular. It sometimes seems as if all this was said by someone else, not by a representative of the authoritarian system of the Histadrut and Mapai. The aim of socialism, Katznelson now maintained, was to achieve "the greatest possible freedom and the least possible domination of one person over another. . . . [The aim] was not to concentrate power in the hands of a single person but to spread it over as wide an area as possible."[160]

In order to give his opinions sufficient authority, Katznelson had to refute some serious accusations made at that period against the labor movement. The classic term of condemnation for those who had strayed from the accepted path was "reformism," but at the beginning of the war, when one saw where certain political developments of the 1930s had led, a shameful new epithet made its appearance: "neosocialism." At the fifth Histadrut convention, in the spring of 1942, Katznelson expended much energy in attempting to clear the movement of that charge. He was aware of the fact that his extreme anti-Marxism laid him open to disturbing comparisons.

Hendrik de Man was the author of *Zur Psychologie des Sozialismus* (published in 1926), translated into English as *Evolutionary Socialism* but better known in French as *Au-delà du Marxisme*. Translated into thirteen languages, including Yiddish, this book was enormously successful and made de Man the most talked-about and controversial socialist writer of the interwar period. The book had one fundamental objective: quite simply, in de Man's words, "the liquidation of Marxism." De Man continued: "[In] order to say *after* Marx, I must first say *against* Marx." *Zur Psychologie des Sozialismus* was, as de Man himself maintained, a "settling of accounts" with his Marxist past.[161] It was followed by a work that complemented his criticism of Marxism: *Le Socialisme constructif*. In the 1930s de Man was the "revisionist" par excellence, the uncontested leader of the anti-Marxist and authoritarian trend in the socialist movement, despised and feared by social democrats such as Léon Blum. Blum, an outstandingly moderate man, was in the habit of stressing his fidelity to Marxism, which he saw as a guide and moral compass.

De Man had always been highly regarded by the right wing of Mapai. Shortly after the party was founded, the journal *Davar* distributed to its readers a booklet whose contents were drawn from the works of the Belgian socialist leader. In 1939, after the death of Émile Vandervelde, de Man became president of the Belgian Socialist Party, and in the summer of 1940 he enthusiastically welcomed the conquest of Europe by Nazi Germany. Now the term *constructive socialism*, with de Man's book *Le Socialisme constructif* in the background, started to become a major ideological burden.

For obvious reasons, Katznelson did not try to defend de Man or his well-known follower, the French socialist leader Marcel Déat, who at the time of the fall of France became an enthusiastic collaborator. The label "neosocialism" had been attached to his faction as a term of contempt in the early 1930s. In reality, de Man's and Déat's views were very similar to Katznelson's, but their positions after 1940 placed them beyond the pale. Thus, Katznelson tried very hard to show that the traitors came not only from the ranks of the anti-Marxists but also from the French Communist Party. Moreover, even the "clean" wing of the French Socialist Party produced one famous traitor, Paul Faure, the party's general secretary. And, before all these, was not Mussolini a faithful socialist, and were there no traitors among members of the Paris Commune? This long and detailed settling of accounts with the European Left had a single purpose: to prevent a general delegitimation of anti-Marxism. "There is a very serious form of anti-Marxism," wrote Katznelson, "which it is difficult to measure oneself against but which is worth knowing. . . . A. D. Gordon had no need of de Man . . . and Brenner did not ask famous leaders for permission to criticize"[162]

This point was very important for Katznelson, but he does not seem to have been aware of the degree to which he had exposed the weaknesses of his own movement. Gordon did not need de Man quite simply because he lived before the Belgian socialist leader: his anti-Marxism was just as violent as de Man's. "Was A. D. Gordon a reformist?" asked Katznelson irritably. "Was Yosef Aharonowitz a reformist?"[163] His answer was unequivocal: "The Eretz Israeli labor movement is not essentially a movement one can call reformist." Moreover, "it's the complete opposite of that. It's a messianic movement: it wants to go the whole way."[164] This raised the great and, at that period, disturbing question: if the movement was not reformist and was anti-Marxist, as Katznelson himself acknowledged, had it not embarked on a dangerous course? If its heroes, Gordon and Brenner, were violent anti-Marxists, was there nothing to be learned from that about the true nature of the movement?

Katznelson did not realize how problematic his answer was. The movement, he claimed, was anti-Marxist but not "reformist." At the same time, its messianism had little to do with universalistic social principles, and its center of gravity, as Katznelson well knew, was the nation. The movement, he wrote, "sees Zionism as part of human redemption, and it regards socialism as flawed if it does not recognize the redemption of the Jewish people. . . . For us, Zionism is organically linked to our socialist vision. This is not something we have agreed to as a compromise. In our eyes, socialism is defective if it does not fully acknowledge our right to exist, grow, and develop. Socialism is a wholly messianic movement."[165]

Thus, socialism was made dependent on nationalism, and the messianism of the labor movement was due to its being a movement of national redemption. In other words, Katznelson's own description of Labor Zionism was the very definition of nationalist socialism. This conception determined Katznelson's attitude to the outside world, the international socialist movement, and the Arab question.

Contrary to the impression one might gain from a cursory reading, Katznelson was not a naive person, and he had few illusions about the relationship between the Jews and the Arabs. He regarded Zionism as a movement for the conquest of the land, and he had no hesitation in bracketing it together with other movements of conquest, although he always insisted on its special quality. "We knew," he wrote, "that one cannot deceive history. We knew that we would not be able to deceive the Arabs, nor did we have any wish to deceive ourselves. We knew that if there was ever an agreement between ourselves and the Arabs, it would be on the basis of not a curtailment of Zionism but the implementation of Zionism."[166]

He said this at the beginning of the 1940s, but ten years earlier, after the Arab revolt of 1929, he had already fixed his attitude toward the Arab problem. First, he declared, one should not approach this question "with a sense of inferiority and a troubled conscience"; there was no intention of dispossessing the local inhabitants. He claimed that after hundreds of years of European colonization in Africa and Asia, the Jews were "the first people who came to one of these countries and said to its inhabitants, 'There is room for you here, and room for us as well.'" Moreover, far from harming the local population, the Yishuv helped them economically "by giving them new means of subsistence."[167] Thus, Zionism "could stand up and say to the socialists: from the time that Europe began to colonize and spread its culture, there has never been a colonizing enterprise as typified by justice and honesty toward others as our work here in Eretz Israel. . . . We have never been a colonialist movement; we are a movement of colonization."[168] The difference between the two was reflected in the absence of a relationship of overlordship and exploitation between the Jews and the Arabs. "The term 'conquest of labor,'" he wrote, "stems from the purity of our desire for a just relationship with the neighboring people." The very existence of a "Jewish working class . . . should be enough to silence all those who wish to lead the Arab workers astray."[169] From this Katznelson drew the conclusion that Zionism had not only the right but also the duty to instill in Jewish youth "the feeling that absolute justice is on our side."[170]

This last point was immensely important to Katznelson. He was sure that without this conviction of the absolute rightness of the Zionist cause the

Jewish national movement could not assume the task of putting its case before the outside world. He thought there was no possibility of reaching a compromise with the Arabs except on the basis of renouncing the ambition of setting up an independent Jewish state in the country. Because he was convinced that Arabs did not accept the Jewish desire for independence, he thought it inadvisable to work for such a compromise. He believed that, in the foreseeable future, Jewish-Arab coexistence would not be possible. That is why he thought it was so important to win the ideological struggle both within the Zionist movement and in the international arena. In the internal sphere, it was necessary not only to overcome "leftist," internationalist tendencies and the doubts that affected many people who had been reared on the principle of proletarian solidarity but also to defeat those who saw the Arab opposition to Zionism as a national struggle. Katznelson went to great lengths to refute the idea that a struggle was taking place between two national movements of equal legitimacy. He felt that accepting such an idea would not only weaken the self-confidence of the Zionist camp but also have disastrous consequences for the Zionist movement's relations with the outside world, for its capacity to mobilize international support, and for its already difficult relationship with the mandatory government.

Thus, Katznelson refused to accept the description of the "disturbances" of 1929 as a "revolt." In his opinion, it was simply a "pogrom," like other disturbances in the area—like those directed against the Armenians, against the Christians in Lebanon in 1860, or against the Jews in Hebron and Safed in 1833. "Calling it a revolt only glorifies the disturbances, whitewashes their perpetrators, and minimizes the significance of our sufferings." In the past, he wrote, when pogroms took place, at least the Jews did not turn their murderers into heroes![171] He claimed that this source of strength should be carefully preserved: "Even when we are wounded or in pain, we should not surrender or bow our heads. We should never agree to call an outburst of robbery and murder a movement of national liberation or an expression of religious feeling."[172] He thus described the "events" of 1929—another euphemism Jews use to this day—as the unruly behavior of "an incited rabble, thirsty for blood and spoil," and not as a rebellion.[173] Katznelson assured the Po'alei Tzion in Germany that "we would have been very happy if the Arab movement had been a movement of liberation, for in that case we would easily have found the way to its heart." He said this not in a naive spirit but based on careful reasoning. Thus, he tried to convince his audience that there were no grounds for claiming that the Arab movement was an "anti-imperialist movement."[174] A movement, he asked, that refused to give the Zionists a "minute province of twenty-six thousand square kilometres" in "an area of four and a half million square kilometres" which it had at its disposal in the Middle East—"could that be called a movement of liberation, an anti-imperialist movement?"[175]

Katznelson felt there was a real danger to the whole Zionist enterprise if the moral superiority of Jewish claims to the country was unrecognized. In practice, this moral and historical right, on which Gordon had already insisted, represented a legitimation of the conquest of the land and, when Jewish settlement required it, the removal of its Arab inhabitants. This principle applied not only to landowners (especially to those who did not live on their land) but also to tenants, and it also applied to Arab laborers who had worked on Jewish farms for many years. Katznelson recognized "the right of each individual Arab to payment, to compensation, to an arrangement," but he totally denied "the right of the Arab people to that particular place of work." Thus, according to Katznelson, the Arabs had no right to the Jezreel Valley: "We have recognized the full right of leaseholders to compensation and a just arrangement, but we have not acknowledged their right to prevent us from settling this area. We do not regard the fact that they live there as a right of permanent occupation."[176]

Here Katznelson formulated a principle that proved to be of permanent value to the movement: the Arab population, as a national entity, has no right of ownership over the land. Moving it from place to place in order to make land available for Jewish settlement is permissible as long as the rights of the individual are respected, but the rights of individuals do not guarantee the right of the Arab people to the land. The transfer of population, provided it was done with the consent of those transferred, was, for Katznelson, a basic principle of Zionism. "Since when have we begun to be ashamed of Zionist principles?" he asked members of the Zionist Executive Committee in November 1942. Katznelson berated the people of Hashomer Hatza'ir who were pleased that Ben-Gurion had "rescinded the transfer."

> What does that mean, to rescind? To rescind means that someone has decided something and then changed his mind. What did Ben-Gurion decide and what has he changed his mind about? Did Ben-Gurion ever speak of forced transfer and "rescinding" that? No! We have never favored a forced transfer, and so we do not have to rescind. From voluntary transfer and agreements between peoples we certainly do not back out, although there are good Jews who have used various terms of disparagement about this idea.
>
> Contemporary history provides examples of a number of transfers that have been carried out in various ways, some bad and some quite good. The Soviet Union, for example, transferred a million Germans, who had lived for several generations in the Volga region, to places far away from there. And we have not heard that those who are so contemptuous of the idea of transfer—Ya'ari [the charismatic leader of Hashomer Hatza'ir] among them—objected to this action, although one may assume that it was not carried out with the consent of those transferred.

For polemical reasons, people suggest that we are planning a monster transfer, and that we believe that without such a transfer no large-scale immigration
is possible. But I have to say that these detractors have never heard this from
our lips, and they merely ascribe these ideas to us.[177]

To prevent a misunderstanding, Katznelson now continued his argument,
attacking his rivals on the Left.

This debate is not timely, for no political situation has arisen that confronts us
with questions of this nature. But since they are forcing us into this discussion
in order to frighten us, since they declare that the concept of an agreed transfer
is unacceptable in a decent society, I have to ask: wasn't [Kibbutz] Merhavia
built as the result of a transfer? Weren't the inhabitants of Fula [the Arab vil-
lage] moved from one place to another? Wasn't this a short transfer carried out
through an agreement? Without many such transfers, Hashomer Hatza'ir
would not have settled in Merhavia, nor in Mishmar Ha'emek, nor in many
other places. If no transfer whatsoever is acceptable, then the settlement activities of Hashomer Hatza'ir are unacceptable. And if what is done for Hashomer
Hatza'ir is acceptable, why should it be unacceptable when done on a larger
scale, not just for Hashomer Hatza'ir but for the Jewish people as a whole?[178]

It is difficult to believe that Katznelson did not know that the tenants'
transfer from the lands at Merhavia occurred without their consent (this was
the result of a deal with the landowner). It is also hard to believe that he was
unaware of the fact that if a transfer such as the one permitting the founding
of Kibbutz Merhavia ever took place on a large scale, it would not be voluntary or by agreement. After the Arab revolt of the late 1920s, no one could
entertain the illusion that an agreement on the vacation of lands by Arabs
was possible. If there were an agreement on a larger scale than the one at
Merhavia, it could only have been between two national movements. But
since it was already clear that such an agreement would not take place, the
only real transfer would be a forced transfer. This was a possibility to which
Katznelson could not give legitimation. He stated:

Just as we believe that aliyah cannot be dependent on [Arab] goodwill, so we
believe that changes of population cannot be imposed. We do not acknowledge
that anyone in the world has the moral right to prevent or obstruct our aliyah,
just as we do not arrogate ourselves the right to force anyone to leave.[179]

Straightforwardly and without inhibitions, constructive socialism was a
socialism of conquest of the land and building the Jewish economy. The
primary aim was to create a strong economic infrastructure; social justice
was never anything other than a byproduct. The labor movement never intended to bring about a social utopia. In its scale of values, economic growth
always took precedence over a fairer distribution of public wealth. The rea-

son for this was very simple: the labor movement believed that implementing Zionism depended not on social justice but on a concentration of political and economic power. Consequently, socialism was understood in terms of production and building.

This was the pride of the founders. Thus, socialism was always depicted as a revolution of labor, the necessary prerequisite for the great national revolution. All moral considerations and universal values were subordinated to the great aim of building the nation. Socialism was never an aim in itself but a tool for the advancement of national objectives, an incomparably effective mobilizing force. Thus, the socialism of the Eretz Israeli labor movement lacked the universal moral characteristics that might have enabled it to bear fruit even after the end of the process of founding the Jewish state.

CHAPTER FOUR

Ends and Means: The Labor Ideology
and the Histadrut

THE BASES OF POWER

The Histadrut, or the General Federation of Jewish Workers, was a unique phenomenon: an autonomous social, political, and economic institution unparalleled anywhere else in the free world. The Histadrut enjoyed full independence, as the colonial government did not interfere with its activities. The government of Palestine authorized it without difficulty to control the whole collective agricultural settlement, and the World Zionist Organization never succeeded in imposing its authority on it. Not even its control of public capital allowed the Zionist Organization to influence the use the Histadrut made of the money it collected. The Histadrut was not only a pure creation of the labor movement but was founded in ideal circumstances. The structure of the Histadrut, the type of relationships that existed within it, the principles by which it operated, and its order of priorities fully reflected the aims of the movement.

In comparison with other labor movements, the Jewish labor movement in Palestine enjoyed immense advantages. Not only did it not have to deal with hostile forces such as a landed aristocracy or a strong bourgeoisie that controlled the state and used its authority to protect its position, but it enjoyed the support of the political and economic institutions that the Zionist movement had set up. The labor movement did not have to uproot entrenched privileges as in England, resort to bloody strikes as in France and Italy, or confront the open hostility of the state as in Germany. Nor did it have to participate in a cultural conflict, which in Europe was often no less bitter than economic and political struggle. In this respect, Palestine—and later Israel—was a tabula rasa, and its geographical distance from Europe plus the general desire to put the diaspora behind only served to emphasize the new beginning.

However, the movement did not have at its disposal a specific working class. On the face of it, this might have been a weakness, but in reality it enabled the founding nucleus to turn the Histadrut into a body embracing all salaried workers in the country. The proletariat in Europe had experienced frustration and hatred due to ruthless exploitation during the industrialization and rapid modernization of the nineteenth century. But this was absent in Palestine, allowing the labor movement to take responsibility for the enterprise of national rebirth in a way that for historical, sociological, and cultural reasons was impossible in Europe. It was no accident that the term *proletariat* soon dropped out of the vocabulary of the Histadrut leadership; it was unsuited to the national goals or the cultural reality. With the liquidation of the Po'alei Tzion Party, the far more neutral term *labor*, or *home of labor*—an expression Katznelson especially favored— came into use. In Europe labor was a necessity, an existential need that was nothing to be proud of or to feel enthusiastic about. This was also the case in Palestine, but the enterprise of national rebirth transformed it into a moral and cultural value.

More than four thousand people took part in the election of delegates at the inaugural convention of the Histadrut. Ahdut Ha'avoda gained 1,864 votes; Hapo'el Hatza'ir 1,324; the new immigrants' list under the leadership of Menachem Elkind, a charismatic leader who was soon to become head of the Gdud Ha'avoda, won 824; and 303 went to the "leftists.". Another 100 votes were classed as "various."[1] With the founding of the Histadrut, all economic institutions created by Ahdut Ha'avoda in order to provide the workers, most of whom were impecunious bachelors, with essential services were transferred to the organization. These included a labor exchange, workers' kitchens, and an enterprise for building and construction—the Bureau of Public Works—which in 1923 became Sollel Boneh, a stock company owned by the Histadrut.

From its inception, the Histadrut was a tremendous success. According to reports by the Executive Committee to the third and fourth Histadrut conventions, in 1923 the organization had 8,394 members—5,435 in cities, 1,331 in moshavot, and 1,621 in collective settlements. Thus, the number of members doubled in its first two years. Four years later, in 1927, there were 22,538 members, of whom 15,325 lived in cities, 4,250 in moshavot (private agriculture), and 2,968 in collective settlements. From the beginning, the Histadrut was the only organized force in the country, as well as the organization with which, in the days of the Third Aliyah, most workers in the country were affiliated via collective settlements and the Bureau of Public Works. In late 1930 and early 1931, the Histadrut had more than 30,000 members, 18,781 in cities (including the industrial enterprises in Nahara'im, Atlit, and the Dead Sea area), 7,783 in moshavot, and 3,496 in collective settlements. According to Ben-Gurion's report, these members included 6,787 women workers and 1,530 working adolescents. On 1 January 1933, the Histadrut had 35,389 members: 21,080 in cities, 10,502 in moshavot, and 3,807 in collective settlements and moshavim. These figures also included women workers and working adolescents. In 1923 members constituted 44.5 percent of the workers as a whole, in 1927, 65.3–70 percent, and in 1933, 75 percent. This was still the percentage in 1939, on the eve of the

Second World War, when the number of members passed the 100,000 mark. In 1940 the Histadrut had 112,000 members, and in 1947, on the eve of the founding of the state, 176,000. At the end of 1949—the end of the War of Independence—the number of members reached 251,000, or 40.7 percent of the adult Jewish population in the country. A year later this number was 330,000, or 46 percent of the adult Jewish population.[2]

In a short time, the Histadrut became an economic giant, the largest employer in the country, the main supplier of health services, and the main purveyor of employment through its labor exchange. At the time of the state's founding, the Histadrut, by means of its Hevrat Haovdim (Society of Workers), controlled 25 percent of the national economy. The term *hevrat haovdim* has two meanings in Hebrew: "community of workers," an egalitarian collectivity of working people in the semirevolutionary sense of the term, and "society of workers," the holding company of all the Histadrut companies, which was registered with the government of Palestine in early 1924. The Histadrut never became a society of workers, but its Society of Workers became, in terms of economic and political power, an extraordinary success story. Bank Hapo'alim (the Workers' Bank)—founded in 1921 by the Histadrut and the World Zionist Organization on the joint initiative of Katznelson and Ruppin—with its associated cooperative loan banks and savings funds, although by no means as large and powerful as it is today, was second (even if only by a long shot) to Bank Le'umi, run by the Zionist Organization.[3] Today Bank Hapo'alim is the largest bank in the country. The founders attached great importance to their main financial instrument. "The bank is the true expression of the workers' will," declared Yosef Aharonowitz, codirector of the bank, a major figure of the Second Aliyah and one of the most important leaders of Hapoel Hatza'ir, in 1922.[4] Very soon new subsidiaries were founded by the Society of Workers in every field of economic activity: housing, planting and food processing, marketing farm produce, insurance, and many others.

The Histadrut was also a trade union, and relative to the total population, the largest trade union in the free world. The Histadrut also founded the Hagana organization, which became the Israel Defense Forces (IDF). According to every criterion—its scale, the number of institutions, or the scope of its activities—the Histadrut was a unique phenomenon. Many people have pointed this out in the past, but two questions still remain: what was the purpose for which this huge empire was set up, and what was the connection between its political and social objectives? Further, what was the purpose of its methods of mass mobilization, the most developed anywhere at that time except in the Soviet Union? Why was there a concern to embrace all aspects of members' lives? Why was it necessary to have such a complex system for supplying services and providing for all the economic, cultural, and spiritual needs of the wage earners?

The Histadrut was never intended to be an instrument of change; its very comprehensiveness rendered it impotent in the social sphere, and the Histadrut society therefore never developed into an alternative to the existing society. Consequently, its economic strength was never used to promote equality. The Histadrut was interested in accumulating wealth and gaining political power, not in creating a socialist utopia. Its founders' intention was not to supersede the capitalist system but to dominate it. Thus, the Histadrut never developed into a counterculture: it never created ideal ways of living that would have shown the weaknesses of bourgeois society, and it accepted the hierarchical system in society. Informal relationships and the obligatory use of the form of address *haver* (comrade) were not enough to conceal differences in standards of living, which were by no means lower than those outside the Histadrut. The movement's leadership enjoyed a position of strength unparalleled in democratic societies; discipline and conformity still prevailed when the rules of the game were challenged during the Lavon affair in the early 1960s. Changes of the guard were almost unknown; a member of the leadership, if he showed loyalty to the organization, could retain his position until he died. Rewards and punishments were meted out according to purely political criteria, and a fall from a position of eminence was generally due not to some action by the rank and file, moral bankruptcy, or administrative failure but to internal disputes and power struggles.

For these reasons, membership did not require ideological affiliation. The Histadrut included a variety of groups and organizations, some of which were not Zionist and a larger proportion of which were not socialist. That is why it was called a general (that is, nonpartisan) Histadrut. The Histadrut was not set up as a socialist body, and a member was expected to observe discipline, not demonstrate ideological allegiance. Despite its control of most aspects of members' lives, ideological pluralism prevented the Histadrut from becoming a totalitarian institution. For the founders, however, the Histadrut always had a special status. These practical-minded people appreciated the importance of the relationships of dependence that developed between the members and the organization. "One can leave the party, but one is tied to the Histadrut with every fiber of one's being," said Ben-Gurion in 1925.[5] The Histadrut's independence from socialist ideology was one of its greatest sources of strength. Ben-Gurion, as its head, opposed any desire on the part of the majority to turn the "General Histadrut into a Zionist-socialist Histadrut." Such a thing, he believed, would probably lead to a "rival Histadrut," which would "destroy the organizational unity of the labor movement in the country."[6] Organizational rather than ideological unity primarily interested Ben-Gurion.

The partnership in the Histadrut of the various kinds of salaried workers with settlers and the self-employed who were not themselves employers was called unity of class. As we have seen in previus chapters, this new concept of class was an "innovation" in the theoretical sphere, and it also differed from the universal ideological significance of the term because membership in the "class" was restricted to Jews. In this way, the general character and ideological neutrality of the Histadrut served the aims of national unity: every worker, regardless of ideological affiliation, provided he was Jewish and "lived on the fruits of his own labor without exploiting the work of his neighbour," could join the ranks of the Histadrut.[7] Accordingly, everyone was welcome: socialists and antisocialists, the religious and the secular. Over time even the last condition, the nonexploitation of one's neighbor, fell victim to the needs of organizational partnership. Ben-Gurion suggested going out and waging a vigorous campaign among the Jewish youth in the diaspora, without regard to ideological affiliation or degree of religious observance, in order to throw the gates of the Histadrut wide open to them. "This is class consciousness, this is the class mission, and this is class fidelity," he declared.[8] For Ben-Gurion, the concept of class unity never meant anything other than this sacrosanct principle of organizational partnership.

He firmly expressed this viewpoint each time the question of Jewish labor came up. At the beginning of the 1920s, and again in the early 1930s, Hashomer Hatza'ir sought to group Arab workers in professional organizations in order to eliminate cheap labor and at the same time replace the concept of "Jewish labor" with "organized labor." The inclusion of Arab workers in the category of organized labor fulfilled the first principle of class solidarity in the usual sense of the term. There is no doubt that the proposal was unrealistic and that Ben-Gurion's criticism of it was politically justified, but the way in which he quashed this naive attempt to reach a minimal compromise between socialist ideology and the harsh realities of the national struggle leaves no doubt about his basic outlook. Ben-Gurion was not simply a pragmatist. By no means! He was a fundamentalist who knew how to choose the most appropriate means of action for a particular time and situation, but his adherence to a rigidly nationalist ideology never faltered. The sarcastic anti-Marxist tone he adopted in this controversy was used in Europe at the beginning of the 1930s only by the enemies of socialism. To Ben-Gurion's great credit, it must be said that he never concealed his opinions. If he had regarded socialism, with its universal values, as being of equal importance to the claims of Jewish nationalism, he would have gone down in history as a revolutionary. But having early in his political career come to the conclusion that there could not be a socialist solution to the Jewish national problem, he was not afraid to say so directly.

> We would like to have a socialist regime, we would like to set up a commune, but although I know that I am liable with these words to give ammunition to those who are only waiting for an opportunity to distort what I say, I say we have no special interest in organized work in this country, we have no special

interest in a socialist regime or a commune in this country, if those involved are not Jewish workers. We did not come here to organize anything, and we did not come here to spread the socialist idea among anyone. We came here to create a home and a place of work for the Jewish people.[9]

In his address to the Po'alei Tzion delegation that, we may remember, visited Palestine immediately after the First World War, Ben-Gurion made it quite clear that "the rights we must all strive for in every possible way are those that will lead to a Jewish state in Eretz Israel."[10] He wished to organize the Zionist movement as a potential state, but because he did not control the Zionist movement and soon after became the unchallenged head of the Histadrut, he began to run it along state lines. "Zionism is the building of the state. Without this, it is a vain idea. The building of a Jewish state requires first the creation of a Jewish majority in the country," said Ben-Gurion at the fourteenth Zionist Congress in August 1925. "The only person who can bring us such a majority," he said, "is the Jewish worker in Eretz Israel."[11] This view dictated Ben-Gurion's policies as the head of the Histadrut. He was not a social reformer; nor was he interested in either the condition of society or the welfare of the individual. He did not regard any social organization, including the Histadrut, as a means of serving the welfare of the individual. Like Katznelson and the other founders, he regarded the individual as existing to serve the nation, and the creation of the Histadrut with all its subdivisions as enabling the individual to carry out this mission. This principle guided Ben-Gurion until the end of his political career. Like all leaders of radical national movements and their ideologists, Ben-Gurion had only limited faith in the individual and in formal democratic arrangements, although, on the face of it, the Histadrut and party system operated according to democratic methods.

It is generally claimed that the Histadrut system was voluntary. This is true only in the most formal sense. Precisely because a state, with its legal institutions, did not exist, precisely because a legislation guaranteeing the rights of the individual was lacking, in the period of the Yishuv social pressure encouraged a rigid conformism and made toeing the line a patriotic virtue. Deviation from the accepted path, a lack of fidelity, and a breach of solidarity on the part of the individual or of a group too small to create its own type of conformism were the only sins considered unforgivable. There was no failure, no transgression that could not be pardoned, including grave deviations from norms of integrity. Maintenance of the internal consensus and obedience to existing institutions were regarded as the only sine qua nons. To the great credit of the movement, these were elected institutions, even if electoral processes were far from meeting the most exacting standards of democratic procedure. But formally, at least, democratic processes did exist, and the leaders of the movement acted accordingly. Thus, within the Histadrut a peculiar blend of conformism, daily social pressure, authoritarianism, and sensitivity to the needs of the members as a whole came into being. The interdependent relationship between the organization and its members was very complex; the organization exerted heavy pressure on its members, but it was also a sort of elixir of life to them. Under normal circumstances, the Histadrut did not take things beyond the point where they were bearable, but in matters regarded as being of vital importance to the organization, such as the episode of the Gdud Ha'avoda (Labor Corps), sanctions were imposed without hesitation and without any consideration of the human price.

Members of the Second Aliyah always had an extraordinary ability to see themselves and their activities on a grand scale. "We are the emissaries of history, the representatives of the Jewish people without a shelter," said Ben-Gurion on one of many occasions.[12] He never tired of declaring his absolute faith in "the dynamics of Jewish history." "I believe in the historical victory of dynamic forces," he said.[13] Those who had not settled in the country spoke in the same vein. "We must decide on a maximalist program, not because we can carry it out immediately, for everything cannot be done at a frantic speed. But the maximum must be a guide for us, even if we begin on a small scale," said the representative of Po'alei Tzion in Lithuania to his fellow delegates at the beginning of 1920.[14] On the same occasion, Yavnieli asked them "to close in on the country from all sides, as we shall have to conquer it as soon as possible."[15] Members of the delegation as a whole hoped to settle a million people within ten years.[16] Syrkin proposed the astronomical sum of sixty million pounds as the amount the movement had to raise to colonize within ten years.[17] Tabenkin said, "There is a need and possibility of settling eight million Jews in Eretz Israel in ten to twenty years."[18]

The leaders of the movement, however, were convinced that no objective could be reached without strength, organization, discipline, and the ability to impose authority without undue concern for democratic niceties. If this involved political coercion, it was a necessary and legitimate element of statehood. They were not prepared to leave much to the individual or to the spontaneous feelings of the masses, whom they regarded as amorphous and lacking in willpower. By contrast, there was no limit to their faith in the energy, the life force, of the activist minorities that organized and led the masses. They believed that a properly led mass was an irresistible force, but a social body that was no more than a collection of individuals was essentially useless.

The Histadrut was held to be "the very embodiment of the process of rebirth of the Jewish people,"[19] and already in 1925 Ben-Gurion was able to describe the form this process should take. At a very early stage, Ben-Gurion understood the nature of the relationship between the organization that provided services and the individual receiving those services. When Ahdut Ha'avoda's economic enterprises and institutions of mutual aid were transferred to the Histadrut, "the party," he said, "was divested of all content. The strong control and influence that the party formerly exercised, and that forced the public to reckon with it, quite apart from its ideas and outlook, that source of strength was taken from it." The party was left only with its "spiritual possessions." Ben-Gurion did not underestimate ideological influence, but he knew that this was not enough to enable the party to regain its power. In order to do that, he said, it had to build up a power base "in public opinion outside it." He recognized the legitimacy of the democratic process. "The personalities and leaders of the party," he said, "have validity only to the degree that the general public gives them its trust and is willing to vote for them."[20] But, at the same time, neither he nor the other leaders of the party were willing to entrust their destiny and that of the Zionist enterprise to the voter.

Most of all, the founders were aware of the supreme importance of economic control. They realized, from their experience in the days of the Second Aliyah, that because of conditions in Palestine economic control was essential to political power. Economics was never an aim in itself; the ultimate goal was political. Consequently, the labor movement was built as a mixed system in which the economic aspect was used to enlist members and as an operative arm. Decision-making power remained with the hard political core. The political figures headed the system as well as its secondary organizations. Ben-Gurion headed the Histadrut from its inception until 1935, Remez controlled Sollel Boneh and then succeeded Ben-Gurion as the head of the Histadrut, and Tabenkin was in charge of collective settlement. In early 1927 Tabenkin's kibbutz, Ein Harod, merged with other kibbutzim, and in this way Hakibbutz Hame'uhad was founded as a countrywide organization. Yosef Aharonowitz headed Bank Hapo'alim, Katznelson ran the newspaper *Davar*.

Yonathan Shapiro has demonstrated how Ahdut Ha'avoda's leadership used the organization to control other bodies in the Yishuv as well.[21] This state of affairs was especially common among communist parties, whereas social democratic parties were generally careful to keep the professional and the political sphere separate. Annie Kriegel, in her classic study of the French Communist Party, has described this operation.[22] The party requires its members to join all socioeconomic and cultural organizations, from trade unions and mutual aid institutions to sporting organizations. Ahdut Ha'avoda, which had never been Marxist and had never supported social revolution, used methods that replicated those of communist parties in democratic societies.[23]

The noncommunist trade unions in Western Europe jealously guarded their independence, and although their members generally voted for socialist parties and most of their leaders were members of those parties, the socialist unions, unlike the communist ones, were never mere rubber stamps for a party. Sometimes there were disagreements between the parties and the unions, resulting in bitter conflicts, a phenomenon unknown in Palestine.

Here I must mention again the main factor that can contribute to an understanding of the complex relationship between the individual, the party, and the Histadrut. The array of services the Histadrut provided created a special connection—material but also emotional—between the members and the organization. There was no other example in the free world of such a dependence on the organization. For the ordinary member, the two organizations, the party and the Histadrut, represented a single system. This feeling grew much stronger after the founding of Mapai, although even in the 1920s there was no real difference between Ahdut Ha'avoda and Hapo'el Hatza'ir. Between the two world wars, the only way for the wage earner unaffiliated with the Revisionist Right to have access to essential services such as a labor exchange and health care was via the Histadrut. Moreover, its members, especially bachelors, needed the workers' kitchen, and they all needed a minimum cultural life, a newspaper, and a publishing house.

The organization also gave its members a sense of belonging, which did not exist outside the communist parties. Through their local branches, the party and the Histadrut represented a kind of extended family. This term is not at all metaphorical, at least in the early years of the labor movement. Many, if not all, immigrants in the days of the Second and Third Aliyahs were bachelors who suffered greatly from loneliness. They needed a framework that could ease their solitude and give them a modicum of warmth. Here, the party and the Histadrut played the role of the communist parties in Europe. Many years ago, several classic memoirs revealed the special relationship that developed between the young party member working in a large industrial enterprise and the party. The local branch, the party cell within the factory, took the place of family for the worker who had arrived from a provincial town or distant village. How much more did this apply to the new immigrant whose family and childhood friends remained overseas! Alone in a strange land, very often without knowledge of the language, cut off from his native surroundings and culture, the pioneer found his home within the political framework. Thus, dependent relationships and feelings of loyalty developed, forming patterns of behavior during the first years. Naturally, over time, as the organization grew, the relationship became less intimate and an estrangement took place, especially in periods of crisis, between the establishment and the ordinary member, and it seems that very often this natural tension was exacerbated by the member's high expectations of the organization.

The feeling of tribal closeness that developed among the members of the extended founding nucleus had a decisive effect on the political culture of the labor movement. Fidelity to the organization became paramount. A party member was like a soldier: a betrayal of the system was unforgivable. That was why people with ideological differences were able to work together successfully in the Histadrut. As long as fidelity to national aims and the organization representing those aims was preserved, divergent or even opposing opinions in social and economic matters were considered secondary.

Shapiro has described the profound understanding between the founders of the labor movement, veterans of the Second Aliyah, and the socialist Zionists who had fled from the Soviet Union but who nevertheless had great respect for the Bolsheviks' methods of operation. The party leadership of Ahdut Ha'avoda and later Mapai arose from the encounter of these two groups. Katznelson never ascribed to the party apparatus the importance that Ben-Gurion did, but he recognized its necessity and did not oppose it, although as early as 1927 he acknowledged that a professional party worker was "necessarily a representative of the party rather than the public."[24] In practice, Katznelson supported the apparatus. The process of creating a professional leadership happened very quickly. As early as the mid-1920s it was clear that a rotation of tasks was not possible. This situation was not new; members of the Second Aliyah, who meanwhile had become the leaders of the movement, had been professional politicians for a considerable period. Whatever Katznelson pretended, he too was a professional politician. The fact that he was head of *Davar* and not of Sollel Boneh does not alter the fact that only a man of the professional political leadership could occupy such a post. As far as we know, Katznelson never suggested changing his position. Shapiro writes that after the third Histadrut convention in July 1927, the labor organization began to function as a normal bureaucratic system.[25] In fact, the change took place after the second convention, in 1923, when all ideas of collectivization were abandoned and emphasis shifted to building the Histadrut power structure.

This should not surprise us. The founders realized that in order to establish a state for the Jewish people they had to create an economic infrastructure capable of absorbing those who came from abroad and a political organization with which to control them. Those who came first—members of the Second Aliyah—were able to pass on their conviction of their right to lead to those who came after the First World War. Thus, a collaboration arose between the two groups, which gradually formed the dominant nucleus in the labor movement, the Yishuv, and the state of Israel. Nobody questioned the ruling elite, except in one case. Some of the people in the left wing of the Third Aliyah, especially those who identified themselves with Gdud Ha'avoda, revolted and generally paid a high personal and political price for their rebellion. Those who repented of their ways were allowed to take their place within the system. David (Dolek) Horowitz, eventually first president of the Bank of Israel (the central bank), was a good example of those who returned to the fold. The outstanding figures among the new immigrants of the 1920s, from the more radical Third Aliyah to the right-wingers of the Gordonia movement who came in 1929—Goldie Meyerson (Golda Meir), Zalman (Ziama) Aharonowitz (Aranne), Mordechai Namirow-sky (Namir), and Pinhas Lubianiker (Lavon)—became pillars of the establishment. They helped run the Histadrut, Mapai, and ultimately the state of Israel. Shraga Nusovitzky (Netzer) devoted his life to the service of Ben-Gurion; he was by no means exceptional. At a very early stage, the founders adopted a natural leadership with the unquestionable right to set the tone and govern society.

Golda Meir described the relationship of the members of the Third Aliyah to their immediate predecessors in the concluding entry of *Sefer Ha'aliya Hashlishit* (The book of the Third Aliyah), published in 1964.

> I believe that the Third Aliyah did not renew the foundations of the movement. Jewish labor, Jewish guarding, the Hebrew language, communal living, working the soil, the desire for the unity of the workers: these were values bequeathed to us by members of the Second Aliyah. But the importance of every example of disseminating a doctrine is twofold: 1. The dissemination of the doctrine itself, and 2. No less important: the finding of people willing to receive and observe it.
>
> I believe that the major importance of the Third Aliyah was its adoption of the doctrine that our comrades of the Second Aliyah handed over to us. We accepted it wholeheartedly and gladly, and we obeyed its precepts.[26]

Anyone who questioned the authority of the leadership was soon regarded as an enemy of the people and was doomed to political extinction. This was a salient feature of the political culture of the Yishuv created by the labor movement. Discipline and the acceptance of authority were inalienable principles. As long as there was unity of action, ideological disagreements had no real significance, as these did not decide policy.

As early as 1915 Ben-Gurion said: "A country is built only by pioneers. The masses do not have historical objectives." He added: "A national or socialist objective can be achieved only through the dedication and self-sacrifice of its first fighters and builders. The expectation of a 'stychic process' is only a hypocritical excuse for sterility and weakness. History is not controlled by a fatal destiny, and life is more than an interplay of blind forces."[27] This idea would guide the labor movement for the next fifty years. Among the Jews, the only ones who counted, in the view of the leadership, were the candidates for aliyah, especially members of Hehalutz. Among the youth, members of the youth movements were highly regarded, and among these the leadership of the labor movement particularly respected the pioneering nucleus, eager to found new settlements. However, there was never any doubt in the minds of the party and Histadrut leaders, self-confident even in times of crisis, about their right to speak not only on behalf of the "workers," or the Zionist movement, but on behalf of the Jewish people as a whole.

Here again the principle on which the system was run greatly resembled that of the communist parties. Supreme authority was given to the highest institutions of the movement: the Central Committee and the Executive Committee, elected by the Central Committee. In the communist movement, this system was known as democratic centralism, and its purpose was to prevent the leadership from becoming dependent on the rank and file. That system was adopted by the Histadrut: the smaller the body that elected the supreme institution the greater the number of Histadrut and party workers, including managers of the powerful economic enterprises, leaders of workers' councils, and others directly dependent on the organization and its leadership. The basic units of the organization were the trade unions, but the method of voting was individual and direct. The organization was countrywide, and all its members theoretically had the right to appoint members of the general convention by vote once a year. In other words, although the organization was made up of trade unions, it was not these basic units that elected the council and executive but the members of the unions as individuals. In this way, both the political leadership's control of the organization and the filtering out in three stages (via the executive, council, and convention) of all demands coming from below were ensured. Union representatives were elected only to the local workers' councils, and these operated under the close supervision of the executive. In addition, the leadership of the movement made sure that members of the Executive Committee were also members of the council that supervised them.[28]

Thus, oligarchic tendencies were present in Ahdut Ha'avoda from the day it was founded. These tendencies, existing in all organizations, trade unions, and socialist parties, were reinforced by the pioneering ideology. In its essential nature this ideology contradicted the basic concepts of democracy. Democracy not only requires majority decisions and a scrupulous respect for the rights of minorities but is based on the autonomy of the individual and on skepticism, namely, the principle that nobody can know the absolute truth, and thus no one has the right to impose his point of view on anyone else. This way of thinking obviously contradicted the pioneer mentality: avant-gardism considered itself not only worthy of imposing its views on the amorphous masses devoid of willpower. In the view of the labor leaders, the activist minority, which knew what was good for the nation, had the right to lead it, even against its will, and without taking the rules of democratic decision-making into consideration. As Ben-Gurion expressed it in 1929:

> For us, democracy is not an empty phrase that is exploited before elections and discarded afterward. Democracy is a necessity of life for us and the sole basis for our development. But we have a principle even greater than democracy, and that is the building of Eretz Israel by the Jewish people. Our great fear for the fate of our undertaking, our great concern in hastening the building of Eretz Israel in the possibly short period that history has placed at our disposal, causes us to infringe on the teachings of democracy, for it is time to act.[29]

Even at the start of their careers, the founders showed disdain for the workings of democratic bodies. In his first volume of writings, Katznelson described his impressions of the 1920 London conference of the World Zionist Organization (one can hardly say one senses any admiration for the decision-making processes of that parliamentary body).[30] Moreover, the leaders of the movement were in the habit of distinguishing between "formal" democracy and "real" democracy. A majority decision was acceptable to them only when it served the right purpose. Ben-Gurion was very much in favor of the principle of decision by a majority in the Histadrut, as his movement dominated the organization. He insistently demanded exclusive control, and he not only expected the minority to accept the decision of the majority but claimed that the majority represented the will of the community as a whole, his argument being that the will of Ahdut Ha'avoda was also the real will of the community.[31] This principle did not apply to the Zionist Organization, where the labor movement was in a minority until the mid-1930s.

The situation necessitated this selective use of the principle of the majority. The Zionist movement represented a minority among the Jewish people, and the form of Zionism exemplified by the Eretz Israeli labor movement was attractive to only a minority of the Jewish proletariat in Eastern Europe and the United States. Most of the manual workers in the factories of Łódź and the workshops of Manhattan embraced non-Zionist socialism, read Yiddish newspapers, and participated in the struggles of the local socialist parties. In addition, the Jewish Yishuv was a minority in Palestine, and its representatives vigorously opposed any attempts to set up institutions of representative government in the country on the basis of majority decisions. In this respect, formal democracy was a mortal danger to Zionism; even the colonialist regime did not ask the Jews of Palestine to honor the principle of majority rule by agreeing to the liquidation of the national home. The justification of Zionism for the Yishuv did not depend on the support of the majority of the Jewish people, just as its implementation could not depend on the goodwill of the Arabs. "We think that the concept of Eretz Israel suits the needs of the Jewish people, and thus we consider the Zionist movement a truly democratic one regardless of whether Zionism is embraced by the majority of the people or not," wrote Beilison in one of the major articles on the subject to appear in the labor press. "We don't insist on formal democracy. When Herzl or Weizmann spoke on behalf of the Jewish people, they were not officially authorized by a majority, and a formal concept of democracy would not have allowed them to speak on behalf of the people." He drew the conclusion that even if democracy were fully in control or "the sovereignty were in the hands of the people[,] . . . the true course of life would nevertheless be charted by an active minority conscious of its objectives."[32]

This view accorded with a concept that was very common in communist parties: collective needs, like correct opinions, are grounded in objectivity. This objective existence cannot depend on the will, which by its nature is subjective. Zionism was produced by the objective needs of the Jewish people, and they determined its path. These needs did not change when supported by only a minority. If only a minority of the Jewish people identified with Zionism, that did not mean that the movement had to submit to the majority; rather it meant that the minority's duty was to lead the movement in the right direction. At the same time, the movement itself was led by a pioneering minority that was "the crown of Zionism," the "supreme revelation" of "all the purity, splendor, and heroism there is in Zionism."[33] This way of thinking had always been typical of a revolutionary mentality. In matters of importance to Zionism, the founders accepted the will of the majority only when it agreed with the objective needs of the nation as defined by the Zionist movement.

This explains why the principle that control of the organization must always remain in the hands of central institutions was consistently upheld throughout the years. The leadership of Ahdut Ha'avoda sought to enshrine this centralization of authority in the legal structure of the institutions. The election system in Ahdut Ha'avoda and the Histadrut was set up in such a way as to ensure that the Central Committee would control the units making up the organization. The difference between a legislative and an executive institution, between the people who had an executive task and those who had to make decisions, was soon obscured. The Histadrut executive performed both functions simultaneously. Similarly, supervision was impossible, because managers of the administrative institutions were the employers of people who through their membership in the Histadrut and in party institutions, such as the council of Ahdut Ha'avoda, were supposed to supervise the administration. This mingling of tasks happened to such a extent that Arlosoroff called the Histadrut an "administrative democracy,"[34] and even the apologetically minded Gorny described it as a "centralistic democracy."[35]

TAKING OVER THE COLLECTIVE SETTLEMENTS:
THE ESTABLISHMENT OF THE NIR COMPANY

The principles of control envisaged by the founders found practical expression in two parallel actions: the liquidation of Gdud Ha'avoda (the Labor Corps) and the establishment of the Nir company. Both actions reflected the founders' constant attempt to centralize political and economic power, especially their ideological struggle against individualistic and pluralistic tendencies on one hand and large-scale collective and egalitarian forms of organization on the other. Ahdut Ha'avoda's war against the Labor Corps was far more than a mere power struggle: the liquidation of Gdud Ha'avoda reflected a crucial ideological decision. The establishment of Nir as the legal owner of the collective settlements and the ultimate decision maker, however, merely reinforced existing tendencies. In those crucial years all that was left of the "community of workers" was the Society of Workers. In the mid-twenties, the Histadrut fixed its attitude toward matters necessary to its proper functioning: the role of moral decisions in political life, the relationship between the individual and society, the proper attitude to utopian socialist manifestations, the role of conformism in strengthening the power structure, and the role of democracy and the principle of self-management.

On 20 December 1925 *Davar* announced that a stock company called Nir would be founded at the agricultural convention, which would be held in a few weeks. Nine days later, Eliezer Yaffe, one of the founders of Nahalal, the first moshav in the Jezreel Valley, launched a sweeping attack in *Davar* on the ways of thinking and methods of control prevalent in the Histadrut. The newspaper particularly stressed the fact that Yaffe's opinions were published "without omissions or retouches." Yaffe made three accusations. First, he wrote that transferring ownership of the settlers' farms and the "means of production," including livestock, to a stock company owned by the Histadrut meant the "socialization of our agriculture" and the victory of "those with a class outlook" over those with a "popular national outlook." Second, he viewed this phenomenon as an attempt by the city to take over the village, and by the majority to dominate the minority. He argued that since the leadership had forbidden farmers to contact the Zionist Organization directly and had decided to transfer ownership of the farms to the Histadrut, why should it not also transfer the property of the urban members of the Histadrut to public ownership? Why should freedom and the right to run one's life in a democratic manner be taken away only from the farmer? Third, Yaffe objected to the extreme centralistic tendency and disdain for democracy reflected in the idea that the Histadrut administration should control the fate of all the "thousands and tens of thousands of agricultural

workers." Indeed, he wrote, "One may perhaps find regulations as democratic and humanitarian as these in an American trust for the exploitation of
coffee or tea plantations, or in South Africa."[36]

Only four days later, a series of articles opposing Yaffe's opinions began in
Davar. This matter was crucial to the Histadrut, and its leaders were enlisted to respond to Yaffe's criticisms. The first to reply was Arlosoroff, who
like Yaffe belonged to the Hapo'el Hatza'ir Party. Most of Arlosoroff's article
was devoted to a refutation of the claim that in founding Nir there was a
desire to replace a "national" concept with a "class" concept. This, wrote
Arlosoroff, was entirely mistaken; it "set up a scarecrow," because the labor
movement was a national movement and its members owed allegiance primarily to the nation, and only "class phraseology," which was "incongrous
and harmful," obscured this basic fact. The danger of "class phraseology,"
according to Arlosoroff, was not that it led or was likely to lead to "acts of
national betrayal but that it encouraged an incorrect and distorted view of
our situation," since "fortunately this view does not reflect the reality of
life in this country and does not correspond to the differences between the
various groups among us." The conclusion to be drawn from Arlosoroff's
words was crystal clear: the socialism of the labor movement in Palestine
was a nationalist socialism. It had nothing to do with a socialization of
the means of production, and the "difference of classes" was a formula without real content.

On this point there was general agreement, and none of the other participants in the debate—Katznelson, Golomb, Aharonowitz, or Lavi—disputed
it. Each one added something to Arlosoroff's argument in his own way. On
one hand, they said, there was no danger of class divisions coming into being
in the urban sector (Golomb); on the other hand, the farmer was the true
"vanguard" of the nation (Arlosoroff), the "foundation of the national edifice"
(Aharonowitz). It was therefore absurd to speak about the city taking over
the village.[37] Arlosoroff agreed with Yaffe about the overcentralization of
the Histadrut and the centralizing tendencies of the proposed regulations of
the Nir company, but in principle he justified establishing the company in
order to ensure the community's control of the individual and the authority
of the movement over all its parts.[38] Arlosoroff, however, was rebuked by
Katznelson for daring to disagree, not with the idea of setting up the company, but with the way it was to be done. In an article signed "Yeruba'el,"
the editor of *Davar* attacked this destructive criticism by a member of the
executive, a man who held a key post in the movement, but there was no
hint of disagreement with Arlosoroff's statement about the meaninglessness
of "class phraseology" in the Palestinian context.[39]

When he appeared at the convention in Haifa at the beginning of February 1926, Katznelson made no secret of the fact that the rationale for establishing the company was to consolidate the Histadrut's power base and

independence and not to create a model of an alternative society. In transferring ownership of the collective settlements to Nir, the Histadrut sought to guarantee its status by creating an irreversible situation. Katznelson explained this very clearly in his opening address. "In recent years," he said, "various attempts have been made in the Zionist movement to attack our position. They do not want to recognize that our autonomy is a prerequisite for building the land. . . . There have been attempts to conduct negotiations with the settlers over the heads of those called 'leaders.'" The idea that there could be direct contact between the pioneers and the suppliers of capital was felt to be fatally harmful to the Histadrut's ability to control the Zionist movement. For its leaders, this represented a deathblow to the project of conquering the land. But the danger was not only external; it was also internal. There was therefore a need for permanent public ownership of the means of production. The possibility that agricultural settlements, especially moshavim, would pass into the private ownership of the settlers had to be avoided at all costs. Moreover, said Katznelson, the farms were not only the product of those who worked on them but resulted from the efforts of the entire "class" or community. It followed that all colonization had to "be controlled by the entire class,"[40] which of course was represented by the Histadrut.

To provide an illustration of destructive processes that could occur after the cooling of revolutionary ardor, Katznelson turned to New Zealand. A man who never ceased extolling the uniqueness of Jewish settlement in Palestine, its pioneering character and moral quality, did not hesitate, when necessary, to use "an example from the general history of colonization." After all, he said, the process of privatization, which had taken place after the original settlers in New Zealand had adopted bourgeois values, could happen in Nahalal as well. People are not so different, and ideology per se was not enough to prevent the disintegration of collective settlement. To the pioneers who were offended by the insinuation that they were about to betray their principles, Katznelson retorted: "This is not a matter of personal trust or of personal insult but a matter of understanding reality and the conditions of the environment."[41] Katznelson's thinking was similar to Aharonowitz's; Aharonowitz insisted on the necessity of resisting the "evil impulse," and thus on the necessity of extending public ownership not only to land and to material possessions such as houses, machines, livestock, and so on, but also to spiritual possessions such as independent labor and mutual aid. Not only did Aharonowitz claim that Nahalal had cost "seventy to eighty thousand pounds" and that it therefore belonged to the entire labor movement, and not only to its inhabitants, but he also wanted human weaknesses to be taken into account.

Like Katznelson and all the other founders, Aharonowitz opposed individualism and had little faith in the instincts of the masses. "To entrust the people with guarding our values is tantamount to abandoning them," he wrote.[42] According to him, Nir's task was to counteract the weaknesses of the individual and hence the limitations of democracy through social and organizational coercion. Yaffe had compared the relationship of the settlers to the Histadrut to the position of children in adult society. Aharonowitz and Katznelson unhesitatingly answered that human nature requires that freedom be carefully circumscribed. Good intentions, they said, are volatile, but the power of organization enables one to cope with changing circumstances. Ben-Gurion summed the matter up in a clear and unequivocal formula: "The main thing is the worker and his willingness to be organized for a common productivity." He claimed that Nir was "in all essentials the Histadrut." It reflected the Histadrut because it was "the means of creating the basis of existence for the Jewish people."[43]

Despite the constant striving for a concentration of power by controlling the lives of Histadrut and party members, the illusion was maintained that the Histadrut was a voluntary organization, and pressures exerted on the individual remained within tolerable limits because these builders of the nation needed disciplined executants and not political saints. This was the reason that such a tremendous effort was put into the system of economic control, whereas workers' education was given a low priority. The founders did in fact recognize the importance of culture as a tool for developing national consciousness, but they never gave education and culture the same weight as economic power. Economic power was used to create relations of dependence between the individual and the community which could have existed only in a society that saw itself as an army mobilized to perform collective tasks and not as a collection of individuals who came together to serve their private interests.

The main decisions at the agricultural convention were made unanimously. Among them was the decision that the Histadrut would own 41 percent of the initial shares of the company. Membership in Nir was on an individual basis, and all kibbutz and moshav members had to belong to it. Ben-Gurion rejected Elkind's proposal that kibbutzim be allowed to join Nir collectively. The majority also supported Ben-Gurion in another controversial matter: his proposal that a normal majority in the general meeting of the company would be sufficient to take measures "to attract private capital to the enterprise."

In order to ensure the dominance of the Histadrut executive, which for all practical matters meant Ben-Gurion, in the current management of the company, it was decided that the initial shares could be voted on according to the instructions of the Administrative Council of the Society of Workers, and not only according to the decisions of the Histadrut convention, as Elkind wanted.[44] This was a practical application of the principle, formulated by Ben-Gurion in the general debate, that "the Hevrat Ha'ovdim and 'Nir' are simply the legal clothing of the Histadrut." "The Hevrat Ha'ovdim and the Histadrut," he said, "must be identical, and the people working, voting, and making decisions in 'Nir' should be the same as in the Histadrut, without any possibility of change or alteration."[45] Katznelson adopted a similar viewpoint in answer to detractors, and he dismissed Elkind's anxieties about a "hierarchy" and his fear, which he shared with Yaffe, that the pioneers might lose their independence.[46]

Ben-Gurion and Katznelson wanted a unity of command and a concentration of all authority in the Histadrut executive. They were not too concerned about small details and formal arrangements. The plan of founding a company that would centralize the ownership of farms had already been discussed in the years before the decision was made—at the agricultural convention at Petah Tiqwa and the second Histadrut convention in Tel Aviv in 1923 (both conventions took place simultaneously), but there was strong criticism of the way in which a question of such decisive importance was brought up at the agricultural convention in Haifa. The complaints of Yaffe and others on this score appear to have some justification. Ben-Gurion claimed at the end of the convention that the question of Nir "has been discussed among us more and better than any other issue," but Katznelson admitted that "there was a need for a deeper examination of the question. There was no forum for it in the Histadrut, for an agricultural convention had not been held for a long time. At any rate, we did everything openly and not in secret."[47] The founders did not feel any need to indulge in procedural hairsplitting, and the question of whether the matter was brought up for discussion by moshav and kibbutz members and not only by party workers, some of whom had long before ceased to do any physical labor or had never done any at all, did not trouble them in the least. In many ways, the opposite was true. Histadrut institutions were built in such a way that there was no need to obtain the agreement of the many who were not politically active. In accordance with the principle that the elite had the right to lead the way, people like Katznelson, Arlosoroff, and Rachel Yannait (Ben-Zvi's wife and a well-known politician in her own right), who lived in the city and whose real profession was politics, were elected at the Haifa convention to the agricultural council with its twenty-eight members. This also applied to Levi Shkolnik (Eshkol), who in theory was a kibbutz member but who was really a professional party worker. After he became a member of the Agricultural Center, Eshkol never again worked in agriculture. Members of the leadership were in need of social myths: the myth of equality, the myth of pioneering activity. In 1931 Katznelson, like all employees of *Davar*, filled in a personal questionnaire. To the question "Do you belong to a farm or a pioneering organization?" he answered in the affirmative, describing himself as a member of Kvutzat (Kibbutz) Kinneret.[48] In the summer of

1939, when he appeared before the Central Committee of Hakibbutz Hame'uhad, Katznelson introduced himself as an "Eretz Israeli worker."[49]

In the final analysis, the founders regarded the establishment of Nir as "a major political conquest."[50] The question of whether a society like the kibbutz, in which private property was eliminated and equality achieved, was better than a system based on private capital and should constitute a model for life in the cities did not come up at the convention at all. On the contrary, Ben-Gurion, Katznelson, and Arlosoroff made it perfectly clear that their intention was not socializing the means of production but only strengthening the position of the Histadrut as the vehicle of national enterprise. "Our institutions have a class form," declared Katznelson, ". . . but they have a national content."[51] If we remember that the term *class* was applied to the entire Histadrut, we realize that a serious demand for socializing the means of production and for equality would have jeopardized the whole system. Any attempt to apply the principles of the rural areas to the cities would have contradicted the task of the Histadrut as builder of the nation and would have led to its breakup. The vast majority of Histadrut members were urban salaried workers or agricultural workers in villages who had no inclination for communal living. The transformation of their private property, which was ultimately derived from capital imported from abroad, into the collective property of a "class" would have required a social revolution. Not only was such a revolution unfeasible, but it was the last thing the founders wanted.

Moreover, when Nir was set up, it was clear that the principle of family wages (see chapter 6) had long before been abandoned and that the Histadrut leadership did not hesitate to provide for itself a standard of living out of all proportion with that of manual workers. Ben-Gurion and Aharonowitz, who were among those who benefited from the situation, and Katznelson, who turned a blind eye to it, saw no reason to object to the tremendous gap between the pioneers in the Jezreel Valley and the office workers in Tel Aviv. They believed that collective ownership of property depended on national requirements and was not an end in itself. It was therefore applicable only to kibbutz or moshav members, who, in Katznelson's words, were "the vanguard of our enterprise and the forefront of the thinking of the entire movement."[52] The pioneer bore a yoke that did not have to be imposed, and in fact could not be imposed, on the urban wage earner. But in order to be quite certain, the performance of duties was not left to ideological enthusiasm, and a rigid judicial framework was created, forestalling any danger of disintegration of the social system.

The functional principle that guided the Histadrut in all its activities was particularly strongly expressed in its relationship with Gdud Ha'avoda. The tension between Ben-Gurion and Elkind was blatant at the agricultural convention in Haifa. Ben-Gurion attacked the leader of the Gdud, the only person capable of opposing him, in every way possible and fought every proposal he made. The former wanted to concentrate power in the hands of the executive, whereas the latter defended the autonomy of the settlers.[53] The decisions arrived at were a victory for the principle of the nation's primacy; values such as individual freedom and the hope for a better society were subordinated to national interests. The Gdud wanted to apply the principles of equality to the urban sector as well, whereas the leadership of the movement wished to restrict public ownership of the means of production to agricultural settlements. There can be no doubt that freeing the urban sector from the yoke of communal ownership put an end to all hope of large-scale social change.

THE CULT OF DISCIPLINE AND AUTHORITY: THE DESTRUCTION OF GDUD HA'AVODA (THE LABOR CORPS)

Gdud Ha'avoda (literally, the labor battalion) came into being at the end of August 1920, more than three months before the founding of the Histadrut, but its inaugural convention at its camp near the village of Migdal, on the Sea of Galilee, did not take place until 17 and 18 June 1921. The Gdud, which was the chief original creation of the Third Aliyah (although sometimes described as a "blend of the Second and Third Aliyahs"),[54] sought to be an independent ideological, social, and organizational unit. Most of its members belonged to the Third Aliyah. Most of the people of the Second Aliyah who joined it were nonconformists, mainly veterans of the paramilitary Hashomer who were unable to find a place in the new organizations created after the First World War. Others who joined the Gdud were members of the Second Aliyah, like Tabenkin, who joined the Gdud in order to try to control the new body, or like Shlomo Levkovitch (Lavi), originator of the idea of the "large kvutza" (for all practical needs *kvutza* and *kibbutz* are interchangeable), who hoped that the Gdud could serve as an instrument for the realization of his ideas.[55] Lavi and his group, who founded Ein Harod in the autumn of 1921 on lands apportioned to the Gdud in an area named Nuris, in the eastern part of the Jezreel Valley (near the Well of Harod, famous in ancient Jewish history), wished to build large kibbutzim with an absorptive capacity in which agriculture would be combined with industry, instead of the small kvutzot of the time of the Second Aliyah. They were not interested in the idea of a single countrywide commune favored by the Gdud; in many respects they were a foreign body in the organization and soon created a split in its ranks, leading to the separation of Ein Harod from Tel Yosef.[56] The "large kvutza" was simply a development of the small kvutza and at the same time was inspired by Syrkin's cooperative projects. By contrast, the Gdud represented a new departure and had real revolutionary potential. Its idea of a single countrywide commune was the only chance of building a true socialist society.

Chronologically, the Gdud preceded the Histadrut, and many of its members regarded the Histadrut as a creation of the new immigrants. "We believe the Gdud created the Histadrut," declared one of its founders to Remez, who defended the seniority of the Histadrut at the Gdud's inaugural convention at Migdal.[57] This opinion, which was generally held by the pioneers of the Gdud, was a cause of friction with the heads of Ahdut Ha'avoda from the time the Gdud was founded. The founding of the Gdud took place during the commemorative ceremony for Yosef Trumpeldor, held six months after his death, on 25 August 1920. The founders comprised about a hundred members of the Crimean Commune—immigrants from the Crimea—or Trumpeldorians, as they were called at that time, who worked on the Tiberias-Tzemah road, on the shore of the Sea of Galilee. It was quite typical that the report in the Ahdut Ha'avoda weekly *Kuntras* appeared only on one page and consisted only of a short sentence stating indirectly that "Gdud Ha'avoda was founded in those days."[58]

The fact that members of Hashomer, which formally disbanded at a meeting at Tel 'Adashim on 18 and 19 May 1920, participated in the founding of the Gdud was in itself a cause of tension between the new organization and Ahdut Ha'avoda. At its convention at Kinneret in June 1920, Ahdut Ha'avoda took over the tasks of security formerly carried out by Hashomer. Hashomer members, led by Israel Shochat, had difficulty resigning themselves to their loss of employment. Shochat lost no opportunity to urge the creation of the Gdud, and his friends from Hashomer joined the new immigrants who were streaming to work on the Tzemah-Tiberias and Tiberias-Tabha roads, the two roads adjoining the Sea of Galilee. Shochat was officially one of the heads of Ahdut Ha'avoda but adopted a position opposed to that of the party and continually clashed with its leadership. He was the only member present at the commemorative ceremony for Trumpeldor and at the ceremony of the founding of the Gdud, and he did all he could to give it an especially colorful and festive character.[59]

Moreover, the Kfar Giladi agricultural settlement, the fortress of the Hashomer veterans, which was founded in October 1916, joined the Gdud, as did most of the members of neighboring Tel Hai. The majority in Tel Hai wanted to amalgamate with Kfar Giladi within the framework of the Gdud. The question of these two northern kibbutzim proved to be a time bomb for the Gdud. In time, it became not only a source of continuous friction with the Histadrut but a means of destroying the Gdud. The desire of Hashomer members to enjoy wide autonomy in defense matters in the Galilee panhandle, their control of their own store of weapons, and their wish to obtain military training in Russia were a thorn in the side of people like Ben-Gurion and Golomb. There is no doubt that this eagerness for independence represented both a challenge to the leadership of the movement and a threat to its capacity to perform essential functions. Ben-Gurion exploited the struggle between the majority in Tel Hai and the minority faithful to Ahdut Ha'avoda, not only in order to neutralize the members of Hashomer, but in order to destroy the Gdud as a whole. The stockpiling of weapons ultimately provided a suitable pretext for expelling about a hundred pioneers of the northern kibbutzim from the Histadrut without a trial through an administrative decision by the Executive Committee.[60]

The first clash between the Gdud and Ahdut Ha'avoda occurred in November 1920, just after the Gdud had been founded and several years before the Kfar Giladi affair had developed into a "security" crisis. The Gdud came into being in the course of the road-laying operations that the British authorities began in the summer of 1920. At the end of that year, 1,100 to 1,350 workers were employed on the roads, most of them new immigrants. Only part of the work was done on the roads of the Sea of Galilee; at that period, roads were laid from Haifa to Nazareth and from Nazareth to Tiberias.[61] There is no doubt that the pioneering enthusiasm of the workers represented a potential that Ahdut Ha'avoda could not ignore, but the Gdud wanted to be an independent contractor for public works, receiving its projects directly from the Department of Public Works of the government of Palestine, whereas Ahdut Ha'avoda, through its Agricultural Workers' Federation, demanded exclusive control in accordance with its usual policy.

The Gdud's demands were discussed at two meetings of the Ahdut Ha'avoda executive and at a joint meeting of the representatives of its executive and those of the Gdud. The Gdud was represented by Yehuda Kopelevitch (Almog), one of the founders of the Hehalutz (Pioneer) movement in Russia; Itzhak Landoberg (Sadeh), the leader of the Gdud on the Tiberias-Tzemah road and later a legendary figure of the Hagana and an IDF general; Menachem Elkind, a powerful figure who refused to bow to Ben-Gurion's authoritarian style of leadership; and Israel Shochat. Before the meeting took place, the Gdud created a de facto situation, which immediately brought it into an inevitable conflict with Ahdut Ha'avoda. The regulations of the Gdud were drawn up in October 1920, and its committee submitted a request for recognition to the mandatory government in accordance with the law of 1920 on cooperative associations. The request carried the signatures of the three founders: Sadeh, Almog, and Shochat. From that moment on, the Gdud was regarded as a dangerous competitor to Ahdut Ha'avoda and met, as might be expected, with stubborn opposition. The tension persisted after the Bureau of Public Works (later Sollel Boneh) was founded at the first council of the Histadrut in Jaffa on 12–19 February 1921. Two days later the council of the Bureau of Public Works met in Haifa, and Katznelson and Remez, who fought the Gdud from its inception, demanded the imposition of Histadrut discipline and rejected the social concepts of the Gdud. They had no interest in the idea of a countrywide commune.[62]

In the months between the founding of the Histadrut and the convention at Migdal, the Gdud gained new members, sent a company to Rosh Ha'Ayin, on the coastal plain not far from Tel Aviv, dispatched people to set things in order in Kibbutz Kfar Giladi, and set up its own internal organization. In this period, Brenner joined its camp at Migdal as a teacher and lecturer. The first issue of the Gdud's journal, *Hasollel*, appeared on 26 December 1920, edited by Brenner.[63] The growth of the Gdud necessitated its institutionalization. Taking advantage of the fact that all the companies were present, the general convention that took place at Migdal on 17 and 18 June 1921 endorsed the Gdud's regulations.

At the beginning of the document in question, the aims of the organization were defined: "To build up the land through the creation of a general commune of Jewish workers in Eretz Israel." This general declaration of intent was followed by five principles.

1. All members are to be organized in kibbutzim that are under the authority of the Histadrut in all matters relating to work and defense.

2. A general fund is to be set up to cover members' needs.

3. All members' needs are to be provided for by the production of the Gdud.

4. Expansion of economic activities and improvement of working conditions are to come about through a reinvestment of profits.

5. The Histadrut should be strengthened and encouraged to adopt the path of the Gdud.[64]

Naturally the last point aroused the deepest suspicions in the Ahdut Ha'avoda leadership, especially as in the opening session of the gathering Elkind spoke of a "conquest of the Histadrut." "It is clear to us," he said, "that the general fund can be used for many purposes."[65] This insistence on imposing the values and organizational patterns of the Gdud on the Histadrut could mean only one thing: the Gdud wanted a different Histadrut. Elkind later said that he had wanted "the whole Histadrut to become a Gdud."[66] Thus, Remez (who together with Ben-Zvi, Golomb, and Shochat was invited to attend the discussions at the convention) warned that the adoption of the proposed regulations "would lead to a total opposition between the Histadrut and the Gdud." He feared that the economic success of the Gdud would mean that this communist organization would overshadow the Histadrut: "It is obvious that if the Gdud makes a profit for years . . . it will become more aggressive and hinder the Histadrut's development." Remez wished to counteract the Gdud's ideological fervor by obliging it to function within the Histadrut framework. "The Gdud," he said, "does not need any institutions of its own, because, if it had them, it would cause a war between us."[67]

But this was not all. Unlike Ben-Gurion, who at that time toyed with the idea of a commune, and unlike Remez, who regarded the idea of a general commune of all workers in Eretz Israel as a long-term alibi permitting economic power and the reserves of manpower to be concentrated in the hands of the Agricultural Center and the Bureau of Public Works, the Gdud, by means of its common treasury, began to practice the principle of collective living throughout the country, from Kfar Giladi to Jerusalem. "The Gdud has a specific path," said Elkind. "It is a communist enterprise. We do not think that the cooperative institutions [set up by the Histadrut] are very efficient, but, where they are, we shall support them." Elkind believed that "only a small portion" of the profits should be distributed among members, and "the rest should be used for building the country according to our ideas."[68] In other words, Elkind denied the basic principles of nationalist socialism, known in the country as constructive socialism. From the viewpoint of Ben-Gurion, who was much more interested in practical solutions than in ideological principles, Elkind's position was acceptable as long as it could contribute to the development of the country, but Remez, Katznelson, Lavi, and Tabenkin, violently anti-Marxist nationalists, soon came to see Elkind and his group as enemies of the people. Before long, however, Ben-Gurion joined them.

At first Ahdut Ha'avoda tried to dominate the Gdud, but it encountered stubborn opposition from the leaders of the new immigrants. Gdud activists were not enthusiastic about Tabenkin's joining them, because they knew that he had come to place the Gdud under the authority of the party that dominated the Histadrut. They were careful not to appoint a man who was one of the main leaders of Ahdut Ha'avoda to the Gdud executive. The only position he was given was on the supervisory committee, and the highest level he reached was that of a candidate for the executive. Lavi was not elected to the executive either but was a member of the committees for budgeting and settlement.[69] Thus, the leadership of Ahdut Ha'avoda, and especially the former nonparty group, which had contributed much to the liquidation of the Po'alei Tzion Party, now found itself faced with a new challenge. For a moment it seemed as if all their work was about to come to nothing.

Nevertheless, in July 1921 the Ahdut Ha'avoda executive decided to permit the Gdud to settle on lands acquired in the Jezreel Valley. On 21 September a first "company" went up to a place near the Well of Harod and founded Ein Harod. It was near this spring that Gideon had set up his camp on the eve of the battle against the Midianites. There, out of the 22,000 men he had assembled, he chose the 300 with whom he went to battle by the way they "lapped, putting their hand to their mouths" (Judg. 7:6).

The first company was followed, a short time later, by a second, and on 13 December Tel Yosef was founded. The Gdud laid claim to all the thirty thousand *dunams* (one dunam equals one thousand square meters, or approximately one-quarter acre) in the Nuris area but had to be content with a little more than half of that. About ten days before they went up to the Well of Harod, another group of pioneers went to the western part of the valley and founded the first *moshav ovdim* (semicollective, cooperative smallholders' settlement), Nahalal. At the end of 1921 and in 1922, the kibbutzim Geva, Hefziba, and Beit Alpha and the moshav Kfar Yehezkel, originally called Ein Tivon, were founded in the eastern valley.[70]

To the question of why Ahdut Ha'avoda decided to let the Gdud settle at the Well of Harod there is no simple answer. The usual explanation given by contemporaries was that at that period Ahdut Ha'avoda still hoped to absorb the Gdud.[71] This explanation seems reasonable, but there are others. In addition, another factor must be taken into consideration. The Labor Corps, which was fashioned in the laying of roads near the Sea of Galilee and was made up of enthusiastic young pioneers, constituted the best material for colonization that had ever existed in Eretz Israel. Nobody was then able to oppose ceding them the lands at Nuris. It is reasonable to suppose that when Ahdut Ha'avoda decided to settle the Gdud in the valley and made Lavi part of the founding nucleus of Ein Harod, it was on the assumption that the Gdud would be absorbed into the party, and that eventually Ein Harod would grow into a large kvutza. In reality, however, Lavi represented a second time bomb for the Gdud. This man, who was one of the nine founders of Hapo'el Hatza'ir[72] and an integral nationalist, was far from sharing the views of the hard core of the pioneers of the Gdud.

The question of how close the Gdud should be to the Histadrut and Ahdut Ha'avoda was the subject of heated ideological debate within the Gdud itself. Most internal disagreements revolved around this point. Before the split into the Left and the Right, and before the common land and property were divided between Ein Harod and Tel Yosef, a minority opposed the regulations of the Gdud as formulated at Migdal. (Among this minority was Lavi, who was to create a crisis leading to the flight of about a hundred people from the Gdud and to the re-formation of Ein Harod as a "large kvutza"). But despite this disagreement, and despite the difference between those who wished to retain a formal connection with the Histadrut (although they were displeased with the direction it was taking) and those who wished to make that connection dependent on certain conditions, there was agreement on the main point: the Gdud had to infuse the Histadrut with its own spirit. From Ahdut Ha'avoda, "as a socialist party," the Gdud demanded staunch support, including a rejection of the establishment of moshavim.[73]

The radicals took up a strong position: "Our way is not submission to Histadrut discipline but bringing the path of the Histadrut into conformity with that of the Gdud. . . . We must say this openly, without making vague statements about the Gdud wanting to strengthen the Histadrut and things of that nature, hiding the truth and causing mental confusion." In addition to strongly worded statements of this kind in *Mehayenu* (the Gdud's journal, which superseded *Hasollel* after the sixth issue), equally forceful articles appeared in the journal urging a peaceful coexistence and collaboration within the Histadrut of "people who want to live a socialist life" and the large masses of workers not attracted by a collective way of living. I must point this out clearly: ideas in favor of preserving the close connection with the Histadrut were given a prominent place in *Mehayenu*, and they were expressed with as much forcefulness as those of the radicals.[74]

The relationship between the pioneer leadership and some of the members of the Histadrut leadership was potentially very explosive, and Gdud members were well aware of it. The most visible immediate source of this conflict was the violent disagreement with the Bureau of Public Works. "Our relations with the bureau are one long series of antagonisms, clashes, and misunderstandings," wrote Sadeh.[75] These struggles were due to the different character of the Histadrut and the Gdud, and not only to the conflicting interests of a contractor for building and road construction and of those who performed the work. Similarly, the conflict between the Agricultural Center and the Gdud was not only about the lands at Nuris. The Gdud objected in principle to settlement in moshavim because it viewed it as a distortion of the Histadrut's purpose and an expression of its refusal to adopt collective policies. Its fight against the bureau, whose director was Remez, who rejected the Gdud's existence, was based on its demand for the implementation of principles of self-management and equal pay. Remez wanted to preserve the existing powers of centralization and control. His motivation was not only economic, however; he opposed the Gdud precisely because he saw it as the nucleus of a new society. The economic success of the Gdud would have endangered the very existence of the Histadrut as conceived by its founders.[76] To prevent this from happening, the bureau used its most lethal weapon: it asked the Gdud to repay the debts it had incurred when it built the roads.[77] The obligation to repay these debts not only prevented the Gdud's settlements in the Jezreel Valley from getting on their feet but turned the entire Labor Corps, with its urban sections and kibbutzim, into a hostage of Ahdut Ha'avoda. The Gdud made a fatal mistake when it agreed to assume responsibility for this debt, whereas the bureau got rid of its own debts (which were considerable) by passing them on to the World Zionist Organization. The leadership of the Gdud realized its error only too late.

The apparent patience of Ahdut Ha'avoda toward the Gdud at the beginning should not deceive us with regard to its aim of ultimately bringing the organization under its control. Ben-Gurion, who had an extraordinary manipulative talent, tried at a certain stage to draw the Gdud toward Ahdut Ha'avoda. When the second Histadrut convention was being prepared and the party's domination of the Histadrut was not yet assured, he approached the Gdud and the other kibbutzim in the valley in an attempt to broaden and strengthen the party's support. When he appeared on 3 December 1922 at a meeting of representatives of kibbutzim at Tel Yosef, Ben-Gurion spoke like a member of the Gdud. He declared his intention to make the kibbutzim his power base. "The opinion of the kibbutzim assembled here," he said, "should be decisive at the convention. What is needed in our work from now on is a strong organized body that will lead the way for the masses of work-ers." Ben-Gurion complained of the weakness of the Histadrut, its lack of a real center of power, and the inability of the organization to dominate its different elements. "The Histadrut," he declared, "can and should be every-thing in this country," but it was "not yet created. Now we must create it." He asked for the support of the kibbutzim in his struggle to control the sources of funding in the hands of the World Zionist Organization, for with-out an independent financial basis, he said, "We cannot hope to achieve autonomy in our activities."[78]

Ben-Gurion knew very well that these views were acceptable to kibbutz members. Although he did not say anything about ideological partnership, kibbutz representatives obviously supported him. The Gdud's platform at the convention reflected this common ground. The first section, referring to the "constitution of the Histadrut," stated that "the Histadrut's sphere of activity will embrace all matters relating to the workers—economic, politi-cal, and cultural." Elsewhere, the platform read: "The Histadrut executive will concentrate in its hands the management of all work carried out in the country (agriculture, building, industry, public projects), the supply of goods, and all other matters relating to the workers."[79]

Ben-Gurion did not ask for more than that. But whereas Elkind and other representatives of the kibbutzim, such as Hillel Dan (a representative of the band of pioneers known as the Emek [Valley] group), wished the Hista-drut to be a "cooperative of organized bodies,"[80] Ben-Gurion felt that a His-tadrut composed of individuals would be much easier to control and would therefore be a more effective operative tool than a Histadrut made up of social forces united by their ideological conceptions. An organized body, as one of the components of the Histadrut, could very easily turn into a com-petitor of Ahdut Ha'avoda. Did not the founders of the Gdud, the new immi-grants under Elkind, tip the scales at the time the Histadrut was founded? A Histadrut in which priority would be given to communes with a socialist ideology, which not only demanded "a total equalization of salaries" but "the delegation of work to organized kibbutzim on their full responsi-bility,"[81] would be a completely different Histadrut from the one that was actually founded and controlled by Ahdut Ha'avoda. When, after the second Histadrut convention, it became clear to Ben-Gurion that the Gdud had no intention of merging with Ahdut Ha'avoda, and that he had nothing to fear from Hapo'el Hatza'ir (Sprinzak, Aharonowitz, and Eshkol had no wish to wage an ideological struggle on behalf of the "collectivists" who opposed the establishment of moshavim), he felt free to eliminate this potential political danger.

This did not prove difficult. The leadership of the Gdud did not have a talent for manipulation comparable with Ben-Gurion's or Remez's; it never acquired the wonderful ideological flexibility of Arlosoroff or Aharonowitz, nor did it learn to close its eyes or look the other way like Katznelson. Gdud members regarded Ahdut Ha'avoda as a political body whose socialist character was in doubt, a quagmire of contradictory trends and orientations. They resented the fact that the party of Ben-Gurion and Katznelson never attempted to realize the principles of sharing and equality that it professed. Unlike Ahdut Ha'avoda, not only did the Gdud adhere uncompromisingly to the principles of equality and mutual aid administered through the common treasury, but its leaders set a personal example. They labored strenuously, first in laying roads and afterward in the fields of the Jezreel Valley. They laid the foundations of Ein Harod and Tel Yosef with their own hands and suffered with the rest from weakness and malnutrition. That was their great mistake. Instead of embarking on a political career, taking over the administrative jobs in the Bureau of Public Works while that was still possible and seizing key positions in the Histadrut, they continued to work hard and realize the principles of equality, autonomous labor, and personal example. While Elkind, Almog, and Sadeh were setting up or re-creating kibbutzim, spreading Gdud companies from the Upper Galilee to Jerusalem, and building and stonecutting, the heads of Ahdut Ha'avoda were making politics into a profession, setting up an apparatus and binding thousands of isolated, unorganized workers to the Histadrut without regarding themselves as being for a single moment obligated to set a personal example. Here, once again, Elkind and Almog recognized their error too late.[82]

When tensions between the Gdud and Ahdut Ha'avoda worsened, Ben-Gurion decided to give favorable consideration to Lavi's old demand that Ein Harod be taken away from the Gdud, as a way of striking at those who were now perceived as political opponents. Lavi wished to break up the Gdud by eliminating the common treasury, and therefore he sought to prevent any possibility that the budgets allocated to Ein Harod would be transferred to other settlements. This stratagem was simple but effective: Lavi accused the Gdud of embezzlement. He did not claim that the treasurer of the Gdud or one of its leaders had taken public money for his personal use. His allegation was simply that the account of Ein Harod was debited to the sum of a thousand pounds to cover a debt incurred by another Gdud commune, and that there were also rumors that various branches in Ein Harod were in deficit. On the basis of these assertions, Lavi turned to the Histadrut authorities and asked that the supply of money to the Gdud's treasury be stopped. On 2 December 1922 he made a declaration about its actions,[83] bringing the crisis to a head.

The next day, the meeting of kibbutzim at which Ben-Gurion asked for their support at the Histadrut convention took place at Tel Yosef. Ben-Gurion, who formally was only a member of the secretariat of the Histadrut executive (the post of secretary-general did not yet exist), did not refer to the Lavi episode either then or in the ensuing weeks, but when he felt the time was ripe, he applied the full weight of the Histadrut steamroller on behalf of Ahdut Ha'avoda.[84] Not only did the Histadrut prevent Lavi and his supporters from being expelled from the Gdud, but it demanded a division of the joint economy. Lavi's group was based at Ein Harod and the Gdud's adherents were gathered together at Tel Yosef. Although supporters of the large kvutza in Ein Harod numbered only 105 and 225 people were at Tel Yosef, the Histadrut decided to divide the joint economy into two equal parts. When the people in Tel Yosef refused to divide the property equally between themselves and Ein Harod, the party retaliated. Ben-Gurion acted swiftly and with cruelty, and he did not shrink from using any means, including withholding medical aid, food supplies, and other necessities.[85] A blockade was imposed on Tel Yosef.

Here it is worth pausing to consider the significance of the sanctions the Histadrut imposed under the direction of Ben-Gurion in light of what it meant to be a pioneer in the Jezreel Valley. Settlement there at that period demanded an intolerably high price. Living conditions required a supreme physical and spiritual effort, and the people in Tel Yosef were at the limit of their capacities. Not only were shoes considered a luxury (they were working tools, acquired first for those unable to work without them), but basic foodstuffs often were in short supply. When the blockade was imposed, Gdud leaders could find no better way to call attention to their plight than to publish the following section of a report, presented to the kibbutz by Dr. Ben-Zion Hirschowitz, the physician in charge of the small Kupat Holim hospital at Ein Harod.

> 1. There is an increasing number of people sick with malaria. 2. The number of relapses is increasing despite intensive medical care. 3. Careful examinations reveal that all the inhabitants of both places have become anemic, which is very alarming. 4. The average weight of the inhabitants is dropping. 5. The number of people complaining of a lack of strength and a general weakness is continually increasing. 6. The number of cases of tuberculosis is increasing at such a rate that we fear the epidemic may spread to the whole camp.
>
> There is no doubt that if the present situation continues for any length of time, only invalids and the chronically sick will be left in the camp.
>
> The causes are: 1. A general lack of food. 2. A lack of special foods and treatment for the sick and for women in confinement.

I know how difficult the situation is in the country as a whole and in the valley in particular, and for that reason I do not wish to touch on this point in this memorandum. I feel it is more important to draw attention to what is happening here. The kitchen of the infirmary does not receive enough health-giving food to enable the invalids to regain their strength, and there is sometimes a shortage of small things of great importance to the sick, such as sugar, tea, lemon, etc.[86]

Under these conditions, nothing could be expected of Gdud members except complete surrender. The Agricultural Center fought against them mercilessly; Sollel Boneh, with the unfailing support of the Histadrut executive under Ben-Gurion, placed a throttle around their neck; and the labor press was closed to them. Since the founding of *Davar* on 1 June 1925, Katznelson denied the Gdud any access to the Histadrut daily.[87] His explanations were lame and hypocritical, but there was no chance that anyone would call the editor to account.

The destruction of the Gdud by Ahdut Ha'avoda took place at a period when there were no disagreements about the overriding importance of national construction. The Gdud's devotion to national aims was outstanding throughout its first years, but its later turn to the Left is liable to cause this simple fact to be overlooked. Ahdut Ha'avoda, under the leadership of Ben-Gurion, declared total war on the Gdud at a time when all its members and leaders saw themselves no less as an advance party in the conquest of the land for the Jewish people than as tracers of a path toward a new society. The language the writers in *Mehayenu* used was entirely normal and acceptable for members of the Histadrut. The overwhelming majority of Gdud members and its leaders, including Elkind (they all expressed themselves a great deal both in speech and in writing), were of the opinion that 'the labor movement has a special character here, connected with the specific aim of the Jewish worker in this country, who, apart from his usual concerns, has the national objective of building the land."[88] When in February 1924, in a rare instance of deviation from this broad consensus, one member proposed introducing 'changes in our principles" to the effect that 'the Histadrut must organize all the workers in this country exclusively on a basis of class affiliation," he was answered by an editorial comment: 'In the regulations of the Gdud, it is written, 'Building the land through the creation of a general commune of Jewish workers in Eretz Israel,' and nothing more."[89] About a year and a half later, at the time of the turn to the Left, Elkind wrote, 'It was a different period in the life of the Gdud, in which the decisive factor in our activity was the national factor."[90]

The assault on the Gdud took place at the height of this initial period. The first blow—the separation of Ein Harod from Tel Yosef through the imposition of brutal sanctions—came in May–June 1923, less than six months after Ben-Gurion appeared at Tel Yosef in order to suggest to the Gdud and the other kibbutzim in the valley that they could play a central role in the second Histadrut convention. In these early years Hapo'el Hatza'ir refrained from supporting Ahdut Ha'avoda's struggle against the Gdud and adopted a neutral position. The integral nationalists in the Gordon tradition, led by Aharonowitz and Sprinzak, would not have hesitated to adopt a hostile position if they had the slightest doubt about the Gdud's loyalty to national objectives. They regarded the struggles in the Jezreel Valley, in Upper Galilee, and in the quarries of Jerusalem as an internal concern of Ahdut Ha'avoda. The leaders of Hapo'el Hatza'ir were not fond of Ben-Gurion's methods, but they were unwilling to quarrel with him over a matter they regarded as secondary.

At the same time, on 27 of August 1926, immediately after the expulsion from the Histadrut of members of Kfar Giladi and Tel Hai, the Central Committee of Hapo'el Hatza'ir published a public statement expressing doubts about the wisdom of expelling the settlements from the organization and preventing their unification. Although Sprinzak and Aharonowitz participated in that decision, and Ben-Gurion was careful to point this out at the third Histadrut convention in July 1927, they undoubtedly had misgivings about Ben-Gurion's ruthlessness. But the leaders of Hapo'el Hatza'ir were already contemplating union with Ahdut Ha'avoda, and although they knew that "were it not for the war waged against the Gdud for several years now, a number of negative things that are happening there today could have been avoided,"[91] they had no interest in engaging in a struggle against the Ahdut Ha'avoda leadership.

The move to the Left was a direct outcome of the war waged against the Gdud by the party. Some members in the Gdud's inner core, led by Elkind (who enjoyed as great an authority among his people as Ben-Gurion had already succeeded in gaining for himself in Ahdut Ha'avoda), came to the conclusion that if the Histadrut was unable to assimilate this experiment in building a new society while striving for national independence, there was no hope of realizing any major social ideals in Palestine.

This was the sole difference—although one that was real and historically significant—between the Gdud and Ahdut Ha'avoda. The Gdud was loyal to the basic goal of Zionism and attracted people who had come to the country in order to put it into practice. But the Gdud also had social aims and stuck to its ideals of equality and mutual aid to the bitter end. By contrast, Ahdut Ha'avoda, a party that from its inception was frightened of too unambiguous a socialist ideology, and that dominated a political economic body that was consciously nonideological, had no interest in universal values. Moreover, this authoritarian party, which throughout its existence was headed by a small nucleus of professional politicians, was unable to come to terms with the democratic and voluntaristic forms of self-administration prevalent in the Gdud: the frequent general assemblies, the long council meetings, the custom of bringing all important questions to a general vote. Nor were the principles of mutual responsibility and absolute equality, the style of leadership through personal example, any more acceptable.

The Gdud demanded a democratization of the Histadrut, which the leaders of Ahdut Ha'avoda regarded as a threat to the dominant position they had succeeded in gaining for themselves in the organization. They knew that if they adopted the proposal "of withdrawing the executive's right of imposing its authority on the conventions" or accepted the principle that "the conventions must have the power of independent decision,"[92] that would be fatal to the party. They soon understood that to prevent the emergence of a political and ideological alternative, the Gdud's economic basis had to be destroyed. All the organizations of the Histadrut were used for this purpose, and Ben-Gurion's efforts were crowned with success. Under his leadership the Histadrut became a brutal apparatus that cast its threatening shadow not only on the individual worker but also on organized bodies. From the mid-1920s on, Ahdut Ha'avoda's, and later Mapai's, control of the sources of credit and supplies made the leaders immune to any real alternative. The episode of Gdud Ha'avoda was a test case, a precedent and a warning to others; Hashomer Hatza'ir, which was close to the Gdud, did not summon the courage to oppose the campaign of punishment and vengeance. Kibbutz Beit Alpha did nothing more than provide Gdud members with horses and mules to help them move from Ein Harod to Tel Yosef, and it only sent a protest to the Histadrut executive. The political leadership of Hashomer Hatza'ir acted very prudently and in practice collaborated with Ben-Gurion. This represented the model of the relationship that henceforth existed between Ahdut Ha'avoda (and later Mapai) and the left wing of the Zionist movement.

With the decision of the Histadrut executive with regard to Ein Harod and Tel Yosef, it finally became clear that Ahdut Ha'avoda had no intention of taking socialist experiments beyond the boundaries of agricultural settlements. This was the reason for the Gdud's turn to the Left. Menachem Elkind and David Horowitz clearly expressed the new thinking during the celebrations of 1 May 1925. Horowitz declared that "there is a clear dividing line between the working-class concept of the nation and that of the bourgeoisie," and Elkind claimed that "the basis of our collectivistic economic organization [is] our class consciousness."[93] This emphasis on class increased to the point where there was a split between the Left and the Right, which soon became so acute that the breakup of the Gdud was inevitable.[94]

From the point of view of the Histadrut leadership, the Gdud was guilty of every cardinal sin of Yishuv politics. In addition to its social ideals and democratic practices, its leaders insisted on their right to be "emancipated from the control of the ideologists . . . of the Second Aliyah," whom they accused of "using their authority to destroy the type of organizations created by the Gdud." Moreover, the Gdud offered a total alternative to "the present path of Hevrat Ha'ovdim [the Society of Workers], the path of state capitalism." The Gdud stated that two systems were preferable to the one chosen by the Histadrut: "The path of cooperatives and of the commune." Even at this late stage, however, Elkind was careful to state that the Gdud had no intention of abandoning the principles of the Second Aliyah. "The Gdud," he said, "did not invent the nationalist and socialist foundations on which its ideology is based but inherited them from the Second Aliyah." That was how Elkind, in October 1925, summarized the report he had presented about three weeks earlier to the council of the Gdud, which met at Tel Yosef to mark its fourth anniversary.[95]

Such a formulation of the Gdud's aims from its leader was already a major step toward compromise with the Histadrut. It was Elkind's way of saying that he did not disagree with the idea that the Gdud sought to realize national as well as social objectives. The statement that the Gdud remained within the ideological tradition of the Second Aliyah was tantamount to holding out his hand to its right wing and an indication of his willingness to accept the authority of the Histadrut.[96] This was the point of contention between the Right and the Left in the Gdud: on the Left there was the Fraction—communists who rejected the principal aims of Zionism and wished to organize themselves as a political body or party with no affinity with the Jewish diaspora or the World Zionist Organization. The less extreme among them agreed "only to participate in those national enterprises which can create a workers' economy."[97] In the first months of 1925, the Gdud gave further evidence of its goodwill. Although at the council at Tel Yosef the Gdud had rejected by a majority of fourteen to twelve a motion to expel the communists from its ranks, at a council in Jerusalem on 15 December 1925 this decision was reversed. Here, the proposal of the Right, slightly amended, received a majority of eleven unopposed, with four abstaining. The decision to expel the Fraction was submitted to the companies for endorsement and was to come into effect within a month.[98]

But all this was not enough to appease those who had decided to destroy the one serious attempt to implement socialism outside the framework of the kibbutzim. After the agricultural convention of February 1926, Ben-Gurion felt he was in a position to launch a new and more sophisticated punitive campaign. The danger that a harsh treatment of the pioneers of the valley and the Galilee would cause a revolt among their neighbors in Moshav Nahalal and the kibbutzim of Beit Alpha or Ayelet Hashahar had now passed. Never before had a campaign of political "purification" comparable to this one taken place in a democratic socialist party. It was unparalleled in the free world, quite simply because nowhere else did a political economic organization exist with the capability to control the lives of its members. A dependence like that of Tel Yosef, Kfar Giladi, and Tel Hai on the Histadrut existed only in totalitarian countries. The Labor Corps may have had a leftist ideology, but Ben-Gurion used Stalinist methods. He exerted economic pressure, resorted to provocations, used libels, and demonstrated a formidable ability in the art of manipulating public opinion: Shabtai Teveth noted the facts from Ben-Gurion's point of view, without attempting to grasp their real significance.[99] The campaign of intimidation and pressure included the expulsion from the Histadrut of members of Kfar Giladi and the majority of members of Tel Hai, a hundred men and women. The process of disintegration was now inevitable, and Gdud Ha'avoda broke up in 1927.

The labor movement, in its struggle with the Gdud, reached the point of no return. Its decision to pursue national goals at the expense of social values was expressed in a concrete manner and with unmistakable vehemence. The conflict would never have reached this point had it not involved a struggle over ends as well as over means.[100] The Gdud was based on the principles of the commune and the common treasury: to each according to his or her needs, regardless of personal contribution. This principle was in contradiction to constructivism, which was concerned with building the economy, not with creating an egalitarian society. The leadership of the Gdud remained true to the principle of equality to the end. The Gdud was a true voluntary organization and showed perseverance in pursuing its social ideals, but it was not a revolutionary body. It did not threaten the existing order, which in any case it was incapable of doing, but sought to function as an autonomous political body and preached communal living through personal example. The Gdud represented the only opportunity that ever existed of creating urban communes, from which perhaps collective settlements based on crafts, industry, and the provision of services might have developed. There is no doubt that if it had been encouraged by the Histadrut, the Gdud could have conferred on the whole movement a totally different quality. Thus, the fact that the leadership of the movement decided to destroy the Gdud, even though the supremacy of the Histadrut was not threatened by Elkind and his associates, is especially significant. From a numerical point of view, the Gdud was infinitesimal; at the end of 1925 it consisted of fewer than six hundred people as opposed to the nearly twenty thousand members in the Histadrut, and there were frequent changes in members because of people leaving the organization. Moreover, the Gdud was not ideologically homogenous and was divided into the Right and the Left.

The threat from the Gdud did not lie in its power or its numbers. The true danger lay elsewhere: the Gdud was all that the Histadrut was not and all that (from a theoretical point of view) it ought to have been. It was a true alternative society, inasmuch as it offered a total moral, social, and economic alternative to capitalist society. It provided a model for the future and the living example of a community that was collective, voluntary, and consequently free. A member of the Gdud was not bound to it by a network of essential services: he or she was free to get up and leave at any moment. The Gdud symbolized the realization of the socialist utopia, and it was here that it represented a danger to the Histadrut and the party that dominated it. Thus, the true threat lay in the area of objectives: Ahdut Ha'avoda had created a system whose purpose was the implementation of Zionism and not the realization of socialism. Socialism was restricted to the kibbutz and never affected more than a negligible percentage of the Yishuv.

If the Gdud had been merely a political party, Ben-Gurion would not have fought against it with any greater determination than he had shown in opposing the Po'alei Tzion leftists. If it had been merely a settlement organization, its relations with Ahdut Ha'avoda would have resembled those between that party and Hashomer Hatza'ir. If it had only objected to the bureaucracy of the Histadrut or accused it of attempting to control the property of its members, as Yaffe had done, the problem would have been solved in the customary manner by one of the institutions of the Histadrut in which the leadership was always assured of a majority. In fact, the leaders preferred dealing with the nationalistic, individualistic, but pioneering Right in the Gordon tradition represented by Yaffe, as it at least left them free to forge links with the leading figures of Hapo'el Hatza'ir such as Sprinzak, Aharonowitz, and Arlosoroff. In the same vein, the controversy with the Po'alei Tzion leftists was purely ideological and thus, from a practical point of view, quite harmless, whereas the members of Hashomer Hatza'ir remained within their kibbutzim and accepted the authority of the Histadrut without difficulty. Meir Ya'ari stood at the head of the committee that represented Ben-Gurion in the final stages of the liquidation of the Gdud. In other words, Hashomer Hatza'ir followed the orders of Ahdut Ha'avoda.

Here let us turn our attention to another matter that casts light on the nature of the Gdud, but especially on the nature of the Histadrut. When the Gdud was in its death throes, before Elkind left the country for the Soviet Union, Tabenkin founded a new organization, which was later called Hakibbutz Hame'uhad. The inaugural convention of the new organization was held at Petah Tiqwa on 5 October 1927. The convention, encouraged by the Histadrut executive represented there by Katznelson, broadened the organizational framework created by Ein Harod immediately after the division of lands and property between Ein Harod and Tel Yosef. Despite the opposition of a group led by Lavi, who rejected the need for a single countrywide collective, Ein Harod, after the split, immediately began to function on a countrywide basis. The absorption, in July 1923, by the settlement of Ein Harod of a band of pioneers known as the Emek group in practice laid the foundations for a second Gdud, called Kibbutz–Ein Harod.[101] The first convention of Kibbutz–Ein Harod took place on 4 August 1923.

Thus, the members of Ein Harod, under the leadership of Tabenkin, set up an alternative Labor Corps. The second, enlarged convention of Kibbutz–Ein Harod on 29 August 1924 authorized the acceptance into the organization of Kibbutz Yagur, near Haifa. More than a year later, in October 1925, Kibbutz Ayelet Hashahar was also accepted. Meanwhile, companies of Kibbutz–Ein Harod were set up in Haifa, Petah Tiqwa, Rehovot, Balfouriyya, Jerusalem, Zikhron Ya'aqov, and Herzliyya. Eventually, these companies settled on the land. The Rehovot company settled at Giv'at Brenner, the Petah Tiqwa company founded Giv'at Hashlosha, and the Herzliyya company established Kibbutz Shafayim. From the beginning, Kibbutz–Ein Harod endowed itself with permanent institutions: a permanent council, an assembly. It moved people from place to place, added companies and disbanded them as needed, and followed the practice of accepting the decisions of the central authority.[102] Anita Shapira concluded that Kibbutz–Ein Harod and Hakibbutz Hame'uhad were organized by Tabenkin "according to principles extraordinarily similar to those of the Gdud."[103] This was true only in appearance, and only with regard to their formal structure, for the aims of the two organizations, apart from collective agriculture and settlement, were entirely different. Tabenkin did in fact regard the Gdud as the source of Hakibbutz Hame'uhad,[104] but here it is worth putting a question that I asked in chapter 2 concerning the foundation of Ahdut Ha'avoda. Just as I asked why an existing socialist party needed to be replaced by a new one, so one may ask now why Tabenkin, a member of the Gdud, engaged in a struggle against one countrywide kibbutz and immediately set up next to it, and after a time in place of it, another organization of the same kind.[105]

The answer lies precisely in the fact that this was not the same type of organization. Kibbutz–Ein Harod, and subsequently Hakibbutz Hame'uhad, did not have a common treasury, and after a short time it focused entirely on settlement. There were, however, experiments, like the one in Yagur, creating a "settlement combining agriculture with salaried labor, with the intention of founding a collective workers' district near Haifa," but the scheme was soon abandoned. The struggle between the Gdud and Ahdut Ha'avoda (let us not forget that Tabenkin was one of the leaders of the latter) was not, as Shapira claimed, a generational problem, a conflict between members of the Second and Third Aliyahs, or between two groups of leaders: one drawing its support from the pioneers of the Third Aliyah and the other deriving its authority from Ahdut Ha'avoda and building a power base through settlement.[106]

The real conflict was between two different conceptions of Zionism, collectivism and the Histadrut. Hakibbutz Hame'uhad did not really want to build the Histadrut society on communal lines and therefore never insisted on setting up a common treasury. It did not fight for equal wages in the cities, and it did not really question (at least until the late 1930s) the bureaucratic practices and antidemocratic tendencies prevalent in the Histadrut. Tabenkin's new formation regarded the kibbutz primarily as a tool in the conquest of the land. Hakibbutz Hame'uhad reflected the official ideology of Ahdut Ha'avoda and did not oppose the principles of constructive social-ism. At the meeting of the permanent council of Kibbutz–Ein Harod, which preceded the inaugural convention of Hakibbutz Hame'uhad, the principle was established that "the kibbutz is a pioneering organization for executing the mission of the labor movement in the country; its function is to support the Histadrut as envisaged by Ahdut Ha'avoda and to follow the path indicated by the party."[107] Katznelson's views on this subject were particularly revealing. At the Ahdut Ha'avoda council on 25 February 1925 dealing with kibbutz affairs, Katznelson made it clear that social factors played no part in his appraisal of the new-style countrywide kibbutz: "I shall decide on my attitude to the countrywide kibbutz when I see the results. It may be decidedly negative or decidedly positive. . . . I will decide on my attitude to it according to its character and its actions. Nothing else will be taken into consideration."[108]

In contrast to this pragmatic approach, the Gdud's aims were very ambitious. If Ben-Gurion had not feared that this would affect the future of the whole labor movement, he would have been satisfied with the Gdud's submission and would not have demanded its destruction. If he had not believed that it constituted a potential alternative to the Histadrut, he would have allowed it to continue in a corner of the Jezreel Valley, in Upper Galilee, or even in Tel Aviv, where one of the companies had settled, as an example and a model for the whole movement. His answer to an apparently innocent question by a middle-level leader in the Gdud as late as the summer of 1923—"Why are they trying to strangle us when we have already surrendered?"[109]—was unequivocal: Ben-Gurion was not interested in social experiments. He wanted a working tool whose principal characteristic was discipline. He did not consider ideological debates as such to have any significance unless translated into practical terms.

This was precisely where the danger lay: the Gdud translated ideology into social practice and sought to provide an example. Its aim was to establish "a general commune of all the Jewish workers in Eretz Israel. The Gdud must be self-sufficient in all the requirements of life and create its own internal economy independently of the world economy or even the local economy."[110] In contrast, Ahdut Ha'avoda did not object to a capitalist economy and never condemned private property. Its leaders favored a complex bureaucratic organization in which important decisions were made by a small body such as the Executive Committee, whose members, because of their domination of the main party, economic enterprises, and mutual aid institutions, like the Kupat Holim, created relationships of dependence between themselves and members of the organization which were almost indestructible. The social utopia of the Gdud threatened to seriously undermine if not destroy this complex apparatus, or to remove the basis of its moral legitimacy.

The labor movement's ideological direction and methods of action were finally determined in the struggle of Ahdut Ha'avoda against the Gdud. It was at that time that it destroyed the only significant attempt not only to combine social with national aims but to question the right of the veterans of the Second Aliyah to dictate the development of the movement in the future. With the collapse of the Gdud, the heroic period came to an end. Already by the mid-1920s it was quite obvious that where the nature of society was concerned, the spirit of the national revolution was conservative.

CHAPTER FIVE

The Triumph of Nationalist Socialism: "From Class to Nation"

WHAT IS A CLASS?

At the beginning of the Third Aliyah, the labor movement still had two options: either to set itself up as an alternative society, first developing its own collective institutions and egalitarian forms of life and then seeking to transform society as a whole, or to accept the existing order. The second option was easier, as the economy being created in Palestine was capitalist. The role of private capital in the development of the country was decisive, and the national wealth that served as the basis of the Histadrut economy, although generally not private capital, could ultimately be traced to the World Zionist Organization.

In the period between the two world wars, private capital represented 75 percent of the funds imported into Palestine, and even in 1940–47 it represented 50 percent. The typical immigrant did not arrive, as is commonly assumed, in total poverty. As Michael Beenstock, Jacob Metzer, and Sanny Ziv have demonstrated recently, the immigrants from Europe came to mandatory Palestine with a great deal of property, and imported capital, private and public combined, was relatively plentiful. In the 1920s the annual inflow of Jewish capital was on average 41.5 percent larger than the Jewish net domestic product (NDP). Although the share of imported capital in the fast-growing economy declined over time, its ratio to the NDP did not fall below 33 percent in any of the pre–World War Two years and was kept at about 15 percent in all but one year since 1941. Owing to this imported capital and the wave of mass immigration, the Yishuv enjoyed an impressive demographic growth of 8.5 percent a year and an economic growth unequaled in the first half of the twentieth century in any other country in the world. Between 1922 and 1947 the NDP grew by an average of 13.2 percent a year, and product per capita at a yearly rate of 4.9 percent. From the beginning of the Third Aliyah to the end of the Fifth (1932–39), the national wealth out of which the Histadrut economy was created accounted for only a quarter of the imported capital.[1]

Another record broken in the days of the British mandate was in the rate of immigration. In those years the Yishuv absorbed a stream of immigrants which relative to the size of the population was unparalleled anywhere else.

Between 1919 and 1947 the country admitted an average of 79 immigrants a year for every thousand Jewish inhabitants. In the peak years of immigration to America from 1820 onward, 16 immigrants entered the country for every thousand inhabitants. In Canada from 1850 onward 15 immigrants entered the country, and in Australia from 1870 onward 11 immigrants entered the country for every thousand inhabitants. Because of the immigration flow, between 1922 and 1947 the Jewish workforce grew by 9.4 percent a year, and the employment rate grew by 8.9 percent a year.[2]

The Third Aliyah lasted from 1919 to 1923. Beginning in 1920, about eight thousand men and women immigrated to the country each year. They were not all pioneers with a socialist outlook; a significant number had been forced to leave Europe because of unstable conditions in the aftermath of the First World War. The rate of immigration during the Fourth Aliyah (1924–28, from Poland) was even higher. Inflation, policies of stabilization and taxation, and measures imposed by the Polish government led to a large-scale exodus. In 1925 the ratio between the number of immigrants entering Palestine and the number of Jews living there reached an all-time record: 318 immigrants for every thousand. The population of the Yishuv, nearly 61,000 in 1920, doubled, and in 1925 it reached nearly 122,000. Between June 1924 and June 1926, 55,000 people immigrated to the country and only 5,000 left it.[3] The Fifth Aliyah brought about a quarter of a million Jews to the country in 1932–39, 162,000 of them in 1932–35. This wave of immigration again doubled the population of the Yishuv in four years. At the end of 1931, 175,000 Jews lived in the country, and at the end of 1935, a peak year of immigration with more than 66,500 immigrants, the Yishuv numbered 355,500 souls. At the end of the British mandate, the Jewish population had grown to a self-governing and economically viable entity of 650,000 members, or about 31 percent of Palestine's total population.[4]

With the end of the Third Aliyah, the initial period of building the Yishuv concluded on a downturn. The Fourth Aliyah gave the Zionist enterprise a new upsurge of previously unequaled proportions. Despite its achievements—and it sometimes seemed precisely because of those achievements—the founders sought to label the Fourth Aliyah as a failure. In the collective consciousness of the labor movement it was associated with the major crisis of 1927 and not remembered for its general contribution to the development of the country. Members of the Second Aliyah who remained in the country and members of the Third Aliyah who were absorbed into the political and economic system of the Histadrut did not like aliyahs motivated by distress. They feared that their monopoly of conquering the country, absorbing immigration, and building the economy might slip out of their hands. "The middle class came and failed. It was bound to fail, because it was not ready for change and was incapable of the transmutation of values necessary for the implementation of Zionism and the building of the land," said Ben-Gurion. ". . . The failure of the middle class to implement Zionism left the country with a material crisis and Zionism with a spiritual crisis. The despair of the failed bourgeoisie poisoned the Zionist soul."[5] In more picturesque language, Yitzhak Laufbahn, Aharonowitz's successor as editor of *Hapo'el Hatza'ir*, deplored "the miserable occupations of petty trading and bar keepers,"[6] which he viewed as characteristic of the Fourth Aliyah.

Faced with the Fourth Aliyah, whose great advantage was its numbers, the heads of the labor movement clung to settlement, which they regarded as the basis of the political and economic strength of the Yishuv. "It is not those who live in Tel Aviv, Bat-Galim [in Haifa], or Beit Hakerem [in Jerusalem] who will decide the political and economic future of the country, nor those who hold the concession for the port of Haifa or for the irrigation of the Jordan Valley, but those who wield the plow in the Vale of Acre and those whose fields imbibe the waters of the Jordan," declared Arlosoroff.[7] Apart from its doubtful political wisdom, this statement contained nothing about the special social character and moral value of collective settlement. Likewise, Sprinzak, in addressing the fourteenth Zionist Congress, made no secret of the fact that the Fourth Aliyah had become a competitor for the domination of the Yishuv. He defended the rights of the labor movement vis-à-vis the tremendous brashness displayed by Menachem Mendel, the Jewish huckster from Poland. (Menachem Mendel, a famous figure of Yiddish literature, symbolized the despised exilic Jew.) "With the coming of the Fourth Aliyah, Menachem Mendel has risen again and expects to take over the redemption of the nation!" he exclaimed.

Indeed, for the labor movement, the Fourth Aliyah constituted a danger. It was unparalleled until that time, and nothing like it ever happened again. This aliyah relied on the strength of the large organized body of Polish Jewry, a Jewry whose voice was heard a great deal in the Zionist Congresses. The Fourth Aliyah was the only one with a real power base and able to compete, at least in theory, with members of the two previous waves of immigration. Therefore it was necessary to subject it to a rapid delegitimization. "When Menachem Mendel smelled the possibility of doing business in Eretz Israel," continued Sprinzak, "he sought impatiently to advance his interests and believed he could do business securely on the paths laid so painfully by the idealistic efforts of the pioneers."[8] When it seemed for a moment that the middle class could be a serious rival in the struggle for political power and economic resources, immigration to Palestine ceased to be regarded as a value in itself.

The political strategy of the labor movement finally crystallized during the Fourth Aliyah. The middle class could enjoy very favorable economic conditions in Palestine and receive an unofficial blessing for coming to build, to be built, and even to enrich themselves in the country, but on condition that they would not compete with it for the use of the public funds collected in the diaspora or for political control of the Yishuv.

Mass immigration accelerated the growth of the Yishuv as a bourgeois society not very different from the developed European societies. The high percentage of people employed in industry(still in its early stages) and in services and the high level of urbanization ought to have required a movement that described itself as socialist to revise its modes of thought and face reality. But because the movement did not deny the legitimacy of private property or seek to change society but wanted only to control it, and at the same time was unwilling to acknowledge the ability of the private sector to implement Zionism, it was obliged to minimize the importance of the Fourth Aliyah and thus to condemn the middle class for its inability to shoulder responsibility for the national enterprise. This was why it had to fall back on the kibbutz. Thus, communal settlement continued to enjoy its moral preference, and because of a handful of pioneers, the Histadrut was able to claim a position of leadership. "The kibbutz is the Jewish form of settlement par excellence. No form of colonization could be more Zionistic; there is nothing like it," declared Ben-Gurion in March 1936, at a time when no more than 8.4 percent of Histadrut members were living in kibbutzim.[9] In the mid-1930s the Plain of Sharon and the Hefer Valley, on the Mediterranean coast, north of Tel Aviv, had long been settled by private farmers and citrus fruits from their groves were the hallmark of Jewish agriculture in Palestine. As Ben-Gurion saw it, the value of the kibbutz was determined not by its social characteristics but by its contribution to national goals, and it also depended on its role as a power base for the political control of the Yishuv and the Zionist movement.

In reality the Fourth Aliyah changed the Yishuv and fixed its character until the War of Independence and beyond it. Dan Giladi, whose pioneering book on the Fourth Aliyah led to an understanding of the period, claimed that both the cultural and the socioeconomic profile of the Yishuv—the makeup of the Jewish labor force and the percentage engaged in productive occupations and services—hardly changed between 1929 and the end of the 1960s. The Fourth Aliyah, which the founders depicted as a perfect example of the impotence of the middle classes and as bearing responsibility for all the misfortunes of the 1920s, brought a larger number of pioneers to the country than the Third Aliyah, and many more agricultural settlements were founded in 1924–29 than in 1919–23. But the main contribution of the Fourth Aliyah was the rapid development in construction, industry, and citrus farming. Progress in industry was continuous, and it took first place in the Jewish economy; the cultivation of citrus fruits was the basis of Jewish agricultural production on the coastal plain.[10]

The Third Aliyah ended in an impasse, and grave doubts began to be voiced about the Yishuv's ability to continue to develop. The Fourth Aliyah brought the crisis to an end and created an unprecedented upsurge of development: this wave of immigration laid the basis for the modernization of Palestine and the infrastructure for the absorption of the Fifth Aliyah. About half of the immigrants were absorbed in Tel Aviv, whose population doubled in less than two years. Two out of three new enterprises founded in 1924–25 were in Tel Aviv. Tel Aviv, a city of forty thousand souls, was the center of economic, administrative, and cultural activity and the true heart of the Yishuv. The growth of the Jewish districts in Haifa and Jerusalem was also very rapid; in 1925 fourteen thousand Jews lived in Haifa and more than forty-two thousand in Jerusalem. These cities absorbed the Fourth and Fifth Aliyahs without much assistance from the Zionist Organization, which concentrated most of its efforts on agricultural settlement. Contrary to the impression that the labor movement sought to create, Jewish Palestine was a country whose level of urbanization stood at 83 percent, among the highest in the world. From the mid-1920s on, the city was the dominant sector, and it dictated the rate of development. It was then that the nucleus of Jewish industry was created, with its main branches: foodstuffs, construction, chemical products, printing, and textiles.[11]

Despite the impression the founders tried to create, mass immigration did not change the professional makeup of the Jewish population, and the number of people engaged in "productive" occupations did not decrease. There were few really wealthy people among the new immigrants. The vast majority of the middle and lower-middle classes who emigrated from Poland were self-employed and set up businesses with a modest independent capital.[12] Although only 17 percent of the immigrants in the 1920s took up agriculture, the Fourth Aliyah developed a new area of settlement between Tel Aviv and Kfar Saba: the Sharon. It founded moshavot such as Herzliyya, Ramatayim, and Magdiel, today well-to-do urban areas in Greater Tel Aviv. In the Jezreel Valley Afula was founded. Most of the lands bought at that period were acquired by private companies. The development of agriculture, including the creation of jobs for thousands of workers, was made possible by the investment of private capital. The number of workers in moshavot doubled in two years and exceeded the number of members in all collective settlements.[13] In the Fourth Aliyah, for the first time in the history of settlement, there was large-scale employment of Jewish workers in the old moshavot, including those based on field crops in the Galilee, which had previously been closed to them. In the new moshavot in the Sharon, Jewish labor was dominant.

At the end of 1925, the Palestinian economy took a turn for the worse. The number of those seeking work increased, and a smaller number of people with capital entered the country. The change in the composition of the wave of immigration began to have effects. In December 1925 the number of unemployed reached two thousand in Tel Aviv, construction came to a halt, the value of plots declined, a large number of bankruptcies occurred in the building trade and among tradesmen and merchants in general, and private deposits were withdrawn from the banks. This crisis, one of the worst the Yishuv had known, could be traced to both internal and external causes. There was an overly rapid growth of commercial activity in which investors, in the hope of making large profits quickly, embarked on risky ventures and went into debt. Also, the economic situation of the Polish Jews deteriorated, with the result that money that was due to arrive in the country never came, causing difficulties for those who relied on capital from Eastern Europe. Bank credit was denied still more, and new immigrants were unable to obtain loans. As a result, the construction of many buildings stopped and a vicious circle was set in motion, with falling prices, bankruptcies, and unemployment on a catastrophic scale. In 1927 40 percent of salaried workers in Tel Aviv—the heart of the crisis—were unemployed.[14]

The crisis affected not only these workers but also the Histadrut as an economic conglomerate. Katznelson blamed the Jewish bourgeoisie: "Twenty years of experience have shown us that we don't receive the wealth of the middle class, but only a middle class without its wealth. Capitalists don't come to us while they have their property."[15] He lambasted the "stock exchange mania—the immigration stock exchange"—which led to excessive investment in construction, to speculation in construction lots, and finally to collapse. The crisis, said Katznelson, was "a crisis of two towns, Tel Aviv and Afula."[16] With an uncharacteristic array of figures, the ideologist of the labor movement sought to demonstrate that speculation and speculation alone was responsible for the fact that there were victims even in the family, such as Sollel Beneh. Despite a last-minute effort by the Zionist leadership, a special loan of twenty thousand pounds, and the creation of a consortium in which Bank Hapo'alim and the Anglo-Palestine Bank took part, Sollel Boneh went bankrupt in June 1927. The situation of Hamashbir, the Histadrut supply and retail company, was not much better, although it did not officially go bankrupt. The fall of Sollel Boneh, the largest Histadrut enterprise, stunned the labor movement. It allowed a glimpse into what was taking place in the Histadrut economy and demonstrated the interdependence of the Zionist movement and the Histadrut in Histadrut's enterprises.

The gradual recovery from the depression (in 1929 wages returned to the level of the last months of 1926, and the unemployment rate returned to what it had been at the end of the boom period)[17] and the founding of new economic enterprises such as Tnuva (farm produce), Yachin (planting and food processing), Shikun Ovdim (housing), and Hasneh (insurance) took place at a time when it had become clear that the Yishuv was developing into a normal bourgeois society. The founding of new moshavot, from Magdiel and Herzliyya to Netanya, and the hunger of the new immigrants, as of the farmers' children in the old moshavot, for land and settlement showed that national feeling and enthusiasm for colonization were not necessarily confined to the Histadrut. Thus the partnership between the labor movement and the middle classes came into being on the basis of an identity of essential aims precluding their power struggles. This tendency already existed in the period of the Third Aliyah, but its final consolidation took place at the time of the Fourth. The people of Ahdut Ha'avoda and Hapo'el Hatza'ir both realized that the development of the economy depended on three factors beyond their control: immigration, the import of capital, and the economic policies of the mandatory government. These three factors objectively favored the growth of the middle and upper-middle classes. Against the economic power of the bourgeoisie, the founders set the political power of an organization controlling the vast majority of the salaried workers and the national importance of collective agriculture.

The accepted principles of action were as follows: "There is no need for any more ideological discussion," declared Ben-Gurion to the members of the council of Ahdut Ha'avoda in January 1925. "I deny the need to revise our ideology, not because everything is clear, but because it will not get any clearer, for our mission is to act." According to Ben-Gurion, the movement should concentrate on only one thing, the creation of a large political force representative of all wage earners.[18] Later, in 1932, Ben-Gurion told the delegates at the fourth Histadrut convention, in the best traditions of "productive socialism," that "the Histadrut teaches its members that work is a very grave and serious matter and the economy is a very grave and serious matter. We want enterprise to be encouraged. . . . We want Lodzia and Nesher [two important private factories] to exist and to prosper."[19] Katznelson, for his part, claimed that "productive socialism"—which he called constructive socialism—unlike "consuming socialism," saw itself as having responsibility for the entire national economy.[20] This "productive socialism" had to act very cautiously in work relationships and obviously implied a new form of social relationships. Thus, for instance, although Ben-Gurion believed that "the purpose of an enterprise was not only to enrich its owners" but also "to provide a decent existence for its workers," he acknowledged that this could be done only "to the degree that the economic capacity of the enterprise allowed."[21]

On the eve of the fifteenth Zionist Congress (1927), Katznelson confessed to the sin of labor egoism, of an indifference to private capital at the time of the Fourth Aliyah. He said: "A socialist, who would have established certain relationships with private capital, should have been put in charge of organizing private industry in this country. We should not have been satisfied with declarations that we do not object to private capital."[22] Another example of this attitude may be found in the articles that Beilinson published in *Kuntras*. "It is not the interests of class warfare that must determine the needs and strategy of the movement, but those of building up the land," he wrote in 1925.[23]

As early as 1920, when appearing before the Po'alei Tzion delegation, Tabenkin had stated: "Our main task is to create the political conditions facilitating our settlement in the land." But to achieve this aim, he said, one had to create economic structures while having a true perception of the relationship between means and ends. "Our main task is an economic one. Only through its fulfillment can we achieve our political aims such as creating a Jewish majority in the country, and so on." Thus, "the economic question is not one of class; it is a national question."[24]

From the very beginning, the movement saw itself as bearing responsibility not only for the fate of the laborer who had immigrated to the country but also for the man with capital who built a house, planted an orchard, or built a factory.[25] Ben-Gurion repeated this idea endlessly, and his struggle with the middle classes was never more than a dispute about control of public funds. Similarly, the middle classes, as Ben-Gurion knew very well, did not deny the value of national funds—money collected by Keren Hayesod (the Jewish Foundation Fund) or Keren Kayemet (the Jewish National Fund)—but objected only to the use that was made of them. In general, one can say that the political representatives of the middle classes objected to the exclusivity claimed by the Histadrut in the use of the national funds.

In explaining the nature of this struggle, Ben-Gurion revealed the significance he gave to the concept of class. "The debate concerning capital," he wrote, "the cause of the strife and opposition between the classes, is only about the *use of capital*. The question is not whose capital, but capital on whose behalf. It is not capital itself that is the subject of dispute, but only its destination."[26] The middle classes wanted national funds to be made available to the private sector, and the Histadrut needed them for its own purposes, especially for collective settlement. Ben-Gurion described this struggle over resources, which was also a struggle for economic control and hence for political control, as class warfare. It is no wonder that the sections of the Zionist Organization concerned with settlement supported the position of the Histadrut with regard to colonization. They all knew that financing the activities of the Histadrut had nothing to do with class warfare in the usual sense or the socialization of the means of production. They all realized that the term *class warfare*, as used by Ben-Gurion, was only a code word for closing ranks in the internal power struggle in the Histadrut and in the struggle for political domination of the Yishuv and the Zionist Organization.

Thus, Ben-Gurion was able to claim that class war was simply a struggle for the wholeness of the people, for its "absolute and complete unity."[27] To those who raised the question of "whether workers must give preference to national considerations or to class considerations," he replied: "This question only demonstrates the ignorance of those who ask it." For it was quite obvious that "in a working class conscious of its historical mission, class interests are identical with national interests." This led him to his conclusion that "the way to achieve national unity is via class warfare."[28]

There is no doubt that this was a new interpretation of the concept, previously unknown in the socialist world. And thus, after declaring that "the socialist pathos of the worker in this country derives from the spirit of the conquerers of the land as a whole,"[29] Ben-Gurion summarized his nationalist socialist principles as follows: "Our movement has always had the socialistic idea that the party of the working class, unlike the parties of other classes, is not only a class party solely concerned with matters affecting the class but a national party responsible for the future of the entire people. It regards itself not as a mere part of the people but as the nucleus of the future nation."[30]

On this basis, there was nothing to prevent one from taking the path that led "from class to nation." In 1929 Ben-Gurion expressed the desire to transform the whole Yishuv "from a working class into a working nation." In the 1930s the word "working" was dropped from this formula. This was not done for the sake of convenience or out of a concern for brevity: Ben-Gurion wanted to give an official authorization to Mapai's policy of national unity. At the time of the publication of his collected articles and speeches in 1933 under the title *Mema'amad La'am* (From class to nation) and with his election to the Zionist executive, Ben-Gurion no longer felt the need to indulge in the camouflage or persuasive exercises of the 1920s. At the beginning of the 1930s, the radical tendencies of the Third Aliyah no longer had to be reckoned with, and its members had been absorbed into the ideological framework and political bodies created by the Second Aliyah.

Thus, the basis was laid for the great alliance with and division of labor in the middle classes. Because of the catastrophic situation of the Jews in Europe, socialism had ceased, from the Zionist point of view, to have any functional value. European Jewry no longer needed a mobilizing myth in order to send its children to Palestine. At the same time, the great majority of those who came had no option but to go to work as soon as they got off the ship.

> The Jew who has no property and cannot remain in exile, and the Jewish youth whose soil has disappeared under its feet, and sees no hope or healing for itself or its people except in working in this country—all these, even if they have not heard of the existence of socialism, will immigrate to this country and become workers. They will create collective settlements, do every kind of labor, and engage in workers' struggles, for that is the one and only way to implement Zionism.[31]

Later Ben-Gurion expressed himself somewhat differently, but in a way that only confirmed the original significance of what he had said: "What we call socialism is only a means to fulfill our desires and realize our aspirations for redemption, resurrection, and liberation." From this he concluded: "The labor movement cannot fulfill its mission wholly and completely if it does not become the movement of the people."[32] "The movement of the people," said Ben-Gurion in his major programmatic address to the Mapai convention at the end of 1933, and no longer the "movement of the working people." At that period, when he was engaged in a struggle for control of the Zionist Organization, Ben-Gurion did everything in his power to find favor with the middle classes. He appealed to the labor movement to remove what he called "the double partition" that existed "to this day between ourselves and the people"—"the class concept that obscures the national character of our movement and gives a false idea of its achievements."[33]

Ben-Gurion did not distinguish between the people who controlled the means of production and those who did not possess those means, but he asked "the working class . . . to isolate the bourgeois minority and to unite the masses of the people around itself."[34] At the same time, Ben-Gurion also, in this context, asked a question that suggests at first that he still entertained the idea of a general transformation of society: "Is the labor movement destined to be no more than a class movement, imprisoned in its class framework, or can or should it be transformed into a people by means of a social revolution?" This sentence, which was meant to find favor with the delegates at the second Mapai convention, was in fact a non sequitur, mere sand thrown in their eyes, for only a class movement was capable of carrying out a social revolution. The retreat from the concept of class so consistently advocated by Ben-Gurion necessarily represented a renunciation of the wish to make changes in the social structure. In his statements both preceding and following this passage, Ben-Gurion made tremendous efforts to appease the middle classes, although he was more vague about the upper bourgeoisie, which in Europe was called the finance bourgeoisie and in Palestine consisted of a thin crust of small industrialists, citrus farmers, and businesspeople. He never hinted at any readiness on his part to touch private property, in the absence of which it was impossible to speak of a social revolution. The same can be said of his statements in the last part of this major speech, entitled "Conclusions."

> The World Zionist Organization is the principal means for organizing the Jewish people and for mobilizing its strength and its moral, political, financial, and human resources for the implementation of Zionism.
>
> No partial enterprise or organization can take the place of this main organization, based on popular foundations, in which all sections of the people participate without exception.[35]

To understand the development of the labor movement at that critical stage, let us reach back a few years and consider the practical political meaning attached to the two concepts of class warfare and the Left and Right. During the entire 1920s, there were discussions in Ahdut Ha'avoda about a union with Hapo'el Hatza'ir, discussions that constituted a continuation of the deliberations that preceded the founding of the party and the establishment of the Histadrut. In the course of these debates, positions were quite naturally clarified. From Ben-Gurion's point of view, for instance, the Ahdut Ha'avoda council, which met in Nahalat Yehuda between 6 and 8 January 1925, was a successor to the party convention of 1922, in which he described socialism as "fooling around." On this occasion, Ben-Gurion was involved in a difficult debate with the leader of the left wing of the party, Shlomo Kaplanski. "The question has been brought up," said Ben-Gurion, "especially by Kaplanski, of whether the union would take us to the left or the right. . . . I see neither left nor right; I only see upward. We must move onto a higher plane. I don't know what right or left is."[36]

A disdain for the categories of right and left and a readiness to ignore them have always been a sure sign of a shift to the right and a retreat from socialism. In the socialist world of 1925 no leader, even among the most right-wing and moderate elements, even among those closest to the liberal center, would have dared to declare that he did not "know what right or left is." The Palestinian context cannot explain everything, unless one presumes that the context was so special that the particular form of socialism that developed within it ceased to be socialistic, even in the most superficial sense of the word.

This impression is strongly reinforced by the fact that Ben-Gurion's position was by no means exceptional. Katznelson supported it without hesitation, but, more important, the concept of class warfare was completely eliminated from the decisions of the council. In its stead came a formula with an entirely different significance: "The political struggle of the worker in this country for his national and class needs," and his struggle "to increase national and class capital."[37] However, these manifestations of goodwill and this readiness to jettison whatever still remained of the ideological assets of socialism failed to satisfy the members of Hapo'el Hatza'ir. Arlosoroff complained about the "firing with blank cartridges" at the council of January 1925, and Aharonowitz, who was present at the discussions, concluded from the "shafts of poison, hatred, and contempt" directed at his party that it was impossible to move toward unification.[38] There were undoubtedly, among the rank-and-file activists in Ahdut Ha'avoda, radical elements that were not enthusiastic about the avowed antisocialism of Gordon's followers.

Moreover, the members of Hapo'el Hatza'ir had many complaints about their partners in the Histadrut. Ada Fishman (Maimon), one of the very few women to have reached an important political standing, complained of their "insatiable power lust" and their unscrupulousness. "There were no means they would not use," she said. Others expressed their resentment of the excessive militancy displayed by the local workers' councils. Similarly, most of the members of Hapo'el Hatza'ir disliked the idea of the large kvutza and the countrywide commune and in 1927 opposed the founding of Hakibbutz Hame'uhad. In view of all this, there were many confrontations between the two sides, especially between Levi Shkolnik (Eshkol), who represented the Hapo'el Hatza'ir position at the third Histadrut convention, and the members of Kibbutz–Ein Harod.[39]

The main point of disagreement, however, was the question of class warfare. When, despite all difficulties, the decision to unite with Ahdut Ha'avoda was nevertheless passed at the Hapo'el Hatza'ir council that met on 21 October 1927, both parties elected negotiating committees. At a meeting of the negotiators on 12 January 1928, class warfare was the only remaining point of divergence between the two parties. The minutes of the meeting constitute an extraordinarily interesting document. At the start of the discussions, Sprinzak declared that "all of us, and even those who are favorable to the idea of unification, agree on one basic point: the class factor has no place in the platform of the united party." For the people of Hapo'el Hatza'ir, this was a sine qua non. The people of Ahdut Ha'avoda knew this perfectly well, and Katznelson therefore immediately explained the true significance of the concept of class warfare as he understood it. Class warfare, he said, meant

1. Strengthening the Jewish worker through organization; 2. Defending workers' interests; 3. Spreading the labor movement's principles and goals in the Zionist movement and among the people.

This is the historical mission of the Jewish worker toward the people as a whole. Consciously or unconsciously, a class war is taking place, but this does not mean it is contrary to the people's interests. In reality, the Jewish worker constitutes a class, and that reality cannot be ignored.

This was followed by another unusually convincing and highly significant argument: "Apart from the question itself, we must also consider its political implications. If we do not deal with this matter of class struggle, it is likely to serve the interests of those elements in this country which are untrue to our constructive national concept of building the land."[40]

Here Katznelson was trying to explain that his use of the term *class warfare* was really intended to counteract the influence of the Left, communists, Poalei Tzion leftists, and Hashomer Hatza'ir in the Histadrut. To prevent the Left from claiming sole possession of the socialist heritage, the majority in the movement had to carry the banner of class warfare. It was essentially a tool in the struggle for power.

After Katznelson had spoken, Ben-Gurion completed the picture: "Three things characterize the working class: an organization, a struggle to improve the workers' condition in the present, and a desire to gain power in the future." Aharonowitz immediately understood the motives of his ally in seeking unification and said that the factors described by Ben-Gurion as characterizing the class "in fact represent us not as a class but as the vehicle of essential Zionism and Judaism on behalf of the whole people."[41] The leaders of Hapo'el Hatza'ir could not have hoped for more. They understood Ben-Gurion's and Katznelson's real intentions. They realized that if not for internal political considerations, if not for the need to struggle for the control of the Zionist movement and the Yishuv, Ahdut Ha'avoda would have had no difficulty dispensing with this bogey, which so frightened Hapo'el Hatza'ir. But as things stood, they managed very well. Because they all shared a profound disdain for speculative matters, Aharonowitz at an early stage in the discussions declared that he was interested not in a "written program" but only in actions, and where action was concerned he was ready for "an unconditional union." Sprinzak, for his part, declared that he had "carefully noted Katznelson's remark about the political strategy of introducing the subject of class warfare. I also note that this explanation changes the meaning of the concept."[42]

On 7–10 October 1928, about ten months after the decisive meeting in January of that year, at a council of Hapo'el Hatza'ir it was made plain beyond a doubt that the party stood firmly by its positions and that unification would take place on its terms. Zvi Luft and Yitzhak Laufbahn expressed the ideological concepts that Hapo'el Hatza'ir brought with it to the union. Luft said that because the concept of class warfare had been reduced "to an economic struggle for improving working and living conditions, its intensity has been further reduced by the spirit of pioneering and dedication to the building of the country." Laufbahn simply and unknowingly repeated the views of Enrico Corradini, almost word for word, when formulating the basic position of his party. "The idea that the Jewish labor movement in Eretz Israel is not a proletarian class party . . . ," he said, "is based on the fact that the Jewish people as a whole is a proletarian people."[43]

Generally speaking, the idea of progressing "from class to nation"—the slogan that accompanied the founding of Mapai—must be viewed against the background of the unification of Ahdut Ha'avoda and Hapo'el Hatza'ir. One of these gradually retreated from its socialist positions, which in any case were very moderate and were always subordinated to national interests, and the other was avowedly antisocialistic.

The leaders of Hapo'el Hatza'ir were well aware of the advantage of employing the slogans "Class warfare" and "From class to nation" simultaneously. Everyone soon understood that in this way one could enjoy the best of both worlds. Socialism could be used as a "mobilizing myth," to activate the urban wage-earning population, the population in the collective settlements, and the pioneering youth arriving in the country, and the principle of "from class to nation" could be exploited to develop collaboration with the middle classes. By about 1930 it was clear to everyone that control of the Yishuv, the Zionist Organization, and the resources it provided for building the country—as well as the development of the Histadrut economy—depended on a division of labor between the labor movement and the middle classes.

Thus, when he appeared at the fifth Ahdut Ha'avoda convention at the end of October 1926, Katznelson angrily attacked those who claimed that "scientifically, in a colonial regime, there is no room for class warfare in a country inhabited by two nations." The guilty party here was Arlosoroff, who had given an exact description of the true nature of the common ideology of Hapo'el Hatza'ir and Ahdut Ha'avoda. But Katznelson knew that without a definition of class warfare in political terms and without ascribing a national significance to the concept, the whole ideological edifice he was erecting with so much care would collapse. "Any attempt," he said, "to obscure the national quality of our pioneering existence would not only be a sin against the destiny of the people but would weaken us and cause us to be swept away by the current. Similarly, any obscuring of our class reality, with its solidarity and power of organization, would not only diminish our strength and power of organization but also harm our national enterprise."[44] In this way, he answered not only Arlosoroff but all those who naively believed that the task of class warfare was to change the bourgeois social order rather than to set it up in order to dominate it.

A socialist party can naturally come to the conclusion that it lacks the power to change the bourgeois system and that it therefore has to compromise with it temporarily. But in the period between the two world wars a socialist movement never turned compromise into a virtue and never made it into the true significance of the concept of class warfare. This was an original invention and did not resemble any definition of class warfare known until that time, but it was in keeping with nationalist socialism. Whereas in Europe nationalist socialism completely rejected the principle of class warfare, in Palestine the majority in the labor movement decided on a more complex solution: it retained the concept but gave it a completely new significance.

At the third Ahdut Ha'avoda convention in 1922, in which, as mentioned earlier, Ben-Gurion abandoned socialism entirely, one sees him making a first attempt at reinterpreting class warfare.

> For Zionism, the struggle of the working class is daily labor, the organization of the workers as a unified body in control of its class affairs, their organization in trade unions for offensive and defensive action in the private sector, their struggle for positions of influence in the economy and the national institutions, the setting up of collective farms, increasing the political power of labor in national

and civic governmental institutions, the struggle of the Jewish working class for its national rights, the struggle to increase aliyah and to direct immigrants toward productive work, socialistic pioneering activities, cultural creativity, and collaboration with the international labor movement. Ahdut Ha'avoda considers it the duty of the Jewish worker to take part in all struggles to impose labor in the life of the people, the land, and the economy. This must be the role of the Jewish worker in creating a socialist Jewish society in Eretz Israel.[45]

Thus, *class warfare* was used as a kind of comprehensive term that included virtually everything in which the labor movement was interested.

If this was indeed the path to socialism, then there was also logic in Ben-Gurion's claim about three years later that "the way to the realization of the unity of the people is via class warfare."[46] Here I should point out that in the period when the Po'alei Tzion party existed, the concept of class warfare was known and was given its customary meaning. For Ben-Zvi it was the core of socialism and a major tool in eliminating class differences.[47] In those days even Ben-Gurion was fairly familiar with such a mode of thinking. At the beginning of the 1920s, however, when he began to decide on his line of action, he asked Ahdut Ha'avoda, in his speech at the party's council that took place on 19 December 1921 and that preceded the Haifa convention of December 1922, to set the workers in the country on a path of "class creativity rather than class struggle."[48] But he soon realized that one could not create a new kind of party, different from the various middle-class organizations, without employing the myth of class warfare, and he consequently accepted the formula that was agreed upon at the Haifa convention. At this early period, Ben-Gurion was greatly preoccupied with the search for the best way of building the nation. He wavered between a dismissal of socialism and the radical idea of an egalitarian workers' community, a sort of communist army of labor. Only when all the disadvantages of these two solutions became clear to him did he begin to choose a third path: collaboration with the middle classes on one hand and the mobilization of salaried workers by means of the socialist myth on the other. Thus Ben-Gurion adopted the middle path chosen at the founding of Ahdut Ha'avoda, when the principle of the primacy of the nation was established once and for all.

From that time on, Ben-Gurion was able to claim that "there is no contradiction, division, or opposition between our Zionism and socialism. . . . Our fidelity to the needs of the entire people, to the historical needs of the entire people, is absolutely and completely consistent with our socialism." To his critics on the Left, members of the Bund who continued to claim that "Zionism and socialism are a contradiction in terms," Ben-Gurion replied with his usual self-assurance: "Our Zionism is whole and complete and profound precisely because we are socialists, because we aspire to total redemption." According to Ben-Gurion, this wholeness was reflected in what he called the class warfare of the labor movement. And of what did this class warfare consist? He defined it as a war on the "conception of class of the man of property, based on minority rule, the lust for gain, exploitation of the worker, denial of the rights of the masses, and the maintenance of class privileges." Thus, concluded Ben-Gurion, "Our class struggle in Zionism, like our class struggle in the Yishuv, is the struggle of a class that fulfills the historical mission of the nation and is concerned with the liberation and renewal of the entire people."[49]

Israel Kolatt has pointed out that in Ben-Gurion's case, "Whenever there was a conflict between Zionism and socialism, socialism was rejected in favor of Zionism," but he is not always aware of the true significance of the passages that he himself quotes. From the extracts he gives from Ben-Gurion's address at the thirteenth convention of Po'alei Tzion in February 1919, Kolatt concludes that Ben-Gurion's language on that occasion was not "particularly Marxist." "Ben-Gurion," he writes, "sought basic connections between Zionism and socialism, such as his idea that a national movement could not be 'healthy,' 'strong,' or influential without socialism, or that socialism could not be 'fruitful among us' if it was not rooted in the 'soul of the nation.'"[50]

No nationalist socialist ever gave a better description of his outlook or the aims of his movement than the one we have here. The Zionism that Ben-Gurion described as "whole" was a Jewish form of European integral nationalism. By contrast, the type of class warfare that Ben-Gurion depicted was merely a political struggle against the bourgeois Right. From the social point of view, this was only a struggle against the excessive privileges demanded by a minority of capitalists. Ben-Gurion contrasted bourgeois class egoism with the role of the worker who bore the whole enterprise of national redemption. It is true that if one defines the political power struggles in the Yishuv and the Zionist movement in terms of class, one can say that the labor movement was fighting a class war. But if one gives the concept of class the significance it usually possessed in the socialist literature of the period, it is obvious that there was no connection between class war and the struggles the Histadrut waged for its share of financial resources and for control of the institutions of the Yishuv and the Zionist Organization. But the concept itself had a great emotional impact, and Ahdut Ha'avoda soon used it as a weapon in gaining power. This was possible because the salaried workers, the members of the Histadrut, and the "people" were treated as identical. If the salaried workers were the people and the struggle for control of the existing social and political institutions was described as a class war, it followed that class war was a war of the entire "people."

From the moment the principle of the primacy of national objectives was finally accepted, a collaboration with the bourgeoisie was solely a matter of circumstances and never again met any resistance in principle. A policy of collaboration already began to bear fruit at the end of the 1920s. In the elections to the sixteenth Zionist Congress in 1929, the liberal-bourgeois General Zionists lost the decisive majority in the Zionist Organization they had enjoyed until then. Ahdut Ha'avoda and Hapo'el Hatza'ir, which already appeared in a joint list, gained only 26 percent of the votes, but they were potential partners in a coalition. In the meantime, Mapai was founded and the momentum was sustained; in 1933, in the elections to the eighteenth Zionist Congress in Prague, it already obtained 44 percent of the votes. In 1931, in elections to the Asefat Hanivharim (the Elected Assembly), the parliament of the Yishuv, more than 40 percent of the voters favored Mapai.[51] Thus, at the beginning of the 1930s Mapai was the dominant party in the Yishuv and the Zionist Organization. Ben-Gurion, the head of the Histadrut, was elected to the Zionist executive, becoming chairman in 1935. Fifteen years after the Haifa convention, the stage of the consolidation of power had come to an end, and more than forty consecutive years of labor domination of the Yishuv, the Zionist movement, and the state of Israel had begun.

THE COLLABORATION WITH THE MIDDLE CLASSES

An especially close relationship soon developed between the labor movement and the liberal or "leftist" branch of General Zionism, and between the labor movement and the part of the Zionist leadership that bore direct responsibility for the Zionist enterprise. The leaders of the Zionist movement held the contribution of the workers, and especially of the settlers who bore the physical burden of Zionist colonization, in the highest regard. Thus, at a very early stage, there was a close partnership with Ruppin, who although in principle was in favor of capitalist agriculture, nevertheless refused to entrust the development of agricultural settlement to market forces. When it was a matter of implementing Zionism, Ruppin was ready to set aside his capitalist principles, just as socialism was disregarded, where necessary, by the workers. Ruppin looked on the workers as an irreplaceable army of labor. As he saw it, the workers in the Histadrut manned the forward positions of Zionism and undertook the most difficult tasks. They constituted a heroic army of conquest that was not to be judged by normal economic criteria. Weizmann and Ussishkin also wholeheartedly supported the demands of Ahdut Ha'avoda and the Histadrut to be granted budgets for realizing the principle of Jewish labor. Everyone agreed that placing national funds at the disposal of the pioneers enlisted by the labor movement was the only formula that had so far proved itself.

At the fourteenth Zionist Congress, which met in Vienna in August 1925, strong criticism of collective settlement was voiced. The leader of the

Mizrahi Party in Poland called the pioneers "Kastkinder," a pejorative Yiddish term meaning "father's boys," or children dependent on their parents.[52] To these critics, and especially those who saw the collective settlements as living parasites of the national funds, Kurt Blumenfeld, leader of the German Zionists, replied: "We shall defend the achievements of the workers in Eretz Israel and protect the national enterprise from the attacks of the Right." Blumenfeld was not a socialist. Weizmann, president of the Zionist Organization, also adopted a strong position in reply to the critics:

> I am very sorry that on this platform I heard the word *Kastkinder*. For years you urged the pioneers in the propaganda of the Left and Right to choose the path of self-sacrifice. When they arrived in the country, they were covered with praise. What has happened at the fourteenth Congress to make them into "Kastkinder"? It is true that there are deficits in the balance sheets of the kibbutzim and moshavim, but don't forget one thing: there is an invisible capital not invested by the Keren Hayesod (Jewish Foundation Fund)—work beyond endurance, a superabundant expense of energy, hunger, and malaria. These are items that do not appear in the budget.[53]

When the Mapai Central Committee convened in March 1931 for a special meeting with Weizmann at a time when his continued leadership of the Zionist Organization was in question, there was no mistaking the atmosphere of family warmth. "We do not need long explanations in speaking to Weizmann," said Katznelson. "We understand one another without much talk." Arlosoroff decribed it as the encounter of the "only two forces in Zionism that have so far demonstrated a true power of creativity."[54]

Weizmann not only appreciated the workers' efforts but also realized that they did not represent any danger to society as a whole. He regarded the labor movement as a pioneering force serving the nation, not a movement of social revolution.

Thus, people such as Weizmann, Ruppin, Ussishkin, and Blumenfeld, acting on behalf of the Zionist movement, encouraged a policy that on the face of it might seem to have been irrational. Although 80 percent of the immigrants of the Fourth Aliyah settled in the cities, collective agriculture swallowed up most of the national budget.[55] On the strength of its position as the representative of national values and their embodiment in the work of the pioneers, the labor movement, as early as the end of the 1920s, gained the support of the entire Yishuv. Nearly all the representatives of the middle classes stood behind Ahdut Ha'avoda in its opposition to the experts' report of 1928. This report was requested by the Zionist Organization in order to examine the use that was being made of the national funds in the country. It was the work of the Joint Palestine Survey Commission, headed by Alfred Mond (Lord Melchett), a major British industrialist and a leader in the Jewish community of England. The commission, in which three other prominent Jewish businessmen were present, was accompanied by experts of international standing. The report was highly critical, and its conclusions were especially damning regarding the agricultural sector in general and collective settlements in particular. The commission especially deplored the influence of the Histadrut on the Zionist executive. The Histadrut reacted strongly to the report and mobilized the support of other political and social forces in the Yishuv.

The Zionist executive, which met in Berlin in the summer of 1928, accepted the Histadrut's positions and said that the commission's recommendations were unsuited to the needs of the country. Weizmann declared that the report was not binding on the Zionist executive.[56] In a speech to the Asefat Hanivharim on 4 July 1929, Ben-Gurion condemned the "experts' report, which contradicts the basic principles of Zionist action," and saw its rejection by the Zionist executive as the basis for establishing an enlarged Jewish Agency.[57] The leaders of the labor movement exploited the opportunity in order to assert their dominance of the Yishuv and to stress the common national interest. They waged a battle against the Zionist Organization's demands for budgetary restraint. Nahum Sokolov, chairman of the Zionist executive, acknowledged the supreme importance of collective settlement, particularly in the kibbutzim. On the same occasion, the executive confirmed by a majority of forty-one to four the support of the Zionist Organization for a principle sacred to the labor movement: the employment of Jewish labor was a sine qua non, overriding all economic considerations.

The moral importance of this victory can hardly be exaggerated. Employers who preferred immediate economic gain to their national duty were now officially excluded from the national consensus. From political and moral viewpoints, the labor movement won a victory on all fronts. The chief editor of *Ha'olam*, the official newspaper of the Zionist Organization, on the day after the meeting of the executive, issued the following statement: "Even those who are not socialists have to support the demands of the workers and concede them a great deal, because at the present time they are the most reliable basis for our future success in this country. They are the symbol of our national effort and spirit of dedication."[58] Before this, the budget for settlement had been presented to the executive for its endorsement. A proposed amendment increasing the budget by more than 30 percent—from 75,000 to 115,000 pounds—was presented jointly by Shlomo Kaplanski and Meir Dizengoff, the "bourgeois" mayor of Tel Aviv.[59]

The middle classes were not motivated solely by national altruism. In matters of income, the principle of national unity worked in favor of the capitalists. In reality, the whole economic system in mandatory Palestine was based on rules that served the interests of the middle classes. From the beginning of the mandate, the government had favored a market economy. The inhabitants of the country were free to carry on international commercial activities, although these were liable to payment of customs duties. The Palestinian pound, which at the end of 1927 replaced the Egyptian pound as the common currency, was until the beginning of the Second World War equal in value to the pound sterling (this had also been the value of the Egyptian pound). The revenues of the mandatory government came from indirect taxation; about 80 percent of the taxes collected were derived from this source. The share of the Jewish population in the tax revenues of the mandatory government was 38 percent in the mid-1920s, reaching 64 percent in the mid-1930s. This situation reflected the increasing Jewish share in Palestine's gross national product (29 percent in 1926 and 57 percent in 1935) and the increasing disparity in product per capita between the Jewish and Arab communities. In the early and mid-1920s, the Jewish per capita product was 90 percent higher than the Arab one, and in the mid-1930s the disparity reached 160 percent. At the same time, the ratio of taxes to income in these two societies remained stable: 16–17 percent among the Jews, and 10–11 percent among the Arabs.[60]

When in 1929–30 the mandatory government announced its decision to impose an income tax, the industrialists protested and declared the proposal a disaster. Matters were shelved until July 1932, when the government again declared its intention to carry out the proposal. The leadership of the labor movement, with Arlosoroff at its head, mobilized itself to avert the catastrophe through procrastination.

At the meeting of the Mapai Central Committee devoted to this topic in November 1932, Arlosoroff presented the plain facts of the case. Of the total revenues of the mandatory government, amounting to about two million pounds, "Most," he said, "is paid by the humble folk, both Arabs and Jews." He said that the middle and upper-middle classes, however, lived in hothouse conditions. The financial institutions, the foreign companies, and the banks were exempted from taxation, and members of the liberal professions did not pay their proper share. These included members of the governmental and urban administration, employees in the private sector, physicians, and lawyers. More than a hundred lawyers in Eretz Israel had an income of five hundred pounds or more, and among them were some who earned between 1,000 and 1,500 pounds, exorbitant sums at that period.[61] Arlosoroff, like Katznelson, Sprinzak, Ben-Zvi, Remez, and Sharett, who were present and took part in the discussion, knew that a socialist movement could not allow itself directly to oppose the imposition of progressive taxation.

When, at that period, the matter was debated by the Va'ad Le'umi (the Jewish National Council), Katznelson used it as a weapon to attack the representatives of the bourgeoisie and condemned the "patriotic panic" of the opponents of the reform. He rightly thought that many among them, even in a Jewish state, would have opposed the imposition of progressive taxation.[62] He decided to wait and see how things would go, for he did not wish the leaders of the Jewish upper bourgeoisie to dictate the Yishuv's policies in a matter of such importance. But when the question was debated in the Mapai Central Committee, the position he adopted was not very different from that of the industrialists and citrus farmers.

> Our main problem is Jewish immigration, which also means the importation of Jewish capital. In this matter, we, the workers, and the capital arriving in the country are bound together by a tragic common destiny. We want the capital entering the country, provided it creates Jewish employment, to enjoy favorable conditions, and we do not want any obstacles to be placed in the way of its investment. From this point of view, with regard to the attractive idea of an income tax, the disadvantages outweigh the benefits. For that would frighten the Polish Jews who are running away from income tax, and who we hope will leave Poland.[63]

Where Katznelson was concerned, this was the decisive argument, and no considerations of justice or equality could stand against it. Arlosoroff added: "At present, the Jewish population, which represents 18 percent of the general population, pays 38 percent of the taxes. We do not want to bear a heavier burden."[64] The Mapai Central Committee therefore decided not to express any opposition in principle to the plan that Sharett could not help but describe as "constructive and progressive," but at the same time to do everything possible to prevent it from being implemented in its proposed form. In practice, it was agreed to freeze the matter and prevent the realization of the program.

The leadership was also ready to go a long way toward meeting the middle classes in what is generally considered to have been close to the heart of the labor movement. From their inception, all socialist organizations fought to preserve the workers' freedom to conduct negotiations about wages and work conditions. A readiness to forgo this freedom of action was regarded as an unforgivable betrayal. But Katznelson was convinced that constructive socialism necessitated an arrangement on labor relations in a spirit of national unity. The proposals he made in *Davar* on 25 March 1927 are extraordinary both in mode of expression and in content.

Katznelson began with an attack on "the wretched type of bourgeois who has an 'appetite' rather than a talent for capitalism, and who cannot conceive of building the economy in any other way than on the basis of the forms of exploitation and bondage which he knew in the remote corners of the earth from which he came, and who, with his hatred and fear of the workers, poisons the atmosphere both in this country and abroad." In order to be evenhanded, however, he immediately, with equal vehemence, attacked "a particular type of 'worker' who does not strike roots in this country, never learns to understand conditions here, and remains attached to the wretched economic traditions he brought with him from the Pale of Settlement. He hearkens to every war cry, without knowing where it can lead, and without being able to distinguish between essential matters and mere delusions, which a worker should treat with contempt." Thus, Katznelson drew a parallel between the "bad" employer and the "bad" worker, between the employer who is out for gain but lacks the practical capabilities of the builders of industrial empires such as Henry Ford—admired by all the nationalist socialists in Europe—and the revolutionary worker who has no sense of responsibility toward the productive process and who seeks profit no less than his employer. Such a person, according to Katznelson, was unworthy of the noble title of "worker" (it was no accident that the term appeared in quotation marks). A true worker was a member of the Histadrut, conscious of his national responsibility and cooperative with the "good" employer, who was also a Zionist who recognized the need to reach an arrangement with his laborers.

Katznelson wanted the private sector to develop as rapidly as possible, and he asked the capitalists only to recognize the Histadrut's monopoly in representing the workers. He was anxious to show them how necessary the workers' organization was to them. The Histadrut, he said, provided a framework that prevented salaried worker from adopting negative patterns of behavior or from developing attitudes that would "poison the general atmosphere and harm both the economy and the workers." The Histadrut was able to keep such wicked thoughts away from the workers. Its sole demand from either the employers or the national institutions was a recognition of organized labor. Finally, in order to consolidate and institutionalize the collaboration with the bourgeoisie for the common aim of building the country, Katznelson proposed a nine-point program. The first point was that "employers who make an agreement with the Histadrut must participate in the labor exchange," and the last was that "all disputes between employers and employees bound by such agreements must be submitted to arbitration."[65] Katznelson wished to submit these proposals to the third Histadrut convention, but they were not discussed there because of the vigorous opposition of the administrative staff.[66] Apart from a natural reluctance to abandon a position of strength, the opposition of the staff had another explanation: the people of the second and third level of leadership were closer to the needs and sentiments of the laborers, and they were not yet prepared to give up one of the main assets of the labor movement.

A notable example of the practical application of the principles that Katznelson brought before the Histadrut convention was the Histadrut's relationship with Pinhas Rutenberg, the legendary founder and first director of the national electric company. In his excellent biography of Rutenberg, Eli Shaltiel paints a picture of an aggressive capitalist with a dictatorial temperament, a great hater of trade unions, strikes, and wage demands. Yet despite his authoritarian attitude to his workers, Rutenberg enjoyed the respect and cooperation of the Histadrut. A good illustration of this special relationship was the behavior of the Histadrut in 1929, two years after Katznelson had proposed limiting the right to strike. During a conflict in the factory producing poles for the electric company (the only major work dispute the company was involved in during Rutenberg's tenure), the Histadrut decided not to call for a work stoppage, even if it meant harming the workers and their rights. Shaltiel writes that in the joint arbitration committee gathered to bring the affair to an honorable conclusion, the representatives of the Histadrut, from Berl Reptor to David Remez, behaved in Rutenberg's presence like schoolboys in front of their headmaster. Indeed, the charismatic Rutenberg, who would briefly head the Va'ad Le'umi, was a man after the labor leaders' own heart. He was made of the same stuff as the leaders of the labor movement. This integral nationalist, who believed only in force and loathed organized labor in all its manifestations, such as the celebrations of the First of May, also described himself as a socialist. The man who was one of the largest employers in the country and who denied the Histadrut the right to speak on behalf of the electric workers was warmly accepted by its leadership on account of his devotion to Zionism, his service in the Jewish Battalions, his practical abilities, his power of leadership, and his connection with the Hagana and matters of security. But most of all, there was a closeness between Rutenberg and the heads of the Histadrut because of their common perception of the aims of the movement. Like them, Rutenberg viewed the movement as an instrument for building the land, an organization whose task was to teach the workers to be content with little and to sanctify labor as the basis of national revival.[67] For him, a good worker devoted his life to the interests of the nation.

On this basis there was no difficulty in achieving a fruitful collaboration not only with Rutenberg but also with other employers. But this unwritten agreement became possible only because the bourgeoisie had come to the conclusion that the socialism of Ahdut Ha'avoda represented no danger to them and that the activities of the Histadrut also served their own interests. Adherents of General Zionism and religious Judaism soon realized that in the term *constructive socialism* the emphasis was on the first word. Constructive socialism did not endanger private property, and its attractions for the private sector were far greater than its disadvantages. Thus, a partnership came into being not only on the basis of shared national objectives but also on an economic basis. It soon became apparent to the industrialists and the citrus farmers that the Histadrut was a stabilizing factor in the economy. The stipulation that labor must be Jewish raised costs in the agricultural sector, and a considerable number of citrus farmers continued to depend on Arab labor. In general, however, the private sector benefited from the presence of the Histadrut. The private sector needed national funds, just as the Histadrut needed private capital. As the country developed and the importance of the cities—especially the first modern Jewish city—increased, the collaboration grew closer. In Tel Aviv and the new moshavot in the Plain of Sharon, the problem of Arab labor did not exist. Here private capital created places of employment, and the Histadrut served as a responsible and disciplined trade union. It was no accident that among General Zionists, those closest to the labor movement were influential representatives of the urban intelligentsia: Meir Dizengoff, mayor of Tel Aviv, and Moshe Glickson, editor of *Ha'aretz*. These people were most receptive to its message, especially as the leaders of the labor movement had demonstrated that they were not content with merely formulating an ideology of national consensus. The way in which they crushed the Gdud Ha'avoda left no room for doubt concerning the seriousness of their intentions. At the end of the 1920s, no realistic person could have suspected Ahdut Ha'avoda or the Histadrut of seeking a socialist utopia or of having revolutionary ambitions.

The fact that nationalist socialism in Palestine served to protect the private sector undoubtedly contributed to a situation that might seem strange. If despite their economic strength the middle classes never became a political force comparable with the labor movement, the reason was that they never felt the need for a unified political structure parallel with the Histadrut. The ideological weakness of the middle classes also stemmed from the lack of any existential need to formulate an alternative to labor's ideology. The middle classes thus allowed themselves the luxury of standing completely aside and avoiding any real participation in the political life of the Yishuv and the Zionist movement.

Yigal Drori has pointed out that the founding of the World Union of General Zionists at the beginning of the 1920s was the consequence not of an identification with a particular idea but of an unwillingness to identify with the two extremes of the Zionist movement, socialist and religious Zionism.[68] The social and political weakness of the Center, particularly noticeable in light of the development of the private sector in the 1920s, made it a natural area of expansion for the labor movement. In the absence of a developed ideology of liberalism, in the absence of a conservative approach that could have been offered during the nation-building process as an alternative to the pioneering ideology, the General Zionist Center became a political satellite of the labor movement. Moreover, General Zionism adopted Weizmann's concept of "synthetic Zionism," a synthesis of the original Herzlian political Zionism and the practical Zionism that gave rise to colonization in Palestine. Adherents of synthetic Zionism, which included most of the great names of the Zionist movement from Ussishkin and Ruppin to Sokolov, were unable to do other than support collective settlement. They were natural allies of the labor movement. They did not endanger its position but strengthened it, and the labor movement, for its part, in accordance with the best nationalist socialist principles, assisted the growth of the free economy. The middle classes renounced the ambition of gaining political power and in return were given freedom of action and the support of the labor movement in the economic sphere. Like all other nationalist socialist movements, the labor movement had no alternative to the liberal economy and thus obviously constituted no threat to the Palestinian Jewish bourgeoisie.

The General Zionists admired the practical talents of the labor movement, its capacity for organization, and its nationalist fervor. Most of the General Zionist leaders and spokespersons who influenced public opinion were not deceived by the revolutionary phraseology, and they soon perceived the true nature of the laborites. Thus, the coalition that brought Israel to independence came into being on the basis of a common nationalism. But General Zionism was not of one piece. Collaboration was natural and easy with the liberal wing of the movement, but not with its conservative wing. The heated disagreements on this account between the left- and right-wing General Zionists only demonstrated the determination of the liberal wing to preserve the alliance with the two main parties of the Histadrut and their successor, Mapai.

Glickson, the principal spokesman of the liberal wing, had an excellent understanding of the labor movement and regarded the Histadrut as the ideal instrument for realizing common national objectives. He stressed the Histadrut's role in uniting national forces, in building up the national economy, and in absorbing immigration. According to Yigal Drori, Glickson was lavish in his praise of Histadrut economic enterprises, which, he said, absorbed the Third Aliyah, created new employment opportunities, and directed immigrants toward productive labor. At the third Histadrut convention in July 1927, he reaffirmed his support. At that time, Glickson was one of the heads of the Union of General Zionists, which called for the establishment of a Center Left in General Zionism. This sympathetic attitude was reflected both in the party platform at the fifteenth Zionist Congress (held in Basel between 30 August and 11 September 1927) and in the way Glickson tried to minimize the harm the Mond Report caused to the labor movement. He praised the "quality of heroism" in the labor-pioneering ideal and said that the report should be regarded as affecting only economic management and not colonization.[69]

Glickson also encouraged labor to continue with its policy of interclass collaboration. One of the chief matters discussed at the third Histadrut convention was the inclusion of Arab workers in the Histadrut. The General Zionist leader urged the labor leadership not to make common cause with the extreme Left on the basis of class conflict, but to concentrate instead on joining forces with the Jewish people at large rather than with the Arab workers. He also urged the two political parties that made up the movement to seek unification for the sake of Zionism.[70] The significance of unification was not lost on the General Zionists. With the founding of Mapai, there was no longer any obstacle to the General Zionists' acceptance of the national authority of the labor movement's leadership. With this final guarantee, the last impediment was removed: a party, one of whose components was Hapo'el Hatza'ir and whose leaders were Ben-Gurion and Katznelson, Sprinzak, Arlosoroff, and Aharonowitz, who never stopped demonstrating signs of goodwill, could not fail—even if it declared itself socialist—to be acceptable to the capitalists.

In January 1927, with the breakaway of most of the conservative wing and the foundation of the National Civic Association, the position of the liberal wing became the official position of General Zionism. This wing had for a long time unhesitatingly backed the labor movement in two matters that the latter regarded as especially important: the sanctity of Jewish labor and the necessity of unconditional support of settlement, regardless of economic cost. This attitude was particularly clearly expressed during the fruit-picking riots in Petah Tiqwa at the end of 1927. On 16 December a demonstration by six hundred unemployed Jewish workers in the citrus groves was dispersed with violence and cruelty by the British police, which had been called in by the farmers. The workers struggled with the citrus farmers, who had refused to employ them and had given the work to Arab laborers. In a biting editorial Glickson declared that "an outrage has been committed against Jewish labor, against our suffering and humiliated brethren, against our whole enterprise, and against our future in this country." But it was not only Glickson who was outraged; other General Zionist leaders also condemned the farmers of Petah Tiqwa in the name of national solidarity.[71] Thus, at least part of the political leadership of the middle class positioned itself next to the labor movement.

In the second matter of decisive importance—unconditional support of agricultural settlement—the General Zionists adopted the position of one of the labor movement's earliest allies, Arthur Ruppin. In 1925 Ruppin published his *Agricultural Settlement of the Zionist Organization in Eretz Israel*, which contained an enthusiastic description of the Histadrut's settlement policies and of experiments in collective agriculture.[72] Two years later, at the fifteenth Zionist Congress, Ruppin praised the system of building up the country through settlement. His speech was much appreciated in labor-movement circles. Shortly after, on Ruppin's fiftieth birthday, Katznelson wrote enthusiastic words of praise for this "perfect example of a good and faithful Zionist." Nearly twenty years later, in January 1943, at a meeting in Ruppin's memory under the auspices of the Zionist executive, Katznelson extolled Ruppin, describing him as "a true friend, both in good times and bad," the father of the kvutza and thus of all collective agriculture. Moreover, he continued, Ruppin had helped found the first moshav and the first large kvutza on purely national grounds. Katznelson particularly liked Ruppin's approach, his way of improvising in response to the needs of the nation, without any ideological bias, but with boundless dedication to national interests. This, he concluded, was a man "who wanted only one thing: the implementation of Zionism."[73]

Glickson never won similar words of praise, but he too enjoyed warm and close relations with the labor movement. In fact, in the collected articles of the editor of *Ha'aretz* it is sometimes hard to discern a significant difference between his approach to Zionism and that of Ben-Gurion or Katznelson. Glickson faithfully represented the opinions of those he called the "popular elements in General Zionism," and he felt he was much closer to constructive socialism than to the "right-wing class principles" of his own movement. Of these, he said that "the interests and ideas he had in common" with his party were no more than those which "existed between all parties and factions in the Zionist movement."[74] He also showered endless praise on the labor movement.

> The workers have brought with them some major ideas and concepts: the historic mission of the working class perceived as the vanguard of the nation in realizing Zionism; the "religion of labor"—the regeneration of the Jew through productive work; the conquest of labor, both in the cities and in the country; the creation of a national economy through national capital and national labor; constructive socialism; the establishment of new social institutions together with the creation of the national economy. These are genuine ideals, whether one likes them or not. And what have we General Zionists contributed to the spiritual heritage of the movement during this period?[75]

Glickson unquestionably recognized the supremacy of the labor movement as the vehicle of national enterprise. At the same time, there is no doubt that if constructive socialism had posed a danger to the existing social order, Glickson would have waged an all-out war against the movement. But because such a danger did not exist, he, like Weizmann, Blumenfeld, Sokolov, Ussishkin, and Ruppin, could praise "the contribution of the Jewish worker to the revival of the Jewish people. No one who does not harbor a secret class hatred . . . ," he said, "can fail to honor and respect the sufferings and sacrifices of the worker in these very difficult times, his tremendous national discipline and self-control."[76] He, too, rejected the idea of the mass transfer of the Jews from the diaspora to Palestine "just as they were," and he, too, was not impressed by "our 'middle class,' whose economic function in its lands of origin was mainly that of an intermediary, and which wanted to have the same function in Eretz Israel and to transfer to this country its familiar social structures." He, too, exactly like the members of the Histadrut leadership, thought that "there is no room in this country for an aggressive class consciousness, whether of the Right or of the Left," and like them he advocated national unity and vigorously asserted that "Zionism will not be implemented without the joint efforts of all classes and social segments."[77]

Glickson was not content to preach but sought to give the Histadrut clear proof of his goodwill and his acceptance of its authority. He condemned "the lockout," which he saw as "an action in danger of making workers go hungry," and when he opposed strikes, he was careful to explain that "we are not objecting to the right to strike as such"; he wanted to judge the strike weapon solely on its usefulness.[78] Glickson also fought against land specula- tion in the Fourth Aliyah with as much determination as the most extreme leftists.[79] He supported national funds to such a degree that *Bustenai*, the organ of the right wing of the General Zionist movement, accused him of opposing private enterprise.[80]

There was only one issue on which Glickson fought labor with great deter- mination: he completely denied the right of the labor system in education to exist. Glickson viewed the Histadrut's educational system as an embodiment of the danger of class consciousness, which he hated. Unable to convince the people of the second and third ranks, who supported labor education, Glick- son turned to Aharonowitz of Hapo'el Hatza'ir, who regarded the schools of the labor system as simply a means of training children for work. He urged him to return to the tradition of Gordon and to follow the basic principles of his party exemplified by such figures as Shochat, Yaffe, and so on.[81] How- ever, when Glickson embarked on his long campaign against labor schools, he knew very well that his cause was not hopeless and that he had allies in the Histadrut. Soon after the founding of Mapai, Ben-Gurion expressed the desire to bring labor education to an end.

THE STRUGGLE OVER WORKERS' EDUCATION

An autonomous educational system for workers would have been logical only if the labor movement had intended to provide an alternative to the existing order. But as there had never been any such intention, labor educa- tion was neglected and fought for its existence from its beginnings until it lost administrative independence in 1939 and was abolished in 1953. At that time, the present national system of education was established.

Officially, the educational systems in Palestine came into being after a decision by the Zionist executive in 1920. Following an agreement reached in London, the Mizrahi Party accepted responsibility for Zionist-religious education; thus the General, or liberal-bourgeois, system and the labor system (zerem ha'ovdim) came into being. The Histadrut began to attend to the education of its workers' children in 1922, after founding the Central Cultural Committee, and the children's education was declared to be one of its chief concerns. But three years earlier a school for the children of Hashomer members had been founded at Tel 'Adashim, in the Jezreel Val- ley, and two years later educational establishments were founded in the pioneering settlements of Ben-Shemen (halfway between Tel Aviv and Jeru-salem), Atarot (near Jerusalem), and Kfar Giladi.

The labor system officially began in 1923 and three years later received full recognition by the Zionist executive, being given the same status as the General system and Mizrahi national religious education. It obtained a budget, pedagogical autonomy, and budgetary and administrative auton-omy. These decisions were confirmed by the sixteenth Zionist Congress in 1929. In 1932 responsibility for education was transferred from the Jewish Agency and the Zionist Organization to Knesset Israel (the Jewish commu-nity in the country) and Va'ad Le'umi.[82] Parallel with this development, the Cultural Committee was replaced with the Committee for Educational Institutions. The latter was originally a body that grew out of the Cultural Committee and served it as an inspecting subcommittee, similar to the parallel institutions of the two other systems.[83] Two years later, in 1934, the Committee for Educational Institutions became the Histadrut Educa-tional Center.

With the establishment of the Educational Center, the struggle over the labor system's existence intensified. War was waged on two fronts. In the Yishuv there was forceful opposition to the system, which was regarded as a manifestation of the tendency toward class segregation, found in some parts of the Histadrut. Glickson, the major spokesman for the opponents of labor education, battled a policy that he described as "blinkered and short-sighted toward anything or anyone outside the 'camp.'" "If the two trends in our educational system become two worlds, separated and divided from one another . . . ," he said, "the World Zionist Organization will have no reason to help them. . . . We do not constitute two peoples, and we do not have two teachings [torot]" (in Hebrew shtei torot also means two Bibles).[84]

At the same time, a struggle between two schools of thought also began in the Histadrut. The first school viewed workers' education as a cultural and ideological asset, an expression of the special character of the labor move-ment. This was similar to the family wage, the foundation of a new social regime, which would eventually replace the existing order. The second school, led by Ben-Gurion and true to the principles of nationalist socialism, saw the organizational independence of this trend as an obstacle to national unity. Opponents of the autonomy of labor education—nationalists to the core—attached little importance to values and principles except insofar as they mobilized the masses for political objectives.

The whole question of education was considered problematic. Immedi-ately after the First World War, the Zionist Organization, which the manda-tory government recognized as representing the Yishuv, established an edu-cational department. The government of Palestine granted the Jewish schools complete autonomy. This independence had its price, and the bur-den of financing the Jewish educational system, unlike the Arab one, which was financed by the mandatory government, fell entirely on the Zionist Organization. The Va'ad Le'umi rejected the proposal that it take responsibility for this, and throughout the 1920s education was regarded as an unfailing source of trouble. Periodical budget cuts by the Zionist executive sometimes resulted in serious crises. The payment of teachers' salaries was always uncertain, and in some cases it was held up for as long as six months. Teachers' strikes were not uncommon. From 1922 on the Yishuv participated in running education, and its role gradually increased. In that year, the government also began to contribute a trifling sum to the Jewish educational sector (2,500 pounds sterling a year), but its share increased from 1.5 percent in the early years to 11 percent in 1927–32. Nevertheless, at the end of the 1920s, the educational system entered a crisis that threatened its ability to function. Only massive contributions from the Rothschild family and Junior Hadassah in the United States managed to rescue it. In these years teachers experienced constant delays in their paychecks and even had to forgo some of them for the system to survive. Only in 1931, following the organization of the Yishuv as Knesset Israel, did the Va'ad Le'umi accept responsibility for education.[85]

We can understand why education was not considered an attractive segment. From the beginning, the labor system was regarded as a burden in both a psychological and an economic sense, although in practice the Histadrut's investment in its schools was minimal. From the point of view of the founders, an investment in workers' education was worthwhile only if the system proved its ability to "deliver the goods" politically. Because the system never included more than a small minority of the salaried workers' children, it was not considered worth investing in. This created a vicious circle. On one hand, the Histadrut was unwilling from the start to invest the sums necessary to make the system attractive; on the other hand, there were endless complaints about the failure of the schools to attract students. An education tax was never imposed on Histadrut members in the cities; such a tax was levied only in kibbutzim and moshavim. Consequently, most of the burden fell on the parents. Moreover, the educational program reflected the conformist outlook prevalent in Ahdut Ha'avoda. Shmuel Yavnieli, a veteran of the Second Aliyah and one of the founders of Ahdut Ha'avoda, a dour party official unable to get a more important job in the Histadrut economy, was sent to lay the groundwork of labor education. As a result, it seems that apart from encouraging agriculture—a subject that was alien to the majority of city dwellers—the system did not propose anything special, and its educational program was not notably different from that of the General system. But, at the same time, the very existence of a labor system constituted a kind of statement, an expression of the movement's special character and its refusal to accept the norms of bourgeois society.

That is why the labor system, from the beginning, was caught up with the fundamental inner contradictions afflicting the whole labor movement. Just as huge sums were invested in collective settlement as a tool for conquering the land, so workers' education could have served as a tool for the conquest of hearts and minds. As such, schools should have been regarded as a precious asset and placed at the forefront of the movement, next to the pioneers, the conquerors of the desert. The reality, however, was different, and the labor system soon became a stepchild of the movement. The primacy of national objectives as well as the fact that the labor movement had swiftly become the establishment *par excellence* led not only to a refusal on the part of the movement to invest the sums necessary for the development of workers' education but to a suspicion of unusual educational experiments.

At the educational council of the Histadrut, which met in early 1923, the opening of an urban Histadrut school was discussed for the first time. When Yehuda Polani, a well-known educator, proposed that the Histadrut take over the private experimental school founded in Tel Aviv by David Idelson and himself, where instruction was based on *amlanut*—education through practical work—his suggestion met with skepticism and opposition. The establishment of the new school was nevertheless entrusted to this pair, but it was not considered a direct continuation of the first one. Already at the end of the first school year, 1923–24, regarded as a probationary year, violent disagreements erupted between the teachers and members of the educational committee set up to supervise their work. Most of the committee members did not accept the new form of education practiced in the school, and the teaching staff handed in its resignation.

After he left the school and realized that the teaching staff, bearers of the new educational gospel, could not work within the Histadrut's framework, Idelson contacted Gdud Ha'avoda, which had given much thought to children's education. Other staff members, however, were of the opinion that in order not to sever the connection with the Histadrut it was better to work in the General school system than with Gdud Ha'avoda. The hostility of the leadership to the rebels of the Jezreel Valley and the Galilee was so great that any connection with them endangered the position of a Histadrut member. Polani, for instance, believing that the Histadrut repressed initiative and opposed any attempt at spontaneous organization, was ready to work in a school of the General system.[86]

Members of the educational committee, headed by Yavnieli, rejected the approach of the representatives of the new progressive education. The conservative approach triumphed. "If you want to make experiments, first make them with your own children and then come to us," said Yavnieli to the chief innovators, Idelson and Sh.-Z. Pogatchov (the latter, who had arrived in the country a short time earlier, had been trained in the new educational methods of the Soviet Union).[87] In the debate in 1926 on establishing a regional secondary school in the Jezreel Valley for the children of the kibbutzim and moshavim, the committee proposed creating a framework that would complete the children's basic education. Pogatchov took a stand opposite to that of Eliezer Shein, one of the leading conservatives. The committee's program, he said, was suitable for a bourgeois society but not for the Histadrut. The educational committee was opposed to the pedagogical experiments that Pogatchov favored, that is, running the school on the lines of an autonomous "children's society." Pogatchov, however, insisted that "those who wish to create a society of workers based on equality and justice must begin by preparing the children as well."[88]

Pogatchov did not realize that the Histadrut had no interest in extending social experiments beyond the boundaries of collective settlements. The collective settlements themselves had not been founded for ideological reasons, and leaders of the labor movement saw no reason to act differently in educational matters. Moreover, normal life continued in the cities, and traditional education was suited to it. To Pogatchov, who had the outlook of a true social reformer, education was a means of laying the foundations of a new human order. This, however, was not the Histadrut's aim; the educational program drawn up by the committee committed itself to no more than developing "an attitude to life that exalts labor and encourages the desire for progress and development in a working Eretz Israel."[89]

After his experiment in Tel Aviv, Idelson continued his innovations and set up a "children's society" at Kibbutz Beit Alpha. Only at the end of the 1920s, however, when the debate between Idelson and the educational committee was over, did the labor system fix its ideological direction. Shimon Reshef has claimed that the debate did not end with the severance of ties between the innovators and the labor system, and that the teaching methods, social outlook, and curriculum of the system's schools were influenced by new ideas.[90] I believe that this was not the case, and that in reality the controversy was settled in favor of traditional education. From the descriptions of later developments, which Reshef provides, it becomes clear that the education of the labor system was not very different from that of the General system. At the educational council that met in the summer of 1928, it became apparent that the majority of those present favored two types of education: agricultural-vocational education, which would facilitate the integration of the graduates into work and society, and what Reshef calls "human-national" education.[91] This education was quite nationalist, with classes in classic subjects such as the Bible, history, the geography of the country, and nature studies. Here labor education reflected the ideological outlook of the Histadrut as a whole.

These subjects, however, were common to all systems and were not especially socialist. The labor system could not have a special ideological direction, as the Histadrut was opposed to any ideology that stressed the class factor, and it thus failed to develop either a distinctive conceptual system or the tool that was supposed to serve it. From the time the educational committee was first set up until it was disbanded in 1931, the Executive Committee did not concern itself with workers' education and took no interest in determining the Histadrut's policies on culture and education.[92] The committee consequently set very modest practical goals for labor education: "Children's health, the acquisition of elementary but practical knowledge, adaptation to village life, the awakening of interest in agriculture, agricultural instruction, fostering allegiance to our movement of revival, and labor in Eretz Israel." There was no suggestion that workers' education had any far-reaching social objectives.[93] Similarly, the school curriculum drafted in the second half of the 1930s did not reflect any real difference between the labor system and the General system. In the labor system, special emphasis was laid on handicrafts, gardening, and agricultural work; in the General system, children learned a little more Bible, Mishna, and English. In the labor system more time was allocated to discussions of social issues.[94]

This does not mean that there were no aspirations to distinctiveness in the Labor system, but the Histadrut educational system was no more homogenous than the organization itself. Among the educators of the system, and especially in agricultural settlements, there were strongly egalitarian socialist elements, and these also existed in the cities, but it was not they who made the decisions. Within the labor system, as in the Histadrut, Ahdut Ha'avoda, and later Mapai, there were various conflicting tendencies, but the power in the movement was in the hands of the advocates of constructive socialism, the builders of national strength, and these had no intention of doing in education what they had refrained from doing in other spheres. The Histadrut executive had no interest in the content of education, because it viewed the labor system as a burden and feared that its educational system might prove to be an endless drain on resources for which more profitable uses might be found. For Ben-Gurion, the trend represented an unnecessary obstacle to *mamlachtiut*; as explained in the introduction, this Hebrew word expressed the primacy of nation and state, of national values and goals above all other objectives. At the beginning of the 1930s, Ben-Gurion initiated a campaign to remove this potential liability. It was potential rather than actual, because the Histadrut did not invest significant sums of money in the education of its members' children.

The Histadrut's lack of interest in workers' education was reflected, first, in a rejection of innovative ideas. The idea of a "children's society" that could provide the infrastructure for a socialist education was rejected in favor of a social education, which would train the child in the realization of national objectives. At the beginning of the 1940s, this form of education involved organizational patterns that were amazingly similar to the institutional hierarchy of the Histadrut, including the post of class secretary. Social education also included group discussions to promote democratic thought and behavior. Although subjects such as solidarity, responsibility, and freedom of expression were debated in these discussions, no attempt was made to instill a socialist conception of human relations. Social education was directed toward "neutral" values, which everyone could accept. The children were asked to provide assistance to the needy and to set up "enterprises of social assistance to needy children," but that was all.[95]

Similarly, the emphasis on physical work could not in itself give the labor system a special character. Its pedagogical origin was the concept of *amlanut* (education through practical work), but even when linked to the "society of tomorrow," where there would be "neither exploiters nor exploited," it could not serve as the basis of an ideological education aimed at changing the social order. The cult of physical labor, isolated from all the other innovative elements in *amlanut*, which were dispensed with, was taken over by the labor system and became one of the main features of its educational system. Moshe Avigal, one of the chief representatives of its ideology, was typically content to define the concept of equality in terms of mutual respect: "Equality of both rights and duties. . . . This equality is possible only if we stop treating physical labor as inferior to intellectual labor."[96] Physical labor, he wrote, created "human, moral, and national values." This equality, he wrote, "gave it its social significance; it also raised the self-esteem attached to all kinds of physical labor on every level and encouraged the people as a whole to produce and to improve its status in the productive system of the society of nations."[97]

The labor system placed great emphasis on the values of national unity, which were considered more important than the interests of any particular sector. It was therefore not eager to develop a separate identity. Thus, despite the fact that as early as 1927–28 the educational council asked for an obligatory minimum program for the labor schools, this program was finalized only in 1937.[98] Until then, the labor educational program was not different in its methods and its ideological content from that of the General system. Throughout that period, labor schools gave a free hand to teachers, most of whom came from the General system. But more important, the Histadrut educational system did not take the trouble to issue special textbooks to the labor system. Workers' children used the textbooks of the General system.[99]

The educational program established in 1937 was based on two main principles: 1. respect for the Jewish people and the need to strengthen it, and 2. the unification of the working class in Eretz Israel and of workers throughout the world in order to create a regime of social justice. But it soon became apparent that social objectives were not ends in themselves but served the greater national interest. The purpose of "instilling the values of the Zionist labor movement," it was stated, was "to give the child the determination to fulfill the pioneering objectives of Zionism." In addition, the program distinguished between subjects that had to be taught in a concrete fashion through "a variety of means . . . through contact with nature in this country and its landscape, and through moral and practical training in participating in the building of it," and theoretical subjects, which enabled the student to understand social problems and "by the study of world affairs and of society's organization" aroused in the student "the desire to improve the social system."[100] When Glickson protested that this meant that children were being taught the theory of class warfare, Yavnieli, in his reply, dwelled at length on this distinction between everyday, practical subjects and theoretical subjects. The most effective defense he could muster was to claim that teachings based on class were not to be taken too seriously.

> With regard to Marx's doctrine of class, it is a theory like any other. Hundreds of youths above the age of elementary school are being educated in our schools today, from fourteen-year-olds to seventeen- and eighteen-year-olds. If these young people are given an idea of Darwin's teachings, for example, the person in question would not think it strange. If the same is done with regard to Marx's teachings, why should he find this so terrible?[101]

In all modern national movements, the study of history has been regarded as crucially important in the the younger generation's education. The teaching of national history has a political and social function: historical studies have the task of forming the consciousness and self-awareness of young people, and the investigation of the past is supposed to develop their sense of the rightness of their national cause. The labor movement's approach was comparable. In 1935, some two years before the minimum educational program was published, the Educational Center's pedagogical committee proposed that history be taught in grades six to eight. The program was to play the classic role required of education everywhere in Europe and later in the Third World: to inculcate a love of the people and the land through a knowledge of their history. Naturally, in Palestine the study of history also had another, supremely important purpose, which concerned the founders in relation to the Bible: to explain and justify the Jewish right to own the land. The heart of the program was not social issues but national history. Even the teaching of socialist doctrines in the eighth grade related to the study of the great national movements: the unification of Italy, the unification of Germany, and the liberation of the Balkan peoples. Even the term *class warfare* appeared in quotation marks.[102]

The nationalist viewpoint was even more pronounced in the study of other subjects. Whereas history required one to grapple with the outside world, subjects such as literature, geography, the Bible, and the history of

Zionism were especially nationally oriented.[103] The Bible and the history of Zionism, however, were included in the study of history. Essentially, the 1937 educational program reflected the conformist nationalist socialist outlook dominant in Mapai.

Even in the celebrations of the First of May, national principles were dominant. The main objective for which the Jewish worker was struggling was said to be the national objective, not the realization of socialism. Yavnieli described this phenomenon beautifully: "While the debate on education has been going on for years, dozens of Jewish settlements have sprung up, bursting with Jewish life, with socialist schools full of the spirit of labor and dedication to the national revival. (The red flag has meanwhile been placed side by side with the national flag as a symbol of the inner unity of our national and socialist aspirations)." In contrast to the fidelity of the members of the labor movement, Yavnieli stressed the erosion that had taken place in "bourgeois" settlements. While those who raised the red flag had been faithful to the nation, "Nes Ziona [a moshava], for example, . . . has become a mixed settlement of Jews and Arabs."[104]

The progressive fusion of the labor system with the General system was in keeping with the policies of the movement as a whole. From the ideological point of view, there was no real obstacle to the unification of the two systems. Both of them served Zionist aims with equal faithfulness, and in the labor system the red flag was a symbol that strengthened the spirit of devotion to the nation rather than weakened it. The settlements of the labor movement, its economic enterprises, and its cultural institutions were a bulwark against any contact with the Arab environment. Nobody fought against the Arab worker more vigorously than the Histadrut; nobody preached national, economic, and social segregation with more determination than the labor movement. Under such circumstances, how could concepts such as workers' solidarity and international brotherhood be taken seriously?

This was the principal weakness of the labor system. Apart from the fact that no immediate political benefit could be derived from it, it did not play a sufficiently distinctive role to justify its preservation. Thus, it was not surprising that the two schools in Tel Aviv that were the standard-bearers of labor education were originally private schools. The first, as we have seen, was Polani and Idelson's school, which the Histadrut took over in 1923. The second, Beit Hinuch North [literally, House of Education, situated in the new northern part of the city], was founded in 1932, and like its predecessor it was run by a group of teachers influenced by progressive educational ideas. The school's policies especially pleased parents from Central Europe, and it met with great success. It was not only the Histadrut people who asked the founders and teachers of the school to join the labor system; a similar proposal was made by Shoshana Persitz, a well-known General Zionist politician, on behalf of the Tel Aviv municipality.[105] This shows that the difference between the two kinds of education could not have been great. In 1934 the school decided to join the labor system, and a year later it moved to Schunat Hapo'alim Alef (First Workers' District) in North Tel Aviv. This district had been founded in 1929 and was the oldest of its kind in the city. It is significant that between 1924, when the first school of the labor system was founded in Tel Aviv, and 1932, or more exactly 1934, not a single Histadrut school was founded in that or any other city. In reality, not even the Beit Hinuch North was founded by the labor system; it was the teaching staff who decided in favor of Histadrut education. The Histadrut, for its part, concentrated all its educational efforts on agricultural settlements.[106]

It is true that the weakness of the labor system in Tel Aviv was also due to the fact that the municipality did everything possible to hinder labor education in the city. "We constitute about half of the city of Tel Aviv. We pay taxes, and the only school run according to our ideas is discriminated against. It has no budget and no building," Katznelson complained bitterly to the Va'ad Le'umi in July 1935.[107] But in matters it really cared about, the Histadrut was not in the habit of giving in and being satisfied with mere complaints. A similar discrimination against the labor exchange or the health care organization (Kupat Holim) would have provoked a strong immediate reaction. Workers' education was simply not regarded as a matter over which it was worth waging an out-and-out war. Moreover, the municipality not only had a policy of hindering the labor system but provided social services, including free municipal education, which competed successfully with Histadrut education. In order to succeed in the competition for the workers' children, considerable sums would have had to have been invested in the maintenance of the schools and in making them attractive, but as it lacked interest in its own educational system, the Histadrut failed to move in that direction.

The labor system might have succeeded better if the founders had thought it could serve as an effective means of mass mobilization, similar to the health services. However, membership in the Kupat Holim was an existential need, whereas workers' education was considered superfluous. The results could have been foreseen. "The comrades as a whole showed no interest in us. The executive did not give us too much attention either," complained Mona Hefetz, an official in the Education Committee, to the Histadrut Council in October 1931.[108] Despite an increase from 153 children in 1922–23 to 2,812 children and 146 workers in fifty population centers in 1932–33,[109] and despite the fact that there were 6,855 students in the Histadrut schools in 1935–36, and a year later, according to the Educational Center, more than 8,000, the labor system comprised less than 15 percent of the total number of schoolchildren, and the great majority of these lived in agricultural settlements. According to the statistics of the Va'ad Le'umi for 1936–37, the labor system had no more than 4,695 students.[110]

In March 1936 Ben-Gurion informed the Histadrut Council that in Tel Aviv only 600 of the 11,000 students in the city studied "in our schools."[111] According to figures given at the fourth Histadrut convention in 1933, 267 children went to the Beit Hinuch North in Tel Aviv, and another 60 children attended the kindergarten for the children of working mothers. In the militant Borochov district, 181 children went to the elementary school, and another 100 attended kindergarten. Thus, in the Tel Aviv area, the labor system in that year succeeded in enlisting only 608 students. In Haifa and its environs, the total number of children educated in the labor system was 331, 172 of whom were from Nesher, another militant working-class district. In Jerusalem 76 students attended the Histadrut school, and there was no kindergarten.[112] If we remember that the inhabitants of the Borochov and Nesher districts and those of the "Haifa workers' district" in any case belonged to the hard core of the Histadrut and Mapai, we can understand why the leaders of the movement did not think that the immediate political contribution of the labor system justified any investment of resources.

The Jewish autonomous national institutions financed at most about 25 percent or less of the total costs of labor education. In 1932–33 the cost of the labor educational system came to 17,500 pounds, but the Histadrut Educational Committee had only 8,382 pounds at its disposal. A little more than half of this sum (4,363 pounds) came from the Department of Education of Knesset Israel (the Jewish community in Palestine). The direct contribution of the Histadrut executive came to 250 pounds,[113] virtually nil.

Although there is a considerable difference between the data from the Department of Education of the Va'ad Le'umi and those of the Histadrut Educational Center with regard to the number of students and the cost of maintaining labor education, the data are the same with regard to the contribution of the Va'ad Le'umi to the maintenance of the labor schools and its significance for the students' parents. According to the Va'ad Le'umi, in 1937–38 the cost of the Histadrut schools came to 37,054 pounds. The Va'ad Le'umi contributed 7,900 pounds, less than 21.5 percent of the cost. However, under the section "Payments to Agricultural Settlements," the sum of 28,824 pounds appears. According to the Educational Center's report, in the previous year (1936–37) the cost of the labor system was 60,000 pounds, and Va'ad Le'umi's contribution was 7,000 pounds. This is how the people of the Educational Center described the situation: "All the institutions [schools] are supported by the agricultural settlements of the Histadrut and the parents' committees in the cities." In Tel Aviv in 1934–35, one out of the three Histadrut schools, the Central Beit Hinuch, needed a contribution of about 250 pounds from the Educational Center's funds, which represented about 20 percent of the sum needed to pay the teachers' annual salaries. The two other schools, Beit Hinuch Bet [School Number Two] and Beit Hinuch North, were, from the point of view of the Educational Center, completely independent. The Borochov district needed assistance amounting to 25 to 30 percent of the cost of educating its children.[114] But we should remember that the Educational Center's resources came from the Va'ad Le'umi. The Histadrut did not participate in financing education but only served as a channel for transferring money.

This situation, in which parents in the cities, in the communal settlements, and in moshavim bore the lion's share of the cost of their children's education (between 85 and 90 percent) was intolerable in view of the fact that in Tel Aviv, at the beginning of the 1930s, school fees had been abolished and elementary schools were financed by an education tax imposed on the city's inhabitants. This arrangement did not apply to the Histadrut schools, and the Educational Center submitted passively to "this cruel discrimination against the children of tax-paying citizens, particularly in Tel Aviv, Hadera, and Petah Tiqwa." In 1936–37 the Tel Aviv municipality allotted the three Histadrut schools 1,500 pounds, or 2.1 pounds per student, a sum that the Educational Center estimated to be "several times" lower than the cost of educating a student in the other schools. And indeed, the municipality's allocation was only enough to cover less than half of the total salaries of the Histadrut schools' teachers. The total sum needed to pay the salaries, according to the calculation of the Va'ad Le'umi, was 3,575 pounds. In Hadera free schooling was introduced in 1937, but the exemption from payment of school fees did not apply to the Histadrut school "because of a deliberate intention to make it shut down." The official reason given for this decision was that the Histadrut school "was no longer registered as an institution of the Jewish community."[115] In 1934 participants in the eighth convention of the workers of the Educational Center had complained that the elementary school teachers' union had prevented the Histadrut schools of Hadera and Petah Tiqwa from obtaining official recognition.[116]

The Educational Center fought on two fronts, and it sometimes seems that the external front, against the right-wing municipalities of Tel Aviv and the old moshavot, was not the most difficult. The internal Histadrut front was hardly easier. The Executive Committee was absolutely opposed to imposing an education tax on Histadrut members as a whole. Such a tax would have provided the only means of developing the labor system and of attracting a significant number of students. In the period after the transfer of managerial responsibility for the Histadrut educational system to the Department of Education of the Va'ad Le'umi, it became obvious that this would have been the only way of developing an autonomous system of secondary education.[117] But the Histadrut leadership was not interested in education, which made the task of the Educational Center impossible. The difficulty of its situation was demonstrated by the fact that in order to help construct buildings for the schools under its control, or in order to move them from rented premises or wooden huts—which happened in Tel Aviv and Jerusa-

lem, in Kibbutzim Ein Harod and Giva't Hashlosha—the educational section of the Histadrut had to obtain six- or eight-year loans from Bank
Hapo'alim, the Nir company, and the Unemployment Fund. In Tel Aviv the
municipality put a plot at its disposal and set aside three thousand pounds,
but the total cost of the building came to eight thousand pounds, and the
Educational Center was unable to raise the rest.[118]

There is no doubt that the Histadrut leadership felt the labor system was
a burden, and the financial aspect was not the most important part. The
economic argument was only a pretext; it was the official, very convenient
excuse Ben-Gurion gave when in 1931 he initiated a campaign to relieve the
Histadrut of any financial responsibility for its educational enterprise. He
also exploited the time factor. Ben-Gurion waited for the expected transfer
of the Jewish educational sector from the Jewish Agency to Knesset Israel in
order to be rid of a millstone that was not only financial but also, and above
all, moral, political, and ideological.

This point needs to be especially emphasized. The Histadrut did not contribute financially to the labor system, but it bore general responsibility
for its existence. It was an address for the endless but justified complaints of
the students' parents, who had to bear the burden, and for the teachers,
whose salaries were always the first casualty of any budget cuts. Pressure
was continually exerted on the Histadrut by people in charge of labor education, who had to deal with parents who asked for more than the system could
give, in terms of both teaching quality and cost. The autonomy of the labor
system also constituted an additional, sometimes conspicuous—and in Ben-
Gurion's view totally unnecessary—focal point for internal tensions in
Mapai. It was no accident that the first concentrated attack on the system
began not long after the founding of the new party.

All these difficulties could have been overcome if there had been the
ideological will to group urban salaried workers into a society with special
values, which then it could have passed on to its children. Because this
motivation did not exist, there was no need to maintain a special educational
system with administrative autonomy. Administrative autonomy would have
had a purpose only if the system had produced a distinctive educational
program and pedagogical approach and had developed the ability to attract
students. By the same token, the creation of a distinctive program would
have been possible only if the Histadrut had constituted an alternative to
bourgeois society.

The opposition to the independence of workers' education, especially on
the part of Ben-Gurion, was ideologically and politically motivated. First,
Ben-Gurion failed to appreciate the value of a workers' educational system
because he had no interest in laying the foundations of a society that would
be basically different from bourgeois society. He wished to dominate society
as it was, as he suggested when he asked a question of an extreme demagogic

simplicity: "Who is interested in unifying education rather than destroying it? Who is interested in national sovereignty rather than anarchy?" The answer was "We are!"[119] Ben-Gurion opposed with all his might what was known as a "class" approach—simply a modest attempt to give the children of the labor system a worldview slightly different from that of the general society. He extolled the principle of "generality" (comprehensiveness), claiming that "we are the generality," and declared once again that the path to victory was "a move from class to nation."[120]

Second, Ben-Gurion intended to eliminate points of friction in the Yishuv. In his opinion, labor education was a major source of unnecessary conflict. It was very conspicuous, and from a practical point of view almost worthless. The leader of the Histadrut therefore proceeded in his customary manner; he began to gradually throttle the system by refusing to provide money for purposes that, according to his scale of values, were unproductive. "At first," he said, "we were told that the money from the World Zionist Organization should be used only for productive purposes such as colonization and building. In my opinion this is right, and it is inconsistent with the policy of setting sums aside for education." He now added another argument, no less instructive than this one. He recognized the fact that in education "we have some major achievements, but we have no right to do anything at the expense of the workers. The workers have sometimes collaborated with this, but despite this, we had no right to buy books or maintain schools out of their wages."[121] This demagogic argument was used only to reinforce the previous one and to stress the fact that unlike the health services or the Histadrut administration, it was not worth imposing a tax on Histadrut members for the sake of education. Education was not a source of power; nor did it serve the primary objective of building the nation.

In opposition to Tabenkin and Katznelson but supported by Kaplan, Ben-Gurion began persistently to seek the liquidation of the labor system.[122] As on numerous occasions, he was ahead of many of his colleagues in the party and was the first to reach conclusions that later became generally accepted. He viewed the transfer of the Histadrut educational system to the Department of Education of the Va'ad Le'umi as not only an appropriate economic solution but also an important step in the creation of the national power structure. He sought to put an end to "our segregation" (here he adopted Glickson's terminology), "which restricts our capacity for action," and also to reassure the middle classes in an area in which he could most easily make concessions, as there was no real danger to the power of the Histadrut. "With regard to the children," he said, "I do not distinguish between the children of workers and other groups. We have achieved whatever we have done with children who did not come from the workers."[123]

After an initial failure, Ben-Gurion waited for an opportune moment, and five years later, in 1936, returned to the attack. He was now chairman of the

Jewish Agency, having taken up the post the previous year. This time his tone was far more biting and aggressive: he rejected the whole system. He claimed that the inability of the labor system to embrace more than 4 percent of the children in Tel Aviv resulted from an ideological perversion. According to Ben-Gurion, its whole outlook was the unfortunate consequence of an attachment to the ways of thinking of the "Po'alei Tzion leftists." The attempt to create a class-based system of education had led to nothing but "failure and bankruptcy." What had been followed in education, he said, was not "the general line of the labor movement in this country" but the separatist line of the Left. He claimed that it was precisely the children of the working class who were discriminated against by this class-based system of education. Not only did the labor movement have no real influence on education in the country as a whole, but owing to the small number of students, its school system was placed at an economic disadvantage. Moreover, he said, workers' education had failed completely even from the point of view of its supporters, for it did not even have a socialist orientation.[124]

The opposition to abandoning the labor system (opponents included not only Hashomer Hatza'ir and Po'alei Tzion leftists but also Katznelson)[125] was sufficiently strong to prolong its decline for a few more years. As happened in other cases, the ideological problem was solved through economic strangulation. No education tax was imposed; nor were Histadrut members given any incentive to send their children to the labor system schools. Here Mapai created an interesting precedent. Anyone who wanted a slightly different education from the usual one had to pay out of pocket. Ideological commitment had to be paid for in full. This situation could not continue indefinitely; consequently, in 1939 the administrative and budgetary independence of the labor system was abolished. Nationalist socialism celebrated another major victory.

The refusal of the Histadrut to assume financial responsibility for labor education had far-reaching consequences. Histadrut elementary education was an expensive commodity, whereas education in the general schools was cheap, and various municipalities began to offer it as a service in the early 1930s (the first was in Tel Aviv). In this period, the Histadrut failed to apply to education the principle of mutual aid on which the health services, for instance, were based, at least in theory. Therefore a lack of funds often meant that the workers' children had to be transferred to the general schools. In addition, the lack of secondary education in the labor system began to undermine primary education there as well. A typical example was the case of the Borochov district and the dilemma confronting the parents there. In August 1939 Dov Zisla, head of the labor system school in the district, appealed to the Educational Center on behalf of the teachers and parents, asking for an allocation of forty pounds toward the sum of 237 pounds. This sum was required to establish a ninth grade for the school year

1939–40 (the ninth grade was the beginning of secondary education). He based his request, among other things, on the fact that the principal of the Gymnasia Balfour in Tel Aviv "has set up a secondary school in Ramat Gan [near the Borochov district] and uses all the means at his disposal to attract children who have finished eighth grade in our school. We see this establishment as a great danger, as it also includes classes on a primary level, and it is liable to undermine our primary education and the social organization we are setting up around our school. If our parents see themselves as dependent on the secondary school for the further education of their children . . ."[126] The rest of the letter is unclear, but the gist of it is probably that "they will prefer to send them to Ramat Gan for their primary education."

Since its founding in 1922, the Borochov district was a party stronghold particularly loyal to the Histadrut, and yet it received no assistance in education, and its inhabitants, devoted to the labor system, had to pay for their children's schooling themselves. The ninth grade, when it finally began in 1939–40, was also financed in such a way that more than half of the cost was covered by the parents and a little less than a third was donated by the teaching staff in the form of hours of instruction and by the parent committees of the two elementary schools in the district. The Educational Center was asked to donate only about 17 percent of the total cost.[127] In the same period, parents fell behind in their payment of school fees, so that teachers failed to get their salaries. The Department of Education ordered the teachers not to begin the new school year unless they received their full salaries of the previous year. Moreover, at the end of September 1938, because of the inability of the Beit Hinuch, the first school in the district (the second was known as Hamakbil, "the other one"), to make its payments to the Kupat Holim, medical inspection was discontinued there.[128]

A problem in itself was the question of secondary education for workers' children. This question preoccupied anyone who believed that a fourteen-year-old child could not be sent out to work. Because of labor's emphasis on agriculture, in 1934–36 three postelementary schools with an agricultural orientation were set up in rural areas: Kfar Yeladim next to Afula, Giva't Hashlosha near Tel Aviv, and Yagur. When they finished the tenth grade, most of the adolescents took up agricultural work, a minority continued to study in agricultural schools, and only a few pursued a general secondary education.[129] This matter was not discussed in the Histadrut until 1939, and an interim report on secondary education was written.[130] There were diverging and even opposing points of view. Moreover, it became apparent in those years that most salaried workers in the cities wanted secondary education for their children. Those who were able to do so sent their children first to the Gymnasia Herzliyya and later to other high schools. At the Histadrut Council in 1936, one of those present said he had heard Dr. Bograshov, principal of the very "bourgeois" Gymnasia Herzliyya and a well-known

General Zionist, boasting at an election meeting that "labor leaders prefer to send their children to me to be educated."[131] And indeed, all three children of Ben-Gurion (the first secretary of the Histadrut), the son of Remez (the second secretary of the Histadrut), and the two children of Yavnieli (the official in charge of the labor system) attended the Gymnasia.

Undoubtedly the increasing demand for secondary education among the growing class of the political management of the labor movement, of those who ran the Histadrut economy, of various officials, as well as of high-level and well-paid specialized workers in the growing industrial and services sectors, led to the founding in 1937–38 of the New High School. This school, which claimed "to educate youth in the spirit of the pioneering Zionism" of the labor movement,[132] soon became a magnet for the children of the Histadrut elite. Toni Halle, the principal and cofounder of the school, a friend of Gershom Scholem, became a legend in this group for many generations.

Throughout the years when Mapai was dominant in the Yishuv, secondary education was a very expensive commodity and was confined to the well-to-do. In the 1930s and 1940s, officials of the Histadrut's economic institutions and political apparatus, party workers, and the management and staff of autonomous Jewish national and local institutions also formed part of this group. In the absence of institutional assistance to secondary education, and in the absence of public secondary education, postsecondary education in Jewish Palestine became a further cause of widening social gaps. The only financial aid was provided by the schools themselves. Thus, for example, the Gymnasia Herzliyya, after giving ninth-grade graduates of the Borochov district a test, agreed, on the basis of their certificates alone, to accept the more talented students, who were promised a special discount in school fees.[133] However, the secondary schools, which were self-supporting and had to balance their budgets, were obviously unable to take their generosity beyond certain limits. In 1940 fees for the secondary classes in the Gymnasia Herzliyya ranged between 21 pounds for the fifth grade and 25 pounds for the eighth and top grade.[134] In the Gymnasia Shalva, fees were lower: 20 pounds a year (or 18 pounds, according to another document found in the same file) for all grades.[135] In the New High School, the pupils paid between 17 pounds a year in the fifth grade and 21 pounds in the eighth grade.[136] In the middle of the decade, fees at the Gymnasia Herzliyya rose to 26 pounds in the fifth grade and 33 pounds in the eighth grade.[137] Students of the Gymnasia Shalva paid between 36.3 and 41.25 pounds.[138] The New High School, for those who paid the full fee, was the most expensive of all; students in the fifth grade paid 36 pounds, and those in the eighth paid 42.[139]

These were very large sums, beyond the means of low-level salaried workers and extremely burdensome for those with middle-range salaries. The fees at the New High School were equivalent to an agricultural worker's six or eight months' salary, or the monthly budget of three modest urban families. (For standards of living, salaries, and so on, see the next chapter.) Even if only 8.4 percent of students paid the full school fees, 52 percent enjoyed a discount of 25 percent, and 34 percent enjoyed an exemption from payment of 26 to 50 percent,[140] it is hard to avoid the impression that the graduates of this "leftist" institution belonged to the top stratum of salaried workers. Similar discounts, if less generous, were offered in the Gymnasia Shalva, where 35 percent of students enjoyed a reduction of 25 percent, and 37 percent were exempted from payment of 26 to 50 percent. The number of those paying full school fees was largest in the Gymnasia Herzliyya: 27.8 percent as against 18 percent in the Gymnasia Shalva.[141]

The contribution of the Va'ad Leumi and municipalities to secondary education was no more than symbolic. In the budget of the Department of Education for 1936–37, the sum mentioned under the entry "Support of Secondary Schools and Seminars" was a ridiculous 1,685 pounds. At that period the mandatory government allotted the Va'ad Le'umi 42,000 pounds.[142] Until 1947–48, when it received 144 pounds, the Gymnasia Shalva did not enjoy any support from the Va'ad Le'umi, and the sums it disposed of for scholarships were ludicrous: for example, 62 pounds for 1943–44 (the first year in which it received a sum from any source except school fees). In the New High School, in 1944–45, fourteen scholarships were recorded, of which six were financed by the municipality. The funding source of the other eight is unclear. In the following year, the municipality contributed 140 pounds for this purpose, and the Va'ad Le'umi provided 354 pounds. The first record of support by the Educational Center is from 1946–47: 500 pounds, compared with 400 pounds provided by other institutions. In that year the school's income came to 6,128 pounds.[143] In the Gymnasia Herzliyya, the contribution of the Va'ad Le'umi and the Tel Aviv municipality to the school's budget in 1943–44 amounted to 1,500 pounds out of a total income of 43,000 pounds. In 1940–41 the Va'ad Le'umi contributed 180 pounds to the 16,156 pounds needed to run the institution.[144] When Mapai was in control in the Histadrut and the Yishuv, not only did it fail to take action to improve the situation of the workers' children, but it even contributed to the perpetuation of their backwardness and economic inferiority.

At the same time, the myth of the superiority of the Jewish laborer was assiduously cultivated throughout the labor movement, and students at the Hebrew University and the Technion warmly embraced this principle. Moshe Sharett, in a meeting with them, formulated this principle as follows: "I think the scale of values fixed by our society, which makes the worker-pioneer the highest class of all, will never be changed." Sharett warned the students, representatives of the party cells in the institutions of higher learning, against "thinking that they are in some way higher than the workers." The students, for their part, assured him that they did not "regard themselves as competing with workers for hegemony." "Our task," they said, "is simply to bring the intelligensia to play a part in the enterprise carried out by the workers."[145] This was said at a period when an already considerable social gap was widening, and this was due, at least in part, to differences in the level of education. At that time higher education was already a path to social advancement and economic affluence. A man without a sought-after profession or without education was merely a laborer, and high school graduates and students at the Hebrew University were not generally counted among these. Even educated new immigrants who in periods of severe economic crisis were sent to do manual labor generally were able, when the crisis had passed, to find their way toward the service sector or private agriculture. Throughout the period of building the Jewish National Home, the myth of the laborer's social superiority served as psychological compensation for his inferior status.

Members of the Histadrut youth movements were recruited from the ranks of the children of the true socioeconomic elite, those who filled the benches of the New High School and other prestigious schools such as Hagymnasia Ha'ivrit in Jerusalem and the Haifa Reali School, and not from the fictitious elite of agricultural, construction, and port workers. The elitism of secondary education and its exclusiveness undoubtedly limited the attraction of these movements. Just as labor education and secondary education had failed to attract the masses, so the Histadrut youth movements embraced only a minute percentage of Eretz Israeli youth. According to figures released by the Mapai Central Committee at the beginning of October 1937, based on the mandatory government's records, censuses of working young adults taken by the Histadrut, and censuses of the youth movements taken by the Youth Department of the Keren Hakayemet (Jewish National Fund), 23,000 young people belonged to these movements. Students at schools comprised 48,000 boys and girls, aged ten to twenty. Of these, only about a third (16,750) belonged to youth movements. Of these, about 12,750 boys and girls belonged to movements unconnected with the Histadrut, such as the politically neutral scouts and the right-wing revisionist Betar. The Histadrut youth movements were made up of 3,500 to 4,000 boys and girls. Thus, only 24 percent of youth movement members and only slightly more than 8 percent of young people attending school received the celebrated ideological training of which the Israeli elite is so proud. "One may conclude," said Zeev Sherf, an expert on the subject in Mapai, "that out of every 100 boys and girls at school, 26 belong to other youth movements and 7 to our organizations. Of these 7, 4 are in Hashomer Hatza'ir and 3 in Mahanot Ha'olim [Mapai]. Two-thirds of the young people in school do not belong to any organization."[146]

Mapai leaders were well aware of their lack of influence on the younger generation. "Our party fails to attract the young people," asserted Sherf, later housing minister in the state of Israel. He gave two reasons for this failure: the "fact that the party does not devote enough resources to this purpose" and "the lack of any intellectual effort on our part." The young people, he said, failed to respond because "we do not provide them with any intellectual challenge."[147] Remez, for his part, viewed the party's ability to deal with youth as a test of its effectiveness, but he did not make any original suggestions. Ziama Aranne, a future minister of education, gave the best explanation. After remarking on the neglect of ideology among workers, on the inability of the movement to organize a seminar on such subjects for them, and on the refusal of Hakibbutz Hame'uhad to contribute to ideological action in the cities, he gave his own reason for the unwillingness of young people to join the youth movements: "All the organizations of the youth movements created by the different sections of our movement were set up to serve the purposes of agricultural settlement. . . . Thousands of boys and girls in school are untouched by our concern or interest because we do not know if, later on, they will settle in kibbutzim or moshavim."[148]

The problems of the youth movements, and especially of Mapai's Mahanot Ha'olim, reflected the weaknesses that afflicted the labor system, from an unwillingness to invest the necessary financial resources to a lack of real ideological commitment. Despite everything, the labor movement controlled cultural matters. Its dominance was assured by the small elite of high school pupils and youth movement members. They, together with members of the collective settlements, produced the best writers, poets, and fighters of the Palmach generation, the generation who founded the state and left its imprint on Israel in the process of formation. The middle classes participated, through the schools and youth movements or their inability to provide the Yishuv with a credible alternative, in the cultural dominance of the labor movement. In general, they accepted it without question.

CHAPTER SIX

Democracy and Equality on Trial

THE HEGEMONY OF THE APPARATUS AND THE POVERTY
OF INTELLECTUAL LIFE

The comprehensive nature of the Histadrut inevitably influenced the parties associated with it. Mapai was founded in 1930 as a composite party, from both an ideological and a social point of view. Mapai's nationalist socialist outlook, the policy of class collaboration, and the principle of the primacy of the nation could be combined with revolutionary declarations, which Ben-Gurion saw fit to make when he thought it necessary. Everyone realized that these declarations had no basis in reality, but they sometimes had a political usefulness. Thus, Ben-Gurion could say he was "committed to a policy of seeking a national coalition in Zionism and the Yishuv," and that "without the national redemption that only such a union can bring about there would be no Jewish working class; nor would there be Jews who created a socialist revolution or a working society." At the same time he could tell Hashomer Hatza'ir: "I am one of those who believe in the necessity of a revolution, and a revolution through force. In my opinion, the workers of Eretz Israel ought to have not only trade unions, agricultural enterprises, cooperative concerns, and cultural institutions but also military equipment and weapons of war, so that when the day comes, they can seize power and maintain it by force."[1] This was said after years of collaboration with the middle classes, after continual attempts to destroy the independence of the labor system in education, after the crushing of Gdud Ha'avoda, and after persistently disregarding the decisions of the Histadrut with respect to "family wages." In view of this deliberate inconsistency, one can hardly be surprised that the only qualification required for membership in Mapai was not ideological commitment but possession of a Histadrut membership card. Essentially, the party was made up of a hard core of Histadrut functionaries and of people from the collective settlements. The latter had an intellectual life of their own, sometimes quite independent of the party. In the cities, the Histadrut and the party provided employment and organizations that wielded considerable economic power. Thus, in difficult times, people came to them for assistance or intervention.

The weakest aspect of the labor movement had always been the intellectual side. The world of Mapai and the Histadrut was narrow and restricted;

the idea that the party fostered an intense intellectual life and conducted deep and stormy ideological debates is, like the legend of equality, purely a myth. No European party called itself socialist and was at the same time as unconcerned with the universal questions of socialism as Ahdut Ha'avoda, and later Mapai. The outside world hardly interested the party; its leaders and thinkers gave little thought to the basic problems of the period between the two world wars. Fascism, Nazism, and the Spanish civil war did not especially preoccupy them outside the Jewish or Zionist context. Mapai was not particularly involved in the events in Europe. When Austrian social democracy collapsed, Mapai's Central Committee ordered protest meetings in the cities and larger moshavot and sent a telegram to the Socialist International expressing a willingness "to come to the aid of the workers in Austria,"[2] but there were no such expressions of readiness to provide assistance—even symbolic assistance—to the fighters in the Spanish civil war. In Austria not very much could have been done, but in the long Spanish war the situation was quite different. Theoretically, Mapai expressed regret for Spain's ordeal, and thunderous applause generally greeted declarations of sympathy, but apart from placards on the First of May or warm statements like the one that concluded the Rehovot convention in 1938, the party did not concern itself with events outside its sphere. Ben-Gurion rebuked France and England for not sending arms or soldiers to Spain.[3] But a movement whose envoys traveled the length and breadth of Europe and America and were present at all important trade union meetings, all socialist party conferences, and all agricultural exhibitions did not send a single delegate to Republican Spain.

In a speech on 1 May 1938, broadcast on the Jerusalem radio, Katznelson claimed that "our tortured land is a brother to Spain, where foreign hands have stirred up civil war, and foreign arms and legions blow up buildings, sowing death and destruction."[4] Like Shlomo Lavi, who drew a parallel between "Spain and Hanita"(a new kibbutz in western Galilee which had to repel armed Arab attacks),[5] making them equally important, Katznelson was incapable of seeing the world in terms other than his own narrow perspective—in this case, through the prism of the Arab revolt of 1936–39. It was the rank and file who wanted to know about the world situation and showed an interest in the international socialist movement, whereas the leadership focused on practical local issues. "We cannot live from day to day in politics," protested the delegate from Kibbutz Ashdot Ya'akov at the fourth Rehovot convention, the day after Ben-Gurion's speech. A member from Kibbutz Yagur followed suit. He asked for "a careful scrutiny of the situation of the world socialist movement." It was necessary, he said, to go beyond "immediate concerns."[6]

The target of all these reflections was Ben-Gurion. The political and polemical speech of the party's leader was warmly supported by Moshe Sharett and was characteristic of the leadership's way of thinking. In this speech, Ben-Gurion looked at things purely from the viewpoint of the movement's interests, the Yishuv and the Jewish people.[7] It is quite possible that no more could have been asked at that difficult period. The specter of Nazism, which was going from strength to strength, overshadowed everything, and in Palestine the Arab revolt was still in progress and unemployment was on the rise. Ben-Gurion was conscious of the fact that these were "terrible times," unparalleled "in world or Jewish history'; he knew that the threat of a world war hung over Europe and that it would not be a repetition of the 1914–18 war. He realized that Nazi Germany had declared "a war of extermination against the Jewish people"—not only against the Jews of Germany, "but against the Jews of the whole world."[8] Tabenkin[9] and other speakers were also aware of the danger of extermination, and they often referred to it. To judge from the record of this convention, the Yishuv leadership well understood Nazi intentions toward the Jews of Europe.

Ben-Gurion's focus on the affairs of the Yishuv was not the result of his lack of understanding of the world situation. In his impressive speech on Saturday night, 7 May 1938, he demonstrated that he understood the situation perfectly well. The narrow perspective he adopted was not a consequence of the Arab revolt of the late 1930s or his obsession with founding a Jewish state but derived from the nature of Zionism and the leader's single-minded pursuit of his aims. This narrow focus was usual with the founders, and it was also the source of their strength. They were not interested in ideological problems, abstract questions, or universal matters. Throughout the world, nationalists hated abstract discussions. To all those at the Rehovot convention who complained about the party's intellectual aridity, its lack of an ideological position, to all those who wanted it to have a "specific ideal," Ben-Gurion replied:

> I see this debate as being concerned with our movement's wholeness and ability to function, its capacity of carrying out its mission in these terrible times.
>
> I want to say . . . that everything depends on party unity. A party cannot live on an ideal alone. We have an ideal, a unique ideal, a specific ideal, a unifying ideal. But, I repeat, a party cannot live on an ideal alone. It needs friendship, it needs comradeship; it needs mutual trust, mutual respect, collective responsibility.[10]

The "specific ideal" was nationhood. If Ben-Gurion asked for "the unity of the working class," it was to serve the national idea. Essentially, Ben-Gurion believed in "comradeship," a code word for discipline and unity of action. He was not interested in ideological debate, however superficial this might be. From his point of view, it was always a time of emergency, and the great virtue of Zionism was that it needed no proof and was a self-contained system. Yosef Shapira, a delegate and a former member of Hapo'el Hatza'ir, expressed this very well. Later Shapira was to write the history of Hapo'el Hatza'ir on behalf of the surviving members of the party. "Today," he said, "we have heard that the party should have a 'specific ideal.' . . . The specific ideal of our movement is aliyah to Eretz Israel."[11]

The last word was spoken by Katznelson. The chief ideologist of the movement was at that time entirely preoccupied with a single concern: the unity of the labor movement, especially the unity of the kibbutz movements. As he saw it, this "specific ideal" was sorely lacking in Mapai. He thus declared the following to the delegates at the conference: "I say to you that nothing in recent years has upset me as much as what has happened in [Kibbutz] Ramat Yohanan and [Kibbutz] Beit Alpha."[12] What shook this spiritual shepherd to the depths of his soul was not the civil war in Spain or the rise of Nazism but an exchange of populations between two kibbutzim because of disagreements among kibbutz movements.

Shallowness of thought and narrowness of perspective had been characteristic of the labor movement from the beginning. By the early 1930s it had become commonplace to regard the absence of a clear ideology as an accepted fact. "Our movement has no specific ideal," Katznelson himself complained at the end of 1931, coining a formula that the delegates at the Rehovot convention repeated more than six years later.[13] In a rare ideological discussion—on the worker in Zionism—at the second Mapai convention at the end of 1932, Katznelson remarked: "This gathering is a rare event in our movement; we are not in the habit of devoting our time to theoretical matters. If we do it at all, we do it in a hurry. Even today we haven't treated the subject exhaustively."[14]

Katznelson's bitter complaint remained ineffective. "For years, there has been no ideological debate among us," declared Fishel Werber, a party worker from Rishon-le-Zion, about five years later, in September 1937. "Our day-to-day activities are not guided by any clear ideological policy."[15] Tabenkin made similar remarks, condemning the party for its lack of a "total ideological conception," which would permit a mobilization of members and offer them a challenge. Y. Freud, of the Agricultural Center, criticized the "spiritual poverty" of the movement,[16] and Yitzhak Ben-Aharon, a future Israeli minister and secretary-general of the Histadrut at the beginning of the 1970s, summed up the situation in the following way: "If we examine the situation, we can say that in our movement today there is no intellectual center, no place for exchanging ideas, for reflection, no place for studying our ideals, for developing and expounding them. Practical life is not accompanied by any ideological activity. Today there are hardly any such centers among the workers." Here Sprinzak interjected: "When did they exist? Can you give any examples?"[17]

The truth, of course, lay with Sprinzak. Even at that time, the lack of ideology was nothing new. Y. Bromberg, a party worker from Hadera, said that "ideological clarity was never the reason for our vast influence. . . . In reality, neither Ahdut Ha'avoda nor Hapo'el Hatza'ir nor Mapai was ever remarkable for what is called a 'program.'"[18] Although this rank-and-file member said that "the source of our strength was the great moral elevation of our movement," and the cause of its present weakness was the fact that "in recent years this elevation has gone," Ben-Gurion did not agree with this analysis. Already in 1931 he asserted: "Our strength lay in organization. Organization means a capacity for collective thought, collective action, and collective responsibility. This organization has been weakened. That is the danger, and not a lack of ideas."[19]

David Remez, Ben-Gurion's successor as the head of the Histadrut, had a similar approach. Remez rejected all solutions to what in the 1930s was called "the crisis among the youth," in other words, the inability of Mapai to attract young people at school or in college. Instead he favored a scheme to set up a new organizational structure—the Youth Center. And in order to strengthen the tenuous relationship between the ordinary Histadrut members and the organization, in 1937 he secured the introduction of the *mas ahid* (comprehensive levy), together with the *mas irgun* (organization tax)—payment for an obligatory membership card—and obligatory membership in the Kupat Holim.[20]

The degree to which ideological matters were neglected over the years was again demonstrated by a remark made by Moshe Baram, later an Israeli government minister and leader of the Jerusalem section, in the Mapai Central Committee in March 1951. The future of the labor educational system was again on the agenda. In the late 1930s, as we saw, the system lost its administrative independence, but now there was a question of eliminating it altogether. "I do not believe," said Baram, "that there has ever been a serious discussion of this question, apart from the one that took place in 1932, when the transfer of the responsibility for education to the Va'ad Le'umi was considered."[21]

Just as the movement's leadership refrained from ideological discussions, so it also carefully avoided another trap: internal democracy. The Histadrut bureaucracy, which at the end of the 1930s numbered twenty-five hundred people, manned the party institutions as well. The party's Central Committee was made up almost entirely of Histadrut officials and kibbutz members. In a census of the party taken on 1 January 1935, ten thousand members were counted, about half of them from collective agricultural settlements. About two years later, the party numbered about twelve thousand people, slightly more than 10 percent of the entire Histadrut membership.[22] In 1937 the number of party members from the city and from the settlements was the same as in 1935. It thus appears that in 1937 only about six thousand people living in cities and small towns owned a Mapai membership card, fewer than half of whom belonged to the Histadrut bureaucracy and economic institutions. It was this segment that in practice constituted Mapai.

In this situation, the usual distinction between executive institutions and legislative and supervisory institutions could not exist. The middle-level workers of the Histadrut were supposed, in their capacity as members of the party's Central Committee or of the various committees and departments connected with the Histadrut executive, to supervise their superiors, and these in turn, again on account of their membership in the party institutions or the Histadrut councils and committees, were supposed to supervise themselves. This institutional arrangement could continue easily and comfortably without frequent elections, and, indeed, from the mid-1920s on, the rule that elections should be held at regular intervals, generally once every two years, ceased to be observed. In 1931 Arlosoroff proposed adopting the German practice (in fact the accepted system throughout Western Europe) of holding a party convention once a year, but he did not even trouble to bring the proposal to a formal debate or to demand a decision. He kept quiet and avoided conflict with his friends in the leadership; Arlosoroff knew that this proposal would never be accepted. In the same vein, in suggesting that one should not "have the same people in both the Histadrut executive and the party," Arlosoroff was not prompted by a democratic instinct. His purpose was to render the work of the institutions more effective, and to breathe life into the party that had just been founded he wanted to transfer people from the Histadrut leadership to the leadership of the party.[23] Arlosoroff proposed a separation of functions, which would also have contributed to a democratization of the Histadrut, but here, once again, he made few efforts to see his suggestions carried out, and in the end he readily accepted this mixing of functions, which contradicted all known democratic arrangements.

An organization whose institutions were entirely made up of professional politicians, or functionaries dependent on each other for their political future, could not be receptive to criticism from the rank and file. These people felt too sure of their position, too protected by their friends who were also their employers or employees to the satisfaction of both sides. They did not have to stand continually for reelection, and over time they lost all sense of the need to struggle to maintain their position. This was the situation in the labor movement since the founding of the Histadrut. At the same time, the top leadership never renounced the humble title of "representatives of the community"; Katznelson always expressed his dislike of the term *leader*, until he came to accept it for lack of an alternative. This man, who had spent nearly all his life—since the time of his immigration—in politics, was so bold as to declare, from the platform of the Rehovot convention: "To this day, I have not learned to be a party man."[24] Similarly, Ben-Gurion insisted, on the same occasion, "I am not a professional politician!"[25]

This playacting by the "comrades" was an integral part of the labor movement's political culture, but nobody was deceived by it. Everyone knew that the party and the Histadrut were led by a handful of professionals appointed by committees. In the 1930s this oligarchic arrangement was a major source of tension, bitterness, and frustration. In the Histadrut and Mapai, the elected person's dependence on voters was replaced by a universal dependence on the system. Thus, as long as the leadership was able to close ranks, there was no means of ejecting people from their positions. There was also a sharply defined limit to criticism. As long as dissensions remained in the ideological sphere and there was no threat to the system, freedom of expression was permitted and practiced, but as soon as there was a real danger, nonconformists were eliminated without mercy. Such threats appeared only seldom, however, as the leaders' authority was derived from their control of the Histadrut economy and later the Zionist movement. Thanks to its domination of the Histadrut, the source of employment, Mapai had no need to function as a voluntary body, dependent on its members' subscriptions. The basis of its strength was the Histadrut and the settlement organizations.

OLIGARCHY AND CONFORMISM

The demand for democracy in Mapai focused on two main points: the holding of elections at regular intervals and with reasonable frequency and the encouragement of a close relationship between party members and party functionaries through the direct election of individual party functionaries. With regard to the first point, there was general agreement in the 1930s that the situation had become intolerable. "We know that our institutions are elected only once every seven or eight years," Beba Idelson, a leader of the Organization of Working Mothers, observed sadly in November 1939. She acknowledged that she had gained her position on the women's workers' council through nomination by the party's Central Committee and not through election. Not only had nobody elected her, but those who appointed her had not, after eight years, even asked her to report on what she had done. "The only thing that can help our movement," she said, "is for people to be publicly elected more often. We do not stand for election. At the Rehovot convention, five members set up the party's Central Committee. I myself was one of those five, and I now regret it. None of us are elected individually. If every candidate for the Central Committee had stood for election at the convention, we would at least know who had been elected."[26]

In fact, four years passed between the second Histadrut convention and the third, six between the third and the fourth, and nine between the fourth (1933) and the fifth (1942). There were no elections for the Mapai convention for five and a half years,[27] and the Central Committee in office at the 1938 Rehovot convention had been set up six or seven years earlier. An agricultural convention had not been held for six years, and in the same period there were no elections to the Tel Aviv workers' council. No office workers' convention had met for eight years, and a women's workers' convention had not been held for a similar period of time.[28]

In the 1930s this situation gave rise to harsh criticism by people of the second and third rank, of all political persuasions. But the leadership, and the people of the second rank who held important executive positions and aspired to the top political leadership, weathered the storms of the period and looked ahead to the final objective: the implementation of Zionism and the establishment of a Jewish state. They realized that the attainment of this objective would not be harmed by oligarchic tendencies in the party or the rule of local strongmen. Nor could the lack of equality or the internal class struggle in the Histadrut really endanger the final goal. Ben-Gurion, Sprinzak, Katznelson, Remez, Kaplan, Eshkol, Aranne, Lavon, Meir, and others were fully aware of the strength of the Histadrut system. They knew that as long as the organic wholeness of the Histadrut was preserved, as long as the Histadrut and the party remained subject to discipline, the system would not be undermined by demands for democracy or equality. Those who ran it—and after the mid-1930s the leaders of the movement also ran the Jewish Agency—knew very well that precisely the lack of internal democracy gave them their freedom of action. They knew how to exploit the tremendous advantages of a system in which the Histadrut was the source of power, providing essential services for three out of four Jewish employees in Palestine. A system in which executive institutions were set up by appointment committees and were sanctioned en bloc by bodies in which most, if not all, members were workers in the Histadrut or its economic enterprises, or representatives of the collective settlements, prevented surprises and perpetuated the control of the Histadrut leadership. Thus, the practice developed of distributing power and its advantages within a closed circle.

The leadership of the movement enjoyed one other great advantage: freedom from criticism by any real internal opposition. The only potential opposition, which in the late 1930s began to gain real power, was Hashomer Hatza'ir. But Hakibbutz Ha'artzi–Hashomer Hatza'ir was completely tied to the Histadrut economic system and did not really fight against the Histadrut society. Conformism and the cult of "natural" leaders were no less developed in Hashomer Hatza'ir than in Mapai. The "election" of Yaari and Hazan to their positions did not differ from the way in which Ben-

Gurion and their associates gained power and held on to it. In major ideological questions such as national goals, there were no disagreements either.
Thus, Hashomer Hatza'ir did not really take issue with Mapai on the question of class warfare. The great difference was with regard to the "dictatorship of the proletariat," in other words, the attitude of the two movements
toward the Soviet Union. "I see Stalin as a kind of nauseating communist
Abdul Hamid," said Ben-Gurion to Hazan and Yaari.[29] He liked to taunt the
leaders of Hashomer Hatza'ir about their fidelity to "scientific socialism,"
about their attachment to ideological collectivism, and especially about
their hypocrisy. He was not far wrong when he told these colleagues on the
Left: "Hashomer Hatza'ir generally acts like Mapai and speaks like the
Po'alei Tzion leftists."[30] Hashomer Hatza'ir rejected the agreement with the
Revisionists and the principle of the division of Palestine, but these matters
had nothing to do with the internal life of the movement. In practical matters—from the affair of the "advances" on salaries to the great corruption
scandal of the 1920s to the imposition of the mas ahid—Hashomer Hatza'ir
supported Ben-Gurion from the mid-1920s onward. It participated in the
conquest of land through settlement and ascribed the relationship that had
developed between the majority and the minority—"a relationship," according to Hazan's enthusiastic description, "that has no parallel in any other
labor movement"—to the fact that they all had "the same ultimate goals: the
redemption of the people of Israel with its wretched multitudes and the
creation in this country of a new way of life in the spirit of socialism."[31] For
the sake of these distant aims, and also for more immediate reasons, such as
a share in budgets for settlement and other Histadrut services, Hashomer
Hatza'ir was prepared to forget the exact times when Histadrut conventions
were supposed to be held.

This situation allowed the Mapai leadership to disregard the harsh criticisms made in the months before the Rehovot convention. The convention
was held only because of the urgent demands of the lower- and middle-
ranking activists, who were always under pressure from the rank and file and
had to deal with the frustration, alienation, and disillusionment that had
sprung up in those years against a background of economic crisis, distress,
and hunger.[32] It was not the economic burden that caused these problems.
Most of them had existeed for many years, some of them since the inception
of the Histadrut and Ahdut Ha'avoda. But there is no doubt that the crisis
exacerbated the feelings of the ordinary members.

There was broad agreement about the nature of the main problem in the
Histadrut and the party: "If we want a cure for our troubles, it's democracy,"
said Aaron Rabinowitz, the secretary of the Jerusalem workers' council.[33]
Like him, many people were conscious of the fact that the methods used in
Mapai and the Histadrut were only outwardly democratic; everyone was
aware of the lack of a real opposition in the Histadrut. The situation that

Ben-Gurion found ideal—the lack of any real alternative to Mapai and the existence of a single Histadrut bloc, which also included Hashomer Hatza'ir and which he wanted to develop into a single Histadrut party[34]—was regarded by an educated and cultured person like Rabinowitz as a major source of evil. This situation undoubtedly helped the Mapai oligarchy to come into being. Zalman Aranne, a man of unimpeachable orthodoxy, described matters as follows:

> One of the most serious complaints that exist in the party is this. You speak about those elected by the party, but we have not chosen them, . . . because the rule in the Histadrut (and also in the party) is not to hold elections for years on end, and even when elections are held, we are not the ones who vote. It is some appointment committee that does the voting. We, the members of the party, vote for a list and not for people. We don't see the faces of those elected by the party. They don't come to us: they have no interest in coming to us either before or after the elections. They don't need our votes; they have no responsibility toward us. A committee elects them even in those rare cases where some elections take place.

He went on:

> With regard to democracy in the Histadrut, I wish to say that the present situation cannot continue. Large segments of the public are convinced that "the emperor is naked," that the formal democracy in the Histadrut has no life in it, and that this system of refraining from holding elections for years on end deprives the public of the possibility of exercising the democratic rights provided by the Histadrut legislation. And not only that, but, as I just said, the public will no longer tolerate the mechanical system of elections by means of a list that denies a party member the right to decide in favor of the candidate of his choice. When I was in England, I was very impressed by the electoral system there. There, every candidate knows that the party may favor him, but it cannot help him if the voters turn their backs on him. The candidate himself must turn to the voters. The candidate himself has to seek out the voter, while with us the voter doesn't see the person elected and the person elected doesn't see the voter. Why should he, when in any case he will be chosen by the party?[35]

Although in 1937 these methods of operation were already regarded as intolerable by a devoted party member like Aranne, another fifty years had to pass before they were changed.

An instructive example of the "electoral system" in the party and the Histadrut was the way in which the enlargement and reconstitution of the Histadrut executive was carried out. At the beginning of February 1937, Ben-Gurion, who no longer was secretary of the Histadrut but who dominated it as he dominated the party, made the following announcement at a meeting of Mapai's Central Committee:

The committee appointed at the last session of the Central Committee to decide on the composition of the Histadrut executive has now met, and it proposes a considerable increase in the number of members in the executive. The executive is at present made up of 14 members [a list follows]. The committee proposes adding 12 more members, and they are [a list follows]. In this way, the executive will be made up of 26 members. The committee recommends that this list be accepted without alteration and without discussion.[36]

This is how an important political decision was made. The entry of Tabenkin and his supporters into the executive reflected a desire to reduce, to some extent, the intensity of the internal struggles in Mapai, and the collaboration of Yaari and Hazan paved the way for exploratory talks concerning a possible unification, which took place a few weeks later. At the same time, a new institution was created, the secretariat of the Histadrut executive, which performed most of the important functions previously carried out by the executive. In this way, another stratum was added to the structure, further distancing those active on the ground level from the apex of the pyramid. As Ben-Gurion had requested, the decision was accepted unanimously and without discussion.

The establishment of institutions without the personal election of candidates had two results: first, "the higher the representative's position in the hierarchy, the less accountable he was to the public,"[37] and second, power was distributed among a small group of people. In the 1930s, when Mapai won the leadership of the Yishuv, this form of control was used a great deal and became one of the salient features of the system. It was no longer restricted to the Histadrut but embraced the national institutions and the institutions of the Zionist movement. The people who controlled the Histadrut Executive Committee and the Mapai Central Committee were also those who directed the Va'ad Leumi and the Zionist executive. "Could it perhaps be decided," asked Fischel Werber of Rishon-le-Zion sarcastically, "whether a comrade can hold no more than two, three, or, at the most, four positions at the same time?"[38] It was particularly unacceptable that the people who concentrated all this power in their hands never had to give an accounting of their actions to anyone except their friends, that restricted elite group whose members divided political power between themselves for years on end and generally until the day they died.

Much of the frustration and bitterness, apart from those occasioned by the widening socioeconomic gap, were due to the fact that as major political problems increased, less attention was paid to internal problems. The leadership of the party, including Ben-Gurion, Kaplan, Sharett, and Sprinzak, was preoccupied with important political matters. Katznelson was preoccupied with insoluble and finally unimportant questions such as the unification of the kibbutz and youth movements, which had ceased to be relevant to the contemporary scene. The people at the top were in the habit of leaving the country for long periods, delegating day-to-day affairs to a professional team led by Remez, Meir (the "coordinator of social activity" in the Histadrut), and Aranne. All this only served to intensify the structural weaknesses from which the movement had suffered since the beginning of the 1920s.

By the end of the 1930s, the idea was well established that the apparatus, the party, and the Histadrut were one and the same thing. The "concealed or open hatred"[39] that, according to Feibush Bendori of the Tel Aviv branch, was the city workers' attitude to the Histadrut apparatus derived from the rank and file's sense of impotence vis-à-vis the leadership. The workers were aware of the alliance forged, at the beginning of the 1920s, between the apparatus and the senior political leadership. Indeed, the senior leadership constituted an inseparable part of the apparatus (from this point of view there was no difference between Ahdut Ha'avoda and Hapo'el Hatza'ir). It cared for it and shielded it from public criticism, even when there were clear signs that it was guilty of corruption and fraudulent dealing. Ben-Gurion, the head of the apparatus, consistently supported the economic leadership of the Histadrut throughout the years when it deliberately distorted the decisions of the conventions and councils or ignored them altogether. It was Ben-Gurion who taught the party and the Histadrut the use of uncontrolled power, and it was Ben-Gurion who promoted the system of "bossism": the Hebrew language of that period had no adequate translation, and the American word was widely used. He was the patron of the first famous party boss: Yosef Kitzis, veteran of the Second Aliyah, strongman of the Tel Aviv workers' council.

"Kitzis's method" (as it was known in Tel Aviv), which began in the early 1920s, was approved by Ben-Gurion. "Who does not remember the dissatisfaction in Ahdut Ha'avoda," asked Ben-Aharon in 1938 (he had been summoned to Tel Aviv in 1932 to repair the damage), "when despite a vote of no confidence in Kitzis by the Tel Aviv branch, Ben-Gurion, acting on behalf of the Ahdut Ha'avoda and Histadrut executives, forced the branch to retain him at its head?"[40] This happened in 1926. According to the historian Meir Avizohar, Katznelson also supported Kitzis, and Avizohar ascribed this as much to the fascination of Kitzis's colorful personality as to an appreciation of his efforts to consolidate the power of the Histadrut in Tel Aviv.[41] It is more probable, however, that Kitzis's effectiveness as a local boss was the chief reason for Katznelson's support. In Tel Aviv, Kitzis practiced the "one-man rule," in the literal sense of the term. He concentrated all power in his hands and, as is usual in such cases, made personal, partisan, and political use of it. During the crisis of the late 1920s, the decision of who would work and who would be unemployed constituted the difference between having a decent existence and going hungry. The Kitzis method was notorious throughout the Histadrut, but it suited the Executive Committee and its head. At the end of the 1930s the fight against Kitzis, the symbol of corruption in public life, was still at the center of the internal struggles in the Tel Aviv branch of Mapai, and of the serious conflict between the majority in the branch and the party's Central Committee.

In reaction to the imposition of the Kitzis method on the party and the Histadrut in Tel Aviv, an opposition movement developed at the end of the 1920s. It was made up of people who ten years later were to become the backbone of the party establishment: Aranne, Mordechai Namir, and Dvora and Shraga Netzer. Only one of them, Yohanan Kushnir, was not promoted, and he remained on the Tel Aviv workers' council. He was to be one of the heads of the second wave of opposition, in the 1930s, and in the summer of 1940 he was even summoned to the Mapai internal disciplinary tribunal in a famous trial, the first in the party's history. At this trial the leaders of the Tel Aviv workers were charged with breaking into the premises of the Histadrut executive and occupying them.[42]

The harsh criticisms by Aranne, Namir, and Netzer, in a memorandum they signed and presented to the Ahdut Ha'avoda executive in 1927, were similar to those the opposition addressed to the leadership of the movement in the late 1930s. The signatories complained about the "terribly dangerous" situation for the Histadrut "resulting from the discrediting of its apparatus" in Tel Aviv. They declared that the apparatus was "largely rotten and very demoralized." A year later Aranne asked for "the great mud pit that has been created in the Histadrut to be drained."[43] Ten or twelve years later, the same story was repeated, with one difference: most of the chief critics in the first wave of opposition had now gone over to the other side. Meanwhile, the problem had spread to Haifa, where the rise of Abba Hushi, secretary of the workers' council and future mayor, had begun. At the end of 1939 Berl Reptor, an important local party worker, painted a bleak picture of the regime of "dependency and fear" that existed in the port city and the center of heavy industry in that period.

> It is no secret that in the Histadrut in Haifa an intolerable regime of "dependency, fear, and factionalism" has been set up. People are frightened of the Histadrut apparatus! And how, may I ask, has the party's Central Committee "solved" the problems of the Histadrut in Haifa? It prefers to leave everything as is! Nothing changes! There is a one-man rule! Do you believe that one can abandon the Histadrut to a one-man rule without its having far-reaching consequences for the Histadrut and the party? Do you suppose that there are no comrades who will fight to change the situation? If the Central Committee pays no attention to the opinion of the loyal nucleus of the party members after party committees have shown that unacceptable practices exist in Haifa, and that for a year and a half there has been no public life in Haifa and the Histadrut is being discredited, what is one to do?[44]

To those, like Sprinzak, for whom Haifa represented a model of "order and organization" for the people of Tel Aviv to follow, Reptor ironically put the following question: "Can it still be said that a 'spirit of comradeship' exists in the Histadrut in Haifa, that the workers enjoy feeedom of expression there, and that there is no dependency or fear?"[45] Twenty-five years later, at the height of the Lavon affair, Moshe Sharett would speak of a regime of "fear and vindictiveness." Reptor forestalled him with his fierce criticism of the cult of personality taking root in the party, the tendency toward a one-man rule, and the regime of "orders and commands."[46]

By the beginning of the Second World War, oligarchic rule in Mapai had become an established fact, which no one attempted to conceal. The violent crisis in the Tel Aviv branch was largely due to the alienation prevailing in the party. The situation in the Tel Aviv branch, which at the height of the crisis numbered about three thousand members—approximately 25 percent of the membership of Mapai and at least half the membership of the party in the cities—was symptomatic of the party as a whole. In the late 1930s political patterns were formed in Mapai which remained unchanged until the Labor Party's long years of opposition in the 1980s.

The founders had two main organizational principles. First, the top of the pyramid should not depend on its base. In communist parties this principle was called democratic centralization and was practiced in a flagrant and extreme manner. In the labor movement the system of centralization assumed a far more moderate form, but from the beginning rules were made enabling officeholders to dispense with the need to stand for election. At the same time the habit developed of failing to hold elections at regular intervals, despite rules to the contrary. By the end of the 1920s, this state of affairs was taken so much for granted that it did not even have to be explained. Only when things became intolerable, as at the height of the crisis in Tel Aviv, was a pretext invented, which over time became the one most commonly used: the security situation. Mapai's two rising stars, Aranne and Lavon, had already learned to make clever use of it.[47]

The heart of the system was the administrative apparatus, which ensured the political leadership's independence from the rank and file, and the leadership constituted an inseparable part of the apparatus. Thus, the apparatus always had the support of the top leadership. The protection of the apparatus was really the protection of the political leadership itself. Ben-Gurion, as the head of the apparatus, stood by it during the storms of the late 1920s and again at the beginning of the 1930s. Later, in the peak years of the struggle in the Tel Aviv branch, the apparatus, which included the everlasting Yosef Kitzis, again had Ben-Gurion's support. At Kitzis's side now stood Mordechai Namir, who at the end of the previous decade had joined the workers' council as a result of the revolt against Kitzis.[48] Ben-Gurion was equally careful not to harm the one-man rule in Haifa. The regime there suited him and the other members of the leadership, as it ensured them both control of the party and internal peace in that city for a whole generation. Ben-Gurion did not feel that the moral price paid for the effectiveness of the Hushi regime was too high.

The system of rule that reached its perfection in Haifa was accepted, in a more moderate form, throughout the party and the Histadrut. This was a necessary consequence of the structures of the two bodies and of the purpose for which they were founded. Less than twenty years after the founding of the Histadrut, the concept of the labor movement as a means of mobilizing men and resources for the national revolution had reached fruition. One can say that the objective was attained; by the end of the 1930s, the labor movement had brought the Yishuv, by then a self-governing and economically viable entity, to the threshold of independence. From the point of view of the founders, the price paid was not too high, quite simply because no price could have been too high.

The second main principle dear to the labor elite concerned the method of dealing with the anti-establishment opposition. An abstract, ideological opposition did not disturb them, but a political opposition with an organizational capability and a real sociological basis had to be fought to the end. Ben-Gurion established the pattern in the 1920s, and Sprinzak and Remez wanted to act in the same manner. Ben-Gurion gave Kibbutz Tel Yosef twenty-four hours to accept his ultimatum. Sprinzak and Remez gave the Tel Aviv branch twice as long: two whole days to set up the Executive Committee of the workers' council from "among those who have accepted the decisions of the Central Committee."[49] But they did not have at their disposal the means Ben-Gurion was able to use with the pioneers of the Jezreel Valley. The Tel Aviv branch was not a kibbutz, and thus it was impossible to deprive the rebels of medical assistance, food, and credit; nor could one expel them from the Histadrut as easily as the members of Kfar Giladi. The only sanction Sprinzak and Remez could use was to expel them from the party. The leadership threatened to do so, but this deep crisis of confidence was now complicated by political factors: the Tel Aviv branch was backed by Hakibbutz Hame'uhad.

In reality, the troubles in Tel Aviv were a crisis of political culture and a crisis of identity. The system of dependency and conformism necessary to build and maintain the Histadrut as a state in the making began to be viewed as a mixed blessing. "For eight years I have been a kind of 'independent listener' in the Central Committee of the party and the Histadrut," said Ada Fishman. "By this I mean that I am not a professional party worker. I am sorry to say that I often feel glad that I am not financially dependent on the organization."[50] She was apparently one of a handful of activists in Tel Aviv who was not an employee of the Histadrut, and she appreciated the resulting freedom and independence.

The bonds of dependence that had developed over the years had an unequivocal aim: to serve as an alternative to the power of political coercion. "We do not have state power," said Sprinzak. "We have neither government nor police nor an army. But we do have another source of power, with which for thirty-five years we have helped Zionism and the Yishuv progress and develop. This source of power is the Histadrut and the party." Thus, the founders never considered coercion illegitimate. They did not look on the party and the Histadrut as voluntary bodies coexisting with other similar bodies in the framework of a pluralistic society. Sprinzak viewed "the Histadrut, this institution that unites us all," as a kind of state, and "the party, this guiding organ, showing the way and conferring authority on those who act,"[51] was like a governing body, making decisions and expecting them to be carried out unquestioningly and without discussion.

By the end of the 1930s, however, it was clear that the system that had developed in the early 1920s had adopted governmental methods without the checks and balances of a democratic regime. While all political and economic power was concentrated in one place, the crest of the pyramid—that is, the top party leadership ruling the Histadrut, the Zionist Organization, and the Yishuv—parliamentary bodies remained without any real authority and without the capability to impose their decisions. Nevertheless, criticism was always directed at the apparatus; the term most commonly used in this connection was "hatred."[52] If the bureaucracy was subject to repeated waves of attack, this was because it represented the establishment. People did not yet dare to call the leadership itself to account.

The root of the trouble was the inability of the Histadrut and the party to deal with the ever-growing social gap within both organizations. The low-level workers' leaders, despite the fact that they themselves worked for the Histadrut, felt that they had the duty of acting as spokesmen for the unemployed. Yet, at the same time, the party expected them to demonstrate loyalty to the system. All this contributed to the growth of the leftist opposition in the Tel Aviv branch of Mapai. When the opposition gained control of the branch, and its representative, David Lifschitz, became its secretary, a situation arose unparalleled in the history of the movement.

The great new development at the end of the 1930s was that social protest was now directed against the Histadrut. The workers' leaders asked it to lead the struggle against the national institutions and against the bourgeois Tel Aviv municipality,[53] but they also attacked Sollel Boneh, whose employment policies were contrary to the interests of the Tel Aviv workers. In this case, the Histadrut's role as an employer was strongly criticized, and this was also one of the points at issue in the famous trial in early July 1940. Five workers' leaders—the most senior among them being Yohanan Kushnir—were brought to trial before the Mapai's internal disciplinary tribunal for occupying the premises of the Histadrut's Executive Committee, where they organized a sit-down. After some remonstrances, the court recognized the justice of their claims against Sollel Boneh. The strikers won the court's sympathy, and despite the secretariat's insistence that the accused be expelled, their membership was suspended for only twenty-four hours.[54]

This trial was a high point in the struggle between the leadership and the rank and file. The struggle continued for months and was remarkable for its verbal violence. Unable to deal with the profound social divisions between its members, the party took disciplinary measures and attempted to delegitimize the protest. All possible derogatory epithets and uncomplimentary metaphors were brought into play. The leadership of the movement feared that the ground was shaking beneath its feet. As long as inequality in the Histadrut was discussed within the organization, there was little danger. But as soon as the revolt of the unemployed came out into the open, it constituted a denial of the comprehensive character of the Histadrut; in other words, it denied its essential nature. The workers' occupation of the premises of the Histadrut's Executive Committee meant the end of the legend that the Histadrut could perform all functions simultaneously and with the same degree of success; that it could be both an industrialist and a trade union; that it could bring together every kind of salaried worker, from skilled and sought-after workers in industry to those chronically searching for employment; and that it could serve as a home for bank managers, lawyers, and small-scale contractors on one hand and for charwomen and agricultural laborers living on subsistence wages on the other.

This blow to the foundations of the Histadrut—both real and imaginary—raised questions about the system's ability to continue to fulfill its main purpose: the achievement of national objectives. The Mapai leaders' harsh reactions were due to their consciousness of the fatefulness of the struggle. When, at the end of November 1939, Golda Meir created a crisis by resigning from the secretariat of the Executive Committee, her intention was to force the junior leadership to close ranks behind the senior leaders.

Her protest, she said, was directed against "the lack of a minimally comradely [haverit] atmosphere" in the Histadrut.[55] Haverut (comradeship), in the language of the movement, meant closing ranks, whatever the cost and in all situations. According to the rules, a "representative of the community" had the basic right, in a difficult situation, to obtain automatic protection. In Meir's opinion, it was the duty of the union secretaries who had presented ultimatums and threatened collective resignation to continue in their tasks for the sake of haverut, and not to leave her, together with Sprinzak and Namir, to face the angry strikers. The task of the lower-ranking functionaries, she believed, was to restrain the workers, not to lead them or to place themselves at their head. Party workers were expected to owe allegiance to those above them, not to those below. The smooth operation of the organization depended on the preservation of the hierarchical system and required every functionary to show "responsibility," in other words, unquestioning allegiance to superiors. "Order and duty, that's our watchword!" shouted Sprinzak to the scores of activists—some estimated the number at two hundred—who had been summoned to impose discipline.[56]

Remez spoke in a similar manner. "Shall we let banditry replace comradeship in relations between party members?" he asked. "We won't let this matter pass, as it is the cause of destruction, just as its solution can be the source of what is good."[57] Sprinzak went so far as to compare the strikers' behavior to the actions of the communist fraction more than a decade earlier. This comparison angered party activists, who regarded it as a vulgar attempt to prevent people from expressing their opinions. Nehemiah Rabin, Yitzhak Rabin's father, a midlevel activist in the metalworkers' union, was shocked at the insensitivity shown by this "comrade who does not ask why this has happened but proposes an 'administrative cleansing,' which he regards as justice."[58] At the trial of the five, Pinhas Tuvin, one of the rebellious workers' leaders, pointed an accusing finger at a long-standing situation: "For years, a regime has grown up in the Histadrut which expects members to submit."[59]

The Histadrut had no use for egalitarian utopians, charismatic workers' leaders, and rebels against the existing order, yet this was the type of people springing up in the Tel Aviv branch of Mapai. From the point of view of the organization, these were dangerous characters who disturbed the smooth functioning of the chain of command. The organization could not fulfill its objectives as a state in the making unless all those within it were ready to serve as a relay belt for policies decided at the top. The decision-making process at the top would remain a dead letter unless those below showed discipline, dependency, and the acceptance of authority that comes with this dependency. After the trial of the five, Aranne expressed appreciation of these qualities. "The apparatus," he said, "has saved Zionism."[60]

Thus, the leadership was suspicious of democracy and felt it was a nuisance endangering the stability of the entire enterprise. Katznelson claimed that the idea of submitting the labor agreement with the Revisionists to a referendum was "abandoning it to blind destiny,"[61] and Ben-Gurion openly demonstrated his disdain for democratic order: "An agricultural convention has not been held for six years. So what? In the last twelve years, there have been only two Histadrut conventions, and yet the organization hasn't been destroyed. At any rate, the lack of conventions has not prevented it from growing."[62] Remez, Sprinzak, and Aranne argued incessantly with the representatives of the unemployed workers in the years before the war, and in the first year of the war they demonstrated neither understanding nor sympathy. Soon the party became totally preoccupied with the formation of Faction B in Tel Aviv.[63] In reducing opposition to an internal matter in this way, the party and the Histadrut avoided having to deal with the real problems it represented.

Another method the founders used to escape responsibility was their habit of placing the blame for difficulties on later waves of immigration. Even those who were sincerely looking for the real reasons of the crisis could not help remarking, at the end of the 1930s, that "many of the new-comers lacked the pioneering spirit" of earlier periods.[64] This disdain for immigrants from the Fourth Aliyah onward was inseparably linked to the myth of the golden era of the early years and was a good excuse for abandoning the socialist dream.

Among the old-timers, self-glorification was second nature and an aspect of the sense of superiority that the pioneers always demonstrated, in relation to both non-Zionists and other currents in the Zionist movement. Among the more perspicacious, however, this attitude was tempered with self-criticism. "We were the leaven in the dough, and we often saved Zionism by our vigilance," said Katznelson in 1932. But he immediately added, "For a number of years, however, we have stopped standing in the breach."[65] Others, who did not share Katznelson's scruples, continued to pour scorn on the labor leaders in America, Bund members in Europe (Aranne), and immigrants from Germany and Poland (Remez) or to loudly declare that with the coming of "the tavern keepers from the shtetls of Bulgaria and Romania," new elements had arrived in the country, with the result that now there was "a great deal of filth in the Yishuv" (Sprinzak).[66]

EQUALITY: PRINCIPLE AND PRACTICE

At the beginning of the 1930s, Histadrut activists of every kind had the feeling that things were turning sour. There was a widespread sentiment that the Histadrut society was on a downward spiral and that the opportunity of turning it into an egalitarian society had vanished. By the end of the decade, this perception had grown even sharper. The late 1930s were years of high unemployment, and thousands of unemployed people rebelled against the movement's leadership. Mordechai Namir, who saw the distress of the unemployed, tried to calm the restive activists (mainly trade unionists) of Mapai's Tel Aviv branch by recalling the situation at the end of the previous decade. The year 1927, he said, was also one of hunger and crisis, "and there was a very grave social and moral situation in the Histadrut due to the fall of Sollel Boneh, following which [the Histadrut] appointed a committee to investigate 'advances' on salaries due to the affair of falsifications in financial assistance to the unemployed in Tel Aviv, and due to the collapse of

Hamashbir. And yet, despite all this, all Ahdut Ha'avoda members, including the unemployed, stood like a wall around the Histadrut and their representatives in the organization, and in the same year we broke the communist fraction." Ten years later, he said, the picture had completely changed. Now it was members of the party who led the rebellious unemployed and told them "to break into the Executive Committee." He came to the conclusion that "such an atmosphere, such uncontrolled behavior, could only appear in our section—so important as an example—because political conduct and political values are not what they were in 1927."[67]

Aaron Ziesling, a member of the left wing of Mapai, who later became one of the dissidents of Faction B and a minister in the Israeli government, responded:

> The truth is that at that time we not only broke the [communist] fraction, but we also destroyed basic principles of the Histadrut, and we suffer the consequences to this day. On the day we abandoned mutual responsibility in the movement—responsibility for each worker, for his day's work—on that day, we too were broken. Those days of unemployment were days of crisis for our movement, a crisis whose consequences are still with us. The ideal of mutual responsibility and equality reflected in the principle of "equal wages" disappeared. Instead, we have had statements warning us against "wastefulness" in the creation of jobs for new immigrants. Thousands of people had no work at that time, yet the standard of living rose in this country, even among ourselves. And, shortly afterward, as soon as unemployment ended, the leadership of the movement adopted the slogan "Get rich!" After this crisis, we had the despicable public atmosphere of "prosperity" [Ziesling used the English word], an atmosphere we largely encouraged. New paths opened out which divided our members. Of course, we also did important things in that period, but we also contributed to social differences. That is the main reason for our social failures, for the lowering of public standards, for the lack of cohesiveness among us.[68]

These were not only two sides of the same coin but two different concepts of what is good and desirable. For the party and the Histadrut establishment, the 1920s were a lost paradise. Those, it seemed, were blessed years in which the movement, united and disciplined, could withstand all the storms that came its way. Apart from the rebels of Gdud Ha'avoda and a few individuals such as Eliezer Yaffe, nobody publicly doubted the leaders' ability and good intentions, nobody dared to challenge their decisions, and no one with a position in the Histadrut and the party had to be accountable to those who appointed him. No misdemeanor, not even acts of open corruption, was sufficient to destroy the political or administrative career of an important official or to remove him from public office. Trade union activists and party workers of the second and third rank took their cue from the leadership: conformism was at its height, and the concept of personal responsibility was unknown. The complex and sophisticated way in which the Histadrut's power structure was built had proved itself entirely.

For this reason, low-level activists were unable to oppose a tacit policy of the leadership: its approval of personal enrichment. Not only did the political and economic leadership not condemn personal enrichment, but it encouraged it as long as rising living standards were the product of economic development. Egalitarian tendencies were strong among the rank and file, but not among those higher up. The higher in the political or economic hierarchy a person stood, the stronger was his tendency to abandon the principle of equality.

Leaders of the second and third rank, who in 1926–27 marched at the head of the unemployed, found themselves on the opposite side of the barricade ten years later.[69] In the 1920s, said Beba Idelson, there was not the "bitterness" that had subsequently developed. "Today," she said, "there is great scorn for the officials who have built up their positions at the expense of those beneath them. We are accused of not being interested in the problems of the members as a whole. . . . Meanwhile, the working population has grown and people's patience is not what it was in 1926 or 1929. The general atmosphere has changed."[70]

By the beginning of the 1930s, it was clear that a socialist society would not come into being in Palestine. Even the greatest optimists had long before stopped expecting that such ideals would have any real influence on the Yishuv or that the Histadrut could be made into an egalitarian society. "The worker in this country has dropped to the level of the worker abroad. He no longer has a pioneering relationship to the Histadrut, and his personal interests are no longer identical with the general interest," declared Ben-Gurion to the members of the Histadrut Council in October 1931.[71] Beilinson, Yavnieli, Tabenkin, and Ya'ari were of the same opinion. A few months before Ben-Gurion made these remarks, Beilinson had complained about the fact that "people do not have the sensitivity with regard to wages that they had a few years ago."[72] He meant that the ideal of equality had disappeared in the Histadrut society. Similarly, in the debate with Ben-Gurion about workers' education, in the autumn of 1931, Yavnieli said that "the concept of mutual aid" no longer existed.[73] In this discussion—on the transfer of administrative control of the Histadrut educational system to the Jewish Agency—Tabenkin regretted the "spirit of the age" and deplored "the loss of our faith in our own capabilities."[74] In the same vein Ya'ari declared: "Once they spoke about a great general commune. But views and beliefs have changed since then, and much has been abandoned as inconvenient." He continued: "One can't speak about the situation in the Histadrut without taking into account what is happening in the country and in the Zionist movement. There is no point in our talking about psychology, feelings, and sentiments if we continue to accept things as they are, for the great danger is that the workers in this country are becoming indistinguishable from immigrants all over the world."[75]

Among the causes of the general decline, the founders always stressed the great change that had taken place in immigration to Palestine. The people of the Second and Third Aliyahs knew how to promote their legend and their superiority to all those who came after them. For many years, even after the founding of the state of Israel, only those who belonged to the two waves of immigration regarded as pioneering, and the native generation, could claim a privileged position. From the Fourth Aliyah onward, only those who went in for collective settlement succeeded in atoning a little for their late arrival. Among the masses of new immigrants who swarmed to the cities and the moshavot, these represented a new elite who had come to join the original pioneering nucleus.

However, the founders were not naive. Despite their sense of superiority, they knew very well that expressions of rebellion and anger not only were the product of demographic changes but had another, far more fundamental, cause: the fact that by about 1930 the Histadrut society itself, apart from the collective settlements, had become an ordinary bourgeois society. Great class differences had developed within it, and instead of representing an alternative to the existing society, it had begun to reflect all the weaknesses of the bourgeois order. Real differences—sometimes enormous—in wage levels and standards of living, between rulers and the ruled, between the bureaucracy and laborers, had become quite common. A party oligarchy had come into being which enjoyed an incomparably higher standard of living than the average worker. Politics was not only a profession but also a highly lucrative one. By the 1930s, great conflicts of interest and feelings of open hostility had arisen between the various strata of the Histadrut: between workers and leaders and between different categories of workers.

During the economic crisis of the second half of the 1930s, social differences in the Histadrut, which by now had become flagrant, gave rise to a bitter open confrontation. At the end of the 1920s, great discrepancies had arisen in the standards of living of the senior Histadrut bureaucracy and the agricultural workers or construction workers in Tel Aviv, but the crisis of the 1930s brought matters to a head. At the end of the decade, there was as much class warfare in the Histadrut as in the society as a whole. Thousands of hungry unemployed people with malnourished children were incensed at the Histadrut bureaucracy and those with permanent jobs. The top stratum of the bureaucracy enjoyed a standard of living that was by no means inferior to the higher bourgeoisie in general. Its members were the object of an animosity often bordering on hatred, due not only to the desperation of the unemployed but also to the deep resentment of those workers whose livelihood was more or less assured. Although tremendous efforts were made in the Histadrut to relieve the sufferings of the unemployed, and its institutions of mutual aid had no equal anywhere else in the Yishuv, the ordinary member of the organization was chiefly impressed by the fact that the Histadrut society was moving farther and farther away from the egalitarian ideals that the political leadership never ceased to advocate. As the years passed, the gap between theory and practice, between expectations and reality, became increasingly obvious. That was the main reason for frustration and bitterness.

The attempt to create equality in the Histadrut had met with many difficulties from the beginning. In the early days after the First World War, the labor movement had put its faith in the principle of cooperation. Labor militants thought that the majority of workers would find their place in the cooperative society, and in this way the problem of hired labor would eventually be solved. The founding of cooperatives was first attempted in the agricultural sector, for only there did the new system play an indispensable role. The creation of collective settlements was the most effective and sometimes the only real solution to the problem of the inability of the Jewish worker to be absorbed into private agriculture. Collective settlements also formed an infrastructure for the absorption of immigrants, although it soon became apparent that the great majority preferred to settle in the cities. The promotion of a progressive or innovative social ideology did not play a major role there, and sometimes it had no importance at all. In the cities, however, no attempt was made to create an alternative to hired labor, for such an alternative was economically unnecessary and could have been adopted only on the basis of an ideological commitment to a struggle against private property. No doubt difficulties were more numerous in the cities than in the agricultural sector, but this does not explain the lack of initiative in this area. Instead, the explanation lies in the absence of any true ideology of struggle against the capitalist order. Thus, relationships of production in the cities continued to be those usual in a capitalist economy. At the same time, there was a strong demand in the Histadrut society for an implementation of the principle of wage equalization.

Here I must draw attention to another point. Some twenty years ago, Zvi Sussman, who investigated economic differences between skilled and unskilled labor, revealed statistics about Jewish workers collected by the statistical departments of the Histadrut, the Jewish Agency, and the mandatory government. These figures prove conclusively that egalitarianism never existed in the Yishuv. All these statistics, which were gathered both continuously and in the context of comprehensive wage surveys in 1922, 1930, and 1937, demonstrate that among the Jewish population, from the time the Histadrut was founded until the Second World War, large differences existed between the wages of skilled workers (academics, officials, and others) and unskilled workers (mainly agricultural laborers and construction workers). The varied data on wage tariffs, real wages, and differences in the standard of living of the various strata of the population led Sussman to the conclusion that a great deal of inequality prevailed among Jewish salaried workers in mandatory Palestine, compared with many other countries and with Israel at the beginning of the 1960s. The main reason for the low wages of the Jewish laborer was the large supply of unskilled Arab labor.[76]

The Histadrut never succeeded in supplanting Arab labor.[77] In the peak period of Arab labor, before the outbreak of the revolt of 1936, at least twelve thousand Arabs worked for Jewish employers. At the same time, five thousand Jews were registered as unemployed, most of them unskilled. In agriculture for every Jewish hired worker there was more than one Arab hired worker. These numbers suggest another reason for the extreme timidity with which workers' councils behaved toward Jewish employers. Trade union representatives knew that a replacement for the unskilled Jewish laborer was at hand, and they feared an increase in unemployment. Their readiness to change their policies in light of strong competition was never in doubt. Sussman gives the supply of unskilled Arab labor as the main reason for differences in salary in the Jewish sector. This also explains the wide gap between the lowest-paid white-collar workers and academicians on one hand and unskilled Jewish laborers on the other.[78]

Because of these conditions, the gap between the wages of unskilled Jewish workers, who were exposed to competition, and those of skilled workers was wide. According to figures from 1928 and 1931, this gap was also great relative to other countries. The gap in wages among Jewish construction workers was the fifth highest among twenty-five countries considered, coming immediately after the United States and a long way before Britain, France, Germany, Italy, and the Scandinavian countries. In metalworking this gap also took fifth place among twenty-two countries and was greater than in the United States. Yugoslavia, Poland, Hungary, and Czechoslovakia came before Palestine, but all Western countries had a smaller difference. In printing the gap in Tel Aviv was smaller than in Warsaw and Tallinn but greater than in London, Berlin, Vienna, and Rome. The figures for 1937 also confirm the existence of significant gaps in wage levels between skilled and unskilled Jewish workers. These differences were greater in 1937 than in 1963. The plight of unskilled productive workers is also attested by the fact that the gap between their salaries and the teachers' salaries was greater at the end of the 1930s than at the beginning of the 1960s.[79]

Differences in Jewish salaried workers' standards of living also confirm these findings. A. Nitzan has analyzed research into Jewish workers' standards of living.[80] The aim of this research was not to examine differences in the standards of living of different strata but to discover the "typical" standard of living. The 1926 investigation is an exception, as it did not include households whose income was less than five pounds a month or above twelve pounds. Even within these limits, one can see great differences in the standards of living of families at the bottom of the scale and of those at the top. The average per capita consumption in families in the second income bracket (from the bottom of the scale) was 1.352 pounds, compared with 4.515 pounds per capita in families in the ninth income bracket (second from the top). Sussman assumed that about 20 percent of the families at either end were not included in the investigation of 1926. Had these been included, the gap would presumably have been even wider. But even without these extremities, it is obvious that very great differences existed. In 1926 families in the ninth income bracket consumed 3.4 times more than those in the second (this figure is the same in 1963–64). Comparing differences in housing yields the same results.[81]

Our primary concern, however, is the Histadrut society, not the Yishuv society as a whole. The problem we have to consider is more difficult and complicated. There can no longer be any doubt that despite its informal manners, the Yishuv was not basically different from any normal capitalist society, or from Israeli society in its first twenty or thirty years. In certain respects, the Yishuv was no better than our present-day society; it is much more bearable to be unemployed in the Tel Aviv of the late 1990s than it was in the Tel Aviv of the late 1930s. Even if we accept the fact that the widespread demand for Arab labor, at least until the revolt of 1936 or the outbreak of the Second World War, depressed the salary of the unskilled Jewish worker, we must still ask: what did the Histadrut do about inequality in sectors that did not depend on Arab labor, such as its own bureaucracy? And, beyond that, there is the key question: to what degree did the labor movement regard equality as a desirable end, something to aim for in a practical sense?

The general belief is that the outlook in the Histadrut was egalitarian, exemplified by the "family wage." The most striking example of the persistence of this egalitarian myth is the teachings of Shmuel Noah Eisenstadt. In his well-known work on Israeli society, on which generations of students were brought up, the doyen of Israeli sociologists wrote: "It sometimes happened that the porter in a Histadrut institution, who had seniority and six children, earned more than the director, who had only two children."[82] It is quite doubtful whether such a Histadrut institution, apart from local workers' councils in their early days, ever existed (by the 1930s, the payment systems of workers' councils already approximated those of other institutions). The family wage was never implemented, as the egalitarian ideology was, from the beginning, subordinated to the nationalist ideology. Its purpose was to serve as a mobilizing myth for the young pioneers of the Third Aliyah, whose imagination was fired by the idea of a social revolution. The egalitarian ideal helped promote national objectives of settlement and the absorption of immigrants, and was therefore adopted by the Histadrut and the party, but the moment there was a conflict between the egalitarian ideal and the political and economic alliances deemed necessary for national reconstruction, the moment there was the slightest doubt about the effectiveness of egalitarian practices in building the nation, the concept was abandoned. For years it was used as a way of political mobilization, without any intention of being put it into practice. This must be obvious to anyone who examines the fate of the concept of equality in the Histadrut.

This concept was abandoned in a way that soon became characteristic of the political culture of the Yishuv and the state of Israel. The Histadrut leadership never admitted the existence of any contradiction. We saw in earlier chapters how the problem of the contradiction between class warfare and the ideal of national unity was solved. In the practical questions of the realization of equality, the movement behaved similarly: it retained the cover while completely changing the content. At the end of the 1920s, after Gdud Ha'avoda was crushed, the Histadrut, under pressure from the second and third ranks, continually made decisions it had no intention of carrying out.

The question of equality was tested daily in setting the wage scale for workers in the Histadrut economy and in negotiations over wages in the private sector. Between the two world wars, the latter was dealt with by the workers' councils. This system also contributed to the widening social gap.[83] If a centralized body such as the Histadrut gave up dealing with such an important issue, and the executive, normally so protective of its own authority, transferred the right to decide to local workers' councils, it was because the leaders thought this was necessary for building the economy. The Histadrut felt it bore national responsibility and was therefore ready to go a long way toward meeting the requirements of those who provided jobs. In fact, as long as the owner of an enterprise accepted the sacred principle of employing Jewish labor, he could count on the full collaboration of the Histadrut. Relations between workers' councils and individual enterprises on a local level were far more agreeable and less antagonistic than collective negotiations on a national level. Direct negotiations between local representatives and local enterprises in the areas in which they lived were in keeping with the policy of class collaboration.

Although one may recognize that external factors such as the availability of Arab labor have to be taken into account, this does not constitute an answer to the question of how seriously the Histadrut related to the problem of equality. For an answer one must look at the Histadrut itself: its economic enterprises, its network of services, its bureaucracy, and the way in which the labor movement carried out its declared aim of extending collectivism to the cities through "workers' districts."

THE FAILURE OF THE FAMILY WAGE

The main subject discussed at the second Histadrut convention in February 1923 was wage equalization, called the "equalization of prices [of labor]." The convention announced its intention "to introduce a single wage level in all Histadrut institutions." It also appointed a special committee, theoretically independent of the executive, to fix this level. At the same time, the convention left a loophole by declaring: "If an institution finds it necessary in a particular case to change the wage level decided on, it must ask for special permission from the committee." The ad hoc committee appointed by the executive to fix the wage scale included Hillel Dan, who later became one of the chief figures of Sollel Boneh, Shmuel Yavnieli, and Levi Eshkol, who were later joined by two other members.

The committee submitted its proposals to the Histadrut Council, which met at the end of December 1923, and the latter approved the scale. The scheme adopted was as follows. The salaries of Histadrut workers were to depend on their family situation. A family allowance was granted to the head of a family, its amount correlating with the number of dependents. The minimum wage was the same in all cases. In the cities the basic wage was fixed at 7.50 Egyptian pounds a month (which until November 1927 was the currency used; the Egyptian pound was equal in value to the pound sterling and was replaced by the Palestinian pound, which kept its value until the beginning of World War II). In the agricultural sector, a certain amount was deducted to reflect the difference between urban and rural rents. In addition to this basic wage, every worker received three extra pounds if married, plus two and a half more pounds if he had a child under the age of three, or three more pounds for a child over the age of three. A sum of two pounds was added for the support of parents who were in the country; parents living abroad were not eligible for support. The upper limit of the scale was twenty pounds; all payments above that sum required the special approval of the wage-fixing committee.[84]

The single wage level was to apply to all Histadrut workers, including professionals such as doctors and engineers. The Histadrut Council declared that all these decisions, "without exception," would go into effect in all the institutions of the organization on 1 February 1924. At the same time as sanctioning the rules, the council allowed for their abandonment in a statement repeating that of the 1923 convention ("An institution that, with good reason, wishes to change the wage level decided on must in each case receive permission from the wage-fixing committee").[85] This injunction, intended to reduce the number of possible exceptions, in fact laid the whole system open to question, and after a few months it was obvious that the institutions of the Histadrut had little intention of adhering to its decisions.

After that, the question of family wages preoccupied the Histadrut for many years and was one of the chief causes of tension, bitterness, and frustration.

A study of the collapse of the family wage in the crucial years between the second (1923) and fourth (1933) Histadrut conventions is particularly instructive, for it gives us a concrete illustration of the nature of the Histadrut as created by its founders. The technique used by the executive under Ben-Gurion to evade responsibility for the decisions made at the second convention, in February 1923, the manner in which the leadership was party to a gross infringement of the very norms it advocated and that it was supposed to maintain, and the eagerness with which all the leaders of the movement—including Ben-Gurion, Katznelson, and Arlosoroff—closed ranks make it abundantly clear that, from the beginning, the Histadrut was not intended to be a framework for an egalitarian society. The movement had no desire to engage in social experiment, which was restricted to collective settlements, and even then permitted it only on condition that those who engaged in it did not demonstrate too much independence. In the cities equality was promoted as a myth, but the emphasis was on the creation of power-building institutions such as Kupat Holim, the Histadrut industrial enterprises, and, of course, Bank Hapo'alim.

After the wage-fixing committee had finished its work, the Histadrut Council assigned a committee of three—Yavnieli, Perlson, and Eshkol—the task of supervising the implementation of these decisions. On the day that the ruling on family wages went into effect, this committee asked for reports from all the institutions of the Histadrut. When reports came in, it was apparent that, with the exception of the Agricultural Center, not a single body in the Histadrut, including the executive, had followed orders in either the letter or the spirit. A good example was Bank Hapo'alim: its management simply declared that "until now, the bank's wage policies have not been those adopted in the Histadrut. Salaries have been fixed in relation to the importance of the task and the salary usual for that position in similar institutions in this country, and the management has fixed salaries in each case in accordance with these principles."[86]

There is no reason that this answer should have surprised party workers as experienced in Histadrut affairs as Yavnieli and Eshkol, for the bank never made any secret of its policies. The management of the bank, in a letter dated 16 June 1923, had already, in a form identical with the report quoted here, described the principles with which it operated. In accordance with these principles, the director of the bank received a salary of 50 pounds a month, and his deputy, who was none other than Yosef Aharonowitz, and the chief accountant were paid 30 pounds each. These three people headed families of three, so that according to the system of family grading, their salary should not have exceeded 13.5 pounds. By contrast, the janitor was paid 6.5 pounds a month, far below the amount required by his family grading, but he also was given an apartment.[87] In the Hamashbir purchasing cooperative, salaries of 25 pounds were quite common. It appears that the family wage system was followed only in the workers' councils, where party functionaries were in direct contact with the militant activists of the Third Aliyah.[88]

The document that the supervising committee submitted to the third Histadrut convention (July 1927) provides an excellent overview. In fact, the committee never succeeded in controlling the various branches of the Histadrut, and it did not even succeed in obtaining accurate reports. The executive, under Ben-Gurion, failed to support it, giving the committee's "independence" as an excuse. This attitude deprived the committee of authority and prevented it from having any influence. The Histadrut leadership merely noted the committee's declaration: "The wage level is not being applied and does not correspond to the true situation." By July 1927 it was clear to everyone that the family wage was vigorously opposed by all major Histadrut institutions.

The committee, whose members could not even agree among themselves, and which meanwhile had gained additional members, was perfectly conscious of the weakness of its position and showed signs of insecurity. In internal discussions in which the majority of members firmly opposed any departure from the wage level, it was unable to do more than point out that "in Bank Hapo'alim they are not paid according to their wage levels, and it is our duty to express our opinion."[89] Finally, Yavnieli resigned from the committee, saying, "It is unable to fulfill the tasks it was given by the Histadrut Council."[90] Although the executive rejected his resignation, it did nothing to prevent the paralysis of the committee and carefully refrained from taking any real action. In practice, the heads of the Histradut refused to implement the convention's decisions.

The same story was subsequently repeated. A committee was again appointed and was given the task of "submitting, within a month, a revised system for grading the salaries of all Histadrut workers." The committee never even met. Another long period elapsed, and at the twelfth Histadrut Council (31 January to 2 February 1927), exactly three years after the family-wage system was supposed to have gone into effect, yet another committee, made up of five senior party workers, was appointed, once again with the task of "examining the compliance of all Histadrut institutions with the wage level and wage policies." This time the committee was also given the task of investigating one of the worst public corruption scandals between the two world wars, the case of the "advances" on salaries, which had come to light in the autumn of 1926. In October of that year, the matter came before the Ahdut Ha'avoda convention, and the executive, under Ben-Gurion, was forced to act. It is doubtful whether the matter would have been debated in the party and Histadrut institutions at all if "certain rumors" had not begun to spread, which, according to a letter dated 6 May 1927 to the editors of *Davar*, "slighted the honor of the workers of the Histadrut."[91]

In its investigations, the committee discovered that not only did the heads of the Histadrut institutions provide themselves with fat salaries through high cost-of-living increases but at the height of a grave economic crisis they augmented these salaries with "advances": loans that were entered in the books but whose repayment was not required. These grave irregularities were described by the committee as involving only a small number of people—about 70 out of the 607 workers whose incomes they had examined (the number of offenders was in fact 100)—but among them, they said, were "a few heads of institutions." In reality, the whole economic leadership and some members of the executive were involved in the scandal. When questioned, the Executive Committee admitted that in some Histadrut institutions, the debts of employees had been simply canceled.[92] In other words, the "advances" were illegal bonuses with which the leaders of the movement had succeeded in raising their standard of living several notches above that of workers as a whole.

In an attempt to calm the anger of ordinary Histadrut members, and especially of the thousands of unemployed, the executive decided to publish the committee's conclusions. On 13 June 1927 a document was published in *Davar* which was inaccurate and which Katznelson censored. The names of the offenders were not given and their identities were concealed from the public. Fearing that the scandal might undermine the Histadrut, Katznelson helped to cover up the affair, and the version offered to *Davar* readers a few weeks before the third convention was the same as the one presented to the convention by the committee. The institutions of the Histadrut were asked to immediately cancel cost-of-living supplements and to refrain from giving "advances" and granting personal allowances without the express approval of the Wages Committee. No criticism was made of the Executive Committee apart from the observation that it "failed to make sufficient use of its right of control."[93]

The crisis of the family-wage system was a crisis of political culture, not a momentary lapse or a manifestation of weakness. The third convention backed the executive. On the eve of the convention and before the publication of the findings of the five-member committee, Ben-Gurion expressed his opposition to the principle of family wages and took up the defense of the administration of Sollel Boneh. Despite the demands of the stricter members of the five-member committee (Ada Fishman, Meir Yaari, and Moshe Beilinson), the principle of personal responsibility was denied and none of the offenders and perverters of morality was brought to account. Not only were their names not published, but the whole affair was treated as if it had never occurred. People who admitted to acts that were dishonest and a gross misappropriation of public funds retained their political and administrative positions and continued to lead a movement that preached a pioneering spirit, a frugal lifestyle, personal example, and a readiness for sacrifice. The only measures taken, on the recommendation of the committee, were collective ones: the payment of cost-of-living increases and the various kinds of special payments and "advances" were forbidden, the canceling of debts was prohibited, and the various bodies were asked to begin collecting on debts immediately.[94]

If not for the fact that in the past the leadership had shown determination in matters it believed to be really important, one might suspect that in this case its meager response was simply a manifestation of undecisiveness. But the executive, which for years had not succeeded in applying the family wage, was the same body that had imposed draconian measures on the people of Tel Yosef, Tel Hai, and Kfar Giladi. The pioneers of the Jezreel Valley and the conquerors of Upper Galilee were thought to deserve every punishment, including the denial of medical assistance to babies and women in confinement, because of their refusal to submit, within twenty-four hours, to the political demands of the Executive Committee. At the same time, the heads of the economic institutions, including the head of the Histadrut, could for years fail to honor the decisions of the conventions and councils without any twinge of conscience. Thus, in the mid-1920s the leadership established norms that were characteristic of the movement in the mandatory period and in the early years of the state.

One of these norms was the principle that the only unforgivable sins were political ones. The goal—Zionism—was sacred, and those who worked on its behalf saw themselves as a company of priests who deserved an adequate reward for their services to society. This aura of sanctity extended to the tools and resources necessary for its achievement; the Histadrut and the party enjoyed special status. Any injury to them was tantamount to withholding redemption. Public criticism of the leaders' behavior and a demand for sanctions against those who acted in an improper manner were regarded as blows to the movement, if not all-out treachery. This attitude permitted the self-righteous preaching of equality and the cult of agricultural labor on the part of political leaders in Tel Aviv, whose standard of living was light-years away from that of pioneers in remote parts of the country.

The most flagrant example of this disregard of behavioral norms was the behavior of Ben-Gurion. The leader of the movement abandoned his early dream of building the Histadrut as a commune as soon as he realized the impracticality of the principle of equality from the national point of view. The health services, labor exchanges, and buying and selling cooperatives existed, in his view, solely for that purpose. It was thus legitimate to use them as a means of pressure, even if it meant driving deviationists to starvation. There was no hypocrisy in this; Ben-Gurion had never thought of the labor exchange and sick fund as mere suppliers of services, just as he did not regard equality or democracy as values in themselves. He also never believed that he personally had the duty of setting a moral example. He studied law in Constantinople together with Remez and Ben-Zvi while his friends of the Second Aliyah were founding Degania and Kfar Giladi. Similarly, the secretary of the Histadrut, who enjoyed a comfortable upper-middle-class existence in Tel Aviv, never stopped publicly complaining that "the bourgeois mentality is taking root among us."[95]

Ben-Gurion never saw any inconsistency in the fact that his apartment in Pinsker Street in Tel Aviv, with its four large, attractive rooms, in which he went to live in 1927 (his family had moved there from Jerusalem two years earlier), cost him ten pounds a month, two or three times the monthly salary of an agricultural worker and three times the rent paid by people like Zalman Rubashov (Zalman Shazar, the third president of the state of Israel) or Katznelson. His children attended the prestigious Gymnasia Herzliyya, where school fees were 2.40 pounds a month, and took piano lessons. Ben-Gurion also spent large sums on books. In the 1920s he had many debts, which were finally paid by the executive in return for promissory notes he had signed. An internal committee under Yosef Aharonowitz, which in July 1926 raised the salaries of certain members of the executive by 45 percent, canceled the leaders' debts to the Histadrut. Of the members of the executive, Ben-Gurion had the largest debt: 283.5 pounds. Next came two other old-timers, Yaakov Apter (260 pounds) and David Zakkai (202 pounds).[96] These were not the largest debts in the Histadrut; there were also two anonymous debts of 536 pounds and another of 450 pounds.[97] At that period, these were enormous sums.

The Histadrut's treatment of these debts was typical of its work methods. Everything was settled among the officials, without any means of control. Similarly, all the committees, bodies, and institutions that dealt with family wages were largely made up of functionaries of institutions that were likewise wholly or largely staffed by Histadrut employees. Only some external factor—public opinion, for instance—could have broken this vicious circle, but the labor press was unconditionally supportive of the institutions. It was closed not only to dissidents but also to excessively strong criticism from bodies such as the central control committee. Only when brought before a Histadrut convention could a question be dealt with by people whose profession was outside the realm of politics. For this reason, the conventions, as mentioned earlier, became more and more infrequent; the third convention was held in 1927, four years and not two years after the second convention, as Histadrut legislation required; the fourth convention was held in 1933; and the fifth was held nine years later, in 1942. The leaders of the movement preferred to work through the Histadrut Council, a body of political professionals, chiefly representatives of the more powerful Histadrut institutions (Bank Hapo'alim, Sollel Boneh, Kupat Holim), plus some left-wing figures such as Ya'ari, Hazan, and Tabenkin, who were also politicians but whose power base was not the Histadrut economy but the kibbutzim. The latter generally showed great understanding for the positions of the Executive Committee and the economic institutions. Meir Ya'ari not only participated in the destruction of Gdud Ha'avoda but also served on the five-member committee that helped the executive, the heads of Bank Hapo'alim and Sollel Boneh, and the editor of *Davar* to cover up the affair of the advances and to withhold much of the truth, especially the most embarrassing part, from the public.

One of those chiefly responsible for the modes of conduct prevalent in the labor movement in the mid-1920s was Yosef Aharonowitz. Outside circles familiar with the history of the labor movement, Aharonowitz's name is hardly known, but in the 1920s and the beginning of the 1930s (Aharonowitz died in 1938), he was one of the most powerful people in the movement, a figure who could not be ignored. In the 1920s Aharonowitz was Ben-Gurion's most important ally in Hapo'el Hatza'ir during the long process that led to the founding of Mapai. Hapo'el Hatza'ir professed to put into practice Gordon's teaching by personal example, and Aharonowitz in partic-ular was considered Gordon's spiritual heir. He was supposed to embody Gordon's ethic of frugal living and personal revolution through labor. Yet Aharonowitz not only headed the committee that canceled Ben-Gurion's debts but also provided himself and his friends in the management of Bank Hapo'alim with a salary six or eight times as large as an agricultural laborer's. He also was one of the chief advocates of lenient treatment toward institu-tions guilty of similar offenses: the Eretz Israel Workers' Fund, which paid its head 35 pounds a month and his deputy 30 pounds, and Sollel Boneh, where most serious cases of corruption were found. Representative allow-ances, global increases, and nonrepayable loans to build or buy homes or apartments were common occurrences among the leadership of this great Histadrut enterprise.[98]

This was the same Aharonowitz who in January 1926 sought to allay the fears of Eliezer Yaffe, when Yaffe, one of the fathers of the moshav, tried to prevent the Histadrut leadership from taking over his property in Nahalal. Aharonowitz assured him that those who were engaged in collec-tive agriculture had nothing to fear; they were the true aristocracy. "The great majority of us city dwellers," he declared, "see ourselves as being of little value compared to the agriculturalists, for we know that the upbuilding of the nation largely depends on you."[99] In the best traditions of nationalist socialism, the lowest sector of society received psychological compensation. Its exalted status was supposed to compensate for difficult living condi-tions, low income, exploitation (in the case of agricultural laborers in the moshavot), and its lack of upward mobility. Urban and rural laborers were honored with hymns of praise but continued to perform grinding labor and had to send their children to work at an age when the children of the "un-worthy"—the leaders, directors, and officials—sat on the benches of Gym-nasia Herzliyya.

The tremendous scandal of the advances revealed the real Histadrut, as opposed to the mythological one. The harsh revelations of the five-member committee were made known to the public, at least in part, at the height of one of the worst crises the Yishuv had ever experienced. About seven thousand unemployed—a huge number, in terms of that period—needed urgent assistance to provide them with a bare subsistence and to ward off starvation. On 26 February 1926 an article appeared in *Davar* whose laconic title told the whole story: "Agricultural Workers Are Going Hungry!" Sollel Boneh, formerly the Bureau of Public Works, in June 1924 became a stock company under the ownership of Hevrat Ovdim. After a long period of presenting false balance sheets, the company was on the verge of collapse. At that period all 128 workers received a variety of bonuses and increases, and the nine members of the management headed by David Remez received all kinds of allowances. According to the committee's report, fifty-seven workers owed 3,084 pounds to the institution. All managers received "advances." In the censored part of its report the investigating committee stated that when all the loans, "advances," and other raises were added up, "The salary of some of the workers doubled or more than doubled." The committee pointed out the fact—which applied to all the institutions—that "those who owed money to the institution" were precisely "those workers in high positions who already received bonuses." In this connection, the committee made another comment of particular interest: "Certain members of the management receive additions to their salaries from both the treasury and directly from the clients of the enterprise." In other words, the directors of this Histadrut enterprise were in the habit of taking bribes. But even more revealing was that according to the report, the benefits the managers received were engineered through a reduction in the salaries of "lower-ranking workers."[100]

Here I should draw attention to what was, from the beginning, one of the salient features of the Histadrut system: the collaboration between the managements and the more influential workers' committees at the expense of the less powerful workers in the same institutions or in the Histadrut as a whole. On the eve of the third Histadrut convention, the Sollel Boneh workers' committee was already a full partner in disregarding egalitarian norms.[101] A system had been created which spread far beyond Sollel Boneh. While the leadership of the institution awarded itself a salary that was sometimes twice or more than twice the amount allowable according to the family-wage system, the salaries of low-grade workers fell below the level required by the wage system, without the workers' committee raising any objections. Thus, by the mid-1920s, great differences had appeared not only between the different institutions but within the framework of each one, from the top down.

All the points that the five-member committee raised and that the third convention approved remained a dead letter, as the Histadrut, as Ben-Gurion said in 1925, had no intention of being an "organization of saints."[102] If he meant that the Histadrut had no egalitarian ambitions, he was correct. The fate of the family wage was not linked to the vicissitudes of the Yishuv economy.[103] Bank Hapo'alim did not wait for the prosperity of the Fourth Aliyah in 1924–26 to avoid imposing the family wage, and Chaim Arlosoroff made his repeated criticisms of the family-wage system in June 1927, at the height of the crisis.[104] Economically, the years between 1928 and 1931 were an intermediate period. In 1931 the question was again brought before the Histadrut Council, with the same degree of urgency as in the period before the third convention in July 1927. The Histadrut was preoccupied with the same problems, used the same methods, and gave the same answers in times of crisis as in periods of affluence or in intermediate periods. It made no connection between the economic situation and the nature of social relationships. The pressure to abandon the family wage was equally strong before periods of prosperity, at their height, and after them, in periods of economic recession. The failure of the family wage stemmed from the fact that from the beginning it never had a strong ideological impetus. There was no willingness to impose the wage and to consider its implementation as the beginning of social change.

As soon as the ink dried on the decisions of the third convention, old practices with regard to wages resumed. In May 1930 the periodical treatment of the problem was renewed, and the twenty-fourth Histadrut Council, which met at the end of that month, decided to make another attempt to impose the family wage. The council ordered the executive to cancel the budgets of institutions that had not received the prior approval of the Wages Committee.[105] As might have been expected, the executive preferred to appoint yet another committee "to examine the existing system of grading in the Histadrut institutions." This time, it was a ten-member committee, headed by Israel Gurfinkel (Guri), later chairman of the Knesset Financial Committee. This new committee took its task very seriously. It made investigations, met with dozens of heads of institutions, and, like the previous ones, obtained reports and collected a great deal of material. The only difference between the Guri committee and the Yavnieli-Eshkol committee of eight years earlier was the improved quality of the paperwork. The first committee had worked in very primitive conditions, and much of the material it assembled, like the protocols of its meetings, was still in manuscript form and sometimes written in pencil. The documents collected by the Guri committee, however, reflected the great advances that had taken place in Palestine: they were typed, orderly, clean, and full of instructive tables. The style and the technical terminology had also improved, but the problems remained exactly as they had been at the time of the second Histadrut convention in 1923.

After collecting information on the salaries of 202 workers in ten Histadrut institutions, the committee reported that there was a great difference in the average salaries in various institutions, amounting to 100 percent or more. The highest salaries, as usual, were paid to Bank Hapo'alim and Hamashbir employees.[106] Similarly, it appeared that there had been no change in the exceptionally high salaries paid to those who had been conspicuous in this respect in the 1920s. Ben-Gurion earned 30 pounds a month, and the directors of Bank Hapo'alim—Aharonowitz, Vogel, and Brodny—received the same. Yitzhak Brodny was one of the ten "hard cases" that the Wages Committee investigating the "advances" had particularly condemned. In the section of the report dealing with Bank Hapo'alim, the person who prepared it attempted to indicate what the salaries of the directors would have been if the family-wage system had been followed. Aharonowitz would have received 18 pounds, Brodny 17.5, and Vogel 12.55. The leadership continued to enjoy special bonuses. Ben-Gurion's salary included a "professional" allowance of 7.5 pounds, which Golomb and Kaplan, whose names appear in the same list of salaries, did not receive in 1928–30. Katznelson also received a bonus, which was given different names in different documents. Sometimes it was called a seniority increment ("stage," in the terminology of the period), sometimes a special increment, and sometimes it was not described at all.[107] Eliyahu Golomb, who earned 13 pounds a month in 1930, received 24.4 in 1936, and Israel Guri's salary climbed from 17.5 to 27 pounds in that period. Among political leaders, salaries depended on status and position in the hierarchy, not on family requirements. In 1936 the executive ceased reporting the makeup of the salaries, being content to give total sums, but pointed out that in addition to their salaries, members of the secretariat Berl Lokker, Israel Marminsky (who already in 1927 had accumulated an exceptionally large debt to the executive), David Remez, and Yosef Sprinzak received a representational allowance of 3 pounds a month.[108]

The inequality prevailing in the Histadrut was commonly known. All attempts to change the situation proved to be ineffective. At the beginning of the 1930s, even the workers' councils, which had followed the rules in the past, abandoned the family-wage levels.[109] The Wages Committee, which had to supervise the application of the system, was at a loss. Weary of promises, the refusal of the institutions to accept decisions, and the executive's consistent evasion of its duty to support the committee, many members of the committee wanted to resign. They made a final appeal to the executive in a letter to *Davar*. "The Wages Committee," they wrote, "continually tries to impose the family wage, but the means at its disposal are insufficient to make it effective." The committee concluded: "All that has been said above proves not the failure of the family-wage system but only the inadequacy of the means for maintaining it." In this approach to *Davar*, the committee was pretending to answer one of the readers' letters, but this was really a cry of alarm, a desperate attempt to mobilize public opinion for the Histadrut Council, which was to meet in March 1931. The letter, an unsigned, undated copy of which was preserved in the archives, bearing the handwritten inscription "not published," was never brought to public attention. It would seem that in accordance with its custom from the time of the "advances," *Davar*, that stronghold of Histadrut conformism, simply refused to cooperate.[110]

The controversies surrounding the deliberations of the twenty-fifth council in March 1931 laid bare all the moral, ideological, and economic inconsistencies and contradictions of the Histadrut society. The labor movement had passed the point of no return.

The council was carefully prepared. This time the very principle of family wages was questioned, and not only its nonimplementation, which had preoccupied the Histadrut in the 1920s. Of the ten members of the committee, which gave its report to the council, only two members, Israel Idelson (Bar-Yehuda, later a minister of the Israeli government) and Meir Ya'ari, supported the family-wage system as it was. The majority, under Guri, wanted to institute a new "synthetic" wage system, one in which wage levels would be determined by profession, with a "family" element. Arguments for and against these ideas filled three detailed memorandums,[111] submitted to the council in the form of three alternative proposals: 1. the annulment of the family-wage system and the institution of a "synthetic" wage scale, which was a "mixed" system (the highest salary would not exceed 22.5 pounds); 2. the institution of a family-wage scale with a minimum salary of 7 pounds and a maximum salary of 22.5 pounds; and 3. the institution of a family-wage scale with a minimum salary of 7.5 pounds and a maximum salary of 13 pounds. These proposals gave rise to the most searching and interesting discussions that had ever taken place on the subject.

At the start of the first meeting, a conflict arose between the agricultural settlements and the Histadrut bureaucracy. The chairman, Ben-Gurion, read out a letter signed by seven kibbutzim and moshavim (Kinneret, Kiryat Anavim, Ginnosar, Nahalal, Balfouria, Tel Adashim, and Kfar Yehoshua) and the Nahalal workers' committee, asking for the standard of living of the Histadrut apparatus to be brought in line with that of "all sections of the [Histadrut] public." The writers of the letter also protested against the size of the Histadrut bureaucracy and asked whether the organization needed "such a large head."[112]

This strong attack by the settlers provoked a reaction from the representatives of the bureaucracy, and from other people as well. Meir Ya'ari came to the defense of those attacked, saying that the workers employed in the Histadrut were no better off than kibbutz members, who "belonged to an institution that guaranteed their security and provided for their needs."[113] This raised a most disturbing question: what, in fact, was the cost of a kibbutz member? Was it acceptable that the cost of keeping members of Degania or Kiryat Anavim was greater than the amount they would be paid according to the family-wage scale? And how could the budget for a kibbutz or moshav member be calculated at all? One member of the ten-person committee commented that in Ein Harod a family of three cost 11.5 pounds a month, whereas in Degania and Kinneret they cost about 20 percent more.[114]

However, these economic factors were not the real cause of the trouble. The heart of the matter, as Golda Meir pointed out, was "the troubled relationship between the ordinary members and the employees of the Histadrut."[115] One activist complained that "the employees of the Histadrut have developed a different spirit from the workers as a whole. A bourgeois spirit has entered the establishment. The labor spirit has gone. Why have the workers in the moshavot been able to save from their earnings and create something, whereas Histadrut employees to this day have not succeeded in contributing anything positive to urban life?"[116]

In one of the many discussions on the subject, the secretary of the office workers' union pointed out that in 1923, "when the office workers did not yet control the Histadrut, the Histadrut Council, which was largely made up of agricultural workers, decided that the minimum wage for Histadrut employees would be 10 pounds for a bachelor and 14 for a married person, 16 for those with one child and 18 for those with two."[117] He intended to demonstrate that when the Histadrut was founded the employees of the organization were already paid a salary several times higher than that of the agricultural workers who had founded it. Although his figures were not quite accurate, he was essentially correct. The leadership of the movement had never thought of equalizing payment for political or administrative work or even office work with that for ordinary physical labor in the city or in the country. The principle that a difference in the standard of living of the political elite and the rank and file was legitimate and even necessary already applied. Thus, when an employee complained that "there is no more equality between the five hundred workers in the Histadrut than there is between them and the workers of the country as a whole," he was only stating the obvious.[118] That, of course, was the reason the family-wage system had "remained on paper, not only with regard to the leaders, but also with regard to the ordinary workers," as Y. Kanievski, coordinator of Kupat Holim and one of its major figures, declared. However, both the supporters of the family wage and its opponents agreed on one point: if the family wage had failed, it was because the leadership, with its various levels, from members of the executive and the heads of institutions to the majority of the major workers' committees, had opposed it.[119]

The family wage continued to exist as part of the egalitarian myth, as a claim unconnected with reality, in order to assuage people's conscience. Even if it was no more than a "fiction," as Guri said,[120] the movement needed this fiction as proof that some connection between ideology and practice still existed. The family-wage system favored the weak and placed the strong at a disadvantage; if it had been applied strictly, unskilled workers with large families would have earned much more than their counterparts in a free-market economy, and skilled workers would have received much less. In the cities the system would have been viable only if the Histadrut had been organized as a "workers' society," a great commune, embodying an egalitarian lifestyle to the same degree as the agricultural settlers, and if it had been scrupulous about maintaining solidarity and practicing mutual aid. But because collectivism was soon abandoned and confined to the narrow boundaries of the kibbutz, the family wage became irrelevant and was never put into practice. Among those who were strict with themselves and others, this gave rise to an uneasy conscience. For the others—the vast majority—it was another one of those principles gravely discussed in moments of reflection by the leaders of the movement. They never stopped preaching pioneer values and a frugal lifestyle while they themselves lived in comfort and affluence in Tel Aviv. Meanwhile, they exhibited to everyone their spiritual agony because their service in the movement deprived them of the opportunity to join the conquerors of the wastelands.

The issue of family wages cast a strong light on the problem of inequality regarding the "comprehensiveness" of the Histadrut—that is, its claim to represent all segments of society. According to the information Moshe Beilinson provided in his report to the twenty-fifth Histadrut Council, the average wage of the employees of the organization was 12 or more pounds a month. The wage of an agricultural laborer on a moshava was 3 pounds a month. In the cities an unskilled worker earned from 5 to 8 pounds, and a skilled worker between 8 and 14 pounds. "Employees in commercial undertakings," as Beilinson called them, earned between 4 and 15 pounds a month, whereas the living expenses of a low-wage earner came to 8 pounds. A family of four could subsist on slightly more than 9 pounds a month.[121]

These figures (similar statistics were given at that time in many other sources) lead to certain conclusions. First, the low wage level of agricultural laborers is rather striking. More than ten years after the founding of the Histadrut, its founders, the agricultural laborers, lived poorly and miserably. Their wage was only a quarter of the average salary of the Histadrut bureaucracy and only a tenth of the highest salaries among them. Even according to the proposal for a family wage with a ceiling of 20 pounds or 22.5 pounds (the professional salary) a month, the agricultural laborer earned only a sixth of the salary of the highest-paid Histadrut functionaries. According to these two proposals, the minimum wage was 7 pounds (the "family" wage) and 7.5

pounds (the "synthetic" or "professional" wage) respectively. It is an interesting point that the gap between the minimum and maximum wages in the two schemes was not large; the difference was in the internal distribution. Advocates of the "professional" wage wished salaries to be fixed according to one's contribution to the organization and one's value in the general labor market, not according to one's needs or the size of one's family.

Advocates of the family wage wanted the Histadrut to represent a slightly more just and egalitarian economic system than existed in the society as a whole. They realized that skilled workers, the heads of the Histadrut institutions, the political leaders, and the secretaries of the major workers' councils could not be expected to have the same standard of living as farm laborers and the unskilled workers in the cities who were exposed to the competition of cheap Arab labor and to the periodical crises of the capitalist market, but they hoped that the movement would at least provide a modicum of equality within the Histadrut system. It soon became apparent, however, that precisely the bureaucracy and the skilled workers, who did not have to suffer from the competition of Arab labor, reaped most of the benefits of the system. Because there was a limit to the wage burden the Histadrut could carry, these benefits were necessarily at the expense of those lower down the ladder.

Thus, labor solidarity in the Histadrut soon became a mirage. It is true that weaker elements such as unskilled workers and clerks without training enjoyed far better conditions in the Histadrut than anywhere else, but the Histadrut economy spurned any "artificial" imposition of equality on the grounds that it was incapable of carrying the economic burden. Skilled workers did not want a narrowing of differences, as their income was likely to suffer. As a result, the degree of inequality in the Histadrut was soon comparable with that in the general society. According to Yitzhak Horin, a director of the Yachin preserves enterprise, the employees of the Histadrut were opposed to any collectivism in their organization. It is therefore not surprising that Horin, on their behalf, asked the council to institute the "synthetic" or "professional" wage system. This was also the position of the representatives of office workers; of Kanievskti and Beilinson, administrators of Kupat Holim; of Abba Hushi, secretary of the Haifa workers' council; and of Eliezer Kaplan, the most influential economist in the movement.

These people claimed that the family-wage system was too expensive and an intolerable burden for economic enterprises such as Tnuva and Yachin. For example, the management of Tnuva, one of the largest commercial and industrial enterprises of the period, declared unequivocally that "salaries must be based on the economic conditions prevailing in the industry. The family-wage system is out of the question where industrial workers are concerned."[122] In other words, skilled workers could find work in the free market and were therefore unlikely to stay in the Histadrut at some sacrifice to themselves. Such people would have to be offered a premium wage. At the same time the salaries of ordinary workers could be reduced to below the family-wage level. The Histadrut economy could have sustained a wage level for unskilled workers appreciably higher than usual in the general economy only if the higher-paid workers had agreed to work for a lower salary than they could have obtained in a private undertaking. That degree of solidarity, however, had never existed even in the earliest days of the Histadrut. In addition, there were great differences not only between the various salary levels but also between the salaries of workers in comparable jobs employed in different parts of the organization. The figures vary, but the general picture warrants the conclusion that great discrepancies existed.[123]

Moshe Beilinson brought up one more argument against the family wage. Like Abba Hushi, he stated that the increase in the competition to the Histadrut economy at home and abroad necessitated a switch to the "synthetic" wage, but that was not the only reason. In his opinion, the family wage was a contribution by the Histadrut to the excessively high standard of living in the Yishuv as a whole. He said that at a time when the vast majority of "artisans, shopkeepers, and peddlers" in Tel Aviv—this uncomplimentary description, so common in labor circles, referred to a broad stratum of the small-business owners—"would be content with 10 or 11 pounds" a month, the average wage in the Histadrut, as mentioned earlier, was 12 pounds a month. He pointed out that part of the money came from contributions from abroad, but "this situation," he said, "is bound to come to an end. It is doubtful if the average Jew in Warsaw is better off than the Jew in Tel Aviv, so how will he be willing to send donations here?"[124]

Beilinson also was one of the main opposers of the very high salary levels that were usual in the national institutions, the Zionist Organization, and the Jewish Agency. Shortly after the appearance of the first issue of *Davar*, Beilinson attacked the Zionist movement in the journal for not preventing the payment of salaries of 30 to 50 pounds a month to "junior officials" and of 120 to 150 pounds a month to senior ones. Some members of the leadership received even more, but their names did not appear in the official lists of the Zionist executive, as their salaries were paid by the institutions of the movement in London.[125] Katznelson, too, had tried to lay down rules and to decide what was permitted or forbidden to the Zionist bureaucracy, but in 1923 he already had to admit the inability of the Histadrut "to act . . . with necessary firmness" against the excessively high salaries paid in Zionist institutions. "We have no right to tell others to do what we are incapable of doing ourselves," he said.[126]

Naturally, the family wage applied only to Histadrut workers, and despite irregularities in practice, it assured them of a much higher standard of living than that of agricultural laborers or unskilled laborers in the cities. Its advocates, however, felt that the Histadrut could have done far more to reduce the glaring inequities of the system. The champions of equality also asked why Histadrut members as a whole had to assure the six hundred people of the administrative staff (which by the end of the 1930s had grown to 2,500) a standard of living far higher than that of most members, especially as they were paid out of the contributions of people who earned much less than they did.[127] On this issue, as in the matter of compulsory arbitration, Ben-Gurion adopted an intermediate position. He said that although the family-wage system "needed to be revised," the synthetic wage system also had its weaknesses, as it failed to meet the requirements of about half the members of the Histadrut. While waiting for a solution to be found, he advocated "flexibility" and wanted to postpone a decision to some unspecified time in the future.[128]

In the view of the family wage's defenders, the system represented an attempt, at the time the Histadrut was founded, "to introduce a few elements of the next social order." What had been achieved, said Bar-Yehuda, "is defective and incomplete and does not represent ideal equality or justice, but it is much more just than anything that exists elsewhere, and that is sufficient reason for us to go to war in order to defend it."[129] By about 1930, however, even the most ardent champions of the system had little hope that it could be defended. Even Bar-Yehuda threw up his hands; he acknowledged that "because the evil had been allowed to go unchecked for so long" a miracle could not be expected. Remez described the synthetic wage as monstrous, and Golda Meir also opposed it. Guri and Ben-Gurion made the distressing admission that in the past "the executive had not been able to find a way to get the decisions of the Wages Committee to be respected."[130]

The decision to institute family wages was the result of pressure by party activists, most of whom did not belong to the leadership of the organization and were not responsible for the Histadrut economy. However, the decision to continue to support this wage system, which they knew would never be applied, just as it had never been applied in the past, was a good illustration of the usual practices in the labor movement. Everyone knew about the great discrepancy between the facts and the egalitarian myth, but the system needed a mobilizing myth. Thus, there was no change following the Histadrut Council of March 1931. New committees dealing with salaries were set up and the debates continued, memorandums continued to flow, and the councils continued to make decisions that were never carried out. In 1935 a committee to investigate the system of grading salaries was again appointed and held its first meeting in May of that year. A month later representatives of the economic bodies appeared before it, saying that "there is not and cannot be any equalization," that "the family wage is not being implemented," and that in fact it never had been.[131] Nevertheless, in January

1936 legislation was published concerning the salary scale of Histadrut workers, and the Wages Committee made a new effort to fix wage levels.[132] The Histadrut continued to behave in its usual manner, and the family-wage system was formally abandoned only at the beginning of the 1950s.

Thus, a sort of division of labor had existed from the beginning. The Wages Committee made its recommendations and tried to implement the decisions of the conventions and councils, whereas the executive stood behind the economic leadership, which refused to apply the family wage. When the management of Yachin handed in its resignation to protest its obligation to apply the wage, the executive rejected its resignation, thus supporting it against the committee and helping it, in practice, to undermine the egalitarian system. In this way, it was made quite clear who controlled the Histadrut. The real power lay at the top of the pyramid and not at its base. The Histadrut was run accordingto the best traditions of centralized democracy. But even more important, in the early 1930s the principle that the creation of economic power always takes precedence over social justice received official sanction. The development of the economic power of the Histadrut constituted the infrastructure of its political strength. From its inception, economic considerations took precedence over social considerations.

CLASS WARFARE IN THE HISTADRUT

The social gaps and differences in standards of living at the end of the 1920s and the beginning of the 1930s were bearable as long as relative prosperity prevailed. In 1926–27 there had been struggles within the Histadrut, but they had been either ideological (the fight against Gdud Ha'avoda) or political (the conflict with the anti-Zionist communist fraction). They were not social. There were plenty of social inequities in the local Jewish society, but dealing with such problems was confined to institutions controlled by professional party workers.

This situation changed completely with the beginning of the long and difficult economic crisis of the second half of the 1930s. If at the beginning of the decade there had been full employment in the country, from 1935 on unemployment began to rise. In 1936, 5 percent of the Jewish labor force was out of work, and in 1939 the rate of unemployment reached 8 percent.[133] In terms of that period, and measured against the relative prosperity of the early 1930s, this was a very grave situation indeed. Because of the distress, inequality was felt to be intolerable.

Between 1930 and 1939 the Histadrut's membership grew from 30,000 to 100,000. In 1937 the organization had a staff of 2,500 members. Data on salary levels in 1937–39 vary. According to one source, in 1937 60 percent of workers earned from 4 to 10 pounds a month, and 70 percent lived on less than 12 pounds a month.[134] According to statistical data presented to the Executive Committee by the Kupat Holim inspection committee in 1939, 51 percent of workers earned up to 4 pounds a month, 10 percent earned from 8 to 12 pounds, and 6 percent earned 12 pounds or more.[135] At the same time, David Remez informed the Executive Committee that nearly 5,000 members earned more than 10 pounds a month. The total number of tax-paying members, excluding the agricultural sector, was 45,000; the secretary of the Histadrut wanted to levy a compulsory loan of half a pound on them until the crisis had passed. In 1939 Aranne reported that 11,000 members of the Histadrut earned more than 6 pounds a month. According to another source, there were 15,000 such people in the Histadrut. In the depressed conditions of that period, these were regarded as privileged.[136]

Whatever the exact figures were, the Histadrut of the second half of the 1930s was a society with great social and economic differences. Against the background of distress, unemployment, and hunger, the differences in standards of living had a particularly disturbing effect. The information on wage levels does not reflect the full situation: the differences were greater than statistical data would lead us to believe because of the work of married couples. A family in which both partners earned a medium or even small sum was regarded as having a high standard of living. The data the Histadrut provided, however, relate to the incomes of individuals, not of families. It was no accident that the abolition of "work by couples" was one of the chief demands of the spokesmen of the unemployed and a bone of contention with the ruling elite. Quite often, the wives of leaders, managers, and various officials receiving their salaries from a public institution were Histadrut workers themselves, earning a good salary.

The difficult problems of that period were not entirely the result of the economic crisis. Structural and ideological difficulties and contradictions that had been present in the Histadrut almost from the beginning finally surfaced. The most basic of these contradictions was the nature of the Histadrut. At the beginning of October 1931, Ben-Gurion recalled the basic conception of its founders. After complaining of the "fictitious relationships" of groups of construction workers in Haifa and Jerusalem who had set up as contractors, thus flouting all Histadrut principles, he condemned the "platonic relationship" of other groups to the organization. Here he meant not only the "workers' wives" but professionals: teachers, doctors, lawyers, architects, and so on. He claimed that the connection to the Histadrut of these people, whose professional interests lay outside it, was "tenuous and lacking any real hold." Their position, he said, was comparable with that of the "members' wives," whose relationship with the Histadrut had "no basis at all." Ben-Gurion wished to create "a special department for all members of the liberal professions," so that "there would not be any purely ideological groups in the Histadrut." "Such a group," he said, "if it existed, would be likely to change the whole character of our organization."[137]

Here one may find the real key to understanding the Histadrut. Its founders saw it as a source of power and as a means of mobilization, and ideological attachment was regarded as secondary, or, at any rate, as insufficient in itself. An ideal Histadrut member was not a socialist eager to contribute to the building of a new society but someone whom the organization could control without interference and without competition from another source. This concept of the Histadrut was a mixed blessing: a source of strength but also a source of weakness. In periods of crisis, it was primarily a source of weakness.

In the days when the organization numbered only a few thousand members, most of them from the Second and Third Aliyahs, the organizational framework served as a sufficiently strong binding force to preserve the unity of the Histadrut during the Fourth Aliyah. But a few years later, when the economic crisis of the 1930s had developed and unemployment had attained dramatic proportions (the Histadrut with its various groups already numbered 100,000 people), the picture changed. Latent tensions and social and ideological contradictions now surfaced. All the limitations of a non-ideological concept of the Histadrut, which saw ideology as a divisive force and common experience as a unifying force, were clearly revealed. In periods of adversity, it became apparent that experience is not necessarily a unifying force. If experience reflects a conflict rather than a community of interests, it can be no less divisive than ideology. However, the Histadrut, created as a tool for building the nation rather than reforming society, was not a socialist body, and its egalitarian ideology was unable to serve as a focus of identity for people of various and opposing interests. This social situation led to the scrapping of the family wage, to the transformation of Histadrut members into virtual employers (as in the case of construction workers, mentioned earlier), and to the emergence of real class differences in its society.

On the eve of the Second World War, the labor movement had to admit that it had no solution to the situation that had arisen. One of the most striking examples of this impotence was the imposition of the mas ahid in 1937. This important reform was intended to create a new unity between the Kupat Holim and the Histadrut. The new tax was imposed both to balance the budget of the Kupat Holim and to strengthen the individual member's ties to the Histadrut. Until then, about 30 percent of Histadrut members did not belong to Kupat Holim. When necessary, those better off consulted a private doctor, which for young people could be cheaper than being subject to taxation, and those on the lower rung of the social ladder could not afford the membership fees. This partial membership was embarrassing for the organization, which conclused that it needed a sort of "ring around the Histadrut."[138]

Because the leadership realized that a socially advanced system of taxation that harmed the privileged would sap the foundations of the Histadrut, the mas ahid that was arrived at was nonegalitarian and unjust. A few people in the Histadrut Council complained, but the great majority understood that a radical approach would antagonize the powerful. "Why did they wait until now to demand progressive taxation?" Remez asked the critics.[139] The secretary of the Histadrut claimed such an idea would be destabilizing, and the delegates at the fortieth Histadrut Council concurred. In his response to the proposal of fixing a maximum family subsistence sum and of paying the surplus into an unemployment fund—a proposal that would have harmed the 11,000 to 15,000 workers who in 1939 earned more than six pounds a month—Aranne said: "In my opinion, this decision will involve the Histadrut in a very dangerous experiment, an experiment whose consequences I can foresee. . . . These extreme proposals, if accepted, will force many workers in the Histadrut to consider not only what the Histadrut gives them but also what it takes from them. Make no mistake: these things will be taken into account tomorrow by the man who is unemployed today, when he begins to work."[140] The proposal to deduct the surplus, in other words, to introduce a progressive income tax in the Histadrut, was a radical demand in those circumstances, but it was the only truly effective policy. All other solutions were mere palliatives.

In addition to the difference between the workers and the unemployed, there were great discrepancies in standards of living. These differences were greater than those reflected in wage levels. In those days there was a tremendous difference between physical work and bureaucratic, technical, or managerial work. Physical labor in a period in which mechanization was still minimal was extremely arduous. In agriculture, where the Jewish laborer was more exposed to the competition of cheap Arab labor than in any other field except construction work in mixed Jewish-Arab cities, his dependency on the farmer was often problematic. Living conditions were often particularly poor and cultural activities were minimal. Agricultural labor was seasonal, and in building, road construction, and public works, supply and demand depended on the economy, the importation of capital from abroad, and the policies of the mandatory government. Office workers, however, worked in far pleasanter conditions and were less exposed to the vicissitudes of the economy. Histadrut workers, in both its administration and its various enterprises, had security of tenure, protecting them from unemployment. It was thus only natural that at the beginning of the 1930s members of the Histadrut bureaucracy, its heads, and those in major positions in Histadrut economic enterprises were among the chief opponents of the family wage. Members of the bureaucracy also enjoyed privileges such as Histadrut housing and trips abroad, which had become such an accepted phenomenon that they even dictated the times of Mapai conventions. For instance, in November 1937 Ben-Gurion decided not to hold the party convention of the summer of 1938 because of the possiblity that the Zionist Congress would convene then. "Many comrades," he said, "will probably be abroad at that time."[141] This comment tells us a great deal about the makeup of the convention, the only gathering that was supposed to include members who were not professional party workers.

Critics of the Histadrut society constantly complained of absences from work due to frequent visits abroad. They claimed that Histadrut housing was available only to better-placed employees and that there was nothing to distinguish it as a labor enterprise: no mutual aid, no schools, no cultural facilities, not even cooperative stores.[142] No less remarkable was Histadrut members' employment of domestic help. According to figures that Ben-Gurion gave in 1931, two thousand domestic workers were listed as Histadrut members. By the end of the 1930s, it appeared that Histadrut functionaries who earned between 20 and 30 pounds a month employed domestic help at 2 to 3 pounds a month. According to Ben-Yeruham, one of the major rebels of the Tel Aviv branch of Mapai, this situation exemplified the revolution that had taken place in the labor movement in the ten years between the crisis of the late 1920s and that of the late 1930s. "In 1927," he said, "I was a worker in Petah Tiqwa; I worked a day a week, I went hungry. At that period, I sometimes visited the apartment of Comrade Idelson [Bar-Yehuda], then secretary of the Petah Tiqwa workers' ouncil, and I saw that he too lived with his family on two to three pounds a month."[143] In many ways this case illustrates the whole problem of the Histadrut as it appeared to the rank-and-file activists.

The years of economic crisis were also years of an identity crisis. Never had there been so much questioning, and never had questions such as, Who are we, and where are we heading? been asked with such earnestness. But the economic crisis did not create the identity problem; it only revealed the complex reality that already existed. In the troubled period of the late 1930s, the full price to be paid for the Histadrut's "comprehensiveness" and for its foundation not on ideology as a model for a new society but on organization and economics as tools in the national struggle became apparent. By that time, the Histadrut embraced about a third of the Yishuv. Thus it is hardly surprising that social struggles and conflicts of class interests developed, no less intense than in the society at large.

Everyone agreed about this in the first and second ranks of the leadership. Despite clear ideological differences between members who were to leave for Faction B and were later to join the independent party that took the historic name of Ahdut Ha'avoda–Poalei Tzion, and the hard core of the members of Mapai, there was a general consensus about facts. Some stressed the "division of members into social strata" (Ben-Aharon),[144] and some denied the existence of conflicting interests in the Histadrut but admitted that the organization had tolerated "the formation of different social strata with different standards of living" (Aranne).[145] It was the lower-ranking party activists, however, who used the strongest terms to describe the situation. They spoke openly about "the classes that have come into being among us," about the shameful situation, about the "chasm that has appeared" among the workers of the Histadrut, which, they said, "is now made up of numerous strata whose standards of living are poles apart."[146] Aranne, however, said that in practice most Histadrut members had now accepted a situation that was "natural, given the regime we live under." In his opinion, the problem came down to the difference between most Histadrut members, who earned between four and ten pounds a month, and the standard of living among the Histadrut bureaucracy. "In the present explosive atmosphere," he said, "this factor is very important."[147]

Israel Guri, who belonged to the center of Mapai and who was usually a conformist, claimed otherwise. The cause of the crisis of confidence, he said, was the fact

> that our movement has committed itself to things that are difficult to accomplish. I mean the promise of equality, which we cannot fulfill. There is a social scale among us which goes from the unemployed to the sort of people who earn twenty-five or thirty pounds a month. . . . This applies not only to the Histadrut bureaucracy but to all our members, who are divided into social strata, ranging from those who subsist on the edge of starvation to those who enjoy a way of life that is above average, with even a little luxury.

And then he came to the point:

> One cannot bridge this gap with expedients. To some extent, it can be bridged with solidarity, but in practice we do not even have solidarity. We ought to be aiming at solidarity, but we can hardly even manage social assistance.[148]

This was the heart of the problem. The rapidly formed class-based society had failed to provide a way of contributing significantly to a reduction in inequality. Social differences within this organization were so entrenched and so glaring that solidarity had become impossible. Here one sees the major weakness of the Histadrut from the social and moral point of view. The Histadrut could impose its will on the weak, it could dismiss ordinary laborers, but it had no leverage against skilled workers, people of the liberal professions, or its own senior administrators. A monthly salary of twenty-five pounds for a member of the Histadrut bureaucracy was not, according to Remez, anything unusual. The number of such people was small, 34 out of 8,000. But Remez failed to provide any information about those who earned twenty pounds or more. Ben-Yeruham estimated their number at more than a thousand, and these included some who earned fifty or sixty pounds a month.[149] These people had reached a position where they were no longer dependent on the Histadrut. In the absence of any ideological attachment, the sense of mutual responsibility was too tenuous to provide the solidarity needed by those on the lower rungs of the social ladder. Moreover, nobody could prevent members of the party and the Histadrut in Tel Aviv, from lawyers with large offices to shop owners, from employing others. In the language of the period, this was called "the exploitation of comrades by comrades."[150]

The call for solidarity was expressed in various demands, none of which was satisfied. The most common demand—one that was considered easiest to fulfill, and that could have rooted out an especially annoying phenomenon—was the abolition of "work by couples." The idea was to prevent married couples from earning double wages, thus making room for the unemployed. The office workers' union further demanded that employment be refused to anyone with an additional source of income—property or another job—and that salaries not exceed the sum permitted by the family-wage level.[151] Among the more radical elements, this proposal took the form of a double demand: in addition to abolishing work by couples, the Histadrut was asked to deposit the surplus income of its employees and those of the national institutions, beyond the amount allowed by the family wage, into a relief fund for the needy. Some asked for all income exceeding the family wage to be abolished for all Histadrut members.[152] But not only did workers of the Histadrut and the national institutions—the Jewish Agency, the Va'ad Leumi—oppose the imposition of this burden, but industrial workers had already shown their indifference to the plight of the needy by refusing to contribute to the Mifdeh, a voluntary fund for the unemployed. These well-established workers had bitter complaints about the lack of equality in the Histadrut, about the luxurious and wasteful lifestyles of the members of the bureaucracy. They wanted to make the fulfillment of their duties contingent on the abolition of work by couples, so prevalent among them.[153] Every sector wanted to pass on the duty of setting a personal example to others.

The dramatic plea heard often in the Mapai Central Committee—"Our party, which preaches equality, ought to do something!"[154]—did not remain without an echo, but neither did it lead to any genuine changes. Among the fifteen to seventeen thousand unemployed, many were literally going hungry.[155] In addition, an unspecified, apparently very large, number of workers needed aid to supplement their very low wages. The greatest shock of all was the revelation of hunger among the children of the unemployed:

> One cannot live in the knowledge that in our community, in our midst, among our workers, there are children who are going hungry. We ask that the first task of the emergency tax be to care for the children. We must first wipe out the shame that a hungry child, a child who comes to school and is hungry,

represents for our community. . . . Making sure that such a child receives one meal at school should be our primary concern, because we do not know whether he receives the other two meals at home. We know that generally he does not receive another two meals at home.[156]

This heartfelt appeal by Golda Meir also failed to produce real results.

Meir was much more sensitive to poverty and distress than many others in the leadership—more than Sprinzak, who was deaf to social or moral demands, and more than Remez, the secretary of the Histadrut, who was subject to intolerable pressures. But she was well aware of the limits of a system based on organizational relationships rather than ideological convictions. She knew that too strong an action against the powerful was liable to cause a rebellion among the bureaucracy and the more important workers' organizations and to lead to general disintegration. Because of its very comprehensiveness, the Histadrut was unable to impose a system of progressive taxation on the income of its members. This explains why, while making her anguished plea on behalf of hungry children, Meir made public a table of patently inegalitarian taxes that Histadrut members were expected to pay in 1940 according to a new scale. In this table the injustice of the Histadrut system of taxation cried to heaven:

Those earning 2 to 4 pounds will pay to the Mish'an and Mifdeh [two relief funds] 0.66 of a day's wages; that is, two-thirds of their salary for a single day per month. Those who earn 4 to 6 pounds will pay 2.2 percent of their monthly salary; those earning 6 to 8 pounds will pay 3.1 percent; those earning 8 to 10 pounds will pay 3.3 percent; those earning 10 to 12 pounds will pay 5.2 percent; those earning 12 to 15 pounds will pay 6.1 percent; those earning 15 to 18 pounds will pay 6.3 percent; those earning 18 to 21 pounds will pay 6.6 percent; those earning 21 to 25 pounds will pay 7 percent; those earning 25 to 30 pounds will pay 7.3 percent; and those earning 30 pounds or more will pay 8.7 percent. Thus, the grading of Mifdeh 4 is from two-thirds of a percent to 8.7 percent.

I want to read out to you one other series of figures: the percentage of his salary that a member would pay to the mas ahid—the Mishan and Mifdeh combined—including unemployment tax. At the bottom level, those earning up to 2 pounds a month will pay 7.5 percent; those earning 2 to 4 pounds will pay 9 percent; those earning 4 to 6 pounds will pay 9 percent; those earning 6 to 8 pounds will pay 10 percent; those earning 8 to 10 pounds will pay 10.5 percent; those earning 10 to 12 pounds will pay 10.79 percent; those earning 12 to 15 pounds will pay 10.89 percent; those earning 15 to 18 pounds will pay 11.59 percent; those earning 18 to 21 pounds will pay 11.69 percent; and those earning 30 pounds and up will pay 13.3 percent. You see that the tax level begins at 7 percent and reaches approximately 13 percent.[157]

We should notice, first, that the second group of figures, which pushes accuracy in the calculation of rates of taxation to one-hundredth of a percent—10.79 percent and 10.89 percent—concludes with round numbers: 7 percent and 13 percent. Was this a rhetorical device? Possibly. One wonders what the reason was for such a niggling exactitude in fixing taxation rates for relatively high salaries (from 10 to 12 pounds a month and up): 10.79 percent rather than 10.80 percent, 10.89 percent rather than 10.90 percent. Did this reflect a kind of commercial psychology? Were the well-to-do less frightened if one stopped at one-hundredth of a percent below the figure? Second, these scales of taxation are grimly ironic for far more serious reasons than those I have just indicated, even if, from a purely arithmetical point of view, they seem to vindicate the sense of social justice of those who prepared them. Did they not ask those with the highest salaries to pay twenty-six times more than those with the lowest salaries, whereas the highest-paid gave "only" fifteen times more than the next highest?

The most important thing to be said about these scales is that they do not take the number of children or dependents into consideration. This is the first grave injustice; the second is that there is no recognition of the fact that a wage of 2 pounds a month was a miserable wage, far—very far—from being able to cover a family's most basic expenses, even if the family consisted of only two people. The rent for one room was about 0.8 to 1.0 pound a month; two rooms cost about 1.2 to 1.5 pounds a month. Fees for secondary education came to at least 2 pounds a month. It is therefore very surprising that those who earned 2 pounds or less were supposed to make any contribution at all. The first scale dealt only with voluntary contributions, and perhaps those worse off were not expected to give a great deal. The taxation rates in the second scale, however, were compulsory. A scale of this kind is never very revealing at either end; it is the areas in the middle that deserve to be studied. Let us not dwell on the table of voluntary contributions; the only interesting point about it is the degree of generosity that people were expected to show. The second table requires our attention. Nine and 10 percent was asked of the majority of wage earners (who earned 2 to 6 pounds and 6 to 8 pounds a month), and only 11 of those who earned 10 to 15 pounds. In Palestine in 1939–40, 11 pounds a month (and, how much more, 15 pounds a month!) was an excellent salary; a cleaning woman earned 2 pounds.

In absolute terms, someone earning 15 pounds a month, according to this scale, would have to pay twice as much as someone earning 8 pounds a month, which would seem to respect differences in salary (15 × 11% = 1.65 pounds, 8 × 10% = 0.8 pounds). Nevertheless, to be fair, a conception of social justice cannot be based solely on arithmetic, and that of the Histadrut purported to take other factors into account. Golda Meir's scale, however, was favorable to those who earned 10 to 15 pounds a month but burdensome for those who earned 4 to 8 pounds. For someone earning 8 pounds a month in 1939–40, 10 percent determined whether a child would receive a secondary education, and for someone who earned 4 pounds a month, 10 percent determined, in the absence of another wage earner in the household, whether one was reduced to penury. Yet, despite this, Golda Meir's scheme was an improvement over the scheme of the mas ahid in 1937. She made tax for unemployment relief compulsory, whereas previously it had been left to the discretion of each Histadrut member. Finally, the scale of taxation presented in 1939 resembled all similar scales in the capitalist societies of the period. It asked far more of the lower middle class than of the upper middle class and the well-to-do.

Golda Meir knew that this was all that could be done. In September 1939, when she appeared before the Histadrut's Executive Committee two months before the Histadrut Council that was to decide on the mas ahid, she could not help declaring with bitter irony that "judging from the discussions of the committee, I can tell you that no revolution will take place in the immediate future." She had nothing more to add and no other suggestions to make, apart from imposing a "large Mifdeh" on all Histadrut members. "As you see," she said, "we have not succeeded in coming up with a proposal that would bring about equalization in the Histadrut."[158] All more drastic proposals, the only ones that could alleviate distress, such as communal canteens for the elderly, confiscation of surplus salaries, or, as Ziesling proposed, the confiscation of one month's pay, were rejected.[159]

These failures were even more striking because of the tremendous efforts that had been made throughout the decade to provide assistance to the unemployed. Since 1933, the year the unemployment fund was created, until the end of 1939, nearly 280,000 pounds were paid into the fund. More than half of this sum was devoted to creating employment and the rest to providing assistance via the Mish'an fund. Half of the revenue came from the regular unemployment tax included in the mas ahid, and the second half from voluntary contributions to the Mifdeh. As contributions were voluntary, sums varied. Mifdeh 1 yielded 60,000 pounds; Mifdeh 2, 38,000; and in Mifdeh 3 the sum was reduced to 21,000 pounds, and the target of 30,000 was not reached. Shraga Netzer, who became known as one of Ben-Gurion's legendary adjutants, reported the refusal of thousands of workers to contribute to Mifdeh 3. At the same time, the unemployment fund provided 6,000 families (about half of them in Tel Aviv) with food as well as financial assistance, and all the unemployed continued automatically to belong to Kupat Holim and to receive free medical treatment.[160]

The only effective solution would have been to impose heavy taxes on all those with large and medium salaries and to mobilize the economic enterprises of the Histadrut for that purpose. Even in the stormy debate between the Mapai Central Committee and the activists of the Tel Aviv branch, this possibility was not discussed, and when on various occasions such things were hinted at, everyone knew that the chances that such a proposal would be carried out were no greater than the likelihood that all Histadrut members would form a commune.[161] The idea that one could expect the Histadrut economy to take economic risks in order to attain social objectives was not acceptable in Mapai. It may be true that the Histadrut economy would have been unable to bear the strain, and that the fear of harming its liquid reserves and of undermining its stability was not unfounded.

Nevertheless, the imposition of an income tax within the organization was a real possibility. The idea had been proposed in various forms with the aim of preventing the Histadrut from splitting up into hostile camps. "I am advocating not equality or a commune but only solidarity between members. Mutual aid should not be confused with social assistance!" cried Ada Fishman when demanding an emergency regime in the Histadrut. Together with Ziesling and Abramovitz, she wanted, as a temporary measure, to grant all Histadrut members a subsistence allowance depending on their family situation. Each member would receive the minimum sum necessary to survive, and the surplus would go into the Histadrut treasury.[162] Ben-Aharon viewed this proposal as "a first step toward creating a minimum degree of equality among us."[163] Aranne, on behalf of the leadership, completely rejected all these ideas. He refused, he said, to "be taken captive" either "by brilliant but unrealistic proposals" or by "proposals that ignore our duty to the unemployed. . . . I accept the dull but difficult path proposed in Golda Meyerson's address."[164]

The leadership's choice to leave things as they were preserved the wholeness of the organization. There is no doubt that any attempt to turn the Histadrut into a commune would have led to its disintegration. The rejection of radical solutions not only demonstrated the refusal of the Histadrut to become an alternative society but was also indicative of the great difference between the ordinary member's concept of the role of the Histadrut and that of the leadership. Except in speeches on the death of Émile Vandervelde, president of the Socialist International, in 1938, the term *socialism* never appeared in the phraseology of the Histadrut or the party. But the demand for equality was still heard, and yet there was also a widespread acceptance of the permanency of the existing order. No one deluded himself that the Histadrut society could still be changed, but in many people this produced a sense of defeat.

Here one sees the ambivalence of the whole enterprise. The ordinary member's demands from the organization were incomparably greater than those of a trade union member in Europe. Indeed, the Histadrut was neither an economic organization nor a trade union: it was the state in preparation. The politically conscious member of the Histadrut, not to mention the trade union or workers' council activist, regarded the Histadrut as an arena where one could come forward with far-reaching demands. They had accepted many hardships in order to build up its political strength and economic power, and thus they expected it to fulfill its moral and social duties. They felt its unwillingness to tackle the problem of inequality as a betrayal. This was the real cause of the bitterness and animosity in the late 1930s.

From the State-in-the-Making
to the Nation-State

THE PEOPLE who brought the state into being also led it during the War of Independence and consolidated it during its first twenty years of existence. The power structures created before the state was founded proved their effectiveness; the state functioned as soon as it was established. The new state also fought a war, the longest and most difficult in its history. Six thousand died, representing 1 percent of the population. Among the fighters were Holocaust survivors who did not yet speak Hebrew and who scarcely understood the orders they were given. Jerusalem was besieged and cut off from the rest of the country, and the Jewish Quarter in the Old City was forced to surrender, like the frontline settlements of Gush Etzion on the way to Hebron. In northern Israel Syrian tanks were stopped at the last line of defense at Degania; in the south the advance of the Egyptian army was halted at the barbed-wire entanglements of Kibbutz Yad Mordechai, founded in 1943 and named after Mordechai Anilewicz, leader of the Warsaw Ghetto Uprising.

Despite the numerical inferiority of its population, which permitted the enemy—both the independent Arab states and the Arabs of Palestine—to hope for a quick and successful campaign, the Yishuv won a brilliant victory. There were many reasons for this: the determination and solidarity of a population fighting with its back to the wall and in danger of being driven to the sea, its ability to adapt and willingness to sacrifice, and the superiority of the Israelis (or the great weakness of the Arabs) both in field operations and in general strategy. Indeed, whenever there was a need for them on a particular front, the Israeli army succeeded at a crucial moment in gathering more men and matériel in better condition, if not in greater quantities, than the enemy. For example, the Egyptian air force, with its eighty-two airplanes in nine squadrons, fighter aircraft and bombers, enjoyed, on paper, an overwhelming superiority. Yet the young state, with its dozen fighter aircraft and a few bombers, at critical moments in the battle for the Negev in late 1948, managed to achieve and maintain almost complete mastery of the skies. The Israeli side made about 240 sorties, compared with only 30 to 50 by the Egyptian side. The Egyptian air force was unable to overcome its chronic shortage of pilots, the poor state of its aircraft, and the deficient training of its ground technicians.[1]

The Israelis' triumph, which became possible only through a mobilization of all the country's resources, was primarily the result of organization and discipline. But it also demonstrated the leadership qualities of the men at the helm and the solidity of the management structures built up during the twenty-seven years between the Histadrut's founding and the beginning of the War of Independence. Heroism and an ability to improvise would not in themselves have been enough to enable the Israelis to repel the combined attack by neighboring countries and then, in the next stage, to launch a counteroffensive. When the armistice was signed in 1949, the frontiers of Israel were far more advantageous to the Jews than those they had agreed to in 1937 and 1947. Now, at the end of the century, they form part of the founders' heritage.

At the end of the War of Independence, Ben-Gurion enjoyed unquestioned authority. No one wanted or was able to challenge him. During the battles, the power to make decisions lay with him, sometimes exclusively. The role he conferred on Chaim Weizmann, elected president of the state, was purely ceremonial. Weizmann enjoyed enormous prestige, but he already seemed to belong to another era. He was the father of the Balfour Declaration, the symbol of Zionist continuity and the Jews' tenacity in surviving the storms of the present century, but he knew that he would never have obtained this honorary position had not another man shown such single-minded passion and obsessiveness. This would never have happened if Ben-Gurion, regardless of circumstances, had not succeeded in persuading everyone to live for the future as if the present did not exist and to regard his personal today as transcended by a common tomorrow.

The institutions that had been established were so solid that the transition from the Yishuv to the state was hardly felt. The country was still ruled by the same people, with the same philosophy of government and the same principles of action. The balance of forces had not changed, and Mapai, as the dominant party, faced no danger of rebellion from anyone, not even a serious opposition. Ben-Gurion succeeded in delegitimizing the Right; it would need thirty years to come to power. In a formal sense, parliamentary democracy seemed to work perfectly from the beginning. Of all societies that gained independence after the Second World War, Israel was undoubtedly the one in which political liberty, a multiparty system, and the supremacy of civil government were most completely assured. But the reality was not always as simple as this brief description might suggest.

To this day Israeli democracy has serious deficiencies, and its weaknesses, for the most part, are those of the prestate Yishuv, where political and cultural life was dominated by the Histadrut. After the founding of the state, as before, the founders were determined not to permit their hands to be tied by abstract principles or to allow the executive's freedom of action to be interfered with. Thus, Israel has no constitution. The resistance of the religious parties (both Zionist and non-Zionist) to a presumed danger of secularization is not the only factor responsible for the absence of a constitution in Israel. By no means. The opposition of the religious, a quite common pretext in Ben-Gurion's day, has not been used as such since the beginning of the 1970s. The danger of secularization, in the sense this concept gained in countries such as the United States and France from the period of the Third Republic on, was never an issue in Israeli society because labor nationalism, as we have seen, was steeped in historical, religious, and semi-religious values.

The Declaration of Independence, read out in the great hall of the Tel Aviv Museum on 14 May 1948, highly liberal and modeled on the French Declaration of the Rights of Man and the American Declaration of Independence, was an article for export, an act of public relations. It had no legal standing in Israeli jurisprudence and thus could not serve as a point of reference with regard to the rights of man, with regard to gender equality (which the religious parties very strongly opposed), or with regard to equality before the law, which, if applied, would have made the Arabs remaining in Israeli territory full citizens. At the end of the war, the Arabs were placed under a special regime, which probably was unavoidable at that period but which had lasting negative consequences. This regime was abolished only nearly twenty years later, in 1966. The special military regime to which the non-Jewish Israeli citizens were subject made the promulgation of a constitution impossible. To this day non-Jewish minorities are still subject to various kinds of discrimination. In the same vein, it is clear that the characterization of the state of Israel in the 1992 basic law "Human Dignity and Liberty," the most liberal piece of Israeli legislation, as both "Jewish and democratic" is highly problematic.

Moreover, colonial emergency legislation remained in force, apart from provisions relating to Jewish immigration, or those which contradicted the existence of a Jewish state. British regulations concerning terrorism, which were directed against the activities of Jewish organizations and imposed a state of siege on Palestine, proved to be a useful administrative tool. Some parts of this draconian legislation were abrogated only in 1979, after labor's fall from power. Other regulations, of Israeli origin, are still in force. These include the celebrated Ordinance Concerning the Fight against Terrorism of September 1948, issued on Ben-Gurion's initiative at the time when the Israeli Freedom Fighters (Lechi), an extreme right-wing group better known in other languages than Hebrew as the Stern Gang, headed by the future prime minister Yitzhak Shamir, assassinated the United Nations' special envoy Count Bernadotte.[2]

In some respects, even today, the country is still managed in a way that is comparable to that would-be state-in-the-making, the Histadrut before 1948. In our time Israel is undoubtedly the Western democracy with the weakest means of control in parliament and the strongest executive branch. Members of parliament are not chosen by the population but are selected from lists presented en bloc. The Israeli voter places in the ballot box a voting slip on which is written only a letter representing the party of choice; the voter has no influence on the identity of the member of parliament. Not until 1988 were labor candidates chosen in conditions of relative openness. They were selected by the Central Committee, a great step forward compared with the system inherited from the period of the Yishuv. Until that time, all candidates for positions of responsibility were appointed by a commission made up of some of the party's leading personalities, which was the best way of ensuring the dominance of the party apparatus. Not until 1992 was this system corrected by the institution of primaries enabling all members of the party to participate in choosing their candidates. However, the election of the prime minister by universal suffrage, which took place for the first time in May 1996, and the additional powers that the head of the executive has at his or her disposal will only reinforce the unfortunate imbalance in favor of the "person at the helm," especially as members of parliament will continue to be chosen from a party list. Thus they will never have the prestige of being true "representatives of the people" in dealing with the head of government. Moreover, these representatives possess neither the legal nor the technical means to supervise and check governmental actions. They have less influence than senior officers in the army or senior officials.[3]

The philosophy and practice of government in Israel are also inherited from the prestate period, dating from the time the leaders of the first Jewish agricultural workers decided to direct the enterprise of rebuilding the nation on its historical territory. In the political system created by the founders, in the Histadrut and the institutions of the Yishuv, the majority had all the rights and the executive was all-powerful as long as it had a majority. These practices gradually became increasingly entrenched, as no change of regime took place in the Histadrut from the time it was founded until recently, and in the society as a whole from the beginning of the 1930s until 1977. For the labor elite, power soon came to be seen as a natural right (which explains the Israeli cultural elite's shock when the Right won the elections of 1977) and parliamentary control as a useless or even dangerous legalistic impediment to the proper conduct of affairs.

In this system, not only was the practice of the alternation of government unknown, but there was also not much accountability. In running the Histadrut and the Yishuv, the labor elite had made conformity a rule of life, the observance of discipline second nature, and secrecy the greatest virtue of the good citizen or responsible leader. These rules of behavior were enforced even more strictly after independence. Official censorship, and especially the self-censorship of the press and the state radio (until 1965 the latter was attached to the prime minister's office), the very frequent appeal to *raison d'Etat* to prevent any real supervision of the state apparatus either by the press or the Knesset, the quasi-sacred status of the army and the other branches of the vast defense establishment, and the subordinate role of justice in essential matters like the rights of citizens, all these contributed to Israel's stifling atmosphere from the War of Independence to the mid-1960s, when Ben-Gurion finally left office (1963).

The Ben-Gurion regime, the supreme expression of the founders' philosophy of government, was a mixed system where a plurality of parties, universal suffrage, and a respect for the basic rules of democracy coexisted with the constant pressure characteristic of a fortified camp. Those revolutionaries, the founders, never regarded democracy, the separation—or rather division—of powers, the right to information, and the right to happiness and well-being as values in themselves. Democracy was considered beneficial or harmful according to circumstances; everything depended on prevailing conditions. The same applied to equality and social justice. The purpose of educating workers' children was not to develop their personalities or enable them to rise socially but to form effective agents of national construction. In 1935 it was in the interests of the nation that the child of an agricultural worker remain a laborer; in 1965 perhaps there was a need for him to become an engineer. But as the country produced or absorbed a sufficient number of engineers, there was no need for free secondary and higher education. This was a familiar and often-repeated argument from the day the Histadrut was created, an argument that was applied in all spheres of social, economic, cultural, and political activity. This way of reasoning derived from the only ambition the founders ever really had: to lead a dispersed nation to independence and endow it with a state. Giving everyone an equal starting point in order to permit social mobility or to change society was not part of their program.

Herein lay the greatness and also the weakness of Ben-Gurion and the labor elite. These people brought the state into being, and once it was created they carried out the gigantic task of immediately absorbing the great waves of immigration that followed (the population doubled between 1948 and 1952). However, they neither wished nor were able to provide the new state with a new society. It was a unique opportunity to innovate; the price was not out of reach, the dream did not require unattainable sums of money, and this was truer of the proposals contained in the Mapai program on the morrow of independence. In the period of the Yishuv, the activists had agreed—some willingly, others reluctantly—to let the society-in-the-making pay the price for a policy aimed at constructing a nation that was capable of becoming a state. But now that the state existed, would the second stage of this revolution, which some people still believed in, be carried out? Would one do the things that one had failed to accomplish in the time of the Yishuv?

The Mapai activists of those crucial years were far more perspicacious than the historian Anita Shapira, who wrote at the end of her biography of Berl Katznelson: "The architect of the socialist society in Eretz Israel was Berl."[4] The reality was undoubtedly less brilliant; because a socialist society had never existed in Palestine, Katznelson could not have been its architect! The activists, for their part, were not nostalgic about the past, even when revised and corrected in hindsight; they knew exactly how things stood. "I will be so bold as to say that the party does not have any socialist program which it intends to carry out," declared Benzion Israeli, a well-known party member, to the Mapai Central Committee in 1949.[5] Two years later Berl Lokker, another important member of the party, confirmed the party's lack of a program: "I think a socialist movement should have some theory, some set of coherent ideas."[6]

On 21 and 22 January 1955, the day after the meeting of the Mapai Central Committee at which Ben-Gurion had celebrated the fiftieth anniversary of the Second Aliyah (see chapter 2), about two hundred party activists, all under the age of thirty-five, held a weekend seminar at the Mapai Training College at Beit Berl. What was interesting here was not the political maneuvers of this young generation eager to gain power but the ideological views expressed at this seminar. After the speeches of Prime Minister Moshe Sharett and some leading members of the party, the meeting was thrown open for discussion. Here is the text of the report published on 23 January in the daily newspaper *Ha'aretz*:

> Many of the young people, reacting to the statements of the ministers and leaders, complained that the party had forgotten about socialism. One of them said that he was very surprised to receive an invitation to a symposium on this subject, as in recent years he had not heard the word "socialism" mentioned at party meetings. Mr. Abraham Ofer [outgoing secretary of the Tel Aviv branch of the party and a future minister] raised a storm at the meeting when he said that "today, the only difference between Mapai and the General Zionists is ten million pounds" (he was referring to the respective proposals of the two parties for the state budget). Mr. Ofer said, among other things, that in fact there was no difference between private enterprises and those of the Histadrut, and demanded far-reaching changes in the Hevrat Ha'ovdim to make its enterprises administratively independent of the Histadrut.
>
> Mr. Sharett disagreed with Mr. Ofer, and in a speech lasting an hour and a half contradicted the assertion that Mapai was no longer a socialist party. He said that socialism was not an end in itself but a process whose characteristics changed according to circumstances, and he enumerated the enterprises and achievements of the labor movement in the country.

Mr. M. Namir, secretary-general of the Histadrut, also supported "socialist pluralism"; that is, continual attempts to realize the aims of socialism in a variety of areas and by different means. In his speech, which like that of Mr. Sharett was apologetic in nature, Mr. Namir said that class war was not at present a war to protect the wage earner from his employer but a war to protect the Histadrut economy from its assailants. Mr. Namir strongly attacked the proponents of the nationalization of Kupat Holim and said that the General Zionists knew very well why they supported the nationalization of the health services. It was because Kupat Holim was the "secret of the strength of the labor movement."

Mr. Namir said that if the British Labour Party had a health care organization and economic institutions like those of the Histadrut, it would remain in power forever."

Indeed, the last sentence of Namir's statement constitutes a faithful summary of labor's philosophy since the first days of the movement's history and an excellent explanation of its ascent to power.

It was no accident that the discussion on the nature and objectives of socialism reappeared within the party with the emergence—via the Lavon affair—of internal opposition to Ben-Gurion's single-handed exercise of power; Pinhas Lavon was minister of defense in the Sharett government in 1953–55, when Ben-Gurion decided to retire temporarily from public affairs. Only when this espionage affair of the early 1950s—in which a number of Egyptian Jews recruited by the Israeli intelligence were captured and comdemned to death or imprisoned—turned, at the beginning of the 1960s, into a major political crisis did socialism become a subject of intellectual debate in the labor movement.

Thus, at first with astonishment and then with annoyance, Mapai, in the early 1960s, saw a small group of intellectuals call for a return "to basics" and propose the application of socialism. The Min Hayesod (Back to Basics) group led by Lavon wanted simply to refresh people's memories. In 1963 the Hebrew University philosopher Nathan Rotenstreich, the intellectual leader of the group, published an essay entitled "Capitalism and Socialism," in which he restated certain basic truths: "An economy cannot cease to be capitalist as long as it is based on the idea that profits must benefit the owners, and not on the idea that they must be used to revitalize it for the benefit of everyone. To free people from dependency: that is the fundamental idea of socialism and the guiding principle on which its analysis of things is based. This liberation not only repudiates a certain idea of property but also completely rejects the idea that profit is both the supreme motivation and the special characteristic of liberty."[7] This was preaching in the wilderness and calling for a revolution, which the founders had never envisaged in the prestate period, feeling it would render the Zionist enterprise futile. They were no more able to accept it when the state was set up, believing it would weaken the state as they conceived of it. The Min Hayesod group broke away and tried to create its own party. Twenty-five years after the founding of the state of Israel, socialism had become solely the concern of the marginalized, the losers and the defeated in the struggle for power among Ben-Gurion's successors.

If nation-building was regarded as the final goal of all political, economic, and social action, there was no reason for the founders, after the establishment of the state, to have abandoned the methods, principles, and modes of conduct that had contributed to that goal. Before the state existed, for want of an alternative, the Histadrut had the role of providing these elements, and it was in and through the Histadrut that the principles and modes of conduct that could bring about the consolidation of the nation had been practiced. That was why the Histadrut, as we have seen, could not be the model of a future society. The same can be said of collective agriculture: the kibbutzim and moshavim (this is an embarrassing truth for all those for whom the kibbutz was a raison d'être for an entire existence) were not a means to a social revolution but tools in forging national sovereignty. For another generation, the kibbutzim continued to guard the frontiers, and their children provided the army with its best elite units. The fatalities the kibbutzim suffered between the Sinai campaign in 1956 and the Yom Kippur War of 1973 were out of all proportion to their numbers in the population. Very few Israelis, however, see a collectivistic form of life as ideal for their society as a whole.

After the War of Independence, the task of consolidating the nation quite naturally fell to the state. The state thus took over from the Histadrut, and in much the same way as the Histadrut, the state used its powers of coercion and prerogatives chiefly to reinforce the strength of the nation, not to establish a better society. Like the Histadrut in the days when it was the main instrument for regulating economic activities, the newly constituted state did not believe that the welfare of the individual could be a value in itself. That was why, contrary to another myth that gained wide credence in its first twenty years, Israel did not have any real social policies. It enabled the poor, the unproductive, all those who had trouble finding their place in the economy, to barely keep their head above water, but a genuine policy of assistance that could have ensured a decent standard of living for the underprivileged was never worked out. As in the time of the Histadrut, Israeli society paid very little attention to those who could not contribute to the accumulation of the national wealth. The UN expert Philip Klein, a well-known professor of social work at Columbia University, who spent more than two years in Israel at the government's invitation at the end of the 1950s, stated that it was not solely or even "chiefly administrative action that calls for revision; it is rather the spirit and objectives behind the administration and its guiding outlook and philosophy. . . . The Welfare State is a Sate for the welfare of workers, producers, builders of an economy and of the national ideal."[8] The development zones and the depressed areas of the cities, most of which were populated by new immigrants from Arab countries who came between 1950 and 1954, were never a focus of attention or financial assistance until the beginning of the 1970s, when protests led by the Black Panthers were organized in the poorer quarters; Black Panthers was the name adopted by groups of young people who demonstrated for the first time on 3 March 1971, in front of Jerusalem's city hall. Prime Minister Golda Meir, who was displeased with these young people, declared that they were not "nice." The expression soon became famous and a matter of derision even for the well-to-do upper-middle classes.

These young people were undoubtedly not "nice." They were even less amenable and disciplined than the unemployed of the late 1930s; they did not speak the accepted language of the Histadrut officials, and they were so bold as to assert that their country had perhaps not done all it could have done on their behalf. Indeed, the protest of the Black Panthers was not the first since the foundation of the state; on 7 July 1959 riots that shocked public opinion broke out in Wadi Salib, one of the most wretched areas of Haifa. Treated as a local problem, the disturbances in Haifa had no national repercussions. In 1971, however, circumstances were different. This time the protest could not be confined to the disadvantaged areas of Jerusalem, and the labor movement sensed trouble. The social problem had become a major political problem, and it had to be taken seriously. That is why at the beginning of the 1970s the leaders of the labor movement began to think about pursuing a less insensitive policy toward the "second Israel" (the non-Western immigrants and their children). The "third Israel"—the Israeli Arabs—still had a long time to wait before any attention was paid to its impoverished condition.

The economic policies of the young Jewish state were characterized by a similar functionalist approach. The centralism and planning inherited from the prestate period were not, as is generally thought, the product of a socialist ideology but corresponded to the needs of national construction. Because society had to mobilize all its forces to achieve its main goal, the creation of a single decision-making center was considered vital. This is why the Histadrut was set up as a highly centralized and authoritarian organization. Nor was there any other reason for the centralism of institutions set up immediately after independence. These deeply rooted characteristics of the prestate period were greatly reinforced both by the necessity of having to cope with mass immigration and by the enormous cost of the War of Independence. The system of rationing and the distribution of resources, like the huge investments necessary for modernization and development, could be managed only by the state, as in Europe.

State economic planning was a method of government in vogue during and after the Second World War, not only in Europe but also in the United

States, where the memory of the Great Depression was still very much alive. In Europe planning was due at that time to the necessity of ensuring full employment and of rebuilding countries ravaged by the war. The same was true in Israel, where the results of this policy were quite good, or, at any rate, were what the ruling elite had hoped for. From 1954 on the country embarked on a course of rapid and continuous economic growth.[9] But at the same time social gaps were widening. Centralism and state planning, accompanied by importation of capital on a very large scale (German money came first, in the form of reparations), finally gave the nation a healthy economic basis but also a society with inequalities on a European scale, and in some cases even more marked than in Western Europe—in education, for instance. The founders were well aware of this phenomenon, but these deep social differences preoccupied them only to the extent that they were harmful to national unity. They felt that social disparities therefore had to be kept within acceptable limits. These men never had any other ideology, and because the policy they had followed since the founding of the Histadrut was highly successful, they saw no reason to initiate dubious experiments.

National construction was a process whereby priority was given to political and economic power. This was the case from the very beginning, and as soon as they had gained any power at all, the founders tried to give it the strongest possible basis, that is, an administrative basis. Therefore one can hardly be surprised at the sustained attention and even affection that the labor elite lavished on its organizations: the Histadrut and the party. In the absence of normal state structures, the founders considered the Histadrut bureaucracy as the administration of the state-in-the-making and expected from it the impartiality and discipline that a "normal" society has the right to expect from its bureaucratic apparatus. Once the state was established, Ben-Gurion transferred his attention and affection to the state's administrative bodies, especially the army. For Ben-Gurion, the army was the ideal melting pot he had always dreamed of. The army had everything: strength, dedication, discipline—all the qualities necessary to serve as an example to the nation. To Ben-Gurion and the other founders, Tzahal (the Israel Defense Force) was more than an army. It also, and to no less a degree, had the function of building the nation. The Israeli army was regarded as a school of national conduct. In Israel the founders wanted the army to be neutral not just to prevent it from interfering in politics but also because it had to be the "army of the people."

Once again this functionalist approach determined the relationships the founders had with the diaspora. In recent years these relationships have been the subject of a debate that has sometimes been highly emotional. This recalls the "historians' debate" in the former Federal Republic of Germany in the 1980s on the nature of Nazism and its place in German history, or the controversy that raged in France in the last months of 1994 about the Vichy regime and its role in the deportation of Jews during the Nazi occupation. In Israel the relevant question is: Did the political elite of the Yishuv succeed in fulfilling the role it gave itself? The Yishuv, as we have seen, claimed a position of preeminence with regard to all Jewish communities of the diaspora, including that of the United States. This claim, however, involved certain responsibilities, especially of leadership. The question, therefore, is not so much to what degree was the Yishuv's desire to "guide" the diaspora sincere but did the labor elite, when it came to power, act in accordance with its ideals, especially during the Second World War.

Before the war, the Yishuv and the Zionist movement did not accord the diaspora any intrinsic value. Zionism was based on a negation of the diaspora. During the war, and especially when the machinery of extermination began to operate, this view gained a terrible implication. Until that time, the Yishuv had considered immigration the only possible solution to the Jewish question. Consequently, the Jewish communities of the diaspora were recognized as having only one function: to serve the Yishuv, and hence the enterprise of national rebirth; at least this was regarded as their principal function. In the Yishuv this "self-evident fact" needed neither moral justification nor material proof. It was simply accepted. However, let us not conclude that this view was responsible for a deliberate policy of disinterest—the more generous say a "wait-and-see" policy, the more critical say blindness—on the part of the Yishuv with regard to Jewish communities in countries under the Nazi heel. It is absurd to even suppose that the Jews of Tel Aviv could have been indifferent to what other Jews were experiencing in Nazi-dominated Europe. It is equally ridiculous to suppose that the Jews of New York took refuge in a policy of "burying their heads in the sand" because they themselves were not in danger. In 1942 Jews in Tel Aviv, New York, and Los Angeles who did not have a grandfather, a father, a sister, or a cousin in Eastern Europe were a rarity. But in New York, as in Tel Aviv, Jews were trapped in a political and psychological dilemma that greatly hindered them. Jews in the United States were Americans above all and were expected, like all other Americans, to support the global policies of Washington. In those years—not only because of the world situation and not only in the United States—minorities were not given the opportunity to express themselves as they have been given in democratic countries in the last twenty or thirty years. In Washington and London, in 1939 as in 1942 and 1944, American and British Jews and Jews of Palestine who attempted to persuade their governments to consider the fate of European Jews were "politely" brushed aside. Never had the Jewish people been so alone. In Tel Aviv they were fully conscious of it, probably more so than anywhere else.

However, this problem unique in Jewish history also has another aspect. Revolutionaries, let us remember, are not usually motivated solely by the need to soothe their conscience. The labor elite thus concentrated its efforts on what had always seemed to them, and which from their point of view remained, of greatest importance: the protection of the Yishuv, the last bastion of the nation. They did not wish to use their resources for purposes for which they would be ineffective. The Zionist movement and the Yishuv knew that the financial and political resources they devoted to helping the Jews of Europe were insufficient or even ludicrous. Yet they did not wish to enter into open conflict with governments or public opinion. They feared that some countries—especially the United States and Britain—would be unable to understand words on behalf of defenseless Jews when the world, they maintained, had other matters to attend to. After all, Zionist leaders believed they would have to appeal to those countries for support in their struggle for a Jewish state once the Nazi scourge was eliminated. On one hand they did not want the war to appear to be a "Jewish" war, and on the other hand it was important not to squander the possibility of future advantages. Today the question of whether everything possible was done to assist the Jews of Europe still troubles the Israeli intelligentsia.[10]

With regard to the higher national interest—the revival of the Jewish nation in its historic land—no price was too high to pay; one was forbidden to calculate the cost. This principle, which had guided the progenitors of the state of Israel for forty years, was the one they continued to follow when the war was over and the first Holocaust survivors disembarked in the port of Haifa. To live up to their ideals, they made the same demands on the emaciated figures disembarking from the ships as they did on themselves and on all immigrants who arrived after them. They had to change, they said; they had to be transformed. How often were these survivors accused of "having gone to the slaughter like lambs"! The newcomers, as pleased as not at still being alive, did not have the strength to argue their case with the Yishuv. They wanted to forget. The most common sentiment among these men and women was the desire to become "new" people, like their brethren "who had the courage to be right" forty years earlier. And who at that time would have dared to argue with those builders of the nation who even in the darkest hours never lost faith in themselves and in the inevitability of Zionism? Their desire was to forget, to become Israelis.

The same demand was made on new immigrants from Arab countries in the 1950s. At first the latter agreed to cut themselves off from their culture, their past. This, they were told, was the only way they could contribute effectively to the national enterprise. But before long these new arrivals felt that the Israeli mold was a violation of their identity. Indeed, the new immigrants from the Arab countries did not know that before denouncing their culture, the founders and pioneers had turned against their own.[11] For the leaders of the Yishuv and later the state of Israel, the cultural revolution had to be total, and no one was exempted. It was the necessary path to national revolution, on behalf of which all major decisions had been made in the days of the Yishuv and which justified all major decisions made since the founding of the state. Before 1948, as after, these considerations governed social policies and policies for repopulating territories. To secure the borders, the new immigrants of the 1950s were settled far from cultural and economic centers, preventing a rapid cultural and economic integration. The leaders of the young state considered it perfectly natural to settle immigrants in harsh and barren regions. After all, Hadera, halfway between Tel Aviv and Haifa, and Petah Tiqwa, today bordering on Tel Aviv—now rich and prosperous towns—were, at that time, in the middle of nowhere. Afula, founded during the Fourth Aliyah, was built under conditions no less difficult than Sderot, Netivot, and Ofakim, three small southern towns that are still vegetating. The thinking of the founders was that building a country and reconstituting a nation required sacrifices. One day, they believed, Sderot, Netivot, and Ofakim would flourish as Hadera and Petah Tiqwa had. Well, it never happened. Today unemployment is highest in the development towns, education is least developed, and there is least social mobility.

The relationship between the labor movement, which assumed the leadership of the national revolution, and its members was first and foremost an empirical relationship and thus subject to modification. In fact, over the years changes did occur. However, Zionism as an ideology of liberation—even when dominated by the labor movement, and even when subject to few socialist or socialist-minded trends that in various periods before and after the founding of the state had demanded the application of certain principles of socialism—never promised to liberate the worker from forms of dependence inherent in the capitalist order. The aim of Zionism was to make the worker the agent of national redemption, to gather the largest possible number of Jews in Eretz Israel, and to give this population a nation-state in the entire historical area of the country. In practice, Zionism, until the last few years, was an unalterable constant, whether the enterprise was directed by the laborites or, later, by the revisionists. This explains why the labor movement, until it relinquished office in 1977, was unable to cope with the consequences of the Six-Day War. The role of occupier, which Israel began to play only a few months after the lightning victory of June 1967, was not the result of some miscalculation on the part of the rulers of that period or the outcome of a combination of circumstances, but another step in the realization of Zionism's major ambitions. If Ben-Gurion accepted the first partition plan of July 1937, it was not because he was motivated by a desire to reach a rational compromise with the Arab national movement but because he wished to give priority to the most pressing matters. The plan, as we know, was rejected by the Palestinian Arabs.

Ben-Gurion knew—and this shows his greatness as a realistic visionary and statesman—that this proposal represented the first real opportunity of creating a state for the Jews. In his view, this was the only consideration that mattered. He wanted to press ahead; he saw how the Arab nationalist movement was gaining strength daily. He also knew that the frontiers of a state were determined by the viability of the society whose territory they defined, its human potential, its industrial and technical capabilities, and its international recognition. The Arab uprising of 1936–39 on one hand and the signs of impending war in Europe on the other convinced Ben-Gurion of the urgent necessity of immediately providing the Jews with a country, no matter how small. For the moment, the Jewish country had to be put on the map and brought into history. The frontiers could be adjusted later, if necessary. Had Ben-Gurion read Hegel? It is most unlikely, but he was instinctively a Hegelian. He believed in the central role of the state in history. A people who did not acquire a state was doomed to disappear.

Israel enlarged its territory after the war of 1948 and, once again, after the war of 1967. When the Golan Heights, Judea, and Samaria were conquered, Ben-Gurion had been out of office for four years, but the Mapai of 1967 was that of 1948, plus or minus a few individuals. In 1967, as in 1948 and 1937, the country's rulers were still convinced that frontiers were created by facts on the ground. After the victory of the Six-Day War, the debate in Mapai was not about whether the doctrine of conquering territory whenever the opportunity arose—put into practice since the first decade of our century—was still valid but about how, and to what degree, the situation created by the Arab defeat could be exploited. This time the disciples of Ben-Gurion and of Tabenkin and Katznelson, of those who had accepted the first partition plan and those who had rejected it, were in the same camp. It is incorrect to assume that it was a case of Prime Minister Levi Eshkol's being unable to resist the combined pressures of Moshe Dayan and Shimon Peres, Ben-Gurion's protégés, and of Yigal Allon and Israel Galili, Tabenkin's followers. The premier, a man of the Second Aliyah, allowed himself to be won over to the position of the four younger activists, and in fact of his whole national unity cabinet, which included Menachem Begin, the Revisionist leader who became prime minister in 1977. For Levi Eshkol, as for the others, the war of 1948 had only just ended. Despite the impression that some of the founders of the labor movement, motivated by internal political struggles, have attempted to create, everyone in the coalition—both the founders and their successors—were united in pursuing a policy of fait accompli in the occupied territories. Despite the divisions in Mapai since the mid-1940s, the family of Mapai remained true to the doctrine of never giving up a position or a territory unless one is compelled to by a superior force.

In 1968 Mapai was re-formed, almost as originally constituted, adopting the name Mifleget Ha'avoda (the Labor Party). This old-new formation was still led by people of the Second and Third Aliyahs, but the generation of 1948 was already well represented and was preparing to take over.

In June 1967 the country had feared for its existence (a fear shared by the West), but at the end of the Six-Day War the geopolitical situation was transformed. Israel had become the major power in the region and enjoyed an economic boom that confirmed this status. The Labor Party, however, had neither learned nor forgotten anything from its days as Mapai. After 1967 everything continued as before. Social and national ideologies were unchanged. Not everyone benefited from rapid economic growth; on the contrary, growth accentuated social differences. Moreover, the nationalism of "socialist" Zionism remained as it had been when Mapai was founded four decades earlier: radical, tribal, volkisch, steeped in the cult of the heroic past, and convinced of the justice of its claims to the entirety of the ancient land, which was formerly the scene of national independence and greatness. This nationalism, together with its symbols, had always been a common enterprise of the Left and the Right. Katznelson described "socialist" Zionism as an enterprise of conquest; Revisionist Zionism never had any other objective. The two forms of Zionism differed only in their methods.

The reason the Labor Party drew the country into an occupation of the West Bank was its nationalism, not its intoxication with the military victory of the Six-Day War or a temporary deficiency in some humanistic values in Zionist thinking. And its denial of the legitimacy of the Arab national movement was not a form of blindness that afflicted only Golda Meir. The prime minister at the time of the Yom Kippur War was chosen as a successor to Levi Eshkol to ensure the perpetuation of a worldview that had begun with Gordon and continued with Katznelson. Like these major thinkers of Eretz Israeli Zionism, Meir appealed to history as proof of the legitimacy, morality, and exclusivity of the Jewish people's right to the country, to the entire country. For her, as for Katznelson, there was room for only one national movement in Palestine. That was also why she prohibited the use of terms such as "Palestinian national movement" and "Palestinian state" on state radio and television.

Yigal Allon also invoked history and historical rights when, as minister of labor in the Eshkol government, he was the chief protagonist of Jewish settlement in Hebron. A kibbutznik and hero of the War of Independence who symbolized the Palmach generation, commander of the southern front and defeater of the Egyptians in 1949, Allon spearheaded the expansion policy. He skillfully exploited the fact that the Israeli government failed to initiate a new national policy, different from the traditional Zionist approach, and for that reason failed to make any clear decisions with regard to Jewish settlement beyond the 1949 cease-fire lines. On 27 July 1967 Allon presented his plan to the government. The plan proposed annexing Hebron and the Mount Hebron area with its population of eighty thousand Arabs to the state of Israel. After presenting his strategic and security considerations, Allon pointed out that in this way "the Cave of Machpela and Rachel's Tomb, precious to us from the national and traditional point of view, would remain within the boundaries of the state of Israel."[12] His celebrated Allon Plan, which included the annexation of the Jordan Valley and the Golan Heights, soon became the official political and settlement plan of Israel under the various Labor governments. In the autumn of 1967 Ben-Gurion also called for settlement in Hebron. "Hebron," he said, "must be settled by Jews, a large number of Jews. This was a Jewish city. One must set up a large Jewish settlement there."[13]

On 14 January 1968 Allon made another proposal: creating an urban neighborhood next to Hebron. Thus the idea of a Jewish town called Kiryat Arba came into being. Today this town has approximately five to six thousand inhabitants and is one of the chief bastions of Jewish extremism. Baruch Goldstein, who on 25 February 1994 murdered about thirty-five Arabs—the exact figure is not known—and who had come to pray at the Cave of Machpela, lived in Kiryat Arba. Goldstein was killed by the survivors of the attack. Today his grave, tended by the inhabitants of the town, is a place of pilgrimage for the extreme religious Right, a kind of monument to a hero fallen in battle. Yigal Amir, Yitzhak Rabin's murderer, also has admirers among students of the national religious system of education.

Prime Minister Eshkol refused to put Allon's proposals to the vote, but at the same time he did not see any "sin" in a Jewish settlement in Hebron and in principle did not oppose the idea of settling in the heart of an Arab town;[14] nor did he take any steps to prevent settlement in Hebron. Consequently, no one could oppose the activistic concept of reviving the Jewish community in the "city of the patriarchs," destroyed in the Arab uprising of 1929. On the contrary, many people in the leadership were ready to support the Rabbi Levinger group, which was made up of extremist elements of Gush Emunim. To this day Levinger displays the most terrible Jewish fanaticism. Thus, on the eve of the first Passover after the Six-Day War, 11 April 1968, his group infiltrated into Hebron deceitfully and on false pretenses. His people received permission from the head of central command to hold a seder in the Park Hotel. After the seder, the group refused to leave. The government was powerless to act, for it dared not take action against Jews who had come to visit the tombs of the Patriarchs and carry out the time-honored Zionist commandment of settling the land. Allon, who appears to have been a party to the secret, immediately arrived in Hebron to visit the group, supported their right to remain in town, and may even have brought weapons from Gush Etzion.[15] The settlements of Gush Etzion, halfway between Jerusalem and Hebron, fell during the War of Independence and were rebuilt on the orders of the government immediately after the Six-Day War.

Allon, the patron of the Levinger group and the initiator of settlement in the Jordan Valley, had the support of Hakibbutz Hame'uhad and of Minister Without Portfolio Israel Galili, one of the outstanding figures of the labor movement, who, like Allon, was a disciple of Tabenkin, the great opponent of the partition of the land. He was also backed by the Revisionist Right under the leadership of Menachem Begin, also a minister without portfolio in Eshkol's National Unity government, and by all religious ministers.

The charismatic minister of defense Moshe Dayan, the legendary chief of staff of the 1950s, also supported the settlement, although in his usual cautious way. Dayan's basic position was similar to Allon's. "All the areas we have taken, including Suez and the Golan Heights, are dear to us," he said in August 1967, "but not like the cradle of our history, Hebron, Shilo, or Anatoth. This is not a question of extending our borders or Lebensraum. It goes much deeper than with areas we have merely conquered."[16] And Dayan expressed himself in similar terms, but even more sweepingly and comprehensively, on 3 August 1967, when he mourned those who fell in the battle for the Jewish Quarter in the Old City of Jerusalem in 1948:

> Our brothers who fell in the War of Independence—we have not abandoned your dream, nor have we forgotten your lesson. We have returned to the Temple Mount, to the cradle of our people's history, to the heritage of the Patriarchs, the land of the judges and the fortress of the kingdom of the House of David. We have returned to Hebron, to Shechem [Nablus], Bethlehem and Anatoth, Jericho and the crossings of the Jordan. . . . Brothers, we carry your lesson with us. . . . We know that in order to give life to Jerusalem, we have to station the soldiers of the Israel Defense Forces and its armor in the mountains of Samaria and at the entrance to the Jordan bridges.[17]

Dayan's attitude was of decisive importance. At that time he was identified more closely than anyone else with the great victory of the Six-Day War and was the supreme authority in Israel in security matters. Thus, on 12 May 1968, one month after the historic seder in Hebron, the ministerial defense committee under Eshkol authorized Dayan to ensure the settlers' security. As minister of defense, Dayan was in practice military governor of all areas conquered in June 1967. On 30 May the same ministerial committee decided not to evacuate the Levinger group from Hebron. The settlers were taken from the Park Hotel, which was under Arab ownership, to military headquarters. This decision led to others, the most important of which was made by the Meir government (Eshkol died in 1969) on 5 February 1970. A majority of twelve ministers decided to found Hebron Illit (Upper Hebron), that is, Kiryat Arba, the beginning of the Jewish settlement in the outskirts of Hebron.

The impotence of Prime Minister Eshkol and other members of the ruling elite was due not—as is often mistakenly attributed—to personal weakness but to an open or latent ideological identification with the settlers' value system. In the summer of 1967 the political fruits of the integral, cultural-religious nationalism of the labor movement had ripened. It once again became apparent, as after the War of Independence, when a way could not be found to give the young state a liberal and secular legislation, that the partnership between the ostensibly secular labor movement and the forces of declared religious nationalism was much deeper than appeared on the surface. Religious and "secular," Right and Left, fathers and sons, still felt that they shared historical and cultural rights based on the sanctity of the Jewish heritage. In 1967 Israel was still very close to the conceptual universe of the shtetl out which the founders had come out.

Thus, Eshkol lacked the spiritual strength to repudiate the great objective of conquering the historical homeland, and in particular its heartland steeped in biblical memories and the deeds of heroes, that great land in which the patriarchs and matriarchs, the kings, the judges, and the prophets had lived and acted. Was this not the goal that he and his friends of the Second Aliyah had set for themselves from the beginning? The strength of Zionist ideology was revealed precisely in Eshkol's indecisiveness. As a realistic and moderate politician, the prime minister feared the problems that might arise from annexation. He did not initiate the settlement either in the Golan or in Hebron, but he had no ideological alternative to offer those who demanded the immediate implementation of the Jewish people's right to their entire historical homeland.

Eshkol (a man of the Second Aliyah), like Meir, (a pioneer of the Third Aliyah), had no response to the argument that if Jews could live in the Arab neighborhoods of Jerusalem and Haifa or in Arab towns lika Jaffa, Ramle, and Lod and consider them their legitimate homes, there was no reason to forbid them from settling in Nablus or Hebron, Gaza or the Golan Heights. If it was permissible to set up kibbutzim or moshavim on Arab lands conquered in 1949, and often on the ruins of villages wiped off the face of the earth, by what moral principle could one justify the prevention of Jewish settlement in the Jordan Valley or the Golan Heights, on Mount Hebron or in the region of Ramallah and Jenin? Did not the people of the northern kibbutzim act in the spirit of their predecessors, the pioneers of Tel Hai, Kfar Giladi, and Hanita, when in June 1967 they started settling on land that had just been liberated from the Syrians? Was not General David ("Dado") Elazar, the head of the northern command, true to the basic principles of Zionism when, after his victory over the Syrian army, he became a patron of the settlers without waiting for the civil authorities' decision? Was this not precisely what one might expect from a military man known for his ideological attachment to the labor movement?

After the victory of June 1967, none of the major leaders of the labor movement thought that Zionism drew its moral authority not from the distant, historical, and mythological past but from its character as a movement of rescue. They did not believe that Zionism simply exemplified the universal right of people to define their own identity and to govern themselves. None of the major leaders of the labor movement believed that the Palestinians deserved the same rights, and that the conquest of land had a moral basis only as long as it was an inalienable condition for creating the infrastructure of an independent Jewish existence. No leader was capable of saying that the conquest of the West Bank lacked the moral basis of the first half of the twentieth century, namely, the circumstances of distress on which Israel was founded. A much-persecuted people needed and deserved not only a shelter but also a state of its own. No one then argued that this objective had been achieved in 1949 and that there was a moral difference between the territories conquered in the War of Independence and those won less than twenty years later. Both had been won from Arabs, but for entirely different purposes. Whereas the conquests of 1949 were an essential condition for the founding of Israel, the attempt to retain the conquests of 1967 had a strong flavor of imperial expansion.

In the years immediately after the Six-Day War, however, few Israelis were capable of making that distinction. Allon and Dayan, the leaders of the younger generation, the war heroes, the exemplars of the "new Israelism," spoke for the great majority. As had happened with other national movements that had struggled to establish a nation-state, the new Israelis, instead of looking ahead, preferred to cling to the past. They were the true heirs of Ben-Gurion and Tabenkin, Gordon and Katznelson, the mentors of that generation and its leaders. For most Israelis, represented by Allon and Dayan, the return to Hebron was the correction of a historical distortion. The first time the natural order of things was upset was when the Jewish people was banished from its land after the conquest of Jerusalem by Titus in 70 A.D., and the second time was when the Jewish Yishuv in Eretz Israel was not strong enough to conquer the entire West Bank in the War of Independence. Tabenkin and Katznelson rejected the first partition plan of 1937, as they were unwilling to give up the whole land, and in 1967 as well Tabenkin was one of the main champions of Greater Israel.

Ben-Gurion, for his part, wrestled with whether the opportunity was not too good to be missed. In November 1956, when the Sinai desert was conquered during the Anglo-French-Israeli campaign, the Israeli attack on the Egyptian army was interpreted as a return to roots. The Gulf of Sharm el-Sheikh was now called Mifratz Shlomo (Gulf of Solomon), and the prime minister declared the whole war to be a "new Sinai revelation." Mount Sinai was where the law was given to the children of Israel who had come out of Egypt, and therefore the revelation at Sinai was regarded as the birth of the nation. The Israel of Ben-Gurion was declared the new kingdom of Israel, extending from the Lebanese border in the north to the islands of Tiran (Yotvata, in Hebrew) in the Red Sea in the south. Only a strongly worded Soviet ultimatum with American support forced Ben-Gurion to change his mind and return to reality. The new kingdom of Israel lasted thirty-six hours.[18]

Ten years after the Sinai campaign, when not only Mount Sinai and Sharm el-Sheikh fell to Israel but the whole land of the judges and kings, the return to Hebron was viewed as another return to the source: the people of Israel coming back to its mythical birthplace. It was in Hebron that Abraham had settled on his return from Egypt. In building this new Jewish town, one was sending a message to the international community: for the Jews, the sites connected with Jewish history are inalienable, and if later, for circumstantial reasons, the state of Israel is obliged to give one or another of them up, this step is not considered final. This was thirty years ago, when few observers and analysts, and fewer politicians, warned of the moral danger of Israel's letting the mystique of the land dictate its territorial policies.

The settlement in the northern part of the West Bank, in Samaria, began in the same way as the settlement in the heart of Hebron. After a number of attempts to settle there, from early June 1974 onward, a group of Gush Emunim members known as the Elon Moreh group gathered in December 1975 in the abandoned Turkish railway station at Sebastia, north of Nablus. Here, too, the extreme national religious Right took the initiative, but it enjoyed, as in Hebron, the sympathy and active cooperation of the leadership of the labor movement and of some of its intellectuals. Many of the political and intellectual elite were impressed by the pioneering enthusiasm of the yeshiva graduates and the disciples of the Bnei Akiva religious youth movement. Among their supporters were a few ministers in the government of Yitzhak Rabin, Meir's successor, who was in office from 1974 to 1977, and particularly Minister of Defense Shimon Peres. Allon could not remain indifferent to any settlement.

The solution found for Hebron was also applied in Sebastia. Rabin, like Eshkol before him, was aware of the grave error of settling in the heart of the thickly populated West Bank, but he too was unable to stand against those who insisted that he should be true to the principles of Zionism. He yielded to Peres, not only out of weakness but because the leadership of the Labor Party did not succeed in resisting the Zionist fervor of people whom many regarded as true pioneers, worthy successors of the builders of Degania and Tel Yosef. Peres not only hoped to reap a political reward for his support of the Right but also saw himself as a sort of successor to Dayan, who following his failure in the Yom Kippur War had been temporarily forced to leave the governement. Thus, the method that had been used successfully in Hebron was adopted near Nablus. Instead of being forcefully removed to inside the green line, the lawbreakers were settled in the army camp at Kadum and gradually set up next to it the settlement of Kadumim. Finally, after the victory of the Right in the 1977 elections, the settlement of Elon Moreh was established. But the taboo had already been broken in the time of the Rabin government, when the path to the creeping annexation of the populated territories conquered in 1967 was first taken.

Whether it was based on an appeal to history or referred to a "divine promise," this mystique always led back to what might be called the histori-cal-religious continuum (in the same way as one speaks of a space-time con-tinuum), invoked by modern Israelocentric Zionism. In this continuum, sec-ularism as conceived by the Enlightenment obviously has no place. It is true that in 1970, as in 1920 and 1940, the mystique of the land was what the various elements of Palestinian Jewish society had most in common. Whether it appealed to history and was supposed to be "secular" or was based on "divine promises," this mystique, since the beginnings of modern Zionism, revealed the limits of secularism in Eretz Israel and later in the state of Israel.

History and religion played the same role in Zionism as they did in all national movements of the nineteenth century. In Western Europe the im-portance of these antiliberal elements was considerable; in Central and Eastern Europe it was always crucial. In the twentieth century Zionism provided the Jewish people with the rationale for a political arrangement that can ensure its survival and relative security, that is, a nation-state. To legitimize their demand for a country of their own, the Jews could not find a better argument than their historical right to Palestine. But no wish, no dream, could even have begun to have been fulfilled had it not been accom-panied by a need to save the body. Long before Europe first went up in flames, all conditions existed to urgently find a solution to the distressful Jewish situation: organic nationalisms, a lack of physical and economic security in Central and Eastern Europe, and increasingly frequent explo-sions of anti-Semitism throughout the continent. In the mid-1930s convert-ing to Christianity was no longer a viable escape. When in the early 1920s the United States closed its doors, Palestine was the only way out, and in 1933 Hitler began to vindicate Zionism.

In fact, from the beginning, a sense of urgency gave the first Zionists the profound conviction that the task of reconquering the country had a solid moral basis. The argument of the Jews' historical right to the land was merely a matter of politics and propaganda. In view of the catastrophic situ-ation of the Jews at the beginning of the century, the use of this argument was justified in every way, and it was all the more legitimate because of the threat of death hanging over the Jews. Historical rights were invoked to serve the need of finding a refuge.

After the Six-Day War, circumstances changed, and certain arguments persisted despite the fact that they were no longer valid. The process of normalization that took over in the mid-1960s, rapid economic development, and a sense of security following the Six-Day War rendered obsolete the argument of the "danger of disappearance"; moreover, the affirmation of historical rights over Judea and Samaria acquired the function that such arguments always had in Europe: to justify territorial claims.

Even the argument based on security was not free from a desire to exploit the occasion and extend the country's borders. The only debate that really took place in the labor movement on the future of the territories until recently was limited to two possibilities: "territorial compromise," which required the annexation of relatively unpopulated areas, and "functional compromise," which meant retaining control of the West Bank without annexing the population. Both conceptions were representative of the conquering nationalism bequeathed to the generation of 1948 by the founders.

The 1993 Oslo peace accords between the Palestinian national movement and the Labor government were meant to bring to an end the historical procees started by the young Polish and Russian Jews who at the turn of the century settled in Palestine with the intention of gaining a country for their people. These people knew that the country would not be given to them and that it would have to be conquered as much through the gun as through labor. That was the basis of Zionism throughout the twentieth century, until that day in December 1987 when local stone-throwing Palestinians decided to take their fate into their own hands. It was probably on that day that the Palestinians reached the point of no return in their progress toward self-government. After a time, the Israelis were forced to recognize this situation. At least slightly more than half of them did, as in 1992 Labor was returned to power by a slim majority after fifteen years in the wilderness. This time the Laborites realized that there could be ways of affirming one's national identity other than by denying the Palestinians the right to self-government, and that there could be boundaries to Israeli territorial identity other than those indicated in the Bible.

If Rabin and Peres agreed to negotiate with the Palestinians, a move for which neither their personal careers nor their convictions only a short time earlier had prepared them, it is not because they believed that the new and probably final partition they hoped to arrive at was the most just and fair solution of a conflict between two nationalisms claiming the same territory, but because this solution was the most rational simply from the point of view of Israeli national interest. Nevertheless, in the history of Zionism the Oslo agreements constitute a turning point, a true revolution. For the first time in its history, the Jewish national movement recognized the equal rights of the Palestinian people to freedom and independence. In the Camp

David agreements of 1978, the Begin government had recognized the "legitimate rights" of the Palestinians but not their equal right to part of Palestine. By contrast, the Oslo accords were signed on that basis, and consequently there was a tacit understanding that when the time came, a Palestinian state would be established in the country. From then on, the Jews were no longer officially regarded as the sole legitimate owners of the Promised Land, and for the first time since they had begun to settle there was equality between the two peoples.

At the end of 1995 many Israelis hoped that when Rabin and Peres would conclude the peace negotiations with the Palestinians, Israel would finally have come of age. The time would then be ripe to tackle the great questions, neglected since the arrival of the first pioneers, questions whose solution could give Israel an open, secular society, more just than the present bourgeois society, a society based on the search for the happiness of the individual rather than the defense of tribal values.

Rabin's assassination on 4 November 1995 was an act of resistance against that process of passage to normalcy. Rabin was a victim of the opposition led by the religious nationalist Right, firmly backed by the hard core of its secular counterpart. Indeed, in more than one respect, the changes we are witnessing in Israeli society today are more significant than those in its first revolution, the national revolution described in this book.

The religious nationalist Right has reasons to represent itself as the guardian of the original Zionism. Today this integrist Right is the only political and cultural movement to offer a different path from the one taken by a large group of the Israeli population and the great majority of the Jewish people. Aware as it is of the changes that have taken place in the world since the end of the War of Independence and since the Six-Day War, Israeli society, for the most part, no longer displays the reflexes of an endangered tribal society which characterized it until the mid-1970s. The new Israeli society is more self-confident and seeks to consolidate its position as part of the liberal West, with the adoption of its values and forms of behavior that this implies.

Until recently all branches of Zionism were guided by more or less the same principles. The difference between religious and secular Zionism, between the Zionism of the Left and the Zionism of the Right, was merely a difference of form and not an essential difference. Its adherents unanimously viewed Zionism as an enterprise for the rescue of the Jews and their transfer en masse to Palestine and, later, to the state of Israel. They all believed that as far as circumstances permitted, the whole land had to be conquered and settled by all possible means. They all recognized that Zionism's task was to bring about a cultural revolution such as the Jews had not experienced since the conquest of Canaan. And all, finally, held the Bible to be the deed to the land, the entire land of their forefathers.

This was the basis of the alliance between the secular and religious Zionists, an alliance that owed nothing to political, circumstantial, or contingent factors. In the Zionism of the Left, secularism was only a veneer. It had a ritual significance, like a prayer repeated automatically. The real emotional center lay elsewhere, in Jewish identity. Chief Rabbi Kook (1865–1935), the leading figure in religious Zionism, regarded the labor movement's reconquest of the ancestral homeland as sacred. A great admirer of the pioneers, he encouraged religious Jews to establish kibbutzim. At that time his spiritual and intellectual proximity to the labor elite prevented the emergence of obscurantism, which in the mid-1970s found its spiritual mentors among some rabbis in the occupied territories of Judea and Samaria. In the time of the Yishuv, there was obviously no need for a religious authority to pronounce a death sentence on a political leader considered guilty of bargaining away a single inch of the God-given land. In those days there was no question of restoring to the Arabs the smallest part of the territory already conquered. The spiritual heritage of the founders, whether Gordon, Katznelson, and Tabenkin or even Ben-Gurion, Eshkol, and Meir, was, largely speaking, identical with that of the leaders of religious Zionism. Even Dayan and Allon, figures born in Palestine and symbolic of the "new Jew," did not really have any terms of reference other than those of their "secular" predecessors, who were wholly the products of the little Jewish townships of Poland and Russia, huddled around their synagogues and rabbinical schools.

In the context of this cultural unity and in the course of a common struggle for independence the de facto alliance of all Zionist movements was forged. The national religious movement and the three movements of secular Zionism (General, Revisionist, and Labor) showed the same determination in combating assimilation and the loss of traditional Jewish identity. At that time all branches wanted as large a country as possible, and they differed only in their views of how it should be attained. For all of them, Zionism was defined in terms of culture, history, religion, and even mysticism. The Jewish people was regarded as a tribe, a tribe that should unite and take its place behind the pioneers who led the enterprise of reconquest and resettlement, and that is why, after the Six-Day War, the difference between the advocates of "territorial compromise" and "functional compromise," whether they belonged to the Center-Left, the Center-Right, or the extreme Right, was only tactical. At that time only a small isolated fringe of intellectuals dared to sound a note of warning. However, voices, including important ones, were raised even on the extreme Zionist Left in support of the "new pioneers" who called for the repopulation of Judea and Samaria in the name of the Jews' historical rights over the whole land of Israel. The overwhelming majority, if not the quasi-totality of the Jewish population of Israel, never questioned the legitimacy of the occupation. Only a minority of Jews in

Israel at the end of the 1960s would have understood the suggestion that perhaps the Palestinians also had national rights over this land.

Like all nationalist movements that came into being at about the same time, Zionism, apart from a few numerically insignificant groups, rejected from the beginning the universalistic aspects of socialism and liberalism. Zionism, like all nationalisms, never considered it its vocation to defend the rights of people or to establish equality among nations. Things could not have been otherwise, its mission having been what it was: to rescue a population in danger of extinction—first a cultural extinction, then a physical extinction. Thus, as long as the Arabs refused to recognize the legitimacy of the Jewish national movement and its emanation, the Jewish state, or to recognize the Jews as a social entity, Israeli society had no difficulty in supporting a nationalism that implied, among other things, the conquest of the whole land of Israel.

This consensus enabled everyone—apart, once again, from a few "eccentrics"—to regard the Six-Day War as the continuation and conclusion of the War of Independence, in which, for circumstantial reasons, the Israeli army was not able to reach the Jordan River and conquer the heartland of the Bible. The Gush Emunim, formally established immediately after the war of 1967, which combines religious fundamentalism with fanatical nationalism in pursuance of its aim of recovering the West Bank through colonization, is therefore right, together with the nonreligious who support it, in claiming that the settlements in Judea and Samaria or in the very heart of Hebron are the natural, logical, and legitimate continuation of Zionism's original intention. It is also right in maintaining that this movement is closer to the spirit of the founders than the "new liberal Zionism," which it does not always recognize as Zionism at all. In effect, the secular Israeli Jew, looking toward the West and receptive to its values, has begun, in recent years, to forge for himself an "independent" identity detached from the mystical ramifications of his religion and the irrational side of his history. This is a revolution that national religious Zionism and radical nationalist (and supposedly secular) Zionism are unable to countenance, and whose development they cannot watch with indifference. The radical nationalist, secular in his daily life and usually lacking a solid Jewish culture, needs the Sabbath, the religious festivals and their ceremonies, and the stones "that are part of our souls" as much as a fish needs water.

He knows that nationalism can exist and develop on the basis of rationalism, individualism, and genuine secularism as well as on the basis of history, culture, religion, and mysticism. The supposedly secular radical nationalism lays claim to Hebron not to bring about the liberation of the Jewish people or the Jewish individual but to renew a connection with a major symbol of Jewish mythical history. In Israel this religious-historical continuum forms the common ground between the religious nationalist and the radical secular nationalist; it underlies their mutual desire to see a Jewish Hebron and is the basis of their claim to this symbolic town and, in fact, to all of Judea and Samaria. The integral nationalist does not view the aspiration to liberty and self-determination as sufficiently mobilizing or unifying. Moreover, he never considers the free expression of this desire a source of legitimacy. People and their aspirations are volatile, but stones are eternal.

The process of liberalization that Israeli society has embarked on is undoubtedly a leap into the unknown; hence the anxiety of nationalist circles. The one-dimensionality of Zionism was one of the reasons for its success. Without giving it the entire credit for the creation of the state of Israel, it is undeniable that the society it created could never have become the united society it soon became, despite the social and economic inequalities that characterized it from the beginning, if Zionism had been pluralistic. Precisely because it represented a single vision did the movement permit the cohabitation and collaboration of religious and secular Zionists. Thus, and only thus, can the famous "historical alliance" of the labor movement and the national religious movement be explained. From 1949 to 1977 the National Religious Party was included in all governments formed by Mapai and its successor, the Labor Party.

As long as the labor movement remained true to the tribal nationalism of the founders, the disciples of Rabbi Kook welcomed and respected it as an ally. But as soon as a truly liberal tendency began to manifest itself in the labor-Zionist camp, as soon as the idea began to gain credence that the individual is not just a soldier in the army of national revolution, as soon as voices began to be heard condemning the aggressive egocentricity that appeared after the Six-Day War, the alliance was no longer possible. And indeed, peace is a mortal danger to the Zionism of blood and soil, a Zionism that cannot imagine willingly returning even an inch of the sacred territory of the land of Israel.

The Jewish settlers of Judea and Samaria and their allies are absolutely right when they maintain that recognizing the legitimacy of Palestinians' national claims marks the end of an epoch. Israel's elites are drawing continually closer to the tradition of the Enlightenment; attitudes alien to the original Zionism are thus becoming increasingly common. Shmuel Yosef Agnon, winner of the Nobel Prize for Literature in 1966, and Nathan Alterman, a towering figure in Hebrew poetry, both founders of the Movement for a Greater Israel after the Six-Day War, were close to the circles in which religious Zionism was formed, but the same cannot be said of the young writers and artists of the present day. Those who count among this new generation are as far from rabbinic teachings as the heavens are from the earth. Similarly, there is an ever-increasing distance between Jewish Israelis who wish to define "Israelism" in political and legal terms and who believe that all individuals are born free and equal, and those who view Jewish Israelis as a tribe that has won a state for itself.

Indeed, the radical but supposedly secular form of Zionism and religious Zionism know very well that they are on the same side. The militants of the settlements of Judea and Samaria, both rabbinical and secular, are convinced that to prevent or halt any social or cultural process they consider dangerous in the long run for the Jewish character of Israel, the occupation must continue, the state of tension must persist, and Israel must remain an entrenched camp.

For years the settlers have prepared for an out-and-out war against what they call the second Hellenization of the people of Israel, a process of cultural assimilation of far greater seriousness in their view than the one the Jewish people experienced in antiquity. These men and women do not dream of a "reconquest" of Tel Aviv, as they know this is beyond their capabilities. Nevertheless, they will not give up without a fight (armed, if necessary, as the more garrulous among them have informed us) the territorial base they have established in the West Bank. For the radical Right, the settler with a gun in one hand and a Bible in the other is the trustee of the people's future. For the radical Right, the repopulation of the occupied territories with Jews is the touchstone of Zionism, and leaving the heights of Judea and Samaria is tantamount to moral suicide.

For this religious Right and this supposedly secular radical Right, a new front against Zionism was opened on the day the Oslo accords were signed. Rabin had become an enemy of the nation, a traitor to his people and its history. As far as they are concerned, the fifth column showed its true colors in Oslo. Rabin's assassination was the work of a very small group, but it gave a tragic dimension to a fact that many people refused to acknowledge until then: Israel too has its Brownshirts, not only consisting of settlers in Judea and Samaria.

But even worse was the fact that the violent struggle against the Oslo agreements enjoyed the passive support and tacit consent of the official, respectable Right. On 5 October 1995, exactly one month before the night of the murder, a large demonstration of all factions of the Right was held in Jerusalem. On a balcony overlooking Zion Square in the heart of Jerusalem, the whole opposition leadership was gathered around Benjamin Netanyahu, from the former prime minister Yitzhak Shamir to members of the government set up in June 1996. Facing the leaders of the opposition—today's government—placards denouncing the "traitor" Rabin dressed in the uniform of an SS officer were waved high above the heads of the demonstrators. Not a word of protest was heard from the speakers' platform, and the man who is prime minister at the end of 1997 never batted an eyelid. For the Right, Yitzhak Rabin and Shimon Peres were comparable to the worst enemy the Jewish people ever had. That is how the matter was understood by those present at the demonstration that night, by those who sat opposite the television screens and watched the leaders of the Right stirring up the crowds, and by those who read about it in the newspapers the next day. That is also how it was understood by the man who four weeks later pulled the trigger. Israel was the first democratic state—and from the end of the Second World War until now the only one—in which a political murder achieved its goal.

Today, more than ever, settlement in the territories endangers Israel's ability to develop as a free and open society. But like all previous attempts at colonialism, the one the Israeli Right wishes to impose on the Palestinians is sure to come to an end. The only uncertain factor today is the moral and political price Israeli society will have to pay to overcome the resistance that the hard core of the settlers is bound to show to any just and reasonable solution.

Notes

The Hebrew titles of works, articles, and documents in the notes are given in an English translation. Where a literal translation was not possible, I made a "free" translation, taking into consideration the content of the work. For the Hebrew titles, please see the bibliography. Page numbers always refer to the original edition.

Preface

1. There is an excellent review of these issues in Gulie Ne'eman Arad, ed., "Israeli Historiography Revisited," a special issue of *History and Memory* 7, no. 1 (spring/ summer 1995). The six contributions contain good bibliographical references. Readers interested in that debate should start here.

The most recent exposé of the official "conservative" approach to the history of Jewish Palestine until the War of Independence can be found in Moshe Lissak, Anita Shapira, and Gabriel Cohen, eds., *The History of the Jewish Community in Eretz Israel since 1882: The Period of the British Mandate*, pt. 2 (in Hebrew) (Jerusalem: Bialik Institute and Israel Academy of Sciences and Humanities, 1994). On the other side of the historiographical fence, post-Zionist ideology is presented by Boaz Evron, *Jewish State or Israeli Nation?* (Bloomington: Indiana University Press, 1995) and the new "critical sociology" by Uri Ram, *The Changing Agenda of Israeli Sociology: Theory, Ideology, and Identity* (Albany: SUNY Press, 1995).

Introduction

1. David Ben-Gurion, *From Class to Nation: Reflections on the Vocation and Mission of the Labor Movement* (in Hebrew) (Tel Aviv: Am Oved, 1976), p. 13.

On Zionism, its history, its vision, and the people who made it, see Walter Laqueur, *A History of Zionism* (New York: Schocken Books, 1978); Mitchell Cohen, *Zion and State: Nation, Class, and the Shaping of Modern Israel* (Oxford: Basil Blackwell, 1987); David Vital, *The Origins of Zionism* (Oxford: Oxford University Press, 1975) and *Zionism: The Formative Years* (Oxford: Oxford University Press, 1982); Ben Halpern, *The Idea of the Jewish State* (Cambridge: Harvard University Press, 1969); Shlomo Avineri, *The Making of Modern Zionism* (New York: Basic Books, 1981); and Arthur Hertzberg, ed., *The Zionist Idea: A Historical Analysis and Reader* (New York: Atheneum, 1977).

2. Dan Horowitz and Moshe Lissak, *Troubles in Utopia* (in Hebrew) (Tel Aviv: Am Oved, 1990), p. 15. Translated into English by Horowitz and Lissak as *Trouble in Utopia: The Overburdened Polity of Israel* (Albany: SUNY Press, 1989). Similar statements appear in the first book written by these two scholars, *From the Yishuv to the State: The Jews of Eretz Israel as a Political Community during the Period of the British Mandate* (in Hebrew) (Tel Aviv: Am Oved, 1977), p. 182. Revised translation into English by Horowitz and Lissak: *Origins of the Israeli Polity: Palestine under the Mandate* (Chicago: Chicago University Press, 1978).

3. Horowitz and Lissak, *Troubles in Utopia*, p. 15.

4. Ibid.

5. Ibid.

6. Anita Shapira, *Going toward the Horizon* (in Hebrew) (Tel Aviv: Am Oved, 1989), pp. 75, 372.

7. Horowitz and Lissak, *From the Yishuv to the State*, p. 193. Anita Shapira expressed the same opinion in *Going toward the Horizon*, p. 7.

8. Dan Horowitz, *Sky and Sand: The Generation of 1948—Self-Portrait* (in Hebrew), ed. Avi Katzmann (Tel Aviv: Keter, 1993), p. 52.

9. Horowitz and Lissak, *Troubles in Utopia*, pp. 145, 170.

10. Eli Shaltiel, *Pinhas Rutenberg: The Rise and Fall of a "Strong Man" in Eretz Israel, 1879–1942* (in Hebrew) (Tel Aviv: Am Oved, 1990), 2:605–6.

11. Anita Shapira, *Going toward the Horizon*, p. 373.

12. Horowitz and Lissak, *Troubles in Utopia*, p. 287.

13. David Ben-Gurion, "Reply to the Critics at the Third Ahdut Ha'avoda Convention" (in Hebrew), *Kuntras* 6, no. 119 (19 January 1923): 29.

14. Ibid., p. 21.

15. Berl Katznelson, ed., *Yalkut Ahdut Ha'avoda* (Ahdut Ha'avoda: A Collection of Texts), 2 vols. (Tel Aviv: Editions of the Socialist-Zionist Union of the Workers of Eretz Israel, Ahdut Ha'avoda, 1929), 1:109. From here on I refer to this as *Ahdut Ha'avoda Anthology* (not to be confused with *Ha'ahdut Anthology*).

16. Berl Katznelson, *Writings of Berl Katznelson* (in Hebrew) (Tel Aviv: Mapai Publications, 1946), 3:142.

17. Ibid., p. 373.

18. Ibid., 6:382.

19. Ibid., p. 381.

20. Ben-Gurion, "Reply to the Critics," p. 21.

21. Ben-Gurion, *From Class to Nation*, pp. 28–29.

22. Katznelson, *Writings*, 1:9.

23. Berl Katznelson, *Neglected Values: Observations on the Problems of Socialist Education* (in Hebrew), ed. Ephraim Broide (Tel Aviv: Ayanot, 1944), pp. 22–23.

24. Chaim Arlosoroff, "Class Struggle and Socialism in the Reality of Eretz Israel: Lecture to the Hapo'el Hatza'ir Convention at Petah Tiqwa" (in Hebrew), pt. 1 of 2, *Hapo'el Hatza'ir* 20, no. 3–4 (18 October 1926): 17.

25. Ibid., p. 18.

26. Chaim Arlosoroff, "The Popular Socialism of the Jews," in *Writings of Chaim Arlosoroff* (in Hebrew), vol. 3 (Tel Aviv: Schtibel, 1933), p. 24. Translated from the German essay *Der Jüdische Volkssozialismus* (Berlin: Hapoel Hazair, 1919).

27. Ibid., p. 37. The original German text reads as follows: "Deshalb muß der jüdische Sozialismus eindeutig und klar national sein" (p. 14). For interesting comparisons, see Enrico Corradini, *Discorsi Politici (1902–1923)* (Florence: Vallechi, 1923), and Zeev Sternhell, Mario Sznajder, and Maia Asheri, *The Birth of Fascist Ideology: From Cultural Rebellion to Political Revolution* (Princeton: Princeton University Press, 1994).

28. Arlosoroff, "The Popular Socialism of the Jews," p. 54. On Barrès see my *Maurice Barrès et le nationalisme français* (Brussels: Complexe, 1985) and *Neither Right Nor Left: Fascist Ideology in France* (Princeton: Princeton University Press, 1996).

29. Arlosoroff, "The Popular Socialism of the Jews," p. 41.

30. Ibid., p. 35.

31. Ibid., p. 73.

32. Ibid., p. 56.

33. Ibid., p. 52.

34. Chaim Arlosoroff, *"Reflections on the Fourth Aliyah (in Hebrew), in Writings of Chaim Arlosoroff,* 3:110.

35. Arlosoroff, "The Popular Socialism of the Jews," pp. 83–86.

36. Ibid., pp. 73–74.

37. Ibid., p. 27. On Gordon, see chap. 1; on Syrkin, see chap. 2. Shlomo Avineri, author of *Arlosoroff* (Tel Aviv: Edanim, 1991) (original version in English: *Arlosoroff* [London: Holban, 1989]), is often unaware of the real significance of Arlosoroff's nationalism.

38. Arthur Moeller van den Bruck, *Das Dritte Reich* (Hamburg: Hanseatische Verlagsanstalt, 1931), pp. 29–78, and Fritz Stern, *The Politics of Cultural Despair* (Berkeley: University of California Press, 1963), p. 243.

39. Oswald Spengler, *Preussentum und Sozialismus,* in *Politische Schriften* (Munich: Beck, 1932), pp. 1–105. On Spengler, see especially Gilbert Merlio's authoritative work *Oswald Spengler: Témoin de son Temps* (Stuttgart: Akademischer Verlag Hans-Dieter Heinz, 1982) and H. Stuart Hughes's *Oswald Spengler: A Critical Estimate* (New York: Charles Scribner's Sons, 1962).

40. Shabtai Teveth, *David's Passion* (in Hebrew), vol. 1, *The Young Ben-Gurion* (Tel Aviv: Schocken Books, 1977), p. 166. This monumental biography, although excessively warm toward the subject in some places and indulgent in others, is indispensable for anyone wishing to understand Ben-Gurion and his career. An abbreviated version of the first three volumes is available in English: *Ben-Gurion: The Burning Ground, 1886–1949,* trans. Shabtai Teveth (Boston: Houghton Mifflin, 1987). On Ben-Gurion, see also Michael Bar-Zohar, *Ben-Gurion* (New York: Delacorte Press, 1978); Michael Keren, *Ben-Gurion and the Intellectuals* (DeKalb: Northern Illinois University Press, 1983).

41. On this early period of Ben-Gurion's career, see Teveth, *David's Passion,* 1:115–68.

42. Labor Movement Archives, section 4, dossier 29: statement by Ben-Gurion, minutes of the Histadrut Executive Committee, 11 September 1939, p. 3.

43. Katznelson, *Writings,* 11:141–72.

44. Arthur Ruppin, *Agricultural Settlement of the Zionist Organization in Eretz Israel* (in Hebrew) (Tel-Aviv: Dvir, [1925]), pp. 97–99.

45. Arthur Ruppin, *Thirty Years of Building Eretz Israel* (in Hebrew) (Jerusalem: Schocken Books, 1937), pp. 28–30. The English version: *Three Decades of Palestine: Speeches and Papers on the Upbuilding of the Jewish National Home* (Jerusalem: Schocken Books, 1936). On the Oppenheimer system, see chap. 2 here. On Ruppin, Oppenheimer, and the settlement of Palestine before World War I, see Derek J. Penslar's innovative work *Zionism and Technocracy: The Engineering of Jewish Settlement in Palestine, 1870–1918* (Bloomington: Indiana University Press, 1991).

Although the model created at Degania was quite special, the idea of collective agriculture was not entirely new. It had an extremely important place in the thinking of utopian socialists, and communities of this kind had existed for many years (for instance, those founded in the United States by Robert Owen and his disciples). With the rise of Marxist socialism, people lost interest in this form of agriculture, except in Russia, where the idea of the commune still had a few supporters. The pioneers of the Second Aliyah sometimes lived together as a community, sharing their income and expenses, before emigrating.

Ruppin allowed those who broke away from the farm at Kinneret to go ahead and supported them subsequently, because he too had been influenced by Oppenheimer's ideas. But although Oppenheimer had recommended that each member of the community be remunerated according to efforts and productivity, these workers demanded an equal wage for all and half of the profits. Oppenheimer's ideas are better exemplified in the moshav and other collective enterprises in Palestine than in the kibbutz.

46. Ruppin, *Thirty Years of Building Eretz Israel*, p. 7.

47. Chaim Arlosoroff, "Class Struggle and Socialism in the Reality of Eretz Israel," pt. 2, *Hapo'el Hatza'ir* 20, no. 5 (26 October 1926): 9.

48. Katznelson, *Writings*, 11:213.

49. Zeev Jabotinsky, *Toward a State* (in Hebrew) (Jerusalem: Ari Jabotinsky, 1953), pp. 299–300.

50. "Hashe'ela Hane'elama" (The unseen question) was the title of an important and very characteristic article, which Yitzhak Epstein, a member of the First Aliyah, published in the journal *Hashiloah* in 1906. The historians of Zionism see this article as a landmark in public discussions of the Arab question. Walter Laqueur used this as the title of chapter 5 (dealing with the Arab question) of his important work *A History of Zionism*. See also Anita Shapira, "A Political History of the Yishuv" (in Hebrew), in *The History of the Jewish Community in Eretz Israel since 1882* (in Hebrew), ed. Moshe Lissak, Anita Shapira, and Gabriel Cohen (Jerusalem: Bialik Institute and Israel Academy of Sciences and Humanities, 1994), pp. 73–75, and Yosef Gorny, *The Arab Question and the Jewish Problem: Political and Ideological Currents in Zionism with Regard to the Arab Presence in Eretz Israel, 1882–1948* (in Hebrew) (Tel Aviv: Am Oved, 1985). Gorny begins his book with Epstein's description. Unfortunately, this book lacks evaluative criteria. It provides some information but has little analytical value.

51. On the Arab national movement, see Yehoshua Porat, *The Emergence of the Palestinian-Arab National Movement, 1918–1929* (London: F. Cass, 1974) and *In Search of Arab Unity, 1930–1945* (London: F. Cass, 1986).

52. Ben-Zion Dinur, ed., *History of the Hagana* (in Hebrew) (Tel Aviv: Ministry of Defense Publications, 1954), 1:66–67.

53. Laqueur, *A History of Zionism*, pp. 225–26.

Chapter One

1. Aaron David Gordon, "On Closer Inspection" (in Hebrew), in *Writings*, vol. 1, *The Nation and Labor* (1911; reprint, Jerusalem, Zionist Library, 1952), p. 124.

Gordon's writings were collected in three volumes by Shmuel H. Bergmann and Eliezer Shohat and published (out of order) in 1951 (vol. 2), 1952 (vol. 1), and 1953 (vol. 3).

Gordon's articles and other writings quoted in this chapter are from the first two volumes of the Hebrew edition: vol. 1: *The Nation and Labor*; vol. 2: *Man and Nature* (these titles are the editors'). In the following notes, I give the title of the Hebrew article in English, the date of its first appearance, the volume in which it appears, and the page number. This note, for instance, would read as follows: Gordon, "On Closer Inspection" (1911), in *Writings*, 1:124. A few essays by Gordon are available in English; see *Selected Essays* (New York: League for Labour Palestine, 1938).

2. Gordon, "The Whole People of Israel" (1920), in *Writings*, 1:260.

3. Ibid.

4. Gordon, "On Closer Inspection," p. 124.

5. Gordon, "The Whole People of Israel," p. 208.

6. Gordon, "Labor" (1911), in *Writings*, 1:136.

7. Ben-Gurion, *From Class to Nation*, p. 13.

8. Katznelson, *Writings*, 5:15.

9. Y. Novomirski, "Our Intelligentsia and Labor" (in Hebrew), in *Ha'ahdut: A Collection of Texts Published in the Newspaper of the Jewish Social-Democratic Party in Eretz Israel (Poalei Tzion), 1907–1919*, ed. Yehuda Erez (Tel Aviv: Am Oved, 1962). From here on I will refer to this as *Ha'ahdut Anthology*.

10. Katznelson, *Writings*, 5:12–13.

11. Ibid., 11:37–38.

12. Ibid., p. 36. Emphasis is in the text.

13. Ibid., p. 222.

14. Ibid., 1:8.

15. Ibid., 11:204.

16. Aaron David Gordon, "Letters to the Diaspora" (1921), in *Writings*, 1:542–43.

17. Aaron David Gordon, "A Clarification of the Basis of Our Thought" (1920), in *Writings*, 2:175. On the concept of the nation in Gordon, see N. Rotenstreich, *The Nation in the Teachings of A. D. Gordon* (in Hebrew) (Jerusalem: Reuven Mass and the Youth Department of the Zionist Organization, n.d.).

18. Aaron David Gordon, "A Definition of Our Attitude" (1919), in *Writings*, 1:218.

19. Aaron David Gordon, "Self-Criticism" (1916), in *Writings*, 1:353.

20. Ibid., p. 348. See also pp. 349–50.

21. Ibid., p. 353.

22. Gordon, "A Clarification," p. 203.

23. Ibid., p. 183.

24. Gordon, "Self-Criticism," p. 328.

25. Ibid., p. 353.

26. Shlomo Avineri, *Varieties of Zionist Thought* (in Hebrew) (Tel Aviv: Am Oved, 1980), pp. 178–79.

27. Gordon, "A Definition of Our Attitude," p. 219.

28. Ibid., p. 220.

29. Gordon, "Self-Criticism," p. 366.

30. Gordon, "A Clarification," pp. 182–83.

31. Gordon, "The Congress" (1913), in *Writings*, 1:193.

32. Ibid.

33. Gordon, "A Clarification," pp. 182–83.

34. Shmuel Hugo Bergmann, "Herder and A. D. Gordon," *Molad* 5, no. 28 (January–February 1973): 322–24. I should note that Herder also influenced the philoso-

pher Martin Buber. See Avraham Shapira, "Buber's Attachment to Herder and to German Volkism," *Studies in Zionism* 14, no. 1 (1993): 1–30. On Herder see *J. G. Herder on Social and Political Culture*, ed. F. M. Barnard (Cambridge: Cambridge University Press, 1969); F. M. Barnard, *Herder's Social and Political Thought: From Enlightenment to Nationalism* (Oxford: Oxford University Press, 1965); Frederick C. Beiser, *Enlightenment, Revolution, and Romanticism: The Genesis of Modern German Political Thought, 1790–1800* (Cambridge: Harvard University Press, 1992).

35. Gordon, "Our Task from Now On," p. 234.

36. Gordon, "The Whole People of Israel" (1920), in *Writings*, 1:209–10.

37. Ibid., p. 208.

38. Eliezer Schweid, *The Individual: The Universe of A. D. Gordon* (in Hebrew) (Tel Aviv: Am Oved, 1970), pp. 82–85. Yosef Aharonowitz relates that Gordon was very pious in the early years after his arrival in this country. It would seem that he ceased all religious practices only toward the end of his life. See Mordechai Kuchnir, ed., *Memories and an Appreciation of A. D. Gordon* (in Hebrew) (Tel Aviv: Histadrut Cultural Publications, n.d.), p. 31.

39. Quoted in Menachem Brinker, *Up to Tiberias: On the Writings and Thought of Brenner* (in Hebrew) (Tel Aviv: Am Oved, 1990), p. 164. On Ahad Ha'am see *Ten Essays on Zionism and Judaism*, translated from the Hebrew by Leon Simon (New York: Arno Press, 1973); *Nationalism and the Jewish Ethic: Basic Writings of Ahad Ha'am* (New York: Herzl Press, 1962); *Selected Essays*, translated from the Hebrew by Leon Simon (Philadelphia: Jewish Publication Society of America, 1962).

40. Gordon, "A Clarification," p. 205.

41. Ibid., p. 177.

42. Brinker, *Up to Tiberias*, p. 140. See also pp. 141–49.

43. Schweid overminimizes the influence of European philosophy on Gordon's thought. He claims that the spiritual progenitor of labor nationalism in Eretz Israel was primarily influenced by Eastern European Jewish traditionalist circles, although he does acknowledge that Gordon was familiar with the great philosophical currents of the nineteenth century. See Schweid, *The Individual*, pp. 9–10.

44. Gordon, "A Definition of Our Attitude," p. 217. Gordon also spoke of "the racial fraternity that binds a people together," but he was aware that this fraternity had not prevented fratricidal struggles and massacres. He pointed out on more than one occasion that the struggles between people of the same race have been no less violent than the wars between people of different races ("Our Task from Now On" [1918], in *Writings*, 2:205). In any case, the racial factor could not have any place (at least not an important place) in Gordon's thinking, because he regarded this element as naturalistic and materialistic.

45. Aaron David Gordon, "Letter from Eretz Israel" (1904), in *Writings*, 1:84. See also pp. 132–33, 171–73.

46. Gordon, "A Definition of Our Attitude," pp. 220, 216–17.

47. Ibid., p. 218.

48. Gordon, "A Clarification," p. 185.

49. Gordon, "A Definition of Our Attitude," pp. 217–18.

50. Gordon, "A Clarification," p. 185.

51. Ibid., p. 186.

52. Gordon, "Our Task from Now On," p. 236. See also p. 223.

53. Gordon, "A Definition of Our Attitude," p. 223. See also pp. 218, 236–37, 242.

54. Aaron David Gordon, "A Worker's Reply" (1909), in *Writings*, 1:107.

55. Gordon, "Our Task from Now On," p. 236.

56. Ibid.

57. Ibid., p. 235.

58. Gordon, "A Definition of Our Attitude," p. 222, and "A Clarification," pp. 188–89.

59. Aaron David Gordon, "On Labor" (1920), in *Writings*, 2:155.

60. Gordon, "A Clarification," pp. 188–89.

61. Ibid., p. 197.

62. Ibid.

63. Gordon, "Our Task from Now On," p. 236.

64. Gordon, "A Definition of Our Attitude," p. 216.

65. Ibid.

66. Gordon, "A Worker's Reply," p. 107.

67. Gordon, "Our Task from Now On," p. 235. Emphasis is in the text.

68. Gordon, "A Clarification," p. 197.

69. Gordon, "A Definition of Our Attitude," p. 226.

70. Gordon, "Letters to the Diaspora," p. 548. See also "On the Unification" (1920), in *Writings*, 1:435.

71. Gordon, "A Clarification," p. 187. The entire passage from which this quotation is taken is worth giving here:

Are we really faced with a class struggle in the commonplace sense of the term? A struggle in which the interests of the two parties conflict? A struggle that places the capitalists on one side and the workers, the proletariat, on the other? The police, the armed forces, and all those who actually force workers to accept the authority of the capitalists, when the former ask the latter for no more than justice and respect for their rights—are they capitalists? Are they not workers and the sons of workers, as proletarian as those they are ordered to fight? I think the war is not between capitalists and proletarians, but between proletarians and proletarians on the orders of the capitalists. And from where do the capitalists obtain their power to give orders? From the wealth they possess? Not at all! The workers have created this wealth just as much as they have! The power of the capitalists does not reside in their wealth, and, indeed, they do not have any real power. Their power is simply the individual weakness of the workers. Let us imagine for a moment that each worker had a self-awareness so developed that he felt with his whole being his responsibility toward all life, all creation— his own and that of others—and that he was able to stand up to anyone or anything that sought to limit that responsibility. Let us suppose that he was able to successfully resist any command to punish, subjugate, fight, or, worst of all, kill a man who labors and lives on the fruits of his labor. What would become of the power of the capitalists? Who would agree to fight their wars? Could one then imagine a class struggle?

72. Ibid., p. 189.

73. Ibid., p. 188. See also pp. 186–87.

74. Katznelson, *Writings*, 11:14.

75. Gordon, "Hebrew University" (1912), in *Writings*, 1:176. Emphasis is in the text.

76. Gordon, "With Impatience" (1914), in *Writings*, 1:140–43.

77. Gordon, "On the Unification," pp. 436–37.

78. Gordon, "Labor" (1911), in *Writings*, 1:132–33.

79. Gordon, "A Definition of Our Attitude," pp. 224–25.

80. Gordon, "To My Defeated Spiritual Brethren" (1919), in *Writings*, 1:418.

81. Ibid., p. 412.

82. Gordon, "Building the Nation" (1920), in *Writings*, 1:257, and "A Definition of Our Attitude," pp. 225–26.

83. Gordon, "On the Unification," pp. 428–29.

84. Gordon, "Our Task from Now On," p. 234.

85. Gordon, "A Clarification," p. 190.

86. Gordon, "The Congress," p. 202. See also p. 195.

87. Gordon, "Hebrew University," p. 170.

88. Gordon, "An Irrational Solution" (1909), in *Writings*, 1:97–98.

89. Gordon, "A Definition of Our Attitude," p. 226.

90. Gordon, "With Impatience," p. 148.

91. Gordon, "Our Task from Now On," p. 246.

92. Gordon, "On Labor," p. 153.

93. Ibid., pp. 156–57.

94. Gordon, "With a Heavy Heart" (1920), in *Writings*, 1:425.

95. Gordon, "On the Unification," 1:432. See also "To My Defeated Spiritual Brethren," p. 416, and "Our Task from Now On" (1918), in *Writings*, 1:242.

96. Gordon, "A Definition of Our Attitude," p. 224.

97. Schweid gives a somewhat different presentation of Gordon's attitude. See *The Individual*, pp. 145–52.

98. Gordon, "Building the Nation," p. 252. Emphasis is in the text.

99. Gordon, "On the Unification," pp. 430, 432. See also "To My Defeated Spiritual Brethren," p. 416; "The Whole People of Israel," p. 208; and "A Definition of Our Attitude," pp. 216, 230–31.

100. Gordon, "A Definition of Our Attitude," pp. 221–22.

101. Gordon, "On the Unification," p. 436.

102. Gordon, "Open Letter to Y. H. Brenner" (1912), in *Writings*, 1:163–64.

103. Gordon, "A Definition of Our Attitude," p. 226.

104. Gordon, "An Irrational Solution," p. 94. See also "On Closer Inspection," p. 130.

105. Ibid., p. 96.

106. Ibid.

107. Gordon, "With Impatience," p. 141.

108. Gordon, "Our Task from Now On," p. 244.

109. Ibid.

110. Ibid.

111. Ibid.

112. Ibid., pp. 245–46.

113. Gordon, "On Labor," pp. 151–52.

114. Gordon, "Our Task from Now On," pp. 243–44.

115. Gordon, "A Few Observations on a Tradition" (1918–19), in *Writings*, 1:384.

116. Ibid., pp. 380–81, 382–83.

117. Gordon, "A Clarification," pp. 187–88.

118. Gordon, "Our Task from Now On," p. 244.

119. Gordon, "Letters to the Diaspora," p. 560.

120. Gordon, "Self-Criticism," p. 366.

121. Gordon, "A Worker's Reply," p. 109.

122. Gordon, "A Clarification," p. 190.

123. Gordon, "A Definition of Our Attitude," pp. 215–16.

124. Ibid., p. 225.

125. Gordon, "Building the Nation," pp. 253–54.

126. Gordon, "From a Barbarous Servitude to a Civilized Servitude" (n.d.), in *Writings*, 1:392–93. See also pp. 393–94.

127. Bergmann, introduction to *Man and Nature*, vol. 2 of Gordon's *Writings*, p. 38.

128. On Gordon's influence on Hapo'el Hatza'ir, see Yosef Shapira, *Hapo'el Hatza'ir: Ideology and Action* (in Hebrew) (Tel Aviv: Ayanot, 1967), pp. 338–39. On the founding of the Gordania Youth Movement, see pp. 460 ff.

129. Katznelson, *Writings*, 9:157.

Chapter Two

1. Beit Berl Archives, file 23/55, meeting of the Mapai Central Committee, 20 February 1955.

2. Ibid.

3. The quotations referred to in this note and in the previous one were taken from the first eight sheets of the reports of this meeting. The pagination of these documents may cause some confusion, as it does not follow any single order. Each of the texts submitted by the various stenographers was given its own pagination

4. David Ben-Gurion, "On the Occasion of the Twenty-fifth Anniversary," in *The Book of the Second Aliyah* (in Hebrew), comp. Braha Habas and Eliezer Shohat (Tel Aviv: Am Oved, 1947), p. 15. The following texts by Ben-Gurion relevant to this book are available in English: *Rebirth and Destiny of Israel*, edited and translated under the supervision of Mordekhai Nurock (New York: Philosophical Library, 1954); *Israel: Years of Challenge* (New York: Holt, Rinehart and Winston, 1963); *Ben-Gurion Looks Back in Talks with Moshe Pearlman* (London: Weidenfeld and Nicholson, 1965); *Memoirs*, comp. Thomas R. Bransten (New York: World, 1970); *Israel: A Personal History* (Tel Aviv: Sabra Books, 1972); *The Jews in Their Land*, rev. ed. (Garden City, N.Y.: Windfall Books, 1974).

5. Israel Kolatt, "Ideology and Reality in the Eretz Israeli Labor Movement, 1905–1919" (Ph.D. diss., Hebrew University of Jerusalem, 1969), pp. 85–86.

6. Beit Berl Archives, file 23/55.

7. Ben-Gurion, "On the Occasion of the Twenty-fifth Anniversary," p. 17.

8. Yehuda Slutzki, *Introduction to the History of the Israeli Labor Movement* (in Hebrew) (Tel Aviv: Am Oved 1973), pp. 161–62. See also Yosef Gorny, "Changes in the Social and Political Composition of the Second Aliyah between 1904 and 1940" (in Hebrew), in *Hatzionut* 1 (1970): 204–46.

9. Beit Berl Archives, file 23/55.

10. See Slutzki, *Introduction.*, pp. 58–59, 124.

11. Ibid., pp. 106–7.

12. Yehuda Slutzki, ed., *The Po'alei Tzion Party in Eretz Israel, 1905–1919: Documents* (in Hebrew) (Tel Aviv: Tel Aviv University Press, 1978), pp. 7–14, 17–19, 33; Yitzhak Ben-Zvi, "The Beginnings of Po'alei Tzion in Eretz Israel" (in Hebrew), in *The Book of the Second Aliyah*, ed. Habas and Shohat, pp. 587–88; Kolatt, *Ideology and Reality*, p. 150.

13. Ber Borochov, *Writings* (in Hebrew), ed. L. Levita and T. Nahum (Tel Aviv: Sifriyat Hapo'alim and Hakibbutz Hame'uhad Publications, 1955), 1:291. Works by Borochov available in English are *Nationalism and the Class Struggle: A Marxian Approach to the Jewish Problem: Selected Writings*, ed. Abraham G. Duker (Westport, Conn.: Greenwood Press, 1973); *Class Struggle and the Jewish Nation: Selected Essays in Marxist Zionism*, ed. Mitchell Cohen (New Brunswick, N.J.: Transaction Books, 1984).

14. Borochov, *Writings*, p. 292.

15. See Jonathan Frankel's remarkable *Prophecy and Politics: Socialism, Nationalism, and the Russian Jews, 1862–1917* (in Hebrew), trans. Amos Carmel (Tel Aviv: Am Oved, 1989), pp. 375–86. The original English edition was published in 1981 by Cambridge University Press. All quotations are from the Hebrew translation. On all these matters, see Matityahu Mintz's informative biography *Ber Borochov: The First Phase, 1900–1906* (in Hebrew) (Tel Aviv: Hakibbutz Hame'uhad Publications, 1976).

16. Ber Borochov, "The Working Class and Territorialism," in *Writings*, 1:323.

17. Frankel, *Prophecy and Politics*, p. 398.

18. Ibid., pp. 404–6. Mintz makes a detailed analysis of the revolution that took place in Borochov's thought between his return to Poltava from Berlin at the end of 1905 and the holding of the inaugural convention of Po'alei Tzion (Mintz, *Ber Borochov*, pp. 233 ff.). A second change of direction, which was a kind of "return to the source" in Borochov's thinking, occurred in 1917. At the third party convention, in Kiev in August 1917, Borochov, who had arrived from New York, repudiated many of the main ideas of "Our Platform" and came very close to Syrkin's constructivism.

19. Slutzki, ed., *The Po'alei Tzion Party*, p. 18. See also Teveth, *David's Passion*, 1:100.

20. Teveth, *David's Passion*, 1:100.

21. Yitzhak Ben-Zvi [Avner, pseud.], "National Defense and the Proletarian Outlook" (in Hebrew), *Ha'ahdut*, no. 16–17 (7 January 1913), in *Ha'ahdut Anthology*, pp. 104–6, 110–5.

22. Teveth, *David's Passion*, 1:100.

23. David Ben-Gurion, "Our Sociopolitical Work," *Ha'ahdut*, no. 2–3 (October 1910), in *Ha'ahdut Anthology*, p. 237.

24. David Ben-Gurion, "The Eretz Israel Workers' Fund and the Section of Po'alei Tzion in Eretz Israel" (in Hebrew), *Ha'ahdut*, no. 4 (18 November 1910), in *Ha'ahdut Anthology*, pp. 399–402.

25. David Ben-Gurion, "First Steps" (in Hebrew), *Ha'ahdut*, no. 46 (15 September 1911), in *Ha'ahdut Anthology*, pp. 411–12.

26. "At the End of the Third Year" (in Hebrew), unsigned editorial, *Ha'ahdut*, no. 47–48 (25 September 1912), in *Ha'ahdut Anthology*, p. 432.

27. Yitzhak Ben-Zvi [Avner, pseud.], "Internationalism and Socialism" (in Hebrew), *Ha'ahdut*, no. 1–2 (4 October 1914), in *Ha'ahdut Anthology*, p. 534.

28. David Ben-Gurion, "A Single Legislation," (in Hebrew), *Ha'ahdut*, no. 25–26 (April 1912), in *Ha'ahdut Anthology*, pp. 75–76; "Questions Concerning the Old Yishuv" (in Hebrew), *Ha'ahdut*, no. 2 (September 1910), in *Ha'ahdut Anthology*, pp. 230–32.

29. Ben-Gurion, "A Single Legislation," p. 75.

30. In addition to the foregoing articles, see the articles by Ben-Gurion included in *Ha'ahdut Anthology*, pp.42–44, 47–51, 159–61, 291–95, 320–21, 333–38, 371–72, 405–7.

31. David Ben-Gurion, "On the Slope" (in Hebrew), *Ha'ahdut*, no. 17 (17 February 1911), in *Ha'ahdut Anthology*, pp. 371–72.

32. Teveth, *David's Passion*, 1:62.

33. Ibid.

34. Shabtai Teveth, "Ben-Gurion, Secretary of the Histadrut," in *David Ben-Gurion: Portrait of the Leader of the Labor Movement* (in Hebrew), ed. Shlomo Avineri (Tel Aviv: Am Oved, 1988), pp. 16–17.

35. Katznelson, *Writings*, 1:12.

36. On Tabenkin as a member of Po'alei Tzion in Poland, see Matityahu Mintz, *Friend and Opponent: Yitzhak Tabenkin in Po'alei Tzion, 1905–1912* (in Hebrew) (Tel Aviv: Hakibbutz Hame'uhad Publications, 1986). Mintz points out that *Ha'ahdut*, Po'alei Tzion's organ, made no announcement and published no message of welcome when Tabenkin arrived in Eretz Israel, on the eve of 1 May 1912 (p. 142).

37. Yosef Gorny, *Ahdut Ha'avoda, 1919–1930* (Tel Aviv: Hakibbutz Hame'uhad Publications, 1973), p. 23.

38. David Ben-Gurion, speech given at the thirteenth Po'alei Tzion convention, in *Ha'ahdut Anthology*, p. 580.

39. Ibid.

40. Ibid., p. 581.

41. Ibid., p. 582.

42. Ibid.

43. Ibid., p. 580. Here Ben-Gurion spoke of the "social" question and not of the "socialist" question. This distinction may have a certain importance. Although he knew the difference between the two terms, Ben-Gurion sometimes used the term *social* to mean *socialist*.

44. Ibid., p. 583.

45. Ibid.

46. Ibid.

47. Ibid., p. 581.

48. Ibid., p. 588.

49. Ibid., p. 592.

50. Ibid., p. 596. David (Ephraim) Blumenfeld was the manager of the Eretz Israel Workers' Fund.

51. Ibid., p. 595.

52. Frankel, *Prophecy and Politics*, pp. 334–36.

53. Shlomo Kaplanski, "The Question of the Agricultural Workers and the Work

Groups" (in Hebrew), *Ha'ahdut*, no. 3–4 (23 October 1914), in *Ha'ahdut Anthology*, p. 219.

54. Ibid.

55. Ibid., p. 220.

56. Frankel, *Prophecy and Politics*, pp. 334–36.

57. Ibid., pp. 337–38.

58. Nachman Syrkin, "Socialist Zionism" (1900), in *Writings of Nachman Syrkin* (in Hebrew), ed. Berl Katznelson and Yehuda Kauffman (Tel Aviv: Davar Publications, 1938), 1:262.

59. Nachman Syrkin, "Race, People, and Nation," in ibid., pp. 264–65.

60. Nachman Syrkin, "The Jewish Question and the Socialist Jewish State," in ibid., p. 44. In English, see *Essays on Socialist Zionism* (New York: Young Poale Zion Alliance of America, 1935). Syrkin's daughter, Marie, has written an interesting biography of her father; see Marie Syrkin, *Nachman Syrkin, Socialist Zionist: A Biographical Memorial, Selected Essays* (New York: Herzl Press, 1961).

61. Syrkin, "The Jewish Question," p. 45.

62. Frankel, *Prophecy and Politics*, p. 348.

63. Syrkin, "The Jewish Question," p. 33.

64. Ibid., p. 47.

65. Ibid., pp. 50–53.

66. Ibid., p. 53.

67. Ibid., pp. 53–54.

68. Ibid., p. 53.

69. Nachman Syrkin, "The People's Fight for Freedom" (1901, in Heberw), in *Writings*, 1:82.

70. Avineri, *Varieties of Zionist Thought*, pp. 151–52.

71. Syrkin, "Race, People, and Nation," p. 267.

72. Ibid., p. 268.

73. Ibid., p. 272.

74. Syrkin, "The Jewish Question," p. 31.

75. Ibid.

76. Ibid., pp. 55–57. Syrkin devotes chapter 5 of the work to a description of the institutions of the Jewish state. See "The Socialist Jewish State" (pp. 47–59).

77. Nachman Syrkin, "Mass Colonization and Cooperatives" (in Hebrew), *Ha'ahdut*, no. 14–15 (24 January 1913), in *Ha'ahdut Anthology*, pp. 199–201. See also "Cooperative Settlement and 'Ha'ahva' Company" (in Hebrew), *Ha'ahdut*, no. 31 (29 May 1914), in *Ha'ahdut Anthology*, p. 212.

78. Syrkin, "Cooperative Settlement and 'Ha'ahva' Company," p. 213.

79. Ibid.

80. Haim Golan, ed., *The Po'alei Tzion Delegation in Eretz Israel, 1920* (in Hebrew), 2 vols. (Ramat Efal: Tabenkin Foundation, 1989). See vol. 1, *The Protocols*, pp. 11–13, and vol. 2, *The Full Report*, p. 17.

81. Ibid., 1:14–17.

82. Gorny, *Ahdut Ha'avoda*, p. 67.

83. Katznelson, *Writings*, 1:73.

84. See Brenner's remarks in the collection of documents compiled by Haim Golan under the title *Zionist-Socialist Union of the Workers of Eretz Israel —Ahdut*

Ha'avoda: Minutes of the Meetings of the Executive Committee, the Council, and the General Assembly (in Hebrew), vol. 1, *December 1919–December 1920* (Ramat Efal: Tabenkin Foundation, 1987), p. 187. See also the quotations in *The Po'alei Tzion Delegation*, 1:17.

85. See the text of his speech and his responses in *The Po'alei Tzion Delegation*, pp. 124–28, 149–51.

86. Ibid., pp. 149–51.

87. Ibid., p. 159.

88. Ibid., p. 47.

89. Ibid., p. 182.

90. Ibid., p. 192.

91. Ibid., pp. 182–83.

92. Ibid., p. 203.

93. Ibid., p. 201.

94. Ibid.

95. Ibid., p. 189.

96. Ibid., pp. 268, 201.

97. Ibid., p. 190.

98. Ibid., p. 47.

99. Katznelson, *Writings*, 2:121, 3:188, 3:7–113. See also Katznelson's booklet entitled *Socialist Zionism* (in Hebrew) (Tel Aviv: Ayanot, n.d.).

100. Kolatt, "Ideology and Reality," pp. 325–26, 328; Yonathan Shapiro, *Ahdut Ha'avoda Hahistorit: Ozmato shel Irgun Politi* (Tel Aviv: Am Oved, 1975), pp. 26–27. This remarkable pioneering work, totally different in spirit, approach, and quality from Gorny's unsophisticated book, is available in English; see *The Formative Years of the Israeli Labour Party: The Organization of Power, 1919–1930* (London: Sage, 1976).

101. Shapiro, *Ahdut Ha'avoda*, pp. 26–27.

102. Katznelson, *Writings*, 1:138.

103. David Ben-Gurion, "From the Debate" at the Petah Tiqwa Convention of 1919 (in Hebrew), in *Ahdut Ha'avoda Anthology*, p. 26.

104. See chap. 6.

105. *Ahdut Ha'avoda Anthology*, p. 1.

106. Katznelson, *Writings*, 11:199.

107. Anita Shapira, *Berl*, vol. 1 (Tel Aviv: Am Oved, 1980), p. 144; see also Ben-Gurion's address at the meeting of the Mapai Central Committee on 20 January 1955 (Beit Berl Archives, file 23/55).

108. Golan, ed., *The Zionist-Socialist Union*, 1:19; Anita Shapira, *Berl*, 1:196.

109. Berl Katznelson, "Ahdut Ha'avoda," address to the first Ahdut Ha'avoda convention at Petah Tiqwa, 24 January 1919, in *Ahdut Ha'avoda Anthology*, p. 7.

110. Ibid., p. 9.

111. Ibid., p. 10.

112. Ibid., p. 9.

113. Ibid., p. 16.

114. Ibid., p. 15.

115. Ibid., p. 22.

116. Ibid., p. 21.

117. Ibid., p. 23.

118. Ibid., p. 8.

119. Ben Gurion's address to the third Ahdut Ha'avoda convention, *Kuntras* 6, no. 119 (19 January 1923): 29.

120. Kolatt, "Ideology and Reality," p. 324.

121. Ibid., pp. 328–29.

122. Katznelson, "Ahdut Ha'avoda," p. 16.

123. Ibid., p. 28.

124. Yitzhak Tabenkin, address to the first Ahdut Ha'avoda convention, *Ahdut Ha'avoda Anthology*, p. 29.

125. Katznelson, *Writings*, 1:124, address to the first Ahdut Ha'avoda convention. Yosef Gorny, for his part, is convinced that the question of whether to add the word *socialist* to the title of Ahdut Ha'avoda was more a tactical matter than one involving fundamental principles (*Ahdut Ha'avoda*, p. 27).

126. Katznelson, *Writings*, 1:123.

127. David Ben-Gurion, "The Party and the Histadrut" (6 February 1925), in *From Class to Nation*, p. 51.

128. Ibid., p. 53.

129. David Ben-Gurion, "The Worker and Zionism" (5 December 1932), in *From Class to Nation*, p. 253.

130. David Ben-Gurion, "The Eretz Israel Workers' Fund and the Branch of Po'alei Tzion in Eretz Israel" (in Hebrew), *Ha'ahdut*, no. 4 (18 November 1911), in *Ha'ahdut Anthology*, p. 399.

131. Ben-Zvi, "The Beginnings of Po'alei Tzion," p. 588; Yosef Shapira, *Hapo'el Hatza'ir*, pp. 28–29.

132. Frankel, *Prophecy and Politics*, pp. 418–22.

133. Slutzki, ed., *The Po'alei Tzion Party in Eretz Israel*, p. 18.

134. Quoted in Yosef Shapira, *Hapo'el Hatza'ir*, p. 65.

135. Frankel, *Prophecy and Politics*, p. 418.

136. Katznelson, *Writings*, 1:164.

137. Frankel, *Prophecy and Politics*, pp. 429–33.

138. Ibid., p. 430. Frankel bases his argument on Gorny's article "Changes in the Social and Political Composition of the Second Aliyah," pp. 208–45.

139. Yosef Shapira, *Hapo'el Hatza'ir*, pp. 181–83; see also Kolatt, "Ideology and Reality," p. 305.

140. The text of these two programs is in the appendixes of Yosef Shapira's *Hapo'el Hatza'ir*, pp. 470 and 477–78 respectively; see also pp. 72–73 and 184–86 of the same work. On the conquest of labor, see Shlomo Tzemah, *Labor and Land First of All* (in Hebrew) (Jerusalem: Reuven Mass, 1950), pp. 47–50.

141. Kolatt, "Ideology and Reality," p. 300.

142. Ibid., p. 306.

143. Shapiro, *Ahdut Ha'avoda*, p. 48.

144. Gorny, *Ahdut Ha'avoda*, p. 78.

145. Quoted by Gorny, ibid.

146. Ibid.

147. Ibid., p. 79.

148. Ibid.

149. See Shapiro, *Ahdut Ha'avoda*, pp. 50–51.

150. See Ben-Gurion's demand that the Histadrut be "the contractor for all the work that the Jewish people carries out in Eretz Israel" in his opening address to the thirteenth—and last—convention of Po'alei Tzion in Eretz Israel (*Ahdut Ha'avoda Anthology*, p. 583).

151. David Ben-Gurion, "Proposals to the Ahdut Ha'avoda Convention" (in Hebrew), *Kuntras* 4, no. 92 (9 September 1921): 3.

152. Gorny, *Ahdut Ha'avoda*, p. 100.

153. Statement by David Ben-Gurion to the Histadrut Council, *Kuntras* 5, no. 107 (3 February 1922): 10.

154. Ibid., p. 11.

155. Ben-Gurion, "Proposals to the Ahdut Ha'avoda Convention," p. 4.

156. Ibid., p. 6.

157. Gorny, *Ahdut Ha'avoda*, p. 80.

158. David Ben-Gurion, at the third Ahdut Ha'avoda convention, *Kuntras* 6, no. 119 (19 January 1923): 29.

159. David Ben-Gurion, "The Administration and the Workers" (in Hebrew), *Ha'ahdut*, no. 22 (24 March 1911), in *Ha'ahdut Anthology*, p. 174.

160. Gorny (*Ahdut Ha'avoda*, pp. 119, 120) comes to a different conclusion. He writes that the relationship of Ahdut Ha'avoda to the Socialist International was a combination of ideological obligation and national interest.

161. Gorny, *Ahdut Ha'avoda*, p. 130.

162. Shlomo Kaplanski, "Open Letter to the Ahdut Ha'avoda Executive Committee" (in Hebrew), *Kuntras* 9, no. 199 (26 December 1924): 9.

163. Ibid., p. 10.

164. Quoted by Gorny, *Ahdut Ha'avoda*, p. 205.

165. Quoted by Shapiro, *Ahdut Ha'avoda*, p. 34. Remez made this statement in January 1920.

166. Moshe Beilinson, "The Jewish Agency" (in Hebrew), quoted by Gorny, *Ahdut Ha'avoda*, p. 283.

167. David Ben-Gurion, "Our Mission to the People" (20 March 1928, in Hebrew), in *From Class to Nation*, p. 195.

168. Shlomo Kaplanski, "The Agricultural Workers and the Working Groups," *Ha'ahdut*, no. 3–4 (23 October 1914): 222.

169. David Ben-Gurion, "The Workers and Eretz Israel" (4 January 1918, in Hebrew), in *From Class to Nation*, p. 21.

170. David Ben-Gurion, "The Crisis in Zionism and the Labor Movement" (2 July 1932, in Hebrew), in *From Class to Nation*, pp. 241–42. Emphasis is in the text.

171. Ibid., p. 42.

172. Ibid., p. 241.

173. See, for instance, David Ben-Gurion, "Two Classes" (24 December 1926, in Hebrew), in *From Class to Nation*, p. 193: "The interests of the propertied class and its national convictions have been in conflict when [the propertied class] has had to deal with national affairs." See also his "Worker and Zionism," p. 258: "An allegiance

to the propertied class is in contradiction to the idea of the nation as an entity. An allegiance to the working class is in keeping with this idea."

174. Ben-Gurion, "Two Classes," p. 192.

175. Ibid., p. 193.

176. David Ben-Gurion, "The Split in Zionism and the Labor Movement" (7 August 1931, in Hebrew), in *From Class to Nation*, p. 220.

177. Ben-Gurion, "Our Mission to the People," p. 200.

Chapter Three

1. Anita Shapira, *Berl, Biographia*. Translated into English by Haya Galai as *Berl: The Biography of a Socialist Zionist: Berl Katznelson, 1887–1944* (Cambridge: Cambridge University Press, 1984). See also her *Land and Power: The Zionist Resort to Force, 1881–1948* (New York: Oxford University Press, 1992). Another example, among many others, of the cult surrounding Berl Katznelson is Zeev Goldberg, ed., *A Man's Path: Three Essays on Berl Katznelson* (in Hebrew) ([Zofit]: Beit Berl Publications, 1968).

2. Kolatt, "Ideology and Reality," p. 313; Anita Shapira, *Berl*, 1:112. On "Berl as a Hasidic rabbi," see Israel Kolatt, "The Man and the Idol," in *A Man's Path*, ed. Goldberg, p. 10.

3. See the text of the speech in Katznelson, *Writings*, 1:60–86. The title, "In Preparation for the Days to Come," soon became a very common phrase, much used on important occasions. The only text by Katznelson available in English is *My Way to Palestine* (London: Hechalutz, 1946).

4. Anita Shapira, *Berl*, 1:121–25.

5. Georges Sorel, *Réflexions sur la violence*, 11th ed. (Paris: Rivière, 1950), pp. 32–36.

6. Ibid., pp. 177, 180.

7. Katznelson, "The Ten Years of Ahdut Ha'avoda" (April 1929, in Hebrew), in *Writings*, 4:39.

8. Berl Katznelson, *The Second Aliyah: Berl Katznelson's Lectures to Socialist Youth* (1928, in Hebrew), ed. Anita Shapira and Noemi Abir (Tel Aviv: Am Oved, 1990).

9. Ibid., p. 9.

10. Berl Katznelson, *"The Miracle of the Second Aliyah"* (1928, in Hebrew), in *The Book of the Second Aliyah*, ed. Habas and Shohat, p. 11. For Ben-Gurion's speech, see Ben-Gurion's address to the Central Committee of Mapai, 20 January 1955, Beit Berl Archives, file 23/55. The tendency to exaggerate the importance of relatively minor events in the history of Zionism and to ascribe to them a weight in the history of the Jewish people which they did not possess has also been characteristic of the school of Israeli historians who accepted at face value the evaluations and assessments (also concerning themselves) of the founders. Thus, Shabtai Teveth claimed that the electoral campaign conducted by Ben-Gurion in Poland from April to July 1933, on the eve of the eighteenth Zionist Congress (held in Prague in August 1933), was "a campaign that decided his political career and was probably of crucial importance for the life of the Jewish people" (Teveth, *David's Passion*, vol. 3, *The Ground Burns*, p. 42). Ben-Gurion had every right to consider the Prague congress "the

decisive congress" (p. 55); that was his personal opinion. But it is very difficult for a historian to maintain that Ben-Gurion's electoral victory was a decisive event in the history of the Jewish people, even if this campaign proved to be his stepping-stone to the presidency of the Jewish Agency, which he took up two years later.

11. Katznelson, *Writings*, 9:193–238.

12. Ibid., pp. 241–66.

13. Ibid., pp. 245–48, 252.

14. Ibid., p. 249.

15. See Katznelson, *Socialist Zionism*; *Neglected Values*; "By the Way: Concluding Discussions of the Histadrut Study Days," in *Deeds and Tendencies* (in Hebrew) (Tel Aviv: Am Oved, 1941); *Being Tested: Conversations with Youth Leaders* (in Hebrew), 3d ed. (Tel Aviv: Mapai Publications, 1950).

16. Katznelson, *Neglected Values*, p. 52.

17. Katznelson, *Writings*, 9:252.

18. Ibid., vol. 5 (2d ed.), p. 73.

19. Ibid., 4:151.

20. Ibid., 3:377.

21. Ibid., 6:161.

22. Ibid., vol. 5 (2d ed.), p. 75.

23. Ibid., 6:161.

24. Ibid., 3:205.

25. Ibid., 7:240–41.

26. Ibid., p. 217.

27. Ibid., p. 220.

28. Ibid., p. 219; see also 12:21.

29. Ibid., 11:130–31, 142–44.

30. Ibid., p. 141.

31. Ibid., pp. 160–62. Emphasis is in the original. On this subject, I recommend Gershon Shaffir's *Land, Labour, and the Origin of the Israeli-Palestinian Conflict, 1882–1914* (Cambridge: Cambridge University Press, 1989), which deals with the question of the agricultural colonization of Eretz Israel considered as one of the aspects of the Israeli-Palestinian conflict. Using an economic approach (an analysis of the struggle for land and for labor), this book significantly modifies some of the hitherto accepted conclusions of Israeli historians. On the question of labor, see particularly Michael Shalev's major work *Labour and the Political Economy in Israel* (Oxford: Oxford University Press, 1992).

32. Katznelson, *Writings*, 11:162–63.

33. Beit Berl Archives, file 23/55. Ben-Gurion's address to the Mapai Central Committee, 20 January 1955.

34. See, for example, Katznelson, *Writings*, 4:39.

35. There are many examples. See some typical cases in ibid., pp. 11, 27; 5:140, 212; 6:76; and 7:192.

36. See the chapter devoted to *Davar* and the year 1925, in *Berl*, by Anita Shapira, 1:241–69. From the facts Shapira gives, one can draw entirely different conclusions, sometimes quite contrary to hers. On Katznelson's tendency to harbor resentment, see, for example, pp. 240, 259, and 287. Yitzhak Luftban, managing editor of the journal *Hapo'el Hatza'ir*, accused Katznelson of using the Histadrut as a forum for

criticizing Hapo'el Hatza'ir. Katznelson neither forgave nor forgot it (pp. 244–45). Nor did Katznelson ever forgive Gdud Ha'avoda for disregarding him and rejecting him as an arbitrator. In Anita Shapira's descriptions, Katznelson emerges as a prima donna who demanded everyone's unconditional admiration and agreement (p. 20). He was touchy and sensitive and was full of complaints against individuals and the world in general, but he also knew how to use all the powers at his disposal to pay off personal and political scores.

37. Anita Shapira, *Berl*, 1:259.

38. Ibid., 2:539.

39. Ibid., 1:230.

40. Ibid., p. 223.

41. Ibid., p. 311.

42. Anita Shapira's conclusion is different from mine (ibid., pp. 285–87).

43. Ibid., p. 285.

44. Katznelson, *Writings*, 3:135.

45. Katznelson, *Being Tested*, pp. 46–49.

46. Beit Berl Archives, minutes of the fourth Mapai convention, seventh session (5 May 1938), p. 7.

47. Katznelson, *Writings*, 5:272.

48. Ibid., pp. 248, 266–69.

49. Ibid., p. 248.

50. See Anita Shapira, *Berl*, 2:496–98. This description expresses the labor leadership's opinion of the workers in general and the labor opposition in particular. Katznelson, for his part, did not conceal the fact that he preferred Yosef Kitzis to Ben-Yeruham. Kitzis, the most important local boss of his time and a competent organizer, whose dealings, according to Anita Shapira, "verged on corruption," had the great advantage, where Katznelson was concerned, of knowing how to maintain order in the ranks. He lived in the same apartment block as Katznelson. In February 1937 the two of them went on a cruise together on the Nile while their families stayed in the same pension near Cairo (Anita Shapira, *Berl*, pp. 543–44), far from the economic crisis of that period, which affected primarily the workers, particularly in Tel Aviv. The crisis, it appears, did not affect everyone: the leaders of the movement who had planned vacations in European spas "took the waters" as if nothing had happened. At that period, Katznelson also resigned himself to his inability to oust Abba Hushi as secretary of the workers' council in Haifa, although he knew that "a regime of 'bossism,' with strong pressure on the workers" (p. 411), was developing in the northern city.

51. Katznelson, *Writings*, 4:156–57.

52. Anita Shapira, *Berl*, 1:133.

53. Gorny, *The Arab Question*, p. 276.

54. Anita Shapira, *Berl*, 1:303.

55. Gorny, *The Arab Question*, p. 278.

56. Minutes of the meeting of the council of Gdud Ha'avoda at Migdal on 17 and 18 June 1921. This document appears as an appendix to *Hasollel: Journal of the Workers in Public Works* (in Hebrew), ed. Haim Golan (Ramat Efal: Yad Tabenkin, 1991), p. 248.

57. Katznelson, *Writings*, 3:338.

58. Epigraph in Zeev Dor's *Role of Kibbutz Hame'uhad in Settling the Country* (in Hebrew), vol. 1 (N.p.: Hakibbutz Hame'uhad Publications, 1979).

59. Katznelson, *Writings*, vol. 5 (2d ed.), p. 217.

60. Ibid., 2:232.

61. Ibid.

62. Quoted by Gorny, *Ahdut Ha'avoda*, p. 192. Gorny found this phrase in the minutes of the meeting of the Executive Committee, held on 1 October 1921.

63. Ibid., p. 181.

64. Ibid.

65. Katznelson, *Writings*, 7:55.

66. Ibid., 4:36–37.

67. Ibid., p. 193. Emphasis is in the original.

68. Ibid., 1:113. See also 6:175–76.

69. Ibid., 1:70–71.

70. Ibid., 6:20–21.

71. Ibid., 3:121.

72. Ibid., 2:123. See also 4:268.

73. Ibid., 3:191.

74. Ibid., p. 117.

75. Ibid., 9:162.

76. Ibid., 4:150. See also vol. 11, and in particular chaps. pp. 13–16.

77. Ibid., 5:243–63.

78. See chap. 2.

79. Kolatt, "Ideology and Reality," p. 369. As Kolatt does not give his source, one should treat this quotation with caution.

80. Katznelson, *Writings*, 3:375.

81. Ibid., 11:205.

82. Yosef-Haim Brenner, "About Terminology" (in Hebrew), in *Writings*, vol. 4 (Tel Aviv: Hakibbutz Hame'uhad and Sifriyat Hapo'alim Publications, 1984), p. 1694.

83. Ibid.

84. Katznelson, *Being Tested*, p. 17. This text was also included in vol. 6 of Katznelson's *Writings*, pp. 375 ff.

85. Katznelson, *Being Tested*, pp. 18–19.

86. Katznelson, *Neglected Values*, pp. 23–24.

87. Ibid., p. 24.

88. Ibid., p. 25.

89. Ibid., p. 27.

90. Ibid., p. 28.

91. Katznelson, *Being Tested*, p. 19.

92. Ibid., p. 49.

93. Ibid., and p. 51.

94. Katznelson, *Writings*, 6:231.

95. Katznelson, *Being Tested*, p. 54; see also p. 49.

96. Ibid., p. 50.

97. *Ibid.*, pp. 50–51.

98. See Enrico Corradini, *Discorsi Politici (1902–1923)* (Florence: Vallechi Editore, 1923). See particularly pp. 100–101, 105–18, 154 ff., and 421.

99. Katznelson, *Being Tested*, p. 56.
100. Ibid., p. 50.
101. Ibid., p. 51.
102. Katznelson, *Writings*, 4:32.
103. Ibid., 3:267.
104. Ibid., 7:111.
105. Ibid., 1:123.
106. Ibid., vol. 5 (2d ed.), p. 67, 6:413.
107. Ibid., 6:418.
108. Ibid., 1:137.
109. Ibid., 2:242.
110. Ibid., 6:173.
111. Ibid., 3:377.
112. Ibid., 6:173.
113. Ibid., 3:378.
114. Ibid., p. 380.
115. Ibid., p. 381.
116. Ibid., pp. 379–80; see also 7:13–14.
117. Ibid., 3:137–38.
118. Ibid., 4:114–18.
119. Ibid., 6:21–22.
120. Ibid., 1:81.
121. Ibid., 4:97–98.
122. Katznelson, *Being Tested*, p. 26.
123. Ibid., p. 25.
124. Ibid., p. 30.
125. Ibid.
126. Katznelson, *Writings*, 6:48.
127. Ibid., pp. 365–67.
128. Ibid., p. 235.
129. Ibid., 9:196–98.
130. Ibid., p. 200. See also pp. 143–90, Katznelson's speeches at the council of Hakibbutz Hame'uhad and at the council of the Union of Kibbutzim. The two meetings were held consecutively in the summer of 1939, the first at Kibbutz Na'an and the second at Kvutzat Degania.
131. Ibid., 3:119, 129.
132. Ibid., 4:70–71.
133. Ibid., p. 217.
134. Ibid., 4:38.
135. Ibid., p. 267.
136. Ibid., p. 31.
137. Ibid., 6:20.
138. Ibid., 4:38.
139. Ibid., p. 37.
140. Ibid., p. 38.
141. Ibid., 6:168.
142. Yitzhak Ben-Zvi, "The Beginnings of Po'alei Tzion in Eretz Israel" (in Hebrew), in *The Book of the Second Aliyah*, ed. Habas and Shohat, p. 587.

143. Katznelson, *Writings*, 2:15.

144. Ibid., 1:220.

145. Ibid., 3:139, 267–69; see also 4:104.

146. Ibid., p. 269. The word *compensation* in the text is in quotation marks.

147. Ibid., 3:136; see also p. 135.

148. Ibid., 2:20.

149. Ibid., p. 15.

150. Katznelson, *Neglected Values*, p. 67.

151. Ibid., p. 68.

152. "Proletarian vision" in the text is always in quotation marks.

153. Katznelson, *Neglected Values*, pp. 19–22.

154. Ibid., p. 27.

155. Katznelson, *Writings*, 3:380; see also p. 438.

156. Katznelson, *Neglected Values*, pp. 33–43, 43–52.

157. Ibid., pp. 42–46, 61–62.

158. Ibid., p. 45.

159. Ibid., p. 115.

160. Ibid., pp. 118–19, 108–14, 55–59.

161. Hendrik de Man, *Au-delà du Marxisme* (Paris: Editions du Seuil, 1974), pp. 35, 38, 351, 354, 418.

162. Katznelson, *Writings*, vol. 5 (2d ed.), pp. 60–62.

163. Ibid., p. 60.

164. Katznelson, *Neglected Values,* pp. 125–26.

165. Ibid., p. 126.

166. Katznelson, *Writings*, vol. 5 (2d ed.), p. 20.

167. Ibid., 4:126–27.

168. Ibid., p. 106.

169. Ibid.

170. Ibid.

171. Ibid.

172. Ibid., 4:95.

173. Ibid., pp. 94–95.

174. Ibid., 4:107.

175. Ibid.

176. Ibid., p. 215.

177. Ibid., 5:112.

178. Ibid., p. 113.

179. Ibid., p. 112.

Chapter Four

1. Slutzki, *Introduction to the History of the Israeli Labor Movement*, p. 290.

2. These numbers are from the following sources: *In the Thirtieth Year: Statistics and Reports, 1921–1951* [in Hebrew] [Tel Aviv: Histadrut Publications, n.d.]), published by the Histadrut on its thirtieth anniversary; the appendixes to the report submitted by the Executive Committee to the Histadrut Council (4–8 October 1931), Labor Movement Archives, file 4/207, pp. 3, 8; and the reports submitted to the second (1923) and third (1927) Histadrut conventions, Labor Movement Archives,

library, D06-34-009, pp. 235–39. This last report is very detailed, although it contains inconsistencies, sometimes on the same page. Thus, three different figures are given for the number of Histadrut members in 1927: 22,538, 23,274, and 23,440. It is possible, however, that these differences indicate changes that took place during that year. Zvi Sussman estimates slightly lower numbers; see *Inequality and Equality in the Histadrut: The Influence of the Egalitarian Ideology and Arab Labor on the Salary of the Jewish Worker in Eretz Israel* (in Hebrew) (Ramat Gan: Massada, 1974), p. 58. According to Sussman, in 1923 the Histadrut had 7,500 members, representing nearly 55 percent of the Jewish salaried workers in Eretz Israel; in 1933 it had 26,000 (76 percent); and in 1939, on the eve of the Second World War, 82,000 (73 percent of the 112,000 Jewish salaried workers).

3. *In the Thirtieth Year* is a gold mine of information on the Histadrut, the trade unions associated with it, the cooperatives, and the Society of Workers. See also Shalev's *Labour and Political Economy in Israel*.

Another useful source of information is the following works of Haim Barkai: "The Public Histadrut and Private Sector in the Israeli Economy" (Jerusalem: The Falk Project for Economic Research in Israel, Sixth Report, 1964), pp. 12–88; "Fifty Years of Labor Economy: Growth, Performance, and the Present Challenge," *The Jerusalem Quarterly*, no. 50 (spring 1989): 81–109; "Economic Democracy and the Origins of the Israel Labor Economy," *The Jerusalem Quarterly*, no. 49 (winter 1989): 17–39; and "The Theory and Praxis of the Histadrut Industrial Sector," *The Jerusalem Quarterly*, no. 26 (winter 1982): 96–108. See also Ephraim Kleiman, "The Histadrut Economy of Israel: In Search of Criteria," *The Jerusalem Quarterly*, no. 41 (winter 1987): 77–94.

4. Yosef Aharonowitz at the fifth Histadrut Council, Labor Movement Archives, file 4/207, p. 4.

5. David Ben-Gurion, "The Party and the Histadrut" (6 February 1925, in Hebrew), in *From Class to Nation*, p. 56.

6. Ibid.

7. David Ben-Gurion, "The First Congress of Working Eretz Israel" (27 September 1930, in Hebrew), in *From Class to Nation*, p. 212.

8. David Ben-Gurion, "Our Method of Action" (15 February 1933, in Hebrew), in *From Class to Nation*, p. 181.

9. David Ben-Gurion, "The Main Question" (8 June 1931, in Hebrew), in *From Class to Nation*, p. 165. See also pp. 164–70.

10. David Ben-Gurion, address to the meeting of 17 March 1920, in *The Po'alei Tzion Delegation*, ed. Golan, p. 203.

11. "Ben-Gurion's Speech," *Davar*, 8 September 1925, p. 2.

12. Ben-Gurion, "Our Method of Action," p. 185.

13. Ben-Gurion, "The Main Question," pp. 169–70.

14. Golan, ed., *The Po'alei Tzion Delegation*, p. 134.

15. Ibid., p. 129.

16. Ibid., p. 190. Ben-Gurion also thought that this figure could be reached easily, and most of the other leaders of the labor movement concurred.

17. Ibid., p. 183.

18. Ibid., p. 195.

19. Gorny, *Ahdut Ha'avoda*, p. 207.

20. David Ben-Gurion, "Class Federation, or Federation of Parties" (9 January 1925, in Hebrew), in *From Class to Nation*, p. 45.

21. Shapiro, *Ahdut Ha'avoda*, pp. 31–32.

22. Annie Kriegel, *Les Communistes Français: Essai d'ethnographie politique* (Paris: Editions du Seuil, 1970).

23. See Shapiro, *Ahdut Ha'avoda*, chaps. 3 and 4.

24. Quoted in ibid., p. 153, from Katznelson's speech at the third Histadrut convention, *Davar*, 10 July 1927.

25. Shapiro, *Ahdut Ha'avoda*, pp. 61–62, 73.

26. Golda Meir, "Wholeheartedly and Gladly" (in Hebrew), speech to veterans of the Third Aliyah at the Habima Theater in Tel Aviv, in *Sefer Ha'aliya Hashlishit* (The book of the Third Aliyah), ed. Yehuda Erez, vol. 2 (Tel Aviv: Am Oved, 1964), p. 910.

27. David Ben-Gurion, "The Gift of the Land" (September 1915, in Hebrew), in *From Class to Nation*, pp. 10–11.

28. Gorny, *Ahdut Ha'avoda*, p. 186; Shapiro, *Ahdut Ha'avoda*, pp. 30–31.

29. David Ben-Gurion, "Why We Are Joining the Jewish Agency" (4 July 1929, in Hebrew), in *From Class to Nation*, p. 207.

30. Katznelson, *Writings*, 1:229–30.

31. Gorny, *Ahdut Ha'avoda*, p. 175.

32. Moshe Beilinson, "The Crisis in Dictatorship and Democracy," *Kuntras* 10 (16 January 1925): 23–24. Gorny (*Ahdut Ha'avoda*, p. 177) is wrong in interpreting this major text as meaning that the Zionist movement has the right to speak for the whole nation "because its calling is in agreement with the true will of the people." Beilinson is speaking not about the people's will but about its needs!

33. David Ben-Gurion, "The Worker and Zionism" (5 December 1932, in Hebrew), in *From Class to Nation*, p. 251.

34. Chaim Arlosoroff, "Questions of the Day" (in Hebrew), quoted from *Hapo'el Hatza'ir* by Shapiro, *Ahdut Ha'avoda*, p. 59.

35. Gorny, *Ahdut Ha'avoda*, p. 185. Scholars agree about the centralistic and bureaucratic nature of the Ahdut Ha'avoda and Histadrut institutions. The differences between them lie chiefly in the tone of their accounts. Gorny simply "confirms" the explanations of the founders and their "official" historians, whereas Shapiro succeeds in preserving a critical perspective. See Gorny, *Ahdut Ha'avoda*, pp. 185–86, 193–94, 227–28, 242–43, 249, 412; and Shapiro, *Ahdut Ha'avoda*, pp. 45–46, 57–60, 124–25. Gorny's work lacks the analytical dimension one usually expects in historical research.

36. Yaffe's long article was published in two parts. See "In Preparation for Our Agricultural Convention" (in Hebrew), *Davar*, 29 and 30 December 1925. A third article was published at the end of January: "Additions to Clarify the 'Nir' Question and That of the Contracts" (in Hebrew), 28 January 1926.

37. Chaim Arlosoroff, "Three Observations" (in Hebrew), *Davar*, 3 January 1926; Eliahu Golomb, "One Anxiety That Leads to Another" (in Hebrew), *Davar*, 6 January 1926; Yosef Aharonowitz, "Concerning E. Yaffe's Article" (in Hebrew), *Davar*, 10 January 1926.

38. Arlosoroff, "Three Observations," p. 3.

39. Berl Katznelson [Yeruba'el, pseud.], "Three Causes of Astonishment" (in Hebrew), *Davar*, 8 January 1926, p. 5. The article was included in vol. 2 of Katznelson's *Writings*, pp. 215–18.

40. "The 'Nir' Question at the Agricultural Convention—Speech by Berl Katznelson" (in Hebrew), *Davar*, 10 February 1926, p. 3. See also Katznelson, *Writings*, 2:218–34, and "Reply to the Comrades' Speeches," in *Writings*, 2:234–46.

41. Katznelson, "The 'Nir' Question."

42. Aharonowitz, "Concerning E. Yaffe's Article," p. 3. See also Shlomo Levkovitch, "The Brotherhood of All Classes" (in Hebrew), *Davar*, 7 January 1926, p. 3.

43. David Ben-Gurion, "Ben-Gurion's Statement in the Debate on 'Nir'" (in Hebrew), *Davar*, 15 February 1926, p. 3.

44. Katznelson, "The Agricultural Workers' Convention" (in Hebrew), *Davar*, 10 February 1926, p. 1.

45. Ben-Gurion, "Ben-Gurion's Statement in the Debate on 'Nir,'" p. 3.

46. Katznelson, "Reply to the Comrades' Speeches," pp. 244–46.

47. Katznelson, "The Agricultural Workers' Convention," p. 1.

48. Labor Movement Archives, IV/228, file 61B.

49. Katznelson, *Writings*, 9:159.

50. Katznelson, "The 'Nir' Question."

51. Berl Katznelson, "Berl Katznelson's Speech in Reply" (in Hebrew), *Davar*, 15 February 1926, p. 4.

52. Katznelson, "The 'Nir' Question."

53. See, for example, the account of the voting at the last session of the agricultural convention, in *Davar*, 10 February 1926, and "Ben-Gurion's Statement in the Debate on 'Nir.'"

54. G. Ostrowski, "What the Emek [Valley] Group Was" (in Hebrew), in *The Book of the Third Aliyah*, ed. Erez, 1:393. On the relationship between the new immigrants of the Third Aliyah and the "old-timers" of the Second in Gdud Ha'avoda, see also Anita Shapira, *Going Toward the Horizon*, pp. 160–62.

55. Shlomo Lavi, "From the Kibbutz of the Select to the Large Kibbutz" (in Hebrew), in *The Book of the Third Aliyah*, ed. Erez, pp. 350–54. The article referred to here was included in Lavi's book *My Account of Ein Harod: Ideas, Memories, and Actions* (in Hebrew) (Tel Aviv: Am Oved, 1947).

56. On the differences between the ideas of the Gdud and the concept of the "large kvutza [kibbutz]," see Menachem Elkind, "The Large Kvutza and Gdud Ha'avoda" (in Hebrew), in *The Book of the Third Aliyah*, ed. Erez, pp. 370–72.

57. See the minutes of the inaugural convention of Gdud Ha'avoda, given as an appendix to the collection of the six issues of *Hasollel*, in *Hasollel*, ed. Golan, p. 247. *Hasollel* (The road builder) was replaced by *Mehayenu: The Journal of the "Yosef Trumpeldor" Labor Corps*.

58. Moshe Shapira, "Commemoration of Yosef Trumpeldor" (in Hebrew), *Kuntras* 2, no. 51 (2 September 1920): 24–25. On the creation of Gdud Ha'avoda, see Haim Kamnecky, "Two Years After the Death of Yosef Trumpeldor, One and a Half Years After the Founding of Ahdut Ha'avoda" (in Hebrew), in *Mehayenu* 1, no. 25 (17 March 1922): 247.

59. Golan, ed., *Hasollel*, pp. 18–21.

60. There seems to be no point in saying more about this complicated question here. The interested reader can refer to Elkana Margalit's book *Commune, Society, and Politics: The "Yosef Trumpeldor" Labor Corps in Eretz Israel* (in Hebrew) (Tel Aviv: Am Oved, 1980), pp. 309–14. This book is essential for anyone wishing to know why and how the Gdud Ha'avoda came into being. See also Aaron Yannai, *History of Ein Harod* (in Hebrew), vol. 1 (Ein Harod: Kibbutz Ein Harod Publications, 1971).

61. Golan, ed., *Hasollel*, pp. 18–21. On the period when these roads were opened, see Erez, ed., *The Book of the Third Aliyah*, 1:247–312.

62. Golan, ed., *Hasollel*, pp. 24–28. See also, as an appendix to this work (p. 262), the regulations of Gdud Ha'avoda, drawn up in October 1920.

63. Ibid., pp. 25–26. See no. 1, pp. 58–64. This first issue was published by the cultural committee of the camps on the Tabha-Tzemah road.

64. See the regulations of Gdud Ha'avoda in ibid., p. 263.

65. Minutes of the inaugural convention of Gdud Ha'avoda, in ibid., p. 241.

66. Menachem Elkind, "Reply to Comrade Dubkin" (in Hebrew), *Mehayenu* 3, no. 59 (17 November 1924).

67. Golan, ed., *Hasollel*, minutes of the council of Gdud Ha'avoda, p. 247.

68. Ibid., p. 249.

69. See *Mehayenu* 1, no. 24 (18 March 1922): 243, 399.

70. Haim Hadari, ed., *Kibbutz Hame'uhad: Decisions and Documents* (in Hebrew), vol. 1 (Tel Aviv: Hakibbutz Hame'uhad Publications, 1977), p. 9.

71. See, for example, Sh. Levitin, "Barter, Barter" (in Hebrew), *Mehayenu* 2, no. 42 (27 July 1923): 177.

72. Yosef Shapira, *Hapo'el Hatza'ir*, p. 29.

73. Haim Kamnecky, "Ahdut Ha'avoda and Gdud Ha'avoda," *Mehayenu* 1, no. 14 (9 December 1922): 109.

74. See the articles by Elisha (no last name given) and H. Friedman, "The Gdud and the Histadrut," *Mehayenu* 1, no. 24 (18 March 1922): 209–11. On the idea of "imposing our principles [the Gdud's] on the Histadrut," see A. H.'s article "Gdud Ha'avoda," Mehayenu 1, no. 30 (18 June 1922): 337–40. See also the articles of two other moderate members, Zeev Isserzon, "An Explanation of Our Intentions and a Statement of Our Requirements," *Mehayenu* 1, no. 29 (19 May 1922): 313–18, 404–6; and Sh. Levitin, "Remarks Before the Gdud Convention," pp. 318–19.

75. Yitzhak Landoberg [Sadeh], "Our Relations with the Bureau," *Mehayenu* 1:403–4. See also Elkind's reports to the Gdud convention at Ein Harod, 16–19 February 1922, in *Mehayenu* 1:233–35, and his statements (in the presence of Ben-Gurion) on 30 July 1922, also in *Mehayenu*, 1:372–73.

76. See Elkind's and Remez's statements on this point at the sixth Gdud convention, *Mehayenu* 1:372–73. See also the convention's decisions, p. 396.

77. See, for instance, the unsigned article "An Examination of the Relations between Gdud Ha'avoda and the Bureau of Public Works" (in Hebrew), *Mehayenu* 2, no. 53 (13 June 1924): 478. See also 1:396–97 and "Memorandum to the Histadrut Executive" (in Hebrew), *Mehayenu* 2, no. 40 (11 June 1923): 147, and "The Gdud's Debt," a section of "Decisions of the Special Council of the Gdud Relating to the Question of Sollel Boneh" (in Hebrew), 11–12 December 1923, *Mehayenu* 2, no. 47 (17 January 1924); and "Open Letter to the Histadrut Executive," *Mehayenu* 3, no. 60 (14 April 1925): 151–53.

78. Ben-Gurion's statements are reported in "Minutes," *Mehayenu* 2, no. 37 (15 December 1922): 92–93.

79. "The Gdud's Platform for the General Assembly" (in Hebrew), *Mehayenu* 2, no. 39 (24 January 1923): 103–4.

80. Elkind's statement, "Minutes," p. 95.

81. "The Gdud's Platform," p. 103.

82. See especially Elkind's self-criticism at the Gdud council held at Tel Yosef on 3 and 4 October 1923, "General Report," *Mehayenu* 2, no. 45 (26 November 1923): 246–51.

83. Shlomo Levkovitch, "Chronicle," *Mehayenu* 2, no. 37 (15 December 1922): 70.

84. On relations between Ben-Gurion and Gdud Ha'avoda, see Teveth, *David's Passion*, 2:195–206.

85. "Memorandum Submitted to the Executive Committee of the Histadrut" (in Hebrew), *Mehayenu* 2, no. 40 (special issue) (11 June 1923): 143. On the division of land and possessions, see also p. 167.

86. Ibid., pp. 143–44.

87. Anita Shapira, *Berl*, 1:258–59.

88. Moshe Shapira, "Our Position in the Histadrut" (in Hebrew), *Mehayenu* 2, no. 54 (4 July 1924): 501.

89. Yehoshua Lanzman, "Reflections on the Gdud's Choices" (in Hebrew), *Mehayenu* 2, no. 99 (29 February 1924): 353.

90. Menachem Elkind, "Our General Direction" (in Hebrew), *Mehayenu* 3, no. 63 (9 September 1925): 209. It is interesting that the destruction of the Gdud terminated at the end of the Third Aliyah. I do not agree with Dan Giladi that the change in the sociological composition of the new immigrants who came with the Fourth Aliyah caused the radicalization of the Gdud, a radicalization that provoked internal dissensions and accelerated the breakup of the organization. See Dan Giladi's important book *The Yishuv at the Time of the Fourth Aliyah, 1924–1929: Economical and Political Analysis* (in Hebrew) (Tel Aviv: Am Oved, 1973), pp. 123–25.

91. Margalit, *Commune, Society, and Politics*, pp. 310–11.

92. "The Structure of the Histadrut" (in Hebrew), *Mehayenu* 2, no. 48 (19 February 1924): 319.

93. "The First of May in the Companies of the Gdud" (in Hebrew), *Mehayenu* 3, no. 62 (24 May 1925): 196, 198.

94. With regard to the history of the Gdud, I again refer the reader to Margalit's important work *Commune, Society, and Politics*.

95. Menachem Elkind, "Letter to the Editor" (in Hebrew), *Davar*, 8 October 1925, p. 3.

96. I owe the account of its lines of division to one of the members of the right wing. See Berl Reptor, "The Currents in the Gdud" (in Hebrew), *Davar*, 14 October 1925. Reptor eventually became an important activist in Mapai and later in Ahdut Ha'avoda.

97. Ben-Ellul, "Impressions of the Gdud Ha'avoda Council" (in Hebrew), *Davar*, 15 December 1925. The reports of Ben-Ellul (no first name given), who was probably *Davar*'s correspondent in the Jezreel Valley, were hostile to Gdud Ha'avoda.

98. "From the Council of Gdud Ha'avoda" (in Hebrew), *Davar*, 27 December 1925, p. 2.

99. Teveth, *David's Passion*, 2:287–300.

100. Yonathan Shapiro writes that the Histadrut's conflict with the Gdud was only a power struggle, and he explains the Histadrut's actions against the Gdud as being motivated by its strategy of gaining complete control of the decision-making process (*Ahdut Ha'avoda*, p. 85). To the question of why Elkind refused to yield in his demand for a common treasury, Shapiro replied: "The idea of a common treasury was the factor that legitimized his comrades' desire to found an organization separate from the Histadrut. This desire for the legitimation of a separate existence had been expressed ever since the Gdud's inaugural convention" (*Ahdut Ha'avoda*, p. 86). By contrast, Yosef Gorny, as usual, accepted the official explanations of Ben-Gurion. "In my opinion," he wrote, "the origin of the conflict should be sought in the general conception of Ahdut Ha'avoda, which wished to set up social organisms capable of functioning" (*Ahdut Ha'avoda*, p. 255).

101. Hadari, ed., *Kibbutz Hame'uhad*, pp. 8–20.

102. Ibid., p. 218; see the calendar and documents in the appendix to the work. See also Zeev Tzur, *The Role of Kibbutz Hame'uhad in Settling the Country* (in Hebrew), vol. 1, *1927–1939* (Tel Aviv: Hakibbutz Hame'uhad Publications, 1979), pp. 19–31.

103. Anita Shapira, *Going Toward the Horizon*, p. 176.

104. Tzur, *The Role of Kibbutz Hame'uhad*, p. 16.

105. Ibid., pp. 11–17. At the time of the inaugural convention of Hakibbutz Hame'uhad, Kibbutz–Ein Harod was made up of four settlements—Ein Harod, Yagur, Gesher, and Ayelet Hashahar—eight companies scattered throughout the country, and several collective groups, including groups of Hashomer Hatz'air. At the preparatory meeting for the inaugural convention, held in Haifa on 27 April 1927, Me'ir Ya'ari was present, representing Hashomer Hatza'ir. Until his death in 1987, Ya'ari was the undiscussed leader of Hashomer Hatza'ir and its ideologist. Ya'ari finally decided not to associate his movement with the merge at the inaugural convention and to form his own kibbutz movement. The Gdud was also present at the Haifa meeting, but it did not respond to the invitation to attend the inaugural convention. Two years after this convention, in 1929, the surviving Gdud kibbutzim, Tel Yosef, Ramat Rahel (near Jerusalem), and Kfar Giladi, finally joined Hakibbutz Hame'uhad.

106. Anita Shapira, *Going Toward the Horizon*, p. 176.

107. Tzur, *The role of Kibbutz Hame'uhad*, p. 16.

108. Katznelson, *Writings*, 3:338.

109. Levitin, "Barter, Barter," p. 178.

110. Hanan Rokhel, "Among Ourselves" (in Hebrew), *Mehayenu* 1, no. 1 (23 July 1921).

Chapter Five

1. Michael Beenstock, Jacob Metzer, and Sanny Ziv, *Immigration and the Jewish Economy in Mandatory Palestine* (Jerusalem: The Maurice Falk Institute for Economic Research in Israel, 1993), pp. 1, 8, 9. On this subject, see also R. Szereswewski's pioneering work *Essays on the Structure of the Jewish Economy in Palestine and Israel* (Jerusalem: The Maurice Falk Institute for Economic Research in Israel, 1968).

2. Beenstock, Metzer, and Ziv, *Immigration and the Jewish Economy*, p. 6.

3. Giladi, *The Yishuv in the Period of the Fourth Aliyah*, pp. 9–11; Beenstock, Metzer, and Ziv, *Immigration and the Jewish Economy*, p. 7.

4. Beenstock, Metzer, and Ziv, *Immigration and the Jewish Economy*, pp. 1, 8.

5. Ben-Gurion, "Our Mission to the People," p. 198.

6. Quoted by Yosef Shapira, *Hapo'el Hatza'ir*, p. 413.

7. Ibid., p. 414.

8. Ibid., p. 416.

9. Labor Movement Archives, IV-207, Ben-Gurion's speech at the thirty-fourth council of the Histadrut, 19 March 1936, p. 35; *In the Thirtieth Year*, p. 33.

10. Giladi, *The Yishuv at the Time of the Fourth Aliyah*, pp. 9–11.

11. Ibid., pp. 38–39, 47, 53, 57.

12. Ibid., pp. 52–53, 66.

13. Ibid., p. 80. See also p. 260.

14. Ibid., pp. 174–75, 180.

15. Katznelson, speech at the fifth Ahdut Ha'avoda convention, 26 October 1926, in *Writings*, 3:40.

16. Ibid., pp. 30–31.

17. Giladi, *The Yishuv at the Time of the Fourth Aliyah*, pp. 194–95.

18. Minutes of the meeting of the council at Nahalat Yehuda, 6 January, 1925, quoted by Shapiro, *Ahdut Ha'avoda*, p. 129 .

19. Ben-Gurion, "Our Method of Action," p. 184.

20. Katznelson, *Writings*, 3:377.

21. David Ben-Gurion, "Arbitration and Strikes" (20 November 1932), in *From Class to Nation*, p. 178.

22. Berl Katznelson, "On the Eve of the Fifteenth Congress" (in Hebrew), in *Ahdut Ha'avoda Anthology* 2:275.

23. Moshe Beilinson, "The Zionist Movement and the Histadrut" (in Hebrew), *Kuntras* 9, no. 192 (7 November 1924): 7.

24. Yitzhak Tabenkin, "Address" (in Hebrew), in *The Po'alei Tzion Delegation in Eretz Israel*, ed. Golan, 1:116.

25. Ben-Gurion, "Our Method of Action," p. 152.

26. David Ben-Gurion, "The Crisis of Zionism and the Labor Movement" (2 July 1932), in *From Class to Nation*, p. 239. See also "Why We Are Joining the Jewish Agency" (4 July 1929), in *From Class to Nation*, p. 208.

27. David Ben-Gurion, "The National Vocation of the Working Class" (2 March 1925), in *From Class to Nation*, p. 187.

28. Ibid., p. 189.

29. David Ben-Gurion, "Changing of the Guard" (16 January 1929), in *From Class to Nation*, p. 207.

30. David Ben-Gurion, "The Parties of the Zionist Movement and the Labor Movement" (7 August 1931), in *From Class to Nation*, p. 220.

31. David Ben-Gurion, "The Worker in Zionism" (5 December 1932), in *From Class to Nation*, p. 249.

32. Ibid., p. 250.

33. Ibid., pp. 250, 257.

34. Ibid., p. 257.

35. Ibid., p. 259. Gorny takes the opposite view. He writes that "the slogan 'From Class to Nation,' when it appeared, meant not the rejection of class values and their replacement by others but the application of these values to the entire people in order to give it a class character" (Gorny, *Ahdut Ha'avoda*, p. 259; see also pp. 322 and 323 of the same work, in which Gorny claims that "at that period the slogan 'From Class to Nation' could be interpreted only in a socialistic way').

36. Quoted by Gorny, *Ahdut Ha'avoda*, p. 317.

37. The text of the resolutions is in *Kuntras* 10, no. 202 (16 January 1925): 18–20.

38. Yosef Shapira, *Hapo'el Hatza'ir*, pp. 436–37. See also Gorny, *Ahdut Ha'avoda*, p. 317.

39. Ibid., pp. 438–41.

40. Ibid., p. 483.

41. Ibid., p. 484.

42. Ibid., pp. 483, 485. On this matter, see also Giladi, *The Yishuv at the Time of the Fourth Aliyah*, p. 252.

43. Ibid., pp. 449, 451.

44. Katznelson, *Writings*, 3:42–43.

45. *Kuntras* 6, no. 119 (19 January 1923): 56–57. We should recall that the convention was held in Haifa, between 17 and 20 December 1922.

46. Ben-Gurion, "The National Vocation of the Working Class," p. 189.

47. Yitzhak Ben-Zvi [Avner, pseud.], "Internationalism in Socialism" (in Hebrew), *Ha'ahdut*, no. 1–2 (4 October 1914), in *Ha'ahdut Anthology*, p. 534.

48. Ben-Gurion's speech to the party's council in Jerusalem, 30 December 1921, quoted by Gorny, *Ahdut Ha'avoda*, p. 49.

49. Ben-Gurion, *From Class to Nation*, pp. 185–86. Israeli historiographers have given this interpretation such an "official" character that even scholars like Dan Horowitz, Moshe Lissak, and Anita Shapira have accepted it without question. Horowitz and Lissak wrote that the labor movement, in contrast to the Revisionist movement, "developed an ideology of allegiance to both the nation and the class" (*From the Yishuv to the State*, p. 193). Anita Shapira, for her part, claimed that "the Eretz Israeli labor movement was a phenomenon that reflected the half-century of Zionist settlement in Eretz Israel. Its socialist qualities enabled it to play a role of the greatest importance in the implementation of Zionism. It was Zionism that made this movement necessary and gave it its originality, so that when it lost its Zionist function, it simultaneously lost its taste for socialism."

50. Israel Kolatt, "Was Ben-Gurion a Socialist?" in *Ben-Gurion: Portrait of the Leader of the Labor Movement*, ed. Avineri, pp. 128–29.

51. Shapiro, *Ahdut Ha'avoda*, pp. 188–90; Gorny, *Ahdut Ha'avoda*, p. 419.

52. Yosef Shapira, *Hapo'el Hatza'ir*, p. 416.

53. Quoted in Giladi, *The Yishuv at the Time of the Fourth Aliyah*, pp. 168–69. On relations between Chaim Weizmann and the labor movement, see Yosef Gorny, *Collaboration and Confrontation: Chaim Weizmann and the Labor Movement in Eretz Israel* (in Hebrew) (Tel Aviv: Hakibbutz Hame'uhad Publications, 1975), p. 62. On Weizmann, see his *Trial and Error: The Autobiography of Chaim Weizmann* (New York: Schocken Books, 1966); idem., *A Biography by Several Hands*, with a contribution by Ben-Gurion (London: Weidenfeld and Nicholson, 1962); and Jehuda Reinharz, *Chaim Weizmann*, 2 vols. (New York: Oxford University Press, 1985–1993).

54. Labor Movement Archives, IV-406, meeting of the Mapai Central Committee on 29 March 1931. Eli Shaltiel writes that "the alliance between the labor movement and Chaim Weizmann is probably the best example of the farsighted pragmatism of the labor movement" (Shaltiel, *Pinhas Rutenberg*, 2:613).

55. Giladi, *The Yishuv at the Time of the Fourth Aliyah*, p. 169.

56. Ibid., pp. 227–29, 236–38. See also Yosef Shapira, *Hapo'el Hatza'ir*, p. 412.

57. David Ben-Gurion, "Why We Are Joining the Jewish Agency" (4 July 1929), in *From Class to Nation*, p. 208.

58. Quoted in Shapiro, *Ahdut Ha'avoda*, p. 187.

59. Ibid.

60. Beenstock, Metzer, and Ziv, *Immigration and the Jewish Economy*, pp. 4–5.

61. Labor Movement Archives, IV-406/5, 13 November 1932, pp. 1–3.

62. Katznelson, *Writings*, 7:305–8.

63. Labor Movement Archives, IV-406/5, 13 November 1932, p. 4.

64. Ibid., p. 2.

65. Berl Katznelson, "Answers to the Questions at Our Third Convention" (in Hebrew), *Davar*, 25 March 1927, p. 2.

66. Shapiro, *Ahdut Ha'avoda*, p. 192.

67. Shaltiel, *Pinhas Rutenberg*, 2:606–12.

68. Yigal Drori, *Between Right and Left: "Bourgeois Groups" in the Nineteen-twenties* (in Hebrew) (Tel Aviv: Tel Aviv University Press, 1990), p. 11.

69. Ibid., pp. 98–99.

70. Ibid., pp. 99–100.

71. Ibid., pp. 101–6. See Moshe Glickson, "The Events in Petah Tiqwa," *Ha'aretz*, 18 December 1927, and "The Demands of the Hour," *Ha'aretz*, 20 December 1927 (both in Hebrew).

72. Ruppin, *Agricultural Settlement*.

73. Berl Katznelson, "Ruppin," *Davar*, 12 March 1926, and "On Ruppin," in *Writings*, 10:222, 223, both in Hebrew.

74. Moshe Glickson, *Changing of the Guard: Collection of Articles* (in Hebrew) (Tel Aviv: Hano'ar Hatzioni Publications, 1938), 1:286–91.

75. Ibid., p. 290.

76. Ibid., p. 289.

77. Ibid., pp. 290–91.

78. Ibid., p. 340. See also pp. 347–49.

79. Ibid., pp. 354–59.

80. Ibid., pp. 376–86.

81. Ibid., 2:503–5.

82. Ministry of Education, *The Book of Education and Culture* (in Hebrew) (Jerusalem: National Press, 1951), p. 6. See also Sh. Reshef, *The Labor Trend in Education* (in Hebrew) (Tel Aviv: Tel Aviv University Press and Hakibbutz Hame'uhad Publications, 1980), pp. 13–16.

83. Labor Movement Archives, library, D.06-34-012(4), report to the fourth Histadrut convention, February 1933, p. 244.

84. Moshe Glickson, "On the Agenda" (in Hebrew), *Ha'aretz*, 7 January 1926.

85. Ministry of Education, *The Book of Education and Culture*, pp. 3–9.

86. Reshef, *The Labor Trend in Education*, pp. 69–75, 91–94, 108. Reshef does not always fully grasp the significance of the facts he relates.

87. Ibid., p. 117. The Educational Council held its meeting at Ein Harod. Reshef refers to Pogatchov's account in "The Regional School in the Jezreel Valley" (in Hebrew), *Hapo'el Hatza'ir* 19 , no. 24 (23 April 1926).

88. Reshef, *The Labor Trend in Education*, p. 120.

89. Ibid., p. 123.

90. Ibid., pp. 128–29.

91. Ibid., pp. 128–30, 140–46.

92. Ibid., p. 191.

93. Labor Movement Archives, library, report of the Educational Council to the Third Histadrut convention, July 1927, p. 342.

94. Labor Movement Archives, IV-215-1387.

95. Labor Movement Archives, IV-215-1495, "Program for the Organization of the Children's Society" (in Hebrew).

96. Moshe Avigal, *Vision and Education* (in Hebrew) (Tel Aviv: Tarbut Vehinuch, 1971), pp. 110–11.

97. Ibid., p. 116. I thank Ayelet Levy, whose master's thesis I supervised, for having brought to my notice the collections of articles by Moshe Avigal and Shmuel Yavnieli.

98. Reshef, *The Labor Trend in Education*, p. 221.

99. Avigal, *Vision and Education*, p. 116.

100. Labor Movement Archives, IV-215-1389, "Introduction to the Program of Studies" (in Hebrew).

101. Shmuel Yavnieli, "An Ill-Timed Controversy," in *In Light of the Concept of Labor: A Collection of Articles on Educational Subjects* (in Hebrew), ed. Shmuel Yavnieli (Tel Aviv: Publications of the Teachers' Union Committee, 1938), p. 88.

102. Labor Movement Archives, IV-215-358, "Proposals for a History-Teaching Program, 1935" (in Hebrew).

103. Reshef, *The Labor Trend in Education*, p. 244.

104. Yavnieli, "An Ill-Timed Controversy," p. 86.

105. Reshef, *The Labor Trend in Education*, p. 233.

106. Ibid., p. 270.

107. Katznelson, *Writings*, 7:204.

108. Labor Movement Archives, IV-207, 4–8 October 1931, p. 76.

109. Labor Movement Archives, library, D.06–34–012(4), report to the Fourth Histadrut convention, Tel Aviv, February 1933, p. 242.

110. Labor Movement Archives, IV-215-1389, "The Labor Educational System in 1937." These facts correspond to those in the Ministry of Education's *Book of Education and Culture*, p. 14. See also the Central Zionist Archives, J-17/190, report of the Department of Education, 1936–37.

111. Labor Movement Archives, Ben-Gurion's speech to the thirty-fourth council of the Histadrut, 19 March 1936, p. 25.

112. Labor Movement Archives, report to the fourth Histadrut convention, p. 243.

113. Ibid., pp. 246–48.

114. Central Zionist Archives, J-17/207, budget of the schools of the Histadrut Educational Center for the year 1937–38; Labor Movement Archives, "The Labor Educational System in 1937."

115. Labor Movement Archives, "The Labor Educational System in 1937"; Central Zionist Archives, J-17/190.

116. Labor Movement Archives, IV-215-1146.

117. Labor Movement Archives, IV-215-1494, minutes of the meeting of the plenum of the Histadrut Educational Center held at Kibbutz Yagur, 20 April 1939.

118. Labor Movement Archives, "The Labor Educational System in 1937."

119. Labor Movement Archives, Ben-Gurion's speech to the thirty-fourth council of the Histadrut, pp. 27–28, 37.

120. Ibid., pp. 31–34.

121. Labor Movement Archives, IV-207, Ben-Gurion's speech to the twenty-sixth council of the Histadrut, 4–8 October 1931, p. 73.

122. About the different opinions expressed on this topic, see ibid., pp. 75–83.

123. Ibid., p. 73.

124. Labor Movement Archives, Ben-Gurion's speech to the thirty-fourth council of the Histadrut, pp. 25–26.

125. See, for example, Katznelson, *Writings*, 7:201–5.

126. Central Zionist Archives, J-17/4389, letter of the school principal to the Histadrut Educational Center.

127. Ibid.

128. Ibid.; see the letters of 21 May 1936 and 11 and 17 August 1939.

129. Labor Movement Archives, "The Labor Educational System in 1937."

130. Reshef, *The Labor Trend in Education*, p. 229.

131. Labor Movement Archives, thirty-fourth council of the Histadrut, p. 41.

132. Central Zionist Archives, J-17/6006, school brochure, summer of 1938. The school was founded by eight teachers as a limited-liability company. See also the report of the general inspector of education dated 17 April 1938 and the report of the beginning of the 1938–39 school year, the school's second year.

133. Central Zionist Archives, J-17/4389, letter of the principal to the Central Educational Administration, 21 August 1939.

134. Central Zionist Archives, J-17/3274, report to the director of the Department of Education of the Va'ad Le'umi.

135. Central Zionist Archives, J-17/3562, report on the school year 1939–40, and letter of 11 March 1941.

136. Central Zionist Archives, J-17/3395, report on the school year 1939–40.

137. Central Zionist Archives, J-17/3274, report on the school year 1944–45.

138. Central Zionist Archives, J-17/3562, report on the school year 1943–44.

139. Central Zionist Archives, J-17/3399, report on the school year 1944–45.

140. Ibid.

141. Central Zionist Archives, J-17/3562, report on the school year 1942–43, and J-17/3274, report on the school year 1943–44. These statistics vary from one report to another, sometimes markedly. Thus, the report for the school year 1942–43 claims that only 5 percent of the students in the ninth through twelfth grades paid the full fee and that 90 percent of the 374 students were given a discount.

142. Central Zionist Archives, J-17/190, budget for 1936–37.

143. Central Zionist Archives, J-17/3274 and J-17/3562, yearly reports.

144. Central Zionist Archives, J-17/3274, yearly reports.

145. Labor Movement Archives, IV-406/5, meeting of the representatives of the Mapai students, 27 February 1932, pp. 4–6.

146. Beit Berl Archives, 23/37, Mapai Central Committee, 6 October 1937, pp. 18–19.

147. Ibid., p. 19.

148. Beit Berl Archives, 23/37, Mapai Central Committee, Remez's speech, 8 December 1937, p. 12; Aranne's speech, 29 September 1937, p. 13.

Chapter Six

1. Beit Berl Archives, 23/37, "Meeting of the Representatives of Mapai and of the Executive Committee of Kibbutz Artzi–Hashomer Hatza'ir to Discuss Unification," 31 March 1937, p. 13.

2. Ibid., 23/34, Central Committee, 14 February 1934.

3. Ibid., minutes of the Rehovot convention, 10th session (continuation), 7 May 1938, p. 3.

4. Katznelson, *Writings*, 8:246. See also Labor Movement Archives, IV-406-94, Mapai file, and Berl Lokker's statement on Spain and China (fourth convention).

5. Minutes of the Rehovot convention, 5th session, 5 May 1938, p. 13.

6. Ibid., 11th session, 8 May 1938, p. 9, and the Sunday afternoon session, 9 May 1939, p. 1.

7. Ibid., 13th session, 8 May 1938, p. 3.

8. Ibid., 10th session (continuation), 7 May 1938, pp. 11 and 7; the pagination is not in sequence.

9. Ibid., 4th session, Wednesday evening, 4 May 1938, p. 4.

10. Ibid., 10th session, 7 May 1938, p. 3.

11. Ibid., 4th session, Wednesday evening, 4 May 1938, p. 4.

12. Ibid., 7th session, 5 May 1938, p. 1 (pts. 1 and 2).

13. Beit Berl Archives, 23/31, Central Committee, 18–19 December 1931.

14. Ibid., minutes of the second session of the second Mapai convention, 3 December 1932, p. 32.

15. Ibid., 23/37, Central Committee, 29 September 1937, p. 32.

16. Ibid., 23/37, 6 October 1937, p. 13. See also the minutes of the meetings of the Central Committee on 29 September 1937, 17 November 1937, and 25 October 1939.

17. Ibid., 29 September 1937.

18. Ibid., 6 October 1937, p. 11.

19. Ibid., 29/31, Central Committee, 18–19 December 1931.

20. Ibid., 23/37, Central Committee, 6 October 1937, p. 14; and Labor Movement Archives, IV-207-34, report on the thirty-fifth Histadrut council, pp. 84–87.

21. Beit Berl Archives, 23/51, Central Committee, 3 March 1951, p. 3.

22. Ibid., 23/37, Central Committee, 6 October 1937, pp. 3, 7, 11, 13; 29 September 1937, pp. 12, 21; 8 November 1937, pp. 2, 9.

23. Ibid., 23/31, Central Committee, 18–19 December 1931.

24. Minutes of the Rehovot convention, 7th session, 5 May 1938, p. 3.

25. Ibid., 10th session, 7 May 1938, p. 3 (pt. 2).

26. Beit Berl Archives, 23/39, Central Committee, 22 November 1929, pp. 46–47; see also Yosef Bankover's statement on 6 October 1937: "We have lost the habit of holding elections for our institutions. We no longer have elections for the Central Committee; we no longer have elections for the Executive Committee" (p. 6).

27. See the statements of Tabenkin, Reptor, and Shorer, in ibid., 23/37, 17 November 1937, pp. 4–5.

28. Ibid., 23/38, statements of Yitzhak Ben-Aharon, Mordechai Namir, and Akiva Globman, secretary of the office workers' union, to the Central Committee, 15 December 1938, pp. 26–27, 38, 39.

29. Ibid., 23/37, "Meeting of the Representatives of Mapai and of the Executive Committee of Kibbutz Artzi–Hashomer Hatza'ir to Discuss Unification," 31 March 1937, p. 14.

30. Labor Movement Archives, IV-207-34, 19 March 1936, p. 25.

31. Beit Berl Archives, 23/37, "Meeting of the Representatives," 31 March 1937, pp. 3, 10–18.

32. Ibid., Central Committee. See minutes of the (major) meetings of the Central Committee on 26 September 1937, 6 October 1937, and 8 November 1937.

33. Ibid., Central Committee, 6 October 1937, pp. 15, 11–12. See also file 23/39, Central Committee, 26 October 1939, p. 44, the statements following the occupation of the premises of the Executive Committee, which led to the trial of July 1940; file 23/37, meetings of the Central Committee on 29 September 1937 and 8 November 1937; and file 23/38, 15 December 1938.

34. Ibid., "Meeting of the Representatives."

35. Ibid., 23/37, Central Committee, 29 September 1937, pp. 12, 14.

36. Ibid., Central Committee, 5 and 6 February 1937, p. 24.

37. Ibid., Central Committee, 6 October 1937, p. 16.

38. Ibid., 29 September 1937, p. 33.

39. Ibid., p. 30.

40. Ibid., 23/38, Central Committee, 15 October 1938, p. 27. This text is quoted in Meir Avizohar, *In a Broken Mirror: Social and National Ideals as Reflected in Mapai* (in Hebrew) (Tel Aviv: Am Oved, 1990), p. 17.

41. Ibid., p. 317.

42. Beit Berl Archives, Central Committee, internal disciplinary tribunal, minutes of the trial, file no. 1 (1940).

43. Avizohar, *In a Broken Mirror*, p. 315.

44. Beit Berl Archives, 23/39, Central Committee, 22 November 1939, p. 43.

45. Ibid. The quotation marks are in the original text. These criticisms were made during the stormy meeting of the Central Committee with members of the Tel Aviv branch of Mapai on 25 October 1939. Following this public meeting, another meeting was held in private. There were no reports on this second meeting. Both meetings were presided over by Sprinzak. He also presided over the meeting of the Central Committee on 22 November 1939, following Golda Meir's resignation. Sprinzak never answered Reptor's question.

46. Ibid., pp. 42–44.

47. Ibid., 23/38, Central Committee, 27 July 1938, pp. 4–5, 8, 10.

48. See, for example, Labor Movement Archives, IV-207, file 26–29, twenty-sixth

Histadrut Council, October 1931, p. 25; and Beit Berl Archives, 23/38, Central Committee, 15 October 1938, p. 37.

49. Beit Berl Archives, 23/39, Central Committee, 25 October 1939.

50. Ibid., 23/39, Central Committee, 22 November 1939, p. 48.

51. Ibid., 23/39, 25 October 1939, p. 3.

52. Ibid., 23/37, 23/38, and 23/39; see the minutes of the meetings of the Central Committee of 3 February 1937, 29 September 1937, 25 October 1937, 27 July 1938, 25 October, and 22 November 1939. Ada Fishman spoke of "hatred among brothers," which is a fair description of the atmosphere of anger and disillusionment in the party in the two years before the Second World War (22 November 1939, pp. 47–48).

53. Ibid., 23/39, Central Committee, 25 October 1939, p. 15 (Dov Ben-Yeruham).

54. Ibid., Central Committee, internal disciplinary tribunal, file 1, pp. 3–5. On Sollel Boneh, see pp. 31–33, 45–52.

55. Ibid., 23/39, Central Committee, 22 May 1939, pp. 42 ff., 37 (Golda Meir's statement).

56. Ibid., 25 October 1939, p. 6.

57. Ibid., p. 20.

58. Ibid., p. 17.

59. Ibid., Central Committee, internal disciplinary tribunal, file 1.

60. Ibid. Pinhas Tuvin quoted the statements Aranne made on the previous day.

61. Labor Movement Archives, IV-406-9-A, Central Committee, 20 December 1934, p. 6.

62. Beit Berl Archives, 23/37, Central Committee, 7 November 1937, p. 6; see also the meetings of 8 and 17 November 1937.

63. Ibid., 6 October 1937, pp. 1–3, 6 (Bankover). On Faction B, see Yaël Ishai, *The Factions in the Labor Movement: Faction B in Mapai* (in Hebrew) (Tel Aviv: Am Oved, 1978).

64. See especially the meetings of the Central Committee of 29 September and 6 October 1937, 15 December 1938, and 25 October and 22 November 1939.

65. Ibid., 23/37, Central Committee, 20 February 1937 (unpaginated).

66. Ibid., 23/37, Central Committee, 29 September 1937, pp. 15–24, 34.

67. Ibid., 23/39, Central Committee, 25 October 1939, p. 10.

68. Ibid. (Aaron Ziesling), p. 46.

69. See, for example, ibid., p. 36, the statement of Feibel Kantor, a leader of the electric company's workers, against Zeev Feinstein and Yosef Kitzis, two leaders of the Tel Aviv branch of Mapai who were among the chief figures of the workers' council in the same city. At the end of the 1930s Feinstein and Kitzis were most strongly criticized by the unemployed.

70. Ibid., statement of Beba Idelson to the Mapai Central Committee, 22 November 1939, pp. 45–46.

71. Labor Movement Archives, IV-207, files 26–29, statement of David Ben-Gurion, Histadrut Council, March 1931, p. 18.

72. Ibid., file 21, statement of Moshe Beilinson, Histadrut Council, March 1931, p. 53.

73. Shmuel Yavnieli, in ibid., Histadrut Council, October 1931, p. 78.

74. Yitzhak Tabenkin, in ibid., p. 82.

75. Meir Ya'ari, in ibid., pp. 32–33.

76. Zvi Sussman, *Inequality and Equality*, pp. 7–9.

77. On Arab labor and the struggle against it, see Anita Shapira, *The Lost Battle: Jewish Labor, 1929–1939* (in Hebrew) (Tel Aviv: Tel Aviv University Press and Hakibbutz Hame'uhad Publications, 1976).

78. Sussman, *Inequality and Equality*, pp. 10, 34–36, 43, 48, 51–52.

79. Ibid., pp. 13–25.

80. Arie Nitzan, *The Standard of Living in Eretz Israel in the Last Twenty Years* (in Hebrew) (Jerusalem: Central Office of Statistics, 1952), pt. 2.

81. Sussman, *Inequality and Equality*, pp. 27–29.

82. Shmuel Noah Eisenstadt, *Hahevra Ha'israelit, Reka, Hitpathut Vebai'ot* (Jerusalem: Magnes Press, 1967), p. 40. This was the Hebrew translation of *The Israeli Society* (London: Weidenfeld and Nicholson, 1967). In his latest book on Israeli society, *Hahevra Ha'israelit Betmuroteha* (Jerusalem: Magnes Press, 1989), originally published in English as *The Transformation of Israeli Society: An Essay in Interpretation* (London: Weidenfeld and Nicholson, 1985), Eisenstadt modified this statement and wrote that this state of affairs existed only in the formative years of the Histadrut. But even in this revised, expanded, and corrected edition, Eisenstadt still writes: "In the beginning, salaries were based on the size of family and partly on seniority, but not on position" (p. 147). This emendation hardly corrects his original generalization. The reality was far from the situation described even in this second version.

83. Sussman, *Inequality and Equality*, pp. 59–64, 69.

84. Labor Movement Archives, library, report of the Executive Committee to the third Histadrut convention, p. 358.

85. Ibid., IV-207, 22–28 December 1923, pp. 133–34. The same formula is used in the report of the Executive Committee to the third convention (p. 358).

86. Ibid., p. 359.

87. Ibid., IV-208-1-81, letter dated 13 June 1923. This file contains mostly documents relating to the Education Committee, but there are also reports submitted to the Wages Committee.

88. Ibid. See the letters and reports dated 6 June 1923 (Executive Committee) and 11 June 1923 (Education Committee). See also the other reports in this file. Some are undated, but all are probably from the same month.

89. Ibid., minutes of the work of the committee, undated.

90. Ibid., library, report of the Executive Committee to the third Histadrut convention, pp. 359–60.

91. Ibid., IV-229-1.

92. Ibid., library, report of the Executive Committee to the third Histadrut convention, pp. 361–63. The five people who signed the document published by *Davar* as well as the Executive Committee's report were Ada Fishman, Meir Ya'ari, Hillel Cohen, Rosa Cohen, and Moshe Beilinson. Rosa Cohen was Yitzhak Rabin's mother.

93. Ibid., p. 362.

94. Ibid., pp. 362–63.

95. Ibid., IV-207, file 26–29, 4–8 October 1931, pp. 17–23.

96. Teveth, *David's Passion*, 2:342–43, 357–59. According to a questionnaire submitted to the employees and journalists of *Davar* in 1932, David Zakkai (who, like the others, was a veteran of the Second Aliyah), Berl Katznelson, and Zalman Rubashov paid rents of 3.50 and 4 pounds a month for two-bedroom apartments (in the Ameri-

can sense of the term). All these men had families. In the Tel Aviv of the late 1920s and early 1930s, one could be decently housed for 3 or 4 pounds (Labor Movement Archives, IV-228, file 61-B).

97. Labor Movement Archives, library, report of the Executive Committee to the third Histadrut convention, p. 363.

98. Teveth, *David's Passion*, 2:354.

99. Yosef Aharonowitz, "Concerning E. Yaffe's Article" (in Hebrew), *Davar*, 10 January 1926, p. 2.

100. Report of the Wages Committee to the secretariat of the Executive Committee, 23 May 1927. This report gave a very detailed picture of the financial situation. See the report of the Executive Committee to the third Histadrut convention, p. 362. See also Teveth, *David's Passion*, 2:360–61.

101. Labor Movement Archives, IV-229-1.

102. Teveth, *David's Passion*, 2:362.

103. In an article entitled "Salaries in the Histadrut in Fluctuating Economic Conditions: The Family Wage and the Economic Situation, 1924–1937" (in Hebrew) (photocopy, Hebrew University of Jerusalem), Yitzhak Grinberg sought to demonstrate that the fate of the family wage was a perfect illustration of the process that the Yishuv economy was undergoing (p. 10).

104. Arlosoroff, "Questions of the Day," *Hapo'el Hatza'ir*, no. 35 (26 June 1927).

105. Labor Movement Archives, IV-207, twenty-fourth Histadrut Council, 24–25 May 1930.

106. Ibid., IV-228, file 57B, and IV-229, file 6.

107. Ibid., files 21, 57A, and 57B.

108. Ibid., files 57A and 65. On Marminsky, see IV-229-1, letter dated 4 May 1927.

109. Ibid., file 57A.

110. Ibid., file 10.

111. Ibid., file 57B, and IV-229, file 6. The final memorandums date from January 1931.

112. Ibid., IV-207, file 25, minutes of the Histadrut Council of March 1931, p. 41.

113. Ibid., p. 51.

114. Ibid., p. 45.

115. Ibid., p. 49.

116. Ibid., p. 44.

117. Ibid., file 40, Histadrut Council of 24 December 1939, p. 95.

118. Ibid., file 25, March 1931, pp. 44–45.

119. Ibid., pp. 48, 51–52. See also p. 43.

120. Ibid., p. 65.

121. Ibid., p. 54.

122. Ibid., IV-208, files 287A and 287B. See also IV-222, files 45, 223, and 532. In the summer of 1932 a committee to study the operation of Tnuva, the Histadrut dairy cooperative, was appointed; Kaplan, Guri, and Namir were members of this committee. See ibid., IV-208-1-181, file 22. On Tnuva-Haifa and Tnuva-Export, see IV-228, file 494; on Tnuva–Tel Aviv, see IV-228, file 233; and on Tnuva-Jerusalem, see IV-228, files 57A and 45A. The findings of the Tnuva Committee, spread out among all these files, may be compared with the data in IV-229, files 6 and 57B.

123. Ibid., IV-207, file 35, March 1931.

124. Ibid., pp. 46, 54.

125. Moshe Beilinson, "Again the Grievous Evil" (in Hebrew), *Davar*, 1 September 1925, p. 2.The title is from Ecclesiastes 5:16: "And this also is a grievous evil, that in all points as he came, so shall he go; and what profit hath he that laboureth for the wind?"

126. Berl Katznelson, Histadrut Council of 22–28 December 1923, p. 48.

127. Labor Movement Archives IV-207, file 25, Histadrut Council, March 1931, pp. 57–59, 62–66.

128. Ibid., pp. 55–56.

129. Ibid., pp. 60–61.

130. Ibid., pp. 49, 55–56, 63.

131. Labor Movement Archives, IV-229, file 11. See also 215-IV-1495.

132. Ibid., IV-229, file 15; IV-228, file 36; IV-228, file 65 (Executive Committee); and finally IV-228, file 219 (*Davar*). See also 214-IV-1495. According to the agreement on the wage scale for Histadrut employees adopted at the fourth convention, the director of each institution was personally responsible for payment of the family wage as stipulated in the regulations. The directors were to be held "personally accountable to the Central Control Committee if a salary was fixed without its express permission or contrary to its decisions." The wage levels specified in the regulations adopted simultaneously with the agreement were:

Basic salary: 7.5 pounds a month.

Maximum salary (without seniority supplement): 17.50 pounds a month.

Salaries of doctors and engineers: 30 pounds a month.

133. See Nachum Gross and Jacob Metzer, *Palestine in World War II: Some Economic Aspects*, Research Paper no. 207 (Jerusalem: The Maurice Falk Institute for Economic Research in Israel, 1993), p. 62.

134. Labor Movement Archives, 23/37. The figure of 60 percent was provided by Aranne at the meeting of the Central Committee on September 29 1939, p. 14. It had already been given by I. Brumberg of Hadera at a meeting of the Central Committee on 6 October 1937. It was again Brumberg who gave the figure of 70 percent for the number of employees whose salaries did not exceed 12 pounds a month.

135. Nehemia Rabin, at a meeting of the Mapai Central Committee on 25 October 1939, p. 18. Rabin was a member of the Kupat Holim Control Committee.

136. Labor Movement Archives, IV-207, Histadrut Council, file 40, pp. 90, 114.

137. Ibid., file 26/29, 4–8 October 1931, pp. 10–11.

138. Ibid., IV-207, file 35, minutes of the meeting of the thirty-fifth Histadrut Council, 7–10 February 1937.

139. Ibid., p. 90. See also the statements of Israel Guri, who was in charge of the mas ahid, p. 86.

140. Ibid., file 40, 24 December 1930, pp. 90–91.

141. Beit Berl Archives, 23/37, meeting of the Mapai Central Committee, 8 November 1937, p. 9. The leaders of the movement had adopted the habit of staying abroad for long periods and found the time to rest in spas. In his article "Ben-Gurion, Secretary of the Histadrut," which appeared in the collective work *Portrait of a Leader of the Labor Movement*, Teveth relates that in 1921 (already!) Sprinzak com-

plained that in the summer of that year "the Executive Committee of the Histadrut did not meet for two months because its members, who were away attending the Zionist Congress [in Carlsbad, Czechoslovakia], had stayed abroad long after the congress was over" (p. 40). It was Teveth again who related that between the end of his election campaign among the Zionist organizations in Poland and the opening of the eighteenth Zionist Congress (held in Prague between 21 August and 4 September 1933), Ben-Gurion took an eighteen-day holiday in the Austrian Alps (*David's Passion*, 3:55). Workers in Tel Aviv never enjoyed the privileges that the leaders of the movement, who never stopped preaching frugality and austere living to their followers, used and frequently abused.

142. Beit Berl Archives, 23/37, meeting of the Mapai Central Committee, 29 September 1937, pp. 29–33 (see the sharp exchange of words between Remez and Bendori, a Tel Aviv activist).

143. Ibid., meeting of the Central Committee, 25 October 1939.

144. Ibid., meeting of the Central Committee, 25 September 1937, p. 3 (Ben-Aharon); see also the statements of B. Reptor and Bendori, pp. 17, 20, 29. Some of Reptor's and Bendori's phrases closely resemble Ben-Aharon's statements.

145. Ibid., p. 13.

146. Ibid., meeting of the Mapai Central Committee, 6 October 1937, p. 11 (Brumberg of Hadera) and p. 23 (Minkowski of Kfar Saba).

147. Ibid., meeting of the Central Committee, 29 September 1939, p. 14.

148. Ibid., meeting of the Central Committee, 6 September 1937, p. 9.

149. Ibid., meeting of the Central Committee, 25 October 1939, p. 21 (Remez) and p. 14 (Ben-Yeruham).

150. Ibid., 23/38, meeting of the Mapai Central Committee, 15 October 1938, pp. 27, 29 (Ben-Aharon).

151. Ibid., 23/39, 25 October 1939, pp. 10, 13, 16, 25, 47, 49.

152. Ibid., pp. 15–16.

153. Ibid., pp. 18–19, 34–35, 50–51.

154. Ibid., p. 51 (Kushnir).

155. Ibid., p. 30; and Labor Movement Archives, file 39 (no other details are given), meeting of the Histadrut Executive Committee, 11 September 1939, p. 53, and file 35, meeting of the Executive Committee, 29 October 1938. The files of the Tel Aviv workers' council are full of letters of supplication and pleas for assistance. The unemployed were chiefly unskilled workers. Among them were long-established immigrants who had arrived at the time of the Second Aliyah, and also some very recent immigrants. There were men whose health had been ruined by many years of backbreaking work (some had tuberculosis), and men who had sold their furniture and could no longer feed their children. Some related their heroic past (road construction, draining marshes, building and enlarging the port of Tel Aviv), and others gave a description—often understated but always heartbreaking—of their families' hunger. See Labor Movement Archives, IV-250, files 408, 358, 360, 250, 454.

156. Ibid., IV-207, file 40, Histadrut Council, 24 December 1939, p. 20.

157. Ibid., p. 16.

158. Ibid., file 39 (no other details are given), meeting of the Histadrut Executive Committee, 21 September 1939, pp. 3–4.

159. Ibid., pp. 4–6.

160. Ibid., IV-207, file 4, 24 December 1939, pp. 11–12, 101.

161. On the various proposals for achieving solidarity, see Beit Berl Archives, 23/39, meeting of the Central Committee, 25 October 1939, pp. 9, 25–27, 32–33, 48–51.

162. Labor Movement Archives, IV-207, file 4, 24 December 1939, pp. 48–49, 68–69.

163. Ibid., p. 74.

164. Ibid., p. 90.

Epilogue

1. In theory the War of Independence was a confrontation between David and Goliath, but in fact the war's results can be explained only by the relative superiority of the Yishuv on the battlefield from the summer of 1948 onward. Hence the victory over Egypt between October 1948 and January 1949, which brought the war to an end. These facts, in their broad outlines, are not entirely unknown. A detailed and accurate account has been given in a recent work—Amitzur Ilan, *Embargo, Power, and Decision in the 1948 War* (in Hebrew) (Tel Aviv: Ma'arachot, 1995)—based on Israeli and foreign archival material and published by the Ministry of Defense.

2. On 2 December 1948 the Supreme Court issued the following ruling: "The Declaration [of Independence] only establishes the fact of the creation of the state in view of its recognition in international law. It represents the will of the people and its profession of faith, but it can in no way be regarded as a constitutional rule by which the constitutionality of laws and decrees can be measured." See Piskei Din (Judgements, High Court), vol. 1, 1948–49, p. 89. On these issues see Menachem Hofnung, *Democracy, Law, and National Security* (Aldershot, England: Dartmouth, 1996).

3. On Israeli politics, see in particular Peter Medding, *The Founding of Israeli Democracy, 1948–1967* (Oxford: Oxford University Press, 1990); Alan (Asher) Arian, *Politics in Israel* (London: Chatham House, 1989); Avner Yaniv, *National Security and Democracy in Israel* (Boulder, Colo.: Lynne Reiner, 1993); Shimon Shetreet, *Justice in Israel: A Study of the Israeli Judiciary* (Dordrecht: Martinus Nijhoff, 1994); Martin Edelman, *Courts, Politics, and Culture in Israel* (Charlottesville: University of Virginia Press, 1994); Ehud Sprinzak and Larry Diamond, *Israeli Democracy under Stress* (Boulder, Colo.: Lynne Reinner, 1993); Myron J. Aronoff, *Israeli Visions and Divisions: Cultural Change and Political Conflict* (New Brunswick, N.J.: Transaction Books, 1989); Yehoshafat Harkabi, *Israel's Fateful Hour* (New York: Harper and Row, 1988); Yitzhak Galnoor, *Steering the Polity: Communication and Politics in Israel* (Beverly Hills: Sage, 1982); Baruch Kimmerling, *The Israeli State and Society: Boundaries and Frontiers* (New York: SUNY Press, 1989); Jacob L. Landau, *The Arab Minority in Israel, 1967–1991* (Oxford: Oxford University Press, 1993); Zeev Schiff, *Intifada: The Palestinians' Uprising—Israel's Third Front* (New York: Simon and Schuster, 1990); Avraham Diskin, *Elections and Voters in Israel* (New York: Praeger, 1991). Since 1972 Alan (Asher) Arian publishes, two or three years after each general election, a collective volume, *The Elections in Israel* (by various publishers), a goldmine of useful information and analysis.

4. Anita Shapira, *Berl*, 2:732.

5. Beit Berl Archives, 23/49, meeting of the Mapai Central Committee, 4 August 1949, p. 2.

6. Beit Berl Archives, 23/51, meeting of the Mapai Central Committee, 3 March 1951, p. 79 (4).

7. Nathan Rotenstreich, "Capitalism and Socialism," in *Back to Basics* (in Hebrew), vol. 2 (Tel Aviv: Kadima, 1963), p. 13.

8. Philip Klein, "Proposals on Programme and Administration of Social Welfare in Israel," Report no. TAO/ISR/29 (New York: United Nations Commissioner for Technical Assistance, 3 January 1961), pp. 5–8. This report, which was deliberately neglected—Klein has been accused of hostility to Israel if not of outright anti-Semitism—is in the possession of Avraham Doron of the Hebrew University. I am indebted to Shoshana Merom, who is writing a master's thesis under Professor Doron, for giving me the Klein report. The study of these questions has only just begun.

9. See Nachum T. Gross, "The Economic Regime during Israel's First Decade," Research Paper 208 (Jerusalem: The Maurice Falk Institute for Economic Research in Israel, 1995).

10. Even the most tolerant works acknowledge that the Yishuv (that is, Ben-Gurion) refused to change its order of priorities; see the exhaustive and very apologetic article by Shabtai Teveth, "The Black Hole" (in Hebrew), *Alpayim* 10 (1994): 111–95. Despite his feud with Tom Segev, author of the harshest attack ever made on Ben-Gurion's behavior during the Holocaust (*The Seventh Million: The Israelis and the Holocaust* [New York: Hill and Wang, 1993]), Teveth was forced to recognize indirectly that Ben-Gurion refused to change the Yishuv's priorities when it became clear that the concentration camps were more than concentration camps. In this connection Teveth, following a brief account of the context, quotes Ben-Gurion from the minutes of a meeting of the Mapai Central Committee in August 1943:

> Some people suggested that the administration of the Jewish Agency should cease all activity in Eretz Israel and should devote all its budgets, including those of the Keren Hakayemet and Keren Hayesod [Jewish National Funds for the acquisition of land and colonization], to rescue actions. To which Ben-Gurion replied, "The administration of the Jewish Agency can use this money only for the purposes for which it has been collected, and it acts on the orders and according to the decisions of the Zionist Congress."

Teveth quotes Ben-Gurion again:

> We all know very well that the administration of the Jewish Agency does not have any general authority over the Jewish people, and it therefore cannot put its hands in its pockets [the Jewish people's] whenever it wants to and in any way it wants. It also has no authority to decide on all questions concerning the [Jewish] people. Unfortunately, there is no organism or general organization of this type. There is the American Jewish Congress, there is the JOINT [American Jewish Joint Distribution Committee] and other organizations. But . . . the Jewish Agency . . . is a general organization of the Jewish people only where the reconstruction of Eretz Israel is concerned. I do not wish to say whether it is more important to build Eretz Israel or to save a Jew in Zagreb. It is possible that in certain situations it is more important to save a child in Zagreb. What should be well understood is that they are two different things.

Was Ben-Gurion right or was he in error in trying to persuade the Yishuv that it should concern itself only with its own affairs? There are different opinions on this matter.

Other questions arise concerning the impotence of the Jewish Agency during the Holocaust years. On reading Teveth's long article, one cannot help being amazed at the passivity of Yishuv leaders; they never protested against the silence of the international press on the Jews' fate in the occupied countries before the extermination began, and especially once it had begun. Teveth is silent about this aspect of the behavior of Yishuv leaders, and when he does say something, it is only in two or three sentences. In light of the fact that the international press ignored Ben-Gurion's address to the Elected Assembly (Asefat Hanivharim) on 30 of November 1944—declared a day of strikes, fasting, and penitence—why did the leadership of the Yishuv not attempt less conventional, tame forms of action? Paid advertisements, for instance. The United States, unlike Palestine, was not under a regime of censorship. Why did they not publish a "black book"? It was a common procedure. The Zionist leadership displayed an exaggerated cautiousness, to say the least, far beyond what was usual in international relations at that period. It seems that in this case Zionist leaders feared the reactions of the allied governments. Teveth is convinced that "Ben-Gurion did all he could where rescue was concerned. If his activities had had the slightest chance of success, he would have devoted most of his efforts to them. To be convinced of this, one need only point to all he did in the last three months of 1942 and the first three months of 1943, a period in which he had not yet lost all hope of a massive rescue operation" (p. 34 of the aforementioned article). What, in fact, were Ben-Gurion's actions during those six months? Teveth relates the following.

1. He made the address to the Asefat Hanivharim of the Yishuv.

2. He sent a telegram to Justice Felix Frankfurter of the Supreme Court of the United States (an important figure in American Jewry at that period), asking him to get American-Jewish public opinion to intervene with President Roosevelt, so that he in turn would intervene with Churchill to open Eretz Israel to Jewish children rescued from the Nazis.

3. He sent directives to Nahum Goldmann, the representative of the Jewish Agency in New York, and to Berl Lokker, its representative in London, asking them to approach Roosevelt and Churchill.

4. He approached the representative of the Polish government in exile in Jerusalem, asking him also to intervene with the British authorities to allow the repatriation of children. (pp. 124–25 of the same article)

"All" this activity does not seem extraordinary for a leader in normal times. It hardly seems commensurate with the problems one was dealing with.

In recent years the question of the Yishuv in the Shoa has become a topic of much scholarly attention. See, in particular, Dina Porath, *Leaders in a Dilemma: The Yishuv and the Shoa, 1942–1945* (in Hebrew) (Tel Aviv: Am Oved, 1986), translated into English as *The Blue and Yellow Stars of David: The Zionist Leadership in Palestine and the Holocaust, 1939–1945* (Cambridge: Harvard University Press, 1990); Yehiam Weitz, *Awareness and Incapacity: Mapai and the Shoa, 1943–1945* (in Hebrew) (Jerusalem: Yad Yitzhak Ben-Zvi, 1993); Hava Eshkoli-Wegman, *Silence: Mapai and the Shoa, 1939–1945* (in Hebrew) (Jerusalem: Yad Yitzhak Ben-Zvi, 1993);

Tuvia Freiling, "David Ben-Gurion and the Shoa of the Jews of Europe, 1939–1945" (in Hebrew), 2 vols. (Ph.D. diss., Hebrew University of Jerusalem, 1990); see also, most recently, Idit Zartal, *Zehavam shel Hayehudim: Hahagira Hayehudit Hamachtartit LeEretz Israel, 1945–1948* (From catastrophe to power: Jewish illegal immigration to Palestine, 1945–1948) (Tel Aviv: Am Oved, 1996).

11. There are many examples of this phenomenon. On 3 January 1951 the censor, at that time attached to the Ministry of the Interior, forbade theatrical troupes, singers, and other entertainers to perform in Yiddish. Only foreign troupes or actors on tour in the country were allowed to use Yiddish. Copies of the letter containing this prohibition were sent to the criminal department of the police in Tel Aviv as well as to the police headquarters (Archives of the Ministry of Culture). I am indebted to Shulamit Aloni, former minister of culture, for giving me a copy of this document.

12. Reuven Pedatzur, *The Triumph of Embarrassment: Israel and the Territories after the Six-Day War* (in Hebrew) (Tel Aviv: Bitan, 1996), p. 229.

13. Ibid., p. 230. Pedatzur is quoting Teveth, *Klalat Habracha* (The curse of the blessing) (Tel Aviv: Schocken Books, 1970), p. 230.

14. Ibid., p. 232.

15. Ibid., p. 233.

16. *Ha'aretz*, 10 August 1967, quoted in Yonathan Shapiro, *Politicians as an Hegemonic Class: The Case of Israel* (in Hebrew) (Tel Aviv: Sifriat Hapo'alim, 1996), p. 112.

17. Shabtai Teveth, *Moshe Dayan* (in Hebrew) (Tel Aviv: Schocken Books, 1971), p. 585.

18. Ibid.

Aliyah

Literally, "ascent'; *aliyah* means a return to Eretz Israel (or Jewish emigration). The act of returning was believed to be a spiritual elevation as well as a physical ascent. *Aliyah* refers to the return of both an individual and an organized group. The first great return ended the exile in Babylon. Mass immigration was renewed in 1882, with the aliyah of the Biluim (*Bilu* is an acronym of *Beit Ya'akov lechu ve nelcha*: "O house of Jacob, come ye, and let us go" (Isaiah 2:5). The practice of numbering the "waves" of immigration was introduced by the immigrants of the Second Aliyah in order to distinguish themselves from their predecessors and successors. The numbering usually ends at five, with the outbreak of the Second World War. Subsequent waves were described either in reference to their sociological and geographical composition (the Children's Aliyah, the Aliyah from the Arab Countries, and so on) or in reference to their status (clandestine immigration, also known as Aliyah Bet, and so on). The following dates are approximate and are intended to serve only as a guide.

First Aliyah, 1882–1902; Second Aliyah, 1904–14; Third Aliyah, 1919–23; Fourth Aliyah, 1924–28; and Fifth Aliyah, 1932–39.

Asefat Hanivharim

Literally, the "assembly of the elected"; the so-called parliament of the Yishuv during the British mandate. Representatives were elected by universal suffrage according to a system of proportional representation. A ballot was supposed to take place once every four years, but because of dissensions in the Yishuv, there were only four between 1920 and 1944 (in 1920, 1925, 1931, and 1944). The first assembly described itself as "the supreme institution for the regulation of the national public life of the Jewish people in Eretz Israel and its sole representative for internal and external affairs." The Asefat Hanivharim met at very irregular intervals for sessions lasting one to four days. The first assembly consisted of only two sessions, and the third of eighteen. The assembly elected in 1944 had its last working session in 1948, a short time before the state parliament (called the Knesset) held its first session (in February 1949). See *Knesset Israel* and *Va'ad Le'umi*.

Biluim

See *Aliyah*.

Brit Shalom

The "Alliance for Peace"; a Jewish organization for rapprochement between Jews and Arabs, founded in 1926.

Eretz Israel

Literally, the "land of Israel"—the land of the people of Israel. The term first appears in 1 Sam. 13:9, meaning "the land where the Israelites dwell."

Eretz Israel should not be confused with the kingdom of Israel, or the northern kingdom, founded by Jeroboam I (933–911 B.C.). The frontiers of the land of Israel changed a great deal over the centuries, from those promised to Abraham (which extended from the "river of Egypt"—the Wadi El-Arish in northern Sinai—to the "great river," the Euphrates, in the northeast) to those included in mandatory Palestine in 1922, comprising a much smaller territory than the one claimed by the Zionists at the Paris Peace Conference of 1919. When Zionists spoke of Eretz Israel at the beginning of the twentieth century, they were alluding to areas included in the map of 1919.

The Scriptures use a number of terms to describe the country: "the Holy Land," the "land of beauty," "the desirable land," "the land of the Hebrews," and so on. The Romans named it Palestine after the Bar Kokhba revolt in 135 A.D.

Galut, or Gola

"Exile." This term led to the adjective *galutic* (exilic). The terms *galut*, *gola*, and *diaspora* can be used interchangeably. In modern Hebrew the adjective *galutic* generally has a pejorative connotation.

Goy

"Foreigner," "gentile" or non-Jew, "nation." Plural, *goyim*.

Hagana

Literally, "defense." The Hagana was a defense organization founded by Ahdut Ha'avoda at its convention on 12 June 1920. It was linked to the Histadrut, which financed it. Membership was voluntary and open to all, regardless of political affiliation. This body replaced Hashomer, which previously had more or less the same functions. The Hagana was always regarded with suspicion by the mandatory government, which explains its semiclandestine character. In the Second World War, however, the British army collaborated with it in organizing assault patrols (see *Palmah*). Before the War of Independence, the Hagana succeeded in training twenty thousand men and women. When the state was founded, the Hagana became Tzahal (the Israel Defense Force).

Hano'ar Ha'oved

"Working Youth"; a pioneering youth movement founded by the Histadrut in 1924. It was run by Ahdut Ha'avoda and Hapo'el Hatza'ir and, after the fusion of the two parties in 1930, by Mapai.

Hashomer

"The Guard"; an organization of Jewish guards formed before the First World War. See *Hagana*.

Hashomer Hatza'ir

"The Young Guard"; a socialist-Zionist pioneering youth movement founded in Vienna in 1916. It became a political party in 1946 and took part in the formation of Mapam (the United Workers' Party) in 1948.

Jewish Agency

The mandate given to Great Britain by the League of Nations in 1920 provided for the establishment of a Jewish agency that would represent the Jewish people before the mandatory government. Article 4 of the text of the mandate (adopted in 1922) gave the World Zionist Organization the status of a Jewish agency and stated that

> an appropriate Jewish agency shall be recognized as a public body for the purpose of advising and cooperating with the Administration of Palestine in such economic, social and other matters as may affect the establishment of the Jewish national home and the interests of the Jewish population in Palestine, and, subject always to the control of the Administration, to assist and take part in the development of the country.
>
> The Zionist Organization, so long as its organization and constitution are in the opinion of the Mandatory appropriate, shall be recognized as such agency. It shall take steps in consultation with His Britannic Majesty's Government to secure the cooperation of all Jews who are willing to assist in the establishment of the Jewish national home.

The initial meeting of this enlarged Jewish Agency took place in Zurich in 1929. Fifty percent of the delegates to this assembly were representatives of the World Zionist Organization, and the rest represented non-Zionist organizations. There were delegates from twenty-six countries. Chaim Weizmann, the first president of the Jewish Agency and president of the World Zionist Organization, became the first president of the state of Israel.

Jewish Battalions, or the Jewish Legion

Units of Jewish volunteers in the British army. There were four altogether. The first (formed in 1916) consisted of Palestinian Jews exiled by the Ottoman government; it was organized in Egypt. The second was largely made up of Russian Jews living in Great Britain but not yet naturalized. The third consisted of volunteers from the United States and Canada. The second and third battalions were organized in Britain. The fourth was organized in Palestine and consisted entirely of volunteers living in the country. After the war the battalions were stationed in Palestine. In 1920 they were disbanded by the British.

Keren Hayesod

The main financial institution of the World Zionist Organization and later of the Jewish Agency. It was founded in 1920. The money collected was used to defray the expenses of immigration, the integration of new immigrants, and the establishment of agricultural colonies (especially kibbutzim and moshavim). Before the founding of the state, the Keren Hayesod also partly covered the expenses of the Yishuv's defense.

Keren Kayemet (Le'Israel)

A fund, based on contributions, established by the World Zionist Organization in 1901. Its purpose was the rehabilitation of land and reforestation in Eretz Israel.

Knesset Israel

Literally, "the community of Israel." Knesset Israel is the title the Yishuv gave iself as an organized body. It was recognized by the mandatory government in 1928. Muslim Arabs refused to organize themselves as a community. Affiliation with a group was voluntary in the sense that the member of a group (Jewish or Muslim) could break away from it, and so reject its authority. Thus, the ultra-orthodox Jews (Agudat Israel) refused as a body to participate in the elected Zionist institutions, whether on the municipal or on the national level. Knesset Israel should not be confused with the Knesset, the parliament of Israel. See *Asefat Hanivharim* and *Va'ad Le'umi*.

Mahanot Ha'olim

Literally, "immigrants' camps"; a pioneering youth movement of high school students, founded by Hakibbutz Hame'uhad in 1927. It set up many kibbutzim.

In 1945 the movement split up. The supporters of Mapai joined the Gordonia (named after Aaron David Gordon) and Young Maccabi youth movements in founding a new youth movement linked to the kibbutz movement: Ihud Hakvutzot Vehakibbutzim (Union of Collective Settlements).

Moshav

Plural, *moshavim*; a type of cooperative agricultural settlement. There are several types of moshavim, ranging from those similar to "private" agriculture to those close to the communalism of the kibbutz.

Moshava

Plural, *moshavot*; a private agricultural settlement. The first moshavot were founded at the time of the First Aliyah or before (Petah Tiqwa is an example). The moshava is not to be confused with the moshav. Most *moshavot* have now grown into towns.

Oleh

An immigrant, or "new immigrant." Feminine, *ola*; plural, *olim*.

Palmah

Acronym of *plugot mahatz*, "assault companies." A unit of nine patrols made up of Palestinian Jewish volunteers, created, armed, and trained by the British army in 1941. During the Second World War the Palmah was part of the British army, with the assent of the Hagana. In the War of Independence, the Palmah, organized in battalions and regiments, was the striking force of the Israeli army. Until the beginning of the 1980s, it provided many of its generals and several of its chiefs of staff, including Yitzhak Rabin. On 7 November 1948 Ben-Gurion put an end to the semi-independent forces within the army, a relic of the prestate period.

Shtetl

A locality (generally a small town or village) in Eastern Europe inhabited solely by Jews; not to be confused with a "ghetto," a quarter to which Jews were confined in European towns and cities.

Tzahal

Acronym of *Tzva Hagana Le'Israel*, the Israel Defense Force, or IDF. It was set up by order of the provisional government a few days after the Declaration of Independence and declared to be "the sole armed force of the state." Lehi (Fighters for the Freedom of Israel) and Etzel (the National

Military Organization)—right-wing military organizations that did not recognize the authority of the Hagana—accepted its authority immediately. Menachem Begin, prime minister from 1977 to 1983, had commanded Etzel (otherwise known as the Irgun), and Yitzhak Shamir, prime minister from 1983 to 1984 and from 1986 to 1992, was one of the leading figures in Lehi (otherwise known as the Stern Gang).

Va'ad Le'umi

Literally, "National Committee." It was elected by the Asefat Hanivharim for one year (in principle) and was a kind of executive committee whose main task was to represent the Yishuv before the high commissioner. The Va'ad Le'umi gradually developed departments responsible for certain public services in the Jewish community: religion, education and culture, health, and the press. There was also a Department for Municipal Affairs. The chairmen of the Va'ad Le'umi, in chronological order, were David Yellin (1920–21), Pinhas Rutenberg (1929–31), Yitzhak Ben-Zvi (1931–44), and David Remez (1944–48). See *Knesset Israel* and *Asefat Hanivharim*.

World Zionist Organization (WZO)

Founded by Theodor Herzl at the First Zionist Congress in Basel in August 1897. The resolution known as the Basel Program, adopted at the congress, remains one of the best definitions of Zionism and of the means by which it intended to achieve its objectives (the WZO being its main instrument).

> The aim of Zionism is to create for the Jewish people a home in Palestine secured by public law.
>
> The Congress contemplates the following means to the attainment of this end:
>
> 1. The promotion, on suitable lines, of the colonization of Palestine by Jewish agricultural and industrial workers.
>
> 2. The organization and binding together of the whole of Jewry by means of appropriate institutions, local and international, in accordance with the laws of each country.
>
> 3. The strengthening and fostering of Jewish national sentiment and national consciousness.
>
> 4. Preparatory steps towards obtaining government consent, where necessary, to the attainment of the aim of Zionism.

In addition to carrying out its function of defending the Zionist cause before the various governments, the WZO devoted most of its financial resources (based on contributions) and energies to promoting Jewish settlement in Palestine and encouraging immigration to the country. See also *Jewish Agency*.

Yishuv

Literally, "settling," "inhabited area," or "small locality." Here the term nearly always signifies "the Jewish population of Eretz Israel," a meaning that the immigrants of the First Aliyah gave the term. The people of the Second Aliyah distinguished between the Old and the New Yishuv, that is, between the Jewish population settled in the country before the 1880s and the people who came from the First Aliyah on. The word can also signify, depending on its context, "political entity" (the Jews of Palestine) or the historical period from 1882 to 1948.

Bibliography

Primary Sources

Archives

Beit Berl Archives, Zofit
Central Zionist Archives, Jerusalem
Labor Movement Archives, Tel Aviv

Newspapers and Periodicals

Davar
Ha'adama
Ha'aretz
Hapo'el Hatza'ir
Hasollel
Kuntras
Mehayenu

Books

Ahad Ha'am. *Nationalism and the Jewish Ethic: Basic Writings of Ahad Ha'am.* New York: Herzl Press, 1962.

————. *Selected Essays.* Translated from the Hebrew by Leon Simon. Philadelphia: Jewish Publication Society of America, 1962.

————. *Ten Essays on Zionism and Judaism.* Translated from the Hebrew by Leon Simon. New York: Arno Press, 1973.

Arlosoroff, Chaim. "Hasozialism Ha'amami shel Hayehudim" (The popular socialism of the Jews). In *Kitvei Chaim Arlosoroff* (Writings of Chaim Arlosoroff). Vol. 3. Tel Aviv: Schtibel, 1933. Translated from German: *Der Jüdische Volkssozialismus.* Berlin: Hapoel Hazair, 1919.

Ben-Gurion, David. *Ben-Gurion Looks Back in Talks with Moshe Pearlman.* London: Weidenfeld and Nicholson, 1965.

————. *Israel: A Personal History.* Tel Aviv: Sabra Books, 1972.

————. *Israel: Years of Challenge.* New York: Holt, Rinehart and Winston, 1963.

————. *The Jews in Their Land.* Rev. ed. Garden City, N.Y.: Windfall Books, 1974.

————. *Mima'amad La'am: Prakim Levirur Darka Veyiuda Shel Tenuat Hapo'alim* (From class to nation: Reflections on the vocation and mission of the labor movement). Tel Aviv: Am Oved, 1976.

————. *Rebirth and Destiny of Israel.* New York: Philosophical Library, 1954.

————. *Zichronot* (Memoirs). Tel Aviv: Am Oved, 1976. Translated into English as *Memoirs.* New York: World, 1970.

Borochov, Ber. *Class Struggle and the Jewish Nation: Selected Essays in Marxist Zionism.* Edited by Mitchell Cohen. New Brunswick, N.J.: Transaction Books, 1984.

Borochov, Ber. *Ktavim* (Writings). Edited by L. Levita and T. Nahum. Tel Aviv: Sifriyat Hapo'alim and Hakibbutz Hame'uhad Publications, 1955.

————. *Nationalism and the Class Struggle: A Marxian Approach to the Jewish Problem, Selected Writings.* Edited by Abraham G. Duker. Westport, Conn.: Greenwood Press, 1973.

Brenner, Yosef-Haim. *Ktavim* (Writings). Vol. 4. Tel Aviv: Hakibbutz Hame'uhad and Sifriyat Hapo'alim Publications, 1984.

Corradini, Enrico. *Discorsi Politici (1902–1923).* Florence: Vallechi Editore, 1923.

Dinur, Ben-Zion, ed. *Sefer Toldot Hahagana* (History of the Hagana). Tel Aviv: Ministry of Defense Publications, 1954.

Erez, Yehuda, ed. *Yalkut Ha'ahdut: Mivhar Hasifrut Haitit shel Mifleget Hapoalim Haivriim Hasozial—Demokratim BeEretz Israel (Poalei Tzion), 1907–1919* (Ha'ahdut: A collection of texts published in the newspaper of the Jewish Social-Democratic Party in Eretz Israel [Poalei Tzion], 1907–1919). Tel Aviv: Am Oved, 1962.

————. *Sefer Ha'aliya Hashlishit* (The book of the Third Aliyah). Tel Aviv: Am Oved, 1964.

Glickson, Moshe. *Im Hilufei Mishmarot: Kovetz Ma'amarim* (Changing of the guard: Collection of articles). Tel Aviv: Hano'ar Hatzioni Publications, 1938.

Golan, Haim, ed. *Hasollel: Kli Mivta Lefoalei Ha'avodot Hatziburiot* (Hasollel: Journal of the Workers in Public Works). Ramat Efal: Yad Tabenkin, 1991.

————. *Hitahdut Tzionit-Sotzialistit Shel Po'alei Eretz Israel—Ahdut Ha'avoda: Haprotocolim Shel Hava'ad Hapo'el, Hamo'etza Vehave'ida* (Zionist-socialist union of the workers of Eretz Israel—Ahdut Ha'avoda: Minutes of the meetings of the Executive Committee, Council, and General Assembly). Ramat Efal: Tabenkin Foundation, 1987.

————. *Mishlahat Po'alei Tzion Be'eretz Israel, 1920* (The Po'alei Tzion delegation in Eretz Israel, 1920). 2 vols. Ramat Efal: Tabenkin Foundation, 1989.

Gordon, Aaron David. *Kitvei A. D. Gordon* (Writings). Vol. 1, *Haouma Veha'avoda* (The nation and labor). Vol. 2, *Ha'adam Vehateva* (Man and nature). Vol. 3, *Michtavim Vereshimot* (Letters and articles). Edited by Sh. H. Bergmann and A. L. Shohat. 3 vols. Jerusalem: Zionist Library, 1951–53 (vols. 2 and 3 appeared before vol. 1).

Habas, Braha, and Eliezer Shohat, eds. *Sefer Ha'aliya Hashniya* (The book of the Second Aliyah). 2 vols. Tel Aviv: Am Oved, 1947.

Hadari, Haim, ed. *Hakibbutz Hame'uhad: Ha'hlatot Vete'udot* (Kibbutz Hame'uhad: Decisions and documents). Tel Aviv: Hakibbutz Hame'uhad Publications, 1977.

Horowitz, Dan. *Techelet Ve'avak: Dor Tashah—Diokan Atzmi* (Sky and sand: The generation of 1948—self-portrait). Posthumous edition edited by Avi Katzmann. Tel Aviv: Keter, 1993.

Jabotinsky, Zeev. *Baderech Lamedina* (Toward a state). Jerusalem: Ari Jabotinsky, 1953.

Katznelson, Berl. *Arachim Genuzim: Sihot al Baiot Hahinuch Lesotzializm* (Neglected values: Observations on the problems of socialist education). Edited by Ephraim Broide. Tel Aviv: Ayanot, 1944.

————. *Bamivhan* (Being tested: Conversations with youth leaders). 3d ed. Tel Aviv: Mapai Publications, 1950.

———. *"Ha'aliya Hashniya": Hartza'ot Berl Katznelson Bifnei Habaharut Hasotzialistit (1928)* (The Second Aliyah: Berl Katznelson's lectures to socialist youth [1928]). Edited by Anita Shapira and Noemi Abir. Tel Aviv: Am Oved, 1990.

———. *Kitvei Berl Katznelson* (Writings of Berl Katznelson). 12 vols. Tel Aviv: Mapai Publications, 1946–1950.

———. *Ma'asim Umegamot* (Deeds and tendencies). Tel Aviv: Am Oved, 1941.

———. *My Way to Palestine*. London: Hechalutz, 1946.

———. *Tzionut Sotzialistit* (Socialist Zionism). Tel Aviv: Ayanot, n.d.

———, ed. *Yalkut Ahdut Ha'avoda* (Ahdut Ha'avoda: A collection of texts). 2 vols. Tel Aviv: Editions of the Socialist-Zionist Union of the Workers of Eretz Israel, Ahdut Ha'avoda, 1929–1932.

Kuchnir, Mordechai, ed. *A. D. Gordon: Zichronot Vedivrei Ha'aracha* (Memories and an appreciation of A. D. Gordon). Tel Aviv: Histadrut Cultural Publications, n.d.

Lavi, Shlomo. *Megilati Be'Ein Harod: Rayonot, Zichronot Uma'asim* (My account of Ein Harod: Ideas, memories, and actions). Tel Aviv: Am Oved, 1947.

Man de, Henri. *Au-delà du Marxisme*. Paris: Editions du Seuil, 1974.

Ministry of Education. *Sefer Hahinuch Vehatarbut* (The book of education and culture). Jerusalem: National Press, 1951.

Moeller van den Bruck, Arthur. *Das Dritte Reich*. Hamburg: Hanseatische Verlagsanstalt, 1931.

Nietzsche, Friedrich Wilhelm. *Beyond Good and Evil*. Chicago: Gateway, 1955.

Ruppin, Arthur. *Hahityashvut Hahakla'it Shel Hahistadrut Hatzionit be Eretz-Israel, 1908–1924* (Agricultural settlement of the Zionist Organization in Eretz Israel, 1908–1924). Tel Aviv: Dvir, [1925].

———. *Shloshim Shenot Binyan Eretz Israel* (Thirty years of building Eretz Israel). Jerusalem: Schocken Books, 1937. English version: *Three Decades of Palestine: Speeches and Papers on the Upbuilding of the Jewish National Home*. Jerusalem: Schocken Books, 1936.

Slutzki, Yehuda, ed. *Po'alei Tzion Be'eretz-Israel, 1905–1919: Te'oudot* (The Po'alei Tzion Party in Eretz Israel, 1905–1919: Documents). Tel Aviv: Tel Aviv University Press, 1978.

Sorel, Georges. *Réflexions sur la violence*. 11th ed. Paris: Rivière, 1950.

Spengler, Oswald. *Politische Schriften*. Munich: Beck, 1932.

Syrkin, Nachman. *Essays on Socialist Zionism*. New York: Young Poale Zion Alliance of America, 1935.

———. *Kitvei Nachman Syrkin*. (Writings of Nachman Syrkin). Vol. 1. Edited by Berl Katznelson and Yehuda Kauffman. Tel Aviv: Davar Publications, 1938.

Tzemach, Shlomo. *Reshit, Avoda Ve'adama* (Labor and land first of all). Jerusalem: Reuven Mass, 1950.

———. *Shana Rishona* (First year). Tel Aviv: Am Oved, 1952.

Weizmann, Chaim. *Trial and Error: The Autobiography of Chaim Weizmann*. New York: Schocken Books, 1966.

Yavnieli, Shmuel, ed. *Le'or Rayon Ha'avoda: Leket Ma'amarim Be'inyanei Hinuch* (In the light of the concept of labor: A collection of articles on educational subjects). Tel Aviv: Publications of the Teachers' Union Committee, 1938.

Secondary Sources
Books and Articles

Arian, Alan. *Politics in Israel: The Second Generation*. Rev. ed. Chatham, N.J.: Chatham House, 1989.

Aronoff, Myron Joel. *Israeli Visions and Divisions: Cultural Change and Political Conflict*. New Brunswick, N.J.: Transaction Books, 1989.

Avigal, Moshe. *Hazon Vehinuch* (Vision and education). Tel Aviv: Tarbut Vehinuch, 1971.

Avineri, Shlomo. *Arlosoroff*. London: Holban, 1989. Translated into Hebrew as *Arlosoroff*. Tel Aviv: Edanim, 1991.

―――――. *Harayon Hatzioni Legvanav* (Varieties of Zionist thought). Tel Aviv: Am Oved, 1980. Translated into English as *The Making of Modern Zionism*. New York: Basic Books, 1981.

―――――, ed. *David Ben-Gurion: Demuto Shel Manhig Tenuat Hapo'alim* (David Ben-Gurion: Portrait of the leader of the labor movement). Tel Aviv: Am Oved, 1988.

Avizohar, Meir. *Bere'i Saduk: Ide'alim Hevrati'im Veleumi'im Vehishtakfutam Be'olama Shel Mapai* (In a broken mirror: Social and national ideals as reflected in Mapai). Tel Aviv: Am Oved, 1990.

Barkai, Haim. "Economic Democracy and the Origins of the Israel Labor Economy." *The Jerusalem Quarterly* 49 (winter 1989).

―――――. "Fifty Years of Labor Economy: Growth, Performance, and the Present Challenge." *The Jerusalem Quarterly* 50 (spring 1989).

―――――. "The Public Histadrut and Private Sector in the Israeli Economy." Jerusalem: The Falk Project for Economic Research in Israel, Sixth Report, 1964.

―――――. "The Theory and Praxis of the Histadrut Industrial Sector." *The Jerusalem Quarterly* 26 (winter 1982).

Barnard, F. M. *Herder's Social and Political Thought: From Enlightenment to Nationalism*. Oxford: Oxford University Press, 1965.

―――――, ed. *J. G. Herder on Social and Political Culture*. Cambridge: Cambridge University Press, 1969.

Bar-Zohar, Michael. *Ben-Gurion*. New York: Delacorte Press, 1978.

Beenstock, Michael, Jacob Metzer, and Sanny Ziv. "Immigration and Jewish Economy in Mandatory Palestine." Jerusalem: The Maurice Falk Institute for Economic Research in Israel, 1993.

Beiser, Frederick C. *Enlightenment, Revolution, and Romanticism: The Genesis of Modern German Political Thought, 1790–1800*. Cambridge: Harvard University Press, 1992.

Bergmann, Shmuel Hugo. "Herder ve A. D. Gordon." (Herder and A. D. Gordon). *Molad* 5 (January–February 1973).

Brinker, Menachem. *Ad Hasimta Hativerianit: Ma'amar al Sippur Vemahshava Beyetzirat Brenner* (Up to Tiberias: On the writings and thought of Brenner). Tel Aviv: Am Oved, 1990.

Cohen, Mitchell. *Zion and State: Nation, Class, and the Shaping of Modern Israel*. Oxford: Basil Blackwell, 1987.

Diskin, Avraham. *Elections and Voters in Israel*. New York: Praeger, 1991.

Drori, Yigal. *Bein Yamin Lesmol: "Hahugim Ha'ezrahi'im" Beshnot Ha'esrim* (Between Right and Left: "Bourgeois groups" in the nineteen-twenties). Tel Aviv: Tel Aviv University Press, 1990.

Edelman, Martin. *Courts, Politics, and Culture in Israel.* Charlottesville: University of Virginia Press, 1994.

Eisenstadt, Shmuel Noah. *Hahevra Ha'israelit Betmuroteha.* Jerusalem: Magnes Press, 1989. Originally published in English as *The Transformation of Israeli Society: An Essay in Interpretation.* London: Weidenfeld and Nicholson, 1985.

————. *Hahevra Ha'israelit, Reka, Hitpathut Vebai'ot.* Jerusalem: Magnes Press, 1967. Originally published in English as *The Israeli Society.* London: Weidenfeld and Nicholson, 1967.

Eshkoli-Wegman, H. *Elem: Mapai Nochah Hasho'a, 1939–1945* (Silence: Mapai and the Shoa, 1939–1945). Jerusalem: Yad Yitzhak Ben-Zvi, 1993.

Evron, Boaz. *Jewish State or Israeli Nation?* Bloomington: Indiana University Press, 1995.

Frankel, Jonathan. *Prophecy and Politics: Socialism, Nationalism, and the Russian Jews, 1862–1917.* Cambridge: Cambridge University Press, 1981. Translated into Hebrew by Amos Carmel as *Nevuah Vepolitika: Sozialism, Leumiut Veyehudei Russia, 1862–1917.* Tel Aviv: Am Oved, 1989.

Freiling, Tuvia. *David Ben-Gurion Vehasho'a shel Yehudei Europa, 1939–1945* (David Ben-Gurion and the Shoa of the Jews of Europe, 1939–1945). Ph.D. diss., Hebrew University of Jerusalem, 1990.

Galnoor, Yitzhak. *Steering the Polity: Communication and Politics in Israel.* Beverly Hills: Sage, 1982.

Giladi, Dan. *Hayishuv Betekufat Ha'aliya Harevi'it (1924–1929): Behina Kalkalit Upolitit* (The Yishuv at the Time of the Fourth Aliyah (1924–1929): Economical and political analysis). Tel Aviv: Am Oved, 1973.

Goldberg, Zeev, ed. *Darkei Ish: Shalosh Massot al Berl Katznelson* (A man's path: Three essays on Berl Katznelson). [Zofit]: Beit Berl Publications, 1968.

Gorny, Yosef. *Ahdut Ha'avoda, 1919–1930: Hayesodot Hara'ayoniim ve Hashita Hamedinit* (The ideological foundations and the political system). Tel Aviv: Hakibbutz Hame'uhad Publications, 1973.

————. *Hashe'ela Ha'aravit Vehabaya Hayehudit: Zramim Medini'im-Ideologi'im Batzionut Beyahas el Hayeshut Ha'aravit Be'eretz Israel Bashanim 1882–1948* (The Arab question and the Jewish problem: Political and ideological currents in Zionism with regard to the Arab presence in Eretz Israel, 1882–1948). Tel Aviv: Am Oved, 1985.

————. "Hashinu'im Bamivnei Hahevrati Vehapoliti Shel Ha'aliya Hashniya Bashanim 1904–1940" (Changes in the social and political composition of the Second Aliyah between 1904 and 1940). *Hatzionut* 1 (1970).

————. *Shutfut Vema'avak: Chaim Weizmann Vetenu'at Hapo'alim Be'eretz Israel* (Collaboration and confrontation: Chaim Weizmann and the labor movement in Eretz Israel). Tel Aviv: Hakibbutz Hame'uhad Publications, 1975.

Gross, Nachum T. "The Economic Regime during Israel's First Decade." Jerusalem: The Maurice Falk Institute for Economic Research in Israel, Research Paper 208 (1995).

Gross, Nachum T., and Jacob Metzer. "Palestine in World War II: Some Economic Aspects." Jerusalem: The Maurice Falk Institute for Economic Research in Israel, Research Paper 207 (1993).

Halpern, Ben. *The Idea of the Jewish State*. Cambridge: Harvard University Press, 1969.

Harkabi, Yehoshofat. *Israel's Fateful Hour*. New York: Harper and Row, 1988.

Hertzberg, Arthur, ed. *The Zionist Idea: A Historical Analysis and Reader*. New York: Atheneum, 1977.

Hofnung, Menachem. *Democracy, Law, and National Security*. Aldershot, England: Dartmouth, 1996.

Horowitz, Dan, and Moshe Lissak. *Metzukot Be'utopia* (Troubles in Utopia). Tel Aviv: Am Oved, 1990. Translated into English as *Trouble in Utopia: The Overburdened Polity of Israel*. Albany: SUNY Press, 1989.

————. *Meyishuv Lamedina: Yehudei Eretz Israel Betekufat Hamandat Habriti Kekehila Politit* (From the Yishuv to the state: The Jews of Eretz Israel as a political community during the period of the British mandate). Tel Aviv: Am Oved, 1977. Translated into English as *Origins of the Israeli Polity: Palestine under the Mandate*. Chicago: Chicago University Press, 1978.

Hughes, H. Stuart. *Oswald Spengler: A Critical Estimate*. New York: Charles Scribner's Sons, 1962.

Ilan, Amitzur. *Embargo, Otzma Vehachra'a be Milhemet Tashah* (Embargo, power, and decision in the 1948 war). Tel Aviv: Ma'arachot, 1995.

Ishai, Yaël. *Siatiut Betenuat Ha'avoda: Sia Bet Bemapai* (The factions in the labor movement: Faction B in Mapai). Tel Aviv: Am Oved, 1978.

Keren, Michael. *Ben-Gurion and the Intellectuals*. DeKalb: Northern Illinois University Press, 1983.

Kimmerling, Baruch. *The Israeli State and Society: Boundaries and Frontiers*. New York: SUNY Press, 1989.

Kleiman, Ephraim. "The Histadrut Economy of Israel: In Search of Criteria." *The Jerusalem Quarterly* 41 (winter 1987).

Klein, Philip. "Proposals on Programme and Administration of Social Welfare in Israel." Report no. TAO/ISR/29. New York: United Nations Commissioner for Technical Assistance, January 1961.

Kriegel, Annie. *Les Communistes Français: Essai d'ethnographie politique*. Paris: Editions du Seuil, 1970.

Landau, Jacob. *The Arab Minority in Israel, 1967–1991*. Oxford: Oxford University Press, 1993.

Laqueur, Walter. *A History of Zionism*. New York: Schocken Books, 1978.

Lissak, Moshe, Anita Shapira, and Gabriel Cohen, eds. *Toldot Hayeshuv Hayehudi Be'Eretz Israel Meaz Haliyah Harishona: Tkufat Hamandat Habriti* (The history of the Jewish community in Eretz Israel since 1882: The period of the British mandate). Pt. 2. Jerusalem: Bialik Institute and Israel Academy of Sciences and Humanities, 1994.

Margalit, Elkana. *Kommuna, Hevra Vepolitika: Gdud Ha'avoda Al Shmo Shel Yosef Trumpeldor Be'eretz Israel* (Commune, society, and politics: The Yosef Trumpeldor Labor Corps in Eretz Israel). Tel Aviv: Am Oved, 1980.

Medding, Peter. *The Founding of Israeli Democracy, 1948–1967*. Oxford: Oxford University Press, 1990.

Merlio, Gilbert. *Oswald Spengler: Témoin de son temps*. Stuttgart: Akademischer Verlag Hans-Dieter Heinz, 1982.

Mintz, Matitiahu. *Ber Borochov: Hama'agal Harishon, 1900–1906* (Ber Borochov: The first phase, 1900–1906). Tel Aviv: Hakibbutz Hame'uhad Publications, 1976.

––––––. *Haver Veyeriv: Yitzhak Tabenkin Bemifleget Po'alei Tzion, 1905–1912* (Friend and opponent: Yitzhak Tabenkin in Po'alei Tzion, 1905–1912). Tel Aviv: Hakibbutz Hame'uhad Publications, 1986.

Ne'eman Arad, Gulie, ed. "Israeli Historiography Revisited." *History and Memory* 7 (spring/summer 1995).

Nitzan, Arie. *Ramat Hahayim Be'eretz Israel Bemeshech Esrim Hashanim Ha'aharonot* (The standard of living in Eretz Israel in the last twenty years). Jerusalem: Central Office of Statistics, 1952.

Pedatzur, Reuven. *Nitzhon Hamevoucha: Mediniout Memshelet Eshkol Bashtachim Leachar Milchemet Sheshet Hayamim* (The triumph of embarrassment: Israel and the territories after the Six-Day War). Tel Aviv: Bitan, 1996.

Penslar, Derek J. *Zionism and Technocracy: The Engineering of Jewish Settlement in Palestine, 1870–1918*. Bloomington: Indiana University Ppress, 1991.

Porath, Dina. *Hanhaga Bemilkud: Hayishuv Nochah Hasho'a, 1942–1945* (Leaders in a dilemma: The Yishuv and the Shoa, 1942–1945). Tel Aviv: Am Oved, 1986. Translated into English as *The Blue and Yellow Stars of David: The Zionist Leadership in Palestine and the Holocaust, 1939–1945*. Cambridge: Harvard University Press, 1990.

Ram, Uri. *The Changing Agenda of Israeli Sociology: Theory, Ideology, and Identity*. Albany: SUNY Press, 1995.

Reinharz, Jehuda. *Chaim Weizmann*. 2 vols. New York: Oxford University Press, 1985–1993.

Reshef, Shimon. *Zerem Ha'ovdim Bahinuch* (The labor trend in education). Tel Aviv: Tel Aviv University Press and Hakibbutz Hame'uhad Publications, 1980.

Rotenstreich, Nathan. "Capitalism and Socialism." In *Min Hayesod* (Back to Basics). Vol. 2. Tel Aviv: Kadima, 1963.

––––––. *Ha'uma Betorato Shel A. D. Gordon* (The nation in the teachings of A. D. Gordon). Jerusalem: Reuven Mass and Youth Department of the Zionist Organization, n.d.

Schiff, Zeev. *Intifada: The Palestinians' Uprising: Israel's Third Front*. New York: Simon and Schuster, 1990.

Schweid, Eliezer. *Hayehid: Olamo shel A. D. Gordon* (The individual: The universe of A. D. Gordon). Tel Aviv: Am Oved, 1970.

Segev, Tom. *The Seventh Million: The Israelis and the Holocaust*. New York: Hill and Wang, 1993.

Shaffir, Gershon. *Land, Labour, and the Origin of the Israeli-Palestinian Conflict, 1882–1914*. Cambridge: Cambridge University Press, 1989.

Shalev, Michael. *Labour and Political Economy in Israel*. Oxford: Oxford University Press, 1992.

Shaltiel, Eli. *Pinhas Rutenberg: Aliyato Unefilato Shel "Ish hazak" Be'Eretz Israel,*

1879–1942 (Pinhas Rutenberg: The rise and fall of a "strong man" in Eretz Israel, 1879–1942). Tel Aviv: Am Oved, 1990.

Shapira, Anita. *Berl.* Tel Aviv: Am Oved, 1980. Translated into English as *Berl: The Biography of a Socialist Zionist: Berl Katznelson, 1887–1944.* Cambridge: Cambridge University Press, 1984.

———*Hahalicha al Kav Haofek* (Going toward the horizon). Tel Aviv: Am Oved, 1989.

———. *Hama'avak Hanichzav: Avoda Ivrit, 1929–1939* (The lost battle: Jewish labor, 1929–1939). Tel Aviv: Tel Aviv University Press and Hakibbutz Hame'uhad Publications, 1976.

———. *Land and Power: The Zionist Resort to Force, 1881–1948.* New York: Oxford University Press, 1992.

Shapira, Avraham. "Buber's Attachment to Herder and to German Volkism." *Studies in Zionism* 14 (January 1993).

Shapira, Yosef. *Hapo'el Hatza'ir: Harayon Vehama'asei* (Hapo'el Hatza'ir: Ideology and action). Tel Aviv: Ayanot, 1967.

Shapiro, Yonathan. *Ahdut Ha'avoda Hahistorit: Ozmato shel Irgun Politi.* Tel Aviv: Am Oved, 1975. English version: *The Formative Years of the Israeli Labour Party: The Organization of Power, 1919–1930.* London: Sage, 1976.

———*Hevra Beshvi Hapolitikaim* (Politicians as an hegemonic class: The case of Israel). Tel Aviv: Sifriat Hapoalim, 1996.

Shetreet, Shimon. *Justice in Israel: A Study of the Israeli Judiciary.* Dordrecht: Martinus Nijhoff, 1994.

Slutzki, Yehuda. *Mavo Letoldot Tenuat Ha'avoda Haisraelit* (Introduction to the history of the Israeli labor movement). Tel Aviv: Am Oved, 1973.

Sprinzak, Ehud, and Larry Diamond. *Israeli Democracy under Stress.* Boulder, Colo.: Lynne Reinner, 1993.

Stern, Fritz. *The Politics of Cultural Despair.* Berkeley and Los Angeles: University of California Press, 1963.

Sternhell, Zeev. *Maurice Barrès et le nationalisme français.* Brussels: Complexe, 1985.

———. *Neither Right Nor Left: Fascist Ideology In France.* Translated by David Maisel. Princeton: Princeton University Press, 1996.

Sternhell, Zeev, Mario Sznajder, and Maia Asheri. *The Birth of Fascist Ideology: From Cultural Rebellion to Political Revolution.* Translated by David Maisel. Princeton: Princeton University Press, 1994.

Sussman, Zvi. *Pa'ar Veshivion Bahistadrut: Hahashpa'a Shel Ha'ideologuia Hashivionit Veha'avoda Ha'aravit Al Secharo Shel Ha'oved Hayehudi Be'eretz Israel* (Inequality and equality in the Histadrut: The influence of the egalitarian ideology and Arab labor on the wages of the Jewish worker in Eretz Israel). Ramat Gan: Massada, 1974.

Syrkin, Marie. *Nachman Syrkin, Socialist Zionist: A Biographical Memorial, Selected Essays.* New York: Herzl Press, 1961.

Szereszewski, Robert. "Essays on the Structure of the Jewish Economy in Palestine and Israel." Jerusalem: The Maurice Falk Institute for Economic Research in Israel, 1968.

Teveth, Shabtai. "Hahor Hashahor" (The black hole). *Alpayim* 10 (1994).

_____. *Kinat David* (David's passion). 3 vols. Tel Aviv: Schocken Books, 1977. Abridged English version, translated by the author: *Ben-Gurion: The Burning Ground, 1886–1949*. Boston: Houghton Mifflin, 1987.

_____. *Moshe Dayan*. Tel Aviv: Schocken Books, 1971.

Tzur, Zeev. *Hakibbutz Hame'uhad Beyishuva shel Ha'aretz* (The role of Kibbutz Hame'uhad in settling the country). Tel Aviv: Hakibbutz Hame'uhad Publications, 1979.

Vital, David. *The Origins of Zionism*. Oxford: Oxford University Press, 1975.

_____. *Zionism: The Formative Years*. Oxford: Oxford University Press, 1982.

Weitz, Yehiam. *Muda'ut Vehoser Onim: Mapai Lenochah Hasho'a, 1943–1945* (Awareness and incapacity: Mapai and the Shoa, 1943–1945). Jerusalem: Yad Yitzhak Ben-Zvi, 1993.

Yaniv, Avner. *National Security and Democracy in Israel*. Boulder, Colo.: Lynne Reiner, 1993.

Yannai, Aaron. *Toldot Ein Harod* (History of Ein Harod). Ein Harod: Kibbutz Ein Harod Publications, 1971.

Zartal, Idit. *Zehavam shel Hayehudim: Hahagira Hayehudit Hamahtartit LeEretz Israel, 1945–1948* (From catastrophe to power: Jewish illegal immigration to Palestine, 1945–1948). Tel Aviv: Am Oved, 1996.

Adler, Max, 29

Afula, 221, 222, 259, 330

Agnon, Shmuel Yosef, 343

Agriculture, 42; agricultural laborers, 296–297, 302, 309; private agriculture, 32–33. *See also* Collective Settlements

Ahad Ha'am, (Asher Zvi Ginzberg), 50, 52, 57, 87

Aharonowitz, Yosef, 48, 74, 193, 195, 244, 296; as co-director of Bank Hapo'alim, 180, 185, 291, 296, 299; and the family wage, 291, 295, 296, 299; as a representative of Hapo'el Hatza'ir, 48, 120, 206, 209, 227, 229, 296

Aharonowitz (Aranne), Zalman (Ziama), 275, 276, 307, 311, 316; on the defects of the Labor movement, 263, 273; disdain for immigrants, 282; as a representative of the apparatus, 188, 277, 281

Ahdut Ha'avoda (Party), 4, 103, 113, 114, 179; and constructive socialism, 9, 153; and Convention of Agricultural Workers (1919), 107; founding of, 19, 34–35, 76, 85, 92, 95–96, 106, 107, 108–110; Kaplanski-Kolton group in, 151; nationalist socialism of, 8–9, 18–19, 22, 73, 112, 113, 121, 125; oligarchic tendencies in, 185–188, 189–190; and socialist ideas, 32–33, 77, 86, 110, 113, 114, 115, 131–132; and struggle with Gdud Ha'avoda, 199, 200, 202, 203, 206–208, 209, 210, 214–216; third convention of, 20–21; unification with Hapo'el Hatza'ir, 226–230. *See also* Labor Movement

Ahdut Ha'avoda-Po'alei Tzion (Party) 4, 310–311

Aliyah, First (first wave of immigration, 1880s and 1890s), 21, 33, 75, 76, 77

Aliyah, Second (1904–1914), 5, 16, 26, 33, 46, 75, 80, 90, 117, 137, 141, 184, 218; Ben-Gurion's view of, 74–76; according to Katznelson, 152; leadership of the Second Aliyah, 79–80, 128; the Marxist group from Rostov in, 80, 90, 166

Aliyah, Third (1919–1923), 5, 78, 117, 128, 198, 218, 220; its relationship to the members of the Second Aliyah, 186–188;

Sefer Ha'aliyah Hashlishit (*The Book of the Third Aliyah*), 188

Aliyah, Fourth (1924–1926), 13, 26, 217–219, 220, 221, 234, 282, 372 n.90

Aliyah, Fifth (1933–1939), 13, 217, 221

Allon, Yigal, 331, 332, 333, 334, 336; Allon Plan, 333

Alterman, Nathan, 343

Amir, Yigal, 333

Anilewicz, Mordechai, 318

Anti-Semitism, 10, 13, 17, 47, 49; according to Borochov, 82–83; according to Syrkin, 100; and assimilation, 16–17, 47; Zionist explanation of, 49, 50

Apter, Yaakov, 295

Aqaba, 44

Arlosoroff, Chaim, 36, 191, 196, 219, 298; on class warfare, 24, 193, 230; on the imposition of income tax, 236; on Jewish nationalist socialism, 24–27, 193, 230; on Jews as a people of proletarians, 24; *Der Jüdische Volkssozialismus* (*The Popular Socialism of the Jews*), 24; as member of Hapo'el Hatza'ir, 26, 35, 227

Ashdot Ya'akov, 265

Atarot, 245

Atlit, 179

Aulard, Alphonse, xi

Austro-Marxists, 25, 91

Avigal, Moshe, 250

Avineri, Shlomo, 53

Ayelet Hashahar, 211, 214, 373n.105

Balfour Declaration, 44, 68, 71, 319

Balfouria, 300

Bank Hapo'alim, 40, 109, 180, 185

Bank of Israel, 188

Bank Le'umi, 180

Baram, Moshe, 268

Barrès, Maurice, 24

Bat-Galim, 219

Bauer, Otto, 25

Beenstock, Michael, 217

Begin, Menachem, 331, 334, 340

Beilinson, Moshe, 127, 191, 223, 284, 293, 302, 303, 304, 363n.36

Beirut, 44

Beit Alpha, 203, 210, 211, 267, 248; children's society in, 248

Ben Aharon, Yitzhak, 267, 275, 310, 316

Ben-Gurion, David, 12, 27, 73, 74, 77, 108, 142, 168; on compatibility between nationalism and socialism, 94, 224, 226, 227, 231–232; on equality and the family wage, 291, 293, 295, 299, 304, 305; and the founding of Israel, 319, 322, 327, 337; *mamlachtiut* (supremacy of the state over civil society), 35–36; *Mema'amad La'am (From Class to Nation)*, 225; as a member of Po'alei Tzion party, 81, 84, 88, 103, 107; nationalist ideology of, 22, 75, 85–86, 87–89, 104, 105, 182, 188, 190, 266; nationalist socialism in, 19, 20–22, 84, 86, 87, 92–94, 99–100, 113, 115, 116–117, 123–124, 128–130, 294–295, 298, 375n.35; and the 1937 partition plan, 330–331; "On the Slope," 87; opposed to the labor trend in education, 244, 245, 249, 256–258; as an organization-man and the head of the apparatus, 22, 30, 85, 116, 121, 184–185, 196, 197–198, 268, 275, 277, 281; "Our Sociopolitical Work," 86; status in the Labor movement of, 74, 273, 274; and struggle for organizational unity, 181–182, 212; treatment of opposition by, 76, 92–93, 168, 223, 278

Ben Shemen, 245

Ben Yeruham, Dov, 145, 310, 311

Ben Zvi (Shimshelevich), Yitzhak, 19, 30, 35, 77, 85, 95, 103, 107, 110, 166, 201, 295

Bendori, Feibush, 275

Benzion, Israeli, 323

Bergmann, Shmuel Hugo, 55, 73

Bergson, Henri, 135

Berlin, 235, 287

Bernadotte, Count Folke, 320

Bernstein, Eduard, 23, 91, 98, 148, 167

Betar, 262

Bialik, Haim Nahman, 50

Biluim, 75

Binyamina, 129

Black Panthers, 5, 326

Bloch (Blumenfeld), David (Ephraim), 83, 108, 110, 151

Blum, Léon, 29, 167, 171,

Blumenfeld, Kurt, 234

Bnei Akiva, 337

Bobruysk, 146

Bograshov (Dr. Haim), 259

Borochov, Ber, 16, 29, 52, 80, 118; Katznelson's views of, 139; *Our Platform*, 82, 83; and Poltava Platform, 81, 83; synthesis of Marxism and nationalism, 17, 19, 28, 73, 74, 89, 93, 106; teachings of, 17, 18, 29, 60, 77, 82, 83–85, 90

Bourgeois, 6, 40, 50, 130, 131, 132; property owner, 13. *See also* Middle Classes

Brenner, Yosef Haim, 38, 44, 58, 87, 103, 153, 172, 201; "Concerning Matters of Terminology," 153

Brinker, Menachem, 58

Brit Shalom, 143

British Labor Party, 29

Brodny, Yitzhak, 299

Bromberg, Y., 268

Budapest, 16

Bulgaria, 282

Bund, 17, 80, 88, 106

Bureau of Public Works, 179, 202, 206. *See also* Sollel Boneh

Bustenai, 244

Cabet, Etienne, 96

Cairo, 44

Camp David Accord, the, 339

Capital, 8, 39–40, 117–118, 129, 217, 221, 239; Katznelson on, 152, 161, 162, 168–169; productive capital versus exploitative capital, 67, 129–130, 161; Public, 40, 129, 130, 217. *See also* Capitalism; Property

Capitalism, 6, 161, 217, 286; Gordon's opinion of, 353n.71

Carlyle, Thomas, 98

Cave of Machpela, 333

Central and Eastern Europe, xii, 11, 28–29; linguistic revival in, 14. *See also* Eastern European Jews

Cities, 25, 106, 221, 240, 286; Gordon's views on, 59

Citizenship, xii, xiii, 11

Class, 169, 181, 197, 232; Ben-Gurion on, 224, 225, 226, 228–229, 231–233; and class collaboration, 22, 23, 33, 34, 39, 40, 42, 128, 129, 131–133, 165, 166, 219, 220, 223, 224, 229, 232, 233–244; and class struggle, 8, 24, 25, 32, 35, 82, 83, 86–87, 91, 132, 251; Gordon on, 66–67, 353n.71; Katznelson's concept of, 228, 230; unity of, 181–182

Collective Settlements, 37, 40, 41, 42, 96–97, 248, 284; allocation of resources to, 234, 241–242; Ben-Gurion and, 121, 124, 125, 142, 220; and control of the Histadrut, 178, 185, 194; criticism of, 233, 234; and the experts' report of 1928, 234; as an instrument of nation-building, 33, 40, 96–97, 105, 106, 109, 117, 122–123, 125, 133, 141, 148; Katznelson and, 33, 138, 141, 147, 152; large kvutza, 198, 203; as the pride of the Labor movement, 40–41, 42, 219, 220–221; Syrkin's views on, 102, 104. *See also* Agriculture; Jewish worker

Communism: communist parties' methods of operation, 185–187, 189; fraction in Gdud Ha'avoda, 211; Katznelson's struggle against, 137, 143, 167–169, 170, 171–172

Communist Manifesto, 84

Constantinople, 85

Corradini, Enrico, 24, 156, 157, 101, 229

Cosmopolitanism, 158, 159

Croce, Benedetto, xi

Crosland, Anthony, 29; *The Future of Socialism*, 29

Czechoslovakia, 16, 287

Damascus, 44

Dan, Hillel, 205, 290

Dashevsky, Pinhas, 50

Davar, 106, 171, 192, 193, 196, 237, 293, 296, 299, 304; Katznelson as editor of, 142, 143, 185, 208

Dayan, Moshe, 331, 334, 336, 337

Déat, Marcel, 172

Degania, 33, 40, 120, 142, 318, 337

De Man, Hendrik, 171, 172; *Evolutionary Socialism*, 171; *Le Socialisme Constructif*, 171

Democracy, 11, 189, 269–279; anti-democratic and oligarchic tendencies in the Labor movement, 17, 183, 184, 185, 189–191, 194, 196, 268–274, 276–279, 281, 285, 294, 306; democratic centralism, 191, 277, 306; Israeli "Human Dignity and Liberty" (law, 1992), 320

Der Yiddisher Kamp ffer, 129

Diaspora, 31, 48–50, 64, 126, 188. *See also* Eastern European Jews

Die Welt, 97

Dilthey, Wilhelm, 98

Dizengoff, Meir, 74, 75, 235, 240

Djilas, Milovan, 43

Dostoyevsky, Feodor Mikhailovich, 98

Dreyfus Affair, 10, 12, 51, 98

Drori, Yigal, 240, 241

Dubnow, Shimon, 50

Eastern European Jews, 4, 12, 47, 219; in the period of the Holocaust, 31, 48–49, 50, 51, 387n.10; as seen by the Labor leadership, 31–33, 36, 42, 48, 50, 51, 265–266; and self-defence, 88. *See also* Diaspora

Education, 244–263; General Educational System, 244, 247, 252, 258–259; Secondary, 259–261; Zionist-religious, 244. *See also* Labor Trend in education

Egypt, 336

Ein Harod, 122, 147, 185, 198, 203, 206, 214, 228, 255, 373n.105; Kibbutz-Ein Harod, 213, 214; and split-up in Gdud Ha'avoda, 206–207

Ein Tivon, 203

Eisenberg, Aaron, 75,

Eisenstadt, Shmuel Noah, 288

Elazar, Gen. David (Dado), 335

Elkind, Menachem, 179, 195, 210, 213; as leader of Gdud Ha'avoda (Labor Corps), 197, 200, 201, 202, 206, 208, 209, 211

Elon Moreh, 337, 338

Emancipation, 12, 16–17, 47

Emek (Valley) Group, 205, 213

Emigration, 5; to the United States, 12, 48

Enlightenment, xiii, 10, 27, 92

Equality, 236, 237, 264, 291, 292, 294, 296, 298, 299, 309, 312, 313, 316, 394; as a mobilizing myth, 196, 214, 229, 230, 261, 262, 264, 288–291, 294, 301, 305, 316, 317, 375n.49; and social gaps in the Yishuv, 39, 261, 279, 284, 286–288, 306. *See also* Nationalist Socialism; Socialism

Erfurt Program, 154

Eshkol (Shkolnik), Levi, 35, 120, 196, 206, 228, 335; and family wage, 290, 291, 292; as Prime Minister, 331

Ezra Zionist organization, 88

Faction B in Mapai, 4, 282, 283, 310

Family Wage, 264, 285, 288, 290–292, 294–296, 298–300, 303–305, 382n.82, 384n.132, 394. *See also* Equality; Histadrut

Fascism, 138

Faure, Paul, 172

Fichte, Johann Gottlieb, 73

Fishman (Maimon), Ada, 227, 278, 293, 316

Fourier, Charles, 96
France, ix, xi, 5, 10, 12, 287, 320, 327; Declaration of the Rights of Man, 320; French Revolution, xi, xii, 10; Vichy regime in, 327
Frankel, Jonathan, 82, 97, 98, 99, 118
Freud, Y., 267

Galicia, 12
Galili, Israel, 331, 334
Gaza strip, 335
Gdud Ha'avoda (Labor Corps), 5, 35, 76, 78, 122, 124–125, 188, 198, 213, 247; Ben-Gurion and, 199, 201, 202, 205, 206–207, 212, 215, 373n.99; building a socialist society, 199, 202, 206, 209, 212, 215–216; celebration of twentieth anniversary of, 214; the communist fraction in, 211; conflicts with the leaders of "Ahdut Ha'avoda," 198–199, 200, 201, 204, 214–216, 373n.100; the Crimean Commune as a nucleus of, 199; and the Histadrut, 203–204, 206, 208, 209, 211; the Histadrut struggle against, 142, 144, 151, 192, 208–209, 210, 212, 240, 278, 294; Katznelson and, 143, 144, 147; regulations of, 201; and roads construction, 199; sanctions against, 183–184, 208, 209; shift to the left in, 209, 210, 372n.90
Germany, xi, 10, 14, 28, 45, 110, 287
Gesher, 373n.105
Geva, 203
Gideon, 202
Giladi, Dan, 220
Ginnosar, 300
Giva't Brenner, 214
Giva't Hashlosha, 214, 259
Glickson, Moshe, 131, 240, 241, 242–244; and opposition to the Labor trend in education, 244, 245, 251
Golan Heights, 331, 333, 334, 335
Goldmann, Nahum, 388n.10
Goldstein, Baruch, 333
Golomb, Eliahu, 31, 107, 108, 126, 147, 193, 201, 299
Gomel, 80
Gordon, Aaron David, 47–73, 76, 352nn. 38 and 43; on biblical culture, 72; "Building the Nation," 65, 66; "A Clarification of the Basis of Our Ideas," 58; and critcism of the Diaspora, 47–48; on historical rights, 68–73; influence of, 52, 73, 119; irrationalism in, 56–59; "Letter From Eretz Israel," 59; on mass mobilization, 58–59; nationalist

ideology of, 16, 36, 32, 52–55, 59, 62, 63, 65–68, 73, 89, 146–147; and negation of liberalism, 58–60; and Nietzsche, 58; "On the Unification," 67; and opposition to socialism, 34, 59–61, 65; on the reformation of man and the value of labor, 26, 63, 64, 65; on religion as an element of national identity, 56–59, 72; suspicion to the outside world, 138–139; on use of force, 71
Gordon, Arieh Lieb, 75
Gorny, Yosef, 90, 118, 123, 124, 191, 373n.100, 375n.35
Gramsci, Antonio, 91
Great Britain, 5, 287
Guri (Gurfinkel), Israel, 298, 300, 302, 305, 311; Committe headed by, 298
Gush Emunim, 333, 337, 342; and Rabbi Levinger's group, 333, 334
Gush Etzion, 318, 333
Gymnasia Balfour, 259
Gymnasia Herzliyya, 108, 259, 260, 295, 297
Gymnasia Shalva, 260, 261

Ha'adama, 103
Ha'ahdut, 30, 49, 86, 87, 97, 102, 115, 116, 128
Ha'aretz, 41, 131, 240, 323
Ha'aretz Veha'avoda, 75
Hadera, 74, 255, 330
Hagana Organization, 107, 180, 200. See also IDF
Ha-Gymnasia Ha-Ivrit, 262
Haifa, 221, 278; anti-democratic tendencies in Mapai branch in, 276–278; Labor trend schools in, 254; workers' council in, 276
Haifa Reali School, 262
Hakibbutz Hame'uhad, 76, 147, 164, 185, 214, 215, 263; and connection with the rebels in Tel Aviv Mapai branch, 145, 283; founding of, 214, 373n.105; Katznelson and, 138, 145, 152. See also Tabenkin, Yitzhak
Halle, Toni, 260
Hamashbir, 109, 222, 291, 299
Hamid, sultan Abdul, 272
Hanita, 265, 335
Ha'olam, 235
Hapo'el Hamizrahi, 76
Hapo'el Hatza'ir, 219
Hapo'el Hatza'ir, 18, 48, 73, 76, 77, 107, 143, 179, 296; antisocialism of, 35, 40, 77–78, 84, 114, 118–120, 121, 140; and Gdud

Ha'avoda, 206, 209; nationalist ideology of, 52, 76; unification with Ahdut Ha'avoda, 4, 117–118, 227–229

Harpaz (Goldberg), Neta, 108

Hashomer, 80, 142, 198, 199, 245

Hashomer Hatza'ir, 164, 182, 258, 262, 373n.105; Katznelson and, 137–138, 152, 164; and the majority in the Labor movement, 4, 151, 210, 213, 271–272

Haskala. *See* Enlightenment

Hasneh, 222

Hasollel, 201, 204

Hazan, Ya'akov, 271, 272, 274, 296

Hebrew University, 14, 104, 261

Hebron, 44, 318, 332, 333, 334, 336,

Hebron Illit (upper Hebron), 334. *See also* Kiryat Arba

Hefer Valley, 220

Hefetz, Mona, 253

Hefziba, 203

Hegel, George Wilhelm Friedrich, 55, 331

Hehalutz organization, 51, 188

Herder, Johann Gottfried, 11, 12, 14, 26, 54

Herzl, Theodor, 12, 51, 80, 97

Herzliyya, 214, 221, 222

Hever Hakvutzot, 164

Hilferding, Rudolf, 29, 91, 138; *Das Finanz Kapital*, 138

Hirschowitz, Dr. Ben Zion, 207

Histadrut (General Federation of Jewish Workers in Palestine), 4, 17, 22–23, 35, 307, 367n.2; and the affair of the advance payments, 142, 143–144, 151, 282, 292–294, 297; as an all-embracing system, 38, 148, 149–152, 178, 179–180, 181, 195; anti-progressive taxation in, 309, 312, 313, 316; Ben-Gurion and, 94–95, 116, 122, 123–124, 144, 184–185; the census of 1922, 79; exceptions and irregularities in, 290, 292, 295, 296, 298–300, 302, 303, 306, 382n.96; and the experts' report of 1928, 234; and the family wage, 288, 290, 291, 303, 305, 382n.82, 384n.132; founding of, 19, 82, 87, 109, 120, 121; and Hevrat Ovdim (society of workers), 20, 23, 122, 169, 195; Katznelson and, 143–144, 145, 147, 150; and the Labor trend in education, 244–259; and mas ahid (comprehensive levy), 268, 309, 315; and mas irgun (organization tax), 268; and mifdeh (voluntary fund for the unemployed), 312, 313, 315; and mish'an (relief fund), 313, 315; political objectives of, 180–182, 183, 185, 197–198; and the principle of equality, 43, 284, 286, 289, 290–291, 299–302, 303, 311, 316; the problem of democracy in, 22, 270–274, 279, 291, 295; and the problem of self-managment, 105–106; and the revolt of the unemployed, 279–281; social differences in, 37, 42–43, 280, 283, 285, 297, 307, 309–312, 384n.141; and the "synthetic" wage-scale, 300, 303, 305; as a system generating power, 30, 34, 79, 105–106, 116–117, 122–124, 127, 151, 183, 191, 195, 196, 205, 210, 271, 277, 278, 307, 310–311; as a trade union, 180, 237–239, 289, 297, 303; and wage-equalization, 285, 290; work of married couples, 307, 312; and youth movements in, 262. *See also* Labor Movement

Historiography, ix–xi, 320, 327

History: Gordon's views on Jewish historical rights to Palestine, 67, 68–73; as a tool of nation building, 16, 251; the Zionist interpretation of Jewish history, 49–50, 362n.10

Hitler, Adolf, 168, 338

Hobbes, Thomas, 61

Holocaust, x, 329. *See also* Diaspora; Eastern European Jews

Horin, Yitzhak, 303

Horowitz, Dan, 13, 14, 18, 20; *From the Yishuv to the State*, 18; *Troubles in Utopia*, 18

Horowitz, David (Dolek), 188, 210

Hoz, Dov, 107

Hungary, 287

Hushi, Abba, 276, 278, 303, 304, 364n.50. *See also* Haifa

Idelson, Beba, 270, 284

Idelson, David, 247, 248

Idelson (Bar-Yehuda), Israel, 300, 305, 310

Ideology, 30; Berl Katznelson's neglect of, 30, 38, 139, 164; Labor's neglect of, 30–31, 75, 76, 113, 127, 228, 267–268

IDF (Israel Defense Forces), 180, 200, 327

Immigration, 3; disdain for immigrants, 282, 285; of Holocaust survivors, 329; mass-immigration, 13, 20, 108, 217, 218, 219, 220; of oriental Jews, 330; Palestine as a land of, 13, 79. *See also* Aliyah, First–Fifth

Income Tax, 236; attitude of Labor movement to, 236–237

Individualism, 31, 59–62, 148; anti-individualism 59, 147, 149–150, 194, 195; Ben-Gurion on, 149–150, 183; Gordon's attitude to, 59, 60, 62; Katznelson's attitude to, 147, 148, 149, 158
Industry, 220, 221
Israeli, Benzion, 323
Italy, ix, xi, 14, 28, 287

Jabotinsky, Zeev, 34, 40
Jaffa, 335
Jaurès, Jean, 25, 29, 91, 98, 136, 138, 148
Jenin, 335
Jerusalem, 221, 318; Histadrut schools in, 254
Jewish Agency, 4, 127, 235, 286
Jewish Battalions, 95, 107, 113
Jewish labor, 16, 23, 103, 119, 125, 128–129, 142, 144, 156, 182, 233, 239, 241–242; Ben-Gurion on, 75, 87, 125, 129; Gordon on, 63, 64, 65, 68, 76; as a moral and cultural value, 27, 36–38, 39, 41, 77, 107, 178, 250; overrides economic considerations, 24, 235. *See also* Collective Settlements
Jewish worker, 42, 125, 128, 129, 132, 239, 284; Katznelson on, 145, 169, 237; and the myth of his superiority, 261–262, 296–297; status of agricultural worker, 296, 302, 309. *See also* Jewish labor; Proletariat
Jezreel Valley, 215, 221, 192
Jordan Valley, 219, 333
Joshua Bin-Nun, 16
Judea and Samaria, 331, 339. *See also* West Bank
Junior Hadassah, 246

Kadum, 338
Kadumim, 338
Kanievski, Y., 301, 303
Kant, Emmanuel, xiii, 11, 25, 98
Kaplan, Eliezer, 35, 257, 274, 299, 303
Kaplanski, Shlomo, 96, 97, 108, 126, 128, 227, 235
Katznelson, Berl, 19, 23–24, 27, 30, 32, 38, 100, 107, 134–177, 180, 224, 258; "Ahdut Ha'avoda," 135; anti-Marxism in, 94, 97, 126; and the Arab problem, 174–176; and Ben-Gurion, 22, 149, 227; as a conservative element, 136, 137, 144, 193, 200; on democracy and majority rule, 190, 195; as editor of *Davar*, 143, 185, 187, 196, 208, 193; and the family wage, 294, 299, 394; *Forgotten Values*, 25; and Gordon, 52, 64, 73; "In

Favor of Perplexity and Against Whitewashing," 137; his influence, 134, 136; "In Preparation for Days to Come," 103, 135, 152, 162, 362n.3; as a leader in Ahdut Ha'avoda, 35, 77, 103, 108, 109, 120; nationalist ideology of, 22, 36, 89, 139, 158, 164, 185; as a nationalist socialist thinker, 32, 76, 110–112, 114, 136, 147, 151, 153–156, 159, 161, 170, 176, 215, 238; and the Nir company, 193–198; persecution of the Zionist left by, 140, 142, 164, 166, 200–201; his personality, 163, 168, 265, 269–270, 363nn. 35 and 36; productive versus consuming socialism in, 159–161; as a representative of the apparatus, 145, 187, 196, 364n.50; on unification of the kibbutz movement, 267, 274; and whitewashing of corruption in the Histadrut, 143–144, 293; writings and lectures, 30, 135, 136–139
Kautsky, Karl, 91, 170
Kfar Giladi, 199, 201, 214, 245, 373n.105; expulsion from the Histadrut, 209, 212
Kfar Saba, 221
Kfar Vitkin, 145
Kfar Yehezkel, 203
Kfar Yehoshua, 300
Kfar Yeladim, 259
Kharkov, 83
Kibbutz. *See* Collective Settlements
Kinneret, 33, 52, 141, 196, 300
Kiryat Anavim, 300, 301
Kiryat Arba, 333, 334
Kishinev Pogroms, 50
Kitzis, Yosef, 275, 276, 277, 364n.50
Klein, Philip, 325
Knesset Israel, 31, 245, 246, 322
Kolatt, Israel, 78, 114, 119, 135, 232
Kook, Chief rabbi, 341, 343
Kopelevitch (Almog), Yehuda, 200
Kraków, 105
Kriegel, Annie, 185
Kuntras, 103, 199, 224
Kupat Holim, 109, 215, 253, 268, 291, 308, 316, 324
Kushnir, Yohanan, 276, 279

Labor movement, 3, 4, 40–42, 178–179, 185; and class collaboration, 22–23, 33–34, 39–40, 42, 128–129, 131, 132–133, 165–166, 219, 220, 223, 224, 229, 232, 233–244; conformism in, 76, 78, 118, 148, 183–184, 187, 188, 283–284, 294, 364n.50; cultural dominance of, 4–5, 232–233, 262–263; democracy in, 17, 183, 184, 189–191, 196, 268–269, 270, 272–274, 279, 281, 293–295; dominance of the apparatus in, 37–38, 186–187, 196, 197–198, 206, 268–270, 274, 275, 277, 280, 295, 304, 306–307, 364n.51; and the five member committee, 293, 296, 297; intellectual life in, 28–29, 42, 131, 264–265, 266–268, 307–308; intellectual opposition in, 324–325; according to Katznelson, 140–141, 162, 163, 164–166, 242; loyalty to superiors, 280–281; myth of socialism and equality, 196, 214, 229, 230, 261–262, 264, 288, 289, 290–291, 294, 301, 305, 316–317, 375n.49; nationalist socialism as the ideological core of, 18–19, 32–33, 34–35, 39, 42, 130–132, 136, 138–139, 153, 216, 306; oligarchic tendencies in, 270–271, 274, 276–277, 279, 285; primacy of national objectives in, 18, 121, 146, 147, 172–173, 176–177, 212, 217; and the principle of dominance of society over the individual, 147, 149–150; relationship with the left wing in, 77–78, 150–151, 210, 272; the shift to the right in, 77–78, 85, 86–87, 90–91, 96, 109, 131–132; struggle against, 270, 276, 279–280, 281–282, 283, 300; its uniqueness according to Katznelson, 141, 142. *See also* Ahdut Ha'avoda; Ben-Gurion; Histadrut; Katznelson; Mapai

Labor Party (founded 1968), 4, 7, 34, 332

Labor Trend in education (zerem ha'ovdim), 244–245, 246, 247–249, 250–252; Ben-Gurion and, 244, 245, 249, 256–258; and Children's Society, 248, 249; Committee for Educational Institutions of, 245; financing of, 253–256, 258, 259; fusion with the General Educational System, 251–252, 258; Ideological content of, 247–253; regional secondary school in the Jezreel Valley, 248; and schools in the cities, 252–254; and secondary education, 247, 258–259, 260; struggle over its existence, 245, 246, 247, 249–250, 256, 258

Labriola, Antonio, 91

Landauer, Gustav, 170

Laski, Harold, 29

Lassalle, Ferdinand, 96

Laufbahn, Yitzhak, 219, 229; on Jews as a proletarian nation, 229

Lavi (Levkowitz), Shlomo, 88, 193, 198, 202, 203, 213, 265

Lavon (Lubianiker), Pinhas, 188, 277, 324; affair, 324

Lechi (Israel Freedom Fighters), 320

Lenin, Vladimir Ilich Ulianov, 91, 126, 138, 170; *Imperialism: Last Stage of Capitalism* (Lenin), 138

Liberalism, xiii, 7, 9, 11, 12, 17, 55, 59; crisis of, 11–12; Gordon's opposition to, 59–60

Liebknecht, Karl, 170

Lifschitz, David, 279

Lissak, Moshe, 13, 14, 18, 20

Locke, John, 11, 61

Lod, 335

Łódź, 190

Lodzia, 223

Lokker, Berl, 299, 323

London, 328

Longuet, Jean, 167

Los Angeles, 328

Luft, Zvi, 229

Lukács, György, 91

Luxemburg, Rosa, 91, 170

Lvov, 14

Maarach, 4

Magdiel, 130, 165, 220–223

Mahanot Ha'olim, 262, 263

Manhattan, 190

Mapai (Eretz Israel Workers' Party), 4, 5, 9, 109, 232, Ben-Gurion's view of, 76; after the founding of Israel, 319, 323, 324, 331, 332; and the founding of the party, 33, 35, 76, 78, 109, 139, 241; internal democracy in, 269, 270–273, 277, 309–310; policy of national unity of, 73, 225, 229, 264; revolt at the Tel Aviv branch, 145, 276, 277, 278, 279–281, 282; socialism in, 19, 34, 86, 132. *See also* Labor movement

Mapam, 4

Marminsky, Yisrael, 299

Marx, Karl, 11, 58, 170, 251

Marxism, 7, 9, 10, 11, 16, 28, 149; Gordon and, 60; in Palestine, 136

Massachusetts, 77

Materialism, 25, 61

Maurras, Charles, 136

Mazzini, Giuseppe, 73

Mehayenu, 204, 208

Meinecke, Friedrich, xi

Meir (Meyerson), Golda, 188, 275, 280, 301, 305, 313, 315, 326, 332

Melchett, Lord (Alfred Mond), 234; the Mond Report, 241
Merhavia, 176
Merlino, Saverio, 27, 29
Metulla, 74
Metzer, Jacob, 217
Michelet, Jules, 73
Michels, Robert, 43
Mickiewicz, Adam, 73
Middle classes: Ben-Gurion and, 130, 219, 224, 225–226; and the Labor Movement, 224, 233–234, 235, 239–244. *See also* Bourgeois
Mifratz Shlomo (gulf of Solomon), 336
Migdal, 198, 199, 201
Mill, John Stuart, 11
Min Hayesod, 324, 325
Mintz, Matitiahu, 82, 83
Mishmar Ha'emek, 176
Mishna, 249
Mitman (Dr.), 95
Mizrahi party, 234, 244, 245. *See also* National Religious Party
Moeller van den Bruck, Arthur, 26; *The Third Reich*, 26
Mommsen, Theodor, xi
Mussolini, Benito, 168, 172
Myth, 135–136

Na'an, 152
Nablus, 335, 337
Nahalal, 33, 120, 148, 192, 194, 203, 211, 300
Nahara'im, 179
Namir (Namirowsky), Mordechai, 188, 276, 277, 280, 282, 324
Nation, 53; according to Herder, 54–55; according to Gordon, 52–59
National Civic Association, 242
National Funds, 40, 129, 217; the struggle over, 224
National movements, 13–14, 15, 47, 114–115, 151. *See also* Zionism
National Religious Party, 343
National Socialism, 7
Nationalism, 9, 10, 15–16, 53–56, 58, 62, 92, 343; in Central and Eastern Europe, 11–12; in Gordon, 54, 62, 73; national languages, 14; and volksgeist, 55; and the reformation of man, 63, 64, 65
Nationalist Socialism, 6–9, 18, 24, 28, 31, 39, 99, 111, 116, 118, 135, 149, 161; in Ahdut Ha'avoda, 19, 22, 73, 112, 113, 121, 125;

Gordon and, 62–64, 67, 73; in the Labor movemnt, 18, 19, 32–35, 39, 42, 130–132, 136, 138–139, 153, 216, 306; in Palestine, 3, 16, 17–18, 19, 21, 22, 23, 24, 25–26, 73, 76, 80, 91, 94, 95, 103, 106, 117, 131, 136, 150, 159, 165, 229; Parasites against producers in, 8, 9, 160–161, 165; in the thinking of Berl Katznelson, 32, 76, 111–112, 113, 114, 115, 135, 147, 151, 154–156, 158–159, 161–162, 169, 176, 238. *See also* Socialism
Nationalization, 11–12, 114, 120, 121–122; Gordon's views on, 66
Negev, 318
Neosocialism, 171
Nes Ziona, 165, 252
Netanya, 222
Netanyahu, Benjamin, 344
Netivot, 330
Netzer (Nusovitzky), Dvora, 276
Netzer (Nusovitzky), Shraga, 188, 276, 315
New High School, 260, 261, 262
New York, 328
New Zealand, 194
Nietzsche, Friedrich, 54, 58, 136; Nietzschean morality, 68
Nir (Rafalkes), Nahum, 83, 104
Nir company, 148, 149, 159, 178; founding of, 192, 193–196, 197
Nitzan, Arie, 287
Nordau, Max, 12, 51, 80
Nuris, 198, 203. *See also* Ein Harod

Odessa, 81
Ofakim, 330
Ofer, Abraham, 323
Oppenheimer, Franz, 33, 96–97; *Cooperative Settlement*, 96
Organization of Working Mothers, 270
Oslo Peace Accords, 339, 344
Owen, Robert, 96

Palestine under the British Mandate, 4, 16, 218; and the economic crisis of the 1930s, 37, 39, 308, 310; economy of, 217–218, 222; revenues of the Mandatory government, 235–236; unemployment in, 221, 222, 242, 282, 297, 306, 307, 312–313, 315–316, 385n.155
Palestinian National Movement, 14–16, 77, 43–46, 146, 236, 339; Ahdut Ha'avoda leaders' attitude to, 146, 182; Arab workers, 16, 242, 287, 288; Ben-Gurion's attitude to, 70,

93, 105, 129–130, 146; and the "distur-
bances" of 1920–21 and 1929, 44, 143, 146,
174, 333; Gordon's views on Arab rights to
Palestine, 67–78; and the Jewish-Arab dis-
pute, 76–77, 363n.31; Katznelson's attitude
to, 140, 143, 144, 146, 147, 155, 173–176;
and the uprising of 1936–1939, 44, 265, 331
Palmach, 332, 263
Partition Plan of 1937, 331, 336
Peel Commission, 45
Peres, Shimon, 331, 337, 339, 340, 344
Persitz, Shoshana, 252
Petah Tiqwa, 74, 242, 330
Pioneering, 36, 50, 52, 68, 77, 89, 117, 119,
191, 207–208; sense of superiority, 282
Plato, 122; *The Republic*, 122
Płońsk, 81, 88, 117
Po'alei Tzion, 16, 17, 52, 60, 68, 80, 81, 82, 83,
88, 107, 118, 119, 184; Ben-Gurion and, 74,
81, 86, 88; the destruction of the party, 19,
35, 76, 84, 85, 92, 106, 107, 108, 109, 146;
Katznelson attitude to, 143, 144, 163; in
Palestine, 80, 82, 84, 88–89, 90, 92; Po'alei
Tzion leftists, 151, 161, 213, 258; Po'alei
Tzion World Union, 81, 102, 104, 108;
Ramle Platform, 81, 84, 85, 118; the Stock-
holm convention, 103, 153; and Workers'
Fund, 117
Pogatchov, Sh.-Z., 247, 248
Poland, 14, 45, 91, 287
Polani, Yehuda, 247, 250
Portugal, 28
Postmodernism, xi, xii
Post-Zionism, xi, xii
Prague, 14
Proletariat, 8, 23, 24, 94, 131–132, 169, 178–
179; as against workers, 353n.71; Dictator-
ship of, 272. *See also* Jewish worker
Property, private, 9, 23, 128, 286; Ben-
Gurion's attitude to, 94, 95. *See also* Capital
Proudhon, Pierre Joseph, 7, 99, 101

Ra'anana, 130
Rabin, Nehemiah, 281
Rabin, Yitzhak, 281, 333, 337, 338, 339, 340,
344
Rabinowitz, Aaron, 272, 273
Rachel's Tomb, 333
Rafi (party), 4
Ramallah, 335
Ramat Gan, 259
Ramat Rachel, 373n.105

Ramat Yohanan, 267
Ramatayim, 221
Ramle, 81, 335
Rattner, Moshe, 75
Red Army, 167
Rehovot, 74
Religion, 56–58, 338, 340–343; Gordon and,
56–57; as an integral part of nationalist out-
look, 56, 57; as a justification for the con-
quest of the land, 57–58; Katznelson and,
56, 163; and role of the Bible as the Jewish
title-deed to Palestine, 58, 72, 73, 249
Remez, David, 34, 35, 127, 239, 257, 263,
281, 282, 295, 305, 311; and corruption in
Sollel Boneh, 143, 151, 297, 299; as head of
the Histadrut, 281, 282; as a leader of
Ahdut Ha'avoda, 73, 107, 109, 120; as a
member of the apparatus, 185, 268, 275,
278, 281, 311; and struggle against Gdud
Ha'avoda, 200, 201, 202, 204
Reptor, Berl, 239, 276, 277
Reshef, Shimon, 248
Reuveni, Aharon, 146
Revisionist Right, 5, 6, 34, 118, 186, 332, 334
Revolutionary Syndicalists, 161
Riga, 14
Rishon-le-Zion, 141, 267
Romania, 91
Rome, xi, 16, 287
Rosh Ha'ain, 201
Rosh Pinna, 74
Rostov, 80, 90
Rotenstreich, Nathan, 324
Rothschild family, 246
Rousseau, Jean-Jacques, xiii
Ruppin, Arthur, 33, 41, 131, 180, 234, 240,
242, 243; *Agricultural Settlement of the
Zionist Organization*, 242
Russia, 28, 91
Rutenberg, Pinhas, 238

Sadeh (Landoberg), Itzhak, 200, 204, 206
Safed, 44
Samaria, 331
Scholem, Gershom, 260
Schopenhauer, Arthur, 98
Schweid, Eliezer, 56, 57
Sderot, 330
Sebastia, 337
Second International, 111
Segev, Tom, 387n.10
Sejera, 142

Sejmists, 81
Shafayim, 214
Shaltiel, Eli, 18, 238, 239
Shamir, Yitzhak, 320, 344
Shapira, Anita, 18, 20, 110, 137, 214, 323, 375n.49; on Berl Katznelson, 116, 134, 135, 142, 144, 363n.36; *Going toward the Horizon*, 18
Shapira, Yosef, 228, 267
Shapiro, Yonathan, 121, 185, 187, 369n.35, 373n.100
Sharett (Shertok), Moshe, 108, 261, 265, 274, 277, 323, 342, 363n.36
Sharm el-Sheikh, 337
Sharon, plain of, 220, 221, 240
Shazar (Rubashov), Zalman, 103, 295
Shein, Eliezer, 248
Sherf, Zeev, 262
Shikun Ovdim, 222
Shilo, 334
Shimoni (Shimonovitz), David, 146
Shochat, Israel, 84, 199, 201, 244
Shochat, Manya, 201
Shocken, Zalman, 41
Simmel, George, 98
Sinai (Mt.), 139
Sinai Campaign (1956), 325, 337
Six Day War (1967), 6, 45, 46, 330, 331, 332, 339, 340, 342
Socialism, 17, 25, 28, 91–92, 111, 132, 148; Ben-Gurion's attitude to, 75, 84, 86, 87, 94, 105, 129, 131–132; Constructive, 6, 9, 30, 36, 68, 90, 103, 104, 128, 130, 133, 153, 159, 162, 176, 223; Democratic, 10, 11, 27, 32, 91–92, 97–98, 99, 111, 118, 132, 148, 161; Experiential, 138, 139, 164; Gordon's opposition to, 59–61, 62–66, 67; Katznelson's definitions of, 158, 169–171, 230; Katznelson's disagreement with, 138, 139, 141, 156–158; Productive versus Consuming, 159–161; Reformist, 171, 172; and unity of class, 181; and unity through existence, 94–95, 113, 114, 115, 116, 266, 308; Utopian, 7. *See also* Labor movement; Nationalist Socialism
Socialist International, 91, 111, 126
Socialist Youth, 137, 170
Sokolov, Nahum, 44, 235, 240
Sollel Boneh, 106, 179, 185, 200, 204, 208, 280; bankruptcy of, 151, 222; corruption in, 151, 282, 296, 297
Sombart, Werner, 26

Sorel, Georges, 20, 98, 99, 135, 136,
Soviet Union, 29, 126, 138, 167, 170, 272
Spanish Civil War, 181, 265
Spengler, Oswald, 26, 27 101; *Preussentum und Sozialismus (Prussianism and Socialism)*, 27
Sprinzak, Yosef, 31, 35, 120, 206, 228, 229, 247, 267, 274, 280; disdain for immigrants, 219, 282; as a representative of the apparatus, 219, 278, 279, 281, 299, 313
Stalin, Josef, 272
Stern Gang. *See* Lechi
Suez Canal, 334
Sussman, Zvi, 286, 287, 288
Syrkin, Nachman, 26, 27, 29, 81, 103, 106, 153, 184; cooperative program of, 96, 97, 101–102, 104; teachings of, 77, 99, 103

Tabenkin, Yitzhak, 34, 73, 83, 122, 184, 257, 274, 284, 295, 334; and the Arab problem, 146; as a fifth column in Gdud Ha'avoda, 198, 202; and founding of Hakibbutz Hame'uhad, 214; as a leader in Ahdut Ha'avoda, 103, 107, 109, 122, 185, 267; nationalist ideology of, 215, 224; nationalist socialism in, 115; as an opposing figure, 76, 164; his view of the kibbutz, 147
Tel Adashim, 199, 244, 300
Tel Aviv, 13, 133, 221, 222, 240, 255; Katznelson's opinion of, 164; Mapai branch in, 145, 276, 277, 278, 279–282; schools in, 250, 253, 254–256, 259
Tel Aviv Workers' Council, 275
Tel Hai, 50, 199, 214, 294, 335; expulsion from the Histadrut, 209, 212
Tel Yosef, 202, 203, 205, 206, 208, 211, 278, 294, 337, 373n.105; blockade of, 207–208
Teveth, Shabtai, 30, 84, 85, 88, 212, 362n.10, 387n.10
Third World, 28
Tiran islands, 337
Tnuva, 222, 303
Tolstoy, Lev Nikolayievich, 54, 58
Trade unions, 186
Treitschke, Heinrich von, 27
Trotsky, Leon (Lev Davidovitch Bronstein), 155
Trumpeldor, Yosef, 44, 50, 149, 199
Tuvin, Pinhas, 281
Tza'irei Tzion, 118
Tzemach, Shlomo, 88, 117, 119

Uganda Plan, 80, 82, 106; Territorialist Organization, 81, 88
Ukraine, 14
Umm-Djuni, 33. *See also* Degania
Union of General Zionists, 240, 241
United States, 13, 79, 320, 326, 328, 338; American Declaration of Independence, 320
Universal Values: in Ben-Gurion's thinking, 140; in Katznelson's thinking, 138–140
Ussishkin, Menachem, 41, 82, 131, 163, 233, 234, 240; *The Question of Zion and Territory*, 82

Va'ad Le'umi, 244, 245, 246
Vandervelde, Emil, 29, 167, 171, 316
Vienna, 16, 287
Virginia, 77
Vogel, Yehuda, 299

Wadi Salib, 326
War of Independence, (1948–1949), x, 3, 5, 6, 45, 46, 220, 318, 319, 322, 325, 326, 335, 336, 340, 342; Generation of, 5–6
Warsaw, 88, 287, 304; Ghetto uprising in, 50
Washington, 328
Weizmann, Chaim, 41, 44, 131, 233, 234, 235, 240, 243, 319
Werber, Fishel, 267, 274
West Bank, 332, 336, 337, 339, 342, 344
Workers' Councils, 289; and the family wage-scale, 291, 299
World Zionist Congresses, 33, 80, 81, 97, 233, 234, 241, 242, 245; Sixth Zionist Congress (1903), 80, 97; Seventh Zionist Congress (1905), 81; Eleventh Zionist Congress (1913), 33; Fourteenth Zionist Congress (1925), 233–234; Fifteenth Zionist Congress (1927), 241, 242; Sixteenth Zionist Congress (1929), 245

Ya'ari, Meir, 213, 271, 272, 274, 284, 296, 300, 373n.105
Yachin company, 222, 303, 306

Yad Mordechai, 318
Yaffe, Eliezer, 148, 192, 213, 244, 296
Yagur, 214, 259, 373n.105
Yannait, Rachel, 196
Yavne'el, 165, 184
Yavnieli, Shmuel, 103, 107, 120, 246; and the family wage, 290, 291; as head of the Labor educational system, 246, 247, 251, 252, 284
Yemen, 79
Yemenite worker, 79, 87
Yiddish culture, 36, 145, 90
Yishuv, 20, 236; economic crisis in, 306; and education, 244–263; social gaps in, 39, 261, 279, 284, 286–288, 306. *See also* Histadrut; Labor movement; Palestine under the British Mandate
Yom Kippur War (1973), 78, 325, 332, 337
Youth Aliyah, 137, 138
Yugoslavia, 287

Zakkai, David, 295
Zangwill, Israel, 81
Zichron Ya'akov, 129, 141
Ziesling, Aaron, 283, 307
Zionism, 12–13, 15–16, 47, 98; anti-rationalist tendencies in, 136; democracy and, 189–191; determinism in, 89, 90; General, 233, 240, 241, 242; as an ideology, 12–13; Katznelson and, 140–141, 165; as a manifestation of absolute justice, 173–174; as a mean of rescue, 338; Messianic trend in, 50, 51; revolutionary aspect of, 77; self-isolation in, 139; socialist elements in, 15, 16, 19–20, 23; the socialist trend in, ix, 27, 115; the "synthetic" school in, 240–241; the utilitarian school in, 50–51; voluntarism in, 89–90
Zionist Organization, 33
Zionist Organization of the United States, 95; educational department, 245
Zisla, Dov, 258
Ziv, Sanny, 217

About the Author

Zeev Sternhell is Léon Blum Professor of Political Science at the Hebrew University in Jerusalem. He is the author, among works in several languages, of *Neither Right nor Left* and *The Birth of Fascist Ideology*, both published by Princeton University Press. His books are now available in French, Spanish, Italian, Portuguese, and Hebrew.